THE WORLD OF FASHION

fourth edition

THE WORLD OF FASHION

fourth edition

Jay Diamond
Ellen Diamond

FAIRCHILD BOOKS, INC., NEW YORK

Director of Sales and Acquisitions:	Dana Meltzer-Berkowitz
Executive Editor:	Olga T. Kontzias
Senior Development Editor:	Jennifer Crane
Art Director:	Adam B. Bohannon
Production Manager:	Ginger Hillman
Associate Production Editor:	Jessica Rozler
Photo Researchers:	Erin Fitzsimmons, Linda Sykes, and Lindsay Aveilhe/Linda Sykes Picture Research, Inc., and Elizabeth Greenberg
Editorial Services:	Newgen–Austin

Fourth Edition, Copyright © 2008 Fairchild Books, Inc.
A Division of Condé Nast Publications

Third Edition, Copyright © 2002
Fairchild Publications, Inc.

Second Printing © 1999
Second Edition, Copyright © 1997
Fairchild Publications, a Division of ABC Media, Inc.

First Edition, Copyright © 1990
by Harcourt Brace Jovanovich, Inc.

Library of Congress Catalog Card Number: 2007933130

ISBN: 978-1-56367-567-6

GST R 133004424

Printed in China
CH11, TP15

contents

extended contents

part three   THE FASHION MERCHANDISE INDUSTRIES

part five MERCHANDISING FASHION

20. Resident Buying Offices and Other Fashion Information Sources for Retailers   482

21. The Fashion Retailer   499

preface

As the fashion industry entered the new millennium, it continued to generate excitement. Career choices became increasingly global as participants were found in every corner of the world. Whether it's apparel and accessories design, textile procurement, product development, retailing, or any other aspect of the industry, fashion's global nature provides limitless opportunities for those whose life ambition is a career in some aspect of fashion. The concept of offshore or nearshore outsourcing continues to dominate the fashion industry.

Whether one has studied to become a professional in the field, gains his or her knowledge from on-the-job experience, or simply has the desire to better understand the industry, *The World of Fashion*, fourth edition, should serve the reader well.

This edition retains much of the information from the third edition while adding a wealth of new concepts and areas of interest. Still organized in five parts, the book has been expanded into twenty-two chapters, with new ones entitled "The Multicultural Consumer and Fashion," and "Outsourcing Fashion Design, Production, and Management." The interest in these areas has so vastly increased that it not only provides other exciting arenas for participants, but it is also bringing increased profits to manufacturers and retailers alike. Each of the remaining chapters has been rewritten to include new information and updated artwork relevant to the recent changes in the industry.

Part One, Introduction to Fashion, includes the evolution of fashion, fashions of the 20th century, the powerful consumer, multiculturalism, ever-changing fashion and its acceptance, and fashion in the global marketplace. Part Two, The Producers of Raw Materials, explores the textiles, fur, and leather segments of the industry. Part Three, The Fashion Merchandise Industries, features apparel for women, men, and children; intimate apparel; fashion accessories; details and trimmings; cosmetics and fragrances; and home fashions. Part Four, Designing and Manufacturing of Fashion Apparel and Accessories, focuses on fashion forecasting for designers and manufacturers, elements and principles of designing and developing a fashion collection, apparel and accessories manufacturing, and outsourcing. Part Five, Merchandising Fashion, concentrates on resident buying offices and other fashion information sources for retailers; the fashion retailer; advertising, special events, publicity, and visual merchandising. The Appendices at the conclusion of the text feature a host of color and fashion trend forecasting services, trade publications for the world of fashion, and trade associations. The scope of the materials featured in these chapters and appendices make *The World of Fashion*, fourth edition, the most comprehensive textbook of its kind.

Another feature of this edition is quotations from renowned people in fashion and the literary world, such as Coco Chanel, Ralph Lauren, Karl Lagerfeld, Oscar De La Renta, and Henry David Thoreau. Each chapter begins with a specific quotation that helps to motivate a discussion between instructor and students.

With the artwork in this edition now in full color, the reader is able to better visualize the excitement that the fashion industry generates.

Popular features have been retained. "Point of View" articles, many of which are new to this edition, bring a sense of industry participation to the text, and "The World of Fashion Profiles" examine people and companies whose presence and talents have made them successful in this very competitive arena. Other pedagogical elements are chapter highlights, important fashion terminology and concepts, questions for review, exercises and projects, and case problems.

Based upon the success of the video series, *The Business of Fashion*, the authors have expanded the video offerings to include The World of Fashion (the same as the name of the text), Promotion: How Retailers Use Special Events to Improve Market Share, Retailing Trends in the New Mellennium, Seventh Avenue: America's Premier Fashion Center, Value Shopping in America, A Retailing Strategy: The Store is the Brand, The Retail Buying Series, The Concepts and Mathematics of Retail Merchandising Series, Retailing: A Career for the 21st Century, Merchandise Sourcing in the Global Marketplace, Leather: The Material That Combines Fashion and Function, Multichannel Retailing, and others. Each of these offerings closely parallels the material in the text and is available directly from Diamond Educational Productions.

An instructor's manual provides additional exercises and projects and a set of exams for each chapter. A PowerPoint presentation can be used in the classroom to highlight topics for lecture and discussion.

acknowledgments

The authors wish to thank the following people and organizations who have significantly contributed to *The World of Fashion*, fourth edition.

Allen Edmond Shoes; American Fiber Manufacturers Association; American Fur Industry; American Wool Council; Committee For Color Trends; Council For Fashion Designers of America; The Doneger Group; Allan Ellinger, Marketing Management Group; Gigi Farrow; Fragrance Foundation; Promostyl; The Fashion Association; Leather Apparel Association; Donna Lombardo, Belk Department Stores; The Larkin Group; Associate Dean Sheri Litt, Florida Community College at Jacksonville; Deirdre Quinn, Lafayette 148; Beth Terrell, Lizden Industries; Joanna Mastroianni; David Wales, FRCH; Rootstein; David Wolfe, The Doneger Group; Gae Marino, The Doneger Group; Sawgrass Mills; Amy Meadows, Director of Visual Marketing, Macy's, Chicago; Brett Wright, CCO and Co-founder, Uptown Magazine and CEO, NuAmerica Agency, Chiqui Cartagena, Managing Director, Meredith Integrated Marketing, COO, Todd Kahn, Sean John Clothing, Burnt Ullman, President, Phat Fashions and Wool Bureau.

Readers of the previous editions, selected by the publisher, were also very helpful in the preparation of this revision. They include Laura Bliss, Stevens College; Carolyn Blount, Shoreline Community College; Suzanne Coil, Baker University; Judith Everett, Northern Arizona University; Yvette Hays–Logan, University of Rhode Island; Pam Kuchenmeister, Illinois State University; Rosemary Leach, Skyline College; Pam Norum, University of Missouri–Columbus; Beverly Olsen, Dakota County Technical College; Christine Pratt, Fashion Institute of Technology; Teresa Robinson, Middle Tennessee State University; George Sproles, GES Associates; Janice Threw, Southern Illinois University–Carbondale; Diann Valentini, Fashion Institute of Technology; Stella Warnick, Seattle Pacific University; Debbie West, Draughons Junior College; Helen Xenakis, Fashion Institute of Technology.

introduction to fashion

Part One discusses the evolution of fashion from the days of couture designers, who created fashions for the few, through the 20th century. Chapter 1 explores this evolution from the beginning of couture through the various inventions of the Industrial Revolution that made fashion available to all classes. Chapter 2 takes a decade-by-decade approach to 20th-century fashion, presenting the historical events that influenced fashion; fashion highlights for men, women, and children; and the designers who influenced fashion.

The success or failure of a fashion product depends on its acceptance or rejection by the consumer, who is the focus of Chapter 3. To create and produce fashion that will meet with success, the industry studies consumers—their motives, social classes, and other characteristics—to determine the types of merchandise important to different groups. A variety of research tools, such as questionnaires, personal observations, and focus groups, are used for the analysis of prospective customers.

In recent years, marketers have taken a new look at consumers and have expanded their efforts in analyzing their makeup and needs. In Chapter 4, the nature of the multicultural consumer and its impact on fashion is thoroughly investigated. Specifically, the purchasing power of African Americans, Hispanics, and Asian Americans are studied, as is the manner in which retailers are refocusing their merchandising efforts to capture the attention of these markets.

As with other professions, fashion has its own vocabulary, and those who participate in the industry must be familiar with these terms. Chapter 5 discusses fashion language, as well as the ever-changing nature of fashion and the potential for each style to remain popular. For example, certain styles may become popular because an influential person wears them. These people are termed fashion leaders, and they can have a significant influence on consumers.

Unlike many industries, fashion occurs in a global environment. As discussed in Chapter 6, fashion is designed and manufactured in a global marketplace. To make U.S. fashion businesses more competitive with businesses in other parts of the world, the U.S. government has enacted specific legislation about which every industry participant should be knowledgeable. To improve their global marketing success, fashion companies belong to international trade associations and attend trade expositions throughout the world.

The fashion arena offers careers in design, manufacturing, retailing, and promotion. Each career affords the individual different monetary rewards and different challenges, as discussed fully in Chapter 7.

the evolution of fashion

I am against fashion that doesn't last. I cannot accept that you throw your clothes away just because it's spring.

COCO CHANEL, DESIGNER

The world of fashion began with individual **couturiers** and evolved, as a result of the Industrial Revolution, into a mass-market industry. By studying this evolution, we become better equipped to understand the organization of the fashion industry and the directions in which it is moving.

THE BEGINNING OF COUTURE

Although the history of fashion may be traced back hundreds of years, it was not until the late 1700s that individuality of design began to emerge. Styles were set by royalty and carried out by the dressmakers who served them. Only the upper class could afford what was fashionable and finely produced. The poor made their own clothing or wore the castoffs of the rich.

By the end of the 18th century, one name had emerged in fashion design—*Rose Bertin*. Initially a milliner's apprentice, she became France's premier designer. As a result of the recognition she received from the Princess de Conti, Bertin was appointed court milliner in 1772. In that position, she was introduced to Marie Antoinette. She soon became the queen's confidante as well as her official designer. Eventually, Bertin became the minister of fashion for the French court. As her reputation grew, she was commissioned to design hats and dresses for the aristocracy. Her fame spread to other countries, and she soon started to export her merchandise.

Garments for the wealthy class were elaborately tailored and trimmed. Each piece was hand sewn, embroidered, jeweled, and embellished to perfection. Aside from Bertin, the names of the dressmakers to the royal families and the aristocracy were generally unknown. Those who employed them jealously guarded their identities to avoid losing them to other families.

During the early 19th century, the opulent designs that dominated the wardrobes of the rich began to disappear; less elaborate dress became the order of the day.

It was not until after 1845, when the Englishman *Charles Frederick Worth* emigrated to Paris, that the world would come to know another designer. In Paris, he first worked for a fabric dealer, whom he persuaded to open a dress department. In 1858, Worth was the first to open a couture house on the rue de la Paix. Along with a list of private clients in Europe and the United States, he was court dressmaker to Empress Eugènie of France. His success would soon motivate others to establish their own couture businesses.

Fed by the magnificent textiles and trimmings of nearby Lyon, it was natural for Paris to establish itself as the world's leading center for couture. The names that followed Worth are legendary and will be discussed in Chapter 2.

THE INDUSTRIAL REVOLUTION

Until about 1770, people worked in much the same manner as their ancestors did. Products were slowly made by hand. Cloth was hand-woven, and a cobbler still used only a hammer, knife, and awl to make a shoe over a last, or form.

During this time, the Western world witnessed the growth of the middle class, which prospered from new avenues of trade and industry and spent money on such luxuries as fine clothing. As the middle class grew in importance, its members created new fashion directions. The business suit, for example, became an important element in a man's wardrobe. Before long, fine tailor shops were opened in London's Savile Row to provide this new business attire.

Changes, however, were taking place in the methods of production. In large part, they could be attributed to the growth of the textile industry, which was revolutionized by a series of time-saving inventions (Table 1.1). In 1733, John Kay received a patent for his **flying shuttle**, which resulted in the manufacture of a loom that produced materials more rapidly. Similarly, spinning was a slow process until 1764, when James Hargreaves, a British spinner, invented the **spinning jenny**. He placed eight spindles on a frame, which could be turned by a single wheel. As a result, one spinner could simultaneously produce eight threads instead of producing one thread at a time. Hargreaves later created a machine that could spin 16 threads at a time. Ultimately, even a child could run the machine and turn out work that had previously required 100 spinners. Then, in 1785, Edmund Cartwright invented the **power loom**, which wove cloth so rapidly that the hand loom was quickly reserved for limited runs of special fabrics.

The increased speed of the spinning machine resulted in demands for large supplies of cotton fiber. This problem was solved by an American, Eli Whitney. In 1793, he invented the **cotton gin**, which separated the cotton seed from the fiber so quickly and expertly that one man was able to turn out the work that once required 300 men.

Because of the competitive advantage these inventions gave to manufacturers, England was very protective of its discoveries and forbade the emigration of textile workers and the exportation of its textile machines. Some workers, however, memorized the details of each machine's construction. These workers left England in disguise, and were able to reproduce the machines in other countries. For example, Sam-

Founders of modern *haute couture* in Paris include Charles Frederick Worth, who was active at the end of the 19th century.

Worth's designs were worn by wealthy patrons such as Mrs. William K. Vanderbilt.

uel Slater left England after learning the construction details for many textile machines. He opened a spinning mill in Rhode Island in 1790, where he introduced the factory system to the United States. During the Civil War, the demand for fabrics to manufacture uniforms helped the growth of U.S. mills, most of which were in New England. By the end of the war, the mills were capable of mass producing textiles. Fashion was now on the way to becoming a major industry in the United States, but one more step was necessary.

Although fabrics were being produced faster than ever before, it was not until the development of the first sewing machine that the world would be treated to a new generation of fashion.

The Sewing Machine

Although Walter Hunt invented a **sewing machine** in 1832, he did not apply for a patent until 1854, when it was denied on the grounds of abandonment. On September 10, 1846, however, Elias Howe Jr. did receive a patent for his sewing machine. As a result, he is generally regarded as its inventor. His failure to market the machine successfully led to attempts by others to further develop the machine. Finally, in 1858, Isaac Singer designed a machine that worked by the use of a foot treadle, thereby freeing the hands to manipulate the fabric. That year, the Singer Sewing Manufacturing Company was incorporated and sales reached 3,000 units. With this invention, women began to sew professional-looking clothes at home, and factories experienced the birth of ready-to-wear apparel.

UNIONIZATION AND THE GARMENT INDUSTRY

These new inventions created what is now known as the garment industry. Coupled with the significant growth of the U.S. population, they led to an increase in the production of apparel. At first, factories were located primarily in Boston and Baltimore. Later, they opened in significant numbers in New York City, the gateway to the new world. Immigrants from Eastern Europe became the mainstays of the sewing industry, as immigrants from Asia and Latin America are now. Their willingness to

Table 1.1		
INVENTIONS OF THE INDUSTRIAL REVOLUTION THAT CHANGED FASHION		
Year	**Inventor**	**Invention**
1733	John Kay	Flying shuttle
1764	James Hargreaves	Spinning jenny
1785	Edmund Cartwright	Power loom
1793	Eli Whitney	Cotton gin
1846	Elias Howe Jr.	Sewing machine

work long hours for low wages made them extremely desirable workers. As the demand for mass-produced goods increased, more and more workers were used to fill every available inch of space in the factories. Working conditions deteriorated and employees often became trapped in unsanitary and dangerous environments.

In an effort to improve working conditions and wages, seven local unions amalgamated to form the International Ladies' Garment Workers Union, known as the **ILGWU**, in 1900. Unfortunately, it was not until tragedy struck that the union made inroads in cleaning up the factories. In 1911, fire broke out at the Triangle Shirtwaist Company in New York City. With the door to the main entrance bolted to keep workers from leaving and a fire escape leading to nowhere, the inferno became a death trap for more than 100 people, most of whom were young women. As a result of this tragic incident, many Americans came to support the garment workers in their struggle against the **sweatshops**. Through the years the union gained significant strength, successfully upgrading working conditions and negotiating fringe benefits and better salaries for its members.

The menswear industry experienced the same sweatshop conditions. The successful strike at the Hart, Schaffner & Marx manufacturing plant in Chicago in 1910 led to the eventual formation of the Amalgamated Clothing Workers Union of America in 1914. Later, the **Amalgamated**, as it was known, merged with the shoe and textile workers to form the **ACTWU** (Amalgamated Clothing and Textile Workers Union).

Today, the garment industry's unions face a new problem—that of decreasing membership. Their numbers have been significantly eroded

The sewing machine was developed by Isaac Singer and changed the course of fashion.

The fire at the Triangle Shirtwaist factory was used by the garment worker's union to make the public aware of sweatshop conditions.

At the turn of the 20th century, John Wanamaker's of Philadelphia was a major retailer.

Sears Roebuck & Company began its business in Chicago in 1893 selling its goods through catalogs.

by the advent of offshore production. To counteract this problem, unions are trying to create jobs by encouraging consumers to buy domestically produced goods. One well-known example is the advertising campaign that reminds consumers to "**look for the union label.**"

RETAILING'S RESPONSE TO MASS PRODUCTION

Until the middle of the 19th century, merchandise, especially wearing apparel, was in short supply. The privileged few had quality clothing that was custom-made by tailors. Others made their own clothing at home, with little concern for questions of fashion.

As a result of the Industrial Revolution, merchandise was produced in quantity in the United States. New facilities were needed to sell this large assortment of apparel and accessory items to the masses. The first were **limited-line stores**, or **specialty stores**, that restricted their merchandise to a narrow classification. Joseph Lowthian Hudson started a small men's and boys' haberdashery (Hudson's) in 1881 in the old Detroit Opera House, and Nordstrom opened its doors in 1901 as a shoe emporium. With the immediate success of these stores, the same companies opened new facilities. This phenomenon started the trend toward **chain store** retailing.

At the turn of the 20th century, the merchandise assortment was becoming more abundant and varied than ever before. Some merchants decided to open new operations that sold more than one type of merchandise, or to expand their limited-line stores to full-line **department stores**. George Dayton built a six-story multiuse building in Minneapolis in 1902, called Dayton's, which eventually merged with Hudson's to become Dayton Hudson. Henri Bendel, established in 1912, started as a small millinery business and eventually evolved into a specialized department store operation, featuring women's apparel and accessories. Other important major retailers who began their businesses during this time were Macy's in New York City, Filene's in Boston, Wanamaker's in Philadelphia, and Neiman Marcus in Dallas.

Although these stores flourished in the major cities, consumers in rural areas had little access to these retailers. In response, companies began to sell merchandise through the mail. The early mail-order merchants were both located in Chicago: Montgomery Ward, which began its business in 1872, and Sears Roebuck & Co., in 1893. Each published a **catalog** offering a wide variety of products that could be ordered through the mail.

Retailing continued to expand throughout the country with branch operations. Although many of the early participants are still in operation, many of those who began the industry, such as Dayton Hudson, Gimbels, and

B. Altman & Co., are no longer in business. And some, such as Marshall Fields and the May Company, were acquired by Federated Stores and now operate under different names. They are both now units of Macy's.

SEGMENTS OF THE FASHION INDUSTRY

Today the numerous segments of the fashion industry include textiles, manufacturers, retailers, licenses, franchises, fashion communications, and market consultants. Although these areas will each be explored later in this book, the following is a brief outline of their roles in bringing the goods from the point of production to consumption. **Designers**, whose talents drive the industry, are explored separately in the next chapter.

Textiles

Before garments can be designed, the most important materials used in their manufacture—**textiles**—must be created. The production of these fabrics involves a variety of different participants as well as processes.

Fibers must be selected to meet the fabric requirements of designers, manufacturers, and consumers. In addition to the natural fibers (cotton, flax, wool, and silk), chemical companies have developed numerous manufactured fibers. Companies such as DuPont, Hoechst-Celanese, and BASF are constantly researching and developing new fibers, improving existing ones, and responding to the demands created by their customers.

The fibers are then transformed into fabrics at textile mills, which are located all over the globe. Some mills limit their responsibilities to one aspect of production, such as weaving yarns; others are **vertical operations** that perform all of the processes necessary for complete production. Burlington Mills is an example of a vertical company.

A converter is the segment of the textile industry that finishes goods according to the specifications of its clients. Brittany and Erlanger are two such companies.

For a more-detailed discussion of the textiles industry, see Chapter 8.

Raw cotton undergoes numerous processes before being made into fibers and then fabrics.

Manufacturers

As evident by their very name, this segment of the industry is responsible for production. Many manufacturers participate in every phase of the construction operation, including designing the line, purchasing fabrics and trimmings, making patterns, cutting and sewing garments, and ultimately marketing the goods to retailers. Today, many manufacturers, such as Nine West, LaCoste, DKNY, Calvin Klein, and Liz Claiborne, have even opted to do their own retailing.

Although some manufacturers run complete operations from the point of production to consumption, the majority function in a more specialized manner. They might hire freelance designers to create their collections, or even fashion consultants, such as the Fashion Service in New York City or Design Intelligence in London, to design the entire line. Some companies design and do their own cutting and use outside contractors to sew the garments. Others use domestic contractors for all of the operations, while a large percentage utilize offshore and near-shore outsourcing partners to perform the actual manufacturing processes.

Whatever the approach, manufacturers are responsible for all phases of production. Many find the benefits of outside contracting so attractive that they are only directly involved in developing the line and distributing it to retailers.

Some of the smaller manufacturers do not even sell their own lines. Instead, they employ **manufacturer's representatives** to sell for them. Known as "reps" or "jobbers" in the industry, they sell a number of noncompeting lines in their own showrooms. They receive remuneration in the form of commissions from the manufacturers they represent. They are technically classified as **limited-function wholesalers**, but they do not take title to or physically handle the goods as **full-service wholesalers** do in most fields.

The typical wholesale component of other industries is conspicuously absent in the fashion industry. Because the goods are short-lived, they must get to the retailers as quickly as possible and not sit on a middleman's shelves.

An important form of manufacturing in the apparel industry is **licensing**. Licensing is an agreement in which individuals and businesses (the *licensors*) give others (the *licensees*), such as fragrance or home fashion manufacturers, permission to use their names on products and companies for a fee or commission. The practice has grown enormously in the past two decades, enabling well-known designers to expand their influence and gain worldwide recognition. Celebrities, entertainers, and corporations are also involved in licensing agreements.

The practice of designer licensing was initiated in the mid-1960s, with such designers as Pierre Cardin, John Weitz, and Ralph Lauren. Licensing arrangements differ from designer to designer. Some designers demand complete control over the individual designs and the right of refusal for substandard offerings; others merely allow their names to be placed on products without significant personal involvement.

Pierre Cardin, one of the world's most famous fashion designers, used this method to capture the attention of consumers all over the world. He began with menswear but eventually contracted with more than 800 licensees, covering such products as children's wear, eyeglasses, home fashions, hats, shoes, and lingerie to expand his empire. Other famous designers who followed with licensing agreements include Bill Blass, Calvin Klein, Christian Dior, and Donna Karan.

In the mid-2000s celebrity designers, such as Jennifer Lopez, Beyoncé Knowles, Sean "Diddy" Combs, and Russell Simmons, who were never associated with fashion have become important players by designing their own collections and entering into

SEAN "DIDDY" COMBS

Few names have hit the fashion industry with such excitement as has that of Sean "Diddy" Combs, as he is currently known. Whether he is referred to as Sean "Puffy" Combs, P. Diddy, Diddy, or any of the other names he has used, it is his persona and talent that have made him into a household name first for young African Americans and, today, for a more expanded audience. But it wasn't fashion that initially helped him make his mark; it was his entertainment talent.

His early training was with record companies before embarking on a career with Bad Boy Entertainment. Performing as Puff Daddy he popularized the East Coast sound of American hip-hop. With huge commercial hits and Grammys under his belt, he became an international success.

In 1998 he founded Sean John Clothing. It soon became one of the most successful clothing brands ever started by a celebrity, and he was named Best Menswear Designer of 2004 by the prestigious Council of Fashion Designers. Starting out with urban hip-hop clothing, he soon set the standard for the latest trends in that genre. His collection of shirts, jeans, hats, and outerwear was geared to the 12–40 age group. His brand soon started to broaden and now includes fine clothing for the discriminating businessman as well as products that he licenses through other companies.

In 2006, Sean John teamed with Estée Lauder and launched his first fragrance, a road that many designers and celebrities take. Few, however, affected the fragrance industry as he has with his Unforgivable scent for men. The enormity of the launch resulted in sales that were more than 200 percent above expectations, and in fewer than two months it replaced Giorgio Armani's Aqua di Gio as the top-selling men's fragrance in the United States. On the horizon is a women's version of the scent and international launches for both the men's and women's fragrances.

Not one to rest on his laurels, Mr. Combs, whose line is featured in Macy's and other well-known retail establishments, is expanding his own shops, the first of which opened on Fifth Avenue in New York City. Factory outlets bearing his name are also opening in Las Vegas and Sawgrass Mils, a mammoth outlet facility in a suburb of Fort Lauderdale, Florida, among other locations.

The marquee status of Sean "Diddy" Combs helped make Sean John a success.

It should be noted that although his fashion career is bringing him accolades, he is still involved in the entertainment industry. His most recent venture is the filming of *A Raisin in the Sun*, in which he again plays a central role, as he did in the Broadway production in 2004.

licensing agreements to expand their product offerings. An exploration of the Sean "Diddy" Combs and the Sean John Clothing empire is presented in a World of Fashion Profile.

Retailer

Once the manufacturers have met their responsibility in the fashion chain, they sell their products to an assortment of **retailers**, who market these goods to customers. Although traditional retailers, such as department or specialty stores, long had a monopoly on fashion merchandise, there is now a great deal of competition from nontraditional retailing formats, such as direct-mail companies, home shopping on cable television, and online Internet retailers.

In examining retailing, we run the gamut from the industrial giants to the smallest entrepreneurs. More and more restructuring is occurring because of mergers and

Macy's—the largest store in the world—is a division of Federated Department Stores.

acquisitions. In 1994, Federated Department Stores, which had already acquired such companies as Bloomingdale's and Stern's, acquired Macy's. As a result it became a giant in the industry. In 1995, Federated expanded even further, with the purchase of the Broadway stores on the West Coast. Today, Federated has become the ultimate department-store retailer with its acquisitions of such organizations as May Company for $17 billion in 2005 and Marshall Fields in 2006, with their units now operating under the Macy's banner.

Even the methods of conducting business are constantly changing. For example, Sears, once a pioneer in the catalog business, has eliminated its general catalog in order to expand its in-store fashion merchandise business. It is also de-emphasizing its private labels in favor of more nationally recognized brands. Sears Holding, owner of Sears, added the Kmart stores to its roster in the mid-2000s, making it an even bigger player in retailing.

The field has also experimented with several new concepts. They include the **spin-off stores**, which are specialty shops featuring a specific collection of the parent department store. Examples of these separate shops include Macy's Charter Club and subspecialty units, exemplified by the Knot Shop, that feature a defined or limited merchandise assortment. Other types of retailing include manufacturer's and designer **outlets**. Originally intended as an alternative for designers and manufacturers to dispose of leftover merchandise, these outlets are now used by such names as DKNY, Ralph Lauren, Gucci, Alexander Julian, and Anne Klein to sell additional merchandise. **Off-price discounters**, such as Marshalls, Kids "R" Us, and Syms, offer manufacturers' irregulars, seconds, closeout goods, canceled orders, overruns, and goods returned by other retailers. These outlets also offer brand-name apparel and accessories at a fraction of their regular selling prices.

The majority of fashion merchandise carried by the retailer is purchased from manufacturers. Today, however, stores manufacture their own goods or have manufacturers produce goods exclusively for them. These products are known as **private**

Mall of America is a mega-mall combining shopping and entertainment.

label merchandise. Private label merchandise sometimes is the only merchandise carried by the retail store in which it is sold, such as Gap, Banana Republic, or The Limited, and is known as "The Store Is the Brand" merchandising. The exclusivity gives retailers an edge on the competition and offers the potential for greater profits, better gross margin, and image enhancement.

The retail business is conducted in a host of venues. The most conventional are downtown or central districts, where most department stores operate their **flagship** or main stores, and the suburban **shopping malls**, which continue to increase in size. Some, such as the Mall of America in Bloomington, Minnesota, are combinations of shopping and entertainment centers. Its success has prompted its expansion over the past several years. Another shopping arena is the **festival marketplace**, which is usually a location once used for other purposes but now transformed into a shopping center that features unique surroundings. Examples are Union Station in St. Louis, South Street Seaport in New York City, and Quincy Market in Boston. Still other venues include **vertical malls**, such as Water Tower in Chicago, which reaches skyward because of the limited space in the downtown area; **enclosed outlet centers**, such as Gurnee Mills outside of Chicago and Sawgrass Mills in Ft. Lauderdale; and **fashion streets**, such as Worth Avenue in Palm Beach, Madison Avenue in New York City, and Rodeo Drive in Beverly Hills, where the most fashionable shops cater to the richest consumers. **Power centers**, where such giants as T.J. Maxx and Marshalls dispose of fashion as well as other merchandise at rock-bottom prices in stores that span several thousand feet, complete the types of venues used for fashion retailing.

Retailing formats also include *leased departments* and *franchises*. Although these formats are explored fully in Chapter 21, their importance warrants definition and a brief mention in this introduction.

Leased departments, owned by outside companies, are operated as departments within a retail store. Leased departments often include restaurants, shoe shops, and

BENETTON

Founded in Treviso, Italy, in 1964 by a sister and three brothers, the Benetton Company has become the most important of the globally positioned fashion franchises. It all began when the sister sold her bicycle to buy a knitting machine on which she could develop unusual patterns. Few could then have imagined that this would be the beginning of a company that would have a sales volume of close to $2.2 billion by 2006.

Initially, the family sold sweaters to local merchants. When the demand increased dramatically, the family decided to enter the retail business. Ten years after the first store opened in 1968, Benetton was operating 1,000 retail outlets in Italy. Today, the product line, which is designed by 200 designers who produce 2,600 styles in 250 different colors, is marketed through 7,000 stores in 100 countries around the world, with the majority in Italy and other European nations. Other stores are in the United States, Canada, South America, Japan, Turkey, Egypt, and Mexico, with China and India gaining visibility for the company as these countries are seen as emerging markets. The stores are either company owned or franchised.

At the beginning of this millennium, Benetton had expanded into the "megastore" concept in the United States.

To keep up with the demand for its products, the company has equipped its facilities with state-of-the-art technology. In addition to completely computerized cutting procedures, the company employs a robot packing system in its warehouses that can ship 35,000 boxes in a single day. Seamless knitting is the method used in knitwear construction, eliminating the need for any sewing in these garments.

To quickly respond to the demands of its retail network, Benetton can ship orders within eight days of their receipt. To guarantee the availability of the colors needed by the stores, merchandise is produced as gray goods and dyed in any of the 250 colors it features.

Benetton has made certain that its appeal is globally appropriate by studying the cultures of every country in the world and producing items that would fit within these cultures. The prices charged by the franchisees are suggested by the Benetton organization, but they may be adjusted as the individual franchisees wish.

The company's advertising campaigns attracted attention throughout the world. Its magazine and television advertisements touched many social issues in a controversial way. Photographs of AIDS patients at their last stages of life and the faces of starving children are just a few of the images used. Today, however, their communications direction has shifted to a tamer commercial approach.

Given the worldwide success of its lines, Benetton has demonstrated that international franchising can be successfully accomplished in the fashion industry. It also should be acknowledged that the total worth of the family is estimated at $10 billion, with a large percentage coming from investments made from the sportswear collections into telecommunications, utilities, restaurants, and other businesses.

Today, Luciano, the group's chairman, and his three siblings are still in control of the empire, with day-to-day CEO Silvano Cassano exercising more autonomy. The taking over of the business is expected to be by Luciano's son, although no date has been set for the change.

fine jewelry departments. An example is Revillon Furs of New York, which operates inside Saks Fifth Avenue.

Franchising is a contractual arrangement that permits an individual (the *franchisee*) to operate a business under the recognizable name of an individual or company (the *franchisor*). Franchising plays a significant role in the fast-food industry, where companies such as McDonald's and Burger King sell the rights to use their names to individuals. The franchisee pays a fee to the franchisor. In addition to the monetary requirement, the franchisees are required to purchase all products and supplies developed by the franchisor. In the fast-food industry, for example, everything from the meat patties to the paper plates on which they are served is specified in the franchise contracts. In the fashion arena, there are franchised units under names such as Ralph Lauren, Yves Saint Laurent, and Lady Madonna. International franchising is growing in the fashion industry. One of the global leaders in franchising—Benetton—is explored in a World of Fashion Profile.

Retail organizations and methods of operation are constantly being restructured to meet the challenges of today's demanding consumer. The methodology employed by today's retailers will be fully explored in Chapter 21.

Fashion Communications

Designing the most exciting collection or operating the most fashion-forward retail enterprise in no way guarantees recognition and success. The messages about the creative new designer, a revolutionizing breakthrough in fiber development, or a new approach to personalized shopping by a retailer only reach the appropriate markets if the **media** choose to pass them on.

Every company in the fashion industry uses either its own advertising or public relations department or outside resources to get its name into print or broadcasting outlets. Publicists write scores of press releases and articles that extol the virtues of those they represent, and they prepare media kits consisting of releases, photographs, and any other material that might motivate the editorial staffs of the media to convey their messages.

The targets of these publicity releases are consumer magazines, such as *GQ, Elle, Harper's Bazaar*, and *Vogue*, as well as trade periodicals such as *Women's Wear Daily* and *California Apparel News*. They are also directed to such alternative offerings as MTV's *House of Style*, which offered news about fashion, lifestyles, and celebrities to a younger market before its cancellation in 2000.

Original television programming and even movies have also peaked the interest of consumers. Programs such as *Project Runway* and *Extreme Makeover* have attracted significant audiences to the world of fashion. In 2006, the highly successful film *The Devil Wears Prada* brought the fashion industry and all of its glamour to the public's attention. With a no-holds-barred approach it also carefully detailed the unscrupulous and manipulative ways in which the business often operates. It gave the everyday consumer a real-life look at fashion and shed light on the industry.

In the fashion industry, there are those whose endorsements often catapult designers into the limelight. One of the most powerful names is Anna Wintour of

Movies such as *The Devil Wears Prada* bring the fashion industry great attention.

the world of fashion profile

DIANA VREELAND

It was the outbreak of World War I that brought eight-year-old Diana from Paris to the United States. In Paris, she had lived in a world in which art, culture, and fashion played dominant roles. Her parents knew such people as Diaghilev and Nijinsky. As a result young Diana felt comfortable mingling in a society that was open to only a few.

In 1924 she married Thomas Vreeland. When they moved to New York City in 1937, Diana accepted a position at *Harper's Bazaar* that was offered to her by then fashion editor Carmel Snow.

Although most people outside of the industry believe that a sure ticket to the inner circles begins with "natural beauty," Vreeland often regarded herself as an ugly duckling. Lacking the conventional beauty often associated with those in fashion, she chose to create a persona that epitomized individuality and style.

She had short black hair, rouged cheeks, and bright red lips that set her apart from the rest. Her writing style was as unique as her dress. In 1939 she became fashion editor, working with Mrs. Snow and Alexey Brodovitch, the art director. In 1963 she left *Bazaar* to work as associate editor at *Vogue*; she later became editor-in-chief, a position she held until 1971.

Unlike those who merely reported on the fashion scene, Vreeland was a significant promoter. Whenever she felt something was important, she prominently placed it in her columns.

From 1972 to 1989 she served as consultant to the Costume Institute of the Metropolitan Museum of Art. Exhibits such as Balenciaga, American Women of Style, Yves Saint Laurent, and The Glory of Russian Costume, to name a few, were among the fashion subjects covered during her tenure at the museum.

Diana Vreeland was one of the most influential people in fashion history.

She was long considered one of the leading players in the fashion industry.

Condé Nast. Former media giants who are worthy of mention here include fashion editors of *Harper's Bazaar* Carmel Snow, from 1932 to 1957; Liz Tilberis, from 1992 to 1999; and Diana Vreeland, who was fashion editor at *Bazaar* from 1937 until 1963 and at *Vogue* from 1963 to 1971. Vreeland's background and influence on fashion is the subject of a World of Fashion Profile.

The subject of fashion communications is explored in depth in Chapter 22.

Market Consultants

A host of different businesses interact with designers, manufacturers, and retailers to assist with the decision-making process. They include *fashion forecasters, resident buying offices*, and *reporting services*. These **market consultants** provide their own expertise and help lead clients in the right direction. Each of these marketing consultants is discussed in detail in Chapter 20.

Briefly, the **fashion forecaster** is someone who, like a weather forecaster, makes predictions long before the designer sets out on the path to creating a new collection. These professionals work as far as 18 months in advance of a season and provide information that helps their clients develop merchandise. By thoroughly investigating some of the primary markets, such as textiles, the forecaster is able to guide designers and manufacturers in their selections of color, texture, styles, and so on. Visiting and analyzing the worldwide fashion centers also enables the fashion forecaster

Fashion magazines help disseminate news of current trends to consumers.

to predict what styles will more than likely appeal to the consumer. David Wolfe, a leading forecaster, regularly visits St. Tropez to study what is being worn on the streets.

Resident buying offices (RBOs) are companies located in the wholesale fashion markets, such as New York City's garment center. They are the eyes and ears of store buyers who, because of their distance from the wholesale markets, cannot make the frequent visits necessary to assess what is new in the industry. RBOs, of which the Doneger Group is the largest, provide everything the retailer needs to make the appropriate purchasing decisions.

Reporting services are similar to RBOs in that they provide pertinent information to retailers. However, they do not purchase merchandise, as the RBO does. Their forte is mainly information.

Regular interaction among the various industry components assures greater success for each of them. Their cooperative efforts foster a better image for the field of fashion and generally assure a more productive future for those who produce the merchandise.

THE FUTURE OF FASHION

At the outset of the 21st century, the world of fashion continues to change. Traditional rules of the game, which included faithfully following the dictates of specific designers on such issues as dress length, continue to be broken. Although globally renowned designers are still crowding the runways with outrageous styles at prices that only a few can afford, new designers are showing fashions that reflect what is taking place on the streets, in the political arenas, in the entertainment field, and in movements to protect the environment.

From 1922 to 1991, the USSR was ruled by the Communist Party. In 1985, Mikhail Gorbachev began a campaign for the country to improve the economy and lessen social constraints. Finally, in 1991, the Soviet Union collapsed. In Germany, the years of East/West separation came to a sudden halt, as symbolized by the tearing down of the Berlin Wall in 1989 and 1990. Early in the 21st century, American headlines were filled with U.S. involvement in Afghanistan and eventually in Iraq. Dissention between President Bush and many prominent congressional Democrats escalated as the numbers of casualties skyrocketed. At the time of this writing, Americans in ever-increasing numbers were beginning to voice their opposition to the United States' involvement in Iraq and called for its pullout.

In the United States in the 1990s, people turned away from the excesses of the 1980s. They began spending money more cautiously and no longer emphasized extravagance in dress, dining, and living. Instead of boasting about purchases made in upscale boutiques, many who still follow high fashion are heading to "off-price" merchants and letting their peers know about the bargains they found. Of course, today this is not always the case. The country has seemed to become a two-tier nation with the vast majority cautiously spending on fashion merchandise, with a significantly smaller percentage spending extravagantly. Designer boutiques are realizing record sales. Shops in major fashion arenas are springing up bearing couture marquee names that cater to the very wealthy.

In addition to the traditional bricks-and-mortar shopping, the rapid growth of the Internet has enabled consumers with limited access to the traditional retailing formats to shop for a wide range of products from their homes. Online retailing also offers budding designers and small companies the opportunity to compete with more established names for consumer dollars through low cost advertising and accessibility.

Those in the fashion business are no longer concerned just with silhouette trends and whether short or long hem lengths will be accepted. They are studying people more closely, in every part of the globe, to learn their style preferences and needs. The streets are providing unlimited ideas to the manufacturers of apparel and accessories. Consider, for example, the biker's leather jacket that turns up as the top of an evening dress; the baseball cap still worn by men, but now with ponytails peeking through the back opening; the exercise clothing that has shifted from the gym to the street; the baggy pants worn very low on the hips and originated by the rappers; the permanent and temporary tattoos that men and women of every age are sporting; and the piercing of parts of the body, in addition to the ears, for the insertion of ornaments. These developments signal that fashion may be born anywhere.

Because designers recognize that fashion is not only for the affluent, they are generating a greater number of **secondary collections**. In the United States, for example, Donna Karan's DKNY line far outsells her designer line. In Europe, the United Kingdom's John Galliano markets a less costly collection, Galliano Girl, and Italy's Franco Moschino produces a line called Cheap & Chic. Others who have taken this

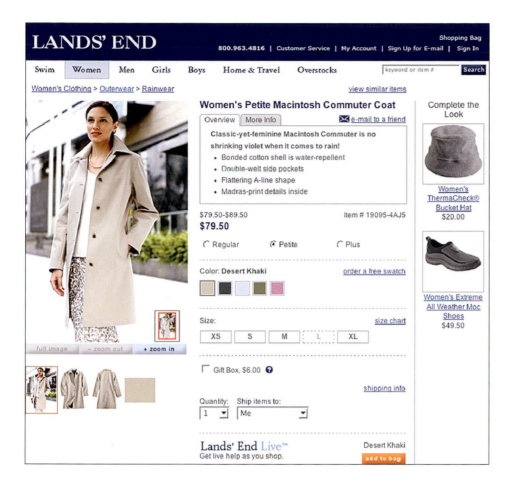

The Internet broadens the consumer market's ability to shop.

road include Bill Blass, Calvin Klein, Sonia Rykiel, Giorgio Armani, and Jean Paul Gaultier. Many of the couture and upscale collections, such as Karl Lagerfeld and Stella McCartney, have joined forces with the likes of H&M and are making their labels available, albeit designs that are far from the couturier collections, and are capturing the attention of the budget-minded crowd that adores fashion.

Fashion continues to expand its horizons with the recognition of designers who have emerged from a variety of ethnic backgrounds. Each brings his or her own experiences to the collections. Rei Kawakubo from Japan continues to capture the attention of fashion's editorial press and the public with avant-garde designs marketed by her own company, Comme des Garçons. Yohji Yamamoto, also from Japan, specializes in oversize clothing in a variety of textures. African-American designer Tracy Reese's lively interpretations reflect her interest in theater, dance, and music. In addition, new corners of the globe are having an impact on fashion. Yeohlee Teng, from Malaysia, uses clear lines and geometric forms for better-priced apparel. Teng and another Malaysian, Yuki (Gnyuki Torimaru), whose designs often feature bias-cut, dramatic silhouettes, are making that part of the world better known to fashion. Gemma Kahng, from South Korea, employs unusual ornamentation and detailing in her collections. Each of these designers has demonstrated that fashion creativity no longer resides exclusively within traditional boundaries.

Another wave of excitement has been the entry of celebrities in the fashion world who have made their marks with their own fashion collections. Leading the pack

Designers' secondary collections (left) far outsell their designer lines (right). Shown here are two lines by Ralph Lauren.

with women's designs are Beyoncé Knowles, Jessica Simpson, Jennifer Lopez, and Nicky Hilton. For men, Sean "Diddy" Combs has created a collection that is capturing significant attention under the Sean John label. Along with his label is the Phat Fashion merchandise, spearheaded by Russell Simmons.

To enhance the fashion designer's creative instincts, the fiber manufacturers have provided a host of products. Lycra spandex is being used in conjunction with natural and manufactured fibers to enhance function as well as beauty, and Teflon, once reserved for the coating on pots and pans, is applied to textiles earmarked for ski parkas, raincoats, and sportswear, as well as to textiles slated for home fashions. Microfibers continue to challenge the luxurious feel of silk, and polyester, in general, has lost its bad reputation and has become a more popular fiber in the apparel industry. The development of new fibers continues, including fibers manufactured from natural materials, such as lyocel (Tencel). New durable press treatments to textiles now permit apparel products to be labelled as "wrinkle-free," "wrinkle resistant," "no-iron," or simply "WR."

Every segment of the fashion industry, from the production of raw materials to the final distribution to the consumer, takes advantage of ever-improving technological discoveries. The most notable are the newest **CAD (computer-aided design) systems**, which eliminate the need for endless paper patterns and the time spent by the designer creating them at the drafting table. Other electronic applications, however, are moving the fashion industry into areas that not long ago seemed like fantasy.

For example, providing **online computer services** has enormous implications for fiber producers, end-product manufacturers, market consultants, retailers, and promoters of fashion. The Internet has gained prominence as a vehicle for communicating, advertising, and selling to suppliers and customers. Information about major retailers is available online. Individuals can download pictures of merchandise over their modem lines and place orders or ask questions via e-mail. Further examples and explanations of the applications of online services are covered in the appropriate chapters.

Another time- and money-saving invention is the use of the fax machine to disseminate designs in a matter of seconds, enabling one that originates in one country to be quickly copied in another. By transmitting the design electronically, the time and effort needed for traditional transmission is eliminated.

No one can predict the future of fashion—who the major players will be or how successful styles will become. By examining the past, one may begin to understand what this industry is all about and the number of variables that interact in the marketplace. Fashion forecasters research consumer preferences and motives. These studies influence the entire fashion industry. This process begins with the textile producers, who generate the fabrics used by the designers and manufacturers to produce apparel and accessories. These decisions influence the trimmings industry, which creates the little "extras" that change a conventional product into one with more appeal; the market consultants, such as the resident buying offices, that help retailers with purchasing decisions; the store buyers, who must make the selections; the visual merchandisers, who display fashion to its best advantage; the fashion promoters, who create special events for professionals and consumers; and the editorial press, which may help to arouse interest in or destroy a particular fashion.

Many people—some famous, some unknown—impact the fashion industry. For example, anyone interested in fashion knows the names of such contemporary designers as Donna Karan, Ralph Lauren, and Calvin Klein and past legends such as Chanel, Balenciaga, and Dior. But who can name a well-known patternmaker, sewer, or trimmer? Although the former group steals the fashion headlines, the designers alone do not create fashion.

Celebrity-designed collections, such as Jennifer Lopez's JLO, play an important role in today's fashion industry.

THE "ENEMY" OF FASHION

While most years generate some degree of excitement in this ever-challenging arena, often a negative force causes unrest as well as a drain on profits for the industry. One recurring theme is the counterfeiting of brands. Whether it is the sunglasses and handbags that are sold from street vendors' carts, back-alley lofts in seedy buildings, or "garages" that are set up to market the fakes and pass them off as the real thing, the practice has reached epidemic proportions. Today, it is estimated that these products account for approximately $600 billion in annual sales across the globe. The fakes sport labels such as Louis Vuitton, Prada, Gucci, Fendi, Coach, Calvin Klein, and any others that the consumer is willing to buy in large quantities.

Fashion signature fakes are reaching epidemic proportions.

In addition to the aforementioned sales venues, the Internet is playing a major role in the marketing of the fakes. For example, eBay accounts for an enormous amount of sales of counterfeit fashion products. Although the company vows to fight the frauds, little has been done to stop the action.

In the global marketplace, where the problem has significantly expanded, the federal government has unsuccessfully tried to curtail the practice. From international litigation at the the World Trade Organization (WTO) to the seizing of goods at border crossings, the hope is that the practice will stop. At this point in time, however, it is still a losing battle for the industry.

THE RISING STARS OF DESIGN

The names that capture the attention of fashion consumers seem to be around for many years, even decades. Whether it is the designers themselves who are still turning out styles that motivate the shopper to purchase, or their design houses when they have been long gone from the scene, names such as Ralph Lauren, Donna Karan, Calvin Klein, Gianni Versace, Coco Chanel, and Yves Saint Laurent still make the headlines. At the same time, it is a field that also introduces new talent every year with the hope that some will emerge as the designers of the future.

The names that make up the list of these hopefuls are at different points in their careers. Some have begun to make their marks, while others are considered to have great potential as the new Lauren or Chanel. Based on expectations and awards from such groups as Ecco Domani with its Fashion Foundation awards, Fashion Group International, and other predictors of fashion, the list, by

Designer hopefuls, such as Derek Lam, are the wave of fashion's future.

no means complete, includes Derek Lam, Doo-Ri Chung, Behnaz Sarafpour, Jack McCollough, Lazaro Hernandez, Laura and Kate Mulleavy, Thakoon Panichgul, Maria Cornejo, Lela Rose, Candice Held, Philippe Naouri, Alexandre Caugant, Kerry Cushman, Alison Zimmerman, Koji Sato, Katia Gomiashvili, Jonathan Riss, Claudia Rosa Lukas, Gemma Kahng, Brian Reves, Sari Gueron, and Frankie Xie.

Only time will tell if the industry's predictors were right.

CHAPTER HIGHLIGHTS

- The evolution of fashion began with the individual dressmaker, who designed clothing for the nobility.

- Fashion reached its present state only after the invention of time-saving machines that made the mass production of ready-to-wear apparel practical.

- The industry grew by employing immigrants who worked for low wages under poor conditions. In the early 1900s, conditions led to the formation of unions, notably the ILGWU and the Amalgamated.

- Increased output led retailers to expand their operations to reach more consumers. In addition to limited-line stores, consumers could now shop in chain stores and department stores, as well as through mail-order catalogs.

- The Internet continues the trend toward multiple-channel retailing formats, with both cataloguers and traditional retailers serving their customers through online Web sites. Shoppers may either go directly to their favorite Web site, or may access any number of them by logging on to search engines, such as Aol.com, Google.com, and Yahoo.com.

- Fashion is now influenced by social and political developments, as well as by the preferences of fashion leaders.

- To meet the demands of economically cautious consumers, designers are developing less-expensive secondary lines.

- The fashion industry is composed of textile producers, manufacturers, retailers, media, and market consultants.

IMPORTANT FASHION TERMINOLOGY AND CONCEPTS

ACTWU	full-service wholesalers	power loom
Amalgamated	ILGWU	private label merchandise
CAD systems	leased departments	reporting service
catalog	licensing	resident buying office
chain store	limited-function wholesalers	retailers
cotton gin	limited-line stores	secondary collections
couturier	look for the union label	sewing machine
department stores	mail-order	shopping malls
designers	manufacturer's	specialty stores
enclosed outlet centers	representative	spinning jenny
fashion forcaster	market consultant	spinoff stores
fashion streets	media	sweatshops
festival marketplace	off-price discounters	textiles
flagship stores	online computer services	vertical company
flying shuttle	outlets	vertical malls
franchising	power centers	

FOR REVIEW

1. Who was the first person in fashion design with a specific clientele?

2. What were five inventions of the Industrial Revolution that led to mass production of apparel?

3. Who were the first workers in New York City's garment center? How did they manage to improve the sweatshop conditions?

4. Which segment of the fashion industry is represented by the Amalgamated?

5. Discuss the concept of licensing and how it has helped some designers prosper.

6. Name an important international franchise operation. Describe how it can react to orders as quickly as it does.

7. List some retailing formats.

8. What are the new rules of the fashion game?

9. What benefits do online computer services provide to the fashion industry?

10. Discuss the role of the media in the fashion world.

11. How do market consultants assist those in the fashion world?

12. Why have some upscale designers chosen to produce secondary collections in addition to their higher-priced lines?

13. How did the movie *The Devil Wears Prada* depict the fashion industry?

14. How has counterfeiting affected the fashion industry?

15. According to the Point of View article, how are counterfeit products affecting the fashion industry?

EXERCISES AND PROJECTS

1. Contact the Singer Sewing Machine Company requesting photographs and information on the history of sewing machines. Using the information, prepare a written report on the various advances in the field from the first machine to the most recent.

2. Select a specific type of retailer, such as an off-price discounter or manufacturer outlet, and trace its history. Concentrate on a well-known store in the selected category.

3. Contact one of the online service companies such as AOL, Prodigy, or CompuServe, and obtain examples of the type of information it provides to one component of the fashion industry, such as designers or retailers.

WEB SITES

By accessing these Web sites, you will be able to gain broader knowledge and up-to-date information on materials related to this chapter.

Union of Needletrades, Industrial and Textile Employees
   www.uniteunion.org
Stylish Vintage Fashion, Clothing and Nostalgia
   www.fashiondig.com

The Case of the Successful Designer

Nancy Park, a young South Korean designer, received positive reviews from the fashion press for her collections designed under the Bravo label. In just four years, Park worked her way up from design assistant to head designer. In that position, she has been responsible for the company's offerings for the past two years. With a flair that is both whimsical and fluid, she is steadily gaining popularity in the United States. As a result, Bravo's competitors have made offers for her services. In addition, a financial backer has offered to finance Park in her own fashion business. Although Bravo has offered to match the salaries proposed by the competitors, it would not give Park a merchandise line with her own name. Unable to come to terms with her employer, Park has submitted her resignation and is now weighing numerous offers being presented to her.

Didier Ltd., a dress manufacturer, has offered to make her the head designer at a guaranteed salary plus 20 percent of sales. Her name would be on a label that reads "Didier Ltd., designed by Nancy Park."

Signal Fashions is a company that manufactures under its own label but also produces lines that bear the names of well-known designers via licensing agreements. Signal has offered a contract to Park that would create a separate division that would have only her name on every label. She would have complete design control, a salary triple her already excellent income, and the potential for part ownership in the company if the line was successful for two years.

Invest Associates, a financial backer with investments in five well-known couture operations, has offered capital that would establish Park in her own first-class fashion business. The deal promises to finance two collections, make available contracting facilities enjoyed by its other interests, and give Park 50 percent of the profits. The label would feature Park's name, and she would have ultimate control over the company's design approaches.

With time drawing near for a decision, Nancy Park is still weighing the merits of each offer.

questions

1. What are the advantages and disadvantages of each offer?
2. Which offer do you think Park should accept? Why?

Global Marketplace Expands Landscape of Counterfeiting

EVAN CLARK

Washington—The Bush administration is wielding an array of weapons in its effort to crack down on fakes, from including intellectual property provisions in trade agreements to seizing goods at the border.

But a trio of Cabinet-level officials speaking at the U.S. Chamber of Commerce's "Countering Global Counterfeiting and Piracy" conference here last week said that despite these measures, intellectual property protection will continue to be a pervasive problem as the global market expands.

Fake goods cost U.S. companies between $200 billion and $250 billion annually and are responsible for the loss of more than 750,000 jobs, according to government estimates. Fashion firms, especially those in the luxury sector where brand name is paramount, have long grappled with the illicit competition.

Commerce Secretary Carlos Gutierrez, U.S. Trade Representative Susan Schwab, and Attorney General Alberto Gonzales addressed the conference, which ran Sept. 28–29, stressing the need for vigilance as the U.S. economy increasingly shifts towards a dependence on innovation and the creation of new technology.

"We're going to make this a priority for many years to come," said Gutierrez. "Globalization just makes the challenge all the more important for our companies. In many ways, ironically, globalization actually facilitates counterfeiting."

As technological advancements and international commerce knit countries closer together, it has become easier to steal other people's ideas.

"Innovation is important today to our economy. It's going to be more important in the future, so intellectual property will be more important as we go forward," said Gutierrez. "We don't treat intellectual property with the rigor that it should have. This is the same as counterfeiting money and it should be treated as such."

The Commerce Department is expanding its intellectual property attaché program, devoting more people and resources to focus on the issue in China, Brazil, Russia, India and elsewhere. Last year, Chris Israel was named the first U.S. coordinator for international intellectual property enforcement to help make sure the various parts of the administration are on the same page.

When other countries prove to be ineffective at protecting intellectual property rights, the U.S. Trade Representative's Office bears part of the responsibility for putting them on track.

"Our enforcement tools range from jawboning at one end to litigation at the [World Trade Organization] and retaliation at the other," said Schwab.

Countries found to be in violation of WTO rules are subject to increased tariffs, or "retaliation," in order to offset the impact of the offense. The agency also negotiates trade pacts, in which it inserts protections for brands and copyrights.

Figuring prominently in the agency's Special 301 report, which Schwab described as an "annual report card on bad actors," were China and Russia. She acknowledged China has made a "fair amount of progress," particularly in the rules area, but lacks follow-through.

"It's all well and good to have the right rules and procedures," she said. "But if you don't have enforcement mechanisms backing them up, the best-laid intentions and best laws and regulations in the world aren't going to help you."

China, which produces a third of all apparel and textiles imported to the U.S., is also the place of origin for 63 to 70 percent of the goods seized at the U.S. border for infringing on intellectual property rights, she noted.

Having already done a fair amount of jawboning, Schwab said it might be time to get tough with China.

"One of the possibilities we've been looking at is taking a case against China to the WTO on intellectual property," said Schwab.

This has its pitfalls, however, since bringing a case to the global body and winning the right to impose retaliatory tariffs does not directly impact counterfeits.

"We will be successful when other countries are convinced that it is in their own best interest to protect the intellectual property of goods that are sold and produced in their countries," she said.

Nils Montan, president of the International AntiCounterfeiting Coalition, said the U.S. approach to the problem of counterfeiting is comprehensive in theory, if not as comprehensive in the results it produces.

"More money needs to be placed on the issue," said Montan, who attended the conference and wants to see more attention paid to keep counterfeits out at the border. "Just because we have a few people coordinating doesn't mean we're putting the resources there."

Still, Montan said the Bush administration deserves "good marks" for its work with China. Looking to the future, the country's top lawman is also trying to get laws with a sharper bite to ward off counterfeiters.

"We are seeking legislation that would, among other things, increase penalties for intellectual property crimes, clarify that registration of a copyright is not required for a criminal prosecution, make attempts to commit copyright infringement a crime, and increase the

tools investigators have at their disposal to track potential intellectual property crimes," said Gonzales, in prepared remarks.

"The theft of intellectual property is not just a cheap bootleg movie or an imitation Gucci bag sold on the street corner, what some might see as a harmless distraction," he said. "Stealing is stealing."

Women's Wear Daily, October 3, 2006

Ethical Fashion Goes Mainstream

ELLEN GROVES

Forget hippy—ethical fashion is hip. Retailer interest in apparel brands that guarantee workers' rights and are environmentally friendly has reached such a peak that manufacturers now worry whether they can keep up with demand.

Until recently relegated to the fringes of the fashion world, ethical brands are fast becoming more mainstream. Widespread media coverage of the movement—plus platforms at events like Paris's Prêt-à-Porter trade show and London Fashion Week—have raised the profile of ethical fashion, so designers are becoming less concerned about how to find distribution than how to manage big orders.

"I don't know how we'll do the quantities," said Peruvian-born designer Judith Condor-Vidal, whose clothing and accessories made by 26 fair-trade cooperatives in South America and Asia will feature in PPR-owned La Redoute's winter 2007 catalogue.

As well as La Redoute, the ethical fashion movement has succeeded in capturing the attention of a broad spectrum

of retailers, including high-end specialty chains.

"We've been watching this movement, looking at eco-type brands which have a strong fashion statement first," said Barbara Atkin, fashion director at Canada's Holt Renfrew, which has picked up Danish socially conscious brand Noir for spring.

"We're of the opinion that you can be fashionable and care about the world," added Averyl Oates, buying director at Harvey Nichols. The British retailer is hunting for other brands to stock alongside Noir, which it has carried for two seasons, and Edun, which it picked up this year. Edun is the socially conscious clothing brand created by Ali Hewson, Bono, and designer Rogan Gregory.

"Provenance is key for consumers," Oates said. "We're finding that like the food market, in the same way as people want to know where their chicken is from, they want to know where their clothes come from."

Sales of ethically sourced clothing, which includes organic cotton, fair-trade

clothes, and recycled items, grew 30 percent in the U.K. to 43 million pounds, or $81 million at current exchange, in 2004, according to the Co-operative Bank's Ethical Consumerism report. Meanwhile, ethically motivated secondhand clothing purchases increased 42 percent to 383 million pounds, or $718 million.

While more recent statistics are not yet available, this year's Ethical Fashion Show, which took place in Paris from Oct. 13 to 16, suggests that growth isn't likely to slow anytime soon. More than 4,000 visitors, including scores of international media, attended the four-day event, a 54 percent jump over 2005. Featuring 60 brands from five continents, the third edition of the trade fair demonstrated how much the ethical category has diversified over the last year. Literally combining grassroots and high-end, designers ranged from newcomers like Yagan, a Chilean jewelry brand made from woven grass reeds, to better-known names such as Edun.

In addition to carrying ethical brands, major retailers are recruiting designers to make collections exclusively for them. La Redoute, for example, has carried its own fair-trade collection for two seasons and this year awarded two designers at the Ethical Fashion Show the opportunity to develop items for its winter 2007–2008 catalogue. Items by the winners, Brazilian brand Tudo Born and Judith Condor-Vidal, will be available to La Redoute's 13 million subscribers next June. While Condor-Vidal had initial concerns about how she'll manage the orders, the designer, who is a member of the International Fairtrade Association and the U.K.'s Ethical Fashion Forum (EFF), is also an economist.

"It's an amazing opportunity. If big companies buy it, there is a much bigger impact," she said. "If I can help more people, well, that's my role."

Condor-Vidal has begun another partnership with hot U.K. retailer Topshop. The chain will take a collection of Bolivian waistcoats shunned by other retailers that have been redesigned by fashion students to create a line of handbags for spring-summer.

And Topshop announced at the Ethical Fashion Show that the winning designs of a Design 4 Life Ghana competition it supported are to be retailed at the chain. The competition was run by EFF in collaboration with the nongovernmental organization Tabeisa. The two winners' batik dresses, produced by Women in Progress, a Ghana-based fair-trade cooperative, will be available this spring.

"EFF on this occasion brought Topshop buyers to the table initially as judges," explained Elizabeth Laskar, director of global communications and events at EFF. "Through dialogue, this led to an even more positive outcome."

The backing of the fast-fashion retailer has lent kudos to the term "ethical" and given new confidence to aspiring designers hoping to tap into demand for fashion-forward yet ethical clothing and accessories.

"Brands need to tell a compelling story," said Holt Renfrew's Atkin. "But consumers have to love it and be drawn to it first. Then when they find out that by buying [a brand] they are making a difference, they feel great."

Those were the motivations behind Numanu Label of Love, a collection created using fair-trade and organic silk, cotton, and wool, which will open a freestanding boutique in Paris's lively Marais neighborhood next month.

Founded by Anglo-French couple Olivia Lalonde and Emmanuel Walliser, the brand is designed "to attract people who are maybe less informed about fair trade who just like the clothes," according to Lalonde.

Consumers then find out that by buying a silk top, they have helped support marginalized communities in India and Cambodia. Lalonde's former career as a children's rights campaigner and Walliser's as an international banker makes for a formidable business objective: "To create as big a commercial base for Numanu as possible in order to maintain sustainable incomes for the largest number of people," Lalonde explained. The brand, which won the Ethical Fashion Show 2006 award, donated two-thirds of its prize money to its cooperatives.

Likewise Les Racines du Ciel (The Roots of the Sky, in English), a year-old brand, takes its name from a 1956 novel by Romain Gary about the environment. The moniker is meant to highlight its commitment to environmental issues. Yet the quality and softness of the recycled kimonos, silk and organic cotton tops, in soft pinks and grays, are designed to draw a fashion-conscious customer who might be surprised to learn the items are naturally dyed with sweet potatoes and mud.

Nathalie Goyette, the brand's development manager, first saw the natural dyeing techniques when on a trip to China years ago. She kept some material, and a chance meeting with a Chinese student in France connected her to a supplier who helped create the environmentally sound collection. Demand has since boomed. "I started out ordering 50 meters of fabric, and now it's more than 1,000," she said.

Similarly, the founders of six-month-old brand Fées de Bengale (Fairies of Bengal in English) place fashion and ethics on a level footing. Their feminine collection of organic silk and cotton tops targets concept stores and ethically focused boutiques, yet the brand's name conjures up images of the women who hand-sew the collection in India.

"It's a mutual exchange. We wanted to make the most of the women's savoir faire," said Elodie Le Derf, the brand's stylist who previously worked at Vanessa Bruno, explaining the couturiers give them feedback and ideas for designs.

Art. 23, founded by the French Fair Trade Co. in September, is also aiming for a chic yet caring image. The trendy collection of minimalist shirtdresses and tuxedo-inspired shirts was designed by Adam Love, who has worked with Karl Lagerfeld and Antik Batik, yet its name pays homage to its social commitments, providing a decent living for the disadvantaged women who make it in India. Referring to Article 23, the universal declaration of human rights, "immediately prompts consumers to think of the respect of human rights," said Art. 23 commercial director Marie Mamgioglou.

As ethical brands multiply both in number and in style, not to mention marketing savvy, so do calls for greater transparency across the entire supply chain. Participants at this year's Ethical Fashion Show had to answer a nine-page questionnaire covering environmental issues and workers' rights, as well as social and business objectives. Each brand's ethical claims were then identified for buyers, either fair trade, traditional skills, recycling, organic, or social projects.

Show organizer Isabelle Quéhé said deciding on a definition of what is in fact ethical is problematic. For Quéhé, pure silk ready-to-wear pieces and evening gowns from designer Torgo based on traditional Mongolian costumes epitomize what is ethical.

"It's about promoting the traditions in less-wealthy southern countries, where the older generation is dying—and that savoir faire with them," she said.

Equally, designers using recycled materials, such as Bilum, which makes funky bags from advertising posters and seat belts, fit her definition. And for the first time the show featured a Canadian designer who employs recycled fur. Quéhé's reasoning: "If it wasn't reused, it would be thrown away in land-fill sites. It's less polluting to recycle it."

The more the ethical clothing category continues to grow, the less it seems another passing fad.

"[Ethics] are part and parcel of modern life," said Harvey Nichols' Oates, pointing to the popularity of Al Gore's documentary on the environment, "An Inconvenient Truth," as evidence of growing sensibilities. "We are not saying that fashion is going to change the world," said Quéhé, "but these amazing stories are just many more drops in the ocean."

Women's Wear Daily, October 31, 2006

Pierre Cardin Museum Chronicles a Legend

ROBERT MURPHY

Paris—Pierre Cardin was like a kid in a candy shop during a preview of the museum dedicated to his 60-year-long career. It opens to the public today.

The 83-year-old couturier rifled through a display cabinet jam-packed with accessories, trying on necklaces and hats while explaining the creative provenance of each.

"This one is from the Seventies, in plastic," he said, holding up a necklace of cascading puzzle-like pieces in front of his double-breasted navy blazer. "You were meant to wear it with a bodysuit leotard—nothing else. You put it on and—voilà—you were dressed. Pretty gutsy, no? I asked Cartier to make it for me and they told me I was crazy."

Cardin said the museum, located in a former garage in the northern Paris suburb of Saint Ouen, would be open three afternoons a week, on Wednesdays, Saturdays, and Sundays. Scholars can visit by appointment.

More than 1,000 pieces are stocked in the archives, with about 140 women's and men's garments on view alongside a

smattering of furniture and a roomful of accessories.

"Now that I'm coming to the end of my career, I want to show people what I've brought to fashion," explained Cardin of his motivation.

"I've never copied anyone," he continued. "Just to look at this [museum] is proof of that. It's difficult to have personality. Anyone can have taste. But not everyone can have a point of view.

"What's Chanel, for example?" Cardin asked in a rapid-fire monologue. "It's a tweed suit. And Yves Saint Laurent? What's he known for? The smoking suit? Marlene Dietrich wore smoking suits well before Saint Laurent did them.

"I was inspired by satellites. By lasers. By the moon. I looked into the future. I was never inspired by a woman's body. My dresses are like sculptures. I molded them and then I put a woman into it. It was more like architecture or art.

"As I look over all of these dresses here, I see a continuity of personality. It's all Cardin. It's all sculpture. It's art."

Cardin has arranged the collection chronologically, starting with his first creations right after he left Christian Dior to strike out on his own. He admitted a pleated red wool coat he created in 1953, for instance, still had traces of Dior's New Look influence. "There's a bit of Balenciaga in it, too. He was my grand master."

But soon after, Cardin said he found his own voice after "a lot of sweat and tears. I spent a lot of sleepless nights in those days. I wanted to be myself."

By the Sixties, he began to be influenced by, as he puts it, "the cosmos."

"One of my dresses from that time was wool formed like a sculpture, as if it had been carved out of marble. These days they make all kinds of incredible [high-tech] cloths. But in those days, I can tell you, it wasn't easy to get the fabric to do that."

Moving to a series of black dresses with metallic necklines from the Seventies, Cardin remembered the grief it took to get them made.

"I loved this idea, of a dress with metal in it, like a necklace holding up the fabric.

But no one would make it. I found a man who made cars to actually get it done."

In the Eighties, he said he was inspired by the innards of computers and radio transistors, which resulted in carapace-like coats and dresses. Later, he worked on blowing up the proportions of the shoulder. "I was inspired by all of those American bodybuilders in the Eighties," he offered.

These days, Cardin said it's mostly nature that he finds intriguing. "I've been to all of the museums in the world," he claimed. "Some people go to find something to copy. I went to make sure I wasn't copying anyone. That's what I understand when I see my work together here. I've always done my own thing."

And he continues to do so. Though speculation surfaces occasionally that Cardin's house is on the block, the feisty couturier has yet to agree to a sale. Sources speculate the snag has been his asking price: close to 1 billion euros, or $1.25 billion. Recently a group of investors headed by the Sultan of Brunei was thought to have made an offer that was turned down.

But then, it doesn't appear that Cardin really wants to sell. He said he just returned from a tour that took him to Qatar, Hong Kong, Taiwan and China.

"I'm not tired," he said. "I can be thankful for that. As long as I feel good, why not continue? I still go to the studio every day when I'm in Paris. One dress a day is what I create. Even on Sundays. People think I'm crazy. But that's my life."

Women's Wear Daily, November 15, 2006

fashions: 1900 to the present

Only the minute and the future are interesting; it exists to be destroyed. If everybody did everything with respect, you'd go nowhere.

KARL LAGERFELD, DESIGNER

During the 20th century, fashion changed significantly. Previously, style and silhouette were dictated by the wealthy. Seamstresses and tailors carried out their client's wishes regardless of their own taste and expertise. It was Charles Frederick Worth who first showed clothing on a mannequin. In 1858, he and his wife opened the first couture house. Other designers who were groundbreakers in the early 1900s are discussed in this chapter.

Although these designers created new and influential styles, their promotion by the fashion industry did not guarantee their success. Other influences on the adoption of a particular fashion include attitudes of the public, social and political issues, technological advances, and world events. Many designers were affected by the social influences and news events of the times in which they worked and produced fashions that reflected these periods. Such events as women's suffrage, World War I, World War II, and the women's rights movement, as well as developments in the world of entertainment, had an impact on women's clothing. For example, women working in factories during World War II wore pants for comfort, a fashion that was adopted for everyday life. Female executives of the 1980s preferred broad-shouldered suit jackets, copied from men's styles, to project the image of equality and power. The tattoos of the 1990s on women's bodies were an expression of individualism.

This chapter discusses the fashions for each decade of the 20th century and the first decade of the 21st century, beginning with 1900 and concluding with the early to mid-2000s, in the following manner:

- *The News of the Times* outlines the various newsworthy events and changes that affected fashion.

- *The Fashions of the Times* examines the specific fashion trends and highlights.

- *The Designers Who Influenced Fashion* provides an overview of those individuals who created the fashions.

After you have completed this chapter, you will be able to discuss:

- Important historical events of the 20th century and how they influenced fashion.

- Different fashion highlights for men, women, and children of the 20th century.

- Important designers of each decade in the 20th century and their influences on fashion.

- Some of the retro looks that surfaced in the 1990s and their sources.

1900–1910

The News of the Times Focused Attention on . . .

the changing role of women. While wealthy women from New York City, London, Vienna, and other cities made their way to the Paris salons of such designers as Paul Poiret to enhance their wardrobes, a new breed of women was emerging. They entered politics, joined clubs, played sports, and went to college. With the expansion of retailing to accommodate the mass production of merchandise that resulted from the Industrial Revolution, many women went to work in the stores and the factories that made these goods as well as continuing to serve the needs of their families. Henry Ford produced his first Model T in 1908.

The Fashions of the Times Were . . .

delicate and still impractical for the changing role of women. Although representing a new era, fashions were a throwback to the late 1800s. A lady's costume was by no means simple. Pinched-in waistlines, exaggerated by tight-fitting corsets, were shown off in one-piece dresses made of chiffon and lace fabrics with leg-of-mutton sleeves and necklines that were characteristically high. The **Gibson Girl look**, born in the 1890s and still very much in evidence, consisted of floor-length skirts and **shirtwaist** blouses. Hats were an integral part of fashion in the 1900s. They were

The Gibson Girl look featured shirt-waist blouses and floor-length skirts.

enormous creations, profusely ornamented with ribbons, feathers, birds, and other elaborate embellishments. Shoes did not play an important role in this decade because the fashions were floor-length. Handbags were small and feminine. Gloves were a significant part of each outfit. Whether it was summer or winter, properly dressed ladies were never without them.

Men had numerous types of outfits, each designed for specific occasions. Upper-class men wore **frock coats** for formal wear and **suits** for less formal situations. The cuts were straight but rather loose-fitting. Laced-up boots were part of every wardrobe, as were **spats** (fabric coverings) worn over regular shoes. Hats were an important part of every man's costume; the type was dictated by the particular function or event. Sportswear as we know it had not yet appeared on the fashion scene. For casual situations, men wore **knickers, blazers** of tweeds and flannels, and less formal hats and shoes.

Children's clothing was an adaptation of their parents' dress. Girls looked like miniature women in their frilly dresses, while boys were small clones of their fathers in their suits, stiff shirts, ties, and hats.

Although there were fashion changes dictated by Poiret throughout this decade, not many chose to shed the formal look of the earlier periods.

The Designers Who Influenced Fashion Included . . .

Paul Poiret, who reigned between 1903 and World War I (1914–1918). He freed women from corsets and designed loose-fitting clothing, but he later designed skirts so narrow at the hem women were unable to walk. *Madame Paquin*, whose claim to fame was that she never made two dresses alike, was the first woman to achieve importance in couture. She designed glamorous evening wear and suits that were adorned with lavish fur. *Jeanne Lanvin* began as a milliner and ultimately branched out into couture that underscored a youthful look as well as styles that were fashioned from costumes worn in her native Brittany. Wedding gowns were one of Lanvin's specialties, as were metallic embroidered garments and other fashions that featured intricate stitching.

Paul Poiret designed in Paris and attracted women, such as actress Joan Crawford, from all over the world to his salon.

1911–1920

The News of the Times Focused Attention on . . .

the events that resulted in the outbreak of World War I. Women continued to gain more independence and were entering universities in greater numbers than ever before. However, all attention was focused on World War I, which the United States entered in 1917. With the large number of men participating in the action, women performed domestic jobs that were once the exclusive domain of men. This set the stage for women to become a force in industries that they had never been allowed to enter. Silent movies offered a new form of entertainment. A particularly controversial film was D.W. Griffith's, *Birth of a Nation*.

The Fashions of the Times Were . . .

a mix of the fashionable and functional. For those whose attention was fashion forward, Poiret's design for a show called *Le Miraret* in 1912 set a trend. His **hobble skirts**, many with slit fronts, revealed women's legs for the first time. The hobble skirt was worn with a wide tunic, and its narrow shape led to the abandonment of petticoats. Other skirts were straight, and lines were simpler than ever before. Tailored suits were extremely popular for daytime wear, and skirt hemlines were very narrow. With these designs, shoes and hosiery became important fashion elements. A side-buttoned shoe was very popular. Ensembles were very much in vogue, with coats that matched the dresses underneath. Furs were used to line coats and trim hemlines.

The decade began with millinery that echoed the earlier years, but it was quickly replaced with less ornate, smaller styles. Parasols became important accessories, as did small handbags.

Although many men continued to embrace the styles of the previous period, a new breed opted for the natural shoulder look. Devoid of heavy padding with narrow lapels and straight trousers, a new silhouette was capturing attention. A simpler form of dress, save for the special occasion, was now the more popular approach.

Children continued to be dressed as scaled-down replicas of adults. Their clothing was fancy, impractical, and anything but functional.

Paul Poiret designed styles that freed women from corsets.

Fortuny's Delphos gowns are composed of narrow pleats and are in costume collections in many of the world's museums.

As the decade moved toward its conclusion, the impact of World War I on everyday life and a sense of practicality pervaded dress. The period ended with a "uniformness" of fashion, with easy and basic forms as the order of the day. What would follow in the next decade was quite a contrast.

The Designers Who Influenced Fashion Included . . .

Fortuny, whose designs were worn by wealthy women and are now collected by museums all over the world. The most famous of his designs is the **Delphos gown**, which is a patented design composed of columns of many narrow, irregular, vertical pleats that are permanently set in silk by a secret process. The shape was enhanced by silk ties fastened at the waist. Another designer of this decade was *Nina Ricci*, who designed graceful, elegant fashions that kept pace with the times but did not break new ground. On the other hand, *Madeleine Vionnet*'s innovations included the bias cut, eliminating the need for fastenings of any kind on dresses, and cowl and halter necklines that still influence fashion. She opened her own couture house in Paris in 1912, which closed during World War I and reopened in 1918. It is also said that she rather than Poiret was the first to eliminate the need for corsets.

Madeleine Vionnet's bias-cuts featured cowl and halter necklines. Her designs continue to influence fashion.

1920S

The News of the Times Focused Attention on . . .

many different things. In the United States, the decade was greeted with an amendment to the Constitution that brought about the era of Prohibition in which alcoholic beverages were forbidden. Speakeasies—nightclubs that sold illegal liquor—were commonplace in the major cities. The music of the decade was jazz. The end of the silent film era was signaled by the release of *The Jazz Singer*, the first film with spoken lines, and the prototype for Mickey Mouse was developed by Disney. In 1920, another constitutional amendment gave women the right to vote. Their vote counted in the election of Herbert Hoover as president in 1920. Women continued to work, but it was their increased participation in sports that led to a casual type of dress. In 1925 F. Scott Fitzgerald's novel *The Great Gatsby* was published and B. F. Goodrich registered the trademark for the zipper. The United States had its first female senator. Charles Lindbergh made the first solo transatlantic airplane flight in 1927. By the end of the 1920s, frivolity, glamour, and excitement were replaced by anxiety and fear created by the stock market crash in 1929.

The Fashions of the Times Were . . .

entirely different from those of the previous decade, with elegance playing a significant role. They reflected the optimism that followed the end of World War I. Fashionable women quickly forgot the functional wear of the previous decade and embraced innovative new styles. As the decade advanced, skirts became shorter. The day of the **flapper** dawned, with knee-length hemlines, long-torso silhouettes with ruffled flounces,

The flapper wore knee-length, flounced hemlines and layers of chains.

layers of chains adorning necklines, and close-fitting hats called cloches covering short hairstyles. Beading and fringes of every type decorated evening wear, and fur wraps lavishly covered them. Stylish women wore silk dresses for daywear under straight woolen coats, and ensembles featured jacket linings matching the blouses that were worn with them. **Sportswear** was introduced, and women wore knickers, **culottes**, and blazers to spectator events.

Men of the 1920s were also introduced to a new look. Bell-bottomed and flared trousers replaced the straight-legged models, jacket waistlines were nipped-in, and shoulders were softer. Men, like women, also began to wear sports clothing. Knickers were fashionable, and the polo shirt was introduced. An air of informality was everywhere.

Children's clothing continued to echo adult styles. Girls wore shorter, less-restrictive silhouettes, while boys donned baggy tweed pants ranging from shorts for the very young to full-length pants or knickers for the older set.

The Designers Who Influenced Fashion Included . . .

Jean Patou, whose flapper dress created a sensation in 1925 with shorter skirts, dropped waistlines, and uneven hems. He was a master of change. In 1929, he was the first designer to bring the waistline back to its normal position and design skirts that were longer. *Captain Edward Molyneux* had couture houses in Paris, Monte Carlo, and London, where his clientele included royalty and theatrical personalities. His clothing was fluid, elegant, uncluttered, and never seemed to go out of fashion. Of course, one of the world's greatest innovators, *Gabrielle "Coco" Chanel*, reigned during this decade. The World of Fashion Profile of Chanel outlines her lifestyle and design inventiveness.

1930S

The News of the Times Focused Attention on . . .

the economic depression caused by the stock market crash. The election of Franklin Delano Roosevelt as president in 1932 and his New Deal philosophy offered hope for relief from the effects of the Depression. Prohibition was repealed. In 1936, Edward VIII of Great Britain abdicated the throne to marry Wallis Simpson, an American divorcée. The growing worldwide economic crisis and concerns about developments in Europe, particularly Hitler's increasing popularity and aggressive behavior, created a more serious outlook. At the beginning of the decade, relatively few could afford the extravagances of the 1920s. Some women tried to make do with what they had by "camouflaging" their old clothing. By the middle of the decade, however, Roosevelt's New Deal generated some optimism, and fashion once again was on the move. Nylon was developed by DuPont. The film industry reached new heights, concentrating on musicals and comedies that provided vicarious pleasure to Depression-

COCO CHANEL

Considered by most fashion connoisseurs to be the 20th century's most important couturiere, Coco Chanel was born in France in 1883. As mistress of a sportsman and horse breeder, she was determined to project a fashion image of simplicity and elegance.

Chanel's career began inadvertently when she started to trim hats for her own use. As people admired them, she began to produce and sell hats at home, eventually setting up a small shop. Her millinery business expanded to include dresses, which became equally successful. A brisk business prompted the opening of boutiques in fashionable Deauville and Biarritz and then an expanded headquarters in Paris. Her clothing was casual but smart, and her followers were quick to embrace these new style concepts. Her collections were simpler and more practical than anything else produced at that time.

Chanel achieved success not only as a couturiere but also as an integral part of the social scene. With simplicity as key to her inventiveness, her collections became broader. Evening wear consisted of simple chemises translated from daytime dresses, but with exquisite fabrics and intricate detailing.

She was a fashion influence from the 1920s until the beginning of World War II, when her presence in fashion collapsed. She closed her couture house, and except for her legendary fragrances, nothing else was produced under the Chanel label. In 1954, however, at the age of 71, Chanel was once again ready for the challenge. Although her new designs were considered "tired" by the press, fashionable women quickly embraced them again. The suit she perfected was produced in a host of new materials and trims, employing color in innovative ways. Pants often replaced suit skirts, and brocades, velvets, and satins were used to create glamorous, understated evening apparel. Simplicity was still manifest in the shape or silhouette of the garments.

Chanel's styles continue to influence fashion and many of today's designers. Whenever the little black dress resurfaces, or when tweed suits embellished with pockets and interesting trim are shown, we are reminded of the genius of Chanel.

Chanel remains a legend for her taste, personal style, and dedication to perfection.

era America. It was the heyday of Fred Astaire and Ginger Rogers's madcap comedies and epic films such as *Gone With the Wind* (1939). When Clark Gable appeared in *It Happened One Night* (1934) without an undershirt, sales of undershirts dramatically dropped. However, by the end of the decade the threat of World War II hovered over people.

Vionnet's wedding gown with its sweeping train was high fashion of the 1930s.

The Fashions of the Times Were . . .

quite different from those of the 1920s. Gone were the flappers and the gaudiness of the 1920s. When the country began to lift itself out of the Depression, an era of elegance emerged.

The short hemlines now dropped to midcalf for daytime and to the floor for evening wear. The **bias cut**, popularized by Vionnet, was an important silhouette; strapless necklines were favorites for the evening, and back-sweeping trains adorned many gowns. Suits, out of favor in the 1920s, made a comeback—this time with padded shoulders and shorter jackets. Colors were subdued, with black, gray, green, and brown the most popular. Fabrics were soft with crepes, jerseys, satins, and soft wools being the favorites.

Men's clothing took on a looser look. Shoulders were broadened and padded; trousers were loose, straight, pleated, and cuffed; and many suits were double-breasted, with wide lapels or revers.

The biggest news of the decade was the growing acceptance of the **spectator sportswear** introduced in the 1920s. Both men and women embraced this leisure wear. Tweed suits, navy blazers worn with white pleated skirts, simple hats, shorter cotton dresses, and even pants found their way into women's wardrobes. While these new styles would eventually be worn for any occasion, in the 1930s they were appropriate only when attending the races or watching other sports events. For the same occasions, men chose the newly introduced knit sport shirts and slacks that were worn with contrasting colored sport coats.

Children's styles were similar to those of the previous decade, with simplicity of design the important factor.

By the end of the decade, lavish clothing gave way to more practical designs. The world turned to more functional dress that would last well into the 1940s.

The Designers Who Influenced Fashion Included . . .

Chanel, who was still in the forefront of couture. *Mainbocher*, an American, who had great success at home and in Europe, appealed to those in the highest social circles. His design of the Duchess of Windsor's wedding dress in 1936 became the most copied style of the decade. *Jean Desses* was noted for the flowing chiffon evening gowns that echoed his Greek ancestry, and *Madame Grés* brought draping to new heights working with chiffon and silk jersey. *Elsa Schiaparelli* changed the shape of the figure by using broad padded shoulders fashioned after the uniforms of London's guardsmen. She also used or-

Menswear in the 1930s featured padded shoulders, double-breasted suits, and spectator sportswear.

naments of unique shapes to enhance her designs, and designed avant-garde sweaters with unusual motifs. She used the first zipper on pockets in 1930. Schiaparelli's collections were always considered elegant and chic. The American designer *Vera Maxwell* designed a **weekend wardrobe** in 1935, consisting of a collarless tweed and gray flannel jacket, a flannel tennis skirt, a longer pleated tweed skirt, and cuffed flannel trousers.

1940S

The News of the Times Focused Attention on . . .

the war against Germany, Italy, and Japan. In the United States, women again worked in factories replacing the men who went off to war. Food rationing added to the discomfort of citizens and residents of many European nations. Because fabric was in short supply, the government regulated its use. General Limitation Order L-85, for example, restricted the amount of fabric used for a garment as well as the number of pockvets and buttons it could have. Nylon was diverted from clothing to use in the production of parachutes, tents, and ropes for the war effort. Other scarce products included wool, silk, and rubber. As a result, civilian use of these materials was limited. The famous fashion houses of Paris closed their doors. Because of this, American

Mainbocher designed the wedding dress worn by Wallis Simpson for her marriage to the Duke of Windsor.

Intarsia handknit like an abstract crusader – in handspun yarns

Sportswear by Bonnie Cashin could be mixed and matched.

Claire McCardell is featured here with some of her separates.

designers were given their first major opportunity in fashion. They were featured in magazines, such as *Vogue* and *Harper's Bazaar*, more frequently. Dorothy Shaver, the president of Lord & Taylor, gave American designers an opportunity to feature their garments in the famous retail organization she headed. At the end of the 1940s, clothing manufacturers in the United States were expanding. The ready-to-wear industry significantly grew.

As the war came to an end in 1945, the world faced the difficult process of recovery. Movies began to flourish with the release of *The Outlaw*, delayed for three years because of its sexual connotations. Television began to emerge as a leading medium.

The Fashions of the Times Were . . .

simple at the beginning of the decade because of the dictates of war. Popular styles included padded shoulders that exceeded those of the 1930s and shorter skirts. American designers, such as Bonnie Cashin and Claire McCardell, designed sportswear and **separates** that could be mixed and matched. The air of casualness lasted well into the 1950s and beyond.

When the war ended, Paris repositioned itself as fashion's standard-bearer. The **New Look**—rounded shoulders, full bustlines, tiny waists accentuated by full skirts—dominated Dior's collection and it was soon adapted by fashion manufacturers everywhere. Skirts grew longer—15 inches off the ground—and jackets were short and fitted. The swimsuit took a new direction as **bikinis** made their debut.

Basics dominated menswear. The suit silhouette most favored was the single-breasted style. By the end of the decade, lapels were narrower. A casual approach to fashion with contrasting sport coats and trousers quickly became popular.

Fashions for the young were more casual. Carefree styles for girls included puffed sleeves and flared skirts. **Jeans** were slowly being accepted, but only for riding bicycles or leisure activities. Oversized sweaters—called **sloppy joes**—were the hot items of the day. Boys wore T-shirts, sport shirts, and styles that were inspired by the military.

The Designers Who Influenced Fashion Included . . .

Americans who joined the ranks of the French as world leaders in fashion. *Adrian*, who had gained a reputation as a designer for films, designed ready-to-wear collections from 1941 to 1952. Tailored suits with large, square shoulder pads were typical of his sophisticated designs. *Bonnie Cashin* was not at all influenced by the dictates of Paris. Her specialty was comfortable clothing for country weekends and travel, made of such fabrics as wool jersey, knits, leather, suede, and tweeds. Hoods, toggle closures on coats and jackets, and leather trim on garments were her trademarks. The toga and kimono were standards. *Claire McCardell* developed casual wear and is credited with what is known as the *American Look*. Simple, clean lines in functional, comfortable clothing were her strengths. She adapted the large pockets, topstitching, and sturdy fabrics of men's clothing to women's wear. *Norman Norell* used simple lines, rich fabrics, and exquisite workmanship for his garments. His evening wear designs consisted of sequined gowns and his sportswear look of sweaters worn over long skirts. He also designed jumpsuits and pantsuits. *Pauline Trigère* used luxurious fabrics, rich tweeds, and artistic prints in very simple, but intricate cuts. *Christian Dior*'s New Look in 1947 was met with wild enthusiasm. Year after year, his creations captured the fashion world's attention—**A-line** and **Y-line** silhouettes in the next decade. *Balenciaga* was the master tailor and dressmaker. His sculptural creations are the embodiment of cut and fit, with each garment architecturally built to mold perfectly to the figure.

Dior's New Look featured tiny waists accentuated by very full skirts.

1950S

The News of the Times Focused Attention on . . .

the Korean War from 1950 to 1953. In the United States, Dwight D. Eisenhower was elected president, and in England Elizabeth II became queen in 1952. Acrylic and polyester fibers became available. The term *teenager* came into general use in the mid-1950s. Teen idols included movie stars James Dean and Marlon Brando, who rose to fame in their respective movies, *Rebel Without a Cause* (1955) and *On the Waterfront* (1954). A new generation of music took hold with the beginning of rock 'n' roll. Elvis Presley's popularity soared. With the publication of *On the Road* by Jack Kerouac, the terms *Beat Generation* and *beatnik* were coined. The economy boomed and the United States dominated world manufacturing. Money was available again for discretionary and luxury purchases. Men became increasingly interested in fashion, opening new markets for manufacturers and designers. Americans who suffered from discrimination demanded their rights. The civil rights movement was sparked by demonstrations in Montgomery, Alabama, and Little Rock, Arkansas, in 1955. *Sputnik*, the first space satellite, was launched by the Russians in 1957. Television became more widely available in homes. More and more women began to enter the job market in careers, such as finance, that were once reserved for men.

The Fashions of the Times Were . . .

extremely diverse. Hemlines were alternately long to short depending on the year and the designer. The first half of the decade was dedicated to elegance, symbolized by the couture collections. Tailored clothing was important for daytime wear; full-skirted, strapless evening dresses were appropriate for special occasions. Sportswear, including slacks, **pedal pushers**, shorts, and halters, was a favorite. Mixing and matching different pieces to create new outfits gained in popularity. Increasingly, apparel was created from the newly developed manufactured fibers.

By the middle of the 1950s a new style developed on American college campuses that reflected a laid-back, nonaggressive way of life. The **beatnik look** had been born. **Leotards** and tapered pants were topped by hooded knits and overshirts; black stockings were the rage. Young men sported beards. **Unisex fashions** began, with men and women sharing the same styles.

Styles that were exclusively for men included charcoal gray suits that featured narrow lapels and natural shoulders and bore the **Ivy League** label. Pants were narrow—many with buckle closures at the back. The standard white shirt was joined by

Elvis Presley popularized a new style of music and influenced dress.

Full-skirted, strapless dresses were worn for such special occasions as proms.

pale pink, which was also considered appropriate for business. Madras was a popular material for sport coats, and shorts were being worn for casual wear. Leather jackets were very popular, especially for the younger set who were enthralled by film stars and rock 'n' roll idols.

Teenage girls began the decade wearing full skirts, often made of felt emblazoned with *poodles*, over stiffened crinolines. The decade ended with many switching to a more relaxed look. Saddle shoes and white bucks were everywhere.

As the 1960s approached, styles never seen before would surface and gain immediate acceptance.

The Designers Who Influenced Fashion Included . . .

those who had been popular in the 1940s, such as Balenciaga, Dior, and Bonnie Cashin. New faces also emerged. *Hubert de Givenchy* was noted for a masterly cut, something that he learned from Balenciaga. His peasant blouse also won him great admiration, as did his collections of elegant evening wear. Intricate cuts, precise seaming, batwing styles, and asymmetrical shapes were among American designer *Charles James*'s many innovations. The stage was set for the 1960s and the emergence of such designers as Mary Quant and Yves Saint Laurent, who first designed for the house of Dior in the 1950s.

1960S

The News of the Times Focused Attention on . . .

the election of John F. Kennedy as president of the United States in 1960. The United States gained in the race for space. Alan Shepard was the second man in space, John Glenn the first American to orbit the Earth, and Apollo 11 the first capsule to land on the moon in 1969. After Kennedy's assassination, President Lyndon Johnson guided the Civil Rights Act of 1964 through Congress, along with significant antipoverty legislation. A second Civil Rights Act, passed in 1965, guaranteed every citizen the right to vote. Despite the passage of these bills, inequalities persisted and riots occurred in Los Angeles (Watts), Chicago, Cleveland, Newark, and Detroit. Both Martin Luther King Jr. and Robert Kennedy were assassinated in 1968. America's involvement in a war in Vietnam—a small country in Southeast Asia—dominated the news, as did antiwar demonstrations on college campuses and city streets. Continuing hostilities between Israelis and Arabs erupted in the Six Day War. The Beatles quickly extended their popularity to American audiences with hit after hit; the term *Beatlemania* was born. In upstate New York, the 1969 Woodstock festival attracted hippies from all over the nation, who came to hear their favorite musicians. The *New York Times* supplement, *Fashions of the Times*, was the first fashion magazine to put an African-

Beatlemania resulted in record-breaking crowds at concerts.

The miniskirt was the rage of the 1960s.

American model on its cover. The National Organization for Women (NOW) was founded in 1966.

The Fashions of the Times Were . . .

no longer dictated by a few designers. Instead, a variety of styles and choices swept the world. The *mod style* was definitely in. Originally a term applied to tailored youth fashions of the period, it was rivaled by the *rockers*, who dressed in leathers and crash helmets.

Probably the greatest fashion controversy of the 1960s centered around skirt lengths. At the beginning of the decade, skirts hovered around the knee, rising steadily until the shortest **miniskirts** were the order of the day. A new fashion capital was born in London, where minis were the popular items. Boots became a standard complement to the miniskirts. Many women discarded their shoes and built complete boot wardrobes.

First Lady Jacqueline Kennedy became an important fashion role model for women, reinvigorating the **Chanel suit** and popularizing the **pillbox hat** early in her husband's presidency. So popular was the Chanel suit that it was produced at every price point and worn by every segment of the population. Dress silhouettes included an **Empire waistline** and A-line or straight-cut shapes that were loose from shoulder to hem. A popular design by Yves Saint Laurent was inspired by *Mondrian* paintings and was constructed of several blocks of color.

The confusion about skirt lengths led many women to wear pants for all occasions. **Pantsuits**, which were introduced in the mid-1960s, were increasingly accepted by women by the late 1960s. Denim and jeans were no longer reserved for the young and those outside the mainstream. What was once considered appropriate only for leisure activities was now making the fashion scene for every type of function.

The phrases "Black Is Beautiful" and "Black Pride" expressed the new feeling of self-confidence and self-worth among African Americans. Traditional African garments, such as **dashikis**, which were often made of **kente cloth** fabrics, were worn. **Afro** hairstyles and **cornrow braids** were widely adopted by both men and women in the late 1960s.

On the beach, Rudi Gernreich's topless bathing suit made its debut. Swimwear was dominated by one-piece loosely fitted blouson styles and two-piece bathing suits, including the bikini model.

Men's fashions were equally exciting. With the popularity of long sideburns to match longer hair lengths, jacket lapels became exaggerated and pants were flared or bell-bottomed. Men wore boots, used jewelry as accents, and shed anything with a traditional look.

By the end of the decade, teenagers and college students dressed more informally than ever. Jeans, ragged **T-shirts**, army boots, ponchos, and long hair became the uniform of the "youth culture." Based on rejection of uniformity—an anti-fashion expression—these styles represented the unkempt hippie look. All types of clothing were acceptable—long and short, new and old. The materials were all natural, and **psychedelic designs** and imagery affected clothing's color and fabrics. Unisex styles continued to gain in popularity.

Mondrian's geometric paintings influenced a collection of Yves Saint Laurent dresses.

The Designers Who Influenced Fashion Included . . .

talented individuals from all over the world. London emerged as a fashion capital with *Mary Quant*'s unique designs. Using the **mod look** of miniskirts to capture the youth market, her materials included denim, vinyl, and colored flannels, all paired with tights. In Paris, *Courrèges* also featured the mini and designed the now famous **go-go boots** that revolutionized the shoe industry. *Yves Saint Laurent* opened his own couture house and treated the world to endless fashion innovations from ballgowns to pantsuits and everything in between. He presented his first ready-to-wear collection, Rive Gauche, which would have wider appeal than his higher-priced couture. *Pierre Cardin* showed his **nude look** in 1966, followed by metal body jewelry and astronaut suits and helmets. He also brought designer fashion to a wider consumer market through licensing agreements. All over the world, clothing and accessories for men, women, and children bore his signature. In the United States, *Anne Klein* was a pioneer in the junior clothing category, transforming juniors into more sophisticated styles. Skirts and blazers were popular items in her collections, as were jersey dresses, pants, and sweaters. *Geoffrey Beene* was winning accolades and awards from the fashion industry. His specialty was simplicity of design, emphasizing cut, line,

Rudi Gernreich specialized in dramatic cuts and color combinations.

and detailing. *Halston*, who began as a milliner at Bergdorf Goodman and eventually gained popularity with his famous pillbox hat design for Jackie Kennedy, shifted to apparel. *Rudi Gernreich* designed more comfortable, unstructured swimwear, including a topless model in 1964. He specialized in sport clothes in dramatic cuts and color combinations.

1970S

The News of the Times Focused Attention on . . .

President Richard Nixon's visit to China in 1972, and his resignation as president in 1974. Oil prices skyrocketed and the first Earth Day was celebrated in 1970. Jimmy Carter was elected president in 1976, the year the United States celebrated its Bicentennial. Egyptian President Anwar Sadat visited Israel, opening the door to negotiations that led to the Camp David Accords in 1979. That same year the Shah of Iran fled to the United States, after which Iran became an Islamic Republic. The Iranian seizure of 63 American hostages caused anxiety in the United States. The movie industry achieved greater freedom with such films as *A Clockwork Orange* (1971), while fashions inspired from *Saturday Night Fever* (1977) and *Annie Hall* (1978) were quickly copied.

Mary Quant and her mod miniskirt designs launched London as a fashion capital.

Two fashion trends set by First Lady Jacqueline Kennedy, a fashion role model, were the pillbox hat and Chanel suits.

The Fashions of the Times Were . . .

more individual then ever before. People were given choices instead of having fashion dictated to them. The designers who had reigned supreme relinquished their holds on the consumer. In 1970, **midi** and **maxi** skirts were introduced. The midcalf length was not embraced by women, who continued to wear their short skirts or opted to wear pants or the longer maxi skirts.

With the rejection of the midi, designers quickly realized the need to satisfy the likes and dislikes of their customers. Women were not ready to rid their closets of comfortable pantsuits, which they continued to wear for all occasions. Manufacturers responded by turning them out at every price point. Some minis caught fire, as did form-fitting **hot pants** and the **platform shoes** with which they were worn. Although young people wore them successfully, the more mature market opted for flared-legged trousers. Granny clothing was in, as was secondhand clothing for those interested in punk rock. Designs by Zandra Rhodes were inspired by the new music. Evening pants were seen everywhere, topped by sheer silks, jerseys, and other dressy fabrics. The preferred blouse was the tunic worn over pants.

The Peacock Revolution made men as conscious of fashion as women.

Unisex clothing, carried over from the 1960s, was still a favorite. Both men and boys wore new, relaxed, and comfortable **leisure suits.**

For men, who had become as fashion conscious as women, the new **peacock look** was the choice. The broad upturned padded shoulders, fitted waistline, long jacket, and flared pants created excitement.

Denim garments were available for all members of the family. Jeans became extremely fashionable, and many sported visible labels to indicate the maker's name. **Designer jeans** became a status symbol for men, women, and teens.

The **layered look** was a fashion innovation that prompted women to buy several pieces of clothing that could be worn one on top of the other.

By the end of the decade, a casualness pervaded the fashion world. Clothing was functional as well as stylish. Knits were in great abundance, in a variety of weights and textures. Those seeking comfort quickly embraced these fabrics. Evening clothing became less important and was worn only by a few. The tailored, less dressy look was now appropriate for most occasions.

The Designers Who Influenced Fashion Included . . .

those from both sides of the Atlantic. **Prêt-à-porter**, or ready-to-wear, which was established in France in the 1960s, began to thrive. In Italy, *Giorgio Armani* was recognized as a masterful designer, who created both men's and women's clothing. An unconstructed blazer in fine Italian fabrics was his specialty and was copied at every price point. *Gianfranco Ferré*, another Italian, became famous for his sculptured designs and beautiful pleating that appeared on comfortable, fluid clothing. In the United States, *Calvin Klein* made simple designs for both men and women and became a household name with his designer jeans. *Betsey Johnson*'s creations were unique. T-shirts in all lengths, vinyl dresses with paste-ons, spandex knits, and tight pants were characteristic of her work. *Norma Kamali* distinguished herself with unusual use of fabric—parachute nylon for jumpsuits and sweatshirt material from gymnasiums

RALPH LAUREN

"I stand for a look that is American," states Ralph Lauren, who is a master at marketing lifestyles. "It is an attitude, a sense of freedom. I believe in clothes that last, that are not dated in a season. They should look better the year after they are bought." These few words summarize beautifully what Lauren and his clothing are all about.

His creative talents were first recognized when he was associated with Beau Brummel neckties. The field was full of narrow, Ivy League ties, and Lauren thought Americans were ready for a new look. He introduced the four-inch-wide tie made of opulent materials; soon it became the status tie to wear. Lauren then began to design a full line of menswear and soon became an international force in the fashion industry.

In 1968, he established Polo, a name taken from a sport that depicted style and grace, and produced a total men's wardrobe. Using fine fabrics in a natural shoulder silhouette, along with expertly crafted shirts, knitwear, outerwear, accessories, and shoes, he quickly achieved a place of importance in menswear. His line has become one of the industry's most distinctive looks.

In 1971, Lauren expanded his empire to include women's clothing. For the active, independent woman, he created an understated elegance that plays equally well in all parts of the country. Beautiful fabrics and attention to well-tailored construction make his suits, dresses, sportswear, knits, and jackets wardrobe mainstays. He soon introduced boys' wear, and later girls' wear of comparable quality. To round out his fashion empire, Lauren added a line of home furnishings, fragrances, luggage, handbags, belts, wallets, scarves, sunglasses, and hats.

Not only does Lauren create beautiful designs, but he markets them as well. From his Madison Avenue flagship

Ralph Lauren's name is a fashion statement in men's, women's, and children's wear, accessories, fragrances, and home fashions.

housed in the former Rhinelander mansion to a network of stores throughout the world, he markets everything he creates.

Designer jeans created by such designers as Calvin Klein became status symbols for the wearer.

to the streets for a variety of ready-to-wear styles. Her innovative use of fabrics carried over into the 1980s and was copied by many manufacturers. *Mary McFadden* used fine pleating in dresses and tunics. *Ralph Lauren* has remained a leading designer since the 1970s. His philosophy and contributions to the industry are outlined in a World of Fashion Profile.

1980S

The News of the Times Focused Attention on . . .

the election of Ronald Reagan as President in 1980. His presidency ushered in an era of conspicuous consumption that his reelection four years later reinforced. The marriage of Diana Spencer and Prince Charles in 1981 supplied the bridal industry with a design that would be extensively copied. Women's roles in the workplace grew, as some rose to executive positions once reserved for men. A new term, **yuppie**, was coined to describe the upwardly mobile young professional. The U.S. space program was set back with

The bridal industry quickly copied the wedding gown of Lady Diana.

the *Challenger* disaster in 1986. The stock market crash in October 1987 sent the U.S. economy into a tailspin. George Bush won election as president in 1988. The Berlin Wall came down, a dramatic step toward the reunification of Germany. China sent shockwaves throughout the world with the Tiananmen Square massacre. MTV began and brought new stars, such as Prince and Madonna, into homes. Nightclubbing emerged as an important part of the life of the young. The television show *Dallas* reached an international audience of more than 300 million, repopularizing the **ten-gallon hat**. Acquired immunodeficiency syndrome (AIDS), which would have a profound effect on the fashion industry, was recognized as a worldwide epidemic. By 1990, a number of top designers (Halston, Perry Ellis, Willi Smith) as well as colleagues who worked in supporting roles in the fashion industry were known to have died of AIDS. Animal rights activists began their campaign against fur apparel. Global concern for the environment continued, with a growing preference for natural fibers.

The Fashions of the Times Were . . .

a revival of earlier styles, with an emphasis on elegant evening wear. The **pouf skirt**, started in the Paris couture shows, was soon adapted by manufacturers all over the world. Miniskirts returned to the forefront of fashion, as they were accepted first by

Lacroix's pouf skirt was the sensation of the Paris runway and soon adapted by many manufacturers.

the youth and later by more mature women who chose to shed the longer hemlines for a newer, younger look.

At the beginning of the decade, licensing arrangements blossomed. As a result, designer label merchandise, sporting the signatures of the world's best couturiers, began appearing on a variety of apparel and accessory products.

New trends in fashion were inspired by the physical fitness craze. The film *Flashdance*, which starred Jennifer Beals and featured torn sweats and aerobic dancing, had a major impact on fashion. Warm-up suits and sneakers (now called **athletic shoes**), previously reserved for sports activities, were now worn as streetwear. By the end of the decade the number of athletic shoe styles stocked by stores was often larger than their stock of traditional shoe styles. Daytime casual shoes were replaced by a wardrobe of athletic shoes; many teenagers never purchased a regular pair of shoes. The uniform of the youth market consisted of a pair of Levi's jeans, a shirt and sweater, and athletic shoes. Before long, adults donned the same outfit. At the same time, the growth in the number of women executives created a need for women's business suits—suits that would be equal in design and quality to menswear. The **power suit**, with its medium-length skirt and tailored jacket, hung in the closets of these new executives. A tailored blouse was usually worn underneath.

By the end of the decade, the fashion world was not in one particular mode. Freedom of choice dominated. Skirts were worn at all lengths and pants were shown in a variety of silhouettes. The Madonna-inspired **bustier** was being worn by the young. Lycra spandex was used not only in exercise wear, but in many other types of garments as well. Torn jeans, once ready for disposal, became a fashion statement.

The Designers Who Influenced Fashion Included . . .

Donna Karan, who started under the tutelage of Anne Klein and was responsible—along with *Louis Dell'Olio*—for maintaining the classic sportswear designs established by Klein. In 1984, Karan opened her own company with backing from a Japanese firm. Her sportswear was characterized by blazers and pants that echoed men's fashions. Sarong skirts and easy, wearable dresses were her signatures. *Perry Ellis* captured the fashion world with both men's and women's designs beginning in the mid-1970s. His influence continued until his death in 1986. Hand-knitted sweaters played an important role in his collections. Japanese designers showed their fashions at the Paris prêt shows in 1983 and immediately stimulated interest with their loose, unconstructed, and oversize silhouettes. *Rei Kawakubo*'s clothes were described as bag lady styles, but throughout the 1980s Japanese designers gained attention in both men's and women's wear. *Christian Lacroix*, the first couturier to emerge in many years, captivated the fashion world in 1987 with his extravagant pouf design. *Gianni Versace* created imaginative styles that were sensuous for women and avant-garde for men. *Claude Montana* introduced biker's leathers to high fashion. *Adrienne Vittadini* used knits in unusual colorations and patterns to establish a niche in the marketplace. *Tommy Hilfiger* produced menswear collections that would be comfortable for both mature and younger consumers.

The women's movement lead many to dispose of their bras.

Torn sweats worn in *Flashdance* inspired clothing for physical fitness activities and casual wear.

In the 1980s, Yves St. Laurent helped popularize suits for power dressing.

1990S

The News of the Times Focused Attention on . . .

the collapse of the Soviet Union in 1991. The strengthening of the European Union and the subsequent creation of the European Monetary Union led to the expansion of companies overseas. The Gulf War between the United States and Iraq ignited a feeling of patriotism among American designers that led to numerous styles that sported designs with flags. The economic recession at the beginning of the decade made consumers more cautious and led to the failure of many businesses. The bankruptcy of Macy's and its takeover by Federated Stores was one major indicator of the economy's downward turn. Bill Clinton's election as president of the United States in 1992 ushered in an economic recovery during the 1990s that contributed to his re-election in 1996. The rapid growth of high-tech industries led to economic expansion at home and abroad. New trade pacts, such as the North American Free Trade Agreement (NAFTA) and the General Agreement on Tariffs and Trade (GATT), promised to improve trade among nations. The Disney Company produced several animated movies, including *The Lion King* and *Pocahontas*. The O.J. Simpson trial was the biggest media event from mid-1994 to 1995. Republicans controlled both houses of Congress for the first time in 40 years. Hong Kong's return to China in 1998 produced a wait-and-see attitude in the international market. Terrorist bombings around the world caused considerable unrest. The world got an inside look at President Clinton's private life when his relationship with White House intern Monica Lewinsky made headlines. Clinton became only the second U.S. president to be impeached, but he was not removed from office.

The Fashions of the Times Were . . .

at first a carryover from the previous decade, but with a strong inclination toward individuality that led to many new styles. Platform shoes reappeared and young people increasingly replaced their athletic footwear with **Doc Martens**. The **grunge look** appealed to many in the youth market. A very casual air was evident in daytime wear. Baggy pants and T-shirts exemplified the **hip-hop style** popularized by movies such as *Boyz 'N the Hood*. As the middle of the decade approached, the look was definitely **retro**. Designers were influenced by every period of the 20th century and inspired by silhouettes of the most famous classic designers. There were Jacques Fath–inspired peplum suits and the mixing of vintage clothing from shops that carried **resale merchandise** with contemporary pieces. Once again, consumers were attracted to updated versions of padded and fitted jackets from the 1950s; pointed pumps and the wrap-dress from the 1970s; narrow suits worn with wedgies; the sheath dress reminiscent of Audrey Hepburn's character, Holly Golightly, in *Breakfast at Tiffany's;* the **Kelly bag**, named for and worn by Grace Kelly in the 1950s; and suits that echoed those worn by Jackie Kennedy in the 1960s. At the close of the century, animal prints were the rage, and heavy embellishments of embroidery, beading, and other detailing were used in apparel. Accessories, particularly pashmina scarves, reached new heights as clothing augmentations.

For men, a more casual look came into vogue as companies established **dress-down Fridays**. It became commonplace for executives to wear **khakis** and **button-down shirts**, without ties, to the office. For the rest of the week, however, the traditional American classic-cut suit and European models were still preferred. Leisure wear now consisted of jeans, work shoes, leather jackets, and active apparel that could be worn for exercise or on the street.

Children continued to wear less formal attire, such as jeans and sweatshirts. The baseball cap was king and crowned most young people's heads.

The Designers Who Influenced Fashion Included . . .

those who had made their mark in previous decades, such as Lagerfeld, Karan, Blass, Gaultier, and Lauren. Others who came into their own included American designers *Richard Tyler*, winner of the CFDA's Perry Ellis Award for New Fashion Talent in 1993, who creates inventive, perfectly tailored clothing; *Anna Sui*, who designs imaginative and adventurous clothing for a younger market; *Isaac Mizrahi*, who produced everything from raincoats to evening wear with a young, inventive air; *Todd Oldham*, who creates simple shapes, often in bold colors, and embellishes them with beading or embroidery; *Tracy Reese*, who creates young designer sportswear including separates and dresses earmarked for career women; *Nicole Miller*, who specializes in unique prints for scarves, men's ties, and garment linings; *John Galliano*, who specializes in bias-cut evening wear and was selected as Givenchy's replacement following the great master's retirement; and *Joseph Abboud*, who excels in menswear with a blend of European styling and American practicality. New European designers included *Herve Leger*, with sensuous and seductive designs, and *Jil Sander*, Germany's premier designer, who specializes in clean design without decoration and cuts that were once out of the ordinary. As the decade ended, *Marc Jacobs* presented his first collection for Louis Vuitton, *Tom Ford*'s Gucci collections premiered, and *Donatella Versace* offered her first collection following her brother's death. Richard Tyler's impeccable tailoring and Anna Sui's whimsical approaches to fashion also characterized fashion at the end of the 20th century.

THE EARLY TO MID-2000S

As the new millennium began, the fashion industry was poised for a great number of innovative ideas. At the time, however, little changed from the previous decade until the middle of this one.

The News of the Times Focused Attention on . . .

George W. Bush and the Republican Party recapturing the White House, along with majorities in the House and Senate, in one of America's closest elections. A switch in parties by one Republican, however, gave the Democrats a slight edge in the Senate until they achieved a majority in 2006. Wars with Afghanistan and Iraq caused a rift in the United States with the majority of Americans calling for withdrawal of troops in 2006 as casualties mounted. President Bush still held out for what seemed to be an unlikely victory. The 2006 election saw the recapture of the House and Senate by the Democrats, and as of this writing, the decision about how to handle the war ef-

The grunge look for the youth market and Jean Paul Gaultier's designs were attention-getting highlights in the 1990s.

fort was still not yet resolved. The new-found wealth of many Americans, which was the result of the unprecedented levels of growth in the financial markets, remained constant.

The Fashion of the Times Were . . .

not revolutionary, as designers followed their own preferences to satisfy the needs of the consumer. Early in the decade, some trends were taken from films such as *Moulin Rouge*, which featured extravagant French fashion, and *Pearl Harbor*, which focused attention on the military look. Skirt lengths and design silhouettes reflected many different styles. Designers continued to focus their designs on their own concepts with no one single trend apparent. Fashion names heretofore associated with upscale collections were also found in value operations such as Target, which featured the Mizrahi label, and H&M, which marketed Karl Lagerfeld and Stella McCartney lines. Many lines designed by ethnic minority celebrities such as Jennifer Lopez, Beyoncé Knowles, Sean "Diddy" Combs, and Russell Simmons made successful debuts.

Summarizing women's fashion trends of 2006, at the time of this writing, *WWD*'s "Lifestyle Monitor" column stated that *Smart = Fashion + Function*. Specifically, some of the success stories focused on longer tunics, skinny jeans, shirt dresses, layering fitted jackets, and exaggerated silhouettes. The one collective theme was "a return of classic garments updated in a fresh way in terms of fabrics and colors," according to Jessica Paruch, a product trend analyst with Cotton Incorporated.

Anna Sui, whose design is shown, is one of the high-fashion designers to come into prominence at the end of the 20th century.

George W. Bush recaptured the White House.

Minority ethnic designers such as Beyoncé Knowles for House of Deréon (left) and Sean "Diddy" Combs for Sean John (right) made their fashion debuts in the early 2000s.

The Designers Who Influenced Fashion Were . . .

the industry leaders from the 1990s. Although several new designers seemed poised on the fashion horizon, it would be the aforementioned ethnic minority group that would capture the headlines of fashion's editorial press.

CHAPTER HIGHLIGHTS

- 1900–1910

  FOR WOMEN:
  Pinched-in waistlines, tight-fitting corsets, leg-of-mutton sleeves, floor-length skirts, shirtwaist blouses, ornate hats

  FOR MEN:
  Frock coats, laced-up boots, spats, knickers, blazers

  FOR CHILDREN:
  Duplicates of adult clothing

- 1911–1920

  FOR WOMEN:
  Narrow silhouette, straight skirts, hobble skirts, matching ensembles, fur trims, smaller hats and handbags

  FOR MEN:
  Natural shoulder look, narrow lapels, straight pants, simple styling

  FOR CHILDREN:
  Duplicates of adult clothing

- 1920s

  FOR WOMEN:
  Shorter skirts, flapper styles, long-torso silhouettes, ruffled flounces, beading and fringes, fur wraps for evening wear, some spectator sportswear

  FOR MEN:
  Bell-bottomed and flared trousers, nipped-in waistlines, softer shoulders, knickers, polo shirts

  FOR CHILDREN:
  Duplicates of adult clothing

- 1930s

  FOR WOMEN:
  Midcalf hemlines for day and floor-length for evening, bias cuts, strapless necklines, suits with padded shoulders and short jackets

  FOR MEN:
  Broadened and padded shoulders, loose trousers with pleated waist and cuffed bottoms, double-breasted suits, spectator sportswear

  FOR CHILDREN:
  Simple styles

- 1940s

  FOR WOMEN:

  Padded shoulders, short-to-long skirts, tiny waistlines, full skirts, short, fitted jackets, bikinis, jeans, oversize sweaters

  FOR MEN:

  Single-breasted suits, contrasting sport coats and trousers, narrow lapels

  FOR CHILDREN:

  Girls wore "sloppy joes" and boys wore T-shirts and sport shirts

- 1950s

  FOR WOMEN:

  Diverse fashions including long and short hemlines, elegant and tailored clothing, sportswear, pedal pushers, the beatnik look for the young

  FOR MEN:

  Dark gray suits, narrow lapels and shoulders, narrow pants, Ivy League look, dress shirts in a few muted colors

  FOR CHILDREN:

  Girls wore full skirts over crinolines and mother-daughter look-alike outfits. Boys wore plaid vests and miniature gray flannel suits like their fathers

- 1960s

  FOR WOMEN:

  Youth-oriented styles, the mod look, miniskirts, hot pants, Chanel suits, chemise dresses, pantsuits, unconstructed swimsuits

  FOR MEN:

  Exaggerated lapels, flared or bell-bottomed pants, boots, jewelry, and long hair

  FOR CHILDREN:

  Jeans and T-shirts were the uniform of teenagers

- 1970s

  FOR WOMEN:

  Pantsuits, hot pants, platform shoes, granny clothing, evening pants and tunics, unisex dressing, designer jeans

  FOR MEN:

  Broad, upturned padded shoulders, fitted waistlines, long jackets, flared trousers, leisure suits, unisex dressing, designer jeans

  FOR CHILDREN:

  Designer jeans

- 1980s

  FOR WOMEN:

  Elegant evening wear, miniskirts, signature merchandise, warm-up suits, athletic shoes, and bustiers

  FOR MEN:

  Physical fitness attire worn for most occasions

  FOR CHILDREN:

  Teenagers wore athletic shoes instead of traditional shoes, Levi's, and a shirt or sweater

- 1990s

FOR WOMEN:

Platform shoes, Doc Martens, grunge casual wear, retro styles and silhouettes borrowed from previous decades

FOR MEN:

Dressing down with khakis and button-down shirts, jeans, work shoes and Doc Martens, leather jackets

FOR CHILDREN:

Jeans, sweatshirts, T-shirts, baseball caps, grunge look, hip-hop style

- 2000s

FOR WOMEN:

Military silhouettes, stilettos and platform shoes, jeans for casual and dressy wear

FOR MEN:

Suits for business attire, luxury fabrics such as cashmere, jeans

FOR CHILDREN:

Jeans, designer labels, T-shirts

IMPORTANT FASHION TERMINOLOGY AND CONCEPTS

Afro
A-line
athletic shoes
beatnik look
bias cut
bikinis
blazers
bustier
button-down shirts
Chanel suit
cornrow braids
culottes
dashikis
Delphos gown
designer jeans
Doc Martens
dress-down Fridays
Empire waistline
flapper
frock coat
Gibson Girl look
go-go boots
grunge look
hip-hop style

hippies
hobble skirt
hot pants
Ivy League
jeans
Kelly bag
kente cloth
khakis
knickers
layered look
leisure suits
leotards
maxi skirt
midi skirt
miniskirts
mod look
New Look
nude look
pantsuits
peacock look
pedal pushers
pillbox hat
platform shoes
pouf skirt

power suit
prêt à porter
psychedelic designs
resale merchandise
retro look
separates
shirtwaist
sloppy joes
spats
spectator sportswear
sportswear
suits
ten-gallon hat
topless bathing suit
T-shirt
unisex fashion
weekend wardrobe
Y-line
yuppie

FOR REVIEW

1. Who were the major designers in the first decade of the 20th century?

2. Contrast the fashions for women during the second and third decades of the 20th century.

3. Discuss the styles of Coco Chanel and the impact they continue to have long after her death.

4. Which two American designers of the 1940s were credited with popularizing women's sportswear?

5. What was considered to be the greatest fashion controversy of the 1960s?

6. How did Mary Quant change the look of fashion for the young?

7. Describe the peacock look in menswear that was popular in the 1970s.

8. In what way did the jeans of the 1970s differ from those that came earlier in the century?

9. Discuss how Ralph Lauren first influenced men's fashions.

10. What types of merchandise were introduced for street wear during the 1980s that had previously been reserved for sports activities?

11. Give examples of retro looks during the 1990s.

12. Which group of designers influenced fashion in addition to the typical creative names?

13. According to Marylou Luther's Point of View article, why do women designers really matter?

EXERCISES AND PROJECTS

1. Select apparel from two consecutive decades of the 20th century and compare them. To locate the apparel, use historic costume books, lifestyle books, fashion and lifestyle magazines, and family photo albums. You can also contact companies for archival photos and press kits. Make photocopies (or use original photos when available) of the apparel and affix the visuals from each decade on one foamcore board. Identify and label garments and accessories.

2. Collect copies of photographs of the retro styles of the 1990s from fashion and lifestyle magazines. Match them to the original styles from which they were adapted. Use your library for reference materials.

WEB SITES

By accessing these Web sites, you will be able to gain broader knowledge and up-to-date information on materials related to this chapter.

Kent Sate University Library
   www.library.kent.edu/fashion_history.html

Metropolitan Museum of Art
   www.metmuseum.org/collections/department.asp?dep=8

The Case of the Insecure Designer

Rick Waters has always been told that he has a "good eye" for fashion. In pursuit of a career in the industry, he enrolled in a four-year college that offered a wide range of fashion majors, including merchandising and design. Although he liked design, he thought that other students in the program had a much greater natural ability than he did for the creation of original designs. As a result, he decided to become a fashion merchandising major.

After graduation, he became an assistant buyer for a major department store. As he combed the markets for merchandise, he always thought that his ideas were better than many he saw. He felt he had the talent necessary to produce merchandise that would sell, even if it was not in the couture category. Generally, he was right on target with the suggestions he made for his department's fashion direction.

Dissatisfied with his career as a merchandiser, he decided to turn to some level of apparel design. After looking for a more creative position, he was hired by Sanders & Smith, a department store that was moving in the direction of private label fashions. His initial responsibility was to research sources that would enable him to style a youthful collection that would retail at moderate price points.

Excited with the opportunity to bring a new line to the market, he enthusiastically set out on his assignment.

questions

1. Where would you suggest Rick look for his inspiration?

2. How might he go about creating styles without drawing upon original ideas?

Why Women Designers Really Matter, 1930–1995

MARYLOU LUTHER

For this discourse, the fashion heroines are women designers. Female designers who changed the course of fashion during the last 65 years. Some of them were better than male designers of the same period. Some were not. All left or are leaving their mark, many of them changing our psyches along with our clothes.

When the Fashion Group was first becoming a presence on the international fashion stage in the 1930s, the two most important female designers were Madeleine Vionnet and Coco Chanel. Both made their mark by molding the dress to the woman rather than molding the woman to—and into—the dress. Both closed their doors in 1939—Vionnet never to return to fashion, Chanel reopening in 1954.

Vionnet's legacy is the bias cut. By designing in the round and cutting fabric on the diagonal, Vionnet took her mannequins out of their corsets into a dress that could be worn without fastenings and underpinnings. Hers was the first true body dress. In her book, *Couture*, Caroline Rennolds Milbank reported that "the first nipple ever shown in the pages of *Vogue* was through a bias-cut white satin of a Vionnet design in 1932—a hint at her modernity and the impact she would have on a whole century."

Chanel brought the *c* word to fashion—*c* for comfort, *c* for casual. She was the first designer to use jersey in women's clothes, the first to be influenced by the street, the first to turn an English sailor's sweater into a high-fashion pullover for women, first to translate a felt Tyrolean jacket worn by Alpine yodelers into the longest-lasting fashion of the 20th century, first designer to create a fragrance, first to use costume jewelry in haute couture, first to mix real jewels with fake, first to invent the little black dress, the rope of pearls, the shoulder bag, and the sling-back pump.

The 1940s belonged to Hollywood, and the most important women costume designers were Irene and Edith Head. Irene, who replaced the legendary Adrian as supervising designer at MGM, created Lana Turner's sweater-and-skirt look (think Prada, 1995, and you've got it) in *The Postman Always Rings Twice*, 1946. Her favorite leading lady was Ginger Rogers, whom she dressed in her signature mitered stripe suits in *Weekend at the Waldorf*, and those amazing dance dresses in *The Barkleys of Broadway* and *Lucky Partners*.

While Edith Head was to reach her greatest acclaim in the '50s, '60s, and '70s, she first made her name with the glamour dresses she designed for Barbara Stanwyck in *The Lady Eve*, 1941; Ginger Rogers's mink dress for the first fashion psychodrama, *Lady in the Dark*, 1943; and Dorothy Lamour's sarongs in *The Road to Rio*, 1947.

Both Edith and Irene predicted that skirt hems would go down when wartime shortages and the infamous L85—the War Production Board's restrictive code on use of fabric for apparel—were lifted, but it took Christian Dior's New Look at 1947 to send skirts plummeting.

In New York, Claire McCardell, Bonnie Cashin, Tina Leser, Clare Potter, and Anne Klein were beginning to carve out the first truly "American" look, defined by the easy, comfortable, casual looks that were later to become known as American sportswear.

In the 1950s, the above-mentioned designers, joined by Vera Maxwell, Carolyn Schnurer, and Jane Derby, continued to define the American concept of easy, colorful, simple dressing, totally uninfluenced by Paris design and totally supported by New York's legendary retail guru, Dorothy Shaver of Lord & Taylor. It is noteworthy that these originators of French-free American design were all women, with the exception of Rudi Gernreich and Tom Brigance.

Anne Fogarty's petticoated dresses with fitted bodices became something of a national uniform with the young, and Edith Head's strapless full-skirted tulle dress for Elizabeth Taylor in *A Place in the Sun* (1951) and her strapless ballgown for Grace Kelly in *To Catch a Thief* (1955) became the prototype for prom dresses from Los Angeles to New York.

In Paris, Chanel reopened her doors in 1954, and "the Chanel suit" became an American status symbol, thanks to the Davidow copies.

In Los Angeles, Margit Felligi was pioneering inventive new swimwear for

Cole of California, who signed Hollywood swim diva Esther Williams to promote them, and Rose Marie Reid was making waves with her own swimwear company. In the 1960s, the mega-trend was the mini, mothered in London by Mary Quant. It was the decade of the Youthquake, the Pill, ecumenics, drugs, rock 'n' roll, Woodstock, and the Age of Aquarius. Paraphernalia was the groovy boutique of this groovy era, and Betsey Johnson was its grooviest in-house designer.

Norma Kamali discovered Swinging London and brought its artifacts to her Fifty-third Street boutique, later adding her own award-winning designs, and in the '70s, becoming the first American to bring real design to inexpensive fabrics—sleeping bags and sweats.

The most important woman of the decade, Jacqueline Kennedy, was not a designer, but her influence on fashion is still being felt—as it was then with her input in Oleg Cassini's clothes for her.

The 1970s brought us the women's movement and pants—pants first as a social protest against mini skirts, later as a sign of sexual equality. Sonia Rykiel invented a new fit—high armholes, shrunken tops, pants with no pleats and round legs—and a new fashion religion, bohemianism.

In London, three women owned the decade. Thea Porter created what came to be known as the rich hippie look—a rags-to-riches idea of getting the rich folks to wear what the poor folks had worn for centuries, but translated into the world's most opulent fabrics. Her fashion seraglio on Greek Street was the quintessential expression of that fashion era's ethnic mode.

Zandra Rhodes, the queen of fashion fantasy, made the most extraordinary dream clothes of the decade, bringing such print motifs as a Las Vegas billboard to gossamer chiffon and an Australian rock to matte jersey—these at a time when evening gown prints were veritably limited to florals and dots. Her "Conceptual Chic" collection, celebrating the safety-pinned punk styles of London's Kings Road, was one of the first examples of high fashion being influenced by the street.

In a decade that became famous for reissuing ideas from the past, Jean Muir proved that modernity was alive and well, at least in her hands. She also promulgated the at-the-time strange idea that it is dishonest to tear up everything every six months just because it's time for a new collection.

The best-selling dress of the decade was Diane von Furstenberg's printed jersey wrap dress with bust darts (male designers had stopped using them). The dress that had sold more than 300,000 models at around $70 each earned her the cover of *Newsweek* in 1976, where she was called "the most marketable female in fashion since Coco Chanel."

The 1970s was also the decade of designer jeans, with best-sellers coming from heiress Gloria Vanderbilt.

Body dressing became a nationwide fashion urge, thanks in part to the disco rage and its celebration of the bodysuit with tie-on skirt in *Saturday Night Fever*. Credit Norma Kamali and Danskin designer Bonnie August for forwarding this fashion cause.

Diane Keaton's vests, ties, chino pants, and men's fedoras in the 1977 Woody Allen movie, *Annie Hall* (many from Ralph Lauren, but all assembled and styled by Keaton), influenced millions of young working women to put together similar getups in a fashion move that became known as gender bending. A few years later, Giorgio Armani called it androgyny.

The message of the 1980s was the emergence of the woman executive as reflected first by fashion androgyny, then shoulder pads, followed by minimalism and comfort-dressing.

Rei Kawakubo was the most powerful woman designer of the 1980s.

She did not, of course, invent black. She just took it from a little black dress to a big black force in global style, creating a look, a mood, and a powerful movement that shook the very foundations of fashion. She continues to see the role of artist as provocateur, and her clothes provoke real passion. Her strong feeling for asymmetry, whereby the right side of her clothes seldom knows what the left side is doing, has had a global impact.

The bodysuit gained new fashion status at the hands of Donna Karan, who made it the base garment of her collections, teaching women its slenderizing, sex-arising virtues. And the jumpsuit jumped into high fashion with its most famous advocate, Pauline Trigère.

The 1990s are mid-way as we go to press, and so far the woman designer of the decade is Donna Karan. Her DKNY collection, her menswear, her pantyhose, her leathergoods, her New York frame of mind, her fragrance, her treatment line, her London shop, her advertising—all have broken new ground. And her signature collection is one of the few today that looks to the future rather than the past. (In 1994 she presented the first interactive fashion show, with the audience flashing miners' headlights on the models so the reflective fiberglass-coated fabrics would glow. And for spring 1995 she offered prom dresses made from the paperlike fabric used in Federal Express envelopes.)

London's Vivienne Westwood is helping define the decade with her quirky, cartoonlike take on retro. Her postpunk revelations began with the crinoline, which petticoated its way around the fashion world, and she was the first to bring real, Victorian-inspired corsets and bustles to the runways, the first to show platforms with six-inch heels—the fore-runners (fore-walkers?) of today's teetering sandals.

Like Karan, Germany's Jil Sander does not believe in putting off the future by putting on the past. Her modern, streamlined clothes are making a definite impact on fashion in the '90s—first with impeccably cut suits and pantsuits, now with more complete collections notable for their fabric invention (the first metallized organzas, the first cotton tweed) and artistic use of color.

Five years from the 21st century, it is interesting to note that while some of the most famous male designers are looking back in a rage of retro, the women continue to forge ahead.

Miuccia Prada is a modernist/minimalist who has created a kind of deluxe bohemian for the fashion intelligentsia. She has made the Prada bag the status symbol of the '90s to date. Rei Kawakubo continues to make waves for Comme des Garçons, reminding everyone that the 21st century is Asia-bound. Rykiel, Muir, and Rhodes evolve their now-famous fashion handwriting. Kamali rediscovers the gym and stakes out new claims on Hollywood glamour. Yeohlee surges ahead as a futurist, her fluid, architectural designs as sane as they are urbane. Cynthia Rowley is Generation X-ercising fashion with wit and fantasy. Betsey Johnson's Youthquake never stops stirring things up. And von Furstenberg is busy reinventing home shopping.

The Fashion Group International, Inc.

the powerful consumer

Modern fashion is about freedom, democracy, and individualism, and this is a development that I, for one, welcome.

GIORGIO ARMANI, DESIGNER

After you have completed this chapter, you will be able to discuss:

- The terms *demographics* and *psychographics*.

- Different buying motives of emotional and rational purchasers.

- Categories of consumers by social classes and explain their differences.

- Differences between observation and questionnaire methods for consumer research.

- How focus groups help businesses learn about consumer wants and needs.

- Some of the legislation that has been enacted by the federal government for the protection of the consumer.

Does the designer or the consumer determine the direction fashion will take? Both approaches have advocates in the business environment. During some periods, a designer's direction, no matter how impressive his or her accomplishments, is totally ignored. At the beginning of the 1970s, for example, the industry "mandated" the midi as the proper skirt length. Across the country, however, customers rejected this new length, and retailers who stocked the midi suffered considerable losses. Rather than accept a style they did not want, many women opted for an alternative—pants. As a result of that experience, many manufacturers and retailers began to be more aware of the wants and needs of consumers.

The 21st century is a time of freedom of choice. Designers have acknowledged that they alone cannot decide what their customers want, and they are offering a smorgasbord of fashion to capture consumers' attention. The 1990s fostered the "retro" look—designs that were adapted from the most successful silhouettes, fabrics, and colors of the world's greatest fashion creators. The mid-2000s featured a return to the sexy look and the military look that echoed the uniforms of people in the armed forces fighting in Afghanistan and Iraq. Was it that designers were playing it safe, or were they judging the wants and needs of consumers by past successes?

To understand what consumers want, it is necessary to understand what motivates them to buy. The study of market segments and various sociological analyses also contribute to consumer assessment. The more attention the producers and retailers of fashion pay to the consumer, the better prepared they will be to meet the challenges of the world of fashion.

MARKET SEGMENTS

To ascertain the wants and needs of the fashion consumer, one must differentiate among the many types of fashion consumers. Income, lifestyle, age, occupation, and other characteristics create different fashion needs. The demands of young, urban business couples certainly differ from those of more conservative members of our society. By separating their clients into **market segments**, or groups, based on these various criteria, professionals in the fashion world better understand what to offer their clients. In this chapter we examine this consumer market in terms of its demographics and psychographics. In the next chapter, the impact that is being made by the ever-growing multicultural consumer will be examined.

Demographics

Demographics is the study of various objective characteristics of the population, such as population size, age, occupation, family life cycle, geographic concentration, education, and income. Market researchers can find this information in governmental sources, such as the publications of the Census Bureau and the Commerce Department, and from original research studies companies sponsor to assess their markets. The importance of each demographic factor is discussed next.

Market research categorizes consumers according to such demographic characteristics as age, income, and lifestyle in order to address their fashion needs.

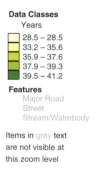

Data Classes
Years
	28.5 – 28.5
	33.2 – 35.6
	35.9 – 37.6
	37.9 – 39.3
	39.5 – 41.2

Features
Major Road
Street
Stream/Waterbody

Items in gray text are not visible at this zoom level

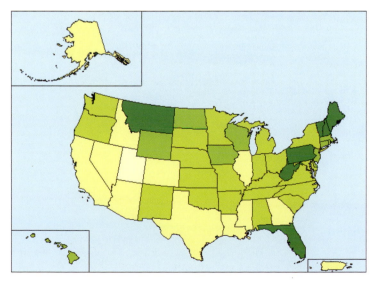

Census data are studied to project future sales.

Population

Population size and location are important considerations. A company does not study an entire population, only that portion directly related to the product being considered. For example, a children's wear manufacturer is concerned with the number of children in the general population. An infants' wear producer, however, needs more specific information about the birth rate to determine the size of the potential market. In addition to sheer numbers, the geographic concentration of people also plays a vital role. For example, the population shifts to the South in the 1980s had positive implications for manufacturers of swimwear. Similarly, the movement to the mountain states in the 1990s and early 2000s created greater needs for hiking gear.

Age

Fashion manufacturers and retailers may emphasize styles that cater to a specific age group. Therefore, to market their product effectively, they need to know what proportion of the overall population fits into each age group. The continued growth of the

Different lifestyle categories account for different needs.

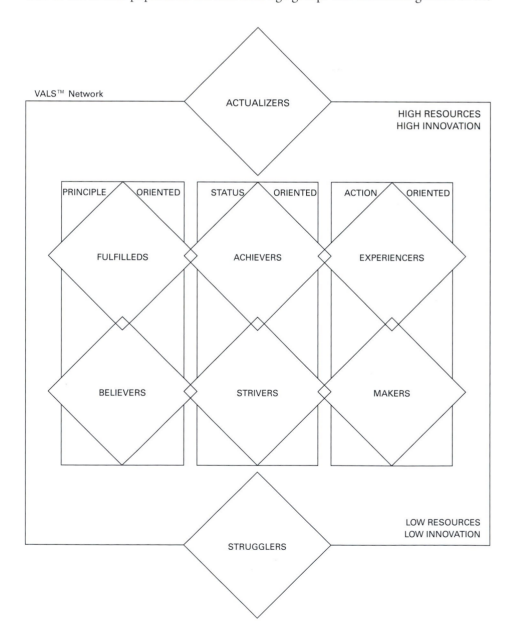

65-and-older market makes them a group that is increasingly important to the fashion industry. This is reflected in the growth of large-sized women's clothing, as women in that age group may wear clothes in that size range. This, added to the continuing demand for large sizes in all age groups, signals the specialized size producer and merchants to expand their offerings. The Limited took heed of these developments and expanded its Lane Bryant division, which specializes in larger sizes. Similarly, Talbots added a line of plus-sized clothing, called Talbots Woman, to its existing lines for misses and petites.

Occupation

Most fashion industry professionals agree that the single greatest factor affecting the women's market is their growing presence in the workforce. Not too long ago, the majority of women did not have professional careers. Today, women are participating at every level of the economy and as a result, their clothing needs have changed. More and more manufacturers are producing fashions suitable for the workplace. Many retailers have expanded their "career dress" departments and have developed personal shopping services that cater to women who have less time to shop because of professional commitments.

Another occupation-related factor—dress-down Fridays—resulted in an increase in the production of casual clothing for work during the 1990s. Many major companies had instituted relaxed dress requirements for all their employees one day a week, with some extending it into other days. This enabled even executives to shed their traditional business clothing and wear casual attire. Although this trend had given the suit manufacturers cause for concern, other manufacturers had gained by making more relaxed, but professional, attire to accommodate this change. While the dressed-down look still impacted menswear production, a return to more formal business attire occurred in the mid-2000s.

Family Life Cycle

Categorizing individuals by groups according to their life cycles is another way to determine fashion needs. Each group has its own special requirements, and a knowledge of them can help those in fashion businesses. The following classifications, which are typical segments of the **family life cycle**, are explored in terms of their potential fashion needs.

YOUNG UNMARRIED Whether they live with their parents, with their friends, or on their own, the members of this group are responsible only for themselves. With the exception of such basic costs as rent, food, and utilities, most of their **discretionary income** is spent on recreation, entertainment, and clothing. On the whole, they are a very fashion-conscious group, eager to accept style changes. Teenagers fall into this group, and they swing with the fashion trends. If the mini is in vogue, they purchase it; if next season the lengths are longer, they quickly accept that change. A great number of designers and manufacturers try to cater to this group. Buying clothing and accessories for work as well as play is an ongoing process.

NEWLY MARRIED Typically, this family unit has two wage earners. They are sometimes called *dinks*, which stands for "dual income, no kids!" Because these couples have two incomes and share household expenses, they can increase their discretionary spending on clothing as well as other purchases. The manufacturers of quality fashions and designer labels find it important to cater to this group.

Those with money to spend and time to shop are considered power shoppers.

FULL NEST I The arrival of children typically causes a temporary reduction in real and discretionary funds. Many women stay home when a child is first born, resulting in a short-term reduction in income. When they return to work, however, the cost of child care significantly diminishes the family's discretionary income. This group's fashion purchasing also radically changes. Less money is spent on clothing for the parents and more on clothing and products for the younger set.

FULL NEST II In this classification, the children are teenagers. Women who stayed home to raise their children now often return to the workplace. Those women who opted for careers are still on the job, but they may now earn substantial incomes. With their increased income, a great deal of money is again spent on fashion merchandise. As more mature women, their tastes are generally more sophisticated and not as easily influenced by trends. They look for better quality merchandise, and manufacturers of both men's and women's higher-priced merchandise target this group. The teenage offspring of this family typically enjoy "trendy" merchandise and are among the best customers for anything new on the fashion scene. These teenagers, for example, were the ones captivated by the grunge look of the early 1990s, and they quickly shed their sneakers when Doc Martens arrived on the scene. Anything new is apt to attract them! Because many teenagers work part-time, earning their own spending money, they are able to buy more expensive items.

FULL NEST III In this classification, both the husband and wife usually work, and the children, aged 17 and older, are still dependent on their parents. Family income is usually higher than ever before, and the spending on fashion merchandise is significant for all members of the family. Bearing this in mind, many manufacturers have directed their efforts toward **bridge merchandise**—goods that are well below couture, but above what is described as "better" sportswear and dresses. Examples of these labels are Dana Buchman and Ellen Tracy. Designer merchandise is directed to a large segment of the group.

Increasingly, however, the traditional **full nests** have been replaced with **single-family households**. In this nontraditional classification, often a single parent is raising the children. In these cases, purchasing fashion merchandise is not the same priority it is in *nested families*. Because total income is lower, less money is earmarked for fashion items.

EMPTY NEST I With the children on their own, much of the parents' financial responsibility has diminished. Although some women retire from their jobs, the number that remain working continues to increase. Income for this classification is generally higher than for the others. Manufacturers and retailers direct quality fashion products for both work and play at this market. Resort wear is also targeted toward this group, because its members now have the funds necessary for travel and for the clothing required for these vacations.

EMPTY NEST II In this version of the **empty nest**, members of the family have retired. As a result, there is a significant decrease in income. Except for a small group whose financial investments guarantee a "good" lifestyle, the majority in this classification are faced with cuts in spending. Thus, less is spent on fashion merchandise. Clothing for the workplace is not necessary and purchases are usually for leisure wear.

SOLE SURVIVOR I This classification includes those who have lost a spouse or life partner; in **sole survivor I**, the survivor remains on the job. Business-oriented clothing is still important. Many in this position eventually seek a new relationship, which puts new demands on fashionable dress. Because financial responsibilities are less demanding and a regular paycheck is ever-present, this group is responsible for quality purchases. Manufacturers of more mature styles find this market has little competition.

SOLE SURVIVOR II More and more people who have lost their mates are retired. Many change their lifestyles as well as their places of residence; they may move to retirement communities. With all of the social activities provided for senior citizens in these communities, more emphasis is on dress than if one lived in a more diverse community. These people become purchasers of leisure merchandise. Others in this group are constrained by lower incomes. They buy little for themselves, but continue to make purchases for family members.

Geographic Concentration

Where people live also determines the clothing and accessories they need. Obviously, a shift in population to warmer climates signals a greater need for lightweight merchandise; a shift northward would necessitate the reverse. Fashion producers must carefully study geographic concentrations to determine not only the extent of the markets for their particular products but also the market's potential for growth. California's significant population growth in the 1970s and 1980s signaled fashion designers to create styles oriented to the casual attitudes prevailing on the West Coast. Because of this shift in population, California became an important fashion resource both for its own retailers and for those merchants all across the nation catering to the needs of relaxed dressers. The state remains a major sportswear manufacturing center.

Education

Money alone does not account for the style and quality of merchandise preferred by consumers. Although many with little or no formal higher education earn substantial salaries, educational level often determines income levels and merchandise needs. As

Casual sportswear lines cater to a laid-back lifestyle associated with California.

the level of education increases, so does the number of people entering business or becoming attorneys, investment bankers, accountants, and physicians. Each profession sets its own dress standards. Individuals need apparel appropriate to their careers. A study of the educational goals of consumers will help reveal how extensive the market will be for fine-tailored clothing and accessories. Stores such as Burberry, Barney's, and Bergdorf Goodman have capitalized on the rewards of education by targeting this rapidly growing group as their primary customers.

Income

A person's income determines the quality and price of the fashion merchandise he or she purchases. Producers and retailers of fashion must be constantly aware of income shifts in their potential markets to determine the price points they will offer for sale. With the two-income family now commonplace, there is more discretionary spending. Many fashion businesses have capitalized on this increase in disposable income by offering additional lines to meet the needs of this group. Designers, such as Donna Karan and Giorgio Armani, who relied on the upper classes for their business, have added lower-priced lines—DKNY and Mani, respectively. They have captured a share of the market that has moved toward quality merchandise but still cannot afford the price points of the couture collections. Most of the major couture houses feature prêt-à-porter, or ready-to-wear, that is often more profitable than their higher-priced offerings.

In the United States, fashion is available at every price point from high-end couture to mass-produced, popular-priced lines. Later in this book, we will focus on the various fashion merchandise classifications according to their price structures.

Psychographics

A more sophisticated approach to the study of market segments is to narrow the groups into even more narrowly defined categories. For example, although age is a factor in determining consumer needs, obviously not all 30-year-old women are the same. Some are at home raising families, whereas others pursue professional careers. Their fashion merchandise needs are distinctly different. Two men earning $60,000 annually have different needs depending on their marital status, career, and type of residence. Perhaps one earns his $60,000 as a plumber, is married, and owns a home, whereas the other is single and lives in an apartment. Their needs are obviously different.

Psychographics is the subjective study of characteristics that describe motivations to buy, such as personality, lifestyle, ethnicity, attitudes, interests, and opinions. The results offer a more complete look at consumers. By identifying particular characteristics, companies can better match their products to the needs of potential customers. Instead of trying to appeal to all 30-year-old women, psychographic segmentation narrows the field to those with similar characteristics so that specific marketing tactics can be more effectively directed.

Table 3.1 is a study by the Newspaper Advertising Bureau, based on a psychographic questionnaire, which categorized men into specific psychographic groups. The essence of the study defines consumption patterns, along with commentaries on each group's fashion purchasing potential.

Table 3.1

CATEGORIES OF MEN IN SPECIFIC PSYCHOGRAPHIC GROUPS

The Quiet Family Man	A self-sufficient, shy individual with little community involvement, who spends much of his free time with his family. He has less interest in consumer goods than most men. He would not be a chief target for the fashion industry.
The Traditionalist	Security and esteem are essential to this follower of conventional rules. He perceives himself as altruistic and considers other people's welfare to be important. He is a conservative shopper and prefers well-known manufacturer's brands. Most likely he is at home wearing classic clothing from manufacturers such as Ralph Lauren, if his income affords him quality merchandise, or lines such as Botany 500 if he is inclined to buy more moderately priced clothing.
The Discontented Man	Dissatisfied with his career, his goals are for a better job, more money, and security. As a purchaser, price consciousness is his characteristic. He is a good candidate for off-price merchants, such as Syms.
The Ethical Highbrow	This man is characterized by sensitivity to others' needs, satisfaction with life and work, and interests in culture, religion, and social reform. Quality is an important consideration and is often a sufficient justification for spending greater sums on a purchase. He would probably be a good customer for lines such as Tommy Hilfiger, where understated, quality merchandise is available at higher than average prices.
The Pleasure-Oriented Man	The "macho" type, he rejects anything that gives the impression of femininity. He is self-centered and a seeker of instant gratification who buys impulsively. His purchases are more likely centered on clothing with a masculine image. He is the perfect customer for athletic apparel, such as muscle shirts, that shows off his physique.
The Achiever	A hard-working man who is interested in social prestige, power, and money, he likes adventure and social activities that revolve around good food and entertainment. He is totally status conscious—a perfect market for designers such as Giorgio Armani and stores such as Barney's.
The He-Man	Action and excitement pervade this man's life. He is a bachelor type, and even if marriage becomes a reality, he continues to conduct himself more as a dominant, single individual. High fashion leather apparel is what would attract his attention.
The Sophisticated Man	An intellectual who admires people of artistic and intellectual achievement. He is the epitome of those whose images are socially cosmopolitan. His tastes in clothing are both unique and fashionable. He would be at home wearing Ralph Lauren and Bill Blass creations and shopping in upscale specialty stores such as Paul Stuart.

A company that manufactures men's apparel and wishes to find a specific market could make meaningful use of the breakdowns in Table 3.1. For example, a designer of men's leather pants and bomber jackets would immediately eliminate several groups based on this study, such as the quiet family man, the traditionalist, the discontented man, and the ethical highbrow. The remaining groups, most notably the pleasure-oriented man, the achiever, and the he-man, would be targeted by this company, as might the sophisticated man.

Although psychographic studies are being used more than ever, they alone should not guide fashion producers and retailers in their pursuit of the best consumer market. They should be used in conjunction with other considerations, such as demographics and factors such as social issues and class structure, which will be examined in the remainder of this chapter.

Buying Motives

Do price and quality motivate a customer to buy designer merchandise? Does the prestige of the label stimulate purchasing? Does the polo pony logo on a Ralph Lauren shirt make it a better product, or does the name increase its desirability? Consumers are motivated to buy for different reasons—some emotional, others rational. To better satisfy the consumer, those in the fashion industry also evaluate potential markets on the basis of motives.

Emotional Motives

Status and prestige are often involved in the purchase of consumer products. Fashion merchandise, in particular, often appeals to **emotional motives**. Throughout history, many people have selected apparel based on the designer's name. A

Standard gear for the youth market includes T-shirts and backpacks.

Dolce & Gabbana creation or a Giorgio Armani suit is sure to attract the attention of many fashion enthusiasts. Often, fabrics used by designers capture the consumer's senses. Denim, for example, prior to the 1970s was an important fabric in the manufacture of jeans. This durable, practical material gave the wearer many years of service. The product was not fashion oriented, but was worn primarily by teenagers and workers who wore denim clothing for practical purposes. Along came Sasson and Calvin Klein, and the designer jeans market was born. Labels were no longer hidden inside the garment, but were displayed for everyone to see. Jeans became a status fashion, and prices quickly escalated. Were the enormous sales due to fine construction, durability, and fair pricing, all rational reasons for purchasing, or was the customer motivated by the prestige associated with a fashion designer?

Although the geniuses of fashion often provide creative styling, expert tailoring, and exquisite fabrics, would their sales be as great if their garments were not identified with world-famous labels? Designers, manufacturers, and retailers are not in business to teach people about product quality and price, but to give customers what they want. If the polo pony logo provides greater profitability for the producer and retailer, then they should market these products as long as customers purchase them. The creations and more notably the "labels" identifying Pierre Cardin in the 1960s and 1970s emotionally motivated shoppers to purchase designer clothing and accessories. In the home furnishings industry, sales have skyrocketed since apparel designers have signed licensing agreements with those manufacturers. Bill Blass, Ralph Lauren, Adrienne Vittadini, and Calvin Klein have had a great deal of success by affixing their labels to bed linens and china. The quality is not necessarily better, but the motives for purchasing have changed.

A World of Fashion Profile of Pierre Cardin reveals how his business astuteness helped the world to become more conscious of designer labels.

Rational Motives

Other consumers base their purchases on careful examination of the products. Is the quality good? Is it competitively priced? Is the material durable? These are all questions considered by the rational buyer. The rational female consumer is not motivated to buy simply because everyone is wearing a new, fashionable skirt length. Her

the world of fashion profile

PIERRE CARDIN

Whether it was restlessness, aggressiveness, compulsiveness, or just good business sense that drove Pierre Cardin to involve himself in so many enterprises, no one else has had his hand in as many fashion ventures.

His name was not necessarily as famous as some of the other couturiers at the middle of the 20th century, when he designed haute couture. He never achieved the stature of the likes of Chanel, Dior, and Schiaparelli. However, Cardin recognized that there was a fashion world of consumers who would love designer creations but simply could not afford the extravagant prices.

Some of his designs, such as the *bubble dress* of the 1950s, caught the public's attention and were quickly copied by manufacturers at many price points. Cardin understood that consumers would eagerly buy designer merchandise if the design bore a couturier's name but was priced below the cost of original designs.

He was certainly the major force behind the licensing of designer labels. For a fee, Cardin allowed a manufacturer of his choice the right to affix the Cardin label to merchandise that the manufacturer would produce. Cardin did not necessarily have a hand in creation of the merchandise, but he had the right of approval before it could be marketed. With this move, the Cardin label was everywhere—on women's, men's, and children's clothing, as well as on watches, jewelry, handbags, belts, wallets, active sportswear, and swimsuits. His name was now visible in every coun-

Pierre Cardin was a major force behind licensing.

try with a fascination for designer clothing. Cardin's licenses numbered several hundred.

He set the stage for others such as Geoffrey Beene, Bill Blass, Dior, Donna Karan, and Emanuel Ungaro. In some cases, the labels were affixed to the outside of the garments on sleeves, collars, pockets, and cuffs for all the world to see. Licensing provided the average person with status and prestige clothing once reserved for the privileged.

In addition to apparel and accessories design, Cardin made an impact with unique furniture designs in the 1970s. With new interest in those designs, he is enjoying a renaissance of the styles, and at age 83 he is planning to open a furniture factory in Vietnam, where his lacquered designs will once again reemerge. A Point of View article in Chapter 15, Home Fashions, explores the interest in his furniture creations.

decision is based on whether or not it is appropriate for her figure. Designer names do not play a major role in the rational purchaser's decision making. Consumers who use **rational motives** when making purchases constitute a sizable segment of the fashion market.

Many retailers who offer private label merchandise that compares in style and quality to the designer lines, but costs less, have found that rationally motivated shoppers will purchase these products. Manufacturers who specialize in knockoffs of designer styles also reach an audience comprised of rational shoppers.

The number of off-price merchants, such as Loehmann's, Marshalls, Filene's Basement, and T.J. Maxx, who carry well-known items but sell them for less, are satisfying the needs of the shopper who likes the notion of wearing designer merchandise but considers price first and foremost.

By knowing their clientele, fashion professionals can move in either direction. Their marketing strategies might include all of the elements that motivate emotional purchasing or those that stimulate rational considerations. Many fashion retailers make this decision by offering a merchandise mix oriented toward both emotional and rational buyers.

Buying Habits

Americans have had certain long-held shopping habits regarding when, where, and how they make their purchases. For most of the past century, stores were the main places in which to shop. Most often, shopping needs were satisfied very close to the time the products were to be used. Except for purchases such as wedding gowns and special-event dresses, women often fulfilled their fashion desires as late as possible. In contrast to the first half of the century, when early purchasing for fashion was the norm, a philosophy of "the later, the better" dominated the decades of the 1970s, 1980s, 1990s, and 2000s.

Purchases were generally made at locations convenient to consumers' homes or places of employment. Once a store satisfied the shopper's needs, repeat business was the usual mode of purchasing. Buying was usually for one item at a time, unless the purpose was for travel, special occasions such as honeymoons, going away to college, or anything that made single purchases impractical.

Late in the 20th century, however, consumer buying habits began to change. With a wealth of catalogs coming into the home, many working and time-pressured shoppers changed their approach to shopping. It was no longer necessary to visit a favorite place to shop for the sake of convenience, nor was it necessary to go from store to store to find a specific product. Every major fashion retailer offered numerous catalogs throughout the year, as did separate catalog retailers. By merely browsing through the multitude of catalogs, just about every shopping need could be satisfied.

By the mid-1990s, when more than 10 million computers were connected to the Internet, consumers' shopping habits had changed once more. In the mid-2000s the number of computers with Internet capability grew significantly, making online shopping even more attractive for retailers and consumers. Subscribers to an online service such as AOL could shop from the convenience of their homes or places of business with complete ease, effortlessly interacting with the e-retailers. Every type of fashion product, at almost any price point, could be quickly viewed, purchased, and delivered in a timely manner. A special shopping trip was no longer necessary, and bucking the crowds was a thing of the past. Some Web sites made purchasing even more practical with the advent of virtual mannequins, which consumers could use to visualize how they would look in a specific item.

The success of online shopping is illustrated by the sales generated during the last seasonal-shopping week of the year. A record number of consumers were trading in their old shopping habits for a new set that afforded them greater comfort and convenience in purchasing. Although these numbers show considerable interest in online purchasing, the sales numbers still pale by comparison with shopping in the bricks-and-mortar venues.

SOCIOLOGICAL CONSIDERATIONS

Other factors to consider in addressing consumer needs are sociologically based. Lifestyle, for example, necessitates changes in clothing design. Students of all ages once dressed more formally. Some dress codes for kindergarten through high school required ties and shirts for boys and dresses for girls. Even footwear was regulated. In sharp contrast, today's younger generation generally wears fashionable clothing such as jeans, T-shirts, and athletic shoes. This, particularly in the public-school sector, has become standard dress for attending class. Given this trend, the producers of formal school attire quickly found their market severely limited. However, in some schools (including public high schools), there is a new movement to require students to wear uniforms. One of the major reasons is to eliminate clothing competition, and this notion is being supported by legislation.

School uniforms are gaining popularity in both public and private schools.

Casual dress is a part of every age group's lifestyle. With the emphasis on relaxation and physical fitness, some merchandise classifications have grown. Sweatshirts and pants, warm-up suits, and athletic shoes had taken dollars away from other product groups. The trend toward dress-down Fridays, as discussed earlier, made casual attire appropriate even in the boardroom. President Clinton gave greater credibility to activewear every time he appeared on television in his running apparel. When did presidents of the United States appear before their public so casually dressed? Going to a restaurant for a casual dinner at one time required somewhat more formal dress. Today, a sweatsuit and athletic shoes can often be appropriate attire.

Another social phenomenon being addressed by the fashion world is the change in the status of women. As already explored, women are in many instances major breadwinners in the family. They earn their own money and spend more than ever before on discretionary purchases. Fashion producers, recognizing this change, have redirected their marketing efforts. Many now approach women as intelligent, independent, educated individuals whose interests are not solely home centered. Merchants and producers specializing in career dress for women are finding this to be a lucrative market.

Those in the fashion industry are best served when they address the social changes in society and market merchandise that best suits these changes.

Social Classes

We often hear about the various **social classes** into which our society is divided. In terms of income, goals, and attitudes, the U.S. population is generally categorized into upper, middle, and lower classes, and then into subdivisions of each. By studying these various groups, fashion merchandisers have yet another barometer by which to judge how best to target their customers.

Upper Class

These are the wealthiest people in our society, about 3 percent of the population. Although money is the primary factor for inclusion in this group, there is a difference in purchasing practices among the different levels within the upper class.

UPPER-UPPER CLASS Those in the upper-upper class have inherited wealth and are the socially elite members of our society. Their purchases tend to be conservative, with quality an important factor; trendiness is not an important consideration. Cost is unimportant to the members of this class. Understated elegance is probably the best way to describe their fashion preferences.

LOWER-UPPER CLASS Although their wealth may exceed that of the upper-upper class, members of the lower-upper class do not have the appropriate family history to join that group. This group is made up of the *nouveau riche* (new rich). They, too, do not consider cost to be important, and their fashion purchases are usually made in the finest shops featuring the best of European and American couture. To this group, the label is everything. Many in this group tell the world of their success, and do it through material extravagances, such as wearing expensive, recognizable apparel.

Middle Class

Approximately 42 percent of the population is considered middle class. Segmentation of the middle class is also important, because the top and the bottom behave quite differently in terms of purchasing.

UPPER-MIDDLE CLASS Although they prefer designer labels and fashion-forward merchandise, this group is a little more cautious about the money it spends than are the members of the upper class. Recognizing this group as an excellent market for designer labels, many of the top fashion producers manufacture separate lines for its consideration. Donna Karan and Perry Ellis, for example, whose couture lines were priced too extravagantly for the middle class, satisfied the needs of these consumers with lines such as DKNY and Perry Ellis Portfolio. These lines were lower priced, but satisfied customers with their status labels. So successful were these innovators that others, such as Isaac Mizrahi, with the Isaac label, and Giorgio Armani with Mani, followed suit.

Many in this class are regular shoppers at off-price stores such as Loehmann's, T.J. Maxx, and Filene's Basement, where they purchase designer labels at lower prices than those charged at traditional department and specialty stores.

LOWER-MIDDLE CLASS Unlike the upper level of the middle class, this group's merchandise selections are geared to lesser-quality merchandise. They are often the purchasers of trendy merchandise copied down to lower price points that they can afford. Stores such as Contempo Casuals, Express, and Pants Place are where they typically shop for fashion merchandise.

Lower Class

This class constitutes the largest segment of the American population, accounting for approximately 55 percent of the total number. Although extremely price conscious, they account for the purchase of a significant amount of the merchandise produced by the industry.

UPPER-LOWER CLASS Price is very important to this group, and purchases are generally made at stores that sell budget merchandise. Most purchasing is done at specialty chains that offer merchandise at minimum prices, such as Lerner New York. They seek fashion items, but their purchases are made when the styles have reached their lowest prices. In addition to the lower-priced specialty chains, they patronize the value discount retailers such as Kmart, Target, Wal-Mart, and Kohl's and off-price stores such as Marshalls and Stein Mart. They are also the targets of the cable shopping networks where inexpensive, low-quality merchandise is available.

LOWER-LOWER CLASS More concerned with survival than fashion, these individuals purchase clothing and accessories as necessities.

FASHION AND CONSUMER RESEARCH

The study of market segments, buying motives, sociological considerations, and social classes provides general information with which the fashion professional can evaluate the potential consumer market. Some producers, retailers, market consultants, and trade associations prefer to learn even more about their prospective customers. Many, therefore, conduct research studies dealing with specifics rather than generalities. They sometimes use investigative techniques, such as observations, questionnaires, and focus groups, to gather information they can use to evaluate the wants and needs of consumers. The type of information gathered can include what styles people are wearing, where they like to shop, whether personal shopping would present a plus for a retailer trying to reach a specific market, which fashion magazines are best suited to promote a collection, and at what price points targeted customers are likely to spend. Online retailers are also benefiting from data about customers gathered on their Web sites. Such information enables them to monitor buying patterns of large groups as well as individual consumers, customizing their approach to each.

The Research Procedure

When those in the fashion industry decide that they must make important decisions concerning their businesses, they sometimes engage in formal research. The majority of companies go to outside sources for these projects. The giants of the industry, such as DuPont, which might want to investigate consumer acceptance of fibers, or The Limited, which constantly needs to assess new locations for expansion, sometimes rely on their in-house staffs to conduct research on an ongoing basis. Whichever approach is followed, the methodology for studying the problems is the same. The following process represents the steps used for successful research.

Identifying and Defining the Problem

Among the situations that might be considered are these: a designer who wants to change price points, a retailer who is considering the introduction of a new division, or a trade association that is toying with the idea of moving its sales exposition to another geographic area. Research studies can help define the problems that might result from these changes.

To make certain that the research concentrates on the specific problem, a further refinement of the problem might prove necessary. For example, a fashion designer who wants to see if other merchandise classifications might warrant future manufacturing considerations must also study these questions: how large is the market for men's active sportswear, and is the timing right to enter such an arena?

Once the problem to be studied has been sufficiently focused, the research project can move forward.

Gathering Data

The next step is to gather the data on which a decision can be based. Data are available from two sources—secondary and primary. Secondary sources are examined first, because they are more readily available, inexpensive to collect, and might satisfy the needs of the research team without the necessity of entering the arena of original or primary research.

Secondary data are available from a variety of places, including those listed below:

1. *Company Records.* Companies offer a great deal of information, including sales reports, product returns, price-point analyses, and so forth. Because this information is on hand at most companies, it is easy to retrieve and examine for decisions that might have to be addressed in the research study. For example, a women's fashion manufacturer that is studying the possibility of adding a companion men's line might study the nature of the retail outlets it already serves to determine if enough of them also sell menswear.

2. *Governmental Agencies.* The federal government, in particular, investigates and publishes information that could be beneficial to a fashion merchant. For example, a merchant who is considering entering the import market would be interested to know that the U.S. Government Printing Office publishes a tariff schedule for imported merchandise that lists the rates of duty as well as the rules of importing. Other regular studies that have implications for fashion business include the various census reports. The Monthly Catalog of U.S. Government Publications lists a wealth of materials on business conditions that provide invaluable information to fashion companies.

Gathering data with personal interviews is an early step in a research procedure.

3. *Trade Associations.* Many associations in the fashion industry deal with matters that could help those in need of research assistance. Associations include the National Retail Federation (NRF), which covers the retailing field, and the Leather Association, which covers the leather industry. The reports they generate could help investigators with their projects.

4. *Periodicals.* Numerous trade papers and magazines regularly engage in research projects or publish stories that cover the fashion industry. Publications such as *Women's Wear Daily* (*WWD*) and *Daily News Record* (*DNR*) are full of such information. Other publications such as *Stores* magazine and *Visual Merchandising* (*VM*) and *Store Design* (*SD*), both retail-oriented, are excellent sources.

Primary data are pursued when secondary research proves insufficient for the needs of the investigators. The data must be obtained by original research. The information is gathered from customers, potential product users, employees, vendors, market representatives, and the media. The major techniques employed in the gathering of data for primary studies are questionnaires, observation, and focus groups.

1. *Questionnaires.* By asking a series of questions, fashion companies may be better able to satisfy consumers. This **questionnaire method** makes inquiries by personal interviews, telephone, or mail. The choice depends on such factors as the size of the market, its location, and how quickly the responses are needed.

    No matter which type of collection procedure is followed, a number of details, in terms of questionnaire preparation, must be considered before the researcher may begin to gather the data.

    - The length of the form must be as brief as possible—limited to one page in most cases. A longer questionnaire could easily discourage the respondent.

    - The language should be appropriate to the respondents. If the questionnaire is directed to industry practitioners, then the language of the trade is perfect. If consumers are the targets, avoid technical terminology. If the form will be mailed, the rule of simplicity is even more important. The interviewer, who might have helped consumers interpret difficult questions, will not be present.

    - The questions should be arranged sequentially so that a smooth transition is made from one to another.

    - Every question should be specific, and words such as "generally" and "usually" should be avoided. Such words might have different meanings to different respondents.

    - Wherever possible, choices should be given for possible answers. In this way, the data will not require interpretation and can be compiled more easily.

    An example of a typical questionnaire used by a fashion retailer is shown on page 78.

2. *Observation.* By merely observing a group of people, one can make some judgments about their fashion preferences. Reporters from *Women's Wear Daily*, for example, often use this **observation technique**. They attend most of the affairs frequented by those most likely to wear high-fashion merchandise. At the annual presentation of the Council of Fashion Design Awards, for example, those who make and wear the most creative designs are assessed without having a single question thrown at them. As each attendee enters the event, photographers and

Typical questionnaire used by fashion retailers.

Dear Preferred Customer:

In all the years of our existence, we have tried to provide you with fashionable merchandise that is timely and represents the creations of the world's major designers and manufacturers. In an effort to offer you even greater exclusivity, we are considering the inclusion of merchandise that will be designed by our own team of product developers. They have had a great deal of expertise in the fashion world. The merchandise, classified as private label, will have a fashion-forward emphasis, and will be priced to suit the needs of many of our customers.

If you would answer the following questions, not only will it help us in our new direction, but we would be delighted to offer you a certificate entitling you to a 20 percent discount on your next purchase.

You may be assured the information you have provided will be confidential and used only for this research.

1. What percent of your fashion purchases are made at one of our stores?
   ___ up to 10%
   ___ over 10% to 25%
   ___ over 25% to 50%
   ___ over 50%

2. What percent of your purchases are designer labels?
   ___ up to 10%
   ___ over 10% to 25%
   ___ over 25% to 50%
   ___ over 50%

3. When you shop in stores that offer their own brands (private labels), what percent of the merchandise is of that nature? _____

4. Would you consider purchasing our own brands? _____

5. Could you suggest a name for our new children's private label merchandise? _____
   _____

6. What is your family income?
   ___ under $30,000
   ___ from over $30,000 to $40,000
   ___ from over $40,000 to $50,000
   ___ from over $50,000 to $70,000
   ___ from over $70,000 to $100,000
   ___ over $100,000

7. What is your family status?
   ___ Single, living alone
   ___ Single, living with roommate
   ___ Newlywed
   ___ Married with children under five years
   ___ Married with children from six to twelve
   ___ Married with teenagers
   ___ Married with older children
   ___ Empty nester (still employed)
   ___ Empty nester (retired)
   ___ Divorced or separated (with family)
   ___ Divorced or separated (no family)

8. What is your occupation? Include "working at home" if you are a homemaker. _____
   _____

reporters quickly record what they are wearing. The news is often reported on the pages of *WWD*, in other publications, and on television newscasts.

More formal observations, or *counts*, are sometimes conducted to provide specific data on just about any fashion category. These **fashion counts** theoretically determine which styles people are wearing. Thus, if a large percentage of men in the study wore suits that were more form-fitting than traditional styles, it might be a signal that men were ready to move into that silhouette.

The fashion count is particularly important in times of radical fashion change. When skirt lengths are being shifted from one extreme to the other, it is prudent for fashion retailers to take a look at what people are wearing, and not necessarily at what the designers are touting. Stocking the wrong length, of course, could be detrimental to the store's profit.

Observation has a distinct advantage over the questionnaire in that it does not require the participation of those being studied. It merely involves the selection of a site in which the people needed for observation purposes congregate. For a look at formal wear, the choice might be the opening night at New York's Metropolitan Opera, where those inclined to show off the latest couturier designs will be present. The beach of a winter resort would be a perfect setting for the swimsuit manufacturer to observe popular styles, so that those with great appeal might be included in the company's next summer collection.

Once the location for counting has been selected, a simple form is used to record the observations. Teams are sent out to do the recording and report back with the collected data.

The example below is typical of a fashion count that a men's formal wear manufacturer might want to use to assess wearer preferences.

3. *Focus Groups.* This technique, which involves a small group of people and a moderator, is being used more and more often. Businesses invite representative members of potential markets to join a panel to evaluate their offerings, methods of advertising, promotional endeavors, services, and so on. Typically, the **focus group** is comprised of 10 to 15 people on a one-time or regular basis. Through active participation, the moderator is able to note the participants' various opinions about what is being studied. The information is recorded and videotaped. A retailer might form a group to determine whether or not a new level of fashion items should be added to the store's merchandise mix. A manufacturer might

Fashion count used by a manufacturer of men's formal wear.

Suit Style	Color	Lapel
single breasted/plain	black	notched
single breasted/vest	dark blue	peaked
double breasted/plain	white jacket	shawl
double breasted/vest	printed jacket	none
other	other	other
_____	_____	_____

Survey Site _____

Instructions: Circle one selection in each category, or write-in those that do not fit any of the preselected choices.

Marketers use focus groups to develop design ideas, advertising plans, and sales strategies.

convene a focus group to consider the expansion of its present couture operation to include prêt-à-porter.

Extremely important factors in the use of focus groups are the selection of those in the study and the choice of a competent recorder who will be able to note even the smallest subtleties offered. This technique produces excellent results for fashion producers and retailers.

Sampling and Collecting Data

After determining the appropriate methodology for collecting data, researchers must determine how many responses are needed for the survey to be meaningful. It is neither necessary nor practical to involve every relevant individual or company in the study in order to come to a meaningful conclusion. A fashion manufacturer with a potential retail market of 1,500 stores, for example, need not gather information from all of those retailers. It need only to investigate a representative portion of that population. The segment that is selected is known as a sample. For the results to be effective, however, the sample must be truly representative of the group.

Among the different **sampling** techniques employed by researchers are the following:

RANDOM SAMPLING In **random sampling**, each individual or business in a predetermined group has an equal chance to be selected. If, for example, a designer wanted to know how retailers would react to his or her line, a list of all of the stores in the market would be needed, but only a small percent would be surveyed.

NONRANDOM SAMPLING **Nonrandom sampling** is similar to random sampling, except that the sample is restricted to, perhaps, one price point. Thus, depending on the criterion, only stores with merchandise price points of more than, for example, $200 might be considered.

AREA SAMPLING In situations where a particular area is being studied, the **area sample** would be restricted to those stores that fall within a predetermined boundary. The actual number to be included is determined by statistical formula.

Once the sample has been decided on, the data are collected. Mail or telephone surveys, personal interviews, or other methods may be used by professionals from marketing research organizations, in-house staffs, or college students who have trained to gather data.

Processing and Analyzing Data

Once the data have been collected, they must be processed. In the case of questionnaire or observation techniques, careful preparation of the forms used will make processing easier. If open-ended questions have been avoided and every conceivable response given a separate category requiring a simple check-off, the task will be accomplished quickly. Using computers, the data are then tallied.

Once the data have been organized, analysis can take place. Some studies, such as those seeking to identify color directions from fashion counts, can be readily summarized. Those that cover more complicated issues may require further interpretation.

This phase of the research is the most important, because it will encourage management to move in a particular direction. Therefore, seasoned marketing analysts evaluate all of their client's options and make recommendations as to which will be most beneficial. Those who conduct research in-house must make certain that their assessments are not biased and are the results of input from many members of the management team.

The final step is a written report that outlines all of the stages of the study. This report, along with charts, graphs, and other materials, will help to explain the research team's suggestions.

The power of the consumer is what makes one store, designer, or business profitable and others unsuccessful. That consumers do make conscious choices is evident from the fact that some products sell in enormous quantities and others fail miserably. So powerful are consumers that only the inexperienced fashion professional ignores their wishes and fails to plan for them.

CONSUMER SAFEGUARDS

Although the consumer is powerful in terms of accepting and rejecting merchandise, he or she may not always be aware of industry practices that diminish the value of consumer selections, making them impractical or even dangerous. The federal government has enacted legislation designed to protect consumers from unnecessary harm. Some fabrics, for example, are flammable and can cause severe burns. These fabrics were once used in children's clothing, such as pajamas. To protect the consumer, the federal government passed the Flammable Fabrics Act of 1953, which restricted the use of the more dangerous of these fabrics. This act and the other pieces of legislation described next reflect the government's role in protecting the consumer.

Wool Products Labeling Act of 1939

This act was instituted to inform consumers as well as product manufacturers of the type of wool and the possible presence of wool fiber substitutes in particular fabrics and garments. Under the jurisdiction of the Federal Trade Commission (FTC), the **Wool Products Labeling Act** has been amended several times. It requires that the label affixed to a wool product indicate the percentage of fiber content by weight and the wool category used in the product. The categories include:

- Wool, new wool, or virgin wool for fibers that have never been previously manufactured.

- Recycled wool for fibers used in a woven or felted material that was never worn by the ultimate consumer and was turned back into a fibrous state.

Fur Products Labeling Act of 1952

Amended several times in 1961, 1967, 1969, and 1980, the **Fur Products Labeling Act** was passed to enable consumers to identify the actual fur used in the garment. Before passage of this legislation, consumers were regularly confused with such "furs" as mink-dyed muskrat or seal-dyed rabbit. Both of these were actually misrepresentations, because the first was not mink and the second was not seal. The act requires that a label indicate the country of origin, if other than the United States; the English name of the animal; whether the fur has been dyed; and whether the garment is made of "waste" pieces. The act also requires the same information to be used in all advertisements.

Flammable Fabrics Act of 1953

Initially, the main purpose of this act was to prohibit the use of highly flammable fabrics in the manufacture of articles of clothing transported in interstate commerce. Fabrics were required to pass a 45-degree-angle rate-of-burning test. The government later concluded that the burning rate alone was an insufficient test. Factors such as molten fiber drippings, smoke intensity, and temperature of ignition were also important. In 1967, therefore, the act was amended to include fabrics used for interior furnishings, as well as such related materials as paper, plastic, rubber, and synthetic foam. On May 14, 1973, enforcement of the **Flammable Fabrics Act** was transferred to an independent regulatory agency, the Consumer Product Safety Commission.

Textile Fiber Products Identification Act of 1960

Enforced by the FTC, the **Textile Fiber Products Identification Act** requires that certain fiber content information be clearly indicated on labels that are securely affixed and conspicuously placed on products. The items included are the generic names of the fiber, the percentage of fiber content by weight listed in descending order of dominance, the country where the product is manufactured, and the manufacturer's name or a registered identification number.

Care Labeling of Textile Wearing Apparel Act of 1972

Enacted in 1972, the **Care Labeling of Textile Wearing Apparel Act** was amended in 1984. Administered by the FTC, it requires that care labels be affixed to most textile apparel products used to cover the body, and most fabrics sold to the consumer for home sewing. The label must be conspicuously and securely placed, as well as indicate one care method, such as washing, and give instructions for doing so.

CHAPTER HIGHLIGHTS

- People in the fashion world approach consumer markets in one of two ways. Some try to dictate fashion, while others try to satisfy consumer wants or needs.
- Marketing research studies demographic and psychographic factors to determine what consumers want, based on a variety of characteristics.
- Consumers buy goods for emotional or rational reasons.
- Every social class has specific characteristics that influence its purchasing patterns.
- To determine how to market products most successfully, manufacturers, designers, and retailers conduct market studies.
- In these marketing studies, data are gathered through secondary and primary sources. Secondary sources include company records, publications by government agencies, and the activities of trade associations. Primary sources include questionnaires, observation, and focus groups.
- After data are collected, they are processed and analyzed to determine consumer preferences.
- The federal government has enacted legislation to protect the consumer.

IMPORTANT FASHION TERMINOLOGY AND CONCEPTS

area sample
bridge merchandise
Care Labeling of Textile
   Wearing Apparel Act
   of 1972
demographics
discretionary income
emotional motives
empty nest
family life cycle

fashion count
Flamable Fabrics Act of 1953
focus group
full nest
Fur Products Labeling Act
   of 1952
market segment
nonrandom sampling
observation technique
psychographics

questionnaire method
random sampling
rational motives
sampling
single-family households
social classes
Textile Fiber Products
   Identification Act of 1960
Wool Products Labeling Act
   of 1939

FOR REVIEW

1. Aside from designers, who else is important in determining which styles will become popular?

2. Define the term *demographics*.

3. What is meant by the term *market segment*?

4. Differentiate between the terms *full nest* and *empty nest*.

5. Explain how the geographic concentration of consumers plays an important role in the manufacture of fashion merchandise.

6. Define the term *psychographics*.

7. Which emotions play a more important role in the purchase of designer merchandise that has easily seen, identifiable labels or logos?

8. What is the major difference between the upper and lower segments of the upper class in terms of how they purchase merchandise?

9. How does the observation method differ from the questionnaire technique?

10. Describe the role of the participants in a focus group.

11. Is it necessary to survey every potential member of a group to come to a conclusion about the group?

12. What is meant by random sampling?

13. What are some of the features of the Fur Products Labeling Act?

14. Why was the Flammable Fabrics Act enacted into law?

15. In the Point of View titled "Whatever Happened to Customer Loyalty?" what conditions led to the demise of such loyalty?

EXERCISES AND PROJECTS

1. Prepare a questionnaire form that explores consumer thoughts on private label merchandise. After the form has been developed, use it as the basis for a research project. Methodology for data collection should be determined and carried out by the class.

2. Develop an observation form that could be used to determine customer preference for a particular fashion product. Swimsuits, for example, would be excellent for warm weather climates and coats for the colder regions. The form should list as many styles of the selected category as possible. The information could be easily obtained from photographs in fashion magazines.

   Once the form has been completed, teams should be assigned to places where the merchandise is worn, and counts of the different styles should be recorded. By tabulating the results, a customer preference determination can be made.

3. Contact a regulatory agency, such as the Federal Trade Commission, for information on the different legislation the agency oversees that protects the consumer. With the information, prepare an oral report for delivery to the class.

WEB SITES

By accessing these Web sites, you will be able to gain broader knowledge and up-to-date information on materials related to this chapter.

The Gallup Organization

   www.gallup.com

U.S. Department of Commerce

   www.commerce.gov

AC Nielsen

   www.acnielsen.com

The Case of the Disloyal Customer

questions

1. Has Granvilles properly defined its problem?

2. What type of research would you suggest Granvilles undertake to solve its problem? Why?

Granvilles is a specialized department store located in the northeastern United States. It has been in operation for the past 50 years, operating first from its flagship store. With significant success, it opened 12 branch operations. Except for the flagship store, which is located in a busy downtown area, the other units are located in upscale, regional malls.

The store has always restricted its merchandise mix to men's, women's, and children's apparel and accessories. The price points are at levels that appeal primarily to upper-middle-class families. Until three years ago, Granvilles had been extremely profitable. Sales continued to increase, and management was satisfied with the showing.

During the past three years, however, there has been a noticeable decline in sales volume and profits. After carefully assessing its method of operation, management concluded that it was not doing anything different now than it had in the past. The only explanation for the decline in sales was competition from a major off-price retailer that was carrying some of the same designer labels at lower prices. Although Granvilles appealed to these manufacturers to stop shipping to its rival, the request was ignored. By selling to the off-price retailer, the manufacturers were able to dispose of leftovers at the season's end.

After numerous meetings, management decided that it could bring back some customers by adding private label merchandise to its inventory. Recognizing that the customer was important to the success of Granvilles, management decided to scientifically study the problem before making any final decision.

Whatever Happened to Customer Loyalty?

As the retail wars intensify and as the markets of the '90s continue to be re-shaped by more value-conscious consumers and radically new systems of retail distribution, a new debate is emerging regarding "customer loyalty." At its nucleus, the issue is the age-old question of what drives consumer purchases the most. Is it price, quality, service, image, or convenience?

The outcome of this debate is of no small consequence since it forms the core selling philosophy of today's retail industry. For manufacturers, customer loyalty has been sought through the development of "brand equity" and "power brands." This is what is achieved, purportedly, through sustained, high-quality, national and global advertising. Such positioning enabled a product or manufacturer to be "top of mind" as consumers considered their purchase needs.

At the retail end, power brands have also been important in a variety of key ways. Retailers initially drew people into their stores by featuring power brands. In so doing, many retailers developed into "brands" themselves, and the strongest became the "anchors" that determined the success of shopping malls.

For manufacturers and stores alike, it is clear that the customer loyalties of the past are gone and that there is a new set of dynamics driving consumer purchasing patterns. Several events occurred to destroy the conditions that had built customer loyalty.

Power Brands Are Everywhere

The days when power brands were the primary drawing cards for department stores have been replaced by ubiquitous availability. Because of a variety of factors—overcapacity in manufacturing, for one—power brands began appearing in mass merchandisers and then discounters and then through the mail and then in factory outlets.

As this occurred, the role and value of "power brands" changed. Not only were they no longer something any outlet could claim to carry with exclusivity, the price consumers had to pay for them varied all over the lot.

The New Category Killers

To capitalize on the changing conditions, "category killer" retailers have emerged, purchasing power brands in specific categories, concentrating on making them available to consumers with the greatest selection at the lowest price.

Intelligent, Value-Conscious Consumers

Over the past decade, consumers have gotten a whole lot smarter about their purchasing and are now naturally attracted to the option that allows them to buy what they need at the "low price."

A sustained period with little growth in disposable income has naturally led consumers toward a position where price has become a more significant component of the overall purchase decision.

These and such developments as product parity, lower disposable income, time pressures, and so on, have eroded both traditional brand loyalty and store loyalty to a large degree. Both still exist, but the lines between brand, store, price, and "service" as the key selling points are blurring.

Brand Loyalty Sways

One of the first victims of these shifts has been brand loyalty. Throughout the consumer product spectrum, few brands have remained unscathed despite their prior levels of loyalty. And, this is not an issue that just affects consumers in the lower income brackets; indeed, this lack of purchasing commitment has affected those in the $50,000-plus range.

A national poll conducted by New York advertising agency Warwick Baker & Fiore last March found that 90 percent of shoppers who go to the store for frequently purchased items go with a specific strategy for saving money. And they are paying careful attention to just how much they save. What is more, this shopping behavior crosses age groups and sexes. Among those "most likely" to believe they save money by using coupons and sales are men, consumers aged 35 to 54, college graduates, working women, and married women.

Shifts in Store Loyalty

Where people are shopping is clearly driven by options that are offering the greatest value relative to price. This has produced the dramatically successful factory outlet malls. The loyalty to regional malls has changed profoundly over the past decade.

Nearly 300 factory outlet malls have opened nationwide since 1990. Why do people go? Is it because of the prices, the brands, or the mall itself? Are these the people who used to go to department stores because they carried the power brands? Or are these people who always wanted power brands but couldn't afford them? Total Research (Princeton, New Jersey) says its research indicates that the typical customer "is a person enamored with brands and saving money." And the average customer seems to be more than satisfied with the outlet shopping experience. A recent survey of 2,100 shoppers in 13 of these centers revealed that the average customer visits them 10 times a year and that one in six visits them four times a month.

How about strip malls? These are opening at the rate of 2,000 a year. Who shops there? These malls are patronized by 89 percent of adult Americans, with 24 percent shopping there exclusively (compared to the 5 percent who shop only at regional shopping centers). The average customer shops seven times a month compared to the two trips a month experienced by the regional malls.

The profile of the people who shop at these places shows a full range of income and education levels. And, with more than half in the $50,000-plus income bracket, strip centers are attracting the group sought after by the more upscale regional malls.

And what is a Bloomingdale's, Macy's, or Nordstrom's clearance center? A discount outlet or a downscaled department store?

Some Answers Surface

Behind all this lies the most important structural change in the economy—perhaps the most significant we have experienced in our lifetime. It goes way beyond any particular format or pricing strategy. To view it as one or the other is a mistake for anyone in the business.

What is going on is akin to the management/organizational strategy of the day, "reengineering": a process that realigns all of the elements within a system so that there is the least possible waste and the highest possible quality outcome.

This restructuring has been generated by the recognition that modern technology is not just a tool to allow us to do what we have always done faster, or cheaper, or better. It is, instead, a powerful tool that enables us to accomplish our objectives in new ways—if we organize the entire system of production, distribution, and sales to maximize the contribution all these technologies can make.

Wal-Mart, Home Depot, Kmart, JC Penney, Levi Strauss, Proctor & Gamble, Taco Bell, Dell Computer, outlet malls, and others are not engaged in some form of pricing competition. They are engaged in innovative attempts to significantly improve the efficiency and quality of getting a product to the consumer through the implementation of systems that utilize the best of modern computer and telecommunications technologies. Retailers are forced to confront and challenge a wide range of "business as usual" aspects within the retail system. The resulting sales mechanics are so new that many of the traditional powers in our economy are having serious difficulty understanding and responding to what they perceive to be some form of pricing or marketing strategy.

Knowing about the many discount options mass merchandisers and discounters provide, consumers want it all: rock-bottom prices, the highest possible quality, the greatest service, and the least hassle. Consumers will, then, reward those places where this set of demands is most reliably met.

Smart retailers have worked hard to create systems that can accommodate this new marketplace reality. They are essentially striving to achieve "store loyalty and enthusiasm" capable of attracting and keeping "smart" customers.

Indeed, retailers need to ensure that they are able to obtain the products their customers want, at the lowest possible cost; they also know this is one buying group that won't stay around long if disappointed. This has created a new type of vendor who will work in partnership with retailers to reduce the time and the costs throughout the entire "system" associated with finally putting the goods in the customers' hands.

Another key to the changes is the renewed importance of the salesperson, whose knowledge and behavior must sustain, rather than contradict, this dedicated effort toward higher customer satisfaction.

What is evolving, then, is an integrated, seamless process from the point-of-sale all the way through to the raw material purchases of the vendors. This opens a whole new set of opportunities and a need to rethink the brand-store-image-price-service equation.

Customers Turn Reviewers

DENISE POWER

With all they gain from customer-written product reviews, online apparel retailers might as well put shoppers on their payrolls.

This growing customer feedback channel gives retailers a salary-free way to police merchandise quality, enhance marketing, refine the product mix, increase sales, and even achieve more favorable rankings on major search sites like Google, Yahoo, and Windows Live Search. Several have added the feature to their sites in time for the critical holiday period, when Comscore Networks predicts November-to-December online sales will top $24 billion.

Without exception, retailers say they post shoppers' unedited (and sometimes typo-ridden) product reviews online as a way to offer unbiased guidance to other shoppers considering a purchase.

"A good customer review goes a long way to convincing that next customer that this is a smart purchase," said Kent Anderson, president of macys.com. Macy's Web site accumulated 10,000 customer-written reviews and product ratings one month after that feature went live in October.

Even negative reviews, which can be difficult to swallow, are essential because they lend credibility to other reviews while alerting retailers to issues needing attention, he added.

"Merchants don't like their products publicly pilloried, like a report card for everyone to see. Nobody likes that," said Bill Bass, chief executive officer at Fair Indigo, a Madison, Wis., branded apparel company. However, posting feedback that a size may run large provides useful guidance to other shoppers, who can factor that variable into their buying decision. "You want no surprises for the customer. You don't want the customer to order a cashmere sweater and it's not quite the right color or the fit they expected," he said.

Shopper reviews led Fair Indigo to correct fit grading on some size 14s and 16s and also to offer size 2 and 0 on some items not previously available.

Other retailers, such as online jeweler Blue Nile and outdoor gear merchants Cabela's and Evogear, also have acted on shopper reviews that spotlight product quality issues. One manufacturer corrected a durability problem with its skis for Evogear, and a jewelry maker whose earring clasps were flimsy replaced all the offending stock at Blue Nile. Retailers also refine Web site images, design, and product descriptions as a result of reviews.

At Blue Nile, merchants initially resisted the posting of negative reviews, especially if the complaint was based on personal taste, rather than quality. "But our CEO said, 'If people don't like it, I don't want to sell it,'" said Darrell Cavens, senior vice president of marketing. As a result of shopper feedback, Blue Nile discontinued some product offerings this fall, proving customers can influence the mix.

The Blue Nile Web site sometimes receives hundreds of shopper reviews in a day, Cavens added, and those comments are circulated daily to 40 people in the company. The company has posted shopper reviews for more than four years now, using homegrown software to manage content and weed out inappropriate reviews containing profanity, for example.

Though he could not cite empirical data, Cavens said customer reviews drive sales, and it's the substance of reviews that bear this out. As an example, he pointed to one review that read, "I purchased this cross for my six-month-old goddaughter's christening based on the feedback from others at this site."

Consumers place more trust in peer-written reviews than expert-authored ones and glitzy marketing come-ons, retailers said. "I want to hear what other people like me think," said Fair Indigo's Bass, "not an ivory tower person." And, remarkably, consumer-written reviews are the most popular form of user-generated content among online shoppers, with 75 percent of Web shoppers using them, far more often than blogs or message boards, according to Forrester Research.

Macy's, Fair Indigo, and Cabela's outsource administration of customer reviews to Austin, Tex.–based Bazaarvoice, whose staff and software screen comments before they are posted. Retailers set their own criteria for vetting reviews. At Fair Indigo, only shoppers who've purchased an item are eligible to review it and no reviews containing the name of a competitor—for good or bad—will make the cut, said Bass.

Cabela's is already achieving the critical mass of reviews it sought, even though the feature was added only two months ago. "We have enough reviews to go to the next level and build merchandising and marketing around reviews," said Vince Stephens, Internet manager, planning and analytics. For instance, e-mail campaigns can now include promotions for top-rated product, according to customers.

Stephens and other retailers said customer reviews can improve their rankings on Google and Yahoo because the content is easier for search engines to find using "spider" programs that crawl the Web to collect information. Sometimes Web site product descriptions do not use language that is spider-friendly, and a Web site goes unseen by the search engine.

While most retailers don't have, or won't disclose, a return on investment for shopper reviews, Cabela's Stephens said he expects to recoup the cost in one year's time.

At Evogear, no ROI was calculated for shopper reviews and the company is allowing the program to grow organically since its launch six months ago, said Nathan Decker, director of e-commerce.

Evogear uses a syndicated customer review program from PowerReviews of Millbrae, Calif., that allows shoppers to post images of themselves using the products. The service is free so long as retailers permit the vendor to post their review content on PowerReviews' own portal, which is due to go live early next year.

Fair Indigo's Bass is not troubled by an unclear ROI for shopper reviews. "There are right things to do and you do them because they are the right things. And you do it on faith that it will have an impact," said Bass, an e-commerce pioneer who headed up Lands' End and Sears' sites before starting his own company this year. He trusts his gut: "I was a helicopter gunship pilot in the Army. And after we shot for a while, we would turn off the fire control computers, because we were better at it with our instinct."

Women's Wear Daily, December 13, 2006

Acting on Impulse

COURTNEY COLAVITA

In the 2000 film *The Family Man,* Nicolas Cage's character, Jack Campbell, stumbles into the men's suiting department of a high-end department store during a routine family outing to a New Jersey mall.

He puts on a $2,400 Zegna suit, checks himself out in the mirror and without more than a moment of thought decides he'll buy it. That's of course until his wife puts the kibosh on his impulse.

Traditional men's retailing windows would consider such a scene just that, a scene—a conceit of fiction that may be perfect for the movies but not applicable on the selling floor. Men, after all, enter a store with a meticulous preparedness or at the least a viable need. They just don't drop down $1,000 on a sweater. Well, at least they didn't until recently.

Men's buying patterns are changing. Retailers and analysts say men are shopping with more frequency and searching out novel items. The result: An increasing number of men are buying on impulse.

"Men aren't shopping just out of need anymore," says Tom Kalenderian, executive vice president and GMM of men's wear at Barneys New York. "The shopping experience has become one of entertainment and that creates a naturally fertile ground for more impulse buying."

Emotional acquisitions are nothing new but until recently this was a phenomenon reserved for the women's market where high-margin items like bags and shoes are often snapped up as easily as chocolates.

And while impulse buying may be at a minimum in the tailored clothing department, it's on the rise in other categories, such as luxury sportswear, furnishings, accessories, and even jewelry, say industry observers.

Andrea Ciccoli, a partner at Bain & Co. here, says a shift away from status symbol items and toward more eclectic ones is helping drive the impulse trend.

"Before it was all about Hermès ties and Church's shoes, and everyone was going after the same status symbols—that is not the trend anymore," Ciccoli says. "The more emphasis for individualism translates into more willingness to search out creative items."

It's only logical that the probability of a sale will increase as men spend more time browsing around stores and the data show it.

Men's wear sales are growing at a faster pace than women's, according to research compiled by Bain. Global retail sales of luxury high-end men's wear reached 20 billion euros, or $24.9 billion, in 2005, according to Bain data. (Figures are converted at the average exchange rate for the period to which they refer.) That number is expected to rise between 11 and 12 percent for 2006.

Retailers and vendors, recognizing the propensity for men to shop less and less restrictively, are implementing new strategies to influence spontaneous buys.

Since an impulse buy derives from a consumer's desire and reaction, it's key, industry experts say, that the product exhibit some kind of singular characteristic—it has to stand out.

"Sometimes companies think they can add a few fashion-oriented items and think that's enough. It isn't," Ciccoli says, adding that graphic T's are a smart way to introduce impulse buying at entry-level price points.

Yet $175 T's aren't the only vehicle to get men to the cash register. Tommy Fazio, men's fashion director at Bergdorf Goodman, notes that men will come in, see a $1,000 Michael Bastian sweater and buy it because it's uniquely appealing.

"The iconic item that best represents the collection is the first to go," says Fazio.

Roger Cohen, Corneliani's U.S. president, says the company's ID Jacket (a sport coat with a built-in center panel vest) has been a runaway success because it's often bought on a whim.

"Whereas a suit is a more thought-out buy—you need a new suit for work or for an evening event—the ID Jacket is much more an impulsive fashion buy," Cohen says. "It's almost like a sweater or an accessory."

Creating great product, however, is just the first step in an intricate cycle designed to get men to spend more freely.

Bob Mitchell, co-president Mitchells/Richards/Marshs, says his stores have begun "to set traps" in a bid to foster unplanned purchases.

"We have created these high-traffic areas where we'll place key merchandise, whether it's a new shipment of Etro shirts or the key outerwear piece from Loro Piana," says Mitchell.

"These products obviously warrant a buy, and are merchandised as a go-to item."

Later this year Ermenegildo Zegna will unveil redesigned flagships in Milan and New York. The Zegnas tapped Peter Marino to design stores that could effectively showcase an array of products, including what Gildo Zegna calls "light items," such as eyewear and fragrances.

Zegna says the stores will have niche areas for different categories and that "will make it very easy for the customer to approach [an item]."

Both Zegna and Mitchell agree that service is the next critical component to trigger a buy.

"One of the key points, though, is getting our staff hyped about the product," says Mitchell. "There has to be a real enthusiasm and, once they have success selling to a few customers, it will just snowball from there."

Zegna agrees although he also stresses the importance of how a product is displayed. "The help of a valid associate is very important," says Zegna. "But the presentation counts very much. It has to play automatically to the customer."

Another pressing issue facing the men's industry is frequency of deliveries and the need for a continual influx of new product. At a conference late last year, Prada chief Patrizio Bertelli said what many in Italian fashion had been thinking for years. He lashed out at highend fashion's inability to compete with its fast-fashion rivals, Zara and H&M, who are able to fill stores with new merch in a matter of weeks.

Barneys' Kalenderian says adopting a quicker cycle is paramount. "Deliveries of fresh merchandise are key for repeat shoppers."

Indeed. Time and time again retailers say new product that gets in early is the first to go.

Bergdorf's Fazio says last month early spring merchandise was doing almost as well as sale items, while Corneliani's Cohen says an in-stock reassortment program allowed the company to effectively restock its ID Jacket when it sold out at Saks Fifth Avenue in New York.

"We stocked it in such depth that Saks was able to get it back into [the stores] fast like in women's wear," Cohen says.

As Bain's Ciccoli says, just because more men are buying impulsively doesn't make them easy targets.

"It's a high-involvement decision," he says. "The consumer is more sophisticated and very aware of what is going on in the market."

Made In Italy, Retail Strategies, *DNR*, January 8, 2007

the multicultural consumer and fashion

Facts do not cease to exist because they are ignored.

ALDOUS HUXLEY, ENGLISH CRITIC AND NOVELIST

After you have completed this chapter, you will be able to discuss:

- The importance of the three major ethnic minorities in the United States to retailers.

- How demographic trends will affect the retailing community in terms of the merchandise they will offer in their inventories.

- The buying power of African Americans, Asian Americans, and Hispanics.

- Fashion products and their growth potential for ethnic minorities.

- How retailers are approaching the multicultural markets to improve their sales positions.

- The development of advertising programs that incorporate minority imagery.

- Why foreign language sales associates are important to today's retailers.

- How merchants are making purchase plans to ensure that their minority base is being satisfactorily served.

Does ethnic diversity play a role in the purchase of fashion merchandise? Up until the end of the 20th century, the answer seemed to be a resounding no! Designers and merchants primarily considered such factors as age, occupation, income, and the family life cycle in their creation and merchandising of fashion products. Today, however, many designers from different ethnicities are addressing the needs of our multicultural population with products that are specifically aimed to capture their attention, and they are making fashion headlines by doing so. Retailers are also beginning to acknowledge the importance of paying closer attention to the ethnic groups in their trading areas by redesigning some of their interior spaces, incorporating multiracial mannequins in their visual presentations, making use of foreign-language signage, using more appropriate advertising, and incorporating collections that have been designed by well-known African American, Hispanic, and Asian American personalities into their merchandise mixes. As a result of these undertakings, the **multicultural consumer** is becoming a more important segment of the fashion world.

MULTICULTURAL MARKET SEGMENTS

The three major ethnic minorities in the United States are African American, Hispanic, and Asian American. These groups make up the **multicultural market segments** in the United States. They are viable segments in terms of their purchasing power and have become very important purchasers of fashion merchandise. Often their needs and wants are the same or similar to the general population, but sometimes their preferences are somewhat different. The differences might be in style, price, or another variable. Whatever the considerations, many **demographic trends** indicate that they will continue to be a driving force in the world of fashion.

By 2010, the minority population is expected to comprise one-third of the overall population.

Demographic Trends

The aforementioned ethnicities that are part of the overall population in the United States are considered sufficiently important by the fashion industry to pay close attention to them. Although collectively and individually they have not reached the same numbers as the white Caucasian population, their numbers are considered significant in terms of buying power. Some of today's multicultural demographic trends imply that the different arms of the fashion industry will increasingly benefit by carefully addressing their needs. Some of the trends that have been identified thus far are the following:

- By 2010, the minority population in the United States is expected to comprise one-third of the overall population. With retailers, in particular, generally using five- and ten-year plans for expansion potential, merchandising adjustments, advertising and promotional approaches, and other business decisions, this date is just around the corner, and it is imperative for them to consider any new company direction.

- By 2010, the Hispanic population is expected to have a cumulative buying power of $1 trillion, much of which will be for fashion merchandise.

- Educational achievement, especially for African Americans, is expected to substantially improve. In 2000, 72 percent of blacks had a minimum of a high school education, as compared to 84 percent for whites. The expected increase in the number of black high school graduates has a potential for greater purchasing power because increases in educational achievement often translate into more purchases.

- By 2020, the three major ethnicities are expected grow six times the rate of the white population. In terms of percents, these populations will grow by 36 percent, with the white population growing by 6 percent.

Lucy Pereda, Venus Williams, and Daisy Fuentes have entered the fashion design field.

- The importance of Hispanics in terms of population must be considered because, for the first time in the United States, they have surpassed the number of African Americans.

- More and more members of minority ethnicities are entering the fashion design arena. Lucy Pereda, who gained fame as a fashion model; Jennifer Lopez, best known for film roles; Daisy Fuentes, former superstar model; and Venus Williams, tennis great, have all entered the field with their fashion collections.

- Growth of minority population in such cities as Miami, Los Angeles, New York, and Houston is making merchants reconsider their merchandise mixes to gain more attention and greater sales from them.

- In overall population numbers, if African Americans, Hispanics, and Asian Americans were considered as a separate nation, they would become the world's fourth largest economy.

- By the year 2050, Hispanic workers will comprise one-fourth of the workforce in the United States.

Demographics, by Minority Ethnicity

Population, buying power, and household mean income provide data that underscore the importance of the three major minorities in the United States to the fashion industry as well as other industrial segments. The following figures, from the most recent Census Bureau survey, which took place in 2000, show that every segment of the fashion industry should pay attention to them as major purchasers.

Population

The general population was estimated to be 293 million with breakdowns according to ethnicities as follows:

White Caucasian	216.9 million
African American	36.4 million
Hispanic	35.5 million
Asian	11.9 million

Buying Power

For the year 2001, the **buying power** of the different groups was estimated to be:

White Caucasian	$6,219.8 billion
African American	$572.1 billion
Hispanic	$452.4 billion
Asian	$12.0 billion

Household Mean Income

The mean annual income for the period studied was reported as follows:

All races combined	$57,045
White Caucasian	$61,237
African American	$40,068
Hispanic	$42,410
Asian	$70,221

It should be noted that these figures are not up-to-date, but are the most current available from which conclusions may be drawn. Of importance from many indicators is the belief that the minority population will continue to increase as a percentage of the overall population.

Language Comprehension

For retailers, foreign language comprehension is particularly important. Specifically, the Hispanics in the United States, with their ever-increasing numbers, are excellent prospects as purchasers. In a report undertaken by the U.S. Census in 2003 and analyzed in the book *Latino Boom!* by Chiqui Cartagena, the subject of a World of Fashion Profile, the figures revealed that although many in this ethnicity understood and spoke English, their fluency was not sufficient to rely on English as the language that will reach the majority of its people.

Studying the figures below, one can see that Spanish-speaking sales associates are necessary to communicate with the Latinos, and that signage should be offered in Spanish.

CHIQUI CARTAGENA

As a media pioneer with more than 20 years' experience developing, contributing to, and launching some of America's most successful Spanish-language products, such as *TV Guide en Español*, Chiqui Cartagena now is managing director of multicultural communications at Meredith Integrated Marketing. Her experience as director of business development for the Ad Age Group, where she was responsible for developing Hispanic business for its leading titles, helped Cartagena emerge as one of the better-known players in multicultural marketing. Another of her accomplishments includes being part of the team responsible for launching the Spanish version of *People* magazine. *People en Español* is still the most successful Spanish-speaking magazine in print today.

Her best-selling book, *Latin Boom!*, explores the Latino market and concentrates on the road to achieving success in business in the United States' Hispanic market. Covering topics that range from a study of the Hispanic demographics, an overview of its top 10 markets in the United States, the media landscape, and the Latino baby boom to the mistakes that businesses should avoid when entering this market, the book has achieved high praise from executives at AOL Media Networks, the Association of Hispanic Advertising Agencies, MTV Español, and Verizon Communications.

Chiqui Cartagena is one of the leading authorities on Latino markets.

Language Usage	Native Born		Foreign Born	
Speak Spanish	14,760,788	100%	13,340,264	100%
Speak English "very well"	10,598,734	72%	3,751,062	28%
Speak English "well"	2,631,784	18%	3,187,624	24%
Speak English "not well"	1,313,595	9%	3,816,895	29%
Speak English "not at all"	216,765	1%	2,584,683	19%

Growth Potential for Fashion Products

Each of the segments of the fashion industry will be sufficiently affected by the population figures, buying power, and household mean incomes of the major minorities. Specifically, the industries of women's, men's, and children's apparel, cosmetics, fragrances, and beauty aids must offer different products from the standard fare produced for the general population. Focused styling by designers and merchandising by retailers have the potential to yield greater sales within these ethnic groups. By paying attention to their ever-increasing numbers and their wants and needs, overall volume will more than likely increase at both the manufacturing and retail levels.

A closer look at the three major **minority ethnicities** reveals they are not identical to one another in terms of such factors as their fashion needs, spending behavior, and other indicators.

African Americans

Once they have satisfied their basic needs for food and shelter, as a group, African American women make apparel and wearable accessories their single most important expenditure. As reported by Cotton Incorporated's *Lifestyle Monitor* report, 38 percent of this segment's women revealed they loved to shop. This is a higher percentage than either their Caucasian or Hispanic counterparts. Also reported was the fact that 28 percent of this population spent more than $200 in the month that preceded the survey as compared with 14 percent of Hispanic women and 12 percent of the female Caucasian population.

Also extremely enlightening was a report produced by the fashion editor of *Essence Magazine*, one of the African American community's leading publications. It indicated that this market is just beginning to emerge as a major purchaser of fashion merchandise. It also revealed that price was not an issue for this market. In agreement with this information was Cotton Incorporated's *Monitor*, which stated 64 percent of African American women would pay more for an item of better quality compared with 57 percent of their Caucasian counterparts and 54 percent of Hispanic women.

Although it is often thought that fashion is primarily a woman's game, trends indicate that the black man is also a major purchaser of fashion apparel and wearable accessories. In numbers that continue to increase each year, black men are spending more on fashion merchandise than ever before, and at **price points** that also continue to spiral upward. Especially important to this consumer segment are designer labels, with leather garments particularly attractive.

African American women are a major force in fashion purchasing.

Teenage African Americans are having a particularly great impact on the clothing markert.

Teenagers are also having an impact on the clothing market. They are emulating the apparel worn by the notable hip-hop and rap stars. Jeans are the major purchases made by this group. The African American teen buys more jeans than either whites or Hispanics of this age group.

African Americans are also spending more than ever on their children's wardrobes. Where basics were once the main consideration, style has become one of the more important considerations when making purchases.

The African American market segment is also a major purchaser of cosmetics, fragrances, and beauty aids. The breadth of the product offerings range from those that are popular-priced to a wealth of others that are higher-priced. In venues such as major pharmacies—for example, CVS and Walgreens—significant floor space is allocated for these products. Department stores are also increasing their main-floor offerings for these products. Together, these retail operations are reaching sales never before realized. Industry analysts currently estimate that more than $6 billion are spent for beauty products, with ethnic minorities responsible for $1.5 billion. Of that number, African Americans account for the greatest amount.

The brands that are specifically directed toward African Americans are either produced exclusively by companies that specialize in ethnic products, such as Flori Roberts, Imam, Interface, and Patti LaBelle, or major midstream companies, such as Bobbi Brown or Adrian Arpel. With people of color requiring specific cosmetic colorations and beauty care products, the number of companies addressing these needs continues to grow, and the number of products continues to increase. Cumulatively, the companies that are catering to these needs are achieving unprecedented sales.

Hispanics

According to a Global Insight study conducted by NBC/Telemundo in 2003, clothing is a major expenditure for the Latino market. Although food purchases account for the largest portion of this group's income, fashion products are significant purchases. "Snapshots of the Hispanic Market," a Global Insight study published in 2003 on brand preferences, showed that Hispanics are also the most important of the three minority groups in brand selection, far outdistancing Caucasians. Of major

African American celebrities, such as Iman, are producing cosmetics.

importance to fashion brand producers and retailers is that in women's and men's clothing, they are more important than non-Hispanics.

As a result of these and other studies many brands are being marketed to this segment. Of significant interest is their loyalty to brands and labels that have been created by Hispanic celebrities. Marquee names such as fashion model Daisy Fuentes; fashion model, journalist, and author Lucy Pereda; guitarist-singer Carlos Santana; and one of the hottest actresses in film and television, Jennifer Lopez, continue to play an important role in fashion design. In addition to the creative talents of these individuals, other names are used simply to attract the attention of this ethnicity. Singer Christina Aguilera, for example, is considered to be one of the most important marketing "tools" to influence the purchases of teenagers, according to *Woman's Wear Daily*. In a list generated by that periodical, she is the number one "name" marketer in a list that includes Cindy Crawford, Teri Hatcher, Hillary Duff, and Jennifer Lopez.

Although they are significant purchasers of cosmetics, fragrances, and beauty aids, Hispanics purchase far fewer specialized products than the African American group. The reason is that their complexions are almost always similar to Caucasians, so they can choose from products marketed to the general population. A trend is developing, however, to produce cosmetics specifically aimed at the Latino market. The leader at this point in time is Zalia, who also produces accessories. Developed by Monica Ramirez, a first-generation American of Peruvian descent and winner of beauty pageants, the cosmetics line flatters Hispanic women with colorations specifically produced for her "Latina sisters," or *chicas*.

Jennifer Lopez and Christina Aguilera are two of the most important marketers to influence teenage purchasers.

Asian Americans

Although they rank third in number after the African American and Hispanic ethnicities, Asian Americans are very meaningful to some fashion designers and merchants because of their incomes. They account for the highest mean income of the three. Also, their population is increasing in percentages, along with Hispanics, at a rate that is greater than the rest of the population. Purchasing power, according to a study by the research group Media Audit, is outstanding. In their most recent study of 86 U.S. markets, Media Audit discovered that 56 percent of the Asian population has household incomes of $50,000 or more. Coupled with these figures is their love

Actor Ricardo Antonio Chavira and company president Monica Ramirez promote Zalia cosmetics.

Asian Americans account for the highest mean incomes of the three major minority groups.

for shopping. *Retail Traffic Magazine* reports that they are the most concerned of the ethnic groups in keeping up appearances.

Asian Americans were one of the first ethnicities to introduce world-famous fashion designers. Initially alone in the industry, Hanae Mori, a couture designer, has been joined by other marquee names such as Anna Sui, Vivienne Tam, and Vera Wang, the most formidable of today's bridal wear couturiers. Through the achievement of numerous prestigious design awards they have become household names in upscale fashion. Others who have joined the ranks of distinction are Maki Doherty Ryoke, Eugenia Kim, Siri Kuptamehtee, Mary Ping, and Jean Yu. Not only have they great appeal to the Asian American market, but they also enjoy a great number of followers from the traditional consumer market.

One of the ways that fashion designers and retail merchants are addressing the needs of this ethnicity is through the offering of collections that are "petite oriented." By skewing their size distributions to small sizes, they fill a void in many inventories.

In terms of cosmetics, fragrances, and beauty aids, specialized products have yet to make it to the marketplace. Few products are available that will enhance their complexions. A lone exception is Zhen Cosmetics, which are available in both bricks-and-mortar establishments and online. Founded by Susan Yee, an Asian American, the company has captured a large portion of the industry. Also involved in the development and distribution of products for this minority is Skinlight Ltd., a mail-order firm that is located in Surrey in the United Kingdom.

Vera Wang is one of today's most important bridal wear designers.

RETAIL APPROACHES IN MULTICULTURAL MARKETS

As noted in the Census Bureau's most recent general survey in 2000, and in numerous private studies, specific regions in the United States are becoming more and more populated by diverse ethnicities. These are called the **multicultural markets**. Specifically, an ethnic population explosion is taking place in various cities. According to the Census Bureau, the percent increase is especially dominant in the following cities:

Miami	81%
Los Angeles	68%
New York	61%
Houston	54%
San Francisco	47%
Dallas	43%
Washington	43%
Chicago	42%
Atlanta	40%
Philadelphia	30%

Using these figures, as well as their own studies, as guidelines, more and more merchants are strategizing to capture the disposable incomes of these groups. Each company must assess the makeup of the ethnic populations in their trading areas to make certain that the fashion products they offer for sale address each group in terms

'LIFE WITHOUT PASSION IS UNFORGIVABLE'

Sean John

UNFORGIVABLE

INTRODUCING THE FRAGRANCE FOR MEN FROM SEAN JOHN

Unforgivable is the largest selling men's fragrance.

Phat Fashions is one of the most dominant fashion collections, as modeled here by designer Kimora Lee Simmons and her daughters.

of specific needs. For example, African Americans and Asian Americans do not necessarily have the same fashion requirements and therefore should be considered separate markets.

Many of the major companies that cater to the working class and middle-income families such as JC Penney, Wal-Mart, Kohl's, and Sears have been paying particular attention to these diverse ethnic groups and have started to merchandise their fashion offerings accordingly. Retailers such as Macy's, which targets middle-income households and more affluent shoppers, are also making significant efforts to attract the multiethnic markets by broadening their fashion offerings. Labels such as Sean John in fashion apparel and men's fragrances such as the Sean John Unforgivable are now important parts of their product offerings.

As discussed in the following sections, retailers are using a wide range of means to capture this market.

Adding Product Lines Directed at the Multicultural Shopper

The once-dominant fashion collections bearing such labels as Ralph Lauren, Calvin Klein, DKNY, and others that became household names are being joined by a host of new lines. Most are aimed at this vastly expanding multicultural market. In addition to the aforementioned Sean John merchandise, labels that dominate include Phat Fashions under the Phat Farm and Baby Phat labels, found in a multitude of retail "doors" both here in the United Sates and in countries such as Dubai and Abu Dhabi; Daisy Fuentes and Casa Cristina by Cristina Saralegui, both sold exclusively at Kohl's; the Wisconsin-based retail giant, Thalia Sodi, a collection that is privately merchandised at Kmart; and Jennifer Lopez.

With these names that were first made famous by their theatrical presence, their recognition in the fashion world has also been enormous. Not only do many African American consumers identify with Sean "Diddy" Combs, founder of Sean John, and Russell Simmons, creator of the Phat Fashion lines, but they have quickly become enthusiasts for the products that bear their signatures as well. Similarly, followers of the Hispanic celebrities such as Jennifer Lopez and Daisy Fuentes also purchase the labels they are identified with.

Using Visual Merchandising That Is Ethnically Oriented

The use of exciting and informative exterior and interior visual merchandising often brings increased sales to the merchant. Store windows, department displays, and signage play an important role in telling the shopper what the company is featuring for their clientele. More and more retailers are using ethnic mannequins in their displays along with the traditional white models. This use is intended to make the minority consumer feel that he or she is being considered in the company's merchandising practices. Graphics that depict a host of different ethnicities also have become important visual merchandising tools. They, along with signage in languages other than English, provide information to those who are not fluent in English.

Developing Advertising Programs That Incorporate Minority Imagery

In both the print and broadcast media, retailers have taken significant initiatives to use African American, Hispanic, and Asian models and other **minority imagery** in their ads. Newspapers, magazines, direct-marketing offerings, billboards, and television advertisements feature average-looking consumers as well as minority celebrities to deliver their messages. While the depicted individuals are representative of different racial backgrounds, advertisers have also introduced language that is more likely

Ethic mannequins are used in many retail displays.

Advertising's use of ethnic models has become imperitive for success.

to be familiar to these ethnicities. The dovetailing of the visual with the message is expected to bring optimum results.

To make certain that the ads are carefully crafted to achieve success with these consumer markets, specialty agencies such as NuAmerica, headed by African American cofounder and CEO Brett Wright, who is featured in a World of Fashion Profile, are being used more and more. Their understanding of the jargon that their constituencies use in everyday communication generally makes the ads more realistic.

Making Foreign-Language Sales Associates Available

The Hispanic and Asian communities, in particular, are comprised of many people who do not have a command of the English language. More and more retailers are employing bilingual salespeople to communicate with this consumer segment. Often, the subtleties of language are missed by those with just a smattering of Spanish, Chinese, or Korean, making the potential for sales losses significant. The practice of staffing foreign-language-speaking employees is important not only in areas where these ethnicities are in abundance, but also in cities where tourism attracts many different ethnicities.

With telephone sales an integral part of a retailer's overall selling approach, it is also important for the company to have representatives who can communicate in different languages on the phone. Some foreign-speaking consumers are reluctant to visit the bricks-and-mortar locations because of their inability to secure travel to them. Thus, many opt for telephone purchasing.

For those who do make the trip to the stores, the coupling of foreign-speaking retail representatives with signage in these languages helps make the store environment more consumer-friendly.

Employing Service Managers with Foreign-Language Competency

Just as it is important for sales associates to "speak the language," so too is it important to staff the store with problem solvers who are fluent in Spanish and other languages. Sometimes problems arise such as product unhappiness, returns that are later than the allotted time period, problems with sales associates, and so forth. If the service manager can communicate in the shopper's language, it is likely that the problem will be more easily solved.

Developing Special Events That Attract Multicultural Markets

Many retailers use a variety of promotional tools to enhance the efforts of their merchandising teams. These are either product or institutional oriented. In either case, the objective is to reach specific consumer groups that the company wishes to target. The emphasis today, for these undertakings, is often directed toward the multicultural audiences.

BRETT WRIGHT

Brett Wright is a leading authority on multicultural marketing.

As cofounder and CEO of NuAmerica Agency, and cofounder and chief creative officer of *Uptown Magazine*, Brett Wright has emerged as one of the United States' leading forces in underscoring the importance of the African American consumer to U.S. retailers. With a background in the music, Internet, publishing, advertising, and fashion industries, he has been able to successfully help businesses reach their African American markets.

The first of his two affiliations is with NuAmerica Agency, based on 125th Street in the heart of the Harlem section of New York City. It was the first agency of its kind with a goal to address the changing urban culture in the United States. While his company represents such fashion organizations as Tommy Hilfiger and Rocawear, they also are heavily involved in promoting companies such as Pepsi and Courvoisier, and the legendary Apollo Theater.

Uptown Magazine, the other company headed by Wright, was established to reach the African American market. It is targeted to the 25–44 age group. Initially it was a New York magazine, but soon it expanded with editions in Washington, D.C., Chicago, and Atlanta. The three editions feature the same basic editorials and information, except for 30 percent of the materials, which is directed to the individual cities.

Giving up a major corporate job, where he earned a seven-figure salary, Wright took the chance on these new companies, and from every indication, he has made the transition a successful one.

One of the more popular special events is the fashion show. Long a mainstay of the retail industry, today's formats are increasingly being used to attract the minority shopper. By concentrating on African American, Hispanic, and Asian collections, retailers are reaching out to the minority population with fashion shows that feature lines such as Sean John, Phat Farm and Baby Phat, Daisy Fuentes, and others. The shows employ ethnic models, music that is popular with the specific ethnicities, and other components that will attract the attention of these much sought-after consumers.

Another tool is the use of in-store appearances by African American, Hispanic, and Asian American designers, and entertainers such as rap artists, who will draw ethnic minorities to the selling floors. The intent is to bring this market to the merchandise that has been created with them in mind.

Planning Purchases

Buyers and merchandisers are considered to be the driving forces behind profitable retailing. As part of proper planning before the actual purchases are made, the merchandising team must carefully study the wholesale markets that produce the goods and make preliminary decisions regarding the merchandise they would incorporate into their merchandise assortments.

Fashion shows are one of the more popular retailing special events.

In-store appearances by ethnic designers help sell thier products.

By reading the wealth of newspapers and magazines patronized by minority consumers, merchandisers can get the pulse of these markets and provide them with products that satisfy any specific needs they might have. Scores of magazines, and to a lesser extent, newspapers, are geared to African Americans, Hispanics, and Asian Americans. In their pages are advertisements that focus on their probable preferences, columns that address these ethnicities, and other news that might give merchants an insight into what products they might purchase. In particular, fashion is generally a big part of the pages of these consumer magazines, and by carefully studying the ads and reports, the buying team may discover the trends that are likely to emerge.

Another way in which merchandise acquisition plans are tailored to fit the retailer's needs is through continuous contact with resident buying office representatives. These companies, which are explored in Chapter 20, provide a wealth of information such as introducing new designers and collections, many of whom are of minority descent.

Of course, the trade publications such as *Women's Wear Daily* and *DNR* feature the most up-to-date news about the fashion industry and alert merchants to the latest trends in the field.

CHAPTER HIGHLIGHTS

- The three major ethnic minorities in the United States are African American, Hispanic, and Asian American.
- By 2010, the minority population in the United States is expected to comprise one-third of the overall population.
- By 2020, the three major ethnic minorities are expected to grow six times the rate of the white population.
- By the year 2050, the Hispanic population in the United States will comprise one-fourth of the workforce in the United States.

- Once they have satisfied their basic needs for food and shelter, as a group, African American women make apparel and wearable accessories their single most important expenditure.
- Many brands have been created that bear the names of African American and Hispanic designers, with each targeted toward minority markets.
- Although the number of Asian Americans pales in comparison to the other minority ethnicities, their high income levels make them excellent prospects for fashion merchandise.
- Retailers are directing their visual presentations toward minority shoppers by using ethnically diverse mannequins in their displays and using signage in Spanish to attract their Hispanic audience.
- Advertising, as with visual merchandising, is being targeted toward ethnic minorities with the use of multiracial models and language that is best understood by these consumers.
- In heavily populated Latino markets, retailers are employing Spanish-speaking sales associates to sell their products.
- Purchase planning that involves the incorporation of collections geared for minority audiences involves the close inspection of the newspapers and magazines read by minorities.

IMPORTANT FASHION TERMINOLOGY AND CONCEPTS

multicultural consumer	minority ethnicities	retail doors
multicultural market segment	buying power	minority imagery
demographic trends	price points	
	multicultural markets	

FOR REVIEW

1. What growth rate is expected for the top minority ethnicities in the United States by 2020?

2. Which of the three minorities in the United States is the largest in terms of buying power?

3. Of the three most important ethnicities, after white Caucasian, which one has the greatest household mean income?

4. After food and shelter, what is considered to be the most important product need for African American women?

5. Why aren't special cosmetics as important to Hispanic women as they are to their African American counterparts?

6. Who, according to *WWD*, is the number one "name" marketer for Hispanics?

7. Why are Asian Americans considered so important as fashion purchasers even though they rank third in number after African Americans and Hispanics?

8. Which city in the United Sates has realized the greatest growth in the ethnic explosion?

9. How has visual merchandising changed to better impact the ethnic minorities in the United States?

10. In addition to using "models of color" in the ethnic-oriented ads, what other approach is being used by advertisers?

11. What types of special events are being used by retailers to attract minority shoppers to fashion merchandise?

12. In what way can retail organizations better prepare their merchandise assortments before making purchase commitments?

EXERCISES AND PROJECTS

1. Visit five major retailers in your city and evaluate their use of ethnic mannequins and other visual devises in their window and interior displays. Develop a list for each company indicating the specific tools used in their minority-oriented displays.

2. Examine the pages of your local consumer newspapers to determine if attention is being paid to ads that address the minority consumer markets. Clip out three of the ads from the papers that best appeal to one or more minorities and explain what methods they use to appeal to these groups.

WEB SITES

By accessing these Web sites, you will be able to gain broader knowledge and up-to-date information on materials related to this chapter.

United States Census Bureau

www.census.gov

Census Factfinder

http://factfinder.census.gov

The Case of the Retailer with an Increase in Minority Shoppers

questions

1. How might the company discover new fashion collections that better appeal to their minority shoppers?

2. What other changes should the store make in order to better serve the needs of their changing clientele?

When Designing Woman opened its doors in 1975, it soon became known as one of the leading fashion retailers in its trading area. The population was predominantly white Caucasian, with a buying power that was upper middle class, and the consumers had a penchant for the latest in fashion merchandise. The product mix was initially designer oriented, but later it included some private labels that were successfully marketed to its consumer base.

As in the case of many geographic areas in the United States, the character of its population began to change. The once all-white clientele slowly showed signs of becoming more racially mixed. Ethnic minorities, including African Americans, Hispanics, and Asian Americans, began to patronize the store and helped it successfully meet sales expectations. In the last year, however, the consumer mix reached a base of 50 percent white and 50 percent other ethnicities. The demographics of income and buying power remained the same.

Recognizing that the "one size fits all" philosophy, in terms of merchandise assortment, might soon be insufficient in maintaining sales levels because of this changing environment, Designing Woman decided that a new merchandising approach might be warranted. In addition to specific product changes, the company also began to examine other concepts that could prevent sales erosion from taking place.

¡Arriba!

According to U.S. Census Bureau projections, by 2050, non-Hispanic Caucasians will make up only 50.1 percent of the total U.S. population. Hispanics will make up 24 percent of the population by that date, with Asians expanding the fastest to 8 percent and African-Americans at 14.6 percent.

As the ethnic mix of the American consumer becomes even more diversified, the idea of a single marketing and merchandising strategy may no longer be applicable. For local merchants, this might require a complete reinvention of their business. National retailers will be required to generate parallel product, display and signage strategies, choosing the option which might fit the dominant local cultural mix.

This idea falls in line with a long-held philosophy that successful retail concepts are responsive to—and presentation reflective of—the local market. While retailers might challenge the effectiveness of delivering different store experiences and products to meet the distinct needs of targeted customers, visionary retailers are giving it a try, as you will see in the examples that follow.

But to be able to accomplish a strategy that caters to the needs and mores of a multiethnic customer base, one must first understand the cultural differences. How are products bought, used and consumed? How are these items disposed of? Answers will provide the basis for customer-centric decisions on store design, display and instore communications.

Knowledge about the ethnic customers and their consuming patterns is becoming readily available, as researchers have also identified this rapidly customer segment. Here are a few highlights:

- Since the last census, 11 percent of the people living here are foreign-born, with more immigration from Latin America and Asia. Of those, there are big differences in family size and education, with 27 percent of foreign-born households having five or more members, and two-thirds having a high school diploma or equivalent, compared to 87 percent of the native-born population. Also, the foreign-born are more likely to live in the western part of the U.S.

- A Coca-Cola Retailing Research Council of North America study titled "Grow with America" compiled a very impressive overview of best practices in ethnic marketing and merchandising for food retailers. The research included such topics as "Define your ethnic merchandising look and organize to execute it," and "Enhance the in-store experience and connect with the community," each of which focused well beyond just identifying the segments and delved into more about the cultural habits of different ethnic groups.

- Sears is reported to be converting selected stores located in areas where at least 60 percent of shoppers are minorities into "multicultural stores" where fashions, signs, color schemes and displays are geared to appeal to Hispanic, African-American and Asian shoppers. Sears discovered that sizing, for instance, was of great concern; Hispanic and Asian women report problems finding small sizes, while some black women stated they found the opposite to be true. The solution: The multicultural stores will stock more petites in Hispanic areas and more plus sizes in predominantly black shopping areas.

- When developing consumer products for specific ethnic groups, the scent has proved to be important. For example, lavender is known to be popular with Hispanic consumers, according to Tom Vierhile, general manager of new-product tracking firm Marketing Intelligence (Naples, N.Y.).

- A 2002 report by the Food Marketing Institute, a Washington-based trade group, found that on average Hispanic grocery shoppers spend $117 a week on food, compared with $87 for the average U.S. shopper, in part because of larger families.

- By 2050, the number of Hispanic women in the United States will reach 48.92 million—an increase of nearly 340 percent from 1990. During the same time, the total U.S. female population will grow only 62 percent, to 206.64 million. At this rate of growth, Hispanic females will make up nearly a quarter of the total U.S. female population by 2050

- Safeway Supermarkets finds that stores that cater to Hispanics reflect the tastes of those consumers, i.e., pork and beef are sliced thinner, there are larger orders of papaya, plantains and yuca root and, at the checkout, the Spanish-language tabloid *Mira* sits next to the *National Enquirer*.

Of course, the challenge of catering to a multiethnic customer base isn't solved by simply putting *Mira* at the checkout, or adding Spanish or Chinese interpretations of English phrases onto signage, or changing the paint colors in stores. Only by fully immersing your company into a thorough understanding of the culturally diverse population of America can you reap the benefits.

Statistics say those benefits are innumerable.

The Planning Stages, *VM&SD*, April 2005

Vision 2020: Integrating Hispanic Marketing and Merchandising Into the DNA of Your Company

RHONDA HARPER

We sit here today at the brink of a newly defined America—one in which the white majority is becoming the minority. But in many ways the world of tomorrow is the same as it ever was.

Population, culture, and commerce have been in constant transition virtually since the beginning of time. Tens of thousands of years ago the earliest humans migrated from continent to continent. And it has continued ever since.

While some people thought that technology and communications would bring us all together in a global economy, we're finding that it may be doing quite the opposite among Latinos in the U.S. Latinos are taking advantage of technology and communications to create new groups and cultural zones. As a result, their old national identities and behavior patterns are proving surprisingly durable. America is not assimilating into a homogenous culture—but rather diverging into lifestyle segments. Examples of this are everywhere, such as segmented music, news, magazines, and television markets.

But let's not miss the bigger point: The Hispanic revolution will impact total U.S. culture!

In the words of Theodore Roosevelt, "Since the beginning of our American history, we have been engaged in change—in perpetual peaceful revolution—a revolution which goes on steadily, quietly adjusting itself to changing conditions."

And we are different today—one in five children under the age of 5 is Hispanic. By 2020, Hispanics will comprise about 25% of the U.S. population. By 2050 minorities will become the majority.

Hispanics have established themselves as a social, cultural, political and economic force. Comprising about 14% of today's U.S. population, they represent about $653 billion in disposable income—and that figure has risen about 30% since 2001! Hispanics have an unprecedented level of influence on the music we listen to (think JLo), the sports we watch (think soccer), and the food we eat. Let's face it: this isn't a niche—it's a market. And this market is going to change America as we know it today.

According to a subcommittee of the 106th Congress, 35% of legal adult immigrants, many of whom are Hispanic, enter America with less than a high school education. Another 600,000 Latinos legally immigrate each year. As the numbers of Hispanics nearly double in the next 20 years, how will this change our laws, our collective social views, the working class and the marketplace?

For example, what happens when America shifts religiously and politically? Consider these facts:

- About 70% of Hispanics are Catholic while only 24% of Americans are, including Hispanics.

- Eighty percent of Hispanics believe legal immigration is good for the U.S.—and a third want more immigration than is allowed today.

- Politically, only 16% of Hispanics are Republican—and this number is dwindling as Hispanics become more educated and gain more tenure in the U.S.

- The Center for Immigration studies calculated that immigration may reduce the wages for native workers, often Hispanic themselves, by $1,915 per year.

- According to PBS's Religion & Ethics NewsWeekly, Hispanic Catholics, overall more traditional than their non-Hispanic counterparts, describe themselves as firmly socially conservative.

So, here we have a substantial future U.S. population that represents perhaps a new mix of elements—socially conservative, politically liberal and personally traditional.

In summary, we are at the brink of a new America, and it will affect everything from our laws, to our society, to our commerce, to our workplace, to our culture. Ironically, 88% of Hispanics believe it is important that they blend into the larger U.S. society—yet they are not assimilating. Acculturation is more the reality.

Today, I speak as a marketer. I speak as a business woman.

As a marketer, I have seen examples of vision, of courage, and of innovation in Hispanic marketing, merchandising and public relations. I have seen industry leaders taking a stand, moving forward, and leaning toward the future.

For example, about eight years ago Wal-Mart started the "Store of the Community" program designed to reflect localized customer assortments and tailor merchandise to each store's demographics. About a year ago, Wal-Mart started printing its monthly ad circulars in Spanish and launched a Hispanic magazine distributed at its 1,300 stores heavily shopped by Hispanics. It has teamed up with Sprint to offer pre-paid wireless service targeted to Hispanics. Last fall it began stocking a line of bathroom and tabletop accessories inspired by Mexican folk art and culture. And its financial services department offers cut-rate fees on money wire transfers—a big lure for immigrants who support families back home And it is paying off. In a recent survey of 500 Hispanic shoppers by NOP World, 36% of Hispanics chose Wal-Mart as their favorite store. But the number-one reason for their choice had nothing to do with Hispanic merchandise. What's the reason? Yes, it is "everyday low prices."

Target Stores has implemented a consortium of nearly 100 associates across its headquarters to ensure that everyone is actively engaged with Hispanic efforts. Additionally, it has a department of influence and action focused intensely on ensuring that it builds and retains leadership among Hispanics.

And less than a year ago Sears put the finishing touches on nearly 100 stores refashioned to appeal to the multicultural markets. They brought in new brands, hired more bilingual staff, produced bilingual signage, and merchandised better-fitting clothes. They even changed their displays, featuring more bright and colorful apparel.

As a business woman, though, I know that this is just the beginning—that we are not prepared for the future. Today, we are an industry awaking to the drums that have been beating for years—those sounding alarms that said that the world was changing. That we needed to take ethnic marketing and merchandising more seriously. That we needed to develop targeted programs, products and services to meet their needs. That this was an area for growth.

Many of us have acknowledged this need, but given the issue lip service. We start ethnic departments but fail to give them the level of leadership and responsibility within the organization to create a difference. We add Hispanic marketing line items to our marketing budgets, using them as marketing insurance, and these are our first lines cut in order to save the mainstream programming. We attend Hispanic conferences, yet go back to our offices and do the same old things. And yet, even if we followed through, these steps would be meager at best.

I'd like you to bear with me now, and complete a simple four-step exercise.

First, I'd like you to hold your pen in your non-writing hand, close your eyes, and write your name. Now, open your eyes and write your name. Next, put the pen in your writing hand, close your eyes, and write your name. Finally, open your eyes and write your name.

Only a few more steps. Next to your first name, write "racism." Next to the second line, write "stereotyping." Next to your third signature, write "ethnic marketing." And, finally, write "unification."

Racism is when you don't know what you don't know. You think that race is the primary determinant of human traits. You may even believe that there is inherent race superiority. Think Ricky Ricardo. Think Archie Bunker. Then ask yourself—do you have your store classified by race? Do you show only Hispanic models in your advertising or signage based on location?

Stereotyping is when you know that you don't know. You think of Hispanics as a race—not a culture. You have a standardized mental picture that represents an oversimplified opinion or uncritical judgment. Think "The Jeffersons." Think "Queer Eye for the Straight Guy." So ask yourself, do you only see Hispanics in your blue-collar positions? Do you have a Mexican section for Hispanics? Do you show women rolling tortillas in your advertising? Do you justify your interest in Hispanic efforts by saying, "Hey, we do stuff around Cinco de Mayo"?

Ethnic marketing is when you don't know that you know. You start targeting Hispanics based on their common traits, language, social views, and customs. Think "The Cosby Show." Think George Lopez. You may have unique advertising "for them." You carry Hispanic Barbie dolls—or Bratz. Hey, you might even change your signage to Spanish.

And, finally, unification is when you know you know. You incorporate Latino marketing and merchandising decisions into all business programs and decisions You mainstream your efforts. You have one brand. One voice. One strategy. Now that strategy plan can be executed in many ways. However, it's integrated and cohesive, because you know that Hispanics in our country are multi-faceted, multi-generational, multi-cultural, multi-lingual, and multi-dimensional. You know that the Latino market impacts general market dynamics and you plan for overall change.

A couple of months ago, we completed original research for this conference and the real truth is that retailers fit into nearly each of the four steps we just covered.

I inserted the following open-ended question into the monthly polling by the VNU Retail Index—a survey of more than 500 retailers in the food, drug, convenience and specialty industries—"What is your company doing regarding identifying, selecting, developing, and retaining high-potential Hispanic talent and how would you rate these efforts?"

As a marketer, I am not proud of our efforts: Seventy-eight percent of retailers say they are making absolutely no effort to hire Hispanics. Why? Let me list the verbatim responses from the survey:

- Our locations do not have Hispanics living in this area.
- Hispanic population in our market is minimal.
- We have recruited people in our HR department who are Hispanic and speak the language. As far as searching out Hispanic talent, we don't focus on it. It really depends on the position.

I am shocked that only 22% of retailers have made an effort to specifically hire Hispanics. Some of the techniques they've pursued include :

- Eighteen percent tried job fairs, college recruiting, and partnering with the Chamber of Commerce.
- Eighteen percent recruit regionally, in high indexing Hispanic markets with success.

- Twelve percent recruit in-store for bilingual speaking.
- Twelve percent have Hispanic employee referral programs.
- Twelve percent advertise in local Latino and Hispanic newspapers.
- Twelve percent engaged search firms and screening processes.

I am shocked on the merchandising front:

- Only 50% of retailers are expanding their product offerings to maximize sales for the growing Hispanic market. Supermarkets are the most aggressive at 58%, convenience store operators are next at 48%, and mass/drug/ specialty outlets pull up the rear at 41%.

As a marketer, I am proud of some of our efforts:

- Some are expanding product lines and sourcing more products from Mexico.
- Some are identifying specific Hispanic groups by store and procuring products for that sub-group.
- And on the tactical front, some are adding out-of-country phone cards, adding Hispanic snack and candy products, and other ethnic foods, greeting cards, party goods, apparel, cooking equipment and tabletop merchandise.

A real truth is that many companies are using the stereotyping and ethnic marketing models. And here are the "seven deadly mistakes" of these models that will derail your success moving forward.

1. **Surname Leadership**: If her name is Rodriguez, we'll put her in charge of Hispanic marketing. She'll know what they want! In fact, we'll have her sit on every diversity roundtable, conference, and task force—and to mentor every new Hispanic we hire. Let's make sure

to keep an eye on her, though—she still has to perform her primary role and responsibility as well as everyone else! Trust me, isolation, discontent and retention will become issues.

2. **Line Item Vetos**: Let's add Hispanic marketing to our marketing budget, merchandising area, etc. Let's see, Hispanics are 12% of the market, so we'll budget 12% of our plan. Hey, wait a minute. They don't generate 12% of our share or sales. So, let's drop that to 5% of our overall plan. Gee, 5% isn't enough to even track the changes—and the headcount to manage it won't pay out. And, we don't even have enough in our budget to handle our mainstream target! OK, let's cut the dollars. Next year will be different.

3. **Divide and Conquer**: Remember Rodriguez from number one. Well, let's have her hire some Hispanic agencies. We'll have them take our plans and make them work for the Hispanic audience. Yeah, that'll take care of it.

4. **Zero-based Planning**: We don't sell to Hispanics, so we don't need to have programs, products, or services. Whew! That saves a lot of time!

5. **Short-term Thinking**: We do Cinco de Mayo and have a Mexican aisle, and, hey, I've attended some conferences! We've got our bases covered!

6. **One-segment Thinking**: Mexican. While Mexicans are about 60% of American Hispanics, there are 40% that are NOT Mexican—and may not even be Hispanic, but Latino!

7. **Lost in Translation**: One of our employees in the finance department is from Argentina so we had them translate all of our signs to Spanish—and even translate our advertising! What a cost savings!

So, what do we do? The real truth is that one day we will understand the *think*, *feel*, and *do* of Latinos and align our marketing and merchandising strategies around them. It is about *who* the Hispanic is, not *what* they are, or the fact that they are Hispanic. It's a matter of learning the community, who the customer is, and finding out what they want to see on the shelves.

When you learn more about the *who*, you will find that it boils down to what we call the fabulous seven:

1. **Family**: The center of life.
2. **Food**: The symbol of unity and love.
3. **Feelings**: Expressing who they are.
4. **Fashion**: Showing respect for events and people.
5. **Femininity:** A nod to their tradition.
6. **Fiesta**: The social environment.
7. **Fitting-In**: The mix between home and country.

So, the next 15 years will bring seven fundamental changes—changes that we need to begin enacting now.

1. **In the future, Hispanic marketing, merchandising, and recruiting will cease being a project—it will simply be a part of your business**. Fact: We are entering the period of negative growth among U.S. workforce. By 2010, there will be more jobs than people, period. Hispanics will become an important element in the job pool at all levels. And that in and of itself will change how we go to business.

2. **In the future, everyone in your company will be a Hispanic marketing and merchandising expert**. Imagine instead of leaving it to a few individuals or a department, everyone from the mailroom to the CEO will be able to speak intelligently on the topic.

3. **In the future, Hispanics will have changed the American culture and people will expect to experience it**. Imagine Hispanic diversity as a value, not just a demographic and how it is important to Generation Y and younger, even if they are not a part of a minority group. Imagine growing up in a multicultural environment—where 20% to 40% of your classroom, your school, your neighborhood, your grocery store, or on your television programming is either Hispanic or African American.

4. **In the future, we will develop personalized marketing directly for the individual Hispanic families and communities**. Imagine reflecting product choices and outreach directly into homes and neighborhoods that reflect the Hispanics' countries of origin, their generations, their acculturation levels and their individual needs.

5. **In the future, bilingualism will not be an option; it will be a part of America**. Imagine Spanish-speaking advertising and programming within mainstream media. Imagine bilingual government signage. Imagine all school children speaking Spanish. Imagine a total bilingual employee base!

6. **In the future, our world view will become more focused on South America instead of Europe**. Imagine enhanced foreign trade and outsourcing to these markets. Imagine the intensity of political forces in Argentina, Colombia, and Mexico deeply affecting Americans.

7. **In the future, the balance of power will change**. Hispanics will become government and business leaders and shift support and programming to a more liberal view. Family values will move front and center—impacting everything from the women's movement to news and entertainment.

This movement has already begun. If you're not already taking steps, your company could be vulnerable. Your Hispanic initiative is too important to leave in the hands of junior employees—it needs to be on your C-suite agenda.

But you cannot expect to have a positive return on investment for Hispanic efforts right away. The market is now forming and credibility and persuasion aren't achieved overnight. I know each of you are wondering what you should be doing. Overall, you need to start moving from . . .

- Market segmentation to holistic marketing,
- Sequential targeting to simultaneous targeting,
- Independent strategies to interdependent strategies,
- Mastering complexity to focusing on simplicity,
- Winning the market to demonstrating experience and validation, and
- Transactions to relationships.

It is up to all of us to rise to the challenge. We dare not fail as our marketplace success demands our attention. We must explore this area, we must invoke focus, we must unite around this effort. Together, we will champion Hispanic marketing and merchandising. It will take the vision of leadership, the capacity to lead, the commitment to make every employee a champion of diversity and inclusion, and the character of an entire generation of business people to ensure we do this not because we have to, but as JFK would say, "because it is right." What we truly need are champions.

My best hope for retailers and manufacturers alike is that you reach to the future and make it your own. That you adopt the changing culture and align it with your strategic plans and actions. It is true that since the beginning of American history, we have been engaged in change. While the future is certain, it is not known who will lead the way. But one thing is clear—success will not find neutrality between those who are visionary leaders and those who are not.

Ketchum South, January 15, 2007

Iman In Charge

JENNY B. FINE

Iman is an extraordinarily passionate businesswoman.

Get her talking about her eponymous beauty brand, and her voice rises and falls with conviction, her eyes lock with yours as she leans in close to make a particularly important point, her finger stabbing the air. But mention the word "ethnic" and it's all she can do to stay in her chair.

"Ethnic," she thunders. "What is ethnic? My. Brand. Is. Not. Ethnic," she continues, clearly enunciating each word to make sure there is absolutely *no* misunderstanding.

"I'm not interested in your ethnic origin, because that comes with culture," Iman declares. "I'm not talking about culture. I'm talking," and she pauses here, "about foundation."

In fact, Iman has a lot to say on the subject of foundation. It is the engine that drives her 12-year-old eponymous beauty brand, accounting for 60 percent of all sales. The sixteen shades, available in three different formulas, represent her vision of a modern-day multicultural line, one targeted to *all* women with skin of color and not just African-Americans.

Iman, dressed today in a black pantsuit and sitting at a glass conference table in her Seventh Avenue office, is not interested in merely paying lip service to the rainbow coalition that is modern-day America. Her goal is to banish the ethnic aisle from mass retailers and create an environment where multicultural brands are merchandised alongside mainstream ones.

"When women shop for bags and shoes and clothing, there is no ethnic aisle," says the supermodel-turned-chief executive of Iman Cosmetics. "Retailers are slicing their own pie too many times. I'm saying get the *whole* pie. It just makes business sense."

America's evolving demographic composition bears out Iman, who studied political science at Nairobi University before being discovered in 1975 by photographer Peter Beard. According to statistics from the U.S. Census bureau, there are about 34.9 million African-Americans in the U.S., or 12 percent of the overall population; 12.4 million Asians, about 4 percent, and almost 42 million people of Hispanic descent, about 15 percent of the overall population. "Women with skin of color represent a huge and growing market opportunity," says Iman. "The multicultural market in the U.S. is $1.5 billion, with the mass market making up to 50 percent of the figure. The future lies with companies who will understand how to talk to her without making her feel she is a minority."

It was those numbers that attracted Procter & Gamble's Marc Pritchard, then the president of P&G global cosmetics and hair colorants, to Iman's business two years ago. In October 2004, Iman signed a multiyear licensing agreement with P&G to design and distribute the brand.

Under the terms of the deal, Iman retains 51 percent of Impala, the company that makes Iman cosmetics, and is the sole active owner and creative driving force. The timing couldn't have been better: Originally launched in 1994 at J.C. Penney, the Iman line was an immediate success. But a series of ruinous business partners combined with Penney's decision to discontinue its beauty business dealt the brand a crippling blow. Iman regrouped, and launched her products in a selective mass distribution in early 2003. Her goal was to deliver prestige quality products and imagery in a mass channel. Price points were slashed by about 25 percent; today, Iman products range in price from $6.99 for a lipliner to $13.99 for foundation.

When asked why P&G, a packaged goods giant whose brands usually hover in the billion dollar sales range, was interested in striking a deal with a fledgling entrepreneur like Iman, Pritchard's answer is immediate. "We're looking to get the right portfolio of brands that target the right fast-growing consumer segments," says Pritchard, who is now P&G's president of global strategic planning. The size of the Iman Cosmetics brand, which industry sources assess will have U.S. retail sales of about $12 million this year and $20 million globally, was less important. "What's important is to be consistently the fastest-growing brand in the market," Pritchard continues, estimating that Procter expects non-Caucasians will make up about 50 percent of the overall U.S. population by 2022.

In 2005 and 2006, Iman Cosmetics saw a 50 percent growth in doors and dollar sales; 25 percent growth is forecasted for 2007–2008, followed by 10 to 15 percent growth the following year and 8 to 10 percent growth in year five. Driving the growth will be new door openings, as well as international expansion. Iman is particularly intrigued by the possibilities presented by India.

"The interest from both of our sides is how to monopolize the market share for women with skin of color," says Iman.

To that end, the companies have hammered out a working relationship, where Iman provides the creative direction and P&G the operational. "Iman has a very clear vision of the business and is the creative and inspirational leader," says Gina Drosos, P&G's vice president, global cosmetics and hair colorants. "We help in the areas where we have a lot of expertise, like operations, retailer relationships and managing a mass cosmetics brand."

Iman's quest for domination of the mass market multicultural beauty scene comes at a time of heightened activity in the market. Milani Cosmetics and Markwins' Tropez brand continue to lead sales, while L'Oréal Paris is also trying to crack the market with its HIP High Intensity Pigments line and CoverGirl with its Queen Latifah collection. What's more, retailers are more results-oriented than ever before. If the merchandise isn't moving, it's out—no matter how innovative the product lineup may be. For proof, look no further than Revlon's short-lived Vital Radiance brand; targeted to women 50 and over, it was on counter for less than 12 months.

To avoid the pitfalls, Iman and senior vice president of brand development Desiree Reid are building the brand door by door. Its primary retail partners are Wal-Mart, Walgreens, Target, Duane Reade and Ulta, but the products are in hundreds of doors of each retailer, rather than thousands. In 2003, Iman started out with about 50 doors. Today, that number is 850, and expected to grow by 1,500 in 2007 and reach 2,500 in 2008.

"In the old days, a retailer would say, 'I'm giving you 200 doors and here they are.' We said we'd like to choose," Iman says. "Why would we want to be in Alaska, for example?"

Among the criteria used when choosing doors: the income level and diversity of a market, particularly of 50-plus and 30-plus customers, as well as the brand's sales history in a prospective region.

Iman and Reid requested—and also received in many cases—prime positioning. "I want to be right next to Revlon and right next to L'Oréal," says Reid. "I know our customer is shopping those two brands because they've courted her."

Iman also assiduously courts her customers. One way is through a national advertising campaign, depicting an Asian, a Latina, an African-American and a Native American. More important to the growth of the brand, though, has been in-store events, including makeup artist visits, sampling, demonstrations and, of course, personal appearances by Iman. "We've covered about 70 to 80 percent of our stores with some sort of activity, and that's what's making the difference," says Michelle Hobson, manager of strategic business development of beauty for Walgreens. "It's all about target marketing. I call it a high-maintenance relationship in a good way," Hobson laughs. "It's not just about getting new products and prepacks on the counter. It's about fulfilling this customer's needs and offering premium quality products in a drugstore environment."

Though Hobson says sales have increased as much as eightfold when Iman makes a personal appearance, Iman, who with husband rock star David Bowie makes up one of New York's glammest couples, doesn't rely on her celebrity to move the merch. "My name helped in the beginning, but today it's about the product," she says. "The product is the celebrity in my company. What I bring to it is integrity." When Iman does make a promotional appearance, the company capitalizes on it by holding multiple events in the same region—if she's in a store in, say, Atlanta, makeup artists are canvassing other key accounts, building on the publicity generated by an Iman visit.

The company puts as much effort into educating retailers as it does educating consumers. "There was a misconception that women of color don't buy over the Internet. At walgreens.com, we're number four," says Iman triumphantly. "There was a misconception that women of color don't like to wear foundation. Well, they don't like to wear foundation that's not right for them. If our business is 60 percent foundation, it shows they *do* wear it when they find the right shade. Retailers erroneously classify many women as non-makeup wearers, rather than customers who have left the market because of a lack of brands meeting their needs."

That's not to say that the transition from Penney's to mass has been entirely smooth. Liquid foundation, the biggest category in the general market, has largely failed to find an audience for Iman in the mass market, ditto with lip gloss in a pot. "Retailers want a certain amount of dollars per square foot," says Reid. "If a product isn't performing, we move it. We have to have a plan for sell-through. Our [problems] may not seem so big because we're not in even door, but we still have the same expectations of every other brand."

Iman is looking to grow the business through both product launches and increased retail distribution. Although foundation comprises the majority of sales, she still sees untapped opportunity in the face category. A new foundation will launch next spring, along with revamped powders and bronzers. Skin care, which currently accounts for about 20 percent of the brand's business, will be revamped for spring 2008. "Skin care is one of the categories that's never really addressed for women of color," says Iman. "We have to be relevant and bring the latest technologies and latest stories to the market. Our intention is to become *the* authority on face when it comes to this market."

If Iman sounds driven, frankly, she is. Ask her why and her voice drops for the first time during a 90-minute interview. "This is my legacy," she says simply. "When I started this, I was a supermodel. Now I'm a ceo. At the end of the day, *this* is what I'll be remembered for. My legacy will be that I have created the best makeup for women with skin of color."

Beauty Biz, *Women's Wear Daily*, December 2006

ever-changing fashion and its acceptance

Every generation laughs at old fashions but religiously follows the new.

HENRY DAVID THOREAU, AUTHOR

As the decade-by-decade review of the 20th century in Chapter 2 illustrates, fashion is ever changing. Styles come into and go out of favor. Sometimes the success of an item is extremely short-lived; other times its success survives from one season to the next. Designers need to understand what motivates consumers to change, because success in the fashion industry means encouraging consumers to discard something old for something new. If everyone wore the same garments year in and year out, the industry would generate far fewer sales.

Designers are the leading players in the field. They must use their creative talents to produce merchandise that captures the consumer's attention. Other players include product developers, merchandisers, and the media. In the end, however, the consumer makes the final decision. If consumers are not ready to change, they will reject new styles. Consumers may choose to wear what is in their wardrobes rather than succumb to a style change that does not reflect their needs.

In some cases, a new style can be rejected in the development process or at the manufacturer's sample stage. Buyers regularly pass over some items in favor of others. Those items that are rejected are withdrawn from the line and sold as **designer's samples** in showroom **sample sales** or to retailers who successfully merchandise such items. Although this is often disheartening to the creators of the merchandise, it is less costly to reject the item at this stage than to sell it to the stores, only to have it become a markdown. Retailers absorb considerable losses from markdowns and often remain distant from the designers and manufacturers who created them.

THE LANGUAGE OF THE TRADE

As with any industry or profession, the fashion business has its own **language of the trade**. To participate in the field or even just to comprehend what the world of fashion is all about, it is necessary to be familiar with the basic terminology. The most frequently used terms are defined below in alphabetical order.

After you have completed this chapter, you will be able to discuss:

- Various terms that comprise the language of the trade.
- Different stages of the fashion cycle.
- Influences on the fashion industry created by individuals or groups, or both.
- Practices of copying and adapting fashion.

This high-fashion design by Carolina Herrera, shown on the runway, is intended to capture the attention of the consumer.

ADAPTATION A garment that uses the main elements of another's design, with variations on such elements as fabric, trim, and ornamentation.

CLASSIC An item that has staying power in the fashion industry. Although some styles fall in and out of favor, classics become **staples** or integral parts of wardrobes. A navy blue blazer is an example of a classic.

COLLECTION/LINE A designer's or manufacturer's offerings for a particular season. Although *line* is often used interchangeably with *collection*, some industry participants reserve the word *collection* for more expensive merchandise, and *line* for the lower price points.

COUTURIER (M)/COUTURIERE (F) French terms for male and female designers of original styles that are made of expensive fabrics using fine sewing and tailoring techniques and materials. Collections are shown twice a year—spring/summer and fall/winter.

DRESS-DOWN FRIDAYS Days on which casual attire is accepted as proper dress in the office. Studies have found that workers are just as productive—if not more so—when they are comfortably attired. Companies such as Levi Strauss, Dayton/Hudson, Marshall Field's, and Neiman Marcus created brochures and help lines to answer questions on what is appropriate to wear on these casual days. John Molloy's revision of his book, *Dress for Success*, includes information on dressing down.

FAD A style that is enthusiastically accepted for a short period of time. A fad tends to gain popularity and acceptance at a brisk pace only to fall rapidly into disuse. *Nehru jackets*, with abbreviated collar and no lapels, were fashioned after the silhouette worn by India's prime minister, Nehru. They swept in and out of the fashion scene of the 1960s. Their quick demise cost millions to both manufacturers and retailers. In the

The main street in New York City's garment district has been appropriately renamed Fashion Avenue.

early 1990s, however, a completely collarless style appeared on shirts. A large segment of the younger market bought these shirts in great quantities. The shirt fit perfectly with the casual direction menswear has been taking.

FASHION A style accepted by the majority of a group. The mini will always be considered a style, as will flared pants, chemise dresses, and turtleneck sweaters. They will only be considered a fashion when a majority of the consuming public accepts and purchases them.

HAUTE COUTURE A French term that means fine dressmaking; in the United States it has come to mean high fashion.

KNOCKOFF A garment that has been copied from the design of some expensive item of clothing. The silhouette and details of the more expensive model are retained, but lower costs are achieved with less-expensive fabrics and construction. The knockoff is sometimes called a *copy*.

PRÊT-À-PORTER/READY-TO-WEAR French for "ready to be carried," prêt-à-porter is used to describe garments that are mass-produced rather than custom-made; synonymous with ready-to-wear.

SAMPLE SALES Periodic clearance sales that manufacturers hold to sell the styles that did not make it into production.

SEVENTH AVENUE The main street of New York City's garment center, but also used to refer to the entire garment district. Also called *Fashion Avenue*.

SILHOUETTE A garment's shape or outline. Although numerous variations of silhouettes are found in fashion, there are five basic shapes in women's apparel. They are the tubular silhouette, which falls straight; the bouffant, which flares out in fullness; the A-line silhouette, which falls from the shoulder extending to the hem; the wedge silhouette, which has greater width in the upper body than the lower body; and the hourglass silhouette, which has equal shoulder and hip width and exaggerated waist indentions. In men's tailored clothing, silhouettes are the American or classic-cut jacket, which employs a fullness to the garment, and the European model, which accentuates a tapering at the waistline and broad shoulders.

STYLE The characteristic appearance of the garment or accessory. Skirts, for example, are a style, as are dresses, shirts, and sweaters. Sometimes there is so much variation within a style that the style actually becomes a classification, with many styles in each. For example, skirts may be flared, straight, pleated, or gored. Styles do not change, although their acceptance by customers changes periodically. Platform shoes, for example, were popular in the 1960s, and again in the early 1990s. Between those two periods, there was little interest in platform shoes, but it was still a style. A simple definition for style is "the characteristics that distinguish one garment or accessory from another."

TASTE A personal feeling about a particular style. When people speak of good taste, they are referring to the appropriateness of a style for a particular use or occasion. What really constitutes taste is often the opinion of some and not adhered to by everyone.

These basic women's silhouettes reappear regularly in designer collections.

FASHION CYCLES

The term **fashion cycle** refers to a style's introduction, growth, maturity, and decline. Styles move through the cycle at different rates. Short-lived styles are called fads and are the industry's nightmare. With the money spent on design, fabric selection, color decision making, garment production, and marketing, the losses from a fad's quick demise can be significant. Styles that last for at least one season are considered fashion. There is no exact time frame for each style to move through the fashion cycle; each lasts as long as there is customer acceptance. The grunge look in the early 1990s lasted a few seasons, while acceptance of athletic shoes as fashion footwear continues.

A-line Silhouette

Hourglass
Silhouette

Wedge Silhouette

Tubular
Silhouette

Bouffant Silhouette

Whatever the duration of a style's popularity, all styles go through the same stages of the cycle.

Introduction Stage

During this period, the designer's new styles are shown to the public with limited exposure. Those with the greatest potential for success, as determined by such professionals in the field as fashion forecasters and the editorial press, are often hyped in the pages of the consumer fashion magazines, whose readers eagerly seek out these styles. Fashion spreads in such publications as *GQ, Elle, Seventeen, Town & Country, Essence, Vogue,* and *Harper's Bazaar* usually arouse the interest of their readers. Other styles may reflect what is current for the new season. Some styles bear labels of distinction and are eagerly awaited by the followers of a particular collection.

The introduction stage is the phase of the cycle at which a style is most expensive. Take, for example, a couturier's creation. It is painstakingly developed using the finest fabrics and hand workmanship and may sell for several thousand dollars. Its introduction is risky and expensive. If it is too radical for acceptance, the designer's reputation may suffer. Of course, if the style finds acceptance at this highest price point, adaptations or copies will move into the marketplace and find wider consumer acceptance.

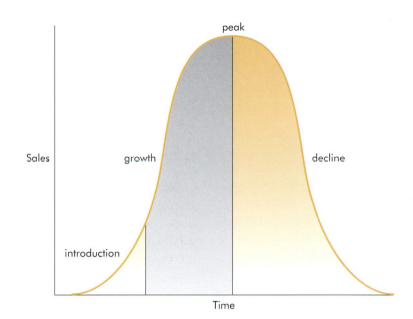

The fashion cycle.

Growth Stage

Once the style seems to catch fire, lower-priced variations and copies are marketed. Those consumers who were attracted to the new silhouettes, shapes, or fabric innovations, but were unable to afford the extravagantly high prices charged for the originals, can now avail themselves of the less-costly models. During the growth stage, the style may be available at a variety of price points. There is, however, a tendency for sales to decline at the highest levels once the market has been saturated with the copies.

Maturity Stage

At this stage, sales achieve their highest potential. The original style is shown at every retail level in many fabrics and adaptations. Stores such as Neiman Marcus, Saks Fifth Avenue, and Henri Bendel might still be featuring the original versions, with the specialty chains selling the lower-priced copies. How long the style remains at the height of its popularity depends on whether consumers will continue to buy more than just one model of the style. In some cases, shoppers make a single purchase of a style, while in other cases more than one purchase may be made. The bell-bottomed and flare-legged pants of the 1970s were bought over and over again and, at that time, became staples in fashion wardrobes. Knickers, however, which were reintroduced in the early 1980s, generally became a one-time purchase.

At some time during this stage, the style's acceptance peaks, sales level off, and the decline stage is reached.

Decline Stage

Usually the decline stage is shorter than the introduction phase. Manufacturers of the style at the higher price level have abandoned production before this period, recognizing that less-expensive copies are taking over the market. They are busy at work on new styles, as another fashion cycle begins. This point in the cycle finds the items drastically reduced in the traditional stores and at very low selling prices at the off-price retailers, who have bought manufacturer leftovers at greatly reduced prices.

When a style has completed the fashion cycle, it does not mean that the public will never see it again. Without question, most styles find their way back into favor, often as more modern interpretations of past designs. It may take anywhere from 10 to 50 years or more for this to happen. Usually only one style recurs at a time. At the beginning of 1995, however, numerous recurring styles made the rounds from a number of previous decades. The styles, shapes, and silhouettes that were once in favor—such as the belted suit of the 1940s, padded jackets and pointy pumps of the 1950s, and the wrap dress of the 1970s—were all resurrected, but in a slightly different way. The wrap dress and the pointy pumps still held favor in the mid-2000s. Good styles do not generally die; they just wait long enough in the wings for someone to bring them back into the mainstream of fashion.

Thus, styles recur or are reinvented, sometimes reappearing as a more accepted fashion than when they were first offered to the consumer.

FASHION TRENDSETTERS AND LEADERS

When the fashion designer creates his or her collections, there is no guarantee that acceptance will follow. A great deal of promotion and fanfare generally surrounds the introduction of the new merchandise, but that only helps get the attention of the prospective market.

One sure-fire way to assure acceptance of a particular style is to have it worn by an admired member of society. These people are **trendsetters** and **fashion leaders**. In the United States, they are generally from the fields of entertainment and sports. Others include members of European royalty and the American first families. The common denominator among trendsetters and fashion leaders is often wealth—a necessity for participation in acquiring new and innovative fashion. In some cases, however, the popularizing of a fashion item may come from people in the spotlight whose notoriety stems from their misdeeds. Two such examples are Bruno Magli shoes, which were frequently mentioned during the O. J. Simpson trial, and the Donna Karan–designed beret worn by Monica Lewinsky that appeared repeatedly in television clips during the Clinton impeachment scandal. During the press coverage of the Clinton-Lewinsky scandal, phones rang all day at Zegna to order the infamous $105 Clinton tie.

Although we are all aware of the fashion innovations that trickle down to the masses after being created by such legendary designers as Saint Laurent, Lagerfeld, Ralph Lauren, and Calvin Klein, we often overlook *street styles*, which are creatively assembled and altered by rappers, ravers, home girls, skaters, deadhead bikers, drag queens, and punks. Many of the fashions created on the street, such as creative buzz cuts, Dr. Seuss–inspired hats, door-knocker earrings, cutoffs, hair extensions, name-plate chains, men's pajamas worn as baggies, tie-dyed T-shirts, neo-hippie patchwork, ethnic jewelry, truckers wallets on chains, tattoos, extreme theatrical makeup, unusually colored hair, body piercing, and latex gear, have achieved significant recognition from the fashion world. These trends all owe their appearance to concrete streets, not runways. Designers such as Todd Oldham, Anna Sui, Jean Paul Gaultier, and even

Punk fashions were created on the streets.

the House of Chanel are continuously revitalized and energized by the street/club scene.

An examination of people from the entertainment world, the sports scene, and the important families of Europe and the United States shows how important these people are as trendsetters, for both **top-down** as well as **bottom-up** fashions.

The Entertainment World

People worldwide have a fascination with the stars of stage, screen, and television. They have influenced clothing, hairstyles, and makeup. Some celebrities have influ-

Madonna in her attire by Jean Paul Gaultier caused a great stir in the fashion world.

GILBERT ADRIAN

A graduate of New York City's School of Fine and Applied Arts, Gilbert Adrian, who dropped his first name when he was discovered by Hollywood, continued his studies in Paris. There he met one of America's foremost composers, Irving Berlin, who assisted him in getting the costuming assignment for Broadway's *Music Box Revues, Greenwich Village Follies*, and George White's *Scandals*.

In 1923, Adrian went to Hollywood to design costumes for Rudolf Valentino, one of the most important early movie stars. From that time until 1939, he was the studio's chief designer. In addition to creating costumes for Joan Crawford, he also designed for such greats as Katharine Hepburn and Rosalind Russell.

His signature designs were sleek, long jackets accentuated by broad shoulders and narrow waists. This silhouette would become Joan Crawford's favorite. For evening wear, his clothing for the films was generally of the "romantic" look, often using flowing organdy as the fabric. His *Letty Lynton gown*, designed for Crawford, was the rage of the day. It was reported that Macy's alone sold more than 500,000 pieces!

He ultimately left the world of entertainment and opened his own studio, where he created both couture and expensive ready-to-wear.

Adrian, primarily known as a costume designer for films, also designed couture and ready-to-wear.

enced fashion through their own style of dress; others have started trends based on the attire worn by the characters they have portrayed.

One of the most popular movie stars of the 1940s was Joan Crawford. Her followers often imitated the styles she wore on and off the screen, particularly the exaggerated, broad-shouldered jacket. Women everywhere wore them. The broad-shouldered look favored by Crawford, as well as other styles that became important in fashion, were designed by Adrian, one of Hollywood's legendary designers. A World of Fashion Profile focuses on the talents of Adrian.

Other stars were also considered fashion leaders. Marlene Dietrich wore suits that resembled those worn by men, and soon she had a rash of followers dressing that way. Katharine Hepburn, who never wore a dress in her personal life, helped make pants standard and appropriate dress for every occasion. Cary Grant favored the drape suit worn by the Duke of Windsor and helped bring it into prominence for men.

When rock 'n' roll took the world by storm, not only was the music new, but so were the styles worn by the famous groups. The Beatles quickly influenced the world with their hit tunes and their fashions. Their mod suits became the rage, and their famous haircuts were soon seen on a great number of their youthful followers.

Today's music stars also influence the way consumers dress. Two stars who were much imitated in the 1980s and 1990s were Madonna and Michael Jackson. Madonna popularized sexy dressing and wore undergarments as outerwear, with a widespread use of lace and a bustier. Michael Jackson's preference for the single glove had teenagers all over the world wearing the solo glove as part of their dress. Rappers continue to influence fashion as well.

Table 5.1

FASHION LEADERS AND THE STYLES THEY POPULARIZED

	Fashion Leaders	Styles Popularized
British Royalty	Duke of Windsor	Knickers, patterned sweaters, drape suit, glen plaids, the "Windsor" knot
	Lady Diana	Wedding dress, slicked hairstyle
First Families	Jackie Kennedy	Pillbox hat, A-line skirts, empire-waist gowns, low-slung pumps, bouffant hairstyle, oversized sunglasses
	John Kennedy	Hatless and coatless appearances led to decline in sales of hats and overcoats; Izod knit shirt worn under sport coat
	Nancy Reagan	Chanel-type suits, the color red
	Barbara Bush	Faux pearls
	Bill Clinton	Nylon running shorts
Entertainers	Joan Crawford	Broad shoulders
	Marlene Dietrich	Male-inspired suits
	Cary Grant	The drape suit
	The Beatles	Mod suits, long hair
	Madonna	Sexy dressing, lace fabrics, the bustier
	Michael Jackson	One glove
	Bruce Springsteen	Jeans, T-shirts, earring
	Cindy Crawford	Face mole as a "beauty mark"

The Beatles' mod attire and hairstyles influenced fashion in the 1960s.

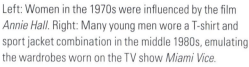
Left: Women in the 1970s were influenced by the film *Annie Hall*. Right: Many young men wore a T-shirt and sport jacket combination in the middle 1980s, emulating the wardrobes worn on the TV show *Miami Vice*.

Even more influential than the stars themselves were the characters they played in films or on television. Annie Hall, a character created by Woody Allen, became not only a memorable film role, but also a major look for the late 1970s. Women all over America wore versions of the Annie Hall outfit seen on Diane Keaton in the film—replete with oversized men's shirts, very long skirts, baggy khaki pants, and men's hats.

As soon as John Travolta wore his white disco suit in *Saturday Night Fever*, young men everywhere adapted the style as their own. It was one of the most popular suits ever worn by the young.

The curly hair fad was popularized by Barbra Streisand in the movie *A Star Is Born*. The movie *Grease*, filmed in the late 1970s, quickly brought leather motorcycle jackets into fashion; *Flashdance*, one of the hottest films of the 1970s, helped to popularize gray sweatshirt fabric as a fashion material; *Risky Business* and Tom Cruise popularized Ray-Ban's Wayfarer sunglasses; and *Urban Cowboy* brought the western look to urban America.

The summer of 1995 was witness to a movie that brought teenage fashions to a new level. Contrasting with typical grunge dress of the time, *Clueless* brought to the screen fashions that briefly influenced the junior market. Parading around in glamorous styles designed by Anna Sui, Dolce & Gabbana, Martine Sitbon, and Donna Karan, the characters were dressed more for Rodeo Drive than the traditional malls. War movies of the mid-2000s brought a wealth of military looks to the fashion arena.

On television, western wear fashioned after the men in the nighttime soap *Dallas* quickly became the rage in the 1980s. All over the country, men were wearing jeans, boots, and western shirts, all topped with Stetsons or other cowboy hats. Don Johnson starred in *Miami Vice*, and his mode of dress included the T-shirt worn under an Armani sport coat in pastel colors, a look that soon became popular with young men. Sockless feet in loafers were also a Johnson trend. Over on the *Dynasty* set, designer Nolan Miller was creating a wide-shouldered silhouette for Linda Evans and Joan Collins, which soon became one of fashion's styles of that decade. Jennifer Aniston's hairstyle in the television series *Friends*, as well as the clothes worn by the entire cast, were influences in the 1990s.

In the 1980s, rock 'n' roll stars, such as Bruce Springsteen, helped make T-shirts and jeans standard dress for the younger crowd. Rap took center stage in the early 1990s, followed by hip-hop, bringing into vogue the low-rise, baggy pants that soon were worn by many teenagers.

In the early 2000s, fashions were influenced by such films as *Moulin Rouge*, which highlighted the French look, and *Pearl Harbor*, which gave us the military look. The public's continued fascination with the fashions worn by celebrities of the entertainment world can be seen each year in the television broadcasts of the Academy Awards and the Grammys. Preshow Oscar programs show the attendees as they arrive, focusing on well-known stars who are wearing the latest designer fashions. At the 2007 Oscars and Grammy Awards, a return to elegance was the highlight. Backless and strapless dresses were the standard. Knockoffs of the most popular dress designs are quickly made available to consumers.

The Sports World

Every sport requires a particular mode of dress for its participants. With the rising popularity of sports and the growing number of spectators, it is easy to understand why many fans have adopted their styles of dress from their favorite sports and athletes.

The hairstyles and clothing worn by the cast of *Friends* greatly influenced the youth market in the 1990s.

At the beginning of the 21st century, *Sex and the City* was watched as closely for its fashions as for its story line.

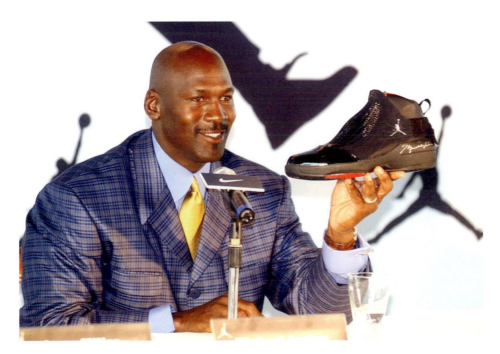

Air Jordans were popularized by basketball great, Michael Jordan.

Tiger Woods has helped bring record sales to golf wear.

French soccer star Thierry Henry is a spokesman for Tommy Hilfiger.

Basketball, for example, has given the athletic footwear industry an enormous boost by popularizing certain models worn by the stars. Michael Jordan and the Air Jordans became the favorite of most teenage boys. Even at prices that approached $200 a pair, they became top sellers. Companies such as Nike manufacture and distribute a whole host of athletic footwear and apparel in stores all over the world, as well as in their own superstores, Nike Town.

Golf, with its fashion-oriented colors and designs worn by the major players, such as Tiger Woods, has encouraged the fashion industry to produce the same styles for street wear. The wide-brimmed hat popularized by golf star Greg Norman has become a favorite on and off the links as has the mock turtle worn by Woods. Designers such as Giorgio Armani and Ralph Lauren have designed golf wear, which is influenced by their signature looks. Several retailers, such as Lands' End, Eddie Bauer, and Talbots, now feature golf wear in a specific section of their catalogs.

Aerobic sports, bicycling, and boxing have also influenced fashion, with leotards, double-layer shorts, bicycle pants, and aerobic shoes.

Football and hockey jerseys, sporting the names of teams and the player numbers, are common among young and old. As soon as a new team surfaces or a new star emerges, the gear worn on the field is quickly translated into wearing apparel.

Skiing, of course, has introduced the world to a whole new wardrobe. Initially, ski apparel was designed of functional fabrics that maintained warmth. The fashion industry, however, immediately benefited when people of all ages embraced the styles for everyday wear.

Now it is soccer that has joined the ranks of the other sports with notables such as French soccer star Thierry Henry. In a deal with Tommy Hilfiger, Henry will be the inspiration of a line designed by the famous American designer.

Even the fishing vest, with its host of pockets, has been embraced by fashion enthusiasts. The bandanna worn by Andre Agassi on the tennis court has become a fashion staple for many, and the red golf shirts and sweaters worn by Tiger Woods on the final day of each tournament gave that color a boost in sales for golf apparel.

As soon as a new sports figure receives the attention of the fans, the fashion industry is sure to follow with apparel that mimics his or her choices.

British Royalty

Although the members of royal families are generally not known for their fashion acumen, some have left their marks as fashion leaders. Most notable have been the Duke of Windsor and Lady Diana, the Princess of Wales.

The Duke of Windsor, a member of the British royal family, was the heir to King George V. After King George's death, the Duke became Edward VIII, but abdicated before his coronation to marry Wallis Simpson, an American divorcée. He began a private life that made him a fashion celebrity. Wherever he went, he was immediately recognized for his keen sense of fashion. He helped to popularize knickers, which he wore for casual dress, and the patterned sweaters that accompanied them. He also wore the English drape suit, which was more comfortable because it had more fabric in the shoulders and chest and fell softly on the wearer to form a wrinkle or drape. Finally, he sported glen plaid woolens, which men all over the world were soon wearing, and the Windsor knot—a wider knot than the traditional tie knot. Not only were his choices popular during his day, but the popularity of some have remained constant.

Princess Diana also emerged as a royal family member to watch. Her youth and regal beauty enabled her to break from the more conservative traditions of dress favored by the British royals. Although her choices sometimes caused consternation among other members of the royal family, her wedding dress was quickly copied and was worn by brides all over the world. In 1995, she was a presenter at the Council of Fashion Design Awards extravaganza. Her appearance was recorded by every important fashion publication and television news broadcast. Her now-famous hairdo was greeted with enthusiasm and was copied by women across the globe. When she put many of her evening dresses up for auction in June 1997, the sale netted $3.25 million for AIDS and breast cancer charities. Even after her untimely death that year, she remains a fashion symbol.

The Duke and Duchess of Windsor were royal fashion style setters after their marriage in 1937.

Princess Diana was responsible for fashions that were unlike those worn by other members of the British royal family.

THE KENNEDYS

John Kennedy was a member of the famous Kennedy family of Boston. As he climbed the political ladder that would eventually bring him to the presidency, he married Jacqueline Bouvier, a young socialite. Increasingly, their pictures were featured in newspapers, in magazines, on television, and on the fashion pages of industry publications, such as *Women's Wear Daily*, that were earmarked for those in the world of fashion.

Jackie would quickly begin to set some of fashion's newest trends. For her husband's inauguration in 1961, she wore a pillbox hat designed by Halston. The style quickly caught fire and was worn by women all over the United States. Before long, whatever she wore was copied. Attending Sunday mass, she often covered her bouffant hairstyle with a mantilla. Both the bouffant hairstyle and black lace mantillas became the rage, as did A-line skirts and low-slung pumps. When she appeared at a ball wearing an Empire-waist gown, that too quickly became a mainstay in evening wardrobes.

John Kennedy was also watched by the public, and immediately received negative publicity from the men's hat industry when he went bareheaded to his inauguration. The hatless Kennedy was held responsible for the decline of hats worn by men. He soon, after much persuasion, carried a hat to show that

The Kennedys were the most emulated political family.

he still used one. He was also criticized by overcoat manufacturers, because he was regularly seen without one. He often appeared only in a suit, no matter how inclement the weather. Men followed his lead and shed their coats.

In a more positive vein, John had some responsibility for moving the Izod knit shirt, emblazoned with the famous alligator, from relatively limited use to new fashion heights. He and the rest of the male Kennedy clan wore the shirt

as a favorite under sport coats for many social events—not just for activewear. It soon became standard dress for many men.

After Kennedy's assassination, Jackie remained a favorite of fashion enthusiasts. In 2001, record crowds flocked to the Metropolitan Museum in New York to view an exhibition of her wardrobe during her years in the White House. Seven years after her death, she is still an influential fashion leader.

America's First Families

Ever since television started to play a prominent role in American politics, we have been able to inspect our leaders more closely. Not only are we able to judge their political strengths and weaknesses, but we may immediately evaluate their appearances.

The influence of television became clear with the election of John Kennedy as president in 1960. For the first time Americans had a closeup view of a first family that was unlike those that had come before them. The Kennedys were young, vital, and charismatic, very different in stature and dress from the Eisenhowers, Trumans, and Roosevelts who preceded them. A World of Fashion Profile focuses on the Kennedys and how they influenced fashion. In 2001, auctions that featured the Kennedy memorabilia were still bringing in great sums.

Nancy Reagan was another First Lady whose interest in and attention to fashion was carefully reported by the press. She was especially fond of James Galanos's evening gowns and Adolfo's Chanel-type suits. She favored the color red, and American women soon chose red as their favorite color too.

Barbara Bush, although an unlikely candidate for fashion distinction, made her own mark on the industry. She was not what fashion enthusiasts would consider the perfect model type. Her matronly figure, was, however, one to which older, more mature women could relate. When she wore the now famous royal blue gown to her husband's inauguration, and later used the color in many other outfits, it was quickly adopted by those women who normally were not considered to be fashion plates. Her preference for oversized, faux pearls quickly caught the attention of manufacturers of costume jewelry. The accessory became one of the most purchased of the decade.

The Clintons were also carefully studied for their personal preferences. Whenever Hillary changed hairstyles—and it was often—they were quickly criticized. Bill, regularly seen jogging in nylon shorts, unintentionally became a fashion influence on active sportswear.

Even the Bushes, not really considered fashion trendsetters, made some marks in fashion. The president reignited the western look, and Laura simple elegance.

Once designers finish their creations and send them down the runways, their success or failure depends on their acceptance or rejection by the consumer markets for which they were designed.

In the world of fashion, acceptance at the highest level comes at the hands of those who influence fashion—those whose choices are imitated by admirers. Those admirers are

Nancy Reagan's fondness for red influenced many American women to wear the color.

As first lady and senator, Hillary Rodham Clinton popularized the pantsuit as business attire. She is shown here as a guest on *The Tonight Show* during her senatorial campaign.

Laura Bush preferred simple elegance.

then known as **fashion followers**. As we have seen, many of the fashion influencers and leaders are from royalty, the political arena, the sports world, and the entertainment world. When an individual has a large following, his or her clothes are often emulated by the fans. Most people lack the time, the confidence, and the money to create their own fashion direction. Thus, they rely on those they admire for direction.

COPYING AND ADAPTING STYLES FOR EVERY PRICE POINT

It should be understood that for the vast majority of consumers to embrace a style, it must be copied or adapted at lower price points. At one time, a style originated at the couture level and eventually made its way down to ready-to-wear. What remained constant was the style; the fabrics, construction, and details changed to fit the different price structure. Today some fashions originate in the street, and then make their way into manufacturers' lines.

A style that originates at the couture level and becomes an accepted fashion generally follows this route:

1. The design originates at the highest price point and is first introduced on the runway.

2. At fashion shows, editors of consumer magazines and trade publications critique the collections and report their opinions. The audiences also include wealthy private clients, invited celebrities, and retail fashion directors.

3. Some retailers purchase the actual couture styles or copies from manufacturers.

4. At this higher price level, the fashion innovators are the purchasers. They wear their selections to places where they will be seen by the press, which will often show pictures of them in their publications or will write about them in their columns.

5. Those styles that seem destined for popularity will be copied or adapted by manufacturers at every price point.

6. The copies are then sold in department and specialty stores to those who follow fashion but are unable to buy at the higher price points.

7. At the end of the cycle, the styles lose their appeal and are often found in off-price and discount stores.

8. As the particular style bottoms out, the couturier is ready to dazzle the fashion trendsetters with a new collection.

CHAPTER HIGHLIGHTS

- People in fashion speak a particular language. To be a professional in the field, you need a working knowledge of that jargon.

- The fashion industry is cyclical in nature. A design moves through the various phases of the fashion cycle, from its creation through its eventual decline.

- Although the designer is credited with creating the latest styles, much of today's fashion originates in the streets.

- No matter where the styles are born, success comes only after they are worn by fashion leaders and trendsetters. The individuals who influence fashion are generally affluent and come from such visible segments of society as the entertainment world, royalty, sports, and politics.

- Once a particular fashion has been created and popularized it filters down to fashion followers.

IMPORTANT FASHION TERMINOLOGY AND CONCEPTS

adaptation	fashion cycle	sample sales
bottom-up fashion	fashion follower	Seventh Avenue
classic	fashion leader	silhouette
collection	haute couture	staples
couturier (-iere)	knockoff	style
designer's samples	language of the trade	taste
fad	line	top-down fashion
fashion	ready-to-wear	trendsetter

FOR REVIEW

1. Define the term *sample sale*.
2. Differentiate between the terms *fashion* and *fad*.
3. Describe the stages of the fashion cycle.
4. From what walks of life do most fashion trendsetters and influencers come? Give some examples.
5. How did the Kennedy family influence fashion?
6. Give examples of styles that were popularized by entertainment celebrities.
7. Where can consumers purchase the styles that have reached the bottom of the fashion cycle?
8. As styles are bottoming out, what is happening to make the cycle begin again?
9. In the Point of View article by David Wolfe (page 134), what importance is given to street style?

EXERCISES AND PROJECTS

1. Find pictures from consumer fashion magazines, newspapers, and trade periodicals that visually describe each term defined in the section "The Language of the Trade." Create an illustrated table. Under each picture list the term.

2. Using a history of fashion text or magazine articles as sources, select a memorable apparel or accessory design that was first successful, fell from popularity, and was then resurrected. Indicate the style, its years in original favor, when it was reintroduced, and the length of time it lasted for each period. Obtain photographs of the original style and describe how it was marketed in later years.

3. Prepare a list of motion picture films and television programs in which the garments worn by characters were considered fashion innovations (include classic and current films). Refer to texts on the history of costume for information. For each film indicated, find a photograph to depict the styles popularized.

4. Compile an illustrated table that features five music stars and the fashions they were responsible for bringing to their fans. Each style should be shown being worn by the entertainer.

WEB SITES

By accessing these Web sites, you will be able to gain broader knowledge and up-to-date information on materials related to this chapter.

Women's Wear Daily

www.wwd.com

MTV

www.mtv.com

The Case of the Calculated Risk

question

Should Tracey go against the traditional fashion cycle used as a barometer for her company and try to "stretch" the cycle for another season with the company's hot item? Defend your answer using the ideas about fashion cycles and the route taken by successful styles presented in this chapter.

Every year since her company began, fashion designer Tracey Gordon has been a success. Creating apparel collections for women at the better price points catapulted her into the forefront of the fashion industry. Season after season, her collections featured styles that pleased her followers. Her designs were often worn by people from the entertainment industry. They include actresses of stage and screen and several of the more successful hosts on talk shows and television news magazines. With well-known women wearing her garments, her styles are regularly seen on the pages of fashion publications, which cover the events attended by her famous clientele.

As with every designer, Tracey is always at work creating next season's line. For her to continue her successful path, new styles are always in the works. Not only will the newer items generate business, but they will be there, ready for sale, when the older styles start to decline in popularity. Being aware of the cycles through which fashion moves and understanding that even the most successful items will eventually fall from favor, she stops the old style's production as soon as it shows signs of lower sales. Rarely does she carry the same design from one season to the next. This is an effort to lower the losses that occur when styles stop selling. She is fully aware of the fact that her best designs will be copied at lower price points, making the originals less likely to sell.

This past season, Tracey created the best-selling item ever produced in her workrooms. It caught fire as soon as it was shown to the public and continues to sell well. With the new season approaching, it is time to abandon the old and concentrate on the new. The aforementioned style, however, is still at the maturity stage and does not appear to be slowing down. Even with copies at lower prices, her original item is still hot in the upscale stores.

She and her management team have been holding discussions for the past three weeks to decide whether or not, for the first time in the company's history, to carry the item over to the next season.

Fashion's Fast Cycle

ANNE D'INNOCENZIO

New York—Hold on tight: the trend machine is setting new speed records.

Powered by technological innovations, particularly the Internet, the globalization of fashion and the savviness of chains like Target Stores and Express to produce immediate designer knockoffs, the trend cycle is moving at an accelerating pace, according to retailers. The life span of a fashion trend is now about five months on average, instead of the year it was just two years ago.

Navigating this frenetic pace of fashion trends has become quite a challenge, and stores are taking a step back to the touchy-feely instinct of retail buyers for the right formula.

The biggest task for retailers is figuring out which trends become fashion basics (like capris and denim jackets), which are flashes in the pan (like pony prints, which hit the stores last fall but quickly fizzled), and which looks will evolve—as in the case of Hippie Chic, which for fall is taking a more exotic form, embracing fur trims.

Retail consultants point to the once-hot Abercrombie & Fitch, whose so-called preppy basics have lost some sizzle, as an example of falling off the pace. A&F is now developing a new store division called Hollister, a West Coast–oriented lifestyle brand.

"Retailers are walking on a tightrope. On one hand, consumers are ready to buy fashion again. On the other hand, they are getting bored so quickly," said Wendy Liebmann, president of the consulting firm WSL Retailing. "Figuring out which trends to merchandise is becoming a huge challenge. You have to be very careful about your inventory. You have to be very flexible in adjusting your buying patterns and cautious about inventory management."

One store that seems to be able to operate at high speed is the hyperactive Hennes & Mauritz, which opened three New York–area stores this past spring. The stores continue to be packed with customers, all jostling for the latest hot item, from red leather pants to ruffled blouses. The stores get replenished with new merchandise daily.

"We are in the forefront of finding trends that are commercial," said Par Darj, president of U.S. operations at H&M.

Hippie Chic, from peasant tops to fringe skirts, has done well, but the retailer is developing it further for fall.

"The trends are happening a lot quicker now. We are communicating a lot faster, with the Internet," said Darj. "There's also MTV and VH1."

"The trends are definitely moving faster," said Julie Gilhart, vice president of fashion merchandising at Barneys New York. "The economy is good. People are swallowing up merchandise really quickly. They want the next big thing. They dive into it. They experience it for a second, and then they want something else."

What complicates matters, she said, is that once a trend hits the runway, consumers are craving to get a taste of it even before it reaches stores the following season—and by that time, the trend is often saturated at all price points.

The frenetic fashion cycle forced Los Angeles consultant Dee Dee Gordon to take her trend consulting to the Internet, after finding that the *L Report*, her quarterly trend digest, was too slow in reaching people.

In August, she and her partner, Sharon Lee, will be launching Look-Look.com, an online youth culture network that offers clients the latest trends on the Internet, from music and film to fashion. Clients can download the latest tunes in London, or see what's hot in denim looks in São Paulo.

"Two years ago, it took somewhere between six months to a year and a half for a trend to move," Gordon said. "Now, because of the Internet, trends can move through different cultures within 15 seconds."

The duo depends on a network of 500 correspondents all over the world to feed them information about emerging styles.

What's a retailer to do? Many buyers agree that there's no set rule to get a handle on which trends to merchandise—or for how long. Many claim that they are just using pure instinct.

"There is no formula," said Barneys' Gilhart. "You just have to feel it. If you *follow* a trend, it will catch you big time when it stops. When you *feel* a trend, then you can maneuver it."

Gilhart pointed out that when her customer sees a key look on the runway, she wants "to satisfy that idea immediately, even though it is next season's trend." The store's strategy is to offer "a hint" of the trend immediately without oversaturating the look.

For example, when python hit the spring runways, Barneys made sure it had python bags and belts immediately in its stores. For spring, it offered selected items in python, such as Yves Saint Laurent's python trench, and developed a linen and python private-label handbag collection.

"What we are trying to do is be aware of trends, but we are not trying to shove it down the consumer's throat," Gilhart said.

She believes that some trends have more staying power and is bullish on the longevity of Burberry plaid, which she believes appeals to both classic and edgier consumers.

"It's not about one particular silhouette," she said, adding that consumers can get their Burberry fix with an umbrella or handbag, not just with pants or a trench.

"Trends are moving faster, in geometric proportions," said Paul Raffin, executive vice president of merchandising at Express, a division of The Limited Inc. "There is no question that you can't have a long view of your line. We are constantly using our fashion radar. Product development used to be static. Now it is agile and fluid."

That's why, over the past two years, Express has beefed up its product development team. Previously, the team was strictly focused on merchandising, and its staff members were "generalists." Express now depends on a team of specialists who monitor specific categories, from denim pants to shorts.

"Our customer is compelled by newness," Raffin said. "We are changing our windows more often and converting our floors with new merchandise."

This past spring, Express took a major stance on brightly colored feminine looks, including pink floral skirts and blouses. The strategy has been successful.

Express has made a few mistakes, like when it invested too heavily last fall in utility looks. Raffin admitted that Express took a loss on that one.

The fashion pace is one of the reasons why contemporary resource Bisou-Bisou is aiming to expand the number of its freestanding stores, according to Marc Bohbot, president. The stores are being used as laboratories to test trends.

"Our own stores give us an idea of what sells, and then we communicate the information to our department stores," he said.

Bisou-Bisou operates 15 freestanding stores. By 2001, the company expects to have a total of 50. Bohbot also pointed out that he has had to change his collection every month to keep pace with trends.

"Two years ago, I would change my collection every three months," he said.

Wendy Red, women's buyer at Up Against the Wall, a junior chain based in Washington, D.C., said that in the junior market, the life span of a trend is about three months. Two or three years ago, it was six months, she said.

"The market becomes flooded with a trend really quickly, and then it kills the trend," she said, noting such examples as python and shiny jeans this past spring season.

Red pointed out that about 50 percent of Up Against the Wall's merchandise is in basics; 25 percent is in fashion; the remainder is in fast fashion. For the trendier items, she depends on smaller vendors, who can produce a hot item quickly.

At least one retail executive—Joseph Mimran, president, chairman, and chief executive officer of Canadian chain Club Monaco—doesn't see a change in the trend cycle.

"Trends have always moved fast," said Mimran. "I think what you see is that some trends come and go, and others are long lasting. The challenge for retailers is which ones do you abandon and go to the next trend? It's hard to say which trends fall in the valley of no return."

Women's Wear Daily, June 15, 2000

Street Style

DAVID WOLFE

Street style is an important fashion force today and likely to remain so. Yet for centuries the term would have been considered oxymoronic and the concept unthinkable. In reality, there was a style in the streets, in that the general population always adhered to some sort of a social dress code. Tinkers, tailors, and candlestick makers all wore clothing of a set mode depending upon the century and the geographical location in which they happened to find themselves. Primitive tribes the world over all conformed to their own style codes. Fashion, such as it was, was formulated by necessity, availability of materials, level of craftsmanship accessible, and of course, affluence. The style of those fashions was not ever created by the masses who wore them. They were most often interpretations of those in a higher social strata; royalty, religious leaders, tribal chiefs, or other such process whereby those less fortunate emulated their betters.

Setting the Scene for the Emergence of Street Style

That theory, a fashion filtration system from high to low, remained a secure system until the last half of the 20th century. Until then, those with money and leisure, the guardians and patrons of culture, were responsible for creating changes in style. When Marie Antoinette, on a whim, stuck feathers in her already towering coiffure, courtiers followed suit and set a style that remained until the English Court was disbanded at the advent of World War II. That same fashionable monarch also provided fashion history with one of the first examples of street style when she fantasized about being a milkmaid and had luxurious versions of peasant garb made. That small glitch aside, the trickle-down system remained intact until the 1950s. Even then, most of the Western world's style was still a watered-down version of the deluxe custom-made haute couture that was shown to great fanfare twice a year in Paris, a city that had long held a monopoly on fashion. However, the seeds of a fashion revolution were being planted, and they thrived in the fertile soil of social discontent that came on the heels of two world wars in quick succession.

Modern Street Style, Born of the Beatniks and Living in Blue Jeans

"Beatniks," as they came to be called, were the first of the rebellious style setters that came from a strata of society other than the privileged echelons. They were writers, poets, and artists known as "the Beat Generation" whose work expressed the disillusionment and sense of disenfranchisement that intellectuals were feeling in the midst of the economic boom that followed the end of World War II. In blue denim jeans and black turtleneck sweaters, the Beatniks lived a lifestyle outside the rigid rules of their time, and they spawned groups with similar attitudes who soon developed similar styles. "Hell's Angels" are direct style descendants of Beatniks. Such style rebels have existed before in fashion history, but usually without affecting the mainstream and certainly seldom changing the entire system. (The Aesthetic movement of the 19th century sought to bring about clothing reform, but without much success.) One item of apparel moved up from the bottom of the fashion food chain to a position of eminence unparalleled in history. The blue denim jean pants originally made for California miners had become a "uniform" for the agricultural and lower class. When stars like James Dean and Marlon Brando flaunted their humble roots by wearing jeans, a major movement was set in place. Blue denim jeans moved up and up until they became high-profile status items in the 1970s, when designers cashed in on their low-brow (and therefore sexual) image. Calvin Klein, Guess?, Jordache, and surprisingly, socialite Gloria Vanderbilt all became famous as names on the labels of blue jeans.

Yves Saint Laurent Sees Style in the Streets

In 1960, one influential designer elevated the street look of the Beat Generation to the very heights of high fashion and in doing so, he reversed the order of the fashion system. Yves Saint Laurent had succeeded Christian Dior following his untimely death and the young genius was viewed as a powerful force. When he created a "street"-inspired collection, the traditional chasm between street and style was bridged. He said, "Motorcycle jackets in alligator, mink coats with sweater sleeves, turtleneck collars under finely cut flannel suits . . . those street inspirations all seemed very inelegant to a lot of people sitting on the gilt chairs of a couture salon. But this was the first collection in which I tried hard for poetic expression in my clothes. Social structures were breaking up. The street had a new pride, its own chic, and I found the street inspiring as I would often again." That statement, a veritable manifesto, has been echoed over and over again by designers ever since.

Demographics and Electronics Explain the Rise of Street Style

Demographics must be studied in order to understand why underground style surfaced and became a major force in fashion. Military men returning from the long duration of World War II simultaneously fathered a generation of babies whose vast numbers added up to a population well known as "the Baby Boom." That generation is responsible for many economic, social, and cultural changes simply because there were so many of them. But their influence cannot be accounted for by mathematics alone. As young people often had done in the past, they questioned the values of their parents and created a new society of self-indulgence that looked attractive to the older generation who felt that wartime deprivations had cheated them of their own youthful good times. So the young generation, which became known quite aptly as "the Youthquake," assumed leadership of mass culture, redefining art, music, and of course, fashion.

Another revolution was occurring that made it possible for street style to emerge. Television spread popular culture to the most remote corners of the world and suddenly everyone, everywhere was exposed to the same fashion forces. The fact that advertisers were often hawking products to the emerging youth market meant that visualization had to be broad enough to penetrate a vast audience. There was no room for elitism. There were more middle- and lower-class kids watching TV than aristocrats, so the fashion images sent forth were targeted far, far below high-fashion taste levels. *American Bandstand* was a phenomenally successful fashion vehicle, although its chief purpose was the promotion of the rock 'n' roll music emerging from the African-American subculture during the 1950s. Young men and women all over America wanted to dress exactly like the Philadelphia kids they saw dancing every afternoon on TV. It is not surprising that singers and musicians soon came to be seen as fashion role models. They were usually not from the upper strata of society and their style came from nontraditional sources. And it was embraced and emulated around the world.

Antiestablishment Rebellion Hits the Streets

The next important chapter in American street style was written by the hippies who were the cultural descendants of the beatniks. The rigid social structure that was in place in the 1950s crumbled under the pressure of a youthful population disenchanted by the older generation's death grip on financial stability and security that the hippies came to view as stifling. They believed in "free love," in mind-altering drugs and total self-expression in terms of a style based upon secondhand and antique clothing, thereby making a big anticonsumerism statement. The American postwar economy was fueled by the consumption of goods with a very short life span, whether automobiles, hit rec-

ords, or fashion. The hippies refuted that economic system and in doing so, they led street style into a fondness for nostalgia that lasted for decades and decades. Until that time, no one except those in dire straits would wear something old and no one would have dreamed of making something new to look as if it were old. But thrift-shop style became chic, and wave upon wave of nostalgia washed over fashion. In the '60s, Victoriana was in style again. In the '70s, there came revivals of the '30s and '40s and '50s. By the middle of the '90s, it was the '60s being revived. Along the way, which seemed to be going backward much of the time, there were some new developments too. In an effort to make blue denim look old and worn-out, French designers Marithe & Francois Girbaud pioneered "stone-washing," a process that broke down fabric fibers and led to years of fashions that were "distressed" and "laundered," all in an effort to make them look used.

Britain Assumes Leadership with a Little Help from the Beatles and the Punks

Music led street style across the Atlantic to England, to London and Liverpool, when the British pop music scene exploded early in the 1960s. The Beatles and other groups worked as hard on their fashion images as on their music. Having suffered far greater deprivations during the war years, it took Britain longer than the United States to recover economically, and when that recovery occurred, pop culture boomed in an atmosphere of affluence and freedom. Designers such as Mary Quant (credited as the inventor of the miniskirt) and Barbara Hulanicki of Biba produced colorful, youthful, and sometimes shocking designs that found immediate favor with the girl on the street. At the same time, young men paraded up and down Carnaby Street

in the most outrageous outfits seen since the time of the dandy more than a century earlier.

How is it that a society usually seen as stodgy could become a breeding ground for outrageous fashions? Perhaps it is simply politeness that keeps Brits from laughing at the eccentrics who have always been accepted and cherished in the United Kingdom, everyone from Dame Edith Sitwell to Quentin Crisp and Zandra Rhodes. Only in such a tolerant environment could the punk style of the early 1980s have been allowed to flower. It was the most rebellious, most intentionally obnoxious fashion statement that had ever been (intentionally) made. Young Britains, feeling deprived of opportunity in the workforce while being supported by a socialist government, became furious and bored at the same time. They drew attention to their emotional angst with an incredibly offensive self-presentation. Heads were partially shaved and the remaining patches of hair were dyed bright colors and made to stick straight up. Safety pins were used to embellish both raggedy clothes and the flesh. T-shirts were partly burned away and pants often featured "bondage" straps to bind the legs together. Vivienne Westwood and Malcolm Maclaren visualized the style that was sold from a shop at World's End, the area at the end of London's Kings Road in Chelsea. A musical expression plaintively shrieked by Sid Vicious went hand-in-hand with the fashions, of course. Amazingly enough, the punk street style showed staying power and held sway over some young people for several decades.

MTV Broadcasts Street Style to the World

The cross-pollination of music and style became stronger still with the advent of "music videos" in the 1980s. To promote their recordings, artists began to make very complex and visually sophisticated visualizations of their music. A new television network, MTV, began in a small way but soon became a world-wide cultural institution. And the clothes the musicians wore while performing in the music videos, which were repetitiously broadcast, were seen by millions around the world, in time almost usurping the influence of fashion magazines in communicating style information. Again, the presentations were aimed at a low taste level because of widespread music distribution and sales. Madonna, Boy George, Cyndi Lauper, and Michael Jackson styled themselves in distinctive and exciting images that were imitated everywhere. As music goes, so goes street style. When rap and hip-hop swept the music charts, suddenly a new street style emerged,

that of the black inner-city young man in hugely oversize jeans (there is no escaping the union of denim and street style).

Is Street Style at the End of the Road?

Street style has become a victim of its own success. Now it is so influential that it is almost instantly swept up-market to more sophisticated and expensive areas. When Karl Lagerfeld picked up the hip-hop influence for a Chanel collection, it became a sign of the times that street style had become a mainstream fashion influence. No longer does it belong solely to the young man or woman on the street. It has become difficult to define, to fence into an identifiable arena. It is, and always has been, the most accurate reflection of society at large, and as the 20th century draws to an end, street style has

become fragmented, almost tribal. Instant electronic communication has made every style rebellion into a mainstream, marketable commodity immediately, thus defusing its appeal to the young person in the street who is forced to discard it quickly and move on. Therefore, it is possible that the end of street style as a universal fashion influence is drawing to a close. Whereas once it represented an attractive, youthful, sexually charged rebellious mode of self-expression, now it can be seen as an insular and segmented reflection of a small and often unattractive sector of modern society. Then again, perhaps that very perception will allow street style to remain on the street, the sole property of the young rebels who use self-presentation as self-expression, the ultimate aim of fashion, whether haute or low.

David Wolfe, Creative Director, DE Doneger Design Direction, the Color and Trend Forecasting Division of The Doneger Group

Hilfiger Signs French Soccer Star

SAMANTHA CONTI

London—Tommy Hilfiger swept into London last week to cut the ribbon on his new Regent Street store, and announce he was joining forces with French soccer star Thierry Henry.

Hilfiger said during a packed news conference at The Royal Academy here that he'd signed Henry—one of the soccer world's most successful strikers—who plays for the Arsenal Football Club. Henry, who's famous among soccer fans almost everywhere except the U.S., will be an international brand ambassador, and be featured in men's formal and underwear ad campaigns for spring and fall 2007.

"It's always been tough for us to find the right guy, someone who personifies the nature of what we stand for," said

Hilfiger. "He's got great personal style, he's a winner, he looks really cool in anything we put him in, and does casual really well. We've been dressing him for a while, and he looks great in tailored clothing in particular.

"And, of course, the PR people love the fact that we both have the same initials, TH."

Hilfiger also plans to design a capsule collection of men's apparel, inspired by Henry's lifestyle. "I'd like to take his look and re-create it for the public," Hilfiger said. The collection will hit the shop floor for fall 2007, and all profits will go to Henry's new charity, The One For All Foundation, aimed at combating racism around the world.

Hilfiger said in a separate interview that the collection would be made up of six to eight items, including shirts, trousers, jackets, ties, jeans and sweaters. The collection, Hilfiger said, will be called TH2 or THTH.

During the news conference, Henry said Hilfiger has been a sartorial inspiration to him.

"In the past, I usually dressed casually, but since I've been in touch with Tommy, I've become more classic—but in a stylish way. Tommy gave me the desire to change my wardrobe, and I put his pieces together in my own way. I think it's important to have your own style," he said.

Earlier that day Hilfiger cut the ribbon on his new Regent Street store, which had a soft opening at the end of November. It's the brand's second flagship, after Sloane Street, and spans 5,500 square feet with a further 9,000 square feet of showroom and offices on the floor above. The store, at 138 Regent Street, is in a newly developed block, next door to Timberland and Brooks Brothers. The style is in tune with the other 600 Hilfiger stores worldwide, and is a blend of English Regency and neoclassical style.

The collection is displayed on two floors, with a more formal look for men's and women's wear on the top floor and a casual look for its dedicated Hilfiger Denim section on the ground floor.

Hilfiger would not give first-year sales projections, but said his English customers were already going for the more fashion-forward items.

He said he was expecting "more international" traffic on Regent Street than Sloane Street, and said he was applying a similar strategy to the U.K.—which represents a small part of the business—as in the U.S.

"We've been in the U.K. for a number of years and view it as most similar to the U.S., which means we've been pulling distribution back—oversupplying is harmful—and going about business in a different way. We only want to offer the brand in premium stores, and through our own stores in premium locations. And I think we've done that with Regent Street—we moved in at the right time."

Newsfront, *DNR*, December 11, 2006

Stars on the Wane: Celebrity Fashion Lines Losing Their Mojo

JULEE GREENBERG

A shakeout is looming in the celebrity designer world.

A few years ago, the fashion industry saw an explosion of music and Hollywood stars who suddenly decided to become designers.

Jennifer Lopez, Beyoncé Knowles and Gwen Stefani were among the first few, but in no time, everyone from A- to Z-listers were turning themselves into clothing and beauty brands. Today, Mary-Kate and Ashley Olsen have everything from sportswear to area rugs; Mandy Moore has T-shirts; Hilary Duff has sportswear and accessories; Jaime Pressly recently introduced a contemporary sportswear collection, and Pamela Anderson, naturally, is pushing her lingerie label. Even Nikki Sixx from metal band Mötley Crüe and Travis Barker from Blink 182 have clothing lines.

Now the winners and losers are starting to emerge. The current leaders are clearly Stefani's L.A.M.B., Kimora Lee Simmons' Baby Phat and Rocawear, according to retailers, while high-profile brands such as JLO by Jennifer Lopez, Nicky Hilton and Jessica Simpson are struggling.

Meanwhile, the jury remains out on such labels as House of Deréon by Knowles, Justin Timberlake's William Rast, Duff and Sean John, which flirted with the women's contemporary market, pulled out and now plans to reenter ready-to-wear with a junior line.

One thing is clear, however: the market isn't what it once was. Rob Smith, executive vice president and general merchandise manager for Macy's East, said overall, celebrity fashion lines have slowed down at retail.

"JLO has softened a lot," he said. "I'm not sure it's because of the product or the fact that Jennifer just isn't out there as much as she used to be, but the line isn't performing like it used to. I think the idea of the celebrity is still huge, it's just that when it comes to fashion, no one has done it well."

Smith said he has yet to see Deréon, Knowles' junior line that just launched in about 500 specialty doors for holiday, but he did try Chick by Nicky Hilton, which didn't perform well.

"It just didn't work, we no longer carry it," he said.

Smith said that, on the flip side, Baby Phat by Kimora Lee Simmons is doing exceptionally well for Macy's and, as a result, the brand's floor space has greatly expanded. In the chain's New York flagship, Baby Phat has taken over prime real estate in the former XOXO space, which has moved to another spot in the rear of the junior department.

"Baby Phat has bridged from an urban brand to a fashion brand that offers really good product and great fashion pieces that appeal to many customers," he said. "It's a terrific brand for us."

Part of the problem is that celebrity lines continue to proliferate at a time when consumers appear bored with the entire concept. They rabidly follow celebrities' personal lives more than ever; they just don't want to wear a Hollywood star's name on their backs.

"The mind-set used to be that a musician was a musician, but when they decided to launch a clothing line, that was big news," explained Michael Wood, vice president and director of syndicated research at Teenage Research Unlimited, a Northbrook, Ill.-based research firm. "Now the novelty has worn off, and it's just not news anymore."

That said, Wood believes the idea of the celebrity is still alive and well, but perhaps not their fashion brands. He said that, while consumers are still interested in reading about stars' personal lives and what they are wearing, that doesn't mean they want to buy a label with a celebrity's name on it. Part of the predicament is that celebrities have no problem putting their names on clothing or accessories; they just don't want to wear it themselves.

"Young people want to wear what the celebrities wear, not the label they have their names on," he said. "Today, there are so many ways for fans to connect with their favorite celebrities, they can log on to their MySpace pages online, for example, they no longer have to buy their fashion brands to be close to them."

Wendy Red, fashion director at Up Against the Wall, a 25-store junior and young contemporary specialty chain based in Washington, said she carries a few celebrity lines, including House of Deréon and Deréon, William Rast (but only for men) and Stars & Straps, a line backed by Blink 182's Barker.

"When House of Deréon launched, I did very well with it," Red said. "The jeans sold out so fast, I couldn't get them in the store fast enough. Since then, they've raised their prices from a $98 jean to a $148 jean, so I think that's part of the reason why the line has cooled off a bit. But now with Deréon, which

I just got in the stores—that is really blowing out."

Red said there is one hoodie in particular from the Deréon line that is selling really well.

"Beyoncé wore it in her video," she said. "I put it on the floor on Friday [Dec. 1] and today [Dec. 4], I only have two left."

Red said she also does well with Stars & Straps and Harajuku Lovers, Stefani's lower-priced line.

"These lines do very well; they are really popular with our customers," she said. "I think that if the celebrity is cool and their line is edgy, there is no reason why it wouldn't do well. With Jessica Simpson's line, for example, it's just not the kind of thing you would put in a cool specialty store."

On the contemporary side, Abbey Samet, contemporary market analyst for the Doneger Group, a New York–based buying office, said some brands perform well, while others are not living up to the hype.

"I've heard that Beyoncé's line [House of Deréon] is not doing well at all, but L.A.M.B. by Gwen Stefani is doing very well," she said. "The thing about it is that nearly all celebrities have stylists that make them look the way they do. It's very hard to translate that look into a product line, which is really what the customer is buying into."

Although fashion lines have seen their ups and downs for celebrities, the beauty business, particularly in fragrances, has not seen the same effect. Rapper/actress Eve Jeffers is the latest example. As she works on her fourth album, Jeffers said she is also on the lookout for a fragrance deal, while her Fetish clothing line, launched a few years ago, went out of business.

The beauty world today is full of celebrities. Coty is arguably the most entrenched, with Gwen Stefani, Jennifer

Lopez, Sarah Jessica Parker, Kimora Lee Simmons, David and Victoria Beckham, Mary-Kate and Ashley Olsen, Shania Twain and "Desperate Housewives" in its stable—with, as reported, perhaps Kate Moss due to sign any day.

Elizabeth Arden's deal with Britney Spears, signed in March 2004, has yielded two top-five hits: Curious Britney Spears and Fantasy Britney Spears. Arden has had teen queen Duff under contract for beauty products since September, and it signed Catherine Zeta-Jones in February 2002 to be the face of its core Elizabeth Arden brand. In addition, NASCAR star Jeff Gordon has been the face of its Halston Z-14 brand since May 2004, and the original celebrity fragrance maven, Elizabeth Taylor, is also part of the company's constellation.

Knowles, too, has dabbled in the fragrance world, as the face of Tommy Hilfiger's True Star fragrance. While her House of Deréon label is still new on the market, some may say that one issue they have with it is fit.

In September, Knowles attended an in-store event at Macy's in Chicago to celebrate the launch of the line and the large shop-in-shop for the collection at the store. When a CBS reporter asked the entertainer if there was indeed a problem with the line's fit, she and her mother and agent, Tina Knowles, cut the interview short, walking away from the reporter.

Chip Rosen, president and general manager at Beyond Productions LLC, the parent company for the Knowles' brands, said it was a misunderstanding and that the fit of the collection is working well.

Samet said she thinks that the denim-based line William Rast, which just launched last year, looks good and has potential to grow.

"I really like the way William Rast looks and I think there certainly is room for it," Samet said. "The denim market can use some freshness, so they have a real opportunity."

Samet said her overall feeling is that the focus of the celebrity-as-designer has shifted to the designer-as-celebrity, which is sparking more interest at retail.

"The newest emerging celebrity is the designer, there was Viktor & Rolf for H&M, Behnaz Sarafpour for Target—these things are what customers like to hear about," she said. "The customer has wised up a lot and, in turn, it's become more challenging for a celebrity to be a designer."

Madonna has a deal with H&M this holiday season called M by Madonna, which she's just renewed for a second season. That line will be in stores in March.

Stefani seems to be the true exception, as retailers and analysts agree her L.A.M.B. brand has continued its strength.

"Gwen has always had that style about her that gives her line that credibility," Wood said. "She wears her own clothes and she really creates what her customers are looking for in a clothing line."

Retailers selling the L.A.M.B. line seem to agree. Nordstrom has recently opened L.A.M.B. shops within its stores.

"L.A.M.B. is one of our strongest vendors in our Savvy department, largely because of our partnership with Ken Erman, the president of SkaGirl [L.A.M.B.'s apparel license]," Ana Swaab, corporate merchandise manager for women's contemporary at Nordstrom, told WWD in September. "L.A.M.B. has selective distribution, and we are proud to be the largest fashion retailer carrying the collection.

"The allure and styling of the fall 2006 line is making it one of the most popular and loved collections with our customers. Customers love the design of the collection, including the vibrant graphic prints, as well as classic and feminine shapes done with a Fifties vintage feel—all reflecting Gwen's own personal style."

While many celebrities are their own marketing machines, being able to wear their own labels and having their photos taken wherever they turn, this business also has given some a fair share of drama. Now, Knowles is facing allegations that she violated a contract related to the founding of her House of Deréon label.

Greg Walker, a businessman based in New York, filed a lawsuit in the Supreme Court in New York this summer alleging that the pop star and actress neglected to pay him money he was owed for helping her find a licensing contract and is asking for $1.5 million in damages. The lawsuit was filed against Knowles and Wear Me Apparel, which does business as Kids Headquarters.

According to court documents, Walker alleged that he and Beyoncé and Tina Knowles entered into an agreement in August 2003 that Walker would help them find a licensing opportunity similar to the Sean John line established by Sean Combs. Walker's obligation under the contract was to obtain proposals and bring them to Beyoncé Knowles. According to court documents Walker facilitated a relationship between Knowles and Wear Me Apparel. Walker received $25,000 from Knowles in July 2004 and an additional $85,000 from Wear Me Apparel between January and June 2004 as part of that contract, according to the lawsuit.

The lawsuit asks for $500,000 in damages against Knowles and $1 million against Wear Me Apparel.

Executives for Knowles did not comment on the suit, which is still pending.

Knowles isn't the only music star to land in court over a licensed apparel brand this year. Simpson faced allegations that she failed to promote her Princy and JS by Jessica Simpson lines. Tarrant Apparel Group sued Simpson and master license holder Vincent Camuto for

$100 million in April. Camuto later filed a countersuit against Tarrant for $100 million. Those suits are also still pending.

But it seems that brands such as these continue on a growth track. Camuto, chief executive officer of the Camuto Group, the master license for the Jessica Simpson brands, said he is working to build a lasting brand. He said that, while Simpson's popularity helps, it's not just about that.

"We are hearing that the product is right on," he said. "Our retailers are very happy with it."

The company just launched a collection of outerwear for holiday selling, will have eyewear in the spring and, in 2007, will look for more licensing opportunities in categories like lingerie, swimwear and even stationery.

At JLO by Jennifer Lopez, executives are confident that one slow season isn't going to break their growth plans.

"Our JLO business has been a little soft this season," admitted Andrea Scoli, president of Sweetface Fashion Co., the parent company for the JLO by Jennifer Lopez-junior brand and Sweetface contemporary label. "But I think that, overall, the junior business has softened."

In 2001, Lopez entered the fashion business with partner Andy Hilfiger and established Sweetface Fashion Co., which now has annual sales of $200 million and includes JLO by Jennifer Lopez junior sportswear, outerwear, lingerie, footwear, watches and jewelry, as well as the Sweetface contemporary collection and four fragrances. Scoli said that, despite the fall in business, the company is poised for growth next year. For the JLO by Jennifer Lopez brand alone, the company will bring in $250 million in sales by the end of this year, she said, and expects 2007 to be even better. Scoli said a great deal of the growth is sure to come from the contemporary brand, Sweetface, which is sold at better specialty stores such as Madison in Los Angeles and Intermix in New York.

"In contemporary, it's cooler to be more select with the distribution," she said. "Jennifer is such a fashion icon. When she's in the press, it's really for her fashion, which is great for the Sweetface brand, since she does wear it."

Scoli said the company also is focused on international expansion, as she plans to pursue more licensing opportunities abroad in the next year.

For Sean John, which closed its Sean by Sean Combs women's contemporary brand earlier this year; Bob Wichser, ceo, said the women's business will be back on track next year. The company has signed a deal with G-III Apparel Group to design and merchandise a Sean John young contemporary line, for a fall launch.

"With Sean by Sean Combs, we just realized that the timing wasn't right and made the decision to exit the market," Wichser said. "But that doesn't mean it won't be back in the future."

The deal with G-III, he said, is different. Sean Combs for women will be set at a lower price point than the contemporary line was, and will be targeted to select specialty and department stores. To test the label, Wichser said select stores are selling a test line of outerwear now, which is selling well.

"We are very happy with the way the outwear is selling," he said. "We thought there was tremendous potential in this market for our brand. We really see it doing very well."

Wichser said that, by the end of this year, the Sean John brand will bring in $450 million in retail sales. Moving into next year; he expects that number to grow by around 15 percent.

Rocawear, the brand backed by Jay-Z, is also on a roll. After the company opened a temporary store in New York last September, the success of it has led it to think more seriously about retail. Now, Jameel Spencer, chief marketing officer at the $800 million company, said it is planning for a retail rollout in 2008.

"Our men's business has always been solid, but the women's is way up this year;" Spencer said. "Our department store business is up by 50 percent."

Spencer said that, for fall, the company will launch Bella Roc, a contemporary brand for women. "Jay has wanted a line like this for a while," he said. "Without him, it would not exist."

The Knowleses also are planning for their growing fashion empire, which includes the House of Deréon and Deréon brands. Deréon just launched at retail for holiday selling and, according to Beyond Productions' Rosen, it is performing very well so far.

"Beyoncé's fans have been asking for a line that's at a more approachable price point," Rosen said. "It's more of what they were asking for, so it's doing well."

At the time of the launch of the company earlier this year, executives projected making somewhere between $30 million and $50 million in first-year wholesale volume. By the end of next year; Rosen said he projects the brand to reach $100 million in wholesale volume. He said this growth will be because of the increase in product for both lines, with a House of Deréon swimwear line launching in February and new licensing opportunities coming up for the Deréon brand.

"It's growing fast, but not too fast," he said. "It's not about how fast or how big we can make this. It's about building a brand that will last."

Women's Wear Daily, December 18, 2006

fashion in the global marketplace

In the fashion business, everything is so temporary. Beautiful for three or four months, then you're tired of it.

TOM FORD, DESIGNER

After you have completed this chapter, you will be able to discuss:

- How governmental legislation affects the importation of merchandise.

- The relationship of governmental trade pacts to the fashion industry.

- Why the United States imposes quotas on imports.

- The most important international fashion centers and their significance to the industry.

- The selling arrangements in the industry that move goods from the producer to the retailer.

The fashion industry has changed considerably over the past 100 years. Initially, the fashion capitals of the world were Paris, where couturiers introduced designs to the world, and New York City, where the industry focused on ready-to-wear. It was not until after the end of World War II that other fashion centers began to emerge. By the 1950s Italian designers such as Emilio Pucci and Mila Schoen were distinguishing themselves in Florence, Rome, and Milan with imaginative creations that rivaled the greats of Paris. London was also waking up to fashion with the designs of Jean Muir, and later, in the 1960s, with Mary Quant. It was not long before the fashion world spread to Japan, Germany, Spain, Scandinavia, Canada, India, South Korea, Mexico, and China. Fashion and its creation are now global.

Where styles are physically designed is only one aspect of the fashion industry. The textile mills that supply the fabrics, the sewers who make the garments, and the trimmings houses that create the enhancements all contribute to bringing the finished product to the ultimate consumer. Each of these industry segments can be based in any part of the world. In fact, most American fashion companies, while based in the United States, do little other than design and distribute the merchandise. Once the individual styles have been created, most often they are outsourced and produced offshore and completed with materials and trimmings that have been purchased in yet another part of the world. It is the exception, rather than the rule, when a garment and all of its elements come from one region.

To understand the complexities of this global marketplace, it is necessary to learn about the role of the U.S. government in the fashion industry, the major international centers, the trade expositions, the trade organizations, and the ways in which the products are sold to merchants.

GOVERNMENT INVOLVEMENT IN FASHION IMPORTING

When American fashion manufacturers confine their production to the United States, no restrictions are placed on how much they may produce, the prices they may charge, or to whom they sell the goods. With the global nature of the fashion business today, however, domestic producers are likely to interface with other countries in the manufacture of their merchandise, most often through **offshore production**.

Once a company decides that it would be more favorable for its operation to use materials from foreign shores or to have the garments constructed offshore, the federal government becomes a major player in that organization's business.

The major reason for government intervention is to ensure that imported goods will not provide unfair competition for goods produced at home. Because foreign labor costs are often lower than labor costs in the United States, the final prices for offshore products will generally be significantly lower than for domestic products. The government tries to protect American business in several ways. These include establishing quotas on imported goods, imposing tariffs, enacting trade pacts with other nations, and using particularly high standards as a restraint measure.

Quotas

A quota is the set amount of merchandise that a country's government allows to be imported in a specific category. Quotas are generally established in numbers of units rather than in dollar amounts. To protect U.S. manufacturers from unfair competition, the federal government has established very specific quotas.

There are two classifications of quotas: absolute and tariff rate. With **absolute quotas**, any merchandise that exceeds the established limit must be disposed of through a variety of means determined by the U.S. Customs Service. If goods are

Offshore centers, such as Hong Kong, account for significant fashion production.

Table 6.1

ABSOLUTE QUOTAS

Each of the following types of cotton has its own quota:

- Cotton having a staple length under 1⅛ inches, except harsh or rough cotton having a staple length under ¾ inch, and other than linters.
- Cotton, other than linters, having a staple length of more than 1⅛ inches.
- Cotton card strips made from cotton having a staple length under 1³⁄₁₆ inches and comber waste, lap waste, sliver waste, and roving waste, whether or not advanced.
- Fibers of cotton woven but not spun.

subject to **tariff-rate quotas**, any merchandise exceeding the specified limits may enter at a higher rate of duty or remain in a bonded warehouse until the opening of a new quota.

Those in the fashion industry must have a complete understanding of the quota system and which merchandise is subject to such restrictions. Silk, for example, does not have a quota restriction, because the United States is not a silk-producing nation. Cotton, however, which is a fiber produced on U.S. shores, is subject to quotas. The specificity of the restriction is best understood by examining Table 6.1, which has been excerpted from the Custom Service's listing.

Duty

Most fashion merchandise imported into the United States is subject to **duty**. The duty rate levied on each item is a percentage of its appraised value. The rates vary according to the individual product and the country of origin. Some fashion items, such as those considered to be antiques, are imported duty-free.

The Harmonized Tariff System (HTS) provides duty rates for virtually every item that exists. The HTS is a reference manual that is the size of an unabridged dictionary and lists thousands of products. The U.S. Customs and Border Protection agency makes the final determination of what the correct rate of duty is that will be applied to a product. Importers receive guidance from them in determining the actual duty.

Trade Pacts

The U.S. government over the years has enacted legislation that affects the manner in which we trade with other nations. Two of the strongest of these **trade pacts** were approved in 1994. They are the **General Agreement on Tariffs and Trade (GATT)** and the **North American Free Trade Agreement (NAFTA)**. In 1995, GATT was replaced by the **World Trade Organization (WTO)** as the world's global trading body.

GATT

The General Agreement on Tariffs and Trade (usually referred to by its acronym, GATT) slashed worldwide tariffs on a variety of products by approximately 40 percent. It established new trading rules between the United States and 123 countries. The agreement was placed under the umbrella of the World Trade Organization, which has the power to enforce the trade accord and assess trade penalties against nations that violate it. Its primary goal is to reduce trade barriers.

In addition to reducing tariffs, the agreement also addresses quotas, by eliminating restrictions on the amount of textiles and apparel that may be imported. These quotas have been phased out in four stages. On January 1, 1995, 16 percent of the quota on all textile and apparel products imported into the United States, based on 1990 figures, was eliminated. On January 1, 1998, another 17 percent became quota free, and in 2002, another 18 percent. In 2005, the remaining 49 percent became quota free.

The reduction in tariffs during this 10-year period initially amounted to approximately 11.6 percent for the United States, because its tariffs were relatively low. As indicated, GATT no longer exists, having been replaced with the WTO.

WTO

Born out of GATT, the World Trade Organization (WTO) is a series of trade negotiations that were aimed at reducing tariffs for the facilitation of global trade on goods. The current set of governing rules stems from the Uruguay Round of GATT negotiations, which took place throughout 1986–1994.

The purpose of the WTO is to ensure that global trade commences smoothly, freely, and predictably. It creates and embodies the legal ground rules for global trading among member nations and offers a system for international commerce. It aims to create economic peace and stability in the world through a multilateral system based on consenting member states that have ratified the rules of the WTO in their individual countries as well. The rules apply to local companies and nationals in the conduct of business in the international arena.

Decisions are made by consensus, though a majority vote may also rule. The Ministerial Committee, based in Geneva, Switzerland, which meets at least every two years, makes the top decisions.

NAFTA

The North American Free Trade Agreement (NAFTA) eliminated quotas and tariffs on goods shipped among the United States, Mexico, and Canada. All three nations hoped to experience economic growth as a result of this new free-market economy.

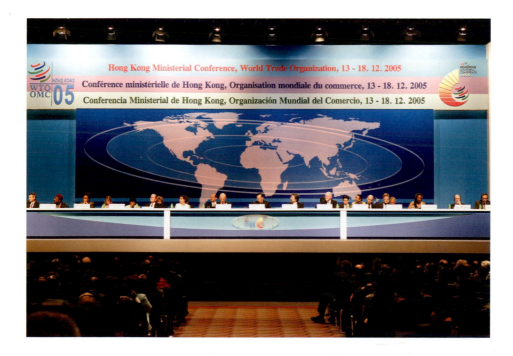

The WTO ensures that global trade commences smoothly.

Mexico has already benefited by becoming a more important resource to the United States. A significant portion of U.S. offshore production subsequently shifted from Asian countries to Mexico to take advantage of lower wages and production costs. Another benefit to the United States is that merchandise flows more quickly from Mexico to the United States than from countries in the Far East.

During the public debate leading up to the passage of the agreement, unions and labor supporters in the United States expressed fears that U.S. employment would suffer as domestic producers shifted their facilities south of the border to take advantage of lower prices. Only time will reveal the long-term implications of the agreement; more than a decade later controversy still surrounds the agreement.

THE INTERNATIONAL FASHION CENTERS

Although Paris and New York City are the centers of fashion, other markets are extremely important. A look at all these markets will help us to understand the scope of the fashion industry.

The United States

All across the country, from New York to Los Angeles, there are designers and manufacturers in the business of fashion. Some of the centers dominate in the industry and serve buyers who come to them from all over the world. Others are regional and serve the needs of local merchants.

New York City

New York City's **garment district** is the United States' most important fashion center. Although it does not compare with Paris in terms of couture, it is, by far, the most significant fashion capital producing ready-to-wear. Known in the trade as Seventh Av-

New York City's garment district attracts buyers from all over the world.

enue, its official boundaries extend beyond that street. Broadway and Seventh Avenue are the area's main streets, but the district runs from Fifth to Ninth avenues and from 35th to 41st streets. In a *Women's Wear Daily* (*WWD*) supplement titled "The Fashion Center," the garment district was reported to be comprised of "approximately 34 million square feet . . . and includes 5,100 showrooms, 4,500 factories, and accounts for $500 million in exported goods."

In recent years, the activities taking place in the garment center have changed. At one time most collections were designed, manufactured, and sold in that area. During the late 1980s and today, however, most companies produce goods at locations away from New York City. They have opened plants in foreign countries where costs are lower. The garment center has become a place where lines are designed and sold to retailers. The hustle and bustle of each day still features the fabric trolleys and racks of clothing being moved through the streets, but the major traffic is generated by the store buyers and merchandisers who regularly visit the market to make their selections.

The most hectic times in the garment district are when the buyers are in town for **market week**. New York's fashion center hosts five market weeks and 65 annual related trade shows. These are periods when designers and manufacturers introduce their new lines. Some manufacturers and designers, who have sufficiently large showrooms, present fashion shows for the buyers. They also wine and dine them. Although some stores have policies forbidding such practices, it is still very much the norm.

Centered in New York City are such upscale companies as Ralph Lauren, Donna Karan, Bill Blass, Calvin Klein, and Oscar de la Renta. Not only do they market their high-end collections, but most also feature their less costly lines, which generally account for the majority of their income.

At the bridge price points, names such as Ellen Tracy, Tahari, and Dana Buchman are housed in the garment district. At lower price points are the likes of the Liz Claiborne empire, which boasts several lines for men and women, and scores of others that do not have the immediate name recognition but nonetheless play an important role in New York City's fashion center.

Since the 1980s, some fashion businesses in New York City have moved from the garment center south to Soho. Competitive rents, availability of large space on a single floor, and an art-and-loft type of environment have lured such avant-garde designers as Todd Oldham and Marc Jacobs away from the more traditional, uptown locations.

Regional Markets

The fashion industry is not confined to New York City. In cities such as Los Angeles and San Francisco, for example, scores of manufacturers operate apparel and accessories companies for all merchandise classifications and every price level. In addition to those companies that are based in these **regional markets**, many feature permanent showrooms that are maintained by New York's manufacturers or showrooms in apparel centers that function primarily during the market weeks.

Los Angeles ranks second as a domestic fashion capital. Its principal offering is sportswear with a casual orientation, although it does feature other types of merchandise. A look at the pages of the *California Apparel News*, the major trade paper for the fashion business on the West Coast, immediately reveals the scope of its industry. Bob Mackie, of film industry fame, and James Galanos, at the couture level,

This trade show calendar is based on information published in *Women's Wear Daily*.

Sunday	Monday	Tuesday	Wednesday	Thursday	Friday	Saturday
					1	**2** Action Sports Retailer, Long Beach, CA / KC women's, children's apparel summer market
3 Action Sports Retailer, KC apparel / JA New York — — / FFANY New York	**4** Long Beach, CA / women's, children's / Women's fall II apparel	**5** summer market → / market — — —	**6**	**7**	**8** / 7th on Sixth — —	**9**
10 7th on Sixth — — / Women's fall II apparel	**11** market — —	**12**	**13** Sunshine Fashion Palmetto/FL	**14** State Exhibitors, Bradenton	**15** →	**16** Off-Price Specialist Show, Las Vegas
17 Women's fall apparel / Off-Price Specialist	**18** market — — / Show, Las Vegas / WWIN Las Vegas	**19** WWDMAGIC MAGICKIDS	**20** Las Vegas	**21** Internat'l Fashion	**22** Jewelry & Accessory / The Imprinted Sportswear / Workshop NY, NYC / American Internat'l Waldorf, NYC	**23** Group Providence, RI / Show Tampa, FL / Sole Commerce, NYC / Designers at the / Pacific Designers Collections NYC / Variety Mdse. Show, NYC
24 Internat'l Fashion Group Providence, RI / The Imprinted Sportswear Show Tampa, FL / Workshop NY, NYC / American Internat'l Pacific Designers / Sole Commerce, NYC / Variety Mdse. Show, / Fashion Coterie, NYC	**25** Jewelry & Accessory / Swimwear Assoc. / Designers at the Collections NYC / NYC	**26** of Fl, Miami / Waldorf, NYC — —	**27**	**28**		

are headquartered in Los Angeles, as are less pricey lines such as Karan Kane, Nancy Heller, Cherokee, Carole Little, Barry Hunter, Miss Liberty, Barocko, and L.A. Gear.

In the northern part of California, the San Francisco region is enjoying its status as the nation's third largest fashion center. Its several hundred manufacturers include Gap, Banana Republic, Old Navy, Esprit, and Jessica McClintock.

Other fashion markets are found throughout the country. Approximately 2,000 showrooms are located in the Atlanta Apparel Mart. Miami, for example, is experiencing considerable growth. Companies cater not only to the retailers in the southern United States, but also to those from South America. Their specialty is sportswear and swimsuits. Dallas is home to designers Victor Costa, Julie and Leonard, Bonnie Boynton, and Jo Hardin. The city also serves as home of the Dallas Apparel Mart, an important center for selling to retailers. Chicago is known primarily for menswear, with companies such as Hartmarx. Its famous Merchandise Mart houses showrooms for manufacturers from all over the nation. Milwaukee is a center for leather with one of the country's most prestigious shoe manufacturers, Allen Edmonds, and producer of wallets, Rolfe, based there.

European Fashion Capitals

All over the continent, designers produce collections that are earmarked for their own populations, as well as for export to the rest of the world. Paris, Milan, and London are Europe's leading fashion producers, with Germany, Spain, and other countries beginning to attract international attention.

The World of Fashion Profile

CHAMBRE SYNDICALE DE LA COUTURE PARISIENNE

In 1868, the Chambre Syndicale de la Couture Parisienne was organized to stabilize and coordinate the activities of the French couture industry. Throughout the years, its position and role in fashion have been strengthened, and it is recognized worldwide as a major fashion trade organization.

Membership is restricted to those who meet the group's stringent requirements. Those requirements include having a workroom; employing a minimum of 20 workers, each capable of providing precision workmanship; completing all work in-house and without contracting out to other factories; custom-making all clothes entirely; and presenting a collection twice a year, as determined by the Chambre, in a live fashion show format.

The services afforded the membership are numerous, including one that offers protection against the copying of designs, a practice commonplace in the United States. To guard against fashion piracy, every design created by a member is photographed and registered. If the design is copied in France, it is punishable by law. With so many couture houses eager to show their collections at a specific time, the group avoids conflicts by establishing a schedule that specifies days and hours when each designer may present his or her line. In this way, buyers have time to view each collection. The Chambre issues appropriate credentials for buyers and the press. It requires that couture houses deliver merchandise within 30 days of purchase. It also provides a training program for everyone in France who demonstrates a talent for sewing. In addition, it negotiates with the government on matters affecting the fashion industry, making certain its membership abides by the established rules.

Nowhere in the world is couture so completely protected by a trade organization.

Paris, France

With the likes of Saint Laurent, Lacroix, Ungaro, Galliano, Gaultier, and Lagerfeld headquartered in Paris, it is no wonder that it remains the fashion capital of the world. With the support of the French government and the resources necessary for design, Paris attracts fashion creators from all over the world.

At one time, Paris was predominantly concerned with haute couture—fine dressmaking, or by American definition, **high fashion**. Today, however, prêt-à-porter (ready-to-wear) takes its place alongside the much higher priced merchandise. Because only a fraction of the market can afford couture designs, it is the ready-to-wear that actually brings the profits to the designers.

Although we are immediately familiar with the names of elite designers, hundreds and hundreds of creative talents work in the Paris fashion industry. Those who have achieved the highest status are accepted as members of the prestigious **Chambre Syndicale de la Couture Parisienne**, a branch of the larger organization Federation Française de la Couture. This prestigious organization is included in a World of Fashion Profile.

In addition to the Chambre Syndicale, there are two more branches of the federation: Chambre Syndicale de Prêt-à-Porter, which represents the ready-to-wear branches of the couture as well as other French prêt designers, and Chambre Syndicale de la Mode Masculine, which represents couture menswear designers. With its rigid rules and regulations, the Chambre Syndicale de la Couture Parisienne recognizes only a handful of designers for membership to the Couture-Creation.

The customers of couture are wealthy people who purchase original designs for their own wardrobes, retailers who purchase them for their inventories or to have them translated into less costly models, and manufacturers who use the designs for

This design from the House of Chanel is representative of the creativity identified with Paris.

inspiration when designing their own lines. Attendance at the fashion premieres, which take place twice a year, requires an entrance or **caution fee** for people in the industry. The amount, established by each house, may come to several thousand dollars but is deducted from purchases made. If a buyer or manufacturer fails to find something to purchase, the fee is forfeited. Private customers attend these fashion shows, as does the press, by invitation and are not charged a caution fee.

With its flair for innovative styling, Paris is likely to remain the world's most famous fashion capital. It is interesting to note that American designers have been contracted to design for well-known French designer houses. In the 1990s, designers from all over the world were named to perpetuate the French fashion industry. American notable Oscar de la Renta began by designing couture and later ready-to-wear for the House of Balmain. British-born John Galliano took over the design responsibilities for Dior. And for the first time since 1968, when couturier Balenciaga retired, the spring ready-to-wear collection designed for that house by Dutch-born designer Josephus Melchior Thimister received favorable reviews.

As the 20th century drew to a close, and the 2000 decade began, a new group of names joined the couturiers' ranks—seven in 18 months, to be exact. These are among the top designers in Paris. The names include Donatella Versace, following in her brother's footsteps; Alexander McQueen, at Givenchy; and Ocimar Vesolato, a native Brazilian. Their creations have price tags that begin at $12,000 and climb steeply once the extravagant trimmings have been added.

This unusually large number of new designers with couture status may be a result of a loosening of the rules established by the Chambre Syndicale.

Milan, Italy

Once known primarily as a source for quality leathers and fabrics, Milan has emerged as a leading fashion center for both men's and women's clothing. While some designers, such as Valentino and Galitzine, have remained faithful to Rome, others have opted for headquarters in Milan. Names such as Armani, Gianfranco Ferré, Krizia, and Missoni design garments earmarked for worldwide distribution. Some, for example Armani, feature both couture and ready-to-wear collections.

London, England

Traditional, conventional ready-to-wear and fine tailoring were the hallmarks of British fashion before the 1960s. At that time, a youth-oriented look, spearheaded by Mary Quant, emerged on London's streets. Her freshness captivated the hearts and pocketbooks of the young, and she, along with other talented designers, prepared Great Britain and the rest of the world for mod clothing.

Although the Quant miniskirts and hot pants caught fire, Quant's popularity declined, as did the excitement over British fashion. Today, however, after many years of neglect by the rest of the fashion world, London is enjoying its status as a fashion

Donatella Versace has continued to keep the Milan fashion house founded by her late brother, Gianni Versace, in the forefront of Italian design.

Designs such as this one by Alexander McQueen make London an important fashion center.

center. Vivienne Westwood, Zandra Rhodes, Betty Jackson, Maxfield Parrish, Wendy Dagworthy, Victor Edelstein, Jeremy Howitt, David Davies, and David Reiss are just some of the talents who have restored London's ready-to-wear market.

Fine-tailored menswear has always been a British specialty, and Savile Row is London's famous locale for fine classic clothing. Turnbull & Asser, Henry Poole, Burberry, and Gieves & Hawkes are some of the leading purveyors of British menswear.

Spain

Always known for leather shoes and apparel, Spain has made important strides in women's and children's sportswear. Through its trade association, **Camara de la Moda Española,** more than 500 firms market their lines. It is through this affiliation that the Spanish fashion manufacturers have been able to gain some recognition outside of the country. The bulk of these companies, headed by such designers as Marce Manuel, Adolfo Dominguez, Marguerita Nuez, and Antonio Alvarado, are centered in either Madrid or Barcelona.

Germany

Germany has more than 2,000 manufacturers of fashion-oriented merchandise located throughout the country. Many of its designers enjoy reputations that reach all over the globe, with the United States a significant market. Leading companies include Hugo Boss, Escada, Mondi, and Jil Sander.

Scandinavia

Denmark, Sweden, Finland, and Norway comprise the important manufacturing countries of this region. The industry is coordinated by the **Central Scandinavian Clothing Council,** which is headquartered in Copenhagen. The best-known merchandise comes from Finland's Marimekko, which produces both ready-to-wear and a full line of home fashions. Although these countries are recognized collectively, each has a distinctive approach to fashion. Sweden's and Norway's contributions are more moderately priced, youth-oriented designs; Denmark's forte is expensive, high-fashion merchandise; and Finland is the leader in original Scandinavian design.

Eastern Europe

With the abundance of inexpensive, skilled labor in countries such as Poland and Hungary, the former Eastern Bloc has become an important center of apparel production. U.S. manufacturers, such as Liz Claiborne, are manufacturing some products there. Macy's has also produced some of its private labels, such as Alfani, in Poland. These nations used to send most of their production output to the former Soviet Union. Now, the Eastern European nations are exporting to countries throughout the world.

South America

South America lags behind the rest of the world in fashion merchandise. The one product, however, that has importance is leather. Garments and accessories, such as shoes and handbags, are produced relatively inexpensively and exported all over the world. Brazil, in particular, is a leader in leather products.

Asia

At the beginning of the 1960s, Asia entered the fashion arena. Japan and Hong Kong (now a part of the People's Republic of China) were the first to become international players. They were later joined by South Korea, Taiwan, and cities such as Singapore in China. Although these countries collectively account for a significant amount of the world's fashion production, China, Taiwan, and South Korea are primarily involved in textile manufacturing and garment construction, with original design occurring mainly in Japan and Hong Kong.

Japan

Although fashion businesses dot the map of Japan, Tokyo is the principal site of production. Japan's role in the fashion industry is in both original design and manufacture of merchandise for foreign companies. Not only does the region produce Japanese designs under their own labels, but Renown, one of the world's leading manufacturers, holds the rights to produce such prestigious American labels as Perry Ellis in Japan for that country's consumption.

Designers of Japanese descent have had an influence in the international fashion industry since the mid-1960s. Hanae Mori was one of the first Japanese designers to capture the attention of the global fashion market, with an aesthetic touch inspired by her Japanese background. Kenzo has worked in Paris since the mid-1960s. His licensing arrangement with The Limited in the 1970s made his designs available to the less affluent consumer. Issey Miyake combines Japanese attitudes toward fashion,

In Hong Kong, fashion is introduced in the Convention and Exhibition Center at the harbor front.

such as wrapping and layering, with exotic fabrics of his own design. One of the more widely acclaimed designers from that region is Rei Kawakubo, who creates collections for Commes des Garçons. Her asymmetrical shapes in cotton, canvas, or linen fabrics are draped and wrapped over the body.

Japanese corporations also provide financial backing for U.S. design firms. In 1984 Takihyo Corporation helped Donna Karan to open her company, Donna Karan New York, which it currently half owns. Anne Klein & Co. is also a wholly owned subsidiary of Takihyo. In 1996, Takihyo decided to discontinue the designer line, which that season was designed by Patrick Robinson.

Hong Kong, China

Although Hong Kong has made significant strides in bringing its own apparel collections to the world of fashion, it is the region's ability to produce garments at low prices that has made it an important player. Famous internationally based companies, such as Armani, Calvin Klein, and Liz Claiborne, often manufacture their goods in Hong Kong. Few locations can offer such expert tailoring at such modest costs.

In the field of original design, companies such as Toppy, Episode, Girdano, G2000, and Goldlion are gaining in international importance. Designers who are emerging as creative forces in the industry include William Tang, Lulu Cheung, Ben Yeung, and Allan Chiu.

When Hong Kong became a part of China in 1997, the transition from a government that believed in free enterprise to one that has a history of tight control on business left many unanswered questions. The joint declaration between the United Kingdom and the People's Republic of China spelled out the following stipulations:

- Hong Kong will enjoy a high degree of autonomy as a Special Administrative Region (SAR) of the People's Republic of China, with socialist policies applied in the mainland not to be applied to Hong Kong. It will maintain its previous capitalist system and lifestyle for 50 years after 1997.

- The Hong Kong SAR will have autonomy in economic, financial, and monetary matters.

- The Hong Kong SAR will determine its own shipping policies.

- There will be the continuing right of free entry and departure from Hong Kong.

There is, however, no way to effectively enforce these stipulations, since China has always acted independently in international matters. Whether China will allow Hong Kong to continue to function autonomously in the future remains to be seen.

Canada and Mexico

Although Canada and Mexico have participated in the fashion industry as both producers of goods for their own countries and exporters to the United States, the passage of NAFTA in 1994 helped to expand their fashion industries.

Canada

With its chief market in Montreal and a second one in Toronto, Canada has more than 2,000 apparel and textile manufacturers. They produce a diverse range of apparel from the highly sophisticated and expensive to the more moderately priced. Among the better known collections are those of Denis Desro, Jean Claude Poitras, Judy Cornish, Roger Edwards, Zapata, and Lida Bada.

Although Canada produces a wide variety of women's and men's apparel, it is particularly noted for men's clothing, and is the second largest supplier to the United States after Italy.

Mexico

With its ability to produce apparel and accessories at modest cost and with the conditions set forth by NAFTA, Mexico has become a leader in the production of

Mexican President Vicente Fox observes workers at the Trans Textil International Factory in San Cristobal de las Casas, Chipas, Mexico.

merchandise for U.S. companies. Many businesses in the United States have set up shop in Mexico to take advantage of the new regulations. One of the problems that has plagued Mexico in the past has been poor-quality construction. With new U.S. interests in the region and quality control a priority, better quality can be expected.

Caribbean Basin Countries

With some of the lowest labor costs in the world and tax and quota exemptions established for them by the United States under the Caribbean Basin Initiative, many countries in this region have become important producers of fashion products. Countries such as El Salvador, the Dominican Republic, Haiti, Jamaica, Costa Rica, and Honduras continue to show significant increases in their exports. They are not the originators of fashion, but serve global fashion businesses by producing merchandise for them.

SELLING FASHION PRODUCTS AROUND THE WORLD

With the size and scope of the fashion industry growing all over the world, designers and manufacturers in the United States use a variety of means to distribute their products.

Selling today takes place in a number of different arenas and formats. In addition to maintaining showrooms for their exclusive use, some producers use road staffs who visit the premises of potential customers and representatives who help sell their lines. Many companies rely heavily on various trade expositions or fairs around the globe to bring their merchandise to the attention of their markets.

Showroom Selling

The larger designers and manufacturers generally maintain showrooms to which buyers may come to make their purchases. These selling arenas are found in every major fashion market in the United States and abroad.

Typically, the home sales office is adjacent to the company's design headquarters, with branches scattered in regional markets. The showrooms run the gamut from large varieties that are not only used to display merchandise throughout the seasons but also double as an arena where fashion shows can be presented, to smaller types that house nothing more than a desk or two and a few racks. Companies such as Liz Claiborne, Perry Ellis, Calvin Klein, Donna Karan, and Anne Klein maintain the larger facilities in the major garment center buildings to accommodate the throngs of buyers who regularly preview their collections. The numerous lesser-known companies opt for smaller offices in less popular buildings to keep operating expenses at a minimum.

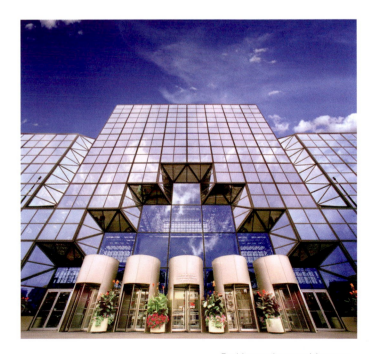

Fashion trade expositions are held in New York City's Javits Center.

To reach customers who do not frequent their home bases, some manufacturers operate showrooms in marts in other parts of the country, such as the Chicago Apparel Center and the Dallas Market Center.

Road Staffs

With many retailers far from the fashion markets and little time to spend in them even if they are within reach, many companies seek business by visiting the buyers.

Traveling sales reps are assigned routes that may take them several hundred miles from their headquarters. They carry sample bags replete with all of the styles in the line and travel from place to place during the season's peak selling periods. Sometimes, the sellers set up shop in a hotel and invite the potential customers to see the line. Some find this a beneficial alternative to in-store selling, because it takes the buyer away from the sales floor where it might be difficult to get the buyer's undivided attention.

Another advantage of **road staffing** is that it enables the seller to witness, first-hand, each store's operation. He or she may communicate with the store's sales personnel, make suggestions about how the line should be presented to the shoppers, advise on visual presentations, and so forth. With showroom visits often limited in terms of time, this personal attention may not be offered.

Manufacturer's Representatives

With the enormous expense of operating a business, many smaller players in the fashion industry are opting for less costly methods of selling their merchandise. Instead of maintaining their own showrooms, some use **manufacturer's representatives** who, in their own facilities, sell several lines. Of greatest importance in this type of arrangement is to choose representatives who sell noncompeting lines. One showroom might sell individual lines of sportswear, sweaters, dresses, and so on that do not compete with each other. For manufacturers using this type of arrangement, one advantage is that a buyer visiting a showroom to see a particular collection might be tempted to buy merchandise from the other represented lines.

MAGIC is the largest men's and women's trade show.

Table 6.2

INTERNATIONAL TRADE EXPOSITIONS

Country	Trade Exposition	Merchandise	Location
United States	Int'l Trimmings Expo	Trimmings	New York
	Int'l Boutique Show	Women's wear	New York
	Kid's Show	Children's wear	New York
	NAMSB	Men's wear	New York
	Private Label Expo	Private label	New York
	FFANY	Shoes	New York
	NADI	Display materials	New York
	Int'l Jeanswear & Sportswear	Sportswear	Miami
	Women's & Children's Market	Women's and children's wear	Dallas
	Int'l Textiles Show	Textiles	Los Angeles
	MAGIC	Men's wear	Las Vegas
	BOBBIN Show	Technology	Atlanta
Spain	Mostra de Tejidos	Textiles	Barcelona
	Feris	Costume jewelry	Barcelona
	BARNAJOYA	Jewelry	Barcelona
	ExpoCalzado	Shoes	Madrid
	IBERPIEL	Furs, leather	Madrid
Italy	Sposaltalia	Bridal	Milan
	Moda-In	Shirting fabric	Milan
	La Moda Milano	Ready-to-wear	Milan
	Prato Expo	Textiles	Florence
	Pitti Bimbo	Children's wear	Florence
	IDEABELLA	Textiles	Cernobbio
France	Premiere Vision	Textiles	Paris
	Indigo	Home textiles	Paris
	SEHM	Men's and boy's wear	Paris
Germany	GDS	Shoes	Dusseldorf
	Interstoff	Textiles	Frankfurt
Portugal	Portuguese Offer	Textiles	Lisbon
Singapore	INTEX	Textiles and trimmings	Singapore
	Fashion Forum	Fashion merchandise	Singapore

The **reps**, as they are called in the industry, are paid on a commission basis by the manufacturer for the merchandise sold. The showroom expenses are their own responsibility.

Trade Expositions

All over the world, trade expositions or **market shows** are held regularly and feature every type of fashion merchandise. They are particularly popular with both vendors and buyers because the industry's participants are able to interface with each other in a very short time. A buyer who has but a few days away from his or her store has the opportunity to review countless collections under one roof. Without these expositions, merchants would have to spend considerably more time going from showroom to showroom in many different geographical locations. With the considerable expense involved in reaching all of the markets, buyers often miss out on lines that they do not have the time to pursue.

Walking through a trade show quickly gives the buyer an overview of the current season's offerings and the ability to quickly compare the offerings of competing companies.

Some of the larger fairs include MAGIC, the largest men's and women's trade show that is held in Las Vegas and **NAMSB** (National Association of Men's Sportswear Buyers), for the menswear industry in New York City. **NADI** (National Association of Display Industries) is a fair of the display industry, and **SEHM** (Salon de'Habillement Masculin), held in Paris twice yearly, attracts approximately 40,000 buyers of men's and boys' fashions from all over the world.

In China, Shanghai is becoming one of the world's leaders in trade expositions. Table 6.2 lists many of the world's fashion-oriented trade expositions.

CHAPTER HIGHLIGHTS

- Fashion, once an industry with limited boundaries, seems to have lost all of its borders.

- Although the majority of the ready-to-wear industry is based in the United States, many of its producers have opted for offshore production facilities to reduce the costs of making the goods. With the design teams based in America, the assembling processes accomplished overseas, and the ultimate customers served all over the world, fashion now is part of the global marketplace.

- To minimize the competition that comes from foreign-produced goods, the federal government places restrictions on imported merchandise by levying tariffs and quotas.

- At the same time, the government recognizes that international trade can be beneficial to U.S. citizens. Thus, it has also enacted legislation to make the United States a better trading partner. The WTO, an outgrowth of GATT, and NAFTA are trade pacts that have solidified these efforts in the global marketplace.

- In addition to Paris, the world leader in couture fashion, and New York City, chief producer of ready-to-wear, other locations have emerged as fashion capitals. Some, such as Italy and London, have become leaders in original design, whereas others, such as Hong Kong, excel as producers of fashion for other nations.

- The selling of the merchandise guarantees a profit for the companies. Vendor sales are accomplished in several ways, including the use of trade expositions.

- Other selling arenas include manufacturer's showrooms and the facilities of manufacturer's representatives.

IMPORTANT FASHION TERMINOLOGY AND CONCEPTS

Camara de la Moda Española	global marketplace	NAMSB
caution fee	high fashion	offshore production
Central Scandinavian Clothing Council	International Boutique Show	regional market
	The Kids Show	reps
Chambre Syndicale de la Couture Parisienne	manufacturer's representative	road staffing
	market shows	SEHM
duty	market week	tariff-rate quota
garment district	NADI	trade exposition
GATT	NAFTA	trade organization
		trade pacts

FOR REVIEW

1. Why do U.S. manufacturers use offshore production facilities?
2. Differentiate between absolute quotas and tariffs.
3. What is the ultimate goal of the WTO pact?
4. Which countries are affected by NAFTA?
5. Distinguish between the fashion strengths of New York City and Paris.
6. Define the term *regional market*.
7. In what way does Hong Kong serve the world of fashion?
8. Why have trade expositions become so popular with vendors and buyers?
9. How does a manufacturer's rep's showroom differ from one that is company owned?
10. In the Point of View article, what trade issues are Congress tackling?

EXERCISES AND PROJECTS

1. Using the Harmonized Tariff System, prepare a table of duty rates for 10 fashion-oriented products. The schedule is available in most libraries.

2. Visit or write a regional wholesale mart, such as Chicago's Merchandise Mart or the Dallas Apparel Mart, and identify the types of companies they lease space to, the expenses involved in acquiring space, the market they serve, and anything else of interest concerning wholesale marts. Prepare a report for oral presentation to the class based on the information you have received.

3. Visit a fashion retailer and examine the merchandise assortment in one classification to determine the country of origin. List each of the countries in the order of overall importance to the store's inventory. Indicate the percentage of foreign-made to domestically produced goods.

4. Select a trade exposition from those mentioned in the chapter and obtain information about it. Find out how often each fair is held, the types of vendors featured, the markets served, the expense of participation, and so on. The information may be obtained through a visit or by contacting the sponsor.

WEB SITES

By accessing these Web sites, you will be able to gain broader knowledge and up-to-date information on materials related to this chapter.

NAFTA Information
   www.mexico-trade.com/nafta.html
Industry Vertical: Garments and Textiles
   www.garments.tdctrade.com
MAGIC International
   www.fabricshow.com

The Case of the Underpublicized Collection

question

What route would you suggest that Gallop and Litt take to guarantee that their line will be seen by the industry's important buyers without the expense of their own showroom in a better location?

For the past five years, Sheri Litt was employed as an assistant designer of children's clothing. Her initial experience was with a traditional line that specialized in infant's wear. After two years with that company, she became an assistant designer, working for Fun in the Sand, a business that manufactured stylish play togs and beach wear for the small set. While working there, she met Caryn Gallop, who started in sales and eventually became national sales manager. The two had an excellent working relationship, and together they helped the company gain industry-wide attention.

Three months ago, Sheri became increasingly interested in starting her own business. She always wanted to be the head designer for a company, but she could not advance because one of Fun in the Sand's partners was the line's creator. She considered moving on to another organization but always felt self-employment was her dream. Not being able to afford the start-up costs on her own and lacking marketing expertise, she approached Caryn about a potential partnership. The two grew increasingly excited about the prospects of ownership and joined forces to open a new venture, Togs for Tots.

With savings of their own and capital obtained from a lending institution, they organized the company. They took a small space in an off-the-beaten-path location, where the designs would be created and an office would be in place for billing. Although it had only a small area to serve as a showroom, its location in the garment district was sufficiently good to gain the attention of many buyers. With a limited advertising budget, they did all they could to promote their new enterprise.

The first line was ready to be shown, but they were still not satisfied that their sales approach was reaching the maximum number of potential buyers.

Congress to Tackle Trade Issues

KRISTI ELLIS

Washington—Congress will get down to legislative business this week under the control of Democrats for the first time in 12 years and its new agenda is expected to have significant ramifications for the fashion industry's sourcing strategies and supply chains.

The Democrats' new goals for trade policy will drive some of the action on Capitol Hill early on, and industry executives are closely watching which philosophy will prevail: free trade, which places an emphasis on lowering barriers for imports and increasing market access for U.S. exports, or fair trade, which focuses on protecting workers' rights overseas while preserving U.S. jobs.

The key issues the new Congress is expected to tackle in the next session, which begins Thursday, include:

- The growing trade deficit with China and its alleged currency manipulation. Apparel and textile imports contributed to the broader trade deficit in goods with China in October, which widened by 6.1 percent to $24.4 billion compared with the preceding month. Observers expect the new Congress to propose a much tougher stance toward the Asian giant.
- The future of free-trade agreements and of the President's trade promotion authority (TPA).
- How to jump-start global trade talks, which have stalled.
- Stricter rules to protect workers' rights, both in the U.S. and overseas.

Overall, the consensus on both sides of the debate is that a new skepticism to-ward trade has taken hold in both parties in Congress. Organized labor's agenda also is expected to gain prominence, and experts said legislative action on new laws governing workers and unions is possible.

House Speaker Nancy Pelosi (D., Calif.) already has laid out her broad agenda for the first 100 hours of the session—and her initial salvo set off alarm bells within the industry. Pelosi has promised that the House will pass legislation raising the federal minimum wage, requiring 100 percent screening of all cargo containers at foreign ports, rolling back subsidies to big oil, and reforming health care and Social Security.

The screening proposal raised an immediate outcry from apparel importers, who said the plan could cause major disruption to shipments.

It is more difficult to gauge the agenda in the Senate, where Democratic leaders have been more circumspect about their legislative priorities in the 110th Congress.

"It will be a big year for trade regardless of other issues, such as the war in Iraq," said Tim Kane, director of the Center for International Trade & Economics at the Heritage Foundation, a conservative think tank.

However, the chances of Congress "actually erecting new trade barriers is unlikely," he said, adding, "A slowdown in trade deals is more likely, since that was already happening with Republicans who were getting nervous about trade."

Kane said there are conflicting forces on international commerce within the Democratic caucus in the House and Senate, which makes it difficult to predict which voices will prevail.

He said experts will be closely watching newly elected Democrats who are coming into office on a wave of anti-trade sentiment and how leaders balance their voices with more pro-trade constituents, such as the Congressional Black Caucus, which has been supportive of trade benefits for sub-Saharan Africa.

Although Pelosi has not unveiled a trade agenda to date, many experts expect several issues to gain traction, including the widening deficit with China and bills targeting its currency manipulation and subsidies, the President's expiring trade-promotion authority, the global round of trade talks, and a push to strengthen labor and environmental laws in free-trade agreements, which could affect the pending Peru and Colombia free-trade deals.

For the 12 months ended Oct. 31, Peru shipped 103.8 million square meter equivalents of apparel and textiles to the U.S., valued at $842.5 million, and Colombia's imports tallied 142.7 million SME, worth $560.3 million.

"We are definitely going to see a China trade bill this year and it's going to be bad," predicted Erik Autor, vice-president and international trade counsel at the National Retail Federation. "Members [of Congress] are chomping at the bit to do a China bill. It's just a question of whether cooler heads can prevail.

"I think they will be under a lot more pressure to whack China. We are keeping a wary eye on the whole situation," Auggie Tantillo, executive director of the American Manufacturing Trade Action Coalition, said. He believes there is already momentum on China, though "how the Democrats choose to deal with this issue is up in the air."

Tantillo added, "First of all, you've got people like (Sens.) Sherrod Brown (D., Ohio) and Jim Webb (D., Va.), who are coming into powerful positions in the Senate and who are vowing to be more aggressive on these issues, and China is at the front of the line for them."

Signaling the possible fight ahead, Rep. Sander Levin (D., Mich.), who will chair the House Ways & Means trade subcommittee, has already said he plans to submit an unfair trade practices case against China's currency manipulation and reintroduce legislation to apply countervailing duties to non-market economies.

In addition, Sen. Max Baucus (D., Mont.), incoming chairman of the Senate Finance Committee, has indicated he is looking for "new tools" to address China's currency policies, other than the Department of the Treasury's semiannual report that has passed on labeling China a currency manipulator.

The President's TPA, which requires Congress to vote up or down on trade agreements without the ability to amend them, expires at the end of June and also will generate a heated debate. The prospects of Congress renewing the author-ity, without any substantive changes to it—such as addressing stronger enforcement mechanism for labor standards—are slim, according to experts.

The global round of trade talks, which has faltered for some time now, will be affected if TPA is not renewed.

"It's hard to say what the prospects for trade-promotion authority are, but it will be a long shot," said Cass Johnson, president of the National Council of Textile Organization. "The election made it more difficult for the administration to get an agreement on TPA through, rather than less difficult. It has given the administration less maneuvering room."

DNR, January 8, 2007

Organizers Adapt Their Show to Attract Customers in a Changing Market

EMILIE MARSH

Paris—While continuing to court markets abroad, French trade show organizers are concentrating efforts to ensure smooth sailing for business back at home.

In order to cater to retailers who are increasingly visiting far-flung locations to unearth stock, French trade show organizers are making sure that Paris fairs are a necessary stop on the textile and apparel show world tour.

"Today, [retailers] are traveling far more than before," said Jean-Pierre Mocho, president of the Prêt à Porter, France's largest ready-to-wear and accessories trade show, which will host some 1,100 exhibitors at the Port de Versailles Feb. 1 to 4. Mocho said that low-cost airfare has helped build buyers' frequent flyer mileage and noted that 70 percent of visitors to The Train and Platform 2, Prêt's New York-based venues, were international, with the majority of European origin.

"The Prêt in Paris gives visitors a preview of what the trends will be in their stores for the following season," Mocho said. The Prêt includes several fashion categories: The Box, the show's accessories section; Atmosphère, for edgy contemporary brands, and Shibuya, a selection of sportswear and denim brands with a younger bent. "We have our local competition in Paris, but our reputation together is what makes Paris an indispensable stop," Mocho said.

Who's Next organizers agreed that the French fashion trade shows offer the ideal balance between commercial brands and cutting-edge young designers.

"Buyers are traveling around the world, becoming more informed and increasing the frequency of their orders," said Xavier Clergerie, organizer of the Who's Next and Première Classe contemporary rtw and accessories shows, which coincide with the Prêt à Porter at the Porte de Versailles.

"Brands like Zara and Mango are able to continuously top up their collections. We have to offer the same service to retailers that are increasingly adding new designers to their collections," Clergerie added.

To meet retailers' demands for unique contemporary brands, show formats are also evolving. "Supersized stands are today being replaced with smaller spaces and more select offerings. Buyers are discouraged by colossal stands. Our stands are small but directional," Clergerie said, noting that Who's Next counts four separate fashion sections, dubbed Fast, Face, Fame and Private.

The less-is-more approach to booths at trade fairs has been driving sales at Tranoi, the uber-trendy fashion fair to be held March 1 to 4 at the Bourse de Commerce and Avenue Montaigne that boasts a niche fair of around 280 exhibitors. "Buyers are very well informed today. As organizers, we take on the role of personal shoppers. We have to know what retailers want and make a careful, limited selection of products," said Michael Hadida, organizer of Tranoi.

Hadida takes a minimalist approach when it comes to optimizing business at the show, advising designers not to overcrowd their stands with too many styles. "Multibrand retailers are diversifying their product range. They are carrying far more brands than in previous years," Hadida said.

To that end, Hadida created a Swedish designer platform that he plans to continue in March. "Retailers are looking for new brands with a creative edge," Hadida said. Looking ahead, Hadida plans to create a showcase for Australian brands next fall.

Meanwhile, organizers at éclat de Mode announced they have shifted dates to Feb. 1 to 4, to coincide with neighboring Who's Next and Premiere Classe. The event will remain in the two-story Hall 5. Project director Sylvie Gaudy said no major changes are planned. "Improved circula-tion and orientation is our main priority, in particular on the upper level," she said.

At Première Vision, Europe's foremost fabric fair—which will be held at the Villepinte exhibit halls Feb. 20 to 23, together with yarns and trimmings fairs Expofil and Mod'Amont—organizers are focusing on optimizing space and ensuring fluidity for buyers at the show. "We try to ensure that every square meter reaches its maximum profitability," said Daniel Faure, president of Première Vision. "We reorganized the salon's layout in order to effectively guide buyers and act as a tool for a successful flow of business."

Sales at Première Vision's first Moscow edition last October were encouraging, according to Faure. "The Russian market is increasingly strong. Buyers are looking for high quality and original products," he said, noting that classic products and designs were less popular with Russian designers.

Running concurrently with Première Vision is Texworld, a fair organized by Messe Frankfurt, featuring less-expensive textiles. The show will be moving from the CNIT complex at La Défense to Le Bourget exhibition hall.

"Traffic at the show will be more fluid," said Michael Scherpe, president of Messe Frankfurt in France. "Having the show in one single terminal will make it easier for exhibitors and buyers to orient themselves." Scherpe said that the show would increase the number of exhibitors to between 750 and 800 in February, noting that the new space will allow for thematic sections for categories such as denim and natural fibers.

Organizers from Eurovet-operated Salon International de la Lingerie confirmed the attendance of those traditional French exhibitors who pulled out from the event's sister trade fair, Lyon Mode City, in September due to factors such as internal restructuring and disaccord with the show dates. The Paris event will return to a four-day stretch, running Feb. 2 to 5, with its Interfiliere section ending Feb. 4. Although its layout in Hall 1 at the Porte de Versailles remains unchanged, one new addition will include the inauguration of the fair's Spicy Boutique, which will host accessories and merchandising exhibitors geared toward the intimate apparel industry.

"[The event will] also cater to developments in distribution in the lingerie sector," said SIL sales manager Cecile Vivier, citing Spanish lingerie chain Women's Secret as a first-time exhibitor.

Meanwhile, a handful of smaller fashion trade fairs throughout the capital will run around the same time as the runway shows. Workshop Paris will be held at Le Cercle Republican and Hotel Regina, while Paris Sur Mode, to be held March 2 to 5, will pitch tents in the Tuileries Gardens to join Atmosphère d'Hiver and the second session of Première Classe.

Women's Wear Daily, November 26, 2006

careers in fashion

A love of fashion makes the economy go round.

LIZ TILBERIS, FASHION EDITOR

After you have completed this chapter, you will be able to discuss:

- Employment opportunities in the various segments of the fashion industry.

- Techniques for a successful job interview.

- How to prepare a résumé and a cover letter.

The world of fashion offers challenging, exciting, and financially rewarding career opportunities. The variety of activities involved in fashion results in diverse jobs that attract people with different backgrounds. Unlike other industries and professions, rigorous credentials and licenses are not required. Although formal education and training are beneficial, successful people in fashion may have studied fine arts, marketing, design, textiles, or just a broad-based program. Many legends began their careers in other fields before choosing fashion. Giorgio Armani studied medicine, as did Geoffrey Beene; Gianni Versace and Gianfranco Ferré studied architecture; and Vivienne Westwood and Bruce Oldfield were teachers.

The types of careers are as numerous as the types of businesses that comprise the industry. The fashion industry is one of the largest employers in the United States. Because of global expansion and offshore production facilities, overseas opportunities are also plentiful. Manufacturers, wholesalers, designers, importers and exporters, retailers, publishers, marketing consultants, and public relations firms are just some of the areas of employment. Classified advertisements in consumer newspapers, such trade papers as *Women's Wear Daily* (*WWD*) and the *Daily News Record* (*DNR*), and numerous employment Web sites present opportunities for those interested in a career in fashion.

SEGMENTS OF THE FASHION INDUSTRY

Some of the positions offered in classified ads are self-explanatory from the job titles; others require more explanation. Trade papers sometimes separate classified ads into two categories—Help Wanted and Sales Help Wanted. Within these classifications, positions are available in all segments of the textile and apparel industries. This chapter discusses the fashion industry in terms of the careers offered in textiles, manufacturing, retailing, market consultants, fashion communications, and modeling.

A growing influence on all of these segments is the Internet. Retailers and manufacturers, using special software and the Internet, now make private B2B (business-to-business) transactions with their suppliers around the world. In addition, specialty retailers provide Web sites that allow customers to purchase their products online. Career opportunities for individuals with fashion skills and technical expertise are likely to expand dramatically with the growth of this medium. Most retailers, for example, use their Web sites for recruitment purposes and are finding greater success than with classified advertising.

Textiles

The textile industry employs technically skilled individuals whose talents and abilities range from creative and artistic to production and sales.

Textile Designer

Textile designers are artists who create particular patterns and present them in a format that can be translated into fabrics. They paint their designs on paper or fabric and prepare the **repeats** that will be used in the finished products. Their extensive use of computers necessitates a thorough understanding of the available software. Some major companies employ designers who simply develop the design concepts and leave the technical developments to repeat artists and painters. Those who usually enter this aspect of the industry are art and design graduates. Their remuneration is generally high.

Colorist

In companies with a great deal of specialization, the **colorist** is responsible for creating the color combinations that will be used in the production of the designer's patterns. The colorist must be an expert in color theory and must understand all of the technical aspects of color utilization.

Grapher

In knitwear, after an initial design has been completed, the design is graphed. These graphs are then used in the production process. In addition to requiring a complete knowledge of knitting construction, the **grapher** must also be computer literate. Computer-aided design (CAD) programs allow graphing to be accomplished more quickly.

Converter

The **converter** oversees the change of greige goods (gray goods), which are unfinished fabrics, into finished textiles. Dyeing, printing, and the application of a variety of fabric finishes constitute converting. Some of the finishes enhance appearance, whereas others are merely functional. The converter's career is a highly technical one that requires a complete knowledge of fibers and fabrics. Additional information on converting is found in Chapter 8.

Dyer

A comprehensive knowledge of dyeing techniques, dye substances, colors, and chemicals is the responsibility of the person who dyes the stock, yarns, or finished fabric. The **dyer** is actually a textile chemist who understands all of the interactions of fabrics and the colors that will be applied. He or she should be a graduate of a textile chemistry program to ably perform the tasks involved in dyeing.

Production Manager

Making certain that every phase in the manufacture of textiles is perfect is the job of the **production manager**. A highly paid career, it involves a complete understanding of every aspect of the textile industry. The production manager oversees plant operations and is responsible for coordination of all activities, including staff management.

Textile Sales Representatives (Reps)

Designers, manufacturers, and retailers are customers of textile companies. Whatever the market they serve, sales reps in textile companies must have a complete understanding of fibers, weaving and knitting, coloring and finishing processes, product care, and fabric end uses. Knowledge is acquired through both formal and on-the-job training. These professionals have the potential to earn substantial incomes.

Manufacturing

At the very core of the fashion industry is the manufacturer. Whatever the product, manufacturing positions cut across all lines.

Designer

Designers are responsible for setting the tone of a line in terms of silhouette, color, fabric, and trim. The most successful have an educational background that includes sketching, draping, patternmaking, and sewing. They are the mainstays of the industry—without their creations, there would be no lines to sell.

Designers must be both technically and artistically competent. Besides preparing aesthetically appropriate sketches of their designs, they must fully understand the

Textile reps sell to manufacturers and designers and must know and understand the benefits of each fabric.

production requirements of each model. Knowing the draping qualities of textiles, patternmaking, construction techniques, and production limitations of their designs is essential. A knowledge of CAD is a must. In some cases, artists are called on to sketch for designers who use the draping approach or to draw designs when the designer is not able to. Sometimes artists paint textile designs according to the designer's instructions so that they can be translated into fabrics; others—especially at the couture level—actually hand-paint designs on fabrics.

Inspiration comes from a variety of events, places, and situations, including movies, television, museum exhibitions, exotic travel, and historical events. The designer must adapt these inspirations into a line of merchandise that will excite the consumer.

Designers are so vital to the company, they are often the principals in the business and have their names on the labels. The major fashion houses are known by the names of their designers; they are equivalent to stars of the entertainment industry.

Occasionally, a designer becomes successful without having followed the traditional path. Sometimes good ideas and good taste are enough—as with Ralph Lauren, who was a tie salesman, and Perry Ellis, who was a store buyer.

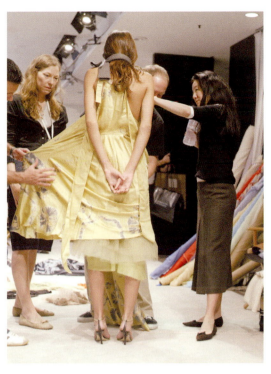

A designer and her assistant discuss details of a new design.

Assistant Designer

The unsung heroes of the design industry are the **assistant designers**. Well versed in all aspects of design, these individuals work as part of a team and are rarely recognized outside of their companies. In many companies, teams of assistant designers actually create the lines. The designer, however, has final approval concerning what will be produced and what will be eliminated, and takes credit for all of the work.

The assistants generally supervise the sewing of the sample garments, select trimmings, shop the textile markets for fabrics, and aid the designer in any way necessary. They are usually not highly paid, especially in comparison to the designer, but hope that with experience they will become head designers.

Merchandiser

The responsibilities of this position vary from company to company, but generally include making decisions concerning the company's line and fabric, performing marketing research, projecting sales, serving as liaison with the sales staff, contacting the mills, reviewing production considerations, and costing the merchandise. In some smaller companies, a **merchandiser** may also serve as designer. In these cases, the merchandiser travels extensively and scouts the market for styles, purchases them, and has adaptations made for the company line. Merchandisers are generally highly paid, especially when product development is within their control.

Assistant Merchandiser

To become a merchandiser, it is necessary to begin as an assistant. This job varies with the needs of the particular merchandiser in a company. Some **assistant merchandisers** are primarily responsible for following and tracking fabric and trimmings orders, initial costing of sample garments, and sales projections, and acting as the intermediary between the merchandiser and other company personnel, such as the designer, colorists, stylists, sales manager, production manager, and quality control manager. This position enables one to learn all the aspects of manufacturing.

Stylist

Companies that do not have a designer or do not give the merchandiser total responsibility for style development may employ a **stylist**. Stylists travel extensively, visiting markets to select styles that will fit the company's line. Rather than just copying the originals, the stylist generally translates each style to fit the manufacturer's needs. A thorough knowledge of textiles and color is necessary so that the stylist can substitute fabrics and colors in the original designs to make the copy cost-efficient.

In large companies, stylists assist designers by researching the market and making suggestions on fashion trends and innovations. Designers and colorists translate this information into specific patterns. To carry out their assignments, stylists interface with fashion forecasters and members of color associations, who are knowledgeable about trends in the industry.

Today's patternmakers prepare their work using CAD systems.

Patternmaker/Grader

Patternmakers use the original design to create the patterns that will be used to produce the finished garments. They must be technically trained in construction, grading of sizes, production, cutting, and fabric use. Because most companies now use computers for patternmaking and grading procedures, patternmakers and **graders** need a working knowledge of computer programs and the use of a **digitizer** for grading patterns.

Salaries for these positions are very high because few people choose to specialize in this area. Although it does not afford the glamour of a designer's career, it provides for excellent, steady employment.

Cutter

As the name implies, **cutters** cut the fabrics and other materials into shapes as dictated by the patterns. This career requires considerable technical skill, including familiarity with computerized cutting. Companies that mass produce merchandise most often use the computerized format; those at the upper levels of fashion might still cut one garment at a time. When a natural material such as leather is being cut, it is the skilled operator who knows how to eliminate the blemished parts while producing the necessary pieces. Even though this skill is very important, remuneration is moderate.

Production Manager

Without a proper production team, the manufacturer's efforts can end in disaster. Anyone who has spent time in the fashion business has had experiences with poor-quality construction, damaged merchandise, and late delivery. The **production manager** for an apparel manufacturer must coordinate and direct all aspects of production so that the designs are carefully executed and the delivery is made as requested on the purchase order.

Cutters must be skilled in all methods of cutting, including computerized cutting.

Several market conditions complicate production. Thus, manufacturers often perform only one aspect of the production process. A company might prepare patterns and cut the materials into the component parts of a product, but subcontract sewing to an outside contractor. In these situations, the production manager must accurately assess the abilities of possible contractors so that appropriate firms are chosen to complete the production. In this way the manager must supervise outside suppliers as well as in-house production.

In today's fashion industry, a significant number of companies produce their merchandise offshore. The distance from the manufacturer's headquarters to the production point complicates the production manager's job. Many find themselves commuting between two countries to make certain that the finished products will be satisfactory and that delivery will be on schedule. For these efforts, production managers are very highly paid.

Quality Controller

One problem that often plagues the manufacturer is poor product quality. Many companies employ **quality controllers** to make certain that the merchandise headed for the retailer is in the best condition to guarantee customer satisfaction. Common errors include the wrong trim on a garment, mismatched sizes in two-piece outfits, poor seaming, faulty zippers, and different dye lots for items that are supposed to match.

Without attention to these details, the merchandise may be shipped to the store, but will soon be returned as unsatisfactory. Not only does this create difficulties for the merchant, who now has an inventory shortage, but it is extremely costly to the producer. Such goods are eventually sold at very low prices to closeout retailers resulting in a loss to the manufacturer.

To evaluate production quality, the controller must know all phases of construction, including familiarity with the quality of materials used. Because much of today's apparel and accessories are produced offshore, many companies hire quality controllers to work abroad so that the finished products need not be shipped back to the factory for the correction of errors.

Quality controllers are well paid because their expertise enables the manufacturer to produce the best possible merchandise.

Manufacturer's Sales Representatives (Reps)

Selling a fashion line can be a financially rewarding career. It is not unusual for sales personnel in apparel firms to be among the highest paid on a company's payroll.

Manufacturer's sales reps are paid basically by two methods. Those who work strictly in showrooms generally receive a salary, while those who cover specific territories are paid on commission. Sometimes, the sales rep receives a guaranteed salary plus a small commission on sales made. The straight commission salesperson, however, has the potential for higher earnings.

The customers served fall into several categories, from small retail operations with limited buying potential to the giants that are capable of purchasing larger quantities. Other buyers represent resident buying offices—businesses that represent retailers and purchase for them or recommend specific lines to them for purchase. Whether it is a small account or a large one, the manufacturer's sales rep performs the same functions: showing the line, helping with merchandising, ensuring goods are delivered on time, handling customer complaints, working with the credit office, bringing customer suggestions to the manufacturer, and fostering better vendor–purchaser relationships.

Retailing

Retailing is a field that offers career opportunities at many levels and in many locations. For those who display the necessary talents, upward mobility is relatively easy.

Most major department stores and large specialty chains offer executive training programs for college graduates. Although the programs vary from company to company, many subscribe to a rotational system in which individuals can explore different aspects of the company's activities. This on-the-job experience prepares the trainees for positions that are challenging as well as financially rewarding. The length of time an individual spends in the training program usually depends on the store's assessment of the individual's progress. Some require longer training periods than others, but once completed, a regular assignment is the next step up the retailing ladder.

General Merchandise Manager (G.M.M.)

This position is the ultimate goal for someone interested in buying and merchandising. Because each company has only one **general merchandise manager**, who is responsible for the store's merchandising philosophy, this is a position reached by only a few.

General merchandise managers supervise the store's several divisional merchandise managers. They allocate dollars to be spent on each division's merchandise offerings and instruct the divisional merchandise managers about the store's markup and profitability goals, image, and other policies with a merchandising orientation.

Candidates for this position usually come from the ranks of the divisional merchandise managers within the company or from other retailing organizations. They are among the highest-paid retail executives.

Divisional Merchandise Manager (D.M.M.)

Each major store employs several **divisional merchandise managers**, who are usually selected from among the successful buyers.

D.M.M.s receive their budgets from the G.M.M. and allocate it to the various buyers under their supervision. D.M.M.s spend considerable time on sales projections, assessing buyer performance, researching market conditions, evaluating industry trends, supervising buyers, and traveling to wholesale markets. Whether accompanying a buyer to a new resource under consideration for a major purchase, attending regional trade shows, or traveling abroad for foreign merchandise acquisitions, the D.M.M. is always on the go.

Most major retailers have policies requiring D.M.M. approval for large buyer purchases. This involves them in merchandise decision making and guarantees that their buyers are not exceeding their purchasing limits.

D.M.M.s are responsible for the coordinating activities with the executives in advertising, sales promotion, and store management. For example, when storewide special events are planned, the D.M.M. must make certain that the promotional activities truly reflect the merchandise presented.

Divisional merchandiser salaries are high. The actual amount is based on the division's sales volume and profitability to the store.

Buyer

Most fashion merchandising students interested in retailing as a career hope to become **buyers**. Buying is seen as the glamour career in the store. Although it does offer the excitement of evaluating new merchandise, attending fashion shows, and traveling to foreign markets, it also requires considerable time commitment and technical skills. In today's retail environment buyers are also involved in product development. Buyers are constantly studying computer printouts, planning purchases, figuring markups, taking markdowns, determining their open-to-buys, and computing the percentage of goods sold in a specific amount of time. Too many college students think that the only skills successful buyers need are good taste and color sense. This is far from the truth. Although a sense of style and color is a necessity, the ability to make quantitative decisions is the utmost important qualification.

Buyers at WWD Magic examine a clothing line.

Most executive trainees who are merchandising oriented can become buyers in as few as four or five years. To determine the accessibility of the buyer position, students need only to walk through a large retail organization and count the different merchandise classifications. Each organization has someone who specializes in purchasing one or two classifications.

The salaries are high and are based on the importance and scope of the specific merchandise to the store.

Assistant Buyer

Most **assistant buyers** begin their careers in executive training programs. Some may have served as department managers before their promotion to assistant buyers. Whatever the track for achieving this position, the assistant buyer's role is very demanding and the salary is comparatively moderate. Assistants make regular visits to the market to place reorders, check on the status of expected merchandise, accompany the buyer to make recommendations on new merchandise, prescreen lines to assess appropriateness for buyer viewing, take markdowns, act as liaison with department managers, and sell during peak periods. The goal of every assistant is to become a buyer; this stage is the proving ground.

Product Developer

Many retailers now create their own merchandise. To meet this challenge, they employ **product developers** who decide which items will be marketed under the store's private labels. Companies such as Macy's, Saks Fifth Avenue, Bloomingdale's, The Limited, and JC Penney participate in these programs. The product developers scout the international markets seeking merchandise that might be adapted into styles for their stores. They might choose the sleeve of one garment, the collar of another, and so on until a specific style has been created. Successful product developers must have an understanding of style, silhouette, fashion trends, fabric, color, and fit. They are most often graduates of fashion merchandising programs and receive high salaries for their work.

Store Manager

Most retail organizations operate their merchandising, control, and promotional divisions from a flagship store or centralized office. Unlike the people in these positions, who perform their activities for the entire organization, **store managers** are needed for each unit in an organization. A large chain requires only one buyer to purchase shirts for 500 stores, but it requires 500 managers.

The store manager's job depends on the size of the unit. In department store flagships and branches, they are often responsible for personnel, service, traffic, security, and maintenance. In the traditional units of chain operations, they are the ones who manage their stores. They hire salespeople, schedule employee hours, handle customer complaints, change displays, keep records, and do anything required to keep the store properly functioning. Many store managers work for a straight salary; others are rewarded with bonuses based on sales volume or profits.

Regional Manager

Most large chains are divided into regions or districts, which are overseen by managers. A **regional manager** may be responsible for as many as 50 stores. His or her job is to make certain that each store is functioning within the policies of the home office by evaluating each store manager's performance and making recommendations for improvements. In some chains, the regional manager may recommend merchandise transfers. Merchandise that is selling poorly in one unit might be shifted to another where it has better sales potential. The job involves making periodic visits to each unit and reporting back to management with a performance assessment.

Regional managers come from the ranks of store managers. They receive straight salaries or salaries plus a bonus for profitability.

Department Manager

In major retail operations, a store is divided into *merchandise departments*. The head of each is a **department manager**, who is responsible for inventory control, record keeping, sales management, employee scheduling, and selling. The department manager receives only average monetary rewards and aims for a promotion to store manager or merchandiser.

Fashion Director

This high-level position in most major department stores often carries the title of vice president. The **fashion director** studies the fashion industry day to day so that the store is prepared to accommodate any fashion innovation.

In the major flagship store, the fashion director works closely with the buyers and merchandisers, alerting them to such details as changing hemlines, color preferences, silhouette trends, and new fabrics. Although each buyer is ultimately responsible for the actual purchases, the fashion director often supplies the information upon which these buying decisions are based. To be successful, directors must work as much as a year in advance of a season to gather information. They travel abroad to assess foreign design trends and textile mill offerings, make regular visits to domestic mills for fabric and color research, scout the tanners for leather information, constantly stay

Designer Pierre Cardin takes a bow alongside his fashion director, Maryse Gaspard (right), after his collection is presented.

abreast of the trade paper forecasts, and are involved in all activities that provide market insights. After all of this detailed study, the fashion director presents to the store's merchandising team an analysis of the upcoming season's offerings and how each buyer's merchandise can be coordinated into a specific, total fashion image.

Many stores use fashion shows to promote their merchandise. Often it is the fashion director who plans the show's format, pulls the merchandise from the different departments, hires models and musicians, prepares the program, and arranges the seating plans. In some stores, the fashion director is called on to select the accessories that will be used to enhance apparel in window and interior displays.

The job is an exciting one. It provides an opportunity to work with many segments of the store and the fashion industry and gives the individual the chance to help mold the store's fashion image.

Advertising Manager

Those with artistic and creative talent might head for a career in retail advertising. Having studied all aspects of graphic design, the **advertising managers** must shape the image of the store's advertising campaigns. They write copy, create artwork, prepare layouts, and direct the specialists.

More and more stores are using **desktop publishing programs** to save money by producing their merchandise catalogs and ads in-house. Therefore, the advertising director must be totally familiar with computer software programs and what they can do.

People who aspire to this position are not the typical students of marketing, retailing, or business administration programs, but rather graduates with majors in advertising or graphic arts.

Visual Merchandiser

Individuals who plan window and interior displays, determine the best way in which merchandise should be presented on the selling floors, and have significant input into store design are called **visual merchandisers**. Their work involves trimming windows, creating props, preparing signage, dressing mannequins, and decorating the store for special events, as well as other responsibilities. They work as members of large in-house teams or as freelancers in their own businesses.

Large stores have visual merchandising managers as department heads, with staff specialists who perform specific functions. The head person sometimes carries the title of vice president and is highly paid. Those in lesser positions receive only moderate salaries. The freelancer is remunerated most favorably; billing clients at $150 an hour is not uncommon. Many who have apprenticed at large stores or who have worked at trimming in those establishments eventually turn to freelancing. With the enormous growth in retailing, this is a career with much opportunity.

The advertising manager shapes the image of the company's campaign.

Personal Shopper

Because today's customers often have many responsibilities, they tend to have less time to shop. Others who have the time are often uncertain of their selections. Retailers have met these needs by employing **personal shoppers**. These individuals, who work as personal or corporate shoppers, must have a thorough knowledge of the store's inventory and a sufficient understanding of fashion to help customers make appropriate selections. Customers may make an appointment to see the merchandise at a specified time. The personal shopper, after consulting with the shopper by phone, preselects those items that will probably meet with approval. The customer may be invited to try on the merchandise in a special area. For example, Bergdorf Goodman uses small, private salons, and Macy's in its Macy's by Appointment (MBA) program, a special facility.

Individuals with good taste and a sense of style, who are willing to provide total service to clients, will be successful personal shoppers. They generally work on a commission basis and are rewarded for their efforts. Many cultivate lists of followers who ask for them again and again, guaranteeing a steady flow of customers.

Interpreters

With the increase in international travel, travelers often shop in places where a different language is spoken. To cater to this clientele, many retailers who are based in cities that attract significant tourism employ **interpreters** to assist these people. At Macy's in New York and Harrod's in London, for example, individuals who speak many different languages are available to accompany shoppers who seek assistance with their selections. The retailers find that these are excellent customers, who often buy quickly and in significant amounts. The basic requirement for such a position is the ability to speak at least three languages fluently. Interpreters are paid a regular wage and sometimes a commission on the merchandise they sell.

A personal shopper assists a customer in choosing a tie.

Market Consultants

Retailers, manufacturers, and designers are always interested in having as much information as possible so that both short- and long-term goals are satisfactorily achieved. Throughout the fashion industry consulting companies function specifically to help such clients. Resident buying offices, reporting services, and fashion forecasters make up the majority of these **market consultants**. For fees, percentages, or commissions, they supply the information needed to achieve success. Each market consulting organization employs a variety of specialists who are responsible for serving their clients' needs. The resident buying offices, the most numerous of the group, assist store buyers with their purchasing requirements; the fashion forecaster predicts long-range trends; and the reporting services prepare press releases concerning every aspect of the fashion industry.

Because all of the marketing consulting companies disseminated materials to their subscribers, this segment offers a great opportunity to those individuals with skills in drawing and writing. For example, flyers containing drawings of the merchandise suggested for the buyer's store must be drawn in a manner that will motivate the retailer to consider purchasing. Individuals are also needed to prepare written promotional pieces describing resources, best-selling items, and fashion notices. Such a position requires the ability to express ideas clearly and simply.

The following positions are just some of the important ones found in many consulting companies.

Resident Buyer

Although the title indicates purchasing, the **resident buyer** is an adviser rather than a purchaser. The major responsibilities are locating new resources, suggesting hot items, handling complaints about vendors, and supplying general fashion information that might help the store buyer formulate purchasing plans. Some buying, specifically reorders and special orders, is part of the job, but not the major part.

The resident buyer helps a client plan the new season.

Unlike the store buyer, who has countless store responsibilities and works long hours to accomplish them, the resident buyer works regular business hours. In cases such as market week, a hectic period when the store buyers visit the wholesale markets, the hours are generally longer. Although the typically short hours may be attractive to some people, the salary levels are much below those of retail buyers. It is easier to become a buyer in a resident buying office than at the retail level, and the formal educational requirements for entry into this career are much less rigorous.

Many people take positions as resident buyers to learn about the fashion industry. Once satisfied that their expertise has been heightened, they transfer to the better paying, more challenging career of retail buying.

Assistant Resident Buyer

An entry-level position, **assistant resident buyers** spend considerable time in the market "following up orders." They check delivery dates and the merchandise status of orders placed by the stores they represent. The job is extremely low paying and serves only as an initiation into the fashion world.

Fashion Forecaster

Resident buying offices and fashion forecasting companies predict fashion trends. **Fashion forecasters** visit the textile mills to assess the fabrics and colors that will be featured in clothing approximately 12 to 18 months later, study haute couture designs that will probably be translated into more affordably priced models, and analyze social, political, and economic events that could become the basis of future fashion trends. Often, they travel to foreign countries to observe the ways in which people there dress—this is sometimes the inspiration for new designs. A fashion forecaster's career requires good verbal and writing skills, a keen understanding of fashion fundamentals, and the ability to participate in research endeavors.

The salaries for such individuals are high, because their forecasts often become the basis for future business decisions.

Fashion forecasters predict trends so that their clients can plan for the future.

Fashion Communications

Print, broadcast, and the Internet media provide exciting careers in fashion. Trade papers such as *Women's Wear Daily*, consumer newspapers and magazines, and television are arenas in which people with strong communication skills can seek employment. In addition to a complete knowledge of fashion, each participant must be able to write about or illustrate fashion in a concise and exciting manner, communicate ideas in a meaningful way, and successfully relate to all segments of the industry.

Most **fashion writers** cover everything with a fashion orientation, from designer openings to gala social events, for a particular publication. Meeting with the designers, attending fashion shows, and playing a part in publicizing fashion are just some of the duties of the fashion writer. They report on who is showing what, who is wearing whose design, what's hot, what's not, and anything else that will appeal to the reader. Writers travel to domestic markets as well as international centers of fashion. Wherever there is a fashion story, a writer will be there to cover it. Those best prepared for entry into this field have degrees in journalism and a full understanding of fashion jargon.

Those with a great deal of experience and industry recognition write regular columns for their newspapers and magazines. Those who achieve "stardom" as fashion writers often become high-profile fashion editors.

Trade and consumer papers and magazines sometimes commission **fashion illustrators** to render fashion drawings. Some artists' styles are so distinct that their work is often as easily recognized as that of a fine artist. Some work for specific publications, while others freelance and sell their drawings to manufacturers, retailers, and the print media. The fashion illustrator must be deft at quick sketching, particularly when the assignment is a fast-paced runway show.

Fashion Editor

To be the **fashion editor** of such magazines as *Vogue*, *GQ*, *Harper's Bazaar*, *Ebony*, or *Glamour* is to have reached the pinnacle of success in fashion communication. These

Fashion photographers must be able to capture the tone and style of fashion designs.

RICHARD AVEDON

Starting in an unlikely environment—the merchant marine—Richard Avedon went on to achieve fame as a fashion photographer. After taking an experimental photography class at the New York School for Social Research, given by the art director of *Harper's Bazaar*, he was invited to join the staff of the magazine in 1945. His tenure at *Harper's* lasted 20 years. In 1966, he moved to *Harper's* rival fashion publication, *Vogue*, where he remained until 1990. After leaving *Vogue*, he worked as a staff photographer for *The New Yorker* until his death in 2004.

Avedon's photography had a style all its own. He incorporated freedom and drama into his works. Those in the industry are always able to recognize his work even if it is untitled.

Avedon's numerous awards include the Art Director's Show (1950) highest achievement medal, the Pratt Institute citation of dedication to fashion photography (1976), the Art Director's Club Hall of Fame (1982), and the Council of Fashion Designers of America Lifetime Achievement Award (1989).

Retrospectives of his photographs have been displayed in one-person shows at the Museum of Modern Art (1975), the Metropolitan Museum of Art (1978), the Whitney Museum (1994), and the National Portrait Gallery in London (1995).

Richard Avedon's photography is noted for its freedom and drama.

positions not only offer significant monetary rewards but also provide an element of excitement. Many editors are extremely influential in helping to promote or destroy a fashion concept. Designers and manufacturers generally try to befriend these people in the hope that it will bring them good press. The requirements of such a position include the ability to write.

Fashion Photographer

Fashion photographers are the dominant forces in print journalism. Catalogs, trade and consumer newspapers, and fashion magazines are full of these photographs. Their subjects are models who either parade the latest designs on runways or model in settings where they must be carefully motivated to show the merchandise to its best advantage. Many photographers work for specific publications, but many freelance and shoot sessions for a variety of clients. The job may be performed in the photographer's or periodical's studio, at trade shows or retailing establishments, or on location.

Richard Avedon, one of the most successful fashion photographers, is profiled in a World of Fashion Profile.

Commentator

In television, fashion information is delivered both visually and orally to the viewer. Although the major emphasis is on the visual, commentary often follows the action. The commentary is, however, generally written in advance by retail or designer fashion coordinators when lines are shown to potential customers. Because most television stations rely on their own regular journalists to read commentary that has been written by someone else, there is little career opportunity for being a **commentator**.

Shopping Network Host

Throughout the United States several cable channels bring merchandise into the homes of the viewer. The programs use a variety of hosts to present the merchandise, the majority of which is fashion apparel and accessories, in a way that motivates the viewer to purchase. **Shopping network hosts** have the looks and personalities necessary to gain rapport with their audiences.

Wardrobe Consultant

The credits at the end of film and television productions often list the names of designers or stores whose clothing was worn by the casts. Most programs use a **wardrobe consultant** whose job is to scout the market for the right merchandise to outfit their stars and then to make arrangements for the loan of the merchandise in exchange for the displayed credit. The consultant must have a full knowledge of the fashion industry, the resources where apparel is available, and the expertise necessary to select the best styles to enhance the wearer's figure. Graduates of fashion programs are best suited for these highly paid positions.

Runway models in a fashion show finalé.

Fashion Educator

A career sometimes associated with the field of fashion communications is that of the **fashion educator**. Many schools from postsecondary to the two- and four-year college level include programs in fashion design and merchandising. Some schools offer a full range of fashion subjects such as retailing, merchandising, designing, and so on; others specialize in just one segment of the fashion industry.

Those with a desire to teach the practices and procedures needed to enter the fashion industry may find employment as instructors. Typically, the requirements for such a career include a master's degree and hands-on experience in the industry.

Fashion Modeling

When it comes to glamour, little compares with the life of a model. The roles range anywhere from those anonymous figures who stroll the aisles in retail venues in informal modeling to the stars of the industry who gain international acclaim and enormous fees walking on the runways. The **informal modeling** assignment is usually the retailer's domain, while the **runway models** are usually employed by a designer or manufacturer.

Informal Model

Walking on the selling floors of many fashion merchants' premises, or strolling among the tables at store restaurants to promote their styles, the participants range

Informal modeling is some-times featured in stores, restaurants, or trade shows.

from those who are employed by the stores in some other capacity and merely have this as an extra assignment to those who are sent by modeling agencies for specific times and events.

Runway Model

The roster of these players, both men and women, sometimes achieve stardom as much heralded as the designers who create the fashions. Often, a particular designer requests a specific model, over and over again, to work the international trade expositions. These are highest paid in the industry and often gain sufficient prominence to enter other fields once their careers are over. Kim Alexis, for example, has become a TV personality and motivational speaker, and Heidi Klum has been successful as TV producer and host of *Project Runway*.

One of the controversies that has surfaced in runway modeling is the "weight" problem. The problem is still being debated at this point in time.

THE INTERVIEW

Securing the Interview

After studying the career choices and selecting those appropriate to one's educational background and practical experience, the route to a job interview should begin. Interviews may be secured in many ways, but the best is networking. Nothing works better than a recommendation from a friend, relative, or acquaintance who knows someone in the field. That is not to say that a recommendation guarantees a job, but it helps gain an interview; the rest is up to the candidate.

A second technique is to carefully review classified advertisements, which are available both in print and through online listings. Candidates can also research the fashion industry at trade shows, in fashion periodicals, and through trade associations and organizations. They can obtain information about specific companies that could be potential employers.

Contacting an employment or recruitment agency is yet another approach. Agencies that specialize in finding employment in the fashion industry are easily found in newspapers, online, and in the yellow pages of local phone directories. They often have leads for positions where fees are paid by the prospective employer.

Whatever approach serves the applicant's needs, specific materials must be prepared before the interview. They are the résumé, cover letter, and portfolio (to show the applicant's special talents).

JENNIFER MURRAY
3930 Stanton Street
Chicago, IL 60616
312-555-6098

EDUCATION:	Bradley Community College Chicago, IL AAS Fashion Merchandising, June 2007 Honors: Magna Cum Laude
SPECIAL EXPERIENCE:	I was one of ten students selected from a group of 95 to participate in an internship with Printemp in Paris as a personal shopper. Being fluent in French helped me considerably.
COLLEGE ACTIVITIES:	Fashion show coordinator President, Retailing club Freshman orientation adviser
EXPERIENCE:	
6/05 -present	LORD & TAYLOR Chicago, IL *Personal shopper and interpreter* • Assist customers with their selections. • Interpret for French and Italian visitors. • Select merchandise for corporate accounts. • Choose accessories for fashion shows.
5/04 - 9/04	THE GAP Chicago, IL *Selling and visual merchandising* • Arranged inventory. • Installed visual presentations. • Responsible for cashdraw tally. • Prepared in-house signage for displays.
6/03 - 8/03	BOOGIE'S DINER Chicago, IL *Selling and inventory management* • Supervised inventory control. • Handled customer returns. • Prepared vendor returns. • Reordered merchandise as per manager's request.
SKILLS:	Computer literacy: Microsoft Office, Internet. Fluent in French.
INTERESTS:	Travel, theater, skiing, aerobics.

Sample Résumé

The Résumé

Those responsible for hiring rarely want to interview every prospective candidate for the job. To determine which individuals have the necessary qualifications for employment, most business executives or human resources managers prefer to have some initial information concerning the applicant's achievements. This personal and professional background is presented in a **résumé**, a historical compilation of a candidate's education and employment record.

Résumés may be professionally written by specialists, for a fee, or may be created by the individual. Many books on résumé writing are available in libraries and bookstores and through local government employment agencies. There are even computerized programs that give the outlines for résumés, requiring only the insertion of specific information. These resources offer a variety of formats to follow, all suggesting that brevity is the best approach. Most résumé writers suggest it should be no more than one page. If it is too long, it might deter the potential employer from reading it.

Cover Letters

The résumé should be accompanied by a **cover letter** that briefly states interest in the company and explains how the sender chose to apply for a position with that particular organization. Perhaps the recommendation of someone with whom the company is familiar or a classified advertisement prompted the application. The company's reputation might be another reason stated in the cover letter. Whatever the motivation, the letter should simply ask the reader to examine the accompanying résumé and arrange for an interview.

Common errors in preparing cover letters are including information that duplicates what is found in the résumé, including so much information that there will be little to discuss at the interview, and addressing the letter "Dear Sir" or "Dear Human Resources Manager." This indicates that the writer spent no time learning the name of the individual responsible for hiring. A telephone call to the company will usually provide the name and appropriate title of the person to whom the résumés and cover letters should be addressed. It is also imperative to correctly spell the individual's name. Any mistake with this simple matter might indicate a sloppy or lazy approach.

Finally, the envelope and the paper on which the letter is written should be the same as that of the résumé. This package is an important means of getting the interviewer's attention. Because each letter might be one of hundreds received by a particular company, it must make a professional impression.

Many employers now ask applicants to submit their cover letters and résumés by e-mail or fax. Although the quality of the electronically transmitted versions does not equal that of traditionally prepared materials, care must still be taken in their preparation and the copy should always be proofread before being sent.

Portfolios

Many positions in the fashion world require creativity. Individuals interested in careers as designers, stylists, product developers, colorists, illustrators, writers, photographers, and visual merchandisers will need to prepare a **portfolio**. At the time of the interview, it will show your artistic and creative abilities.

The portfolio, which will quickly give the interviewer an impression of your accomplishments, should be presented in a professional format. This may be achieved

3930 Stanton Street
Chicago, IL 60616
312-555-6098
December 3, 2007

Ms. Emily Winters
Human Resources Manager
Lord & Taylor
1525 Fifth Avenue
New York, NY 10007

Dear Ms. Winters:

At the suggestion of Mr. Anthony Finch, Director of Executive Development at Lord & Taylor in Chicago, I am writing to you about possible employment as a personal shopper in your New York City flagship store.

I completed my two-year degree in Fashion Merchandising, in June, 2007, and am currently anticipating enrollment at New York's Fashion Institute of Technology for a bachelor's degree. The program is given in the evening, which will allow me to work full time.

The time spent at your company's Chicago store enabled me to apply what I learned in college to the real world of retailing. It was an excellent experience.

Enclosed is a copy of my resume, which gives you some background information about me.

Sincerely,

Jennifer Murray

Jennifer Murray

Sample Cover Letter

by employing the services of an expert or by your own careful preparation. A design portfolio should include sketches with color and fabric swatches for all of your designs and any other materials illustrating your creativity. For a writing position, articles in trade or consumer publications should be carefully organized and displayed. Notice of any prizes should also be highlighted.

With a perfectly executed package, you are ready to prepare for the interview.

Preparing for the Interview

Once an interview is arranged, prepare to sell yourself to the organization by dressing appropriately and learning something of the company's background and goals.

Researching the Company

All too often candidates are rejected because they know little about the organization to which they are applying for a job. By researching the company, an individual demonstrates that he or she is not merely applying for any job, but is being selective.

Major companies, such as DuPont, Calvin Klein, Ralph Lauren, The Limited, and Macy's, for example, are the easiest to learn about. They prepare annual reports for their stockholders, in which the company's assets, specialties, and goals are generally summarized. These are available just for the asking. Major businesses are often the subjects of articles in the trade papers and consumer newspapers, all of which are easily obtainable in libraries or via the Internet. The companies' own Web sites are frequently good sources of direct information, but a firsthand glimpse of a company may be achieved through an actual look at it. When applying to a major retailer, for example, a visit to one of its stores will immediately reveal its inventory emphasis and the code of dress demonstrated by its employees. When the career choice is editorial in nature, familiarize yourself with that company's periodicals to learn about the style of writing and the areas of interest.

As much research as possible will benefit the applicant by making him or her feel more comfortable and confident during the interview.

Role Playing

Many career hopefuls show up at an interview totally unprepared for the questions that may be asked. Although researching the company will provide information, it will not provide the questions or techniques that might be employed during the interview. **Role playing** is a technique that might help. It involves two people, one who plays the part of the interviewer, the other the interviewee. Although this will not be identical to the actual interview, it can usefully simulate the meeting between the business executive and the job applicant.

Ideally, role playing would involve a friend or relative with business experience or a teacher with interviewing experience. If these sources are unavailable, another student could perform the interviewing task. Whoever the participants might be, it is necessary to provide the mock interviewer with any company information gathered during the research stage. Having participated in this role playing, the applicant is better prepared to handle the real thing.

Appearance

All too often, hopes for a position are dashed by having worn the wrong outfit for an interview. Although the terms *good taste* and *appropriate dress* are bandied about, many people simply do not understand their meanings. A good method for choosing the right interview outfit is to visit a retailer that specializes in corporate dress or business attire, or a service, such as personal shopping, where individual attention is provided. Another approach is to visit the company to which you are applying and observe the type of clothing worn by the staff. For a fee, there are specialists who will help you with your total appearance, including personal grooming and wardrobe selection. Many books written on the subject are available in the library.

Whatever resources are used to determine the appropriate dress, its importance cannot be overemphasized. When the door is opened to the interviewer's office and the applicant enters, it is this first impression that may make or break the interview.

Postinterview Practice: Letter of Appreciation

After the interview is concluded, the candidate should send a **letter of appreciation** that expresses gratitude for the time the interviewer spent with the applicant and indicates continuing interest in the company. Emphasis should be placed on what was

3930 Stanton Street
Chicago, IL 60616
312-555-6098
December 10, 2007

Ms. Emily Winters
Human Resources Manager
Lord & Taylor
1525 Fifth Avenue
New York, NY 10007

Dear Ms. Winters:

Our meeting on Friday with you and your assistant made me realize that working for your company would be an exciting and rewarding experience. Not only did you both make me immediately feel at home, but your enthusiasm for Lord & Taylor has made me believe working for the company would be a wise choice. I believe that I can fit comfortably in your organization and would like to have the opportunity to do so.

While I was told that others were being considered for the position, I believe, if chosen, my contributions would be at the highest level.

If you have any other questions you would like answered, please feel free to contact me.

Sincerely,

Jennifer Murray

Jennifer Murray

Sample Letter of Appreciation

learned during the interview, as well as the enthusiasm the applicant has to work for the company. It might also be beneficial to relate how, if successful in obtaining the job, one would be an asset to the organization.

CHAPTER HIGHLIGHTS

- The fashion industry offers a variety of career opportunities in textiles, manufacturing, designing, retailing, marketing, and communications.

- The fashion industry accommodates people with diverse educational backgrounds. There are, however, some technically oriented careers that necessitate a mastery of particular skills.

- Because the fashion world is global in scope, employment opportunities are not limited to one geographical location.

- Candidates for jobs in the fashion field should prepare a résumé, cover letter, and, if appropriate, a portfolio.

- Prepare for the job interview by researching the company background, role playing, and assembling an appropriate wardrobe.

IMPORTANT FASHION TERMINOLOGY AND CONCEPTS

advertising manager
assistant buyer
assistant designer
assistant merchandiser
assistant resident buyer
buyer
colorist
commentator
converter
cover letter
cutter
department manager
designer
desktop publishing
   programs
digitizer
divisional merchandise
   manager

dyer
fashion director
fashion editor
fashion educator
fashion forecaster
fashion illustrator
fashion photographer
fashion writer
general merchandise
   manager
grader
grapher
interpreter
letter of appreciation
manufacturer's sales
   representatives (reps)
market consultant
merchandiser

open-to-buys
patternmaker
personal shopper
portfolio
product developer
production manager
quality controller
regional manager
repeats
resident buyer
résumé
role playing
shopping network host
store manager
stylist
textile designer
visual merchandiser
wardrobe consultant

FOR REVIEW

1. In what situation would a manufacturer generally employ a stylist?

2. Why is it necessary for patternmakers to understand the use of a digitizer?

3. Why are quality controllers used in fashion manufacturing?

4. How does the general merchandise manager's job differ from that of the divisional merchandise manager?

5. Describe the role of the fashion director for a major retailer.

6. How does the job of a product developer differ from that of a designer?

7. Why have retailers developed personal shopping programs?

8. How does the resident buyer's job differ from the store buyer's job?

9. Is the fashion editor important to the success or failure of a designer? In what way?

10. What is the job of a wardrobe consultant for television?

11. Describe the role of a converter.

12. For a creative position, what besides a résumé is necessary to show an individual's talents?

13. According to the Wini Rider-Young Point of View, what are some of the areas of expertise needed for success as a fashion writer?

EXERCISES AND PROJECTS

1. Using the example in the text or one of the other suggested sources, prepare a résumé to use when applying for a full-time position.

2. Write two sample letters, one to accompany your résumé, the other to show appreciation for an interview.

3. Using the classifieds in a trade paper such as *Women's Wear Daily* or *DNR*, chose a career opportunity that motivates you to seek further information. Research the company in terms of size, geographical location, merchandise specialization, and so on. The information can be obtained from the sources outlined in the chapter.

WEB SITES

By accessing these Web sites, you will be able to gain broader knowledge and up-to-date information on materials related to this chapter.

Fashion Careers

www.fashion-careers.com

Monster.com

www.monster.com

The Case of the Successful Job Candidate

Stacey Peters will graduate from college in two months with a degree in fashion merchandising. In addition to the required liberal arts courses, she has studied a number of fashion-related subjects, such as retail management, textiles, advertising, fashion coordination, and fashion publicity. Her cumulative grade point average is 3.7 out of a possible 4.0, which will enable her to graduate with honors. Because she comes from a family that has been in the fashion industry at various levels, Stacey brings a great deal of enthusiasm to a prospective employer.

Like any diligent prospective graduate, Stacey has done her investigative homework. She has researched numerous manufacturing companies and retail organizations, preparing a résumé appropriate to each. To her credit, her time and effort have paid off. She was invited to interview with three prestigious fashion-oriented retail organizations and five manufacturers. The interviews resulted in three firm offers:

1. Smith and Campbell, a department store with 15 branches, offered her admission to their executive training program, which could lead to either a merchandising or management career. The starting salary is $25,000 with future raises based on her ability to perform.

2. Design Images, a high-fashion chain organization, offered her a position as an assistant store manager in one of the company's 35 units. For a starting salary of $21,000, Stacey would assist the store manager and have such decision-making responsibilities as employee scheduling, visual merchandising, handling customer complaints, and inventory replenishment. Within two years she could become a store manager.

3. The Male Image, a menswear designer and manufacturer, has agreed to hire Stacey as a sales representative. Initially she would sell the company's line in the showroom for a salary of $27,000 and eventually become a "road" salesperson with compensation based on straight commission.

Each of the companies is based in Stacey's general geographical area and provides potential for a successful career.

questions

1. What aspects of each job should Stacey investigate before making a decision?

2. What are the disadvantages, if any, of each job?

3. Which position would you suggest she accept? Why?

Advice to Aspiring Designers:
Get Smart Before Getting Started

VALERIE SECKLER

Talented designers too often underestimate the importance of business skills when seeking financing for their young businesses.

This was the consensus of factors, the most common source of funding for designers whose companies are in early growth stages. These entrepreneurial ventures are often rich in design and sales talent, said factors interviewed by WWD, but sorely lacking in crucial back-room support like production proficiency, accounting expertise and sales organizations.

Such shortcomings typically undermine a designer's efforts to obtain financing and often explode the fledgling enterprise, factors noted.

Miles Stuchin, president of Access Capital, a factor that counts apparel designers among its clients, said, "We sometimes see design expertise but weak production skills. Often a company can produce, but is weak on bookkeeping. In smaller companies with limited funds, these can be big problems."

Observed Walter Kaye, president of Merchant Factors, "We don't see lots of designers going into business as we did in the past. Many who try don't know how to go beyond line development."

"They're not as able to market themselves and find funding as their predecessors," added Kaye, who founded Merchant 10 years ago at age 57.

In order to win the confidence and financing of factors, a young designer firm must build the proper business foundation and get at least one successful retail season under its belt.

After sinking $10,000 to $15,000 of their own money into their businesses, designers' next infusion of funds can come from a variety of sources, factors explained. They include family members, investors with roots in the apparel business, contract manufacturers seeking to boost production to cover overhead and joint ventures established with apparel companies that are looking to segment or trade up.

"All too often designers lose their initial investment because the new company doesn't have staying power," cautioned Kaye. "We've seen budding designers with lots of ideas but little capital, and we discourage them. They need adequate capital to develop their samples line, buy supplies and stay afloat until the money from their first season comes in."

A joint venture is one of the best ways for young designer firms with limited capital to get started, according to Kaye. The joint venture partner gets "very big leverage" in exchange for its business and financial support, resulting in "many deals that work out very well," he noted.

"Existing Seventh Avenue companies tend to be frequent and good sources of money," Stuchin agreed, assessing the joint venture route. "Complementary businesses and players tend to know and trust each other."

The good news for young designer firms is that their gross margins of 35 to 40 percent are far stronger than, say, the 15 to 20 percent achieved by mass market startups. So if they can survive the first season or two, designers' chances of finding funding from factors brighten considerably.

Factors lend money to young designer companies against their accounts receivable, typically offering financing for firms with sales ranging from $1.5 million to $5 million.

"Our average client has sales of about $2 million, but we've started funding $800,000 companies that are doing $15 million today," said Kaye.

Such firms can generally borrow 75 to 80 percent of the face value of their credit-approved receivables from factors. The fee is usually the prime rate plus a single-digit percentage. The percentage is determined by the principals' previous experience and the quality of the company's receivables and retail accounts, among other considerations.

Gary Wassner, president of Hilldun Corp., a niche factor for designer apparel resources, said his firm lends anywhere from $50,000 to $700,000. "The majority of our loans are about $150,000," he stated.

Assuming the business basics are in place, the criteria factors used to determine lending fees also help them to decide whether to lend money to a designer company in the first place. The most crucial: the ability to produce well-finished clothes that fit properly and deliver them on time to a range of quality retailers.

"We look for designers who are able to sell to a number of stores rather than to a guardian angel," said Stuchin.

For this reason, he noted, "We greatly prefer designers selling to department stores than to specialty boutiques. They take about the same amount of time to sell, and the department store has the much bigger pen."

When Hilldun's thinking about lending to a designer company selling $1,000 suits, for instance, "We have to be certain about the fit, finishing and timeliness of delivery," said Wassner. "The only way to know is if they've shipped for a season and the stores liked the merchandise."

As for on-time deliveries, the chief culprit creating slowdowns is the late arrival of supplies. "Designers have to be careful about their fabric suppliers," Wassner stressed. "This is where most of their delivery problems lie.

"Designers also have to know their factories will produce on time for them and not push them to the bottom of the heap," he added. "They need to use smaller shops where their orders carry more clout and to put an employee on site to monitor operations."

Another plus for designers seeking financing, said Stuchin, is the employment of an accountant specializing in the apparel business. "Credit suppliers look to see who's preparing a company's financials," he noted.

Most factors said it's usually harder for designer firms to secure funding than it is for other apparel businesses, because their higher cost results in a greater concentration of sales on fewer items.

"The odds of getting paid by a company making 10 dresses for $100 apiece are better than for a company making a single dress for $1,000," reasoned

Stuchin. "If there's one rip in the $1,000 dress, that's it."

Moreover, even if factors are paid consistently, the size of the factoring volume generated by designers is far smaller than that of moderate or mass resources.

"Lots of factors avoid designer companies due to their lower overall sales volumes—factors won't do $50 million in volume with clients making $1,000 garments," said Wassner.

Nevertheless, Merchant's Kaye insisted, "It isn't necessarily harder for younger designer companies to get financing, but they often lack the business acumen to secure the funds.

"Many times they get bad advice," he added. "They can only get started seeking loans from factors after their first season of orders are in from good retailers."

Women's Wear Daily, March 27, 1995

Primer for a Would-Be Fashion Writer

WINI RIDER-YOUNG

So you're mad about fashion and think that being a designer is the only way to go.

Imagine this.

You are sitting on a gilt chair in the grand salon of a *pallazzo* in Rome and watching Valentino present his *alta moda* collection.

Or—

You are sipping a glass of wine in Bob Mackie's living room in Beverly Hills and hearing about the dress he's designed for Cher to wear to the Oscars.

Or—

You have just flown to Mexico with two models and are posing them wearing white dresses in the doorway of a Spanish mission.

This is the way you go if you are a fashion writer.

What It Takes

To be a fashion writer you must have two interests: a passion for fashion and a love of writing. You wouldn't be reading this if the first weren't true. As for the second, fashion writing doesn't require the talent of an Ernest Hemingway or a Dorothy

Parker, but you do have to be able to write and communicate.

Most newspapers now require a degree in journalism; however when you have an expertise like fashion, the knowledge supersedes the craft.

Fashion writing can take you in several directions: copy writing, advertising, catalogs, TV, magazines, and newspapers.

You question that a television fashion reporter needs writing skills? Believe me, Elsa Klensch of CNN's *Style* writes everything down and memorizes it before she looks into the camera and delivers her fashion coverage. She is the epitome of a fashion reporter.

Being a fashion reporter/editor for a magazine or newspaper can take you everywhere you want to go.

Learn the Tricks of the Trade

Like all good jobs, it takes a while to get there but here are some pointers for what to do along the way.

Expose yourself to fashion to the maximum; read all the fashion magazines, go to fashion shows, look for fashion on TV, shop stores for fashion, but above all, sell fashion for a while. There is nothing like working in hands-on fashion sales to understand that no two tastes are alike. A customer may think an outfit is the bee's knees while you wouldn't be caught dead in it. This is a big point to remember when reporting fashion.

Learn that fashion writing is not about describing fashion, it is about seeing fashion with words. No one was better at it than Eugenia Shepherd, the late fashion writer for the *International Herald Tribune*. In reporting an Yves St. Laurent collection, where the designer showed models wearing narrow ankle-length skirts, matching narrow hip-length sweaters and small matching berets, Ms. Shepherd wrote,

"This year Yves St. Laurent is making women look like tubes of toothpaste."

Is that coat yellow? Or is it mustard or lemon?

Do swirls of white satin cord trim a white satin collar? Or does the collar look like a wedding cake?

See it. Get it?

Learn how to spot trends and where to look for them. The best place is in fashion magazines and especially in cosmetic advertising. The clothes on models in cosmetic ads have to be both up to the minute and enduring.

Go to back issues of fashion magazines at the library and follow a silhouette or a color for a year. Watch it grow or diminish. You'll soon be able to spot the momentum.

The Importance of Styling

For a while, try to get a job as a stylist. Learn how to put jewelry and scarves and accessories with outfits. Learn what to add and what to take away. One of the best routes to knowing fashion is to work as a stylist (a glorified goffer) for a fashion photographer.

A fashion editor needs a lot of experience in styling as she collects, coordinates, and accessorizes clothes for photography and supervises fashion photo shoots.

Developing Taste

The taste level for your job will develop with your experience. After seeing designer fashion shows and store merchandise, after watching society women, CEOs, rock musicians, MTV celebrities, movie stars, television personalities, businessmen and women, body-pierced youths, and chiseled models (notoriously ill-dressed when off the runway), you will find your own professional fashion center.

You should not write a personal opinion about the fashion you are reporting, anyway. (More about this later.)

Know Your Readers

You must get to know your readers and to whom you are writing. What do they want to know? Do they want to know the current trends? Do they want to know about the latest Paris *prêt-à-porter*? Do they want to read about career dressing? Do they want to know where to buy the fashion, and if so, how much? Do they want makeup and beauty tips?

If you are writing for a high fashion magazine, the focus is evident. If you are writing for a city newspaper you will probably write a little bit about everything.

And how will you report *prêt-à-porter* and the New York designers' collections to the readers in a town where there are no high-fashion stores?

An example of good reporting in such a town is the fashion supplement of a Florida newspaper where slides from *prêt-à-porter* and the New York collections (available through The Fashion Group) were used to help readers find the fashion locally. For example, a slide of a slip dress from a designer runway was published side-by-side with a photograph of the closest thing to it found in town.

Fashion Phonetics

And if you are talking fashion, you should learn how to say it. Nothing reveals fashion naivety more than mispronouncing a designer's name.

Job Responsibilities

When you finally get that coveted job as fashion editor, there are responsibilities that require maturity.

With the job comes power: power to make a star or declare a dud, power to build a designer or ruin his reputation, power to control a manufacturer's business with praise or dissention.

A fashion editor should report not critique fashion.

Critiquing, perhaps, should come with omission. If it isn't good, don't picture it, don't write about it.

The message here is to responsibly handle the power that comes with the job.

Temptations and Ethics

If a fashion editor has this kind of power there are those who will try to tempt her with gifts. Nothing like a beautiful new dress or a leather jacket for free if you write about their line.

Just say, "No."

Ethics in this job are a priority and top notch asset.

Attending Collections, Here and Abroad

Attending the designer's collections here and in Europe is pure theater. You see the most beautiful clothes on the most beautiful models in the world, with productions staged and choreographed like a Broadway show. All are by invitation only. As the collections are attended by both buyers and press, there is a clamor for seats.

There is a pecking order. Big store buyers usually get the first invitations (Neiman Marcus, Saks Fifth Avenue, Bergdorf Goodman), then top drawer publications—*Vogue*, *Harper's Bazaar*, Fairchild Publications (i.e., *Women's Wear Daily* and *W*). Next come the big newspapers: *U.S.A. Today*, the *New York Times*, *Washington Post*, the *Los Angeles Times*, *Chicago Tribune*.

The designers also like to sprinkle their audiences with celebrities and society women. Entertainment personalities like Lauren Bacall, Kathleen Turner, Barbara Walters, and Ivana Trump and society women like Chessy Rayner, Nancy Kissinger, Pat Buckley, and Blaine Trump are often seen sitting in the best seats in the house.

The best seats are close to the side of the runway or fifth-row-center at the front of the stage.

Editors from small newspapers must call the designer's public relations department and request a ticket. They can be hard to get. One famous designer will not give a ticket to an editor unless his *design collection* is sold in the town where her newspaper is published. Another designer

is loathe to let in the riff-raff, small town newspaper reporters.

A reporter can see as many as eight shows in a day and her copy probably will contain trends in silhouette and color spiced with a bit of show business. She will go back to her hotel room, usually dead tired and late at night, to write and file.

Laptop computers with built in modems and fax machines make sending copy back to the newspaper a breeze, a far cry from the old days when, from Paris, copy was telegraphed at fifty cents per word.

Let the Show Begin

The shows have a general format, taped music and running time of less than an hour. The mood of the show—from music to tempo, from model to hair and makeup—reflect the mood of the collection: elegant or funk, soft or tough. All shows are paced accordingly, with models appearing one right after the other, often two or four at a time.

At the end of the collection, all of the models remain on the runway while the designer appears to receive his accolades. They clap. They kiss. It is *his* moment.

The traditional European designer's show ends with a bride before the accolades.

Don't Miss the Side Show

In thriving, sophisticated cities like New York and Paris, there are things going on other than the collections.

Are all Parisian women dying their hair red?

Is wearing a purple scarf with matching beret the latest fad on the Champs Elysées?

Are New York society women really wearing jeans and blazers shopping on upper Madison Avenue?

Have Aerosol Fishermen replaced Nikes in walk-to-work comfort in New York?

No one is better at spotting street trends than Bill Cunningham, the fashion photojournalist for the *New York Times*. He reports trends from bare mid-riffs to wide-brim black fedoras (the kind Madeleine Albright wore overseas) and supports these trends with photos.

And think of all the people you can interview, not only a designer, but the American model who is in Paris for the first time or the producer of Macy's Thanksgiving Day parade.

There's always a side show going on. Don't miss it.

Getting Down to Business

When a fashion editor isn't reporting on the collections or new fashion trends, when she isn't coordinating clothes and dressing models for a fashion shoot, what does she write about?

Anything, but with an angle.

Hair color—"Do Blonde's Really Have More Fun?"

Hair cut—"Will Short Hair Short Circuit My Sex Appeal?"

Beach hats—"Turkeys In the Straw."

Tattoos—"Tattoos Are Forever. Or Are they?"

Modeling—"Models for the New Millennium."

What about giving fashion advice? On the telephone, yes. But unless a fashion editor has a *personal column*, like Eugenia Shepherd's column *Inside Fashion*, she should not be subjective. Authority is attributed to others: designers, make-up artists, hair stylists, doctors, readers.

What about the story "Will Short Hair Short Circuit My Sex Appeal?" Interview a bunch of men from a CEO to a professional football player. They will tell you whether they like long hair better than short and why.

The Rewards

A fashion writer doesn't get top dollar in this high-finance world we live in. But if you love fashion, where it comes from and the excitement that surrounds it, fashion writing could be for you. Reporting fashion takes you to New York, to Europe, to designers' showrooms, to tropical locations, to chic restaurants and throbbing night spots. Best of all it keeps you *au courant*, on the cutting edge, in pace with the times.

What a way to go.

Weighing the Weight Issue

What qualifies as too thin is a debate raging from New York to Milan, and no matter where one stands, there is one thing almost everyone agrees on: enforcing any kind of body-type rule for models is nearly impossible.

Following the much-ridiculed move last fall by officials in Madrid to ban what they considered too-thin models and the death last month from anorexia of 21-year-old Brazilian model Ana Carolina Reston, the issue is forefront once again because Italy's Camera Della Moda plans to promote a nationwide campaign against anorexia, recruiting the fashion industry as a key ally. The Council of Fashion Designers of America also said it is considering drawing up guidelines for American designers, editors and stylists.

At a time when size zero is becoming increasingly common, many in the industry said that the plans to regulate model size are a noble effort but are impractical. They point out that every body type is different and that in many cases, models are thin either because they are young and not physically mature or it is in their genes and not necessarily indicative of an eating disorder.

"People forget that many of these girls are very young, and they are thin because they are very young," said Paul Smith. "When you look at your nieces and nephews, they look skinny. It's kind of the same thing."

Didier Grumbach, the president of France's Chambre Syndicale, believes that though anorexia is a "serious public health problem," it won't be solved by regulating the size of girls allowed to walk in shows.

"The best way to solve the problem is to talk and write about it," said Grumbach, adding that imposing rules on the size of girls would become "too subjective" and tricky to manage. "It's a false remedy to think that by slapping down a bunch of rules that you're going to solve a serious problem. Paris isn't interested in creating those types of rules."

Even the man who is stimulating the latest debate—Mario Boselli, president of the Camera Nazionale della Moda Italiana—admits the difficulties. "The idea is that a doctor certifies a model's health based on different parameters even if they're skinny, because skinny doesn't mean anorexic," he said Wednesday. "Take Gisele [Bündchen]: She's thin but in great shape and healthy. It's like the doctor's certificate that you need to get

your driver's license. We want to push a healthier and sunnier woman."

Boselli and Giovanna Melandri, the Italian minister for sports activities and youth-driven programs, unveiled the plan Tuesday to promote a nationwide campaign in Italy against anorexia. The idea is to develop a manifesto with support from designers, top brands, model agencies and photographers that would seek to ban the use of emaciated models in advertising and on the catwalks.

"Details [of the proposed manifesto] are still to be defined, but we hope that designers, photographers and model agencies will embrace it. For designers that don't, we may have to penalize them by not assigning a slot on the calendar or taking them off the official calendar." He said this should also apply to the big-league designers.

"It's still early to talk about the manifesto because it should be ready by the end of January, in time for the ready-to-wear shows in February," added Boselli. "However, I think it's very positive that we joined forces with the minister of sports and youth policies because it reinforces the message."

And designers and industry executives generally are fully behind the ideal. Giorgio Armani said, "I am in line [with minister Melandri]. For my shows, I've never wanted girls that were too thin. I prefer models that know how to wear my clothes."

Following the Madrid proposal last fall, Donatella Versace told *WWD*, "I support completely what happened in Madrid. We shouldn't promote models that are too slim. Anyway, models cannot be overweight as well. You work in fashion, so it's tricky."

Diane von Furstenberg, president of the CFDA, said in a statement, "It is undeniable that fashion has a huge impact on young women. Therefore, it is important that, as an industry, we encourage good health and self-empowerment as beauty. The entire industry has to remain sensitive and aware of this issue, but not discriminatory."

Steven Kolb, executive director of the CFDA, said the association has started looking into ways to promote working with healthier models. He hopes there will be a development before the New York shows in February that will involve the entire fashion community, from designers to agencies and magazine editors, as well as health professionals who are experts in eating disorders.

However, Kolb noted, "I don't think we would ever mandate or regulate the situation, but we can suggest or recommend healthy alternatives and bring the issue more to the forefront."

Derek Lam underscored the importance of promoting a healthy look, but the designer does not necessarily believe in legislating model standards. "Then you start to pigeonhole an ideal," Lam said. "Some people are 5 feet 10 inches and have an incredible metabolism and genetic makeup."

Lam said that he always makes a conscious effort to cast healthy models. "There is really no way you can hide it when someone is unhealthy on the runway."

Sally Singer, fashion news and features director at *Vogue*, said, "I do think it's a serious issue, and it's not a place for political grandstanding. It's one thing to say you'll police this, but where's the line between an emaciated versus really thin model?"

Singer said that at *Vogue*, editors want the girls to be healthy and not suffering from eating disorders. "It's better for the industry when the girls are healthier and not emaciated, and clothes look better on them. There's a reason why the supermodels [in the Nineties] were so successful," she said, since they projected a healthy image and looked terrific in the clothes—from the curvaceous Christy Turlington and Cindy Crawford to the athletic Naomi Campbell.

Singer said she's observed on the runways that "the girls are increasingly young and small and not terribly persuasive as models. We would welcome designers and casting people to choose girls who project a more healthful image. We try to use girls who really project a personality. We don't use the newest girl of the moment."

Cathy Gould, director of Elite North America, said, "This disease is being approached the wrong way. It is an illness, but there is no scientific proof that having thin models or actresses makes people become anorexic or bulimic. I would rather see all this money and attention being spent on research as opposed to pointing fingers at models who are naturally thin and tall."

If an Elite model shows any sign of either illness, the problem is addressed immediately but such instances are "very rare," she said. In addition, healthy Elite models are often referred to nutritionists and personal trainers for their well-being, Gould said. "With the schedules they keep and the travel they do, we have to be sure that they take care of themselves. If they don't, they are over in a season, and we definitely don't want that."

One leading model's agent, who requested anonymity, said "It's not about the models—it's about the designers who make the size-zero samples. The problem comes from the people who set the rules. The people who really need to do something is the designers. If a girl is a size two, she can't do the show."

"The models have nothing to do with it. Those poor girls are being blamed. A lot of them are really naturally skinny because they are 17 years old," the agent said.

Vittorio Missoni, sales and marketing manager of the family-owned company, said, "I think models are not really a point of reference for young girls as much as ballerinas, showgirls, starlets. The Italian Chamber of Fashion has always been unanimous on one point: that models should look healthy, and the trends today work in this sense. Male models, too, a few seasons ago were too scrawny. Now they look healthier. They look like they work out at the gym.

"Russian, Ukrainian girls are all quite pale and slim, it's simply how they are. We had a show in Moscow, and at the casting, there maybe were 300 of them, and they were all really alike: pale and slim.

"I've seen plenty of models in our showroom, and they eat a lot, believe me. No, we've never had problems turning down models who were unwell."

Lucy Danziger, editor in chief of Self, said, "My position is that women who are too thin don't look healthy. There's a borderline, and you know when you have crossed it: when you see the huge collarbones sticking out. We've sent models home if they're too skinny, and when we hire them we tell them, 'Do not lose weight.' They obviously need to fit into a sample. We once had to cut the sample. We won't send the model home, but we'll cut the sample."

Danziger said last season she saw more super-skinny girls on the runway than ever before. "Now it's a critical mass. This year seemed to be a preponderance of too-thin body types." She said that by today's standards, Kate Moss, in her early modeling days, would be fuller than these girls today. "Too skinny doesn't look healthy. As an editor, I'm an advocate of healthy women. We won't show women who are unhealthy or at either end of the spectrum," she said. She said if she wants to show a fuller figure, size 10 or size 12, she has to cast a plus-size model.

Amy Astley, editor in chief of *Teen Vogue*, said, "While the details of the Italian manifesto are not yet known, Teen Vogue certainly agrees that anorexic girls belong in treatment, not on the runway. We always seek to promote a healthy body image to our readers, both through extensive articles about proper nutrition and by not knowingly booking anorexic or eating-disordered models for photo shoots."

"It is difficult to mandate weight as every body is, of course, different, and slimness is generally a requirement in the profession. However, as models tend to be young, it is the responsibility of those adults around them—bookers, family, designers, editors and others—to ascertain whether a model is respecting her health or whether she is in need of assistance," she said.

Charles DeCaro, partner in Laspata/DeCaro, the ad agency in New York, said the naturally thin models "are mutant creatures who have this ungodly ability to eat whatever they want, and they show up and do a good job. We don't hire a girl based on their body fat. It's just who they are. I've never been with one of these people who hasn't eaten as much, if not more, than everyone else. They're just lucky."

A spokeswoman for the National Association of Anorexia Nervosa and Associated Disorders, a Highland Park, Ill.-based not-for-profit organization, said, "The media and fashion industry use role models that are very slender and petite. It is our hope that the fashion industry can promote positive body image and that individuals come in all shapes and sizes. There is absolutely no such thing as an ideal body size or weight or height. In addition, this extreme focus by designers on the super-skinny model is not healthy for the professionals on the runway and . . . the young girls and teens who view them."

Women's Wear Daily, November 7, 2006

The Overachievers: Modeling Success

ROSEMARY FEITELBERG

It used to be that landing an endorsement deal or a walk-on role in a B-level flick was the best that models could hope for once their runway days were over. No longer. A batch of entrepreneurial models who rose to fame before the millennium continue to reinvent themselves.

With careers as divergent as their personalities, Kim Alexis, Tyra Banks, Helena Christensen and Heidi Klum have been developing multiple vocations. But they are far from the only opportunists. When Janice Dickinson was approached for this article, her frontwoman had one question, "Is there any pay or is it self-publicity?"

Forthcoming as they were about their plans and their prospects, Alexis and Christensen were the only ones willing to address the ongoing controversy about Madrid banning underweight models from its runway shows. Alexis said, "It is about time that someone recognizes that too thin is not sexy. Banning is extreme, but effective, and will make a positive statement on health over looks."

Christensen said, in some instances, the responsibility falls to mothers and agents, who should tell an aspiring model "very early on that her body just isn't the right type for this industry and that it would be wrong and unhealthy to try to change it." Should an agency sign her, the company should "be sure to support the [girl] 100 percent with any weight issues, follow her diet and eating habits and build up her self-confidence, so she can deal with the pressures of the business."

"Many of the girls who end up having weight issues usually come into the modeling industry with very low self-confidence and very little support from their family. If an agency decides to employ a girl, it is their full responsibility to make sure she is healthy, physically and mentally," said Christensen.

In addition to the Madrid controversy, here's what the models had to say on a host of other topics, ranging from the highlights of their modeling careers to their latest entrepreneurial endeavors:

Kim Alexis, motivational speaker, author, TV personality, seven-time marathoner

What's new?: "I've been speaking [publicly] for the last five years. Now I'm interested in getting my ideas presented in different ways: books, TV shows, a magazine concept. My message is to encourage women. At 46, I'm running my eighth marathon in New York this fall for Team for Kids, which helps schools set goals. Women my age ask, 'Is it OK for me to have a life now?' I've just sent my son off to college. I want them to know you're so much more beyond the mother of your children."

Who were some of your favorite designers to model for?: "Azzedine Alaïa, Perry Ellis, Ralph Lauren and Calvin Klein."

Do you have a favorite runway moment?: "A few years before Perry Ellis died, he had Kelly Emberg, Nancy Donohue and me go down the runway together being light, carefree and young versus the untouchable girl."

Is there one you would like to forget?: "I had gone over to Italy and tried to get fitted for a dress, and the designer canceled me. He said I was too big. In high school, I swam five-and-a-half hours a day."

Models today need to be more : "Professional and conscientious. I've heard over and over again they do what they want to do. They sit in their clothes and wrinkle them. They scratch their head, and someone needs to redo their hair."

Who had the best parties?: "I didn't do a ton of that. I found I was happy to wake up the next day and say, 'I feel good

about myself.' But the first night I came to New York, I took my shoes off while dancing at Xenon and stepped on some glass and ended up fainting into my dad's arms. I was all in white, and he was in white, and there was blood everywhere. People said years later they thought I'd had a drug overdose, but I was like, no, I was dancing barefoot."

Big break: "I was taking college courses and planned to go to [the University of Rhode Island] to study pharmaceuticals. I was really into sports and played the clarinet. I didn't know how to pluck my eyebrows or do my makeup. This [local] modeling school wanted to send pictures of me to one in New York. I kept saying, 'No, I don't want to be a model.'"

Tyra Banks, creator, host and executive producer of "America's Next Top Model" and creator, host and producer of "The Tyra Banks Show"

What's new?: "I have five television shows in active development and a feature film with Nickelodeon Movies being produced with Wendy Finerman. Her feature film credits include 'The Devil Wears Prada' and 'Forrest Gump.' 'ANTM' is in its seventh cycle, and there will be even more celebrity guests for the second season of 'The Tyra Banks Show.'"

Who were some of your favorite designers to model for?: "Christian Dior fashion shows were always exciting for me. The designs were so over-the-top and absolutely glamorous when Gianfranco Ferré was designing, during my days in Paris."

Memorable runway show: "The Yves Saint Laurent shows were incredible, when I was modeling. Yves Saint Laurent himself was actually still designing, and he would book us all day for a fitting.

He wanted to see a complete vision, so he'd have us all in full hair and makeup— all for just a fitting! [Those] bright-red lips, those tight chignons . . . we'd wait around in our white robes. It was old-school artistic couture. I can still remember the smell of the lipstick, like crushed red rose petals."

Do you have a favorite runway moment?: "The Anne Klein fashion show—Louis Dell'Olio was designing— where I was given a full-length black crocheted dress to wear down the runway. I remember slinking down the runway like a cat and getting a huge ovation. My mom was so proud."

Is there one you would like to forget?: "An Isaac Mizrahi fashion show where I got into so much trouble for swinging my cape too much—Isaac yelled at me for going overboard. But what Isaac didn't know was that the guy who stands with the model right before she goes onto the runway told me, 'Tyra, you better swing that cape like I know only you can!' The guy saw Isaac digging into me, but kept mum. So did I. I took the fall for that guy. But CNN's 'Style With Elsa Klensch' ended up using that footage of me swinging that Mizrahi cape at the top of her style show for years!"

Who had the best parties?: "I never went to the parties. I went to work and then went home. I always had my eye on business, not fun."

What was the funniest or strangest thing you saw backstage?: "The craziest behind-the-scenes spectacles were at Thierry Mugler shows. It was like a circus of freaks and flavor—absolutely over-the-top wild."

What was your big break?: "My big break was when I first moved to Paris and booked 25 shows: Chanel, Dior, Lagerfeld, YSL. It was the first time in history any model had done that. It was incredible."

Helena Christensen, photographer, co-owner of Butik, a TriBeCa boutique, and co-designer of its new clothing line

What's new?: "I just got back from a small exhibition of my photos in Tokyo, and I'm working on a big show opening at the Locust gallery in Rotterdam at the end of November. So far, we're not planning any other Butik stores, but you never know. We just presented our own clothing line, Christensen and Sigersen."

Who were some of your favorite designers to model for?: "Always Karl Lagerfeld at Chanel, because the clothes were beautiful and he is exciting. Also, it felt very special to be working for one of the most legendary houses in fashion history."

Do you have a favorite runway moment?: "I did a Thierry Mugler show once where a big porn star was walking on the catwalk before me. When I started to walk, he came back, pulling off his pants and showing off. Well, the reason he was such a big porn star . . . well, it was an odd sight to look at strutting up there."

Is there one you would like to forget?: "The one where I fainted in the final lineup because my corset was extremely tight and it was 104 degrees."

Who had the best parties?: "Versace had some pretty decadent soirees . . . and Galliano! But the girls had their own best parties, really."

What was the funniest or strangest thing you ever saw at a show or back-stage?: "Oh dear, just about everything was rather strange. Most of it has been erased from my memory. There was too much to remember."

What was your big break?: "Meeting Peter Lindbergh and Lagerfeld the first week I was in Paris . . . and probably Herb Ritts directing me in the 'Wicked Games' video."

Today's models need to be more . . . : "Can't finish that one. The ones I know are very cool and so beautiful. No complaints there."

Heidi Klum, producer and host of "Project Runway" and "Germany's Next Top Model," jewelry designer

What's new?: "It feels like so much is new all the time. We had the 'Project Runway' finale during fashion week, and I've started having meetings with my German TV show, 'Germany's Next Top Model,' [which] starts shooting next year. We are on our second season, and it's been a great success in Germany. I've designed an exclusive jewelry collection for QVC called the Heidi Klum Collection for Mouawad and was on QVC earlier last month to introduce that. Being at home with the kids is wonderful. Trying to teach them everything from potty training to 'please' and 'thank you'—it's a lot of work, patience and fun."

Who were some of your favorite designers to model for?: "I have a lot of favorites, but, really, it depends on the occasion. I wore Michael Kors for the Emmys this year; for CFDA, I wore J.Mendel. On 'Project Runway' this season, I wore everyone from Donna Karan and Catherine Malandrino to Roberto Cavalli and Zac Posen."

Do you have a favorite runway moment?: "My favorite runway moment was during last year's Victoria's Secret fashion show when my husband [Seal] was performing 'Love's Divine,' as I walked the runway in angel wings that had megawatt lights on them, as well as on the bra and panties—it was fabulous!"

A show you'd like to forget: "When you are on the runway, all you want is for it to be perfect. I remember slipping badly and almost falling at the Millennium Fashion Show in Times Square. I *just* caught myself."

Who had the best parties?: "I am not big on the party circuit. I'm more the type to chill with friends at dinner. I do remember, though, when I first came to New York being dragged to the Tunnel, watching people dance in nothing but a G-string in these cages . . . then being dragged to the Vault, watching things that I can't even repeat."

What was your big break?: "Signing with Victoria's Secret was a big break in my career. I got a ton of visibility from the campaigns, which they started using me in right away and walking in the fashion show. Right around the same time, getting the cover of *Sports Illustrated* Swim and all the press that surrounded it, that helped raise my profile as well. This was the beginning, so it was a big break, but everything after that up to this day is still important."

Today's models need to be more . . . : "Nah, I'm a live-and-let-live girl."

Ready to Wear Report, *Women's Wear Daily*, October 3, 2006

the producers of raw materials

Before a designer can finalize plans for a new collection, all of the available raw materials that go into making the various products must be explored. These raw materials are the subject of the chapters in Part Two.

Of particular importance is the variety of fibers and fabrics that might be used. The appropriate choice is based on construction, methods of coloring and decoration, and the decorative and functional finishes that enhance appearance and use. As emphasized in Chapter 8, a complete knowledge of the textile industry is necessary to assure the selection of the most appropriate fabrics.

Other raw materials are fur and leather, the focus of Chapter 9. By themselves, furs are used for coats, other outerwear, and trimmings. There are numerous types, each providing a different look and price point. Today's fur manufacturers, while still producing products in record numbers, must confront animal rights protesters who believe that animals should not be killed for their skins. The fur producers have expended great energy in efforts to inform consumers about the humaneness of the industry.

Leather is a raw material that continues to receive a lot of attention from designers of fashion merchandise. It is used in the construction of garments, as well as for such accessories as shoes and handbags. As with other materials, leather comes in a wide range of qualities and prices.

Having learned all of the technical aspects of these materials, the reader should be ready to explore each of these components of fashion merchandise in Part Three.

the textile industry

Isn't it wonderful to unpack wool jersey and thumb your nose at an iron?

SALLY KIRKLAND, FASHION EDITOR

After you have completed this chapter, you will be able to discuss:

- Natural and manufactured fibers.

- Major fiber classifications and the advantages of each.

- Various dyeing and printing techniques used in textile coloration and the advantages of each method.

- The importance of the finishes that are applied to fabrics.

- Some of the methodology used by the industry in the marketing of textiles.

Exciting fashion design is not simply the result of a creative mind sketching innovative silhouettes. To best serve the consumer's needs, the professional apparel and home fashions designer must completely understand the raw materials that will be incorporated into the final product.

The major raw material for the fashion industry is textiles. Today's market is vast, with globally based centers and complex operations that make use of technological advances in production. Thus, fabric users must constantly check that their final choices are appropriate. A designer developing a garment intended for extensive wear while traveling, for example, must consider the fiber's ability to shed wrinkles. The wrong choice of fiber content could quickly result in an unsuccessful product.

Although the United States is a leader in world textile production, considerable competition comes from other countries. Just as apparel producers have gone offshore to manufacture their garments, many designers regularly scout foreign markets for fabrics. In an effort to curtail imports and protect domestic production, the United States empowers a quota on those fibers, such as cotton, that pose the greatest threat to domestic production. Trade agreements, such as the General Agreement on Tariffs and Trade (GATT), which has been replaced by the World Trade Organization (WTO), and the North American Free Trade Agreement (NAFTA) have raised more serious considerations for U.S. producers. Their effect on the domestic textile industry remains to be seen.

SCOPE OF THE TEXTILE INDUSTRY

As far back as 25,000 B.C. individuals made fabrics from fibers found in nature. By contrast, present-day manufacturers operate in a technologically advanced environment that affords more accurate production at incredible speed. In the United States alone, more than 30,000 people are employed in the manufacture of synthetic and cellulosic fibers,

Left: Today's textile industry employs enormous sales staffs to cover the needs of the marketplace. Below: Color cards and swatches are used to sell fabrics to manufacturers and designers.

as well as hundreds of thousands more who produce natural fibers that collectively manufacture enough yardage to travel to the moon and back 23 times and circle the globe 14 times! According to the American Fiber Manufacturers Association, Inc. (AFMA), procedures that once took several months now take as little as a few minutes. The sophisticated looms can turn out as much as 100 yards of cloth in an hour. According to the American Textile Manufacturers Institute (ATMI), 9 billion pounds of fiber that result in $10 billion in sales are produced annually. The textile industry is capable of producing enough yardage in one minute to make 2,000 dresses; 24 hours later there will be sufficient yardage for 3 million dresses. The industry invests more than $2.37 billion on new plants, equipment, and computer systems that monitor all of the processes. According to ATMI statistics, of the total amount of fabric produced, 38 percent is used for women's, men's, and children's apparel; 27 percent for home furnishings; 8 percent for floor coverings; 23 percent for industrial and miscellaneous consumer products; and 4 percent for export.

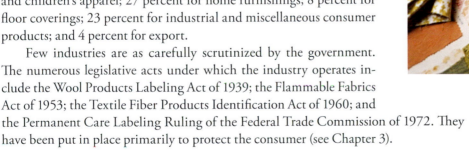

Few industries are as carefully scrutinized by the government. The numerous legislative acts under which the industry operates include the Wool Products Labeling Act of 1939; the Flammable Fabrics Act of 1953; the Textile Fiber Products Identification Act of 1960; and the Permanent Care Labeling Ruling of the Federal Trade Commission of 1972. They have been put in place primarily to protect the consumer (see Chapter 3).

PRIMARY AND SECONDARY SOURCES OF FABRIC

The textiles industry is made up of primary and secondary sources. Primary sources, such as mills or converters, make or create the materials; secondary sources, such as jobbers and retailers, are merely responsible for selling fabric.

Mills

Mills are the giants of the industry. They are **vertically integrated**, which means that they not only manufacture the fabrics, but also produce the yarns and apply the necessary finishes (functional and decorative enhancements) to improve the fabrics. These operations produce woven or knitted fabrics, or both. The larger U.S. mills are primarily located in the South, with the major ones in North and South Carolina.

The major vertically integrated mills include Avondale Mills, Cone Mills Corporation, and Milliken & Company.

The mills sell their goods to a variety of users, including converters, manufacturers, and designers of apparel and home fashions; jobbers or wholesalers; and retailers.

Converters

Converters are the intermediaries between the mills and their customers. These companies buy **greige goods** (gray unfinished fabrics) from the mills and then have them dyed, printed, and finished according to the specifications and directions of designers and manufacturers of apparel and home fashions. Their flexibility allows them to address the current needs of the fashion industry in terms of colors, patterns, and finishes.

Importers

As with finished garments, fabrics are being produced in many parts of the globe and are then imported into the United States. There are two types of textile importing companies: the **direct importer** and the **import mill**. Direct importers buy finished fabrics or manufactured textile products, such as clothing or soft luggage, and bring them into the United States. An import mill is a foreign company that owns textile machinery and makes the fabric (or yarns) that is then exported to the United States.

Although the greatest amount of fabric is imported from the Far East, fabrics are imported from other parts of the world as well.

Jobbers

This industry segment buys fabrics primarily from the mills and converters, with occasional purchases from garment manufacturers who no longer have the need for goods that were purchased. **Jobbers** deal in small quantities and are able to dispose of **mill overruns**, a term used to describe more fabric than was originally specified, fabric no longer needed by garment producers, discontinued fabrics, and some current materials. Their customers are the custom tailors whose needs are limited, furniture upholsterers, and manufacturers who produce very small quantities. Jobbers are primarily located in large textile and garment centers such as New York City, Atlanta, Chicago, Dallas, and Los Angeles.

Retailers

Although the home sewing business has declined in recent years, there is still a need for stores that sell to the ultimate consumer. They buy in small quantities that include mill overruns, closeouts, and the newest fabrics. Many of these retailers are mom-and-pop stores, with some chain operations found in the industry.

FROM FIBER TO FABRIC

Five elements are involved in the production of fabrics: fibers, yarns, structure, color, and finish. Fibers are usually twisted together and spun into yarns. Yarns are either woven or knit to form a fabric (structure). Color is added to enhance the fabric's appeal, and a finish is applied to make the fabric suitable for its intended use.

It is important for a designer to understand that each of these elements provides the fabric with certain basic characteristics or properties. If any part is changed, the result would be a different fabric—perhaps making it unsuitable for the specific end use. For example, by blending or combining two or more fibers, characteristics of each may be achieved in a single fabric. A blend of cotton and polyester provides the wearer the coolness of cotton and the ease of laundering of the polyester. Table 8.1 includes the four classifications of properties: aesthetics, durability, comfort, and safety.

Fibers

Fibers are the basic ingredients of fabrics and are classified into two broad categories: **natural** and **manufactured**. Natural fibers are derived from plants, animals, or minerals, and include cotton, flax, wool, or silk. Manufactured fibers are chemically produced through petroleum-based cellulosic or rubber and mineral bases. Each fiber has characteristics that makes it suitable for various uses. The popularity of a fiber at any given time is determined not by its inherent characteristics but by demand.

Natural Fibers

Cotton and flax are the major vegetable fibers used in the production of apparel and home fashions. **Wool** and **silk** are the two most important fibers derived from animals. Other natural fibers include **hemp**, **ramie**, and **jute**. **Specialty hair** fibers, such as cashmere, alpaca, vicuna, camel's hair, angora, and mohair play less important roles because of their high cost.

COTTON Consumer purchases of cotton merchandise continue to increase at record levels. Once threatened by the manufactured fibers, consumer demand has made

Table 8.1

CATEGORIES OF FIBER PERFORMANCE PROPERTIES

Aesthetics	Durability	Comfort	Safety
Properties relating to visual effects as well as those perceived by touch	*Properties relating to resistance to wear and destruction in use*	*Properties relating to physical comfort*	*Properties relating to avoidance of danger or risk of injury*
Flexibility	Abrasion resistance	Absorbency	Nonflammability
Hand (feel)	Chemical effects	Cover	
Luster	Environmental conditions	Elasticity	
Pilling	Strength	Wicking	
Resiliency			
Specific gravity			
Static electricity			
Thermoplasticity			

Leading producers of cotton include the United States, the People's Republic of China, Russia, India, and Egypt.

it today's most widely used fiber. Most cotton comes from the southern part of the United States, but significant amounts are being produced in other countries. China ranks second in the world, and Russia third. India, Egypt, Mexico, and Brazil are also important cotton-producing nations.

Seedlings emerge about one week after planting and flower in approximately four to six weeks. The flowers ripen and fall off the plants in a few days, leaving a small ovary that matures into a cotton boll. Once the boll expands, it splits and produces a fuzzy, puffy substance. When the cotton is ready for picking, it is mechanically harvested. Ginning, the next stage, separates the fiber from the seeds. After ginning, the fiber is classified and graded. The class of fiber depends on its length, which runs anywhere from ⅜ to 2½ inches, quality, and fineness. The fiber is then turned into fabric using many of the various techniques discussed later in this chapter.

FLAX The long fibers taken from the stems of flax plants are processed and made into the fabric called **linen**, the oldest known textile fabric. Unlike cotton, linen is not produced in the United States, but the United States is a chief user of the fiber. Russia, France, Belgium, Ireland, Egypt, Poland, and Italy are the major linen-producing countries. Linen's prominence was rivaled only by the introduction of cotton, which was less expensive and more versatile.

The flax fiber is removed from the stalk through a process that is called **retting**. Retting is achieved by natural means, such as placing the stalks on the grass (dew retting), submerging them in water, or using chemicals. Once loosened, the stalks are broken and *skutched*, a term that describes taking the flax from the stalk. They are then separated according to fiber lengths by a hackling process that combs and straightens the fiber, which is then spun into yarn.

Even though it wrinkles easily, linen remains a favorite for clothing worn in warm climates because it is extremely cool and lightweight. Manufacturers now offer softer "washed" linens, which have a relaxed texture that requires less care.

WOOL The Wool Products Labeling Act defines wool as "the fiber from the fleece of sheep or lamb or the hair of the angora or cashmere goat." The most significant quan-

Flax comes from the stem or stalk of the flax plant and is harvested by pulling the entire plant from the ground.

The best-quality wool comes from the sides and shoulder of the sheep; the poorest comes from the lower legs.

tity of wool comes from domesticated sheep. Wool is particularly easy to produce because approximately one year after shearing, the sheep is again ready to deliver a brand-new crop of raw material.

Sheep are raised all over the world, with Australia, South Africa, Great Britain, Russia, and the United States as major wool-producing countries.

After the fleece has been sheared and is ready for processing, it is graded according to the length of its staple, which generally ranges from 1 to 16 inches, and fineness. It is then sorted and separated into grades, cleansed by a scouring process, and combed to increase smoothness and strength. Any wool that is sheared at eight months or earlier is classified as lamb's wool, an extremely soft and lustrous fiber.

Properties such as absorbency, elasticity, and density help to provide warmth and make wool a favorite cold-weather fiber.

Silk is a continuous strand of two filaments cemented together, forming the cocoon of the silkworm.

Pashima, a blend of the finest cashmere and silk, in a 70/30 combination, is one of the most luxurious fabrics in the world. It has become the fiber of choice for high-quality scarves of all sizes and shapes. The best characteristics of cashmere and silk give this fabric a soft and drapable hand like that of no other textile.

SILK The only natural fiber that is several hundred yards long is silk. It is a filament fiber produced by the silkworm during the building of its cocoon. Strands measuring as long as 1,600 yards can be unwound or reeled and used to produce fine silks. A coarser, short-fiber silk, which must be spun to produce yarn, comes from a wild species and is called *tussah silk*. By far the greatest amount of silk is cultivated, and its vast production is carefully controlled to ensure fine yarn. Other varieties of silk include *douppioni*, a rough, uneven textured fiber, and *waste silk*, short fibers that come from damaged cocoons and must be spun into yarn like cotton or flax.

Silk fibers are extremely strong, have a high lustrous appearance, and provide elegance to any garment designed for a silk fabric.

Japan continues to be the world's leading producer of silk, followed by China, Korea, Italy, and India. Silk is one of the few fibers not produced in the United States.

Manufactured (or Man-Made) Fibers

As early as the mid-1800s the quest for laboratory-created fibers had begun. Hilaire de Chardonnet, a native of France, experimented and ultimately developed an **artificial silk** known as **rayon**. Through the purification and breaking down of wood pulp and cotton linters (the fuzzy by-products of cotton) into liquid form, scientists formed this new, cellulose-based fiber.

Manufactured fibers are made when a thick chemical substance is forced through tiny holes in a metal device called a **spinnerette**, which resembles a shower head. The fine streams of liquid are extruded into a bath and solidified into filament fibers. The number of holes in the spinnerette ranges from as few as 10 to as many as 10,000. The shape, number, and size of the holes in the spinnerette vary with the desired filament fiber and yarn.

As the filament emerges from the spinnerette, the fibers are solidified. Three methods are used to extrude and harden the fibers, depending on the chemical composition of the solution. These methods are **wet spinning**, **dry spinning**, and **melt spinning**. As the filament hardens, it is stretched to reduce its diameter. This also increases the strength of the fiber and stabilizes its ability to stretch without breaking.

One of the trailblazers in the production of manufactured fibers is E.I. DuPont de Nemours & Company, Inc. Its development of nylon and other fibers revolutionized the textile industry. A profile of the company is included in a World of Fashion Profile.

Manufactured fibers are referred to by the **generic name** established by the **Federal Trade Commission**. The fiber manufacturer identifies a **trademark** in order for its fibers to be distinguished from generic fibers produced by other fiber manufacturers. Acetate, acrylic nylon, rayon, and spandex are examples of generic names. Creslan® is the registered trademark for acrylic produced by American Cyanamid Company, and Lycra is the registered trademark for spandex produced by E.I. DuPont. Table 8.2 lists trade names, generic class, and manufacturers.

MICROFIBERS During the 1990s, technological advances made it possible to produce fibers, such as polyester, nylon, and acrylic, in diameters finer than silk. The fine fibers are called **microfibers**. Fabrics made from microfibers are extremely soft and drapable and are almost indistinguishable from silk.

LYOCEL: FIBER OF THE FUTURE Produced from the cellulose of wood pulp, lyocel (known commonly by its trade name of Tencel) is natural in origin. It has unique properties and is

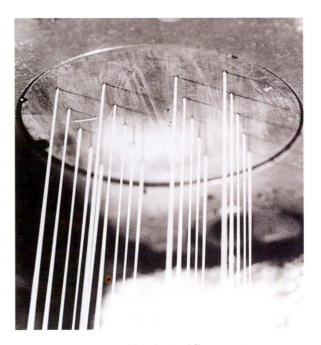

Manufactured fibers are produced by forcing liquid through a device called a spinnerette.

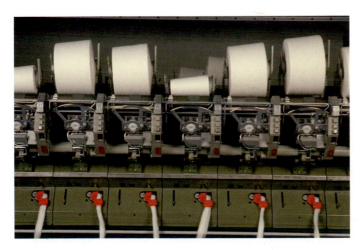

Manufactured yarn is placed on spools ready for further processing.

Yarns being processed for use in fabrics.

THE DUPONT COMPANY

On October 28, 1938, at a *New York Herald Tribune* forum at the soon-to-be-opened New York's World's Fair, DuPont announced the name of a new fiber—nylon. This discovery soon dramatically changed the world of fashion. Not only did DuPont revolutionize the hosiery industry, but it went on to develop other fibers with major implications for the textile industry.

In 1951, it offered Orlon and Dacron. In 1952, these fibers were successfully blended with cotton to give the world never-before-known comfort and ease of care. It was not long before French fashion designers began to utilize nylon and Orlon in combination with high-quality natural fibers. This was the type of

recognition that the manufactured fiber industry needed to market its products to the fashion industry.

To demonstrate the benefits of these new fibers, DuPont promoted them in many unusual ways. To convince the menswear market of the value of Dacron, it had one of its marketing men wear a Dacron polyester suit for 67 days without pressing it. When it was time to launder the suit, DuPont had the man jump, suit and all, into a swimming pool. When he emerged from the pool, the suit was tossed into a dryer from which it emerged wrinkle-free. The rest is history.

Before DuPont's introduction of Lycra spandex, stretch control of fabrics was difficult. With the stretch and recovery

characteristics of the new fiber, the swimsuit and undergarment industries were revolutionized. Soon, renowned designers were using Lycra fabrics in their collections. Today they are regularly used by Donna Karan, Nicole Miller, and Norma Kamali.

Other fiber innovations included Teflon, used not only for cookware but also as a coating on rainwear, and Micromattique, a fiber that most closely resembles silk.

DuPont's pioneering discoveries in the fiber field have led the way for fashion producers to utilize manufactured fibers in their collections and to treat them with the same "dignity" afforded natural fibers.

available in a wide variety of fabric constructions. Its key feature is its soft and luxurious drape. Produced by Acordis, Tencel promises to launch a new era in fiber manufacturing that bridges the gap between nature and technology.

Yarns

Yarns are groups of fibers twisted together to form a continuous strand. All textile fabrics are produced from yarns. The process is called **spinning**. Yarns are woven or knitted to form a textile fabric. Before the actual spinning takes place, the fibers must be cleansed and refined to rid them of impurities or oils that will affect appearance and durability. Once the fibers have been cleansed and refined, they may be spun into yarn.

There are two main categories of yarns: **spun** and **filament**. Spun yarns are short lengths of fiber twisted or spun to hold them together. Filament yarns are composed of continuous strands of fiber that may be miles long. Manufactured fibers can be produced in any length desired.

Various spinning methods are used, with ring spinning the most common in the United States. Open-end spinning is a newer system that is three to five times faster, with air jet being the fastest, at a rate that is seven to ten times that of the conventional ring technique.

Constructing Fabrics

Two major methods are used in the process of turning yarn into fabric: **weaving** and **knitting**. For some fabrics, known as **nonwovens**, the fiber or stock is turned into a fabric without first producing the yarn. The most important of these processes are **felting** and **bonding**. The former matts fibers into a web that is held together with additives;

Table 8.2

SELECTED FIBER TRADE NAMES

Trade Name	Generic Class	Producer
A.C.E.	polyester	AlliedSignal Fibers
Acrilan	acrylic	Monsanto Chemical Company
Anso	nylon	AlliedSignal Fibers
Antron	nylon	E.I. DuPont de Nemours & Company, Inc.
Biokryl	acrylic	Mann Industries, Inc.
Caprolan	nylon	AlliedSignal Fibers
Celebrate	acetate	Hoechst Celanese Corporation
Chromspun	acetate	Eastman Chemical Products, Inc.
Cordura	nylon	E.I. DuPont de Nemours & Company, Inc.
Crepeset	nylon	BASF Corporation
Creslan	acrylic	American Cyanamid Company (Cytec Industries, Inc.)
Cumuloft	nylon	Monsanto Chemical Company
Dacron	polyester	E.I. DuPont de Nemours & Company, Inc.
Estron	acetate	Eastman Chemical Products, Inc.
Fortrel	polyester	Wellman, Inc.
Glospan	spandex	Globe Manufacturing Company
Golden Glow	polyester	BASF Corporation
Golden Touch	polyester	BASF Corporation
Hollofil	polyester	E.I. DuPont de Nemours & Company, Inc.
Hydrofil	nylon	AlliedSignal Fibers
Lurex	metallic	Metal Film Company
Lycra	spandex	E.I. DuPont de Nemours & Company, Inc.
Micromattique	polyester	E.I. DuPont de Nemours & Company, Inc.
MicroSpun	polyester	Wellman, Inc.
MicroSupreme	acrylic	American Cyanamid Company (Cytec Industries, Inc.)
Modal	rayon (HWM)	Lenzing Fibers Corporation
Nega-Stat	polyester	E.I. DuPont de Nemours & Company, Inc.
Pa-Qel	acrylic	Monsanto Chemical Company
Pil-Trol	acrylic	Monsanto Chemical Company
Resistat	nylon	BASF Corporation
SEF	modacrylic	Monsanto Chemical Company
Silky Touch	nylon	BASF Corporation
Softglow	nylon	BASF Corporation
Stainmaster	nylon	E.I. DuPont de Nemours & Company, Inc.
Supplex	nylon	E.I. DuPont de Nemours & Company, Inc.
Tactesse	nylon	ICI Fibers, Inc.
Tencel	lyocel	Acordis
Timbrelle	nylon	ICI Fibers, Inc.
Ultron	nylon	Monsanto Chemical Company
WearDated	nylon	Monsanto Chemical Company
Worry Free	nylon	AlliedSignal Fibers
Zefkrome	acrylic	Mann Industries, Inc.
Zefran	acrylic	Mann Industries, Inc.
Zeftron	nylon	BASF Corporation

Top: Textiles being handwoven on a simple loom.
Bottom: Today, the computer plays a major role in weaving textiles.

the latter forms webs from either filament fibers that are then layered, or loose staples that are plied together by numerous means.

Weaving

Interlacing two or more sets of yarns at right angles produces woven fabrics. The stronger yarns are called **warps** and are placed lengthwise on the loom. The **fillings**, or cross-wise yarns, also called **wefts**, are then interlaced with the warp yarns. The range of weaves runs from the plain weave, which is the simplest, to the **jacquard**, from which the most intricate patterns are created.

The different techniques not only produce fabrics that have different appearances, but also impart different characteristics.

PLAIN WEAVE The most often used weave, the **plain weave** produces fabrics that range from sheer to heavy. Well-known fabrics include gauze, gingham, taffeta, burlap, and canvas. Each warp yarn passes alternately over and then under one filling yarn. A variation of the plain weave is the **basket weave**, which interlaces two or more sets of yarns as one yarn. If a two-by-two basket is desired, two sets of yarns are interlaced with two sets of fillings. This variation of the plain weave imparts a decorative effect in the fabric. Because of the frequent interlacings of the yarns, plain woven fabrics tend to wrinkle more.

TWILL WEAVE When the need for durability is important, such as for work clothes, the **twill weave** is often the choice. The construction produces a diagonal line that runs upward to the right or left. This creates a **herringbone pattern**. Denim is produced using the twill weave.

a. The plain weave is the simplest method of weaving.
b. The basket weave is a variation of the plain weave.
c. The satin weave is used when a shiny fabric is desired.
d. The twill weave produces a diagonal design.

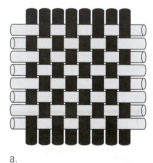

a.

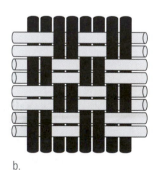

b.

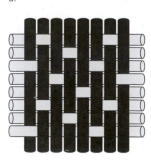

c.

d.

SATIN WEAVE If a smooth, shiny-surfaced fabric is desired, it may be achieved with the **satin weave**. By floating one yarn over as few as 4 or as many as 12 yarns before interlacing them, a lustrous surface results. *Satin* is the name of the fabric woven by this method using filament yarns. It is lustrous and smooth. *Sateen* is a durable cotton fabric made with spun yarn, but is not as lustrous. Although the shiny surface has been achieved, long floats of the yarn create a fabric with inferior wearing quality. In addition, the use of filament yarns create a rough surface and contribute to filaments breaking. Satin-woven fabrics are used in apparel where durability is not important, such as evening wear and dresses.

PILE WEAVE When a plush surface is desired, the **pile weave** is used. Its production requires three sets of yarns: a regular set of warps, a regular set of filling yarns, and an additional set—either warps or filling yarns—that form the dimensional surface. The raised surfaces are either left alone, leaving a looped appearance as in terry cloth, or cut, as in the case of velvet.

DOBBY WEAVE If the desired fabric is to feature a small, geometric pattern, the **dobby weave** is the construction choice. Using a dobby loom, fabrics such as birdseye piqué, found in some cotton apparel, is produced.

JACQUARD WEAVE The most intricate weave is the jacquard. It is a complicated procedure that requires a special loom called the jacquard loom, originally invented in 1805. A series of punched cards were laced together to control the warp yarns and achieve the desired pattern. The jacquard loom required a large space and a very high ceiling. Today, the computer has simplified production. Although computerized jacquard looms are faster than the original, they still operate more slowly than other looms. As a result, fabrics produced this way, such as brocades and damasks, are generally quite expensive.

Knitting

Interlooping yarns produces a knitted fabric. Specifically, loops are formed and new loops are then drawn through the preceding ones. The continuous addition of loops creates a knitted fabric. Knitting may be accomplished by hand or machine, each producing a different type of knitted material. Unlike weaving, which requires two or more sets of yarns, knitting is accomplished by using one continuous, single yarn. The appearance of a knitted fabric is accomplished by the type of machinery used, the density of the yarns, the size of the needles, and the spacing of the stitches.

Basically, there are two types of knitting techniques: **weft knitting** and **warp knitting**. Knitted goods that are produced horizontally are weft knitted, with the stitches running from side to side for the width of the fabric, and are interlooped with each succeeding row. Examples of weft knits are the fabrics used for sweaters and hosiery. Construction takes place on either flat or circular knitting machines.

The jacquard loom produces intricate patterns.

Sophisticated machines knit fabrics quickly and efficiently.

In warp knitting, large numbers of yarns are used to make the fabric. Each yarn is looped around a single needle to form loops that are vertically attached to other loops.

The sophistication of today's equipment enables manufacturers to produce a vast array of goods using yarns that run from the finest to the densest. Single jersey, double jersey, and intricate jacquard knits are easily manufactured with state-of-the-art knitting machines. Computer-controlled and electronic machines enable the industry to design a vast array of fabrics within a few minutes.

Computer-Aided Design (CAD)

In the fashion industry, a wealth of patterned materials are made available to apparel and home furnishing designers for use in their collections. Often, the fabric's patterns give the garments and home fashions their appeal. To meet the demands of the apparel and home fashions industries' creative forces, the fabric industry is always involved in the development of new designs that would enhance the finished products.

Until recent years, fabric designers painstakingly hand rendered their designs. With pen and ink and a vast array of paints, they produced the patterns on paper. This was a time-consuming task, because the patterns had to be depicted as repeats on a large board to show how they would look as fabric.

Today, technology enables the process to be significantly shortened. With the use of the computer and a number of different software packages, the designs can be accomplished in a matter of a few hours. These systems, known as **CAD**, or **computer-aided design**, have revolutionized the industry. They are available in a broad range of programs, from the simplest to the most sophisticated.

Some of the systems used in the textile industry include Monarch Computex, the leading provider of Macintosh-based CAD systems, Pointcarré Weave, Monarch Design Studio, Primavision, Arabesque, and Weavette. Although they each provide

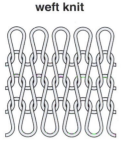

weft knit

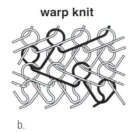

warp knit

a. Weft knitting produces a horizontal material. b. Warp knitting involves producing fabric in which loops are vertically attached.

b.

a.

Designs can be created on CAD, or computer-aided design, systems in a matter of a few hours.

specific features that are unique to their systems, collectively they are used for every aspect of the design process.

Coloring Fabrics

The most important element in a textile product may very well be color. A wrong color could easily hamper sales. Color can sell an inferior fabric or make the most desirable fabric unmarketable. There are two methods of applying color during the various stages of fabric production: **dyeing** and **printing**.

Dyeing Fabrics

Solid-colored fabrics and sometimes multicolored designs, such as plaids, are achieved by dyeing. Today's textile industry has a large number of dyes available to satisfy every company's requirements. Aside from the ability to properly impregnate color with specific intensities, each dye has specific characteristics that determine its most appropriate uses.

The dye selected must be the best suited for the ultimate use of the product by the consumer. For example, when laundering is a chief benefit of a garment, its **colorfastness** must be guaranteed. That is, the color must not bleed or run. **Fading** is yet another factor to be considered, especially when exposure to sunlight is likely, as

Table 8.3

GENERAL CLASSIFICATIONS OF DYES AND THEIR IMPORTANT CHARACTERISTICS

Type of Dye	Dye Characteristics
Acid	Excellent for bright colors, not fast to washing, withstands dry cleaning.
Basic	Good to achieve bright shades, generally colorfast to laundering and light, crock resistant.
Chrome	Excellent colorfastness, dull color.
Direct	Poor colorfastness to light and washing, generally dry cleanable.
Disperse	Colorfastness varies according to fiber used, colorfast to crocking, generally dry cleanable.
Fiber reactive	Perfect for bright colors, good fastness to color except when used in chlorine.
Napthol	Bright colors, color fastness to light varies, colorfast to sunlight and laundering.

with fabrics used for draperies. Without careful attention to the specific end use, customer returns can be assured. Table 8.3 lists some of the general classifications of dyes and their important characteristics to the apparel and home fashion industries.

Dyeing can be accomplished at any stage during textile manufacturing.

- Fibers may be dyed—stock dyeing.

- Yarns may be dyed-yarn dyeing.

- Fabrics may be dyed—piece dyeing.

- Garments may be dyed—garment dyeing.

FIBER OR STOCK DYEING When short fibers, or stock, are placed in a dye bath before they are spun into yarn, they are being fiber or **stock dyed**. This process is generally restricted to woolen materials. Its advantage is the degree of color penetration that can be achieved. The color is locked into the yarns, making them colorfast. One problem with fiber or stock dyeing is that color is selected in the earliest stages of manufacturing, before consumer demand has been assessed.

Adding color directly to the chemical solution used to produce manufactured fibers is a special method of coloring fibers, called **solution dyeing**. Fabrics made from solution-dyed yarns are practically fade proof and are therefore suitable for draperies. However, because solution-dyed materials are available in only a limited range of colors, the method is not widely used on fabrics slated for fashion apparel.

YARN DYEING Color can also be added after the fibers have been spun into yarn. This allows a little more time for fashion considerations to influence selection. **Yarn dyeing** is less expensive than stock dyeing, but more costly than piece dyeing. Examples of yarn-dyed fabrics are gingham, madras, and brocade.

Occasionally solid-colored fabrics are yarn-dyed instead of piece-dyed because yarn dyeing results in better dye penetration and improved colorfastness. A good example is fabrics used for upholstery.

PIECE DYEING Adding color to a fabric is called **piece dyeing**. Coloring at this stage eliminates some risk because you are dyeing the piece goods to order for a definite sale. Its advantage is to postpone the color decision as long as possible, but the penetration of the dye is not as dense as in the techniques discussed earlier.

Fabric from the dye bath is ready for additional finishing.

When a fabric is made of two or more different fibers and two color effects are desired, the results may be achieved by a process called **cross-dyeing**. Because dyes react differently with different fibers, the dyes can be put into the same dye bath so that one dye will color one fiber and another the second fiber. In a fabric that is rayon and polyester, for example, one dye in the dye bath will have affinity for the rayon, the other for the polyester. The major advantage of cross-dyeing is that it is an inexpensive technique when compared with yarn dyeing, which would have otherwise been used to achieve the various patterns.

GARMENT DYEING When it is necessary to apply color as late as possible, entire garments may be dyed. In this way when a retailer wants a specific color within a modest time frame, the manufacturer can dye the garments to order. For example, Benetton stocks its inventory, void of color, and within a matter of three weeks or less, they can accommodate any color asked for by its stores. By using **garment dyeing**, Benetton avoids the possibility of being left with colors that do not sell.

Printing Fabrics

Patterns may be applied to fabrics by a number of printing processes. Artists carefully prepare designs on paper or with the aid of computer programs, which must then be adapted for use on fabrics.

The oldest technique for pattern application is painting designs directly on fabric. Although it is not frequently used, it is found in the collections where limited quantities are produced. Maria Snyder, a New York-based designer of couture-quality merchandise, is known for her hand-painted applications. Each one is painstakingly reproduced on silks and other fibers by craftspeople who follow her original design.

The majority of patterns that appear on fabrics are printed by one of three commercial methods: screen printing, roller printing, and heat-transfer printing.

SCREEN PRINTING Although it is one of the oldest printing processes, **screen printing** is still extensively used today in the production of fashion-oriented fabrics.

Fabric being hand-screen printed.

The goods may be hand- or roller-screen printed, the latter providing the speed necessary to accommodate large-scale fabric production. At some manufacturers who use screen-printed materials in their garments, the automated roller-screen method is used when production requirements are significant. Hand-screening is the choice when limited quantities are ordered.

In both cases, an artist designs the print and transfers it onto one or more screens made of nylon, polyester, or metal tightly mounted on a wooden or metal frame. Because screens were originally made of silk, the process was called **silk screening**. A film that adheres to the screen is cut away wherever the color must penetrate. Print paste is poured into the frame and forced through the screen onto the fabric passing under each screen. This is repeated until all of the colors have been applied. The number of screens depends on the different colors in the pattern. For a six-color job, six screens would be needed.

There are three ways of making screen prints: **hand-screen printing**, **automatic-screen printing** (flat-bed screen printing), and **rotary screen printing**.

Rotary screen printing, which is used today, is capable of printing more than 100 yards of cloth in one minute. Dye is fed inside the screens and forced through tiny holes onto the fabric. Each cylinder on a printing machine adds a different color and a different part of the pattern. Modern technology enables the textile industry to print high-quality fabrics in this manner and, with carefully selected dyes, colors will not fade.

ROLLER PRINTING In **roller printing**, copper-plated rollers are engraved with patterns for each color. If eight colors are to be used in the design, eight different rollers will be engraved, each representing a different part of the pattern. The rollers, which have been etched with a photoengraving process, rotate through a dye bath and transfer dye onto the fabric. After all of the colors have been applied, the print is complete. Roller printing is best suited for long production runs of the same pattern. It is used primarily for woven fabrics and not for knits because of the resulting fabric tension.

For large production needs, rotary screen printing is employed.

HEAT-TRANSFER PRINTING With **heat-transfer printing**, patterns are first printed onto paper and then transferred onto fabric. The paper and the fabric are rolled together under pressure at high temperatures to achieve the transfer.

The main advantage is cost. It is less expensive to use than the other techniques because it requires a considerably smaller investment in equipment. Heat-transfer printing involves printing designs on fabrics, garment parts, or whole garments. Individuals who have purchased patterns and have transferred them onto T-shirts at home with an iron have basically performed heat-transfer printing.

Finishing Fabrics

Finishing is the final treatment of the fabric that will enhance both its performance and its aesthetics and make it suitable for its intended end use. Fabrics can be made shrinkproof, softer, water repellent, or wrinkle resistant. Finishes can be grouped as either chemical or mechanical.

A chemical finish can consist of bleaching or mercerization for cotton. Mercerization of cotton will improve luster and add strength to the fabric. A mechanical finish includes brushing or napping to produce a fuzzy surface.

Computers are used to apply functional and fashionable finishes to fabrics.

Shrinkage-resistant finishes, such as Sanforization, provide comfort by helping to maintain the fit of a garment. Scotchguard is the name of a soil-resistant finish for upholstered furniture, and Zepel is the name of a water-repellent finish for raincoats. Some finishes, such as glazing, polishing, or embossing, improve the aesthetics of a fabric.

Table 8.4 lists some of the finishes that enhance appearance.

Finishes provide the consumer with easy-to-care-for fabrics that require a minimum amount of ironing or pressing after the garment is worn and cleaned. Durable

Table 8.4

FINISHES TO ENHANCE APPEARANCE

Finish	Process
Calendering	An ironing process that produces a smoother, stiffer, polished fabric.
Delustering	Removing unwanted sheen with chemical treatment.
Embossing	Creating a dimensional design with engraved rollers.
Flocking	Using adhesives to apply short fibers to fabrics, giving them a plush effect.
Fulling	Scouring and laundering wool to make it more compact.
Mercerization	Using sodium hydroxide to increase sheen, strength, and absorbency in cotton fabrics.
Moireing	Achieving a watermarked effect by using etched rollers.
Napping	Brushing the surface of the fabric to raise the surface.
Plisseing	Adding a crinkled effect by pasting sodium hydroxide onto fabric, resulting in shrinkage and thus a crinkled look.
Shearing	Evening pile-woven fabrics through the use of a machine that resembles a lawn mower.
Singeing	Smoothing a fabric's surface by carefully passing it over a gas flame to burn off tiny fibers.

Table 8.5

FINISHES TO IMPROVE OR INCREASE FUNCTION

Finish	Process
Antistatic	Chemical application that prevents clinging.
Durable press	The use of resins and heat to help keep a garment's shape, even after laundering.
Flame retardency	Chemical treatment to make fabrics resistant to burning.
Permanent press	An application of heat, resins, or liquid ammonia to permanently hold creases or pleats.
Preshrinking	Different processes used to reduce shrinkage; best known is Sanforizing.
Sizing	Applying starches to add stiffness, body, and weight to fabric.
Water repellent	A special finish that helps fabric repel water but still lets air flow through.

press or permanent press is a well-known care finish. Table 8.5 identifies finishes to improve or increase function.

MARKETING TEXTILES

As with any other segment of the fashion world, textiles must be marketed to capture the attention of fabric buyers and designers, and the ultimate user of the product—the consumer. Of significant importance to the textile industry are the trade associations and trade expositions. They each assist the producers in reaching appropriate markets.

Trade Associations

Trade associations are groups that are responsible for publicizing the efforts of their industries and providing research materials for their members. A complete list of trade associations is included in Appendix 2.

Cotton Incorporated and the National Cotton Council are concerned with the U.S. cotton industry. The former organization is responsible for increasing the retail

THE INTERNATIONAL WOOL SECRETARIAT

In 1937, the wool growers of the southern hemisphere founded the International Wool Secretariat (IWS). Its goal is to promote and improve the performance of wool all over the world. Headquartered in London, the organization has fully staffed offices in 32 countries. It is the broadest based international fiber network supplying technology to the industry.

The U.S. branch, the Wool Bureau, Inc., is headquartered in New York City, with a technical research facility in Woodbury, New York. Other centers are found in Italy, Holland, Japan, and Great Britain. The IWS uses computer links to rapidly disseminate information on new wool developments and to address processing problems.

In addition to technical research centers, the IWS maintains an International Wool Men's Wear Fashion Office in London, an International Wool Fashion Office for Women's Wear in Paris, and a Knitwear Styling Service in Delft, Holland. These offices offer significant information for fashion designers who use woolens.

The Woolmark symbol was created in 1964 to identify for the consumer wool yarn and wool products that meet high standards for strength, colorfastness, mothproofing, shrink resistance, and other qualities. More than 14,000 manufacturers in more than 50 countries are licensed to use the symbol. It has become an international standard of quality.

By working with spinners, weavers, knitters, and manufacturers, the IWS helps to expand public knowledge and use of wool, to develop new products and processes, to encourage the economical production of high-quality wool goods in apparel and home furnishings, and to coordinate the marketing of wool and wool products.

market share of U.S. cotton fiber, with its goal of enhancing the American consumer's preference for cotton and cotton-containing fabrics. The latter is the unifying force of the U.S. cotton industry's seven segments: producers, ginners, warehouse workers, merchants, cottonseed crushers, cooperatives, and textile manufacturers.

The Wool Secretariat, on the other hand, is an internationally based organization that promotes wool all over the world. Some of the group's activities are outlined in a World of Fashion Profile.

Trade Expositions

With the vast number of fiber producers, fabric manufacturers, and wholesalers in the world, the need to bring them together for the purposes of showing and selling their lines has become increasingly more important. Because they are located throughout the world, it is generally too costly and time-consuming for purchasers to visit all of the important textile centers. The trade exposition has become an important vehicle for enabling the various components of the fashion industry to interface with each other. At these shows, row after row of vendors are housed in booths that feature their sample lines. Sales representatives benefit from this centralized meeting place by reaching prospective customers they might not have ever known to be potential users of their products. The buyers, on the other hand, can, in a short time, compare the offerings of several competing vendors.

The number of textile expositions that are held all over the world continues to grow. A look at Table 6.2, International Trade Expositions, immediately reveals that these events are held in every corner of the globe. In cities such as Barcelona, Singapore, Florence, Paris, Frankfurt, and New York, the textile expos are in full swing.

ADVERTISING AND PROMOTING TEXTILES

Advertising and promotional endeavors are directed toward both the industrial purchaser and the consumer. The efforts put forth by the industry are numerous and include both print and broadcast advertising.

a.

b.

c.

d.

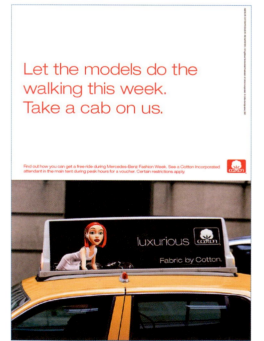

e.

a. Yarn cards show availability of colors and are used for marketing. b. Boards suggest ways in which fabrics can be used by potential purchasers for their collection. c. Presentation boards make dramatic statements for fabric usage. d. Line drawings, accompanied by fabric swatches, show end uses for fabrics. e. Industry advertisements are directed at manufacturers, designers, and consumers.

In terms of advertising, the fiber producers regularly develop campaigns that are found in both trade and consumer newspapers. In the trades, such as *Women's Wear Daily*, *Daily News Record*, and the *California Apparel News*, the targeted audiences are the designers, who select the fabrics to be used in their creations, and the retailers, who merchandise fashion items. Fiber producers are also advertising on television. By showing their fibers in television commercials, they are reaching the consumer market that might seek a particular fiber if sufficiently motivated.

Many companies also participate in cooperative advertising, in which they share the expense of a designer's ad, for example, when the fiber producer's name is mentioned. In this way, the fiber producer can "ride the coattails" of a famous designer or manufacturer.

Many promotions are also part of the fiber producer's marketing plan. DuPont, for example, produces a runway show featuring its Lycra spandex fiber and invites the designers to see how they can work it into their apparel collections. Cotton Incorporated regularly presents a fashion show at the Council of Fashion Designer's Seventh on Sixth event, in which it features full lines of clothing specially designed for the show. The attending designers and manufacturers are then able to see the potential for the fiber in their own lines. Not only do the fiber producers reach those in attendance, but the publicity received through media coverage gives them even more coverage.

The major fiber producers maintain their own staffs for advertising and promotion. When special events are planned, they often use outside resources.

CHAPTER HIGHLIGHTS

- The textile producer is the primary supplier of the fashion industry.

- The textile industry is comprised of industrial giants that perform all the processes necessary to produce fabric and are vertically integrated. Smaller organizations specialize in one specific aspect of textile development.

- Fibers are classified as natural, such as cotton, flax, wool, and silk, or manufactured, such as microfibers, polyester, and spandex.

- Fibers are spun into yarn or made into filaments.

- Yarns are primarily woven or knitted into fabric through a variety of means, the most widely used of which is weaving.

- Fibers, yarns, fabrics, or garments are then dyed; some fabrics are printed with designs that have been created by textile artists.

- A variety of finishes may improve fabric durability and attractiveness.

- To successfully market its offerings, the textile industry has established trade associations, each representing a specific subdivision of the field, and trade expositions, where vendors and purchasers meet to buy and sell.

IMPORTANT FASHION TERMINOLOGY AND CONCEPTS

artificial silk	greige (or gray) goods	printing
automatic-screen printing	hand-screen printing	ramie
basket weave	heat-transfer printing	rayon
bonding	hemp	retting
CAD (computer-aided design)	herringbone pattern	roller printing
	import mill	rotary screen printing
colorfastness	jacquard weave	satin weave
cotton	jobbers	screen printing
cross-dyeing	jute	silk
direct importer	knitting	silk screening
dobby weave	linen	solution dyeing
dry spinning	manufactured fibers	specialty hair fibers
dyeing	melt spinning	spinnerette
Federal Trade Commission	microfibers	spinning
felting	mill	spun yarn
filament yarn	mill overruns	stock dyeing
fillings	natural fibers	trademark
finishing	nonwovens	twill weave
flax	piece dyeing	vertical integration
garment dyeing	pile weave	warp knitting
generic name	plain weave	warps

weaving   wet spinning   yarns
weft knitting   wool
wefts   yarn dyeing

FOR REVIEW

1. Discuss the concept of vertical integration in textiles.
2. Where is the textile industry primarily located in the United States?
3. Differentiate between spun and filament yarns.
4. What type of loom is used when a large intricate pattern is needed for a fabric?
5. Distinguish between weft and warp knitting.
6. At which stage will dyeing provide the greatest amount of penetration for fibers?
7. Describe the procedure used in screen printing.
8. Why are finishes applied to fabrics?
9. What is the major advantage of linen to the wearer?
10. Why does the textile industry use trade expositions to sell its offerings?
11. How does Cotton Incorporated use the Seventh on Sixth promotion?
12. In the Point of View by David Grant Caplan how does he explain the relationship between nylon and spandex?

EXERCISES AND PROJECTS

1. Using narrow strips of paper, ¼ inch wide and 6 inches long, construct a plain weave, a twill weave, and a 5-float satin weave.
2. Scan the pages of fashion magazines and find five fashion-oriented cooperative ads that feature the fiber producer's name.
3. Contact one of the many textile trade associations to learn the specifics of its membership. Prepare a report featuring the services it offers.

WEB SITES

By accessing these Web sites, you will be able to gain broader knowledge and up-to-date information on materials related to this chapter.

Textile/Clothing Technology Corporation
   www.tc2.com/index.html
American Textile Manufacturers Institute
   www.americantextile.com
American Fiber Manufacturers Association, Inc.
   www.fibersource.com

The Case of the Fiber with an Image Problem

The rayon industry has always spent a great deal of money promoting its fiber. In its early years, the trade association responsible for building rayon's image concentrated on the product's appeal to the industrial market. Through extravagant theatrical productions, fashion manufacturers, designers, and retail merchandisers were made aware of the advantages of the rayon fiber. Many fashion producers and store buyers jumped on the bandwagon and included rayon in their merchandising plans.

Although the industrial market has accepted the merits of rayon, many household consumers still consider rayon a low-cost fiber used only to imitate natural fibers in the production of inexpensive garments. The industry is thus faced with an image problem.

At its last major conference, the association's membership had as its prime agenda item, "The Selling of Rayon to the Consumer." If top designers use the fiber and understand its advantages, how can the message be delivered to the public? There was a general agreement that the approach used to motivate market professionals could not be employed to attract consumer attention. There is simply no arena large enough to house the masses for such industrial extravaganzas. By the meeting's end, a solution to the problem had not been found.

question

How can the household consumer be motivated to consider rayon as a quality fashion fiber?

Pulling at Stretch Fibers' Roots

DAVID GRANT CAPLAN

New York—Aside from aerodynamic automobiles from General Motors and tiny televisions from RCA, another toy of tomorrow was on display at the 1939 New York World's Fair: women's stockings made from nylon, widely regarded as the first stretch fiber.

Although a patent had been issued to DuPont in 1938 for the new polymer, the synthetic fiber's splashy debut occurred at the chemical giant's "Wonder World of Chemistry" exhibit.

Led by Harvard University graduate Wallace Carothers, a team of DuPont researchers invented nylon 6,6—made from a chemical base known as polyamide 6,6.

Soon after nylon was introduced, it replaced silk and cotton as the fiber of choice for women's hosiery. Nylon may have cost more than silk, but it was more durable and easy to care for.

Nylon's run as the preeminent stretch fiber lasted until 1958, when DuPont chemist Joe Shivers invented "Fiber K," the world's first spandex, which the company later trademarked Lycra.

In 1959, spandex started to replace rubber in corsets. Women were bowled over by the fiber's ability to stretch up to 600 percent its original size and then spring back to its original form.

"The first end use that it revolutionized was pantyhose, allowing it to be more sheer than rubber would allow for," said Linda Kearns, DuPont's global brand manager for Lycra spandex. "In fact, I'm not sure if pantyhose were even possible without Lycra."

Shortly after Lycra spandex hit the stores, DuPont's competitors followed suit.

Globe Manufacturing Corp. (now RadiciSpandex Corp.) in 1962 began producing spandex, marketed as Glospan, at its facility in Fall River, Mass.

Two years later, Bayer Corp. in Germany began production of spandex under the Dorlastan moniker. The company's U.S. spandex production facility, located in Bushy Park, S.C., opened in 1995.

Jan Nolen, the Goose Creek, S.C.-based marketing and merchandising manager for Dorlastan, said spandex was rapidly accepted by shoppers.

"Consumers began to demand more of it because the rubber would deteriorate with age, as well as with wear and laundering," she said.

Prior to the launch of Glospan, Globe, which was founded in 1945, had primarily produced rubber thread.

Bill Girrier, vice president of sales and marketing at RadiciSpandex, said "the 15-year run we had with rubber thread had been good for us" but the advent of spandex upped the ante.

The company produced its last spool of rubber thread in 1998.

"Spandex enabled manufacturers to make a lighter-weight, sheerer fabric, so in the early Sixties we realized that we had to develop spandex of our own," he said.

Once corset manufacturers began using spandex, the fiber—which is always used in blends with other fibers—began its infiltration into other categories.

For example, DuPont said that Lycra spandex started to catch on in support

hose in 1962, swimwear in 1974, sheer pantyhose in 1979, activewear in the early-Eighties and ready-to-wear by the Nineties.

While DuPont was the first off the block in the race to turn the new fiber into a moneymaker, its competitors have followed at its heels.

"With great respect and humility to our big competitor, which is a market-maker, they created a lot of markets by showing people how they can do it," said RadiciSpandex's Girrier.

DuPont's Kearns said spandex has experienced "exponential growth in terms of its first use to now.

"For the first two or three decades of Lycra's existence, nylon was generally the companion fiber," she said. "Then, when it emerged into ready-to-wear its companion fibers became cotton, wool and polyester."

Kearns said Lycra was quickly embraced by consumers during its early years but encountered some resistance as it expanded into new categories.

"People really adopted the benefits of fit and comfort in its first uses of swimwear, hosiery and girdles and it was welcomed again with activewear," she said. "There was some uncertainty initially in the ready-to-wear area because it was a whole different paradigm—it was new companion fibers like cotton, wool and polyester."

Kearns said some consumers frowned upon spandex for sportswear and rtw because they considered the fiber appropriate only for foundation garments and activewear.

"When people thought of Lycra they thought of tight and shiny, whether it be bike shorts or bathing suits, but that's truly the nylon construction that makes things tight and shiny and not the Lycra at all," she said. "Just a little bit of Lycra in denim dresses, women's or men's shirts and suits really can maintain the overall look and feel . . . and add just a little bit more comfort and freedom of movement."

Despite spandex's growing presence in a number of categories, its makers believe there's still room for the business to grow.

"There is still rubber that is out there in some uses—in baby diapers, in socks—so there is still an opportunity for a rubber replacement," Kearns said. "We've got a lot of growth in diapers and we've got new technologies for these markets, in terms of film and polymers."

While spandex may have stolen the spotlight from its stretchy predecessor, nylon, the two enjoy today a symbiotic relationship.

"Nylon and spandex are absolutely complementary," said Rognoni Umberto, the Cesano Maderno, Italy-based marketing manager for nylon maker Nylstar. "The spandex gives [the garment] the stretch, but the nylon gives it the appearance and the touch."

Nylstar, which has a facility in Greensboro, N.C., is a joint venture between France's Rhodia and Italy's Snia created in 1994.

Bill Scott, business director of textile and automotive products for nylon maker BASF Corp. in Charlotte, N.C., said "nylon combined with Lycra is technically a very good marriage."

"Nylon takes dye well," he said. "You get the rich colors that intimate apparel wants to use so it's a very comfortable fit with spandex garments."

BASF began producing nylon in Germany shortly after DuPont's World's Fair launch and entered the U.S. market in the Fifties.

RadiciSpandex's Girrier said another synthetic fiber, acetate, meshes well with spandex.

"One of the big markets that added to the popularity of stretch was the acetate fabrics that so many blouses and skirts were made out of in the mid- and late-Nineties," he said.

On the polyester front, Wellman Inc. in 1965, then known as Wellman Combing Co., started to produce nylon and polyester staple fibers and plastic resins from recycled raw materials.

John Anderson, the vice president of marketing for Wellman's fibers groups, pointed out that the company is able to produce stretch properties in fibers other than spandex.

"In a lot of the textured woven offerings that are out there," he said, "our customers are achieving stretch through using the stretch potential inherent in regular polyester."

Women's Wear Daily, June 12, 2001

Fiber Development in the 21st Century

SHARON BURKE AND KATHY SMITH

In barely a century, synthetic fibers revolutionized the textile industry. Man-made fiber research was initially focused on mimicking the natural fibers they replaced. But today, rapidly expanding know-how and extensive R&D have reinvented our expectations of fiber, fabric, and clothing. Engineered fibers of the future will have unique qualities all their own.

The exciting challenge for the twenty-first century is to design, produce and deliver—"to order"—solutions to consumer needs. The seeds for development and commercialization of "smart" fibers have

been sewn, and the trends are already underway.

An example of the evolution of fiber development specific to consumer needs in intimate apparel is DuPont's Lycra. Lycra was first introduced as fiber K in 1959, and shapewear manufacturers were immediately impressed with its unique elasticity, recovery, and durability compared to those qualities in the rubber fiber then in use. Women loved the new level of lightweight support that Lycra brought to lingerie. Today, rubber has all but been replaced by this modern elastane fiber.

Lycra technology has evolved since its early days, and a new generation of shapewear, called Lycra Soft, with exceptionally soft, nonbinding fit, was introduced at Sears in time for the 1997 holiday season.

Gone is the notion that garments are smart only because they make the wearer look fashionable. Today's smart clothes perform well. Consider the antistatic or antimicrobial fabrics now available. But however impressive all this present fiber technology is, tomorrow we'll see advances that we can scarcely begin to imagine. Biotechnology may form the basis for fiber feedstocks. Imagine comfortable, easycare apparel made with fibers spun from solutions fermented from sugar. Or corn, beets, rice—even potatoes—might make great feedstocks.

Advanced computer simulation techniques are being explored to develop synthetic spider silk. New knowledge in materials science, biotechnology, and electronics are causing fundamental changes in the way we work with materials. We are moving from adaptation, refinement, and shaping of what is available, to designing and producing materials-systems to specification.

Synthetic fibers have come a long way over the past 100 years. But with biotechnology, we have a long way to go. The twenty-first century will certainly extend our visions to new vistas.

Sharon Burke, Textile Research Laboratory Manager, DuPont, and Kathy Smith, DuPont Lycra Marketing Manager for Intimate Apparel. September, 1998.

chapter 9

furs and leather

If you don't want to wear furs, don't. If you love it, wear it. It's about freedom of choice.

MICHAEL KORS, DESIGNER

Like the textile industry, the fur and leather industries are primary markets. By themselves, their products serve no purpose in the consumer market. However, when manufactured into apparel, accessories, or home fashions or when used as trimmings for fashion items, they achieve popular appeal.

These two industries serve the tastes of people at many income levels. Leather shoes are available at both expensive and inexpensive price points, the wide range being the result of variations in quality, styling, and construction, and sometimes the inclusion or omission of a designer name. Once reserved for the affluent members of our society, furs are now within reach of a larger number of consumers. The price differential for this product depends on the availability and quality of the skins, the intricacy of construction, the color popularity, the designer signature, and the importance of the fur as a fashion statement.

Both furs and leather must undergo extensive treatment before they can be manufactured into garments or accessories. In addition to designers, technical experts are needed. Whereas textiles are relatively easy to transform into fashions, leather and fur products require painstaking craftsmanship.

Both industries will be explored in terms of

- Market scope

- Production procedures

- Materials

- Style

- Marketing

After you have completed this chapter, you will be able to discuss:

- Changes in the consumer market for garments made of fur.

- Stages involved in the processing of furs.

- Various techniques of fur construction.

- Furs such as mink, ermine, sable, fox, rabbit, muskrat, and Persian lamb.

- The necessity for the Fur Products Labeling Act of 1952.

- The process by which leather hides are transformed into usable materials.

- The origins of leather and its uses.

FURS

Often, the gala social events covered by print and broadcast media attract attention, in part, because of the apparel worn by attendees. Whether it is the opening-night festivities for the Metropolitan Opera or the annual award presentations of the Council of Fashion Designers of America, what the people wear is often bigger news than the events themselves to the editorial press and photojournalists. Because the photographers are often restricted to locations outside of the arenas where the galas are held, their pictures often show the guests arriving in their evening wraps. If the events take place during the colder times of the year, fur garments receive the camera's attention.

Although fur has long been associated with special occasions, it is not exclusively used for such events. Today, while style and fashion are often foremost in the minds of consumers, function is also a consideration. The warmth a fur garment provides, along with its long-term use, makes fur a practical purchase. Women rushing to their offices or shopping in their favorite stores may be seen wearing anything from a sweeping mink to a casual raccoon coat.

Some individuals feel that the taking of skins from animals for the purpose of adornment is inappropriate—in part because it is endangering some animal species; in part because of the perception of how these animals are raised and killed. **Animal rights activists** and environmentalists have made their cause known throughout the world with a variety of demonstrations. They have assaulted wearers of fur garments and picketed fur salons. An attack on the Fifth Avenue offices of Karl Lagerfeld is an example. A well-funded organization, **PETA (People for the Ethical Treatment of Animals)** spent $11.5 million in 1994 to discourage the purchase of furs. Supporters, led by vocal celebrities such as Kim Basinger and Ricki Lake, and supermodels such as Kate Moss and Cindy Crawford, caused significant setbacks in the industry.

Left: Luxury furs are used primarily for special occasions. Right: Casual furs are worn for shopping, business, and everyday use.

Some consumers have responded by refusing to buy any furs; others are only buying furs from animals that are not endangered. Several fashionable retailers with global recognition, such as Harrods in London, closed their fur salons as the efforts of these groups succeeded in reducing demand for fur garments. Others were forced into bankruptcy. Faced with the adverse press initiated by these demonstrations, the industry decided to take a stand and publicize its right to freely sell furs. Through position papers developed by trade associations and advertisements by individual fur manufacturers that respond to the arguments of animal rights activists, the industry has continued to market furs. It no longer concentrates merely on the beauty of the product and the prestige given to the wearer, but it makes every effort to allay the fears of those who might abandon the idea of a fur purchase because of the controversy that surrounds the industry. The industry's actions appear to be winning back some consumers. In spite of the actions of those opposing the use of furs, many fashion designers continue to make significant use of furs as trimmings on apparel, and design collections of fur garments.

Components of the Fur Industry

Before a fur garment is offered for sale, it passes through the hands of different specialists. The process begins with those who raise or trap the animals, then moves to the processors who transform the skins of the animals with the hair intact, and finally ends with the designers and manufacturers who create the finished products.

Farmers and Trappers

Fewer than one-quarter of the furs produced in North America come from animals that run in the wild. The majority of the furs come from animals raised on fur farms. The vast majority are centered in Wisconsin, Minnesota, and Utah in the United States and Ontario and Quebec in Canada.

To produce the pelts in a humane way for garment use and to dispel any arguments about mistreatment of animals, the farmers have developed standards that are

The animal rights activists demonstrate to deter the use of furs for garments.

administered by the Fur Farm Animal Welfare Coalition in the United States and by the Mink Breeders Association in Canada. Every aspect of these farms' activities including methodology, nutrition, veterinary care, and humane harvesting procedures are outlined in their guidelines. Those who raise the animals today are a different breed from those of the past. More and more often, they are young farmers with college degrees in agriculture, biology, or business, who serve apprenticeships on established farms to learn the complete fur-production cycle.

When the pelts are obtained by trapping, a great effort is made to guarantee humane treatment. **Endangered species** are no longer sought and captured in the United States. Wildlife managers oversee the operations, establishing quotas and trapping seasons when necessary. In addition to learning about trapping from their predecessors, current trappers take specific educational courses, learning the latest methods of trapping.

Trappers sell the **pelts**—undressed skins with the hair intact—to agents who auction to wholesalers, manufacturers, and designers. In contrast, fur farmers usually omit the agent stage and sell directly to the garment producers.

Global **fur auctions** are held in such major areas of the United States as New York City, Minneapolis, St. Louis, and other world centers such as St. Petersburg, London, and Toronto.

Processors

After the auction, the pelts are brought to processing companies that transform them into skins that can be turned into garments. Many different processing stages must be undertaken. They include dressing, dyeing, bleaching, and glazing the pelt, all of which are fully discussed later in the chapter.

Designers and Manufacturers

Once the pelts have been processed, craftspeople turn them into garments. As with other apparel and accessories, the designer creates the styles that will be marketed. In

Fur auctions are held globally to sell pelts to manufacturers.

FENDI

Fendi furs are always lighthearted and fun.

Five sisters—Paola, Anna, Franca, Carla, and Alda—direct one of the world's major fashion houses that emphasizes leather and furs. The business was opened in 1925 by their parents—Edoardo and Adele Fendi—as a small leather and fur workshop.

A new boutique on the Via Pave in Rome, Italy, and the entry of the five sisters into the business paved the way for its ultimate recognition. In 1965, Karl Lagerfeld joined forces with the Fendi family and combined his creative genius with their business expertise. Their collaboration gave a particular style to fur coats. Stitches, inlays, interwoven fabrics, and lacquering changed the furs from the traditional, functional item to a more creative and fashion-oriented item. Beginning with made-to-order fur garments, the company strengthened its position with a ready-to-wear fur line in 1969.

Their leather goods underwent a similar evolution. Handbags were printed, interwoven, dyed, and tanned.

In 1977, the company expanded its efforts to include ready-to-wear. By 1984, Fendi became an international name.

In 1985, the Gallery of Modern Art of Rome celebrated Fendi's 60 years as a fashion house and its 20-year collaboration with Karl Lagerfeld with an exhibition. In that same year, the company launched its first fragrance.

In 1987, the third Fendi generation, sensitive to market needs, created the Fendissime line of fur and sportswear. In 1989, Fendi opened its first American flagship store on New York City's Fifth Avenue. During the same time the company launched the Fendi Uomo fragrance to accompany its newest endeavor, the Fendi Uomo line, a collection of menswear.

By 1992, the Fendi company was headquartered in one central building in Rome, which also housed all of the fur workrooms. Today, in addition to fur and leather products, Fendi licenses many items throughout the world. Sixty percent of its production is exported all over the globe. There are more than 100 Fendi boutiques worldwide, as well as 600 in-store shops.

the past, there was little creative styling for furs. The designs were basic or classic, with the fur itself being the most important element in the construction. Today, however, fur styling is as varied as any other garment. No longer are consumers limited to purchasing just one fur, which by necessity was generally simple and long-lasting, but many have several furs in their wardrobes. With style and silhouette now so important, notable designers have come to the forefront and are creating complete lines of furs. Glancing at fur advertisements immediately reveals names that once were associated only with the women's apparel industry. They include Valentino, Fendi, Yves Saint Laurent, and Oscar de la Renta for "high chic" designs and Michael Kors, Marc Jacobs, and Dolce & Gabbana for "cool" fur designs. The use of these and other famous names on labels is usually the result of licensing agreements between the designers and fur manufacturers. By marketing furs with such recognizable fashion names, the industry has been able to more easily justify the high prices to these garments. One of the most successful fur designers is Fendi, which is profiled in a World of Fashion Profile.

Once designers have fashioned the styles, the next stage involves matching the skins to the designs and turning them into salable garments.

Processing of Fur

The three operations necessary to prepare the pelts or skins for construction are **dressing**, **dyeing**, and **bleaching**.

Dressing

Pelts are initially soaked or mechanically treated to render them soft. The inside skins are fleshed to remove any unwanted substances. To make the "leather" portion of the pelts more workable, they are **tanned** or **aged** by means of chemicals. The tanning process tends to remove some of the natural oils from the skins, which must be replaced through **kicking**. This involves beating the furs against each other. If too much excess oil remains, the furs are placed in a drum filled with sawdust until some of the oil has been removed. After this stage, some fur pelts are further processed. The long guard hairs may be removed by a shearing process, as is done with sheared beaver, or by plucking, as is sometimes done with raccoon. After a final cleaning, they are ready to be used naturally or to be color enhanced.

Dyeing

Fur pelts are dyed for a variety of reasons and by several means. Sometimes the purpose is to improve the natural color or to give the bundle of skins a uniform appearance. If there is the slightest variation of color among the skins to be used in a garment, the final product will not have a perfectly matched look. Other times, furs are dyed to give them a fashion flair. It is not unusual for some of the more avant-garde designers to use the fashion colorations of the season for their furs, as they do in their apparel collections. If the fashion industry is touting purple, then purple it might be for some fur garments.

The dyes can be applied most easily by totally immersing the bundle in a dye bath; this is called **dip dyeing** and can be recognized at once because both the fur and the leather side will receive the color. If the choice is to color enhance or deepen the natural shade, brushing the edges of the fur with dye, or **tip dyeing**, is the method used. In cases where a pattern might be the designer's decision, as is the case when imitating other fur markings is desired, **stencil dyeing** is used. No matter how the furs are dyed, the fact that they have been colored must be indicated on the tag. This protects the consumer from purchasing a fur that he or she thinks is natural, but actually has been enhanced with color.

Bleaching

White furs are often tinged with yellow, which detracts from their appearance. To eliminate this unpleasant coloration, the pelts are bleached. In other cases, just to guarantee the even distribution of dyes, the furs might first be bleached. This is particularly true for dark furs that will ultimately be lightened. Excessive bleaching, while producing the desired light color, however, may be harmful to the fur and could shorten its life.

Glazing

The last process before manufacturing is **glazing**. The fur is sprayed with water and chemicals and pressed with special irons to improve luster and smoothness.

Constructing Fur Garments

Pelts are now sent to the manufacturer to be made into garments. The stages of construction vary according to the inherent characteristics of the fur, the intended appearance of the garment, and the eventual price at which it will be sold.

Matching the Skins

Skins are carefully arranged on the pattern to conform with the designer's plan and to the customer's measurements if the garment is to be custom made. It should be noted that most furs are being mass-produced, rather than customized for each purchaser. Only in cases where expense is not of primary concern is the garment made to exact customer measurements. The stock sizes enable stores to carry a wider assortment, giving the shopper wider selection and immediate wearability.

Top: The letting-out process elongates fur and avoids cross-seamings.
Bottom: A technician resews skins that have been let out.

To achieve the best appearance, the skins are matched and placed according to length and texture of hair, color, and other characteristics. Of course, if the skins have been dyed, there is no color-matching. So subtle are the markings and features that only a trained craftsperson can satisfactorily perform the task of matching.

Cutting and Sewing the Skins

After placement of pelts has been determined, the skins are cut to fit the pattern. Fine garments are hand cut; inexpensive ones may be cut by machine. The method of cutting depends on the characteristics, price, and the ultimate appearance of the fur.

There are several techniques used to cut and sew the pelts into a fur garment.

SKIN-ON-SKIN CONSTRUCTION Producers of inexpensive furs often use the method called **skin-on-skin construction**, in which each skin is placed and sewn next to subsequent skins to form a garment. Unless the furs are long-haired or naturally curly, as in the case of Persian lamb, it is almost impossible to conceal the resultant seaming.

LETTING-OUT CONSTRUCTION Fine furs, such as mink, are generally constructed by the **letting-out method**. This is a costly technique that requires time and skilled craftsmanship. Its purpose is to elongate the fur to the full length of the desired garment, eliminating horizontal joining marks, a characteristic of the less-expensive joining methods. The process involves cutting each skin vertically down the center of the dark stripe and then cutting the strips diagonally ⅛ of an inch wide. The narrow strips are then resewn to form the longer skin. After the lengthening procedure, the skins are rematched, sewn to fit the pieces of the design, dampened, stretched, and stapled onto a board until dry. The expert takes care not to stretch the furs too much because they might eventually split if overstretched. The various components are then sewn to complete the garment.

SPLIT-SKIN CONSTRUCTION Although female minks are generally favored because of their silkier appearance and lighter weight, they cost considerably more than male skins. For less expensive garments, the male skins might be manipulated to resemble the female skins by using **split-skin construction**. The operator slices the skin down the center, creating two pieces of fur. Each piece is then let out and elongated for use in the garment. Although this construction technique is still costly, it reduces the ultimate price of the garment because it requires fewer skins and uses less-costly male skins.

WHOLE-SKIN CONSTRUCTION In cases where smaller garments, such as jackets, are to be produced, elongation of the fur is unnecessary. A full skin will have the length needed without resorting to skin-on-skin joining. The full skin is merely cut to fit the pattern. This is known as **whole-skin construction**.

LEATHERING In cases where bulky furs, such as fox, are used, it is sometimes desirable to insert strips of leather or other material between the rows of skins to eliminate bulkiness. Each skin is sewn to a strip, which is then sewn to another skin until the process is completed. If the skins are very bushy, the inserted strips will not be seen. In addition to eliminating bulkiness, **leathering** also reduces the number of skins necessary to make a garment. Sometimes, the inserts are intentionally visible as part of the designer's styling.

Assembling Fur Garments

The pieces that have been assembled from the skins are then sewn together by hand in an operation called **closing**. This requires expert workmanship by expert technicians.

Finishing Fur Garments

At this point, the lining is sewn to the coat or jacket. Snaps, buttons, hooks and eyes, or zippers are sewn in place. The garment is now finished except for a possible lining monogram that identifies its owner.

Types of Furs

The many different types of furs used in the manufacture of coats, jackets, and enhancements are classified according to specific families. The weasel family group represents some of the world's most desired and costliest furs, including ermine, sable, and mink.

A look at the vast amount of fur advertising reveals that mink is the most popular fur among consumers and that it is available at many price points. Although quality and construction contribute to the price variation, it is the color that often accounts for the biggest difference. Considerable cross-breeding has produced a great number of mutations with many different colors. A garment in a color that is rare, or promoted by the fashion industry as the newest, garners the highest prices. Thus, when a color loses its popularity, garments in that color will probably fall in price.

The cat family is characterized by specific markings and patterns. It is a favorite of fur designers who create the unusual and includes lynx and leopard. The family of furs known as rodents offers a wide range of prices, from the most expensive to the very inexpensive. This family includes chinchilla, beaver, nutria, muskrat, and rabbit. The canine group is primarily dominated by the fox. It is easily distinguished by the long guard hairs and lush fur fibers. It is a showy fur

A variety of fur coats are shown for buyers.

that is often used for special occasions. The density generally calls for leathering to eliminate some of the bulkiness. The varieties of fox include red, white, blue, silver, and gray. The ungulate or hoofed-animal family produces fur that is tightly curled and includes Persian and South American lamb. See Table 9.1 for a more complete list and description of types of furs.

Regulations in the Fur Industry

Before 1952, the fur industry was less than truthful in describing its furs. Inexpensive pelts such as muskrat were sometimes misrepresented as a type of mink, and advertisements heralded mink-dyed muskrat as a popular fur. In an effort to protect the consumer, federal legislation now requires proper identification of fur garments. The **Fur Products Labeling Act of 1952**, which has been amended many times, requires the following:

1. Furs must be advertised and labeled using their English names.

2. The name of one fur may not be used to describe another.

3. The country of origin, if not the United States, must be clearly stated in ads and on labels.

4. Garments made of waste or scraps must be labeled as waste or section furs.

5. Furs that are dyed must be noted as such in ads and on labels.

The **Endangered Species Conservation Act** was passed to protect animals from extinction. If an animal species is threatened because of declining numbers, it cannot be hunted for its pelts. These restrictions are intended to help the species continue to breed and increase its population. Leopards and tigers are among these endangered groups.

Selling Furs to the Consumer

Furs are sold in a variety of places, such as fur manufacturer's facilities, retail establishments, and temporary sales arenas.

Fur Manufacturer's Facilities

Many fur manufacturers open their doors to the public. Individuals are invited to purchase from an inventory that has already been produced or to avail themselves of the company's designer who will custom-tailor a coat or jacket. It is the latter approach that patrons of furriers generally prefer. They are shown a variety of styles or may have one made from their own design, choose from the many bundles of skins on hand, have a muslin made to their exact measurements, and select the lining that would finish the garment. Buying this way, of course, is more expensive than off-the-rack purchasing.

Retail Establishments

Throughout the world, retailers have long sold furs directly to their customers. Some stores belong to a chain that carries only furs, such as The Fur Vault; others are department stores with fur salons, which are most often leased departments. With leased departments, the retailer invites a fur manufacturer to open a department in the store and to completely merchandise and manage it. The store charges for the space and often receives a percentage of the sales.

Table 9.1

TYPES OF FURS CLASSIFIED ACCORDING TO SPECIFIC FAMILIES

Family	Types of Furs	Description
Weasel	Mink	Finest variety comes from the northern part of the United States where it has been farmed. Female skins are more desirable than males because of their suppleness and lightweight quality.
	Sable	The coldest part of Russia produces the finest sables. The intensity of the weather causes the animal to grow the densest fur. Similar in appearance to mink, its fuller, longer guard hairs give it a bushier look. One of the world's rarest furs, a prized Russian sable coat can cost in excess of $100,000.
	Ermine	Extremely expensive; a white fur accentuated by natural black-tipped markings on its tail. Rarely used commercially any longer. Seen as part of dress for royalty in state processions. Occasionally, pieces are used as apparel enhancements.
	Stone marten, kolinsky, fitch, wolverine, otter, skunk	Lesser known furs; found occasionally in designer collections.
Cat	Lynx	Easily recognized by long, bushy guard hairs and slightly spotted markings. Best quality is from the coldest parts of Russia and Canada. Although it often plays a role in fashion, its tendency to shed makes it a problem for wearers.
	Leopard	Once the favorite fur of the cat family, no longer used for garments because it is on the endangered species list.
	Lynx cat	Slightly less costly than lynx.
	Ocelot	Similar to leopard, but not as strikingly marked.
Rodent	Chinchilla	Most expensive fur in this family. Extremely rare as well as extremely perishable. Generally has a gray coloration, but through mutation fur farming, other colors have been achieved.
	Beaver	Often the consumers who want this fur ask for "sheared" beaver. The reason for this is that during the processing of the pelts, the long guard hairs are sheared leaving the soft, downy fur fiber undercoat. Available as a natural fur in shades of brown, beaver may also be dyed in a host of shades in designer collections.
	Nutria	May be sheared as is beaver, but more often shown with the guard hairs intact. Extremely serviceable and provides years of wear.
	Muskrat	One of the most widely used furs to imitate the look of more costly skins. Resembles mink when it is dyed and let out; resembles beaver when sheared. To produce this fur as inexpensively as possible, the typical method of construction is skin-on-skin.
	Rabbit	Inexpensive and processed to imitate other furs. Often dyed the latest fashionable colors or bleached white. While rabbit garments have a luxurious appearance when new, the phenomenon is short lived because of significant shedding and low durability.
Canine	Red fox	Orange-red color; caught in the wild. Generally reserved for trimming on coats and suits.
	White fox	Often the choice for a dramatic entrance. Whitest species from the northernmost parts of the United States and Canada.
	Blue fox	Actually brownish with a blue cast. Fox with a real blue color is Norwegian blue fox, a mutation developed in fur farming.

(continued)

Table 9.1 (*continued*)

	Silver fox	Silvery guard hairs and blue-black fur fibers. Most silvery variety is called platinum fox, a mutation of the silver fox.
	Gray fox	Least desirable of the family; relatively inexpensive; often dyed to imitate silver fox.
Ungulate	Persian lamb	Raised on farms; fur is tightly curled and lustrous. Majority are black, but some are available in natural gray and brown.
	Broadtail	Pelts from newborn Persian lamb; characterized by a flat, watermarked pattern. More expensive than Persian lamb.
	South American lamb	Inexpensive and durable; used to produce mouton-processed lamb. Fur is sheared and electrified to relax the pattern.

Temporary Sales Arenas

One of the ways manufacturers attract large crowds of potential fur purchasers is to lease temporary space in a hotel or convention center. There, for a few days, consumers can examine merchandise and make their purchases. Large print advertisements and television commercials are used to announce these events, which are most often touted as special sales. Sometimes a group of fur manufacturers will combine their efforts and bring together the merchandise from their respective factories. By doing this, they share in the expense of such an operation.

A fur boutique owner helps a customer try on a white mink sweater and white fox hat.

LEATHER

Consumers are more interested in leather today than ever before in fashion history. Once used primarily as a fashion accessory for shoes, handbags, and small purses, designers from around the globe now use leather to create suits, coats, jackets, and sportswear for every member of the family in a variety of styles and price points. One need only to walk through regional malls to find such stores as Tannery West and Wilsons, which feature significant assortments of leather garments.

As with furs, different skins have different characteristics. Calfskin is unlike pigskin or sheepskin in appearance, and nothing like rawhide. The variety of skins available to producers is large, and the methods of production are numerous. As a result, the finished products are quite varied. Although often imitated by synthetic materials, nothing yet available has the natural feel and beauty of leather.

Characteristics of the Leather Industry

Each year, the industry makes technological advances in the production and processing of leather, including the application of silk-screen designs and the creation of textures that are softer than ever. With these and other innovations, the industry continues to expand. The major centers of cattle production for the leather indus-

Leather apparel can be enhanced by decorative details such as the design on this jacket by Dolce & Gabbana.

try are the United States, the countries that formerly made up the Soviet Union, and Western Europe. Other producers include Argentina, Brazil, India, and Mexico. The United States alone accounts for more than $1.5 billion. U.S. tanning activities are concentrated in the Northeast, Midwest, Middle Atlantic states, and California. The shoe and leather goods industries in the United States employ more than 200,000 workers.

Processing of Leather

The processing of leather involves 20 individual stages. Once the hides and skins are removed from the dead animals, they must be pretanned or cured. **Hides** are the pelts taken from large animals, such as horses and cows, and **skins** are the pelts taken from the smaller animals such as calves, sheep, and goats. After curing, which involves the use of salt as a primary agent, the pelts begin the 20 stages of processing.

1. *Receiving and Storage.* The pelts are received, sorted according to size and weight, and packed in bundles that will travel to the tannery as a unit.

2. *Soaking.* To restore moisture that is lost during the curing stage, the pelts are soaked for 8 to 20 hours. The process makes them softer as well as cleaner.

3. *Unhairing.* Most hair removal is accomplished by the use of chemicals that have little effect on the leather itself. Manufacturers who wish to sell the hair for use in other products remove the hair mechanically.

4. *Trimming and Siding.* This next stage removes the unusable perimeter areas of the pelt. The process is accomplished with a circular blade.

5. *Fleshing.* This process removes excess flesh from the underside of the pelt by a mechanical operation employing sharp, rotating blades.

6. *Bating.* After the hair and flesh have been removed, it is necessary to remove the chemicals used in earlier stages. This removal is accomplished by washing the hides and skins in large cylindrical drums filled with chemicals.

7. *Pickling.* Prior to the actual tanning operation, the pelts are salted and placed in an acid bath to make them more susceptible to tanning. This is actually a preserving operation.

8. *Tanning.* Preserving or **tanning** leather can be accomplished in a number of ways. Most leather is now chrome tanned, a four- to six-hour process that produces leather best suited for the majority of product uses. Other tanning agents include barks, roots, oils, and minerals. Each takes longer than chrome tanning and each produces leathers with unique characteristics.

9. *Wringing and Sorting.* Excess moisture is removed during this stage. Pelts are then sorted according to thickness.

10. *Splitting and Shaving.* Pelts vary in thickness and must be **split** or sliced for uniformity. To do this they are fed into a splitting machine that slices off the

a.

a. Leather processing involves making pelts uniform in thickness. b. Pelts are set out to dry after they have been made uniformly thick. c. Pasting of skins and hide to vacuum them dry.

b.

c.

underneath or flesh layer. If a large area of the flesh layer or split is thick enough, it can be further processed for product usage. The remaining pelt is then fed into a shaving machine that levels the overall thickness to exact specifications.

11. *Retanning, Coloring, and Fat Liquoring.* Retanning is a second tanning done to impart desirable properties to the leather not accomplished through primary tanning. Coloring of leather is now achieved by applying water-soluble dyes. Hundreds of dyes are available today, each with different properties. Factors such as penetration and color density must be considered in dye selection. **Fat liquoring** lubricates the leather's fibers and makes them softer and more flexible.

12. *Setting Out.* The first of the drying processes involves smoothing the leather grain and removing any excess moisture before the actual drying phase is begun.

13. *Drying.* A variety of techniques can be chosen to dry leather. The simplest, *hanging*, is a procedure similar to that of clothesline drying; *toggling* is a means of stretching with clips; *pasting* is the most popular method. In pasting, skins and hides are pasted on six- by eleven-foot plates and vacuum dried, a process in which water is extracted by machine.

14. *Conditioning.* After drying, some pelts are too hard for use in merchandise production and require conditioning—the introduction of controlled moisture.

15. *Staking and Milling.* To make the leather soft and pliable, machines stake the leather by pounding it with "fingers" or pins.

16. *Buffing.* To improve its appearance by removing scratches or blemishes, the grain or surface of the leather is lightly buffed. The operation involves a sanding cylinder that is rotated against the leather.

17. *Finishing.* The natural beauty of the leather is protected by means of a finishing system. The leather might be coated with transparent materials allowing the grain to show through or covered with opaque powders to achieve a coloring effect. Surface coatings are achieved through polyurethanes and other chemicals. The finishing department carefully selects the right ingredients for specific, desired results.

18. *Plating.* The final appearance-improving step is plating. Leathers are smoothed to improve their feel or grained through embossing.

19. *Grading.* Unlike fabrics, which are uniformly produced, leather quality differs from pelt to pelt. Leather is graded according to such factors as color, thickness, and defects. The better the quality, the more expensive the ultimate products.

20. *Measuring.* Because leather hides are irregularly shaped and because price is based upon area, each piece must be measured.

Origins and Uses of Leathers

Each type of leather is suited to particular uses. Because of their suppleness, some are used extensively for gloves; others, because of their durability, are headed for use in upholstery and shoes. Table 9.2 identifies the types of leathers and uses.

Characteristics of Leather

Just as different fibers have specific characteristics and properties, so do the hides and skins of animals. In addition to the beauty offered the wearer, leather also is functional.

Table 9.2

TYPES AND USES OF LEATHER

Types of Leather	Uses
Cow and steer	Used extensively in shoe production for parts such as uppers, soles, insoles, and linings; coats and jackets; gloves, belts, and handbags; luggage and upholstery.
Calf	Shoe uppers; handbags, wallets, gloves; garments.
Sheep and lamb	Sueded for use in shoes and garments; extremely soft, also used for gloves and linings.
Goat and kid	Apparel, shoe uppers, gloves, and handbags.
Pig and hog	Fancy leather goods, such as shoes and billfolds; different types come from the peccary and carpincho pigs.
Deer	Softness makes deerskin a favorite for dress gloves and moccasins.
Horse	Shoe uppers and soles; gloves and sometimes garments.
Reptile (alligator, crocodile, lizard, snake)	Handbags, shoes, and belts; reptile skins are among the most costly to use.

Leather has extremely high tensile strength—it can withstand a great deal of stress without tearing apart. It is also extremely flexible, thereby avoiding the potential for cracking because of cold and heat. Because it also absorbs moisture, breathes easily, and has the ability to conform to specific shapes, it is the perfect material for shoes.

Its versatility makes it a much sought-after material by the consumer.

Fashion Leathers

A look through the large assortment of leather merchandise immediately shows that there are many different fashion-oriented leathers. They are basically derived from the categories described in Table 9.2, but have been specially treated or finished to impart different looks. The following alphabetical list is composed of the more popular fashion leathers.

ANALINE LEATHER A product that is colored with transparent dyes and shows the natural characteristics of the leather.

DISTRESSED LEATHER A material with a weathered appearance.

LAMB LEATHER The softest leather of the group.

NAPA A shiny, smooth, or pebbly surfaced material.

NUBUCK A lightly buffed leather with a fine nap that appears smoother than suede. It is used for shoes, blazers, skirts, and pants.

SHRUNKEN LAMB Leather with a pebbly, grained surface.

SUEDE A velvetlike leather that is produced by napping the skin's underside.

Promoting and Marketing Leathers

The widespread use of synthetic leather has provided competition for the leather industry. Large numbers of consumers have been persuaded to purchase less-costly products that have characteristics similar to leather.

The leather industry has several trade associations, such as the Tanner's Council, the New England Tanner's Club, Leather Industries of America, and the Leather Ap-

ANDREW MARC

Although the fashion industry has heralded its major designers for many centuries, the emphasis has been on names that design a whole host of apparel and accessories. Recognition is generally reserved for those who present apparel collections for women and, less frequently, for men. Rarely is an individual who is associated with one basic material singled out for special attention. In the leather industry, however, this has been the case for a few individuals.

Andrew Marc has achieved fame through the exclusive design of leather apparel for men and women. Although most shoppers merely look for a particular leather style and quality, few ask for a specific designer name. The exception is Andrew Marc.

In 1981, the Andrew Marc label rose into prominence as a subsidiary of the company founded by Fred Schwartz, the famous chairman of the Fur Vault and uncle of Andrew Marc Schwartz. Andrew Marc combined form and function for his signature style—and a classic—the leather bomber jacket. The garment featured a leather outer shell that was lined with fur. It quickly became the industry's leading seller. From this unique concept evolved a collection of diversified silhouettes including motorcycle styles, anoraks, crop styles, and leather sportswear. All of the items are designed with clean understated lines and authentic detail.

Today, the company is owned and operated by Andrew Marc and his wife, Suzanne. They are committed to bringing the public a superior quality product with unsurpassed craftsmanship. By consistently updating their styling and by designing garments with customers' lifestyles in mind, Andrew Marc has become one of the leading leather outerwear companies in the United States.

An Andrew Marc design always is fashionable.

Left: The menswear industry is a major consumer of leather. Right: Leather pants are easy to wear and are a practical luxury.

parel Association, to promote the image of leather and its importance to the consumer. Unfortunately, these associations do not have the same recognition as associations in the textile industry. Unlike Cotton Incorporated and the Wool Bureau, which regularly present their messages in the print and broadcast media and are immediately recognized by the consumer, the names of the leather associations are not readily known.

Recognition is greater when tanners persuade major designers to include leather in their collections. The use of designer names in advertising helps to focus attention on a leather product.

Selling is accomplished primarily through trade shows, among which Leather World, the Wolburn Show, the St. Louis Show, and the Accessory and Garment Leather Show are the most popular in the United States. Semaine du Cuir, in Paris, is the world's largest international fair.

CHAPTER HIGHLIGHTS

- Both the fur and leather industries have continued to increase their presence in the fashion world.

- The fur industry has had to confront opposition from animal rights activists and environmentalists who use a variety of methods to discourage consumer purchasing.

- The leather industry is facing competition from synthetic products that rival its use.

- Fur prices have become much more reasonable because of increases in fur farming and the popularity of less-recognized furs.

- To be manufactured into garments, furs undergo several processes, from dressing the pelts to various construction techniques and finishes.

- The federal government continues to play an important role in the marketing of furs through key legislative acts, the most far reaching of which is the Fur Products Labeling Act.

- The fur industry continues to increase sales each year. Marketing efforts include ads that try to allay concerns raised by industry opponents.

- Fur licensing agreements with famous designers have also helped fur sales.

- Leather processing is a painstaking, time-consuming venture that involves 20 different steps.

- The leather industry is promoted through trade associations.

IMPORTANT FASHION TERMINOLOGY AND CONCEPTS

animal rights activists	fur auctions	skin-on-skin construction
bleaching	glazing	splitting
closing	guard hairs	split-skin construction
dip dyeing	kicking	stencil dyeing
dressing	leathering	tanning
dyeing	letting-out	tip dyeing
endangered species	pelts	whole-skin construction
Endangered Species Conservation Act	PETA (People for the Ethical Treatment of Animals)	
fat liquoring		

FOR REVIEW

1. What major undertaking in the early 1990s caused considerable difficulty for the fur industry?
2. How has the fur industry fought the accusations of PETA?
3. Why are there such large price differentials in the fur market?
4. Describe the three industry segments involved in the production of fur.
5. In what way has the Fur Products Labeling Act helped the consumer?
6. Explain how letting out improves the appearance of some fur skins.
7. Differentiate between skin-on-skin and split-skin construction.
8. What are the three major types of outlets used to sell furs?
9. What is the difference between a leather hide and a skin?
10. What method of tanning is preferred by the leather industry? Why?
11. What is meant by the term *splitting*, as it applies to leather?
12. Collectively, which group of leathers is the most costly?
13. In what way does analine leather differ from other leathers?
14. In what format does the leather industry sell most of its goods?
15. Who are some of Anton's clients as discussed in Point of View, "The Leather Man?"

EXERCISES AND PROJECTS

1. Call or write to a fur manufacturer asking for permission to record the various stages of fur production. The task might be performed with a still camera, in which case slides would be taken, or a video camera. Using the slides or video, prepare a talk to accompany the visual presentation to your class.
2. Prepare an oral presentation about the furs currently being marketed by the industry. Pages may be used from fashion magazines and mounted on femecore board for presentation to the class.
3. Take the position of an animal rights activist and prepare a talk that would support your cause.
4. Select three items of leather from your wardrobe such as belts, shoes, apparel, and handbags, and try to determine their animal sources.
5. Write a report on the status of the leather industry. Information may be obtained from the various associations mentioned in the text, as well as from trade periodicals and consumer publications.

WEB SITES

By accessing these Web sites, you will be able to gain broader knowledge and up-to-date information on materials related to this chapter.

Leather Industries of America
   www.leatherusa.com

Leather Apparel Association
   www.leatherassociation.com

Fur Industry/Fur Information Council of America
   www.fur.org/furind.html

The Case of Uncertain Expansion

A&R Furriers, Inc., has been manufacturing furs for the past 30 years. The company, founded by Paul Kim, has always enjoyed a fine reputation and its profits have regularly increased, providing Mr. Kim with a comfortable lifestyle.

Last year, Cathy, Mr. Kim's daughter, joined the company. Fresh out of college, she brought great enthusiasm and a wealth of ideas that could improve the company's present position. She spoke about the possibility of merging with another company that would give the newly expanded organization a greater competitive edge. Because her father was aware of the pitfalls of merging, the proposal fell on deaf ears. She then suggested expanding the business by opening a retail division. By manufacturing their own garments, she proposed, the company could offer furs at a lower price than most stores and still make an admirable profit.

The senior Kim has thus far vetoed all of his daughter's suggestions. He agrees that expansion in some direction might be beneficial, but he is afraid of jeopardizing the company's position. Mergers are not in line with his thinking and retailing requires efforts not within his expertise.

Although the company's products are successfully sold to stores that insert their own labels on the garments and to individuals who come to the company for custom-designed garments, there does not seem to be another route for increasing business. He is still open to ideas for expansion, but the proper direction seems to elude him.

question

Bearing in mind Cathy Kim's two proposals, how might A&R expand its operation and increase profits?

point of view

The Leather Man

ELENA ROMERO

You've seen his work in music videos, in magazines and on award shows. But chances are his name will not ring a bell. That's because leather craftsman Anton is one of the fashion industry's best-kept secrets.

Working out of a 500-square-foot showroom in the heart of New York's garment district, Anton diligently creates what he considers to be his works of art, which have been worn by entertainers including Lauryn Hill, Eve, Lenny Kravitz, Samuel L. Jackson, Cheryl Crow, Marilyn Manson, and Keith Richards of the Rolling Stones.

Interestingly enough, Anton never went to fashion design school.

"I actually started sewing when I was 12," he begins to explain. "My brother, Sheldon, started sewing at home. He's five years older than I am, so he was about 17 when I started making stuff. It was that whole younger brother thing. You know, I saw him doing something and automatically I was gonna do it—but do it even better."

Like his brother, Anton was a natural. "What it amounts to is that as an artist, you can teach yourself," he says. "It just so happened that I was an artist too. I taught myself."

Developing his talent, the Chicago native began by making clothes for himself on a home sewing machine. "Back then, it was about being slick," he recalls of his teen years. "Silks, wools, sharkskin suits, some linen, and polyester shirts. There was no leather in the picture. It was not about leather at all."

By the time he was 18, Anton began to experiment with the fabric that would be his trademark for years to come. "It was really just something else to show," he admits. "I didn't really know the power of leather then. I would take jackets apart that were already made and remake them using the opposite side."

Anton would purchase leather jackets from thrift shops, bring them home, deconstruct them and recut them into something else. "I was using the wrong side, which was preserved," he notes. "That's how I really started putting my hands on leather. It really taught me a lot about the construction of garments and the way things are made."

The reversibility aspect of his apparel, for which he is now known, happened almost by accident. "I was making a pair of leather pants for somebody," he recalls. "I wanted to use the leather side. He wanted to use the other side. I was looking at the other side and I said, well that's kind of cool too. So I ended up making them so he could wear them on both sides."

And so it began. But it wasn't until the mid '80s that Anton realized he would actually design for a living. He was 26 at the time, married for four years and in Chicago. He began to make frequent buying trips to New York and finally relocated there in 1994. "I found this guy I had met at a seminar at FIT and he decided that he liked my work," he says. "He wanted me to design a line. So we ended up developing this line—spending a lot of money—and it went nowhere."

About a year later he met a woman over the Internet who was a promoter at The Tunnel nightclub. She would later introduce him to a friend with whom he would go into business. "She had a store down on St. Marks [Place]," he says. "This was when St. Marks hadn't really gotten where it is today. It was, like, her store, my product."

That's when Anton's work began getting media exposure in *The New York Times* and on Fox's *Good Day New York*. Coincidentally around that same time, Anton met Lauryn Hill's stylist, Deborah, at the store. It wasn't long before Anton was commissioned to create pieces for Hill's first solo album, *The Miseducation of Lauryn Hill*, which won multiple awards including five Grammys.

"We made about six pairs of pants for Lauryn, some capri pants, and we did a long dress for her," he says. "She was the first celebrity to wear my stuff. It was my first big hit." Word quickly spread through the industry and other stylists soon followed suit, bringing with them a client roster that included Stephen Baldwin, Halle Berry, Eric Benet, Lenny Kravitz and Maxwell.

"We've also been working on Aerosmith for the past year," Anton says. "It's been one project after another. Stylists have been a big part of our flow. But now we have people like this wardrobe guru who dresses regular people."

According to Anton, he currently has a clientele base of about 300 and his prices range from $300 for a leather top to $15,000 for an ostrich or alligator trench coat. "We custom-make to whatever size you need it to be," he says. "It only takes about two weeks to do that. But a lot of the projects we've taken on we've done in less. The stuff we made for Eve for the Essence Awards we produced in one day."

Just don't be surprised if the next time you see Anton's work you have a strange craving for pepperoni; he has just finished dressing Carmen Electra for a Pizza Hut commercial.

Daily News Record, June 18, 2001

How Trade Associations Benefit Their Membership

LILI KASDAN, LAA MANAGING DIRECTOR

A core group of America's most progressive leather garment manufacturers, retailers, tanners and professional leather cleaners founded the Leather Apparel Association (LAA) in 1990, realizing that there was much to be gained by working together. As a non-profit professional service organization catering specifically to industry needs, LAA has been able to create a comprehensive marketing program and sales support system that many businesses would find cost-prohibitive or impossible to do on their own. The goal of LAA is to promote sales of leather apparel in the American market through public relations, education, advertising and market research. By stimulating demand and increasing the size and scope of the market for leather clothing, LAA is helping every company in the leather apparel business grow stronger, broader, and more profitable.

Members are dedicated to fostering cooperation and working together to improve garment quality, durability and customer satisfaction. Membership is open to all businesses wishing to see the leather apparel business grow in the United States. LAA unites buyers, suppliers and industry peers alike. Members, therefore, also include producers of leather garment accessories, insulations, water-repellent and garment care products, as well as international tanneries and factories who produce for the American market. Membership represents a public commitment to quality and service.

LAA's national marketing campaign has two distinct targets. The first objective is to stimulate consumer demand, utilizing newspaper and TV publicity, and educational brochures. Maintaining that demand is imperative to the success of the second objective, to promote the sales of products and services made by LAA members specifically. Sales for all types of companies dealing with leather apparel are ultimately dependent on consumer demand.

For example, LAA spends thousands of dollars trying to get retailers to buy garments made by its manufacturing members through trade advertisements, catalogues and other industry promotions. Likewise, LAA tries to influence manufacturers to buy skins from its member tanners. If consumers were not interested in buying leather, LAA's efforts to promote its members would have little effect because retailers would have no incentive to buy garments from leather manufacturers, and consequently, manufacturers' orders to the tanneries would be down as well.

In order to stimulate consumer interest in leather, LAA creates press kits for newspapers and magazines containing photographs and the latest information on leather fashion trends and garment care. This annual national publicity campaign generates an average of 500 stories in the press every year. LAA spokesmen may also appear on TV news and talk shows to promote leather fashions created by members. Keeping leather in the spotlight serves an additional purpose. When retailers see such publicity in their area, it helps build confidence in the product.

Consumer satisfaction with the performance and durability of leather garments is of great importance to the potential for sales. In an effort to improve garment quality, LAA has issued guidelines for manufacturing which identify the sources and solutions to potential problems that often precipitate consumer complaints. Another set of guidelines help prevent garment owners from making mistakes with cleaning and care. Should consumers or businesses have a problem with a garment, or need help finding a cleaner or vendor, LAA serves as a referral service and information center. LAA maintains a state-by-state listing of its professional leather cleaning members in order to assist the public and the trade.

At the trade level, LAA helps members increase their company profile and publicity through participation in seminars, fashion shows and direct mail campaigns. Trade advertisements and brochures publicize the names and products of LAA members. These marketing vehicles tell buyers what LAA is doing to drive sales up, and why buying from LAA members is good for business.

For sales support, the association offers consumer booklets and retail sales training brochures that explain manufacturing, shopping tips and common leather terminology. LAA garment hangtags containing care instructions serve to increase customer confidence with every item shipped, sold or cleaned. Members also make use of the LAA logo in their own ads, in-store and on displays to enhance their company's prestige and credibility.

LAA gives the industry a united, public voice, making it possible to lobby Washington to protect the industry from international trade politics. Since well over 90% of the leather garments sold in the U.S. are imports, preventing damaging tariffs requires constant vigilance. Dealing with the media on these and other issues is another prime responsibility, which the association handles on a daily basis. Interviews with reporters and researchers run the gamut from industry sales to questions about animal rights extremists. A bi-monthly newsletter keeps members abreast of international industry developments, issues, trends, and business opportunities.

The association gets its funding almost entirely from membership dues, unlike other apparel industry groups who are funded through various tariff systems. Therefore, industry support is the key to providing the kinds of programs and services that will build a stronger, broader and more profitable leather apparel business.

Lili Kasdan, Managing Director, Leather Apparel Association, Inc.

the fashion merchandise industries

Women's, men's, and children's wear make up the apparel components of the fashion industry; other components are intimate wear, trimmings, wearable accessories, cosmetics and fragrances, and fashions for the home. Each component includes a variety of different products within its lines, and those who work in each area must be aware of specific circumstances that are unique to each, such as size classifications and marketing methods.

The largest of these groups is women's wear. Within this group, manufacturers generally cater to specific product classifications, such as dresses and sportswear, and price categories, such as couture, designer, bridge, moderate, and budget. They market their goods for four or five different seasons, longer than any other segment of the fashion industry.

The men's fashion industry is considerably smaller than the women's. It generally produces two major lines a season, and companies usually restrict their offerings to one type of merchandise. The goods are most often sold to retailers at trade expositions. One of the crazes to hit men's and women's wear in the late 1990s was *Fridaywear*, a term used to describe a relaxed style of clothing worn to work on Friday. It had taken some business away from tailored clothing and had added interest to casual merchandise that was worn for this dressed-down day. Today, however, more and more businesses have returned to tailored clothing as the appropriate dress for the entire week.

The children's wear field closely parallels the women's segment, although it only features two seasons. The women's, men's, and children's wear industries are the focus of Chapter 10.

Chapter 11 looks at intimate apparel from a historical perspective, describing the evolution of various undergarments, and the fibers and materials that made these styles possible. Today, manufactured fibers such as spandex provide designers with an opportunity to develop body-molding undergarments that are an essential part of the fashion scene. The in-store shop is increasingly being used to merchandise these intimate apparel collections.

Trimmings play an important role in the business of fashion, as discussed in Chapter 12. They are both decorative and functional. The simplest garment may be magnificently enhanced with exciting trim. Designers can choose from a wealth of adornments to give their garments and accessories unique looks.

Shoes, handbags, gloves, jewelry, and other accessories are produced all over the world. A complete overview of each accessory item is featured in Chapter 13, which presents the range of possibilities available to professionals and consumers as wardrobe enhancements.

Cosmetics and fragrance sales are skyrocketing all over the globe. As Chapter 14 explains, apparel designers have entered the market through licensing agreements, and many have made fortunes in this way. The cost to launch a new fragrance may by more than $40 million, but with profits so high, it is considered good business to do so. Celebrities from the entertainment and sports arenas have jumped on the fragrance bandwagon by joining major companies to produce and market their own brands.

One of the fastest-growing segments of the industry produces fashions for the home. This area is the focus of Chapter 15. More and more apparel designers are producing bed and bath products, dinnerware, and other products for the home bearing their famous signatures. Very large specialty retailers are expanding their businesses to handle these home fashion items.

After studying each of the different fashion merchandise classifications, it will be time to move on to the manufacturing of the products. This is the focus of the chapters in Part Four.

apparel: women's, men's, and children's

Fashions fade; style is eternal.

YVES ST. LAURENT, DESIGNER

After you have completed this chapter, you will be able to discuss:

- The major classifications of women's wear.

- The various size ranges of women's wear and their unique characteristics.

- The seasons in women's apparel and the importance of each in the industry.

- A comparison of menswear before the 1950s with today's fashions.

- Where the major menswear markets are in the United States.

- The various product classifications in menswear.

- The effects of Fridaywear on men's and women's apparel.

- How children's fashions have changed since the 1950s.

The apparel business is the most important segment of the fashion industry, accounting for more companies, employees, and sales volume than any other segment. Although it is dominated by the industrial giants, there always seems to be a new company on the horizon ready to make its entrance. Some, through hard work and creative ideas, prove that there is room for a newcomer; others, because of inexperience or undercapitalization, fail. Success depends on the uniqueness of the line, astute buyers, sound financial resources, and creative marketing.

Although there are parallels among women's, men's, and children's wear, there are also distinct differences. Each is available at a wide range of price points, each is produced all over the globe, and each appeals to a variety of consumers. In terms of marketing, they also follow similar paths. But when it comes to designer recognition, the women's wear industry plays the dominant role. While menswear designers are receiving more attention than ever before, it is the designers of women's wear and their collections that garner most of the press coverage.

Today, manufacturers of women's, men's, and children's wear and their product offerings have changed significantly. Operating in a highly competitive, global environment, all three segments face daily challenges to create the right products for the marketplace.

WOMEN'S WEAR

The hype generated by the women's wear industry is often compared to that of the film industry. Openings of designer collections in Paris, Milan, and New York receive as much attention and press coverage as the release of a major motion picture. Such reigning designers as Lagerfeld, Armani, Donatella Versace, Lacroix, Sui, Klein, Karan, and Ford are treated with the same amount of awe reserved for the world's greatest entertainers. Although the marquee names of the industry are often idolized, most industry employers never receive public recognition.

Women's wear includes merchandise in a number of classifications and price points. Participants in all levels of the industry cater to a specific market segment and must consider a host of factors before embarking on the production of a line. It is an enormously competitive segment of the fashion industry. Those who work in it must understand its goals and how to achieve them.

Throughout the decades, women's wear has undergone more changes than men's and children's wear. From the fashion designs of Poiret and Paquin at the beginning of the 20th century to Chanel, Dior, Balenciaga, and later to Quant, Courrèges, Lagerfeld, Lauren, Armani, and Karan, silhouettes were changed, hemlines were raised and lowered, and innovative styling continuously redirected the fashion scene.

Today's designers and manufacturers operate with the same vigor and verve as their predecessors. They must address the needs of potential customers by producing lines that will turn a profit for the industry.

Markets

The women's wear industry is truly a global business. Although Paris still reigns as the world's leader in haute couture, affluent and sophisticated women also converge on other European capitals to buy the originals of Lagerfeld, Dolce & Gabbana, Galliano, Westwood, Armani, and the other leading designers. The haute couture business may grow smaller every year, but it still sets the stage for designers' secondary design lines and serves as a source of ideas for American fashion.

An innovative design from a Prada haute couture collection.

In New York City, ready-to-wear holds center stage. From the higher price points of Donna Karan and Calvin Klein to the more modestly priced lines, no city in the world has as much to offer retail merchants. In its famous garment center, thousands of manufacturers and designers produce new lines, season after season. Some buildings are known for specific levels of fashion; others house the newcomers waiting for their companies to be recognized. Regional markets in the United States are in cities such as Chicago, Dallas, Los Angeles, and Atlanta, where apparel centers and marts are filled with branch offices of New York's manufacturers as well as the headquarters for those of regional producers.

Product Classifications

The U.S. apparel industry is composed of manufacturers who specialize in a particular product line and those whose offerings cut across numerous categories. The bulk of the industry works at what it knows best. Dresses range from the one- or two-piece variety to the fanciest ballgowns, with a range of prices that begin very low and climb very high. Dress manufacturers concentrate either on daytime dresses or evening wear. Evening wear includes after-five lines, prom and party dresses, and bridal wear, including the mothers of the bride and groom.

The U.S. sportswear market came into its own as early as the 1930s and 1940s. American designers such as Claire McCardell, Norman Norell, Pauline Trigère, Thomas Brigance, Bonnie Cashin, and Anne Klein developed a strong following and influenced a unique style of dress. Two-piece dressing that utilized skirts, pants, blouses, and sweaters was the order of the day then and has remained the favorite of

Two-piece dressing by U.S. designers like Anne Klein (on the right in this 1974 photo) is still an important fashion category.

This design from Michael Kors collection exemplifies contemporary casual sportswear.

women everywhere. This classification includes separates, which enable the wearer to mix and match various elements to form many different outfits.

Coat and suit manufacturers usually restrict their merchandise to this classification, because it requires highly skilled workers and machinery not necessary for other apparel products. There are, however, some manufacturers who cut across other product classifications, such as Jones New York and Ellen Tracey. The market for coats and suits has remained a solid one, with more and more women needing such attire for their careers.

Once identified as active sportswear in the sportswear classification, **activewear** has become a large classification of the apparel industry. The physical fitness craze and concerns about weight have caused many women to join exercise clubs, where particular types of apparel are standard. Sweatshirts and sweatpants, sport bras, bicycle pants, tank tops, and similar apparel are found in every color and pattern. Warm-up suits and jogging outfits complete these wardrobes.

Since the early 1990s, a growing number of women have been playing tennis and golf, activities that continue to gain in popularity. This has given manufacturers an entirely new market. Pro shops and specialty stores are filled with assortments that are worn on as well as off the playing fields. One reason for this change has been the television coverage of professional women's sports. Many athletes endorse the apparel they wear and influence the average woman's choice in such items.

With the demand for golf sportswear reaching new heights, some marketers of these products are increasingly relying on the Internet to sell merchandise. Pivot Rules, a distributor of moderate golf wear, launched a Web site in 1998 to sell an assortment of brands, including Polo, Hilfiger, Nike, and Nautica, bypassing the traditional retail channels. The brand-name merchandise is offered at discount prices.

Swimwear, once relegated to a short season, now functions year round. Although spring and summer are still the dominant sales periods for swimwear, resort and cruisewear lines have significantly added to profits. Many manufacturers preview their next season's collections at summer's end to get a feel for market changes and a jump on the styling that they will introduce in their resort collections. Swimwear manufacturers are comprised of companies that have been in the industry a long time, such as Jantzen, Catalina, and Gottex. Other swimwear manufacturers have made the assortment more fashion oriented through licensing agreements with famous apparel designers. The introduction of this new method of marketing swimwear caused prices to rise.

Swimwear is a dominant factor in the fashion industry all year round.

One of the fastest-growing merchandise classifications is intimate apparel, or lingerie, often called by its new name, **innerwear**. Merchants such as Victoria's Secret operate full specialty stores limited to lingerie. Designers such as Calvin Klein have made undergarments even more appealing. Department stores that once considered lingerie a less important item are now expanding their operations to carry fuller assortments. Chapter 11 focuses on the intimate apparel industry from a historical perspective, outlining trends from the origins of the industry to the present day.

Some of the fashion industry giants diversify their lines and cover a wide range of ready-to-wear items. For example, Liz Claiborne designs sportswear, dresses, menswear, sunglasses, and shoes within the company and under licensing arrangements.

Whatever the arrangement, collectively the women's apparel market includes the following classifications:

- Sportswear/Coordinated Separates
- Knitwear/Sweaters
- Activewear/Sports
- Coats/Suits
- Daytime Dresses
- Evening Wear
- Intimate Apparel

Table 10.1 lists the various women's wear markets within each classification.

Fridaywear

The term **Fridaywear** describes the less traditionally structured clothing that is now acceptable in many offices, particularly on dress-down Fridays. Although there has been a return to more formal dress in some companies, this casual approach to business

Table 10.1

CLASSIFICATIONS OF WOMEN'S WEAR MARKETS

Sportswear/Coordinated Separates	Career
	Misses
	Junior
	Casual/Weekend
Knitwear/Sweaters	Bulky
	Pointelle
	Intarsia
	Jacquard
	Novelty
	Sweater sets
	Pullovers
	Outerwear
Activewear/Sports	Golf
	Tennis
	Ski
	Swimwear/Cover-ups
	Bicycling
	Rollerblading
	Exercise/Aerobics
Coats/Suits	Dressy
	Casual
	Wardrober: Jacket/Skirt/Pants
Daytime Dresses	One- or two-piece
	Dress and jacket
Evening Wear	After-five/Cocktail
	Country-club wear
	Gowns
	Prom/Party
	Special Occasion
	Bridal/Mother of the bride/Bridesmaid
Intimate Apparel	Foundations
	Daywear (camisole, tap pants, slips, teddys)
	Sleepwear (nightgowns and pajamas)
	Sleep sets
	Sleepshirts/Nightshirts
	Robes

dress is still accepted in many business organizations. Even on other days of the week, women are dressing more flexibly, with pantsuits and separates forming a larger part of their wardrobes. This more relaxed wear easily makes the transition from work to play. Retailers already in the business of merchandising casual wear, such as Banana Republic and Gap, are reaping the benefits of this approach to fashion. Major retailers, such as Bloomingdale's, Lord & Taylor, and Macy's, have repositioned their inventories to address these new needs of women. With the growing popularity of the dress-down concept, more and more retailers are rethinking their merchandise mixes.

Price Points

Fashion merchandise is available in a number of different price points or ranges. In the women's wear industry, manufacturers usually concentrate on one of them—or sometimes two. Donna Karan, for example, produces two collections, one at the designer level, which labels its designs Donna Karan, and the other at the bridge level, bearing the DKNY label. By doing that, the company is able to reach a segment of the population familiar with the famous signature, but unable to afford its prices.

At the top of the price ladder is couture, followed, according to cost, by designer, young designer, bridge/better, contemporary, upper moderate/lower bridge, moderate, budget, and private label.

Couture

With prices as high as $5,000 for a jacket and $20,000 or more for an evening dress, **couture** merchandise is not within the reach of most shoppers. According to some of the more savvy fashion trade periodicals, consumers who purchase an item from a couture collection number only in the hundreds. The merchandise is one-of-a-kind, custom-tailored, and made of the finest fabrics. It is the only level of fashion where truly innovative styling is available.

Designer

Even designers who produce couture have turned to prêt-à-porter, or ready-to-wear. **Designer** merchandise carries labels similar to those at the top price points. Average price points for a jacket is $750 to $1,500 retail. The clothes are generally found in major fashionable department stores such as Saks Fifth Avenue, Barneys, and Neiman Marcus, in spaces described as in-store designer shops.

Young Designer

This price point appeals to a trendy customer who is very status conscious. The average jacket price at retail is from $300 to $800. Although some department stores have **young designer** shops, clothing is more likely to be found in specialty stores. Designers includes Gemma Khang, Marc Jacobs, Todd Oldham, Cynthia Rowley, and Anna Sui.

Bridge/Better

The sportswear merchandise that falls between the designer levels and the more moderately priced lines are known as **bridge collections**. This price point also encompasses the secondary lines of designers such as Christian Lacroix and Donna Karan, hence the name *bridge*. Unlike the designer jacket, which retails from $750 to $1,500, a jacket in a bridge collection would sell from $400 to $650. Bridge collections, such as DKNY, RRL, Anne Klein II, and Mani, are recognized by their company's names rather than specific designers. Examples of better lines include Dana Buchman, Tahari, and Ellen Tracy.

Contemporary

This is the category of sportswear that appeals to the widest audience. Prices for a jacket range from $150 to $225. Sold in department stores and sometimes in freestanding stores, examples includes Liz Claiborne, Carole Little, Jones New York, and Evan Picone.

Left: New York designer Donna Karan's couture label carries very expensive price tags and appeals only to a small market. Right: Her bridge collection—DKNY—with lower price points, has wider consumer appeal.

Liz Claiborne designs apparel for several classifications in the women's wear market including sportswear and suits.

Upper Moderate/Lower Bridge

This is a price point that is more fashion forward and updated than traditional merchandise. Jackets range from $100 to $120. **Upper moderate/lower bridge** clothing, with labels such as Chaus, Karen Kane, and Evan Picone, is sold in department stores.

Moderate

This large and extremely price conscious category consists of moderately priced groups of merchandise. It represents the offerings of such leaders as Guess and Esprit. The prices are more affordable to middle-income consumers. Prices generally range from $70 to $100 for jackets.

Budget

At the lowest level of the price structure are the dresses, sportswear, coordinates, and other apparel items that rarely bear nationally advertised labels. These garments are usually reproductions or adaptations of higher priced goods in low-quality fabrics. Designers such as Isaac Mizrahi have contracted with Target to produce lower-priced collections that have the pizzazz found in higher-priced merchandise. The **budget merchandise** is serviceable, but generally not as well constructed. More and more department stores are disbanding the budget classification, leaving it to stores such as Target, Kmart, and Wal-Mart.

Private Label

Private label is a term used to describe merchandise that is manufactured by retailers themselves in collaboration with a branded manufacturer. An unlikely participant in this branding approach is Ralph Lauren, considered by many to be the ultimate of label recognition. He is now involved in producing products for department and specialty stores that will feature neither his famous polo pony nor his signature, but will include quality produced fashion featuring the retailer's own private brand. Private labels cover all markets from bridge to moderate and cost as much as 25 to 50 percent less than if the same item were a brand label. Examples of stores and their private labels include The Limited, Macy's (Charter Club), Kmart (Jaclyn Smith), Kohls (Daisy Fuentes), and JC Penney (Arizona denim, Hunt Club).

Size Specialization

Before the 1950s, the purchase of a dress meant considerable alterations for many customers. Size ranges were dominated by the misses customer, who was generally unable to find anything off the rack at sizes smaller than 8; for her junior counterpart, size 7 was the smallest available. Except for some higher-priced lines, the size problem cut across most dress styles.

In the 1950s, Anne Fogarty, a designer who dressed the younger figure, broke new ground by promoting the famous Anne Fogarty Five, a dress one size smaller than was normally available. It was an instant success and smaller-figured juniors were able to buy dresses that were better proportioned to their bodies. Other manufacturers followed suit. Before long, size 1 became available for the tiniest junior figures and size 2 for the fuller, but small, misses figure.

As more and more women purchased the better-proportioned sizes, fewer alterations were necessary. Today, increased size specialization is evident. A female shopper can choose from a variety of size ranges that include misses, juniors, petites, and women's sizes, as well as specialized categories such as maternity and tall sizes.

Misses

The majority of women fall into the misses size range of 6 to 16. The misses figure is fuller-figured and longer waisted. Some manufacturers specialize in the smaller figure and begin with a size 2, but only go up to size 12. Other manufacturers begin with size 8, but produce up to 18 for the larger figure. Often, the size range is determined by the particular manufacturer and the specific style.

Juniors

In fashion, the word *junior* refers to size and not age. Although many manufacturers produce clothing that has a youthful look, junior-sized garments are proportioned to fit those who are slender and shorter waisted. The size range typically found in this category is 5 through 13, although sizes 1, 3, and 15 are generally available.

Petites

Recognition of the specialized needs for a shorter woman has resulted in this smaller-proportioned size range. Typically, petite sizes are manufactured for those women measuring 5′4″ and under. The length of the skirt or pants and the proportionate structuring of the sleeves minimize alterations. Petite sizes are odd-numbered, beginning with size 1 and ending with size 13. Some manufacturers have also introduced shorter versions of their misses sizes, which are even-numbered.

Women's

The larger, fuller figures of average heights wear women's sizes. They are even numbered and most frequently available in sizes ranging from 14 to 24. Recent years have seen a tremendous increase in the number of stores that carry this size range. Chains such as Lane Bryant and Lerner Woman, both belonging to the Limited organization, and Elizabeth, part of the Liz Claiborne empire, have many outlets catering to this clientele. What has made the category even more appealing is the styling. Once relegated to "dowdy" looks, the new women's sizes now feature the most fashionable silhouettes.

The shorter, fullest-figured women wear half sizes. The clothing is proportioned for the short-waisted heavier figure and generally comes in sizes from 12½ to 26½.

Tall Sizes

Available in even sizes that begin as small as 8 and range up to 20, tall sizes enable the tallest woman to purchase clothing perfectly proportioned for her figure. Not only are the hemlines longer, but so are the sleeves and waistlines.

Maternity

This size range duplicates the regular misses and junior sizes except that the construction allows for the expansion of the garment. At one time pregnant women had to settle for larger-sized regular clothing or less fashionable maternity wear. Today, with most women remaining on the job until their delivery dates, fashionable apparel is a necessity. Business suits and dresses that rival the stylings of regular-sized clothing are available in many maternity shops, such as Lady Madonna, Reborn, and Pea in the Pod. Even the most fashionable, narrow-legged jeans and knitted pants, swimsuits, and shorts are available.

Selling Seasons

The women's wear industry has the most selling seasons. Typically, this segment of the industry is represented by four or five collections a year, namely fall, holiday, spring, summer, and—for those who choose to participate—resort or cruise wear. Some fashion leaders, such as Liz Claiborne, break the seasonal norm and introduce new groups of merchandise as frequently as every six weeks. This approach is only appropriate for companies with enormous distribution and production facilities that can keep up with the pace. Some retailers, such as Gap, which manufactures its own merchandise, follow an even faster pace with their fashion items. The use of more than the traditional number of seasons has both advantages and disadvantages. On the plus side, it provides the store with a continuous change of merchandise that can enliven the usual slow or down periods. On the minus side, it sometimes adds merchandise to inventories that still need to be disposed of before the new can be successfully merchandised.

Whatever the decision, each season has its own personality and sales potential.

Fall

Generally, this season is the most profitable for the manufacturer. It lasts longer than the others and usually provides a new fashion story or unusual emphasis. It can be a dangerous season, however, if market research has indicated a radical change in fashion. The introduction of the briefest miniskirt coming on the heels of a longer skirt might be greeted with little enthusiasm. At the same time, fashion is a changing business that must take some risks if change is to occur.

Some manufacturers produce two lines at this time, Fall I and Fall II, with the former earmarked for earlier delivery and the latter for later delivery.

Holiday

The so-called holiday season is brief and manufacturers offer a new, but abbreviated, line. Some silhouettes that met with success in the fall reappear in more luxurious fabrics. The fall's flannel blazer with pearl buttons might repeat for the holidays as a satin model accented with rhinestone buttons. Companies that concentrate on dressy apparel might receive the greatest attention at this time. At the start of the new year, holiday merchandise is marked down to make room for the next season's apparel.

Resort

Resort wear, which is sometimes referred to as cruise wear, is a seasonal line that many producers bypass. Those who do invest in these collections often use the line as a barometer for testing fashions that will be shown during the summer. It is traditionally a proving ground for the swimwear industry. As a rule, resort wear belongs to the higher-priced designer and bridge collections, because their customers are the ones who can afford the luxury of a winter vacation. Manufacturers of lower price points closely follow the high-fashion designers at resort time, using their silhouettes and styles as the basis for their own summer lines.

Spring

The season that often provides the greatest difficulties for manufacturers and retailers alike is spring. At one time, it was a season for lightweight coats, suits, dresses, and sportswear. Fabrics were less bulky than those used in fall apparel, but heavier than the cottons and linens used for the summer lines. Recent years, however, have proved to be a disaster for many manufacturers and merchants who followed this traditional road. Today, most consumers shed the heavy garments of winter and move directly into summer attire. As a consequence, many producers have relegated the once-successful spring season to a partnership with summer. It means heavier, textured linens, cottons, and blends that can easily sell in the summer months if necessary.

Summer

With the traditional spring apparel of yesteryear only a memory, the suits and dresses of fall often step aside to make way for sportswear and swimwear. The season that used to start after Easter in the stores now begins right after the President's Week clearances. The season slows down in June, with retailers beginning to clear away their summer inventories to make room for fall merchandise. This is often a down time for regularly priced merchandise. Some manufacturers produce interim or transitional collections that sell when summer is waning and fall has not yet begun. The fabrics for these lines are lightweight, but of colorations that are darker and more subdued than the summer items.

Selling Women's Wear

The primary method of selling women's wear is in the manufacturers showrooms. In New York City's garment center and the many regional markets throughout the country, the large manufacturers operate their own selling spaces. Smaller organizations often engage a manufacturer's representative to show their merchandise in showrooms that feature several, noncompeting lines. The manufacturers and designers also maintain road staffs that travel designated territories and visit retailers in the hopes of selling the line.

The Council of Fashion Designers of America (CFDA), the subject of a World of Fashion Profile, has been known for its many promotional endeavors, including the now-famous tent show, Seventh on Sixth, for the women's wear industry in New York City's Bryant Park.

More and more fashion producers are taking their cue from the menswear industry and participating in trade expositions. With the National Association of Men's Sportswear Buyers (NAMSB) and Men's Apparel Group in California (MAGIC) expositions so successful for men's merchandise, expos featuring women's merchandise are becoming increasingly popular. MAGIC now also includes women's wear. See the World of Fashion Profile on MAGIC.

Promoting Women's Wear

Promotion is a necessary tool that is used to alert both the industry's professional buyers and consumers to the season's latest innovations. The ways in which the word is spread are numerous.

Fashion show presentations are the industry's best promotional tool. They start with the much heralded runway shows for the press, stores, and private clientele that take place in Paris, and move on to the more routine entries that are found in retail operations and mall centers. Fashion shows give the attendees firsthand knowledge of what is new for the coming season in a format that generates excitement. Other approaches include designer personal appearances, awards receptions, workshops, contests, fashion clinics, and so forth. A fully detailed exploration of women's wear promotion is offered in Chapter 22.

MENSWEAR

Whereas women have been showered with fashion choices for many decades, men have generally been presented with lackluster, traditional attire. Influential designers were preoccupied with enhancing the female figure—camouflaging it, glamorizing

MAGIC

MAGIC was founded in 1933 and quickly became the world's largest trade event to exclusively market menswear. It was an annual event hosted by the Men's Apparel Group in California. Today, the event is featured twice a year in Las Vegas, drawing buyers from all over the world.

Its sponsor, Magic International, soon expanded the exposition to add women's and children's lines to the men's offerings, as well as a segment that concentrates on sourcing for those retailers wishing to contract with private label contractors for their own collections. Retailers representing the smallest boutiques to the largest chains converge on the event that showcases 3,600 manufacturers and more than 5,000 brands.

At the Las Vegas Convention Center, and other venues in that area, the event is segmented into four separate shows: MAGIC, which features menswear; WWDMAGIC, which concentrates on women's apparel and accessories; MAGIC kids, exclusively marketing children's wear; and Sourcing at MAGIC, the arena that addresses the needs of private label retailers.

MAGIC, the menswear segment, concentrates on every major category in menswear, including designer clothing, contemporary collections, casual wear, streetwear, active sportswear, accessories, young men's, and kids. It is the buying event of the year for this market.

WWDMAGIC has become the largest trade event for women's apparel and accessories in the world. In conjunction with *Women's Wear Daily*, the fashion industry's chief authority, it has become the major event of its classification in the world. It connects the buyers with such markets as contemporary clothing, juniors, junior accessories, casual lifestyle, women's sportswear, dresses, swimwear, resort wear, and a host of wearable accessories.

MAGIC kids is the largest of the trade fairs representing the children's wear industry. The show features product classifications from layette and toddler to teen. Designers and manufacturers from around the world descend on Las Vegas semiannually to offer their collections to the largest number of buyers under one roof.

Unlike the other classifications, Sourcing at MAGIC

(continued)

MAGIC (continued)

addresses the needs of manufacturers and retailers in the improvement of their supply chains. Emphasis is placed on private label merchandise that retailers of these products can assess and learn how they may market them more profitably. A wide range of topics are explored such as trend forecasting, sourcing practices, and others that will help those interested in this market function. It has become the largest expo of its type in North America.

In just four days, twice a year, buyers are able accomplish their purchasing needs without having to visit the individual vendor showrooms to view the latest collections.

WWDMAGIC (opposite and above) is the world's largest trade show, held twice yearly in Las Vegas. The show features women's apparel and accessories and caters to both manufacturers and buyers.

it, and through creative silhouette engineering, reshaping it. The likes of Chanel, Dior, Balenciaga, and other international greats captured all the attention, leaving the menswear industry in a dull state.

Menswear has generally consisted of well-tailored clothing; the upper end of the spectrum produced the finest tailoring money could buy. Style simply remained constant—the same suit selling for years and years with no fear of fashion obsolescence. Many, in fact, adopted a "two pairs of pants" philosophy, preserving the same suit for even longer periods of time.

Suddenly, in the very early 1960s, men's fashion began to change radically. England was a forerunner in this new movement with the mod look of Carnaby Street, whose shops attracted the attention of young men with jackets with very wide lapels and bell-bottomed trousers. These changes closed the doors on the single-mindedness of men's fashion. European designers, who heretofore had concentrated only on female dress, embraced the male's newfound freedom of choice in fashion and began to create new silhouettes for men. Pierre Cardin's peacock look was accepted by men who were excited by these innovative stylings. Cardin, who first made his mark with innovative women's collections, was foremost in the introduction of

The mod look originated in London and took the fashion world by storm.

THE COUNCIL OF FASHION DESIGNERS OF AMERICA (CFDA)

The purpose of the CFDA is to promote the image of fashion and the people who are important to the industry. The council organizes a number of activities, including award presentations, centralized fashion shows, and charity benefits.

Each year, at New York City's Lincoln Center, celebrities from the world of fashion, entertainment, and the media gather to honor those in the fashion industry who have either made their mark in a specific merchandise classification or who promise to become leaders in the field. Among the awards given are those for continuous outstanding design, the Perry Ellis Award for the most promising designer, and achievements in the accessories field.

The CFDA tries to capture the attention of the media and the public with its awards ceremonies. It uses famous people from theater, television, and other walks of life as presenters. Perhaps the most dazzling presenter to date was Lady Diana, the Princess of Wales. Her appearance was recorded by all the media and shown on television broadcasts all over the world. It is coups like this that make the council a leading publicity agent for the industry.

The CFDA also sponsored the Seventh on Sale event in which leading designers donated merchandise that was sold to raise money to fight AIDS. The items were sold and money was raised in such fashion centers as New York City, San Francisco, and Los Angeles.

In 1993, the organization began Seventh on Sixth. With the support of its corporate sponsors and designers, the event established centralized fashion shows

CFDA's American Fashion Awards are the industry counterpart to the Oscars; recognition by one's peers is the ultimate honor for a fashion designer.

in New York City's Bryant Park that were similar to those in Paris. The event is now sponsored by Mercedes-Benz.

The CFDA is regularly called on to promote the fashion industry, and year after year it does so in many innovative formats.

the newest, high-fashion shapes for men—broad, peaked shoulders, fitted waists, and flared trousers. His entry into men's ready-to-wear helped transform men from the standardbearers of traditional dress to what we see today.

No longer are the gray flannel suit, white shirt, and tie the order of the day for proper business attire. Suits of every texture and color in a variety of silhouettes are accessorized with patterned shirts and enhanced with a wide assortment of ties. Today, a more relaxed approach is evident even in the most formal business environments. On Fridays, in particular, some companies are opting for more casual dress. Even some of the large corporations have relaxed their dress requirements and accepted a more casual look for every day of the week.

Who wears what, and for which occasion, still plays an important role in appropriate dress, but the parameters are broader than ever before.

Markets

Although the menswear industry is internationally based, New York City remains the major player. From the most elegant custom-tailored suits meticulously produced by the finest tailors to the ready-to-wear that accounts for the lion's share of the menswear business, New York City is the place where it is all available.

Any man interested in a custom-tailored suit that costs more than $3,000 can easily find a small operation that will design, cut, and sew the garment to his exact measurements. Many of the finest merchants who specialize in better off-the-rack clothing, such as Barneys, Paul Stuart, and Bergdorf Goodman, will also custom make clothing for those willing to pay the price. Some designers, such as Alan Flusser, have forsaken the route of mass-produced better ready-to-wear for custom-tailored clothing, along with a lower-priced collection that is exclusively marketed at Steinmart stores. Except for Hong Kong, which specializes in hand-sewn suits, few cities, if any, can rival the handcrafted models turned out in New York City.

In addition to New York, with menswear manufacturers producing at every price point, there are other centers that figure prominently in the industry. In the United States, Chicago, Baltimore, Los Angeles, San Francisco, Boston, Rochester, and Philadelphia are the men's manufacturing centers. Some of the companies are based in these cities, using their facilities for designing, patternmaking, and warehousing. The production, however, is generally accomplished offshore in places such as Hong Kong and South Korea, where the cost of labor is significantly lower. No matter where the companies are located, most often they maintain showrooms in New York City for the buyers. Unlike the women's industry, which covers New York City's entire garment center, menswear is more concentrated, with most major manufacturers having showrooms in one building, 1290 Avenue of the Americas. Later we will discuss the temporary showrooms used by the industry at trade expositions.

Product Classifications

The menswear industry is made up of several separate classifications. Some manufacturers concentrate on only one apparel group, such as casual wear, or even a subclassification, such as pants; others have various company divisions producing merchandise that crosses several classifications. Hartmarx, for example, is an industry giant that includes numerous merchandise groups under different labels.

Tailored Clothing

Collectively, coats, suits, sport coats, and dress trousers comprise the tailored clothing category. For many years, this group dominated the industry. Men were expected to wear suits and coats to their places of work and on many social occasions. Other items of apparel were needed to round out their wardrobes for less formal environments and events. The average businessman owned a number of suits that he rotated throughout the year. With the relaxation of the dress code, many tailored clothing manufacturers began to experience hard times. Some redirected their merchandising efforts to include less formal attire; others were forced to close their doors.

Menswear is no longer relegated to lackluster fashions. The range of fabrics and colors has broadened since the days of the gray flannel suit.

At the end of the 1990s, Italian companies such as Canali, GFT, Ermenegildo Zegna, Corneliani, and Lubiam began to promote a new fashion emphasis in tailored clothing. They are working to bridge the gap between relaxed designer fashion and traditional models of menswear. Waistlines have become narrower, less padding is used in the shoulders, the armholes are higher, linings are lighter, and softer fabrics

Relaxed business dress codes seemed to threaten the tailored clothing segment of the men's fashion industry in the 1990s, but a return to more formal office attire began to emerge around the turn of the century.

Casual business dress and suits now coexist in the office, even on dress-down Fridays.

have entered the picture. According to Anna Zegna, of Ermenegildo Zegna, "Tailored clothing can never go back to what it once was—heavy fabrics and stiff construction." The dramatic sales increase in the "new" tailored clothing seems to confirm the direction that menswear is taking at the start of the 21st century.

Fridaywear

The menswear industry has also had to adjust to dress-down Fridays. In addition to the conventional American- and European-cut suits, more casual attire is being worn in the workplace. Casual suits made of tweeds and other sporty fabrics, sport coats and contrasting trouser combinations, and even pants and shirts alone have become acceptable for at least one day a week. Often, even the sacred tie has been eliminated during this dress-down period.

Manufacturers such as Tommy Hilfiger and Claiborne are capitalizing on this concept by featuring comfortable apparel appropriate for both work and leisure activities.

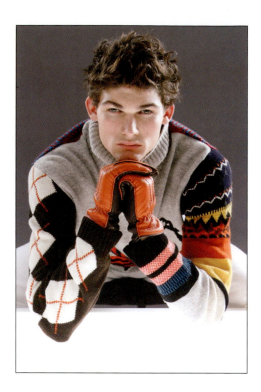

Men's furnishings, such as belts, ties, and gloves, have become more important since fashion and functionality have merged.

Men's Furnishings

The catch-all category that includes shirts, neckwear, underwear, belts, socks, and pajamas is the furnishings group. It is an important classification that capitalizes on designer licensing agreements. When names such as Pierre Cardin, Bill Blass, Calvin Klein, Yves Saint Laurent, and Geoffrey Beene appear on shirts or undershorts, the price points move upward. Today, even ties that hover around the $100 mark have become staples in some men's wardrobes. With suits often "nondescript" in design, it is the tie that distinguishes one man's appearance from another's.

Gloves, scarves, hats, braces, and other items round out the menswear classifications. Gloves remain the dominant item in this group because of their functionality. Hats, once commonplace in a man's wardrobe, are not popular. The only exceptions are baseball caps, knitted caps worn for skiing and during cold weather, and the tweed and suede sportier types worn with casual attire. Scarves, too, are an insignificant entry. They are generally worn only on the coldest days. The one fashion item that captures a small part of the market is braces, or suspenders. Men with careers in finance, investment banking, and law often choose this accessory as part of their standard dress. Their popularity has resurfaced because CNN talk-show host Larry King sports scores of different braces. Although Larry King will probably not make the lasting fashion impact that someone like the Duke of Windsor made, or even Andre Agassi with his bandana, he has given braces a great deal of exposure. Of course, only those that actually button on are considered appropriate; clip-ons are a fashion "no-no."

In addition to all of the brand label furnishings, there is also considerable growth in private labeling in this category.

Casual Wear

This merchandise group came into prominence during the 1970s. The relaxed dress code for some businesses coupled with the requirements of leisure activities resulted in a tremendous increase in market share for sweaters, knit shirts, jeans, and unstruc-

Casual wear, especially garments made of denim and leather, came into prominence in the 1970s and has remained a favorite.

tured sport coats. Although the leisure suits of the 1970s are no longer in vogue, the other items remain in favor.

Active Sportswear

The physical fitness craze that took the United States by storm during the 1980s has remained very important. Sweatsuits, jogging apparel, running shorts, tank tops, tennis shorts, golf pants and shirts, and athletic footwear have provided comfort both on and off the field. This type of apparel is worn to restaurants, movies, for shopping, on campus, and for leisure activities. Companies such as Reebok and Nike continue to expand their product lines to capture a larger share of this market. Both companies have opened large retail operations that exclusively feature their entire product lines of active sportswear.

Outerwear

Merchandise such as jackets, ski wear, and parkas constitute the outerwear category. Clothing that was once destined only for the coldest climates and for use in winter sports is now being produced with fashion in mind. One need no longer head for the slopes to wear a ski jacket; any casual destination will do. One of the indicators of the change in this once functional merchandise is the choice of colorization. The brightest and boldest color schemes, reflective of the color choices of the times and selected by the fashion designers, are utilized in outerwear. Many miracle fibers, such as Thinsulate, have helped reduce the bulkiness once associated with these products and made them lighter weight.

Because the season for this type of merchandise is limited, its manufacture has been assumed in many cases by the producers of active sportswear and rainwear.

Work Clothes

Once relegated to use by those in construction-type jobs, the styles have been adapted for other uses. Jeans, for example, are not just functional clothing that affords the wearer long-lasting use (so important for laborers), but are a fashion product on their own. As a separate category, jeans are one of the major classifications of apparel. Worn with denim shirts, sweatshirts, and workshirts, they have become the uniforms for many, especially students at every educational level.

Jeans first caught the attention of the masses when embraced by companies like Sasson and designers such as Calvin Klein. The name on the back pocket identified the manufacturer of the product and gave prestige and status to the wearer. Although the designer jean has not maintained its popularity, the denim pant is still an extremely important category. This is evident from observing inventory produced by Levi Strauss, the largest of the jeans manufacturers, Lee's, and Wrangler, and the full selections retailed by stores such as Gap.

Together with cargo pants and painter's-style pants, jeans are the common uniform for young adults worldwide.

Rainwear

From basic models designed to repel water to the most important classic creations, rainwear has become a significant part of menswear. Many men choose the all-purpose raincoat, with a zip-out lining, in place of the traditional overcoat. Coats of this nature are not only functional but also appropriate for any occasion. Luxury and prestige are also parts of the rainwear market, as seen by the now famous Burberry raincoat. The detachable woolen collar and lining and inner plaid fabric are indicative of this raincoat. While styles fall in and out of favor, the Burberry, with a price tag of $850, has helped rainwear achieve a status all its own.

Although the raincoat has become a mainstay in most men's wardrobes, its popularity has spelled disaster for the traditional winter coat. So many men have opted for all-weather raincoats that many manufacturers have dispensed with the production of heavy, winter coats.

Size Specialization

Men can choose from a variety of size ranges, particularly in tailored clothing. The vast array enables them to purchase proper-fitting clothing, without the need for major, costly alterations. This not only helps the retailer minimize clothing adjustment but also enables consumers to feel comfortable about the final fit of their purchases.

Although the size variations offer benefits to the purchaser, they often present merchandising problems for the merchant. The need to stock varied size ranges requires a considerable amount of space, as well as large outlays of money.

Tailored Clothing

Coats, suits, and sport coats come in several size ranges to accommodate the tallest to the shortest male, with physiques that range from the athletically fit to the slightly built.

REGULAR The majority of tailored clothing garments are produced for men considered to be of average height—between 5'8" and 5'11". The sizes usually run from 36 to 44, but some manufacturers cut both smaller and larger regulars. The measurement is based on chest size. Typically, the greatest volume is in the 40 to 42 range.

Many stores limit their inventories to the even sizes, with some offering only a small number of odd sizes.

LONG Designed for men who are from 6' to 6'3" and are proportionately built, these sizes are most often available from 38 to 46.

SHORT This size accommodates men who measure from 5'5" to 5'7" and are proportionately built.

EXTRA LONG For individuals who are 6'4" and over, garments in the extra-long size typically range from 38 to 48.

PORTLY These sizes are targeted at men who are in the same group as regulars, but with thicker waistlines.

STOUT This size fits men with heights of 5'5" to 5'7", who wear size 50 or over.

EXTRA LARGE This size accommodates men who wear size 50 and over and are at least 6' tall.

ATHLETIC CUT In the past, men with expanded chests and narrow waistlines often required considerable alteration to their clothing. Some manufacturers produce the athletic cut, which addresses this type of physique. The sizes generally are available from 40 to 44 and accommodate heights of 5'8" to 5'11".

Shirts

Shirts are produced in two distinct size designations: one for sport shirts and the other for dress shirts. Sport shirts come in sizes that range from small to extra large, whereas dress shirts come in sizes that take into account a man's neck measurement and sleeve length.

Dress shirts are the most difficult to merchandise because of the two size requirements they must address. For the average customer, neckband sizes range from 14½ to 17 and sleeve lengths from 32 to 35. Retailers catering to customers who require special sizes because of their height or weight carry even broader selections. The complexity of merchandising may be best understood when one considers how many different actual sizes there are for one neck measurement. Size 15, for example is available in sleeve lengths of 32, 33, 34, and 35. If different colors are available, the number of shirts necessary to complete a full size range becomes enormous. Many manufacturers, especially those that produce at modest price points, have gone to dual sleeve lengths. That is, they produce a 32/33 or a 34/35 to cut down on the amount of inventory. This, of course, does not necessarily suit discriminating purchasers. Those who want specific sleeve lengths must often pay more for the shirt.

In addition to these shirt measurements, there are other variations. Regularly proportioned men wear the regular cut; thin men, the tapered cut; and heavy-chested men, the full cut.

Sweaters

The stretchability of knitwear makes sweaters one of the easier groups to merchandise. Stretchability enables the manufacturer to produce in sizes that range from small to extra, extra large.

Selling Menswear

Two seasons, spring/summer and fall/winter, dominate the menswear industry. Most manufacturers present their major collections for these two seasons, with some adding interim lines if their offerings are more fashion oriented. Spring collections are shown from the middle of July to the end of September; fall presentations take place from mid-January to the end of February. Secondary lines are sold in the March/April period for winter and holiday merchandise and in October for late spring and summer apparel.

Although many mensweaer companies maintain year-round permanent showrooms in the major markets such as New York City, the vast majority of the industry's companies sell their lines at trade expositions.

Trade Association Expositions

The major trade associations sponsor expositions on a regular basis. These expositions bring buyers and sellers together under one roof. The most important of these events are those coordinated by the National Association of Men's Sportswear Buyers (NAMSB), the Men's Apparel Group in California (MAGIC), the Designer Collective, Salon de'Habillement Masculin (SEHM), and IMBEX.

One of the larger of the U.S. entries is NAMSB. The organization was founded in 1953 to increase the visibility of the men's sportswear market. Before its formation, tailored clothing received the most attention in the industry. Today, the association's original purpose has been expanded to include all categories of menswear. Three times a year, NAMSB presents three show weeks in New York City. More than 1,000 menswear lines are exhibited and more than 30,000 retail organizations of every size come to make their purchases for the following season.

MAGIC is the West Coast version of NAMSB, but is significantly larger. It was originally established to promote that area's sportswear market but has grown significantly and features lines from other locations. Like NAMSB, it attracts buyers from all over the country. The exposition, although still using California in its name, is now held in Las Vegas.

As NAMSB grew into an enormous trade show, a small segment of the menswear industry believed that the format no longer suited its needs. The group consisted of designers whose strengths were quality and originality at a price point above the rest of the market. In 1979, a few of the industry's talented designers formed what has become a showcase for the best in menswear fashion, the Designer's Collective. Membership is gained only after careful screening of an applicant's work and not by a willingness to pay dues. Those who are selected may exhibit their collections at the group's expositions.

SEHM and IMBEX are European-based groups that market their participant's lines in the same manner as their U.S. counterparts. Designers and manufacturers from all over the world converge on Paris for SEHM and London for IMBEX to show the latest in menswear.

Promoting Menswear

The menswear industry promotes itself to its retail customers and the editorial press in a number of ways. In addition to using the trade papers, such as the *Daily News Record* (*DNR*), a number of different groups have become part of the promotional packages. One of these is the Council of Fashion Designers in America (CFDA).

Council of Fashion Designers of America (CFDA)

The success of selling women's wear encouraged the CFDA to adapt the format for the menswear industry. In 1995, the CFDA brought together many men's fashion collections for runway presentations in various New York City environments, such as the Sony sound center. Designers such as Alexander Julian and Tommy Hilfiger presented their collections in productions that rivaled the excitement generated by their women's wear counterparts. The coverage by the press finally brought much-needed attention to the industry. With its success, such presentations have become regular events.

CHILDREN'S WEAR

Early in the 20th century, children's wear echoed the styles worn by their parents. In fact, children looked very much like miniature adults. The clothing worn was dictated by the parents, with children having little to say about dress preference.

Beginning in the 1950s, a significant change was noted in children's wear. Rock 'n' roll music and television helped to separate the younger generation's tastes from those of their parents. Teenagers, in particular, wanted the right to exercise their opinions in terms of dress and eventually broke away from traditional dress expectations. Girls wore full skirts that were exaggerated by petticoats, as well as loose shirts and oversized sweaters that went with skirts and pants. Boys took to more casual wear that featured knits and jeans. Gone were the days when copies of adult clothing were the only apparel for children's wear. A new world of fashion for the youth of America was born.

Today, some children's wear is again emulating adult clothing. Many manufacturers of adult clothing, such as Tommy Hilfiger and Ralph Lauren, produce little boys items that echo their fathers' clothing. Stores such as Gap, with GapKids, Talbots, with Talbots Kids, and the Limited's Limited Too, produce lines that resemble their adult offerings.

Bright colors are attractive to both the children who wear the apparel and the adults—often doting grandparents—who buy it.

Product Classifications

Children's wear classifications are as numerous as those for the men's and women's wear markets. For girls, dresses, skirts, pants, blouses, sweaters, suits, swimwear, active sportswear, outerwear, and the like are fashioned to fit specific needs. For boys, the breadth and depth of the product line is just as diverse.

Some manufacturers, such as Healthtex and OshKosh, produce a variety of products in their collections. Others restrict their offerings to one classification, such as knitwear. Within both of these merchandise approaches, there is also a need to decide whether to address all children's sizes, from infants to preteen, or to cater only to one or two size categories.

Size Classifications

Children's wear has a much broader range of styles than does men's and women's apparel. This is because of the different age groups through which children pass. From the infant stage through the preteen period, many different styles are required.

Infants' and toddlers' wear is designed to meet the special needs of these age groups.

The children's wear market has greater appeal today with its broad fashion offerings.

Infants

Most lines are produced in a range of "month" sizes, beginning with newborn or 3 months and moving up to 24 months. The sizes selected for the individual child do not necessarily reflect the child's true age, because each child experiences a different rate of development. The size is merely directed to an average stature for that particular age.

Toddlers

T2 through T4 is the size range for toddlers, children who are crawling and beginning to walk. A large infant can sometimes wear a small toddler size.

Children's

Girls' clothing in this classification ranges in size from 3 to 6X and boys' from 3 to 7. Once a toddler has stopped wearing diapers, he or she usually progresses to children's sizes and stays with this range until the first or second year of school.

Girls

Having outgrown the children's classification, girls enter the 7 to 14 sizes.

Boys

When they can no longer wear the children's sizes, boys move into a range from 8 to 20, which serves this group until they are ready to wear some of the specialized student or teen sizes.

Preteen

No longer satisfied with the styles of the girl's range and still insufficiently developed to enter the teen or junior market, girls may wear preteen clothing in sizes 6 to 14. The merchandise generally reflects the styles of the teen market, but is proportioned to fit preteen bodies.

Price Lines

Although the men's and women's industries offer merchandise at all price points, children's price lines are not as diverse. Children's clothing is viewed as a perishable item because of the rapid growth of its wearers, the beating it often takes from just plain wear and tear, and constant laundering. These factors make buying new clothes in larger sizes a necessity. To have greater appeal, most manufacturers stay within a price range that appeals to a wide audience. Of course, some children's wear manufacturers deal with a small, upscale market and produce more costly merchandise. An example is Ralph Lauren with his Polo label. Parents who prefer these products for themselves often choose the same labels for their children.

Selling Children's Wear

The methods of operation parallel those of men's and women's fashions, using individual showrooms, manufacturer's reps, road staffs, and trade expositions. With lines generally produced twice a year, there are two major selling seasons. More and more manufacturers are opting to sell at the trade expos, such as Pitti Bimbo in Florence, and Salon de la Mode Enfantine in Paris.

Promoting Children's Wear

Children's wear requires less expensive promotion than either men's or women's fashions. In addition to fashion shows at trade expositions, manufacturers advertise in children's trade publications, such as *Earnshaws* and Fairchild Publications' *Children's Business*. As with the other segments of the fashion industry, promotion activities will be explored later in the text.

CHAPTER HIGHLIGHTS

- The men's, women's, and children's wear industries parallel each other in a number of ways. Their merchandise is available at many different price points, it is produced internationally, and the appeal is to very broad markets.

- The women's wear industry receives greater attention from the editorial press than either men's or children's wear.

- Women's fashions come in a variety of price points, classifications, and size ranges.

- The major markets for the women's industry are found throughout the world. Paris is still the center for couture, while no place is a match for New York City's ready-to-wear market. Of course, all over the world other fashion capitals and regional markets coexist and offer merchandise of every style and shape.

- Women's wear has the largest number of seasonal collections.

- Women's apparel is promoted through a variety of endeavors, the most important of which is the fashion show.

- Menswear styling, after remaining constant for many years, finally came alive in the early 1960s with the mod look from London's Carnaby Street.

- The peacock look, popularized by Pierre Cardin, featured broad, padded shoulders, nipped-in waistlines, and long jackets.

- Men's clothing is available in a range of sizes tailored to fit a variety of physiques without necessitating a great deal of alterations.

- Promotion of menswear is accomplished through a variety of means, with trade shows and associations playing major roles.

- The children's wear industry came into its own in the 1950s and 1960s when the youth of America began to express their own opinions about dress.

- Children's sizes range from infant to preteen, with each range featuring appropriate styles for the ages of the wearers. At the preteen level, the styling is similar to that found in junior collections; only the proportions differ.

- In all three apparel classifications, trade expositions play an important role in the selling of the lines.

IMPORTANT FASHION TERMINOLOGY AND CONCEPTS

braces
bridge collection
Carnaby Street
Council of Fashion
   Designers (CFDA)
cruise wear
Designer Collective
electronic press kit
The Fashion Association
   (TFA)

Fridaywear
half sizes
holiday season
IMBEX
Men's Apparel Group in
   California (MAGIC)
misses figure
National Association of
   Men's Sportswear Buyers
   (NAMSB)

off the rack
peacock look
petite sizes
price points
resort wear
Salon de'Habillement
   Masculin (SEHM)
selling season
tailored clothing
toddlers

FOR REVIEW

1. Where is the center for women's couture located?
2. Name three classifications of women's wear and the importance of each to the industry.
3. Explain the bridge price point.
4. Is the junior size necessarily directed to the young? Explain.
5. In what way are women's sizes different from half sizes?
6. When and where did the menswear fashion revolution take place?
7. List five major merchandise classifications in menswear and indicate one product in each.
8. Describe the differences between regular and athletic cuts.
9. How do dress shirt sizes differ from those of sport shirts?
10. What are the major seasons in menswear?
11. Discuss some of the activities undertaken by the Council of Fashion Designers of America that have benefited the fashion industry.
12. What events led to the change in children's clothing styles?
13. Why are children's price lines more restricted than women's and men's?

14. What is the major method used for promoting fashions?
15. Summarize the key concepts in the Point of View article titled "Ralph to the Rescue."

EXERCISES AND PROJECTS

1. Prepare an oral report on a famous apparel designer for presentation to the class. Information is available from the designers or from periodicals available in most libraries.
2. Contact a women's wear buyer to learn about the various seasons in the industry. From the information collected, prepare a table showing the seasons, dates of purchasing, and delivery dates.
3. Visit a men's tailored clothing department in a major store and, through inspection or questioning of the manager, determine the percentages of each subclassification of the category.
4. If you are in a city that hosts a trade exposition, such as NAMSB or MAGIC, write to the sponsor to request tickets for the event. Most organizations will honor student requests. Write a report outlining the various observations made at the event.
5. Prepare a booklet on children's wear for one season using pictures found in mail-order catalogs and magazines. Concentrate on only one size range. Summarize the fashion highlights that are apparent in the selected styles.

WEB SITES

By accessing these Web sites, you will be able to grain broader knowledge and up-to-date information on materials related to this chapter.

Fashion Group International
   www.fgi.org
DNR
   www.dnrnews.com
Women's Wear Daily
   www.wwd.com

The Case of the Disagreeing Partners

Lilliputian is a children's wear company that specializes in infants, toddler's, and children's size ranges. It has been operating successfully for eight years. Unlike most manufacturers, the company began to earn a profit only 14 months after its doors were opened.

The two-team partnership began with knitted items for infants. The articles were hand constructed by women who worked in their homes. Using this approach, neither a factory nor showroom was needed. Lilliputian sold its goods by calling on better-priced specialty stores.

With significantly favorable reaction, the owners kept expanding. First, they leased a small facility in which they added other lines. A complete line of infant wear was later joined by toddler's and children's groups. In a short time, they gained a national reputation.

As each period of growth proved successful, one of the partners, Donna Barrie, expressed a desire to expand once again. This time she feels the preteen market would be an appropriate choice, because mothers would recognize the Lilliputian label and purchase this next size range for their youngsters. Beth Jansen, the other company principal, is opposed to the idea. She believes the new market is significantly different from the one they know, and that it is smaller, because many stores do not carry as much variety in preteen merchandise. Furthermore, she thinks older children might reject the new line simply because Lilliputian has always been associated with younger children's wear.

The partners are now making a decision.

question

With which partner do you agree? Why?

Ralph to the Rescue:
Lifestyle Guru Creates Private Brand Division

MARC KARIMZADEH

New York—Ralph Lauren is about to enter a new, private world. Today, the Polo Ralph Lauren Corp. is expected to unveil the formation of Global Brand Concepts, a group that will focus on developing lifestyle brands in exclusive partnerships with department and specialty stores. The collections could range from women's and children's wear to accessories and home furnishings. But make no mistake: They will not carry a Polo label, nor will they in any way be marketed to suggest Ralph Lauren is behind them.

But Polo would own the trademarks developed under any deals, giving the corporation the potential to significantly boost its revenues and gain control over more real estate in department and specialty stores, including distribution channels he may not yet be in. And in another unusual twist, the stores would own the product, sparing Polo any headaches over inventory.

The new division's mission is to develop non-Ralph lifestyle brands that are exclusive to its retail partners using Polo's extensive resources and brand-building expertise, from design to manufacturing, marketing and advertising. After 40 years in business, there is no doubt in Lauren's mind that he has what it takes—the Rx—to give a boost to department and specialty stores.

"I look at this industry and walk around the stores to see what is going on," Lauren said. "I think one of the things stores need is an ability to be individual, the ability to say, 'This is mine.' They have to be able to say, 'Come to my store because we have something you don't have.'"

The idea for Global Brand Concepts came from the designer's recent observation that many large stores are plagued by sameness, with little to set them apart from one another.

"In this day and age, there are a handful of designers and brands that are very strong," Lauren observed. "They can grow, but at a certain level, they start to overlap. Consumers are looking for something new, retailers are looking for something new and the brands are looking to grow their business."

With Global Brand Concepts, Lauren is making an aggressive push into the arena of exclusive retail brands. The move raises the question whether talks with J.C. Penney for an exclusive lifestyle collection under a different name, first reported in WWD last June, triggered this new concept, which could set the stage for a deal with the mid-market retail chain in the near future.

Lauren is tight-lipped about any such partnership, other than to say, "I have spoken to them, and I have spoken to other companies. I have companies that wanted me to do the whole store and give them a whole image."

The designer has already had a taste of exclusive retail brands with Chaps. Polo inked an exclusive deal with Kohl's to sell Chaps branded apparel in 2005. Until 2003, Chaps was marketed as Chaps Ralph Lauren, but although it still embodies the preppy, Anglo-Saxon sensibility Lauren has made his trademark, there is no longer any indication the designer is behind the brand. The introduction of Chaps was the biggest launch in Kohl's history.

More recently, exclusive retail brands have been gaining traction elsewhere, even though almost all of them carry an established designer's name. This spring, Oscar de la Renta is relaunching his better-priced O Oscar sportswear collection exclusively at Macy's, which is already home to the T Tahari line that is exclusive to Federated. And Vera Wang signed a deal last year to create an exclusive line for Kohl's.

Observing the retail scene overall, Lauren said, "There are a lot of things that need to be addressed. The large stores . . . sometimes don't see what they need or they want a new brand that says something about their company and gives them an identity, the way you need a face that says, 'Who am I, what do I stand for and what separates me from this other guy across the street?' We are big enough and have a team that is strong enough to develop individuality for these stores."

By creating Global Brand Concepts, Lauren is moving a notch closer to what many (jokingly) assume is his ultimate goal: world domination, at least in floor space. The new division gives his company an opportunity to gain significantly more real estate at retail, and it's not limited to luxury stores. Since Lauren will offer the brands under a different guise, the concept could, in theory, be expanded to retailers at any tier, from class to mass. It allows the designer to dodge the dangers of downgrading or diluting the Polo moniker.

"There is a world out there that I don't want to put Ralph Lauren in because Ralph Lauren is exclusive," Lauren said. "It is a luxury brand, and all our brands have their designations. But there is more business, more growth. And there's a lot of potential in the stores that really need help, and they want what Ralph Lauren is about and see what we can do."

He certainly has the track record to back up his confidence. Today, Polo is one of the healthiest and fastest growing fashion and luxury businesses, with revenues of $3.75 billion in its most recent fiscal year. In the runup to its 40th anniversary year, Lauren and president and chief operating officer Roger Farah have created a business model based on a multitude of Ralph Lauren related labels; a strategy of buying back licenses to gain better control, and a focus on freestanding retail, from bringing Ralph Lauren stores to Tokyo and, this spring, Moscow, to new store concepts like Rugby and Double RL. Polo has been stepping up brand recognition efforts by becoming the official sponsor of high profile sports events like the U.S. Open and Wimbledon tennis tournaments.

"If you look at our company, you see Ralph Lauren, Polo, Purple Label, Black Label, Lauren and children's," the designer said. "These are all concepts that grew out of a tie. It's all done under these offices. And there's Rugby retail and Ralph Lauren retail. There will be Lauren retail. They are all different concepts with a soul that has to do with Ralph Lauren."

"This is a place that is designed on every level, and we develop our advertising," he added. "It is like a school here.

We do our own branding, our own planning as to how we're going to advertise. That kind of flexibility, that sort of dimension, says, 'What can we do that would be interesting?'"

Farah said in a statement, "This fits into our overall strategy of continuing to invest in the breadth of our unique offering. We are setting up a structure which can basically be a one-stop shop for companies in need of nice opportunities to meet customer's demands."

In its premise, Global Brand Concepts resembles a private label development business, though Lauren hopes to create brands that will offer more than the own label assortment usually found in department stores.

The group's strategy is flexible, and each arrangement will be customized, the details depending on the nature of the relationship. Retailers can approach Lauren about developing an exclusive line for their stores, or, if he sees an opportunity in a retail chain and envisions a particular brand concept, he can suggest it. The designer will be involved in each brand and will work closely with his design teams.

Hypothetically, a chain like Penney's could contact Lauren about developing a new lifestyle collection. Global Brand Concepts would then enter a contract agreement with Penney's, and Lauren and his team would develop the brand from scratch, a process that would include concept, design, sourcing the fabrics and contracting out production. Then the group would work on brand-building through advertising and marketing, all of which the retailer would finance.

The organization's structure would loosely resemble a wholesale operation. A retail client would be required to carry the entire product line, which it would then own and would be responsible for inventory issues such as markdowns. Polo

will oversee its presentation at retail. If the lines proved successful enough to merit stand-alone stores, it would be up to the retailer to finance such an extension. Legally, however, Lauren would own the brand's trademark since Polo Corp. would manufacture and ship the product as part of the arrangement, but the company does not plan to deal with markdowns or excess inventory.

"I love breaking the rules and the ability to have other niches," said Lauren. "There's no limit. I think this is very important for retail. Can they do it by themselves? Maybe and maybe not. Many retailers have tried to, but they are in the retail business. It's very hard to develop a brand internally. You can develop a name and say, 'OK, we will make this a private label,' but is it a leader? How do you promote it, advertise it, build that brand and market it? Our sense is to develop a new concept with a partner. We would say, 'This could be interesting for your store.'"

The designer said it was too early to disclose the kind of lines he envisioned at retail but noted they could be at any tier as long as they were "within the world of what I am seeing and what I think is missing," Lauren said. "It doesn't matter if that's hip-hop. Maybe I am thinking I want to do a new jeans brand or a new career look, a young look or home. It can have that diverse sensibility, but it has to be something I really want to do within this company."

Skeptics may wonder if Lauren runs the risk of creating lines that will directly compete with Ralph brands on the selling floor, but he downplayed the notion.

"The goal is to make them all individual. The goal is not to make them copies," he said, adding that while they could compete on some levels, there would be plenty of nuances and details to differentiate them.

He added that Global Brand Concepts would be positioned to develop brands for retailers around the world. As chairman and chief executive officer of Polo, Lauren will oversee the operation and assemble a separate team of executives that will work at Global Brand Concepts to develop the new exclusive brands.

Lauren wouldn't disclose projections for Global Brand Concepts but indicated the division would fit in with the company's momentum.

"This is a public company and a company that has to perform, so we sharpen up. We try and look at the future and see what we haven't done, what no one else has done and where we can be original," Lauren noted. "That's the premise. The fun for me is the newness."

Despite this push to build non-Ralph brands, the market for Polo extensions has not been saturated. Far from it, said Lauren, "but I am not going to build a brand unless I have a reason."

"I want to take this company to greater heights than I have," he added. "This is my baby. It started with a tie, out of a drawer in the Empire State Building. I was the only one in the company and had to pick up the phone. One year, for Thanksgiving, my wife, my father-in-law and my mother-in-law were sewing on labels in a warehouse downtown. I can't even believe that ever happened. The most important thing for me is building this company and this brand."

Women's Wear Daily, January 8, 2007

Those Zeros Keep Adding Up

ROSEMARY FEITELBERG

New York—Zero could be the new six.

Not restricted to painfully thin runway models, Hollywood celebrities or Tom Wolfe's famed Social X-rays, size zero is gaining ground with everyday women and designers alike. For some women, being a size zero is something to brag about; for others, even that isn't small enough.

While some might be all too familiar with what a shopping challenge zero-ness poses, many—presumably larger people—didn't even know such a size existed until Madrid Fashion Week's organizers agreed to ban zero-sized models last month. Yet Robert Duffy, president and vice chairman of Marc Jacobs International, recently said Marc Jacobs sells more zeros than any other size in its collection and, truth be told, he has never seen a cutting order for a size 14.

While some designers have aggressively gone after zeros as a way to compensate for the near nonexistence of petite departments in many department stores and major chains, that was not why Lela Rose got into the game. Rose said she started offering her collection in

that diminutive size two years ago, when a handful of customers found themselves swimming in her size 2 pieces. To her surprise, zero has become one of her label's top-selling sizes.

Zero-sized merchandise is doing so well for Nicole Miller that she plans to introduce a subzero size next season for even smaller women. The new size would be geared toward women with a 23 ½-inch waist and 35-inch lower hip. (That waist size is said to be the one Victoria Beckham has, which also is said to be the circumference of a soccer ball.) Sizes zero and 2 are always the first to sell out in Nicole Miller stores. "Zero is too big for a lot of girls and I wouldn't say they are anorexic girls. There are many very petite girls and very small Asian women," said Miller.

Another factor that may be contributing to the zero craze is the prevalence of vanity sizing among some brands. "I've noticed that other companies are sizing up. I used to go buy pants and would wear a 6, but they started to be too big. Now a 4 is too big," Miller said.

Some fashion executives speculated about how the tabloids' analysis and full length photos of the extralean frames of Nicole Richie, Kate Bosworth, Ellen Pompeo and other celebrities might play on Americans' never-too-thin mind-set.

Ed Bucciarelli, chief executive officer and president of Henri Bendel, said, "Clearly, there has been much discussion about models and celebrities being too thin. That's tabloid fodder. We live in a very celebrity-conscious world, especially in the U.S. Maybe some are trying to emulate the girls they see on the [magazine] covers."

While Lela Rose, Marc Jacobs, Cynthia Rowley, and Nicole Miller may be on board with zero sizing, many high-end American designers are not. Bucciarelli said, "I wonder if it's an American phenomenon. I don't know there is an equivalent size in Europe."

Petite shoppers were up in arms last spring when Saks Fifth Avenue announced it was dropping its petite department. The news caused such an uproar the retailer has since said the department will be reinstated. As things stand, zero is "one of the sizes that sells out pretty quickly" at Saks, a company spokeswoman said. Theory, which also offers items in a double zero, and Alice + Olivia are among the popular labels with size-zero customers, she said.

Olympic skater Kristi Yamaguchi, a zero-wearing shopper, said she usually checks out Nordstrom, Saks Fifth Avenue and Neiman Marcus, but small sizes tend to sell out quickly. Further complicating things is the fact that buyers tend to buy only a few size zeros of a particular style, compared with plenty of 8s or 10s.

"If I find something I kind of like, I feel pressured to get it. I know if I wait, it will be gone. Stores need to carry more small sizes," she said.

At Bendel's, zero-sized merchandise comprises about 5 to 10 percent of the total business. The prevalence of superslim silhouettes such as leggings and skinny jeans should only make more women size down whenever possible, said Bucciarelli. Diane von Furstenberg, Sass & Bide, J Brand, Alice + Olivia and LaRok are a few of the labels that are popular for their zero sizes, he said.

Sometimes zero isn't small enough. Jennifer Hoppe, a zero-sized New Yorker, said she spends "hundreds and hundreds of dollars" annually on alterations. She often finds herself shopping at Gap, Banana Republic and Old Navy—sometimes in the children's department—to try to find clothes. "I don't have a destination. In fact, that's been my dream—to open a store for small people, even though I know it's so politically incorrect."

The 110-pounder is so adamant about the dearth of diminutive sizes, she once wrote an essay that was published in *For Me* magazine about the reverse discrimination she faces. "People often think it's perfectly OK to comment about how I'm really small and the fact of the matter is they would never say that to an overweight person."

More contemporary resources are offering size zero, said Hoppe, who buys Rebecca Taylor pants and Joe's Jeans. Wrap dresses are a mainstay in her wardrobe because of obvious reasons.

"I can find things, but it takes me longer than most people," she said.

Boston-based technology writer Stefanie McCann, who buys zero and

double-zero clothes, said finding casual clothes is not a problem, but "the work stuff is almost impossible, which is tough when you are almost 40 and you are really limited to what you can wear." Suits are out of the question, as their alterations could easily run $150, and dresses aren't much better. She often winds up shopping at Saks Fifth Avenue, Arden B., outlet stores and "even Marshall's."

During her twice-a-month business trips, McCann tries to seek out boutiques, which tend to carry smaller sizes.

That means shoppers like McCann buy more full-priced merchandise since they don't really have the option of waiting for something to go on sale. She said she has mentioned the lack of proper-fitting clothes to salespeople in stores, but they have shown little sympathy. "They'll say, 'Isn't that a great problem to have?' "

New York-based publicist Jennifer DeMarchi also noted that finding jackets is tough because the shoulders never fit properly and sleeves are always too long. "I think plus-size women have more options than zeros these days. Wal-Mart and Target have plus-size departments, but no petites," she said.

Ready to Wear Report, *Women's Wear Daily*, October 6, 2006

Men's a Bright Spot for YMA Panel

JEAN E. PALMIERI

New York—Men are more willing to step out in terms of fashion, opening a window of opportunity for retailers and wholesalers.

At a roundtable sponsored by the YMA Fashion Scholarship Fund prior to its annual fundraising dinner next month, top executives took on a series of topics affecting the industry, including the growing importance of fashion to the male consumer.

Ken Hicks, president and chief merchandising officer of J.C. Penney Co., who will be honored at the dinner on Jan. 10, said that five years ago 70 percent of men's wear purchased at Penney's was bought by women. But today, 70 percent of it is purchased by men. "That's a huge change," he said. "It shows guys give a damn."

Karen Murray, group president of men's wear, mid-tier, international alliances and licensing for Liz Claiborne

Inc., another dinner honoree, has also noticed a switch. Five years ago, she said, 75 percent of Claiborne men's wear purchases were "made or influenced by women," but that number has definitely decreased.

Nevertheless, Murray said fashion firms must continue to push the envelope. "Men don't change much in what they wear," she said, noting that most of their purchases are "replacement" items. "We have to give men a reason to buy and get them more interested in fashion."

At a post-roundtable press gathering, Murray added: "Once you get out of New York, the average men's wear customer doesn't want to be a metro-sexual and only goes to a store for an event, an occasion, or to replace an item. They're afraid to reveal that they care about what they're wearing. Sure, the young guy is better, but the problem we all face is how to get the average man interested in how he looks and feel comfortable about it."

Hicks said that, in consumer research, male customers were proud to think they could wear a treasured new shirt 300 to 400 times. "That's a problem," Murray interjected.

Chris Kolbe, president of Original Penguin, said that among the "20- to 30-somethings," fashion is becoming more important. "Men are more sensitive to fashion and wearing things differently. The playing field is expanding."

He believes there is a "big hole in the men's business and it's all about the guy in his thirties who wants to dress better, but not like his dad. And he also wants to shop in a different kind of store where he'll feel comfortable in a relaxed, cool shopping environment."

Another hot topic was private label, which continues to grow in importance and change the dynamic of relationships within the industry.

Noting that many of Penney's private labels, including the Arizona Jeans Co., are $1 billion businesses, Hicks said budding designers should be open to working in this segment of the industry. Unlike a designer brand, private-label creators can find their products on the floor in a few months.

Murray said that "defending, protecting and building brands" will become more important over the next few years as labels such as Arizona continue to grow in importance. "Five years ago we thought retailers couldn't live without wholesalers. Today, retailers are good wholesalers and the days are gone when we can do things better."

Hicks said the continued consolidation among retailers and manufacturers means private and proprietary brands will become even more essential in the future as consumers choose where to shop by the "destination" brands offered.

In addition to private brands, other opportunities for growth in the future include brand extension into products that are destined to become more popular, such as children's and baby wear, as well as international expansion, Kolbe said. "Commerce without borders."

Tim Gunn, chairman of the department of fashion design for Parsons and co-host of *Project Runway*, asked the panelists if they looked at "design through the lens of commerce," and all agreed that they do.

Murray said that "great product is wonderful, but if you're not figuring out how to make money, it's over."

Hicks agreed that "product and commerce support each other," and Kolbe said young people tend to get into the fashion business "for a love of product, innovation and creativity," but they also need to consider ROI—"return on imagination," or "the intersection of product and business." He said it's also smart to know "what opportunities not to pursue."

That was a lesson that April Singer, designer and founder of Rufus Apparel, understands well. She said that after starting her men's line three years ago, it had been suggested often that she also take on women's wear. But she opted to put that on hold until "all the kinks" were worked out, she said. Now that the men's business has taken off, she will launch a women's collection for fall 2007, she revealed.

At the post-event, Hicks said Penney's men's business continues to be good and for the past several months has been among the chain's top performers. "We think 2007 will be a good year with a lot of exciting things coming up." He pointed to the expansion of J. Ferrar and the introduction of Concepts by Claiborne, as well as the opening of 50 new stores and the hiring of a new ad agency as among the reasons for his optimism.

And that's without any "external factors" such as Penney's picking up market share from the former May Co. stores that were converted this fall to Macy's, which can help Penney's perform "even better," he said. "We can't control the outside world. We just have to make sure we have the best portfolio going forward. And we feel good about it."

The YMA Fashion Scholarship Fund dinner will be held at the Marriott Marquis in New York. It will also honor *American Idol* judge Paula Abdul.

Newsfront, *DNR*, December 11, 2006

chapter 11

intimate apparel

Luxury need not have a price; comfort itself is a luxury.

GEOFFREY BEENE, DESIGNER

After you have completed this chapter, you will be able to discuss:

- The evolution of intimate apparel and types of innerwear that have been worn.

- The various products that comprise the intimate apparel market.

- The internationally famous couturiers who designed intimate apparel.

- The relationship between intimate apparel designs and ready-to-wear.

- The fibers and fabrics used for intimate apparel.

- The manner in which intimate apparel is being marketed by manufacturers and retailers.

Today, the intimate apparel industry is a major entity in the world of fashion. New styles of women's undergarments, foundations, and shapewear are constantly being introduced and new fabrics are developed to enhance them. This fashion category has become one of the fastest-growing segments of the fashion industry.

The great amount of interest that surrounds intimate apparel today is by no means new. Although many of us think of **undergarments** as inventions of the modern-day world, their use can be traced back to antiquity. Many contemporary products, such as corsets, are adaptations or variations of those that were first worn thousands of years ago; others are more recent innovations.

The dress of ancient eras, and the periods that followed, generally dictated the types of **innerwear** that women would be required to endure. From ancient times through the early 1800s, the emphasis was on items that either enhanced or concealed the breasts. Today, of course, the designs and styles of intimate apparel are vast, with bras, corsets, petticoats, pajamas, and robes offered by a significant number of designers and manufacturers. The intimate apparel industry is growing faster than most of the other segments that comprise fashion.

THE EVOLUTION OF WOMEN'S UNDERGARMENTS

Styles from Antiquity to Medieval Times

The images of the ancient world that we see in the artwork and statuary of Crete, Egypt, Greece, and Rome provide a wealth of evidence that as early as 2000 B.C., clothing reflected a fascination with women's breasts. As in modern times, the breasts were often the focal points of the figure. The women of Crete wore corsets that molded their figures and supported their breasts in a manner that accentuated them.

Around 1000 B.C., in Greece, women wore strips of cloth, called *apodesmes*, that were rolled just below their breasts. This was probably the first type of undergarment.

The purpose of these cloths was not to accentuate the breasts but to prevent as much movement as possible when women walked. Many of the Greek statues and mosaics displayed in museums throughout the world feature the female figure clothed in varied designs of this nature. Eventually the Greeks began to use a band of cloth wrapped over the breasts, called an *anamaskhaliter*. This was the forerunner to the modern brassiere.

At the beginning of the Roman Empire, women bound their breasts with an article called the *fascia*, a sort of fabric bandage intended to control movement and prevent the breast from developing too much. Women with very large breasts wore the *mamillare*, a leather band or bra that minimized the size of their breasts.

In the early Middle Ages, fashion continued to minimize the breasts by binding them and concealing them further within dresses constructed of vast yardages of material. This style continued until the 12th century, when clothing began to give more definition to the female figure. Clothing that clung to the body necessitated new types of undergarments. Women wore the *cotte*, a laced tunic that held the figure in shape; the *bliaunt*, with side or back laces, which helped to shape the bust; and the *surcot*, a design that fit over the dress and was tightly laced. The laced-up models helped slim the figure and mold the bust. In the late Middle Ages, the figure-fitting fashions led to the use of corsets. Ultimately, corsets were stiffened, boned, and tied, helping to accentuate the waistline. This type of undergarment produced a shapelier silhouette.

Styles from the 1400s to the 1800s

During the early 15th century, the breasts were held very high with the support of a wide belt placed directly below them. Some women began to show more of their breasts with deeply cut necklines. Also in evidence in paintings of this period were breasts that were thinly disguised with sheer fabrics.

A prominent element in fashion of the 1500s in England was the **chemise**. This simple undergarment, which dates back thousands of years, was loose fitting, slipped over the head, and was often embellished with a pleated bottom. In contrast to the figure-defining corset, it was a comfortable undergarment that was worn under loose-fitting dresses.

During the 16th century, the busts of aristocratic women were presented in cone-like designs. The corset, a descendant of the *bodice* worn in the 15th century, was constructed much like a straight jacket, of extremely rigid materials. It was worn under a dress and over a soft, cotton shift. Women often fainted because of breathing difficulties caused by the rigidity and tightness of their corsets. Undergarments and other intimate apparel styles became increasingly important from the 16th through the 18th centuries. Many of these garments are still very much in fashion today.

With the death of Louis XIV of France in 1715, women began to have more influence over the design of their clothing. The armored undergarments they had previously worn were cast aside and they began to wear more comfortable supports under their costumes. The corset was still the domain of aristocratic women, who wished to distinguish themselves from women of the lower classes. These commoners did not subscribe to foundation garments, using only *corselets*, which laced over their skirts and blouses and supported the breasts. As the end of the 1700s drew near, the corset was used to push the breasts upward, causing many fashionable women to almost pop out of their dresses.

During the early 1800s, in both France and England, more relaxed clothing gave rise to different undergarments. Lightweight cloth brassieres were worn, and corsets were less confining. Unlike the harnesses of earlier times, these versions were devoid of boning or were only lightly boned to give the figure shape.

Introduced in the 1840s in England, the **camisole**, or **cami**, slipped over the head and ended at the waist, where it hung over the top of the corset. It was fitted with fine shoulder straps. When some women discarded corsets, the camisoles were worn without them. Many were richly embroidered and trimmed with lace. When sheer dress bodices became fashionable, the camisole was intended to be seen through them.

The **crinoline** was another undergarment popular in the 1840s. It was made of horsehair and the wearer slipped it over the head and positioned it at the waist. The stiffness of the horsehair gave extra fullness to the wide skirts of the times. An adaptation of the horsehair version was the wire cage crinoline that was introduced in 1856. This newer model gave extreme fullness to skirts.

Women in this period wore various types of garments under their skirts, including drawers, petticoats, farthingales, and pantalettes. The **petticoat** was an underskirt that hung from the waist to give fullness to the wide skirts. It was generally adorned with ribbons and had two or more layers. Some petticoats were hooped when the dress called for extra fullness. The **farthingale** was a petticoat with many graduated hoops. **Drawers** were long, baggy knickers that were originally seen below the hems of skirts. Some were just loose designs that were worn under skirts and dresses and were not meant for exposure. With the advent of slimmer dress silhouettes, drawers disappeared from the fashion scene. Longer than drawers, **pantalettes** were full-cut pants that extended below the calf and were intended to be seen. They were, therefore, often intricately decorated with frills, ribbons, and laces.

Between the early and mid-1800s, when dress designs often employed "back interest," the **bustle**, a large pad stuffed with cotton, down, or cork, was tied around the waist under the overskirt or dress to give extra fullness to the back of the garment. The **bustier**, which originated in the 1800s, was a deep-waisted bra and camisole that fit over the ribs and ended at the hips.

Women in this period wore nightgowns to bed. The **bed jacket**, first designed in the 1800s, is a short jacket that ends at the base of the ribs. It was generally worn over a nightgown for additional warmth.

Styles from 1900 to the Present

As the fashions of the times changed with each decade, the garments that women wore underneath their clothing also changed. Different types of bras and corsets were introduced, along with new kinds of innerwear. By 1900, alluring negligees, fancy petticoats, elegant corsets, lacy slips, and other styles came into vogue, and a new era of inventive undergarments and accessories was born.

First seen at the turn of the 20th century, **cami-knickers** combined a camisole and knickers. The top had thin straps, and the pants varied from straight lines to those with great volume.

In 1916, the **brassiere**, or bra, replaced the camisole. Initially, boneless designs were used to flatten the bust and push it downward. From the 1920s until today, a wealth of bra styles have become important to fashion. In 1925, adjustable straps were added to the design; 1930 saw new models that were boned and stitched into different cup sizes; the late 1930s witnessed the boned, strapless model; during the 1940s, padding was added to give extra shape and fullness; during the 1950s, wired and circularly stitched patterns came into prominence. Lycra made the bras of the 1960s more flexible, and bras in many different styles have been created from the 1970s until today as the perfect undergarment for most types of apparel. The **sports bra** is a recent variation that is designed to be worn by women during physical activities. It is often

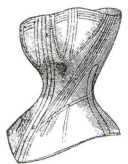 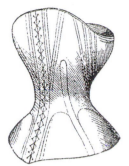

Woman's corset, front and back views, 1862

Women's undergarments from the nineteenth century provided a foundation for small-waisted, full skirts and later, for the bustle.

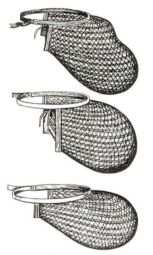 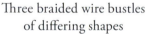

Horsehair bustle

Three braided wire bustles
of differing shapes

constructed from a combination of fibers, such as cotton (for comfort), polyester (for easy laundering), and spandex (for support).

In 1923, the corset and brassiere were introduced as a one-piece design, called the **corselet**. The **bra-slip**, which first appeared in the 1930s and regained popularity in the 1960s, consisted of a bra that was attached to a slip at the waist. This garment eliminated the need for separate bras and slips. Panties replaced drawers or knickers in the 1920s.

Akin in many ways to the corset, the **girdle** was first worn in the 1920s. It was boneless and lightweight, made with elastic, and featured garters to which stockings could be attached. Worn by women throughout the 1950s and 1960s, the girdle lost its popularity in later decades as women opted for a more natural look.

Derived from the 19th-century *maillot*, a one-piece configuration that was similar to a bathing suit, the **body stocking** was introduced in the 1960s to be worn under transparent dresses. Generally it is flesh colored to give a nude impression and is constructed from fine, knitted fabrics. It has a low front and back and very narrow straps.

Shapers, or shapewear, is a term given to a type of garment designed to control the figure, much like a girdle, but constructed without the use of rubber. These garments are generally made with fibers such as spandex, which provides both stretch and shaping. The most important of the spandex fibers is produced by DuPont under the trademark name of Lycra®.

Sleepwear is a major segment of the intimate apparel industry.

Thongs are a type of high-cut, tight-fitting panty that is generally constructed with fabrics that utilize spandex in combination with other fibers. Borrowed from men's underwear, **boxers** are loose-fitting, short pants that generally end just below the thigh. Usually made of cotton, silk, or rayon fabrics, they became popular in the 1980s and remain popular today.

Several types of sleepwear came into fashion in the 1900s. **Pajamas**, two-piece pants and shirt sets used for sleeping, made their appearance. First introduced in 1950, the **baby doll** is a very short, trimmed nightdress. It was popularized in the movie of the same name that came to the screen in 1956. The baby doll is often trimmed with ribbons, bows, laces, and other ornamentation. The **teddy** is a one-piece design that originated in the 19th century. It combines a bodice and short knickers and is narrowly shaped. The **negligee**, a lightweight dressing gown adorned with laces and ruffles, is usually constructed from fine, sheer fabrics. The **peignoir** is a similar type of robe that derives from a 16th-century garment worn by women before they dressed for the day. In the 1900s, it was usually worn over a nightgown. Trimmed with laces and ribbons, peignoir sets were often part of a bride's trousseau.

CONTRIBUTIONS OF HAUTE COUTURE DESIGNERS

At the turn of the 20th century, Paul Poiret, considered by many to be the foremost couturier of the time, created a new fashion silhouette. The lines he chose to focus on were natural. Although the corset was still very much a part of proper dress for women, he was determined to go against tradition. As he revealed in his own writings,

> It was the era of the corset. I declared war on it. The last of the rotten gadgets was a thing called the Gaches-Sarraute. Of course I have always known women to be encumbered by their own endowments and anxious to hide or distribute them. It was in the name of Liberty that I advocated against the corset in favor of the brassiere, which has gone on to become extraordinarily successful.

Although many women embraced the newfound freedom of Poiret's designs, others continued to wear corsets. Madeleine Vionnet, another couturier of the period, also chose to rid her clients of their dependence on corsets. Her bias-cut, freed-up silhouette, based on that of ancient Greece, permitted more freedom of movement and less restrictive corseting. Soon afterward, Madame Grès, with her draped designs, also freed women from the confines of the traditional corset.

In the 1950s, Balenciaga, perhaps better known as a master couture tailor, created scores of intimate apparel designs. These creations were as carefully constructed and planned as the haute couture original dresses and ensembles of France's master "architect" of fashion.

Mary Quant was a major force in fashion in the 1960s. Although she is perhaps best remembered for her youthful designs, which included the miniskirt, skinny rib knits, and hipster belts, she had a significant impact on intimate apparel design. Her "spotted pajamas" were an instant success when *Harper's & Queen*, a London magazine, featured them. Other intimate apparel designs included a host of youthful underwear products and a vast collection of stockings.

In the 1980s, Calvin Klein became a major force in the intimate apparel industry with his introduction of boxers for women. Using the same styling of boxer shorts that men wore, he revolutionized underwear. His efforts soon turned to other intimate apparel products, ranging from bras to hosiery.

With the popularity of Calvin Klein's intimate apparel designs, other notable designers joined the innerwear bandwagon. Americans Ralph Lauren, Donna Karan, Rudi Gernreich, and Norma Kamali and such couturiers as Europe's Emanuel Ungaro and Oscar de la Renta have successfully ventured into this fashion arena. Modern-day designers have periodically reinterpreted traditional undergarments as part of women's innerwear and outerwear fashions. Examples of some current reinterpretations are presented in Table 11.1.

THE RELATIONSHIP BETWEEN INTIMATE APPAREL DESIGNS AND READY-TO-WEAR

Through the centuries, intimate apparel styles have both influenced and responded to women's outerwear fashions. A look at the various designs created in the intimate apparel collections shows that there is generally a connection between those styles and the ones being shown in ready-to-wear. This is particularly true in such categories as bras, slips, panties, and the like. The reason for this connection is quite simple: to ensure that outerwear is shown to its best advantage by the wearer, the proper undergarments are needed.

As far back as antiquity, undergarments were fashioned to complement the clothing of the times. When fitted styles appeared during the Middle Ages, laced-up undergarments were

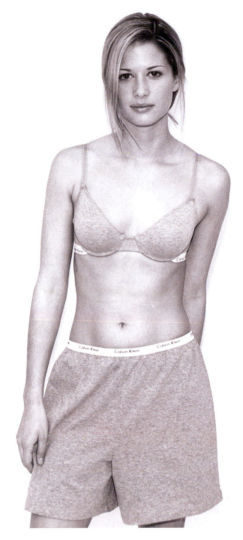

Boxer shorts for women, introduced in the 1980s by Calvin Klein, were a new intimate apparel item that quickly became popular as loungewear and sleepwear.

Table 11.1

TWENTIETH-CENTURY REINTERPRETATIONS OF TRADITIONAL INNERWEAR

Innerwear Article	Modern-day Reinterpretation
Bustier	In the 1950s and again in the 1980s, this undergarment reappeared in the guise of evening outerwear; Madonna's adoption of this style in the 1980s began a fad among young women who copied the look.
Cami	An extremely fashionable innerwear item today.
Cami-knickers	Today's designs are lightweight, unobtrusive, and very short; they are often referred to as "step-ins" because of the manner in which they are put on by the wearer.
Crinoline	This design has reappeared from time to time, as in the 1950s when U.S. designer Anne Fogarty created her very full-skirted dresses.
Farthingale	Generally seen today only under specially designed gowns, such as wedding gowns.
Petticoat	During the 1970s, this design experienced a renaissance with Ralph Lauren's "prairie look."

employed to ensure that outer garments fit smoothly. At the turn of the 20th century, corsets with bust supports were used to enhance the fashionable hourglass dress silhouettes of the time. Later in the century, undergarment specialists introduced a variety of different styles to make the fashions of the times fit better. Examples of these, along with the outer garments they were designed to enhance, include the following:

- The one-piece corselet with low back, which was a perfect companion for the bias-cut crepe evening dresses featured in the 1930s.

- The fitted satin slip in 1935, which was designed to be worn with straight-line dresses.

- The elasticized one-piece corselet shown in 1953, which was designed to be worn under princess-line dresses such as those designed by Christian Dior.

- The long-line bra, which was worn under strapless dresses in the mid-1950s.

- The halter-neck bra, featured in 1967, which was worn under dresses that followed the same neckline.

The changing shape of the bra over the course of the twentieth century reflects the changing silhouette of women's wear.

Woman's corset, 1907   Women's corsets, 1917   Woman's corset, 1923   Brassiere and girdle, 1930s

Brassier and garter belt of the 1940s   Girdles of the late 1940s and the 1950s   Bikini pants and bra, 1969   Uplift Wonderbra, 1994

- The mini-length, nylon bra-slip, which was designed to be worn under the mini-dresses of the 1960s.

- Wired half-cup bras, popular in the late 1970s, which were designed for wear under dresses that showed a woman's cleavage.

- Individual, glued-on breast supports, introduced in the late 1980s, which were worn under clingy, laced-up-the-front designs.

- Spandex, often in combination with other fibers, which was used in undergarments that were devoid of zippers and fasteners, and firmly molded the figure in a natural way when worn under form-fitting garments.

Couturiers have long been known for designing showstoppers for the fashion shows at the Chambre Syndicale–sponsored openings of internationally famous couturiers. Often, the designs have been outrageous creations based on intimate apparel styles. Unlike many couture designs, which are destined to be copied at lower price points by fashion manufacturers, these showstoppers are presented merely for their shock value. Issey Miyake's molded plastic bustier was high-tech dressing at its best. It came complete with a bellybutton and breasts with nipples. Designed to shock the audience, it catapulted Miyake to fame.

Other designers have used intimate apparel silhouettes and fabrics as the basis for ready-to-wear styles. Many of these styles have become popular components in the apparel collections of manufacturers and retailers. In the late 1980s, for example, one of the hottest items was transformed from the ranks of intimate apparel to ready-to-wear. It was the lace bustier, fashioned after a style that Madonna wore in her record-shattering concert performances. Of course, this was not the first design that was adapted from intimate apparel. However, it was particularly important because it used both a design (bustier) and a material (lace) that were characteristic of intimate apparel. Apparel designs may borrow just the silhouette or shape from an intimate apparel item, or they may concentrate solely on fabrics borrowed from undergarments.

Many of these designs were fashion newsworthy, either for their shock value or for their ability to persuade consumers to accept them as new fashion ready-to-wear.

- The string bikini, an enormously successful item that has been capturing the attention of women for decades, was fashioned after the bra and panty. It was introduced in Paris in the mid-1940s and was thought to be just a passing fad. Few knew the impact it would ultimately have on swimwear.

- Jane Fonda popularized shorts and bras, borrowed from innerwear styles, in the movie *Barbarella* in 1968. Not long afterward, numerous designs of this type were being purchased by women to be worn when exercising. These garments were made of shimmering stretch fabrics, similar to those worn by Fonda.

- The slip dress has been a mainstay in many women's wardrobes for several decades. Calvin Klein made a significant splash with slip styles for evening wear in 1992. The silhouette featured a bra-shaped bodice with thin straps, constructed of Chantilly lace over chiffon.

- In 1984, the corset dress and girdle dress were popular designs of couturier Jean Paul Gaultier. The former featured a cone bust and back lacing and was as tightly fitted as the corsets worn by many women in prior centuries. The latter model featured a tightly backlaced design with a sheer, see-through top. A variety of the corset and cone bra was designed specifically for Madonna. Shortly after her appearance in this outerwear bra, Annie Lennox, lead singer of the Eurhythmics, wore a red lace bra and leather pants in her concert appearances. The attention given to these bras motivated several manufacturers to produce decorative adaptations, which unexpectedly proved to be tremendous sellers in the stores.

- Azzedine Alaïa used spiral seams, curves, and darts embodied in stretch fabrics, much like those found in corsets. The extremely tight-fitting garments created ultrafeminine silhouettes. Later on, his designs with synthetic stretch fabrics made the clinging, corset-like designs more comfortable for the wearer.

- The 1992 bondage collection of Gianni Versace featured a number of leather bras and scanty underpants. Although his designs brought attention to these styles, many had been present for decades as "street styles" in London.

- Moschino's rayon and spandex bra dress of 1994 was the epitome of a dress design based on intimate apparel. It featured a tight-fitting corselet to which a pouf skirt, made up of dozens of lacy bras, was attached. Although it was not designed for the general consumer, it made a distinct fashion statement.

- Thierry Mugler's leather corsets reflected sadomasochistic influences. These corsets were not worn as intimate apparel, but rather as outer garments. Many were adorned with spikes and nipple rings. They, of course, made fashion headlines, but appealed to only a tiny segment of the market.

FIBERS AND FABRICS USED FOR INTIMATE APPAREL

Until the middle of the 20th century, cotton and silk were the mainstays of intimate apparel. Cotton was the more popular choice because of its easy care characteristics and comfort. Silk was generally restricted to more affluent purchasers because of cost. In 1910, rayon, the first of the manufactured fibers, joined cotton and silk as another important innerwear fiber. Adorning innerwear fabrics were trims made of various types of laces, such as Alencon and Chantilly, satin ribbons, and fabric ruffles.

DuPont's introduction of nylon in 1938 revolutionized the hosiery and intimate apparel industries. The new fiber was extremely strong, easy to launder, and very serviceable. The advent of World War II restricted nylon's use for wearable items, but once the war was over it became a prominent component of innerwear products. Later, acrylics and polyesters were added to the roster of fibers used by the industry.

Since the introduction of nylon and the other manufactured fibers, the textile industry has made significant advances, producing variations of these fibers as well as others. Many of the newer manufactured fibers are now mainstays of the various product lines, such as slips, bras, sleepwear, panties, and shapewear, that comprise intimate apparel.

LYCRA This is DuPont's brand name for spandex, the ultimate stretch fiber used in blends with nylon, silk, polyester, or cotton in most bras, shapers, control garments, and panties. The fiber is incredibly flexible, stretching up to 700 percent with the ability to bounce back to its original shape without sags or bags. It also offers great freedom of movement, superior comfort, a stay-put fit, and easy care.

In addition to the traditional **Lycra** fiber, LycraSoft® has been introduced for intimate wear. This is considered to be a breakthrough in spandex technology with

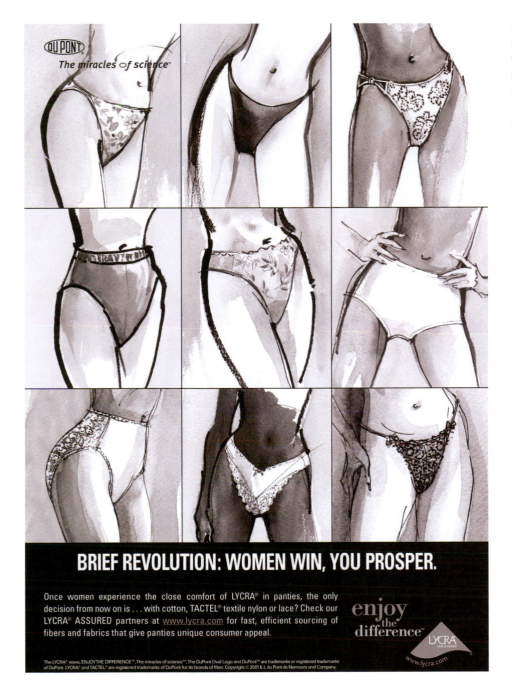

DuPont's trade advertisements of Lycra® focus on features such as softness, durability, and gentle control, all of which are important to manufacturers of intimate apparel.

features such as unprecedented comfort, resilience, softness, durability, and resistance to heat degradation and hydrolysis. It is the ideal rubber replacement.

Although lace has always been a popular intimate apparel trim, wearers often complained about its stiffness, scratchiness, and itchiness. Lycra has given birth to a new generation of romantic, feminine laces that combine a host of functional features with decorative uses. This has led to a resurgence in the use of "soft-to-the-touch" laces in Europe by both designers and manufacturers. Lace composed of Lycra® is being used in loungewear made with Dacron® polyester, bra and panty sets, pajamas, and bodysuits.

MICROMATTIQUE This is a revolutionary microdenier polyester that gives one the sensation of wearing fine silk. **Micromattique** has a soft suppleness that makes it perfect for use in sleepwear and slips.

ANTRON A lustrous type of nylon that gives fabrics a dry hand, opacity, and improved print clarity, **Antron** is found in panties, shapewear, and sleepwear. A variation is Antron III, which is one of the most widely used fibers for slips and sleepwear. Its appearance is smooth and satiny, with a pearlized luster. It was the first antistatic and anticling fiber on the market. Even with repeated washings and dryings, these characteristics do not wash out. To round out its benefits, Antron III is stain resistant and releases soil.

COOLMAX This is a high-tech performance fabric that keeps the wearer dry and comfortable because of its ability to speed evaporation away from the skin. In intimate apparel, **CoolMax** is used in the linings of sports bras and the crotch of leggings to help avoid chafing and irritation.

SUPPLEX Made from nylon, **Supplex** is cottony-soft and supple and combines a natural look and feel with performance benefits such as colorfastness and fuzz resistance. Used in feminine foundation garments, it is often blended with Lycra® to provide shape retention and freedom of movement.

TACTEL This is a silky-soft nylon that has a rich hand and is incredibly light on the body. It holds color extremely well, is easy to care for, and, when combined with Lycra, offers excellent shape retention and freedom of movement. **Tactel** is used in intimate apparel such as shapewear and foundations.

MARKETING OF INTIMATE APPAREL

Similar to other segments of the fashion industry, such as ready-to-wear, accessories, and home furnishings, intimate apparel has become increasingly competitive in recent decades. Manufacturers and retailers use a variety of strategies to gain market share. High on the list of these endeavors are licensing agreements between innerwear producers and apparel designers that give significant exposure to their products. Other strategies include establishing separate in-store shops to highlight particular designer labels, and the expenditure of enormous advertising and promotion budgets to bring product lines to the consumer's attention.

Manufacturers

In the hope of capturing a major portion of the innerwear market, manufacturers make use of many different marketing strategies, such as licensing agreements with well-known designers, and major advertising and promotional programs, among others.

Licensing Agreements

High-profile apparel designers are entering into licensing agreements with intimate apparel producers in record numbers. Although many manufacturers have been in the innerwear game for decades, producing bras, panties, sleepwear, and other products under their own names, their marketing approach has shifted in recent decades. One need only enter the section of a store devoted to these items to see that the names of fashion luminaries such as Calvin Klein, Ralph Lauren, and Donna Karan are prominently displayed.

Such partnerships between manufacturer and designer quickly bring new attention to the lines. Given the popularity of designer labels for dresses, sportswear, suits, handbags, hosiery, jewelry, and other fashion items among consumers, these names affixed to intimate apparel products often give them the necessary exposure to make them sell faster than without the benefit of the label.

Although the general public might not know the degree of involvement of the marquee-name designer in the creation of the products, the identifying logo or signature is sufficient to motivate them to purchase. In most cases, for example, the apparel designer's innerwear products are designed by people other than the name on the label. The agreement may call for the designer to have final approval of the creations, but little more than that. In some situations, a high-profile designer does not even require approval rights. If one considers the large number of product lines bearing a particular designer label, it is quite easy to understand the inability for personal participation by that designer. A good case in point involves one of the earliest entrants into licensing agreements, Pierre Cardin. At the peak of his popularity, the designer had his signature or logo affixed to more than 600 global fashion lines, most of which he had little to do with except to collect the royalties for the use of his name.

Another point to consider is the fact that the designer associated with the line might not even be living. Such is the case with Christian Dior. At the height of his career, in the 1940s and 1950s, the French designer was a legend in his own time, creating innovative styles that are clearly recorded in the history of fashion. Several decades after his death, his name continues to be prominent in intimate apparel collections. The power of the label still commands significant attention from today's manufacturers. Table 11.2 lists some of the major names in intimate apparel, with their manufacturer affiliations.

In addition to the designer connection, other high-profile licenses are big business. What is more appealing to the youth market than a label or logo identifying

For intimate apparel manufacturers, the licensing of designer names adds fashion appeal to their products. The licensing agreements allow designers the opportunity to extend their lines into a new market segment. Josie Natori and Bestform Group have such an agreement.

Table 11.2	
DESIGNERS AND THEIR INTIMATE APPAREL AFFILIATIONS	
Designer	**Manufacturer Affiliation**
Christian Dior	Bestform Group
Tommy Hilfiger	Cypress Apparel Corp., Jockey International
Donna Karan, DKNY	Wacoal America
Calvin Klein	The Warnaco Group
Ralph Lauren	Sara Lee Corp.
Mary McFadden	Boutique Industries
Josie Natori	Bestform Group
Nike	Vanity Fair Intimates
Oscar de la Renta	Bestform Group, Carole Hochman
Valentino	The Warnaco Group

itself as a Disney or Barbie product? The answer is, probably nothing! When the Lion King, Mulan, or a new juvenile character is introduced, hundreds of products, not only underwear and sleepwear, bear the logos. This is often a guarantee that the products will have immediate recognition and appeal.

Advertising and Promotional Endeavors

The scope of the advertising programs that manufacturers are undertaking in the intimate apparel field highlights the need to call attention to their products. The leading intimate apparel categories, under the banners of Calvin Klein, Ralph Lauren, and Donna Karan, for example, spend millions of dollars promoting their lines in the United States and abroad. Their activities include newspaper and magazine advertising, the broadcast media, direct marketing, billboards, and a wealth of special events.

Calvin Klein has been the most aggressive of the promoters. In the United States, for example, his use of billboard advertising is extravagant. In high-traffic areas such as Times Square in New York City, a larger-than-life billboard stretches endlessly, featuring models in a variety of innerwear designs. It is surely an eye-catcher.

With the market for his and other American designers' products so significant overseas, Klein has targeted other countries in the promotion of underwear. In 1998, he employed the services of high-fashion model Christy Turlington, who appears regularly in his magazine ads, to make personal appearances in key European markets. In Paris, at Galeries Lafayette, Christy appeared before huge crowds, and each customer received an autographed poster with a purchase. The same event was repeated in London at Selfridges to great success. Other stops on the tour included photo shoots at the Salon International de la Lingerie exhibition and at the Calvin Klein Collection store on Avenue Montaigne in Paris. Promotions were also planned for Italy, Germany, Spain, Austria, Holland, and Luxembourg to try to capture the largest segment for designer innerwear abroad.

With the tremendous increase in dollar volume for direct marketing by retailers, intimate apparel manufacturers are spending a great deal of money to place their products in these mailings. Using the concept of cooperative advertising, they share

Calvin Klein's advertising has a reputation for being controversial. This ad was part of a campaign for children's underwear in 1999; the campaign was abruptly terminated when some consumer groups complained that the poses of the models were provocative.

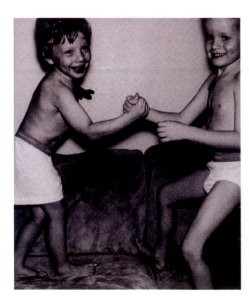

the expense of promoting their products in the retailer's direct-mail pieces. An examination of these mailings shows that the innerwear products command a great deal of the space.

Runway shows featuring intimate apparel are also becoming commonplace for manufacturers. Whether it is a small show at the company's headquarters during market weeks, or in larger arenas such as the trade shows, which are discussed in the following section, these special events are gaining in popularity. Also import to the industry is the effort of the Intimate Apparel Council, whose goal is to stimulate the growth of the intimate apparel business. Table 11.3 features the members of the council.

One of the faster-growing ways in which innerwear manufacturers are bringing attention to their collections is through the extensive use of trade shows. Two of the more important entries are Lingerie Americas and Curvexpo. Both compete in Las Vegas, which has become the trade show capital in the United States ever since MAGIC took up residence there. Since Lingerie America was organized in 2002, the number of brands exhibited has grown from 75 to 270, indicating that the trade show is the arena that brings results to innerware manufacturers.

The Victoria's Secret spring fashion show has become a major media event with virtual front-row seating on TV.

In-Store Shops

The concept of the in-store shop had been the domain of couturiers and upscale fashion designers, who used it to feature their apparel collections. Today, the better-known intimate apparel collections are being merchandised in the same manner. Innerwear bearing such labels as Calvin Klein, Ralph Lauren, and DKNY is being featured in these in-store shops. Stores such as Neiman Marcus, Nordstrom, Macy's, and Saks Fifth Avenue are meeting the demands of the giants in the industry such as Warnaco and Sara Lee, producers of some of these "marquee" intimate lines, to merchandise their collections in this way.

Table 11.3

2006 MEMBERS OF THE INTIMATE APPAREL COUNCIL

Barry Ross Intimate Connections	Invista
Bendon NA/Elle Macpherson Intimates	Jockey International, Inc.
Biflex Intimates Group, LLC	Lovable World Trading Co., Inc.
The Bromley Group, LLC	Movie Star, Inc.
Carole Hochman Designs Group	Nilit America
Chantelle Lingerie, Inc.	The NPD Group
Charles Komar & Sons, Inc.	O'Bryan Brothers, Inc.
Chelsea design Group	Rago Foundations LLC
Delta Galil Ltd., USA	Russell Newman Ltd.
Eileen West	Sara Lee Branded Apparel
Fashion Forms	Spotless Enterprises
Hanky Panky	VF Intimates
Hanro USA, Inc.	Warnaco Inc.

The intimate apparel department at Macy's West has separate in-store shops for national brands, such as Joe Boxer; designer brands, such as Donna Karan; and INC, a private label of Macy's Inc.

Retailers

With competition among retailers at its highest point, the need for proper marketing is more important than ever before. Each merchandise classification requires special attention to make certain it is achieving its sales potential. Intimate apparel is one of the key areas in which retailers are placing a strong marketing emphasis. The emphasis for these product lines is expressed in special events, advertising, efforts to heighten consumer awareness of private label products, and inclusion of special in-store shops.

Special Events

Many in the intimate apparel industry credit one company with heightening consumer awareness of these products. That company is Victoria's Secret. Each year, Victoria's Secret produces a major spring fashion show in New York City to publicize its newest collection. The guests, who number about 600, include fashion editors from every major publication. TV camera people and paparazzi are also on hand to record the event for use in magazines, newspapers, and television shows.

Many department stores are using on-premises fashion shows to create interest for their innerwear merchandise. For example, Younkers, based in Des Moines, Iowa, has used this format to promote its line of junior sleepwear. One of the retailer's shows, in the spring of 1998, generated a one-day increase of $150,000 for its innerwear department, as compared with the previous year.

Another in-store event that is extremely popular is the appearance of representatives from bra companies. They often present a trunk show of the latest designs and meet with shoppers who have specific undergarment needs. These events generate immediate sales for the stores and often motivate the attendees to become regular wearers of the line.

Advertising

The use of advertising is the retailer's major tool for bringing shoppers into the store or selling to them via direct-mail pieces. The use of newspaper ads, direct mail, and radio continues to grow for intimate apparel. Many of these ads are cooperative ventures in which the manufacturer and retailer share the cost. The aforementioned fashion show by Younkers department stores was advertised in the newspapers as the "Slumber Party at Younkers," which helped to bring in a large audience. To appeal to teenage shoppers, the company also places ads in school newspapers and targets radio commercials to that group.

Private Label Awareness

The use of a retailer's own brand has made important inroads in all innerwear categories. These items are produced by manufacturers and are merchandised as store brands. To compete with the highly publicized designer labels, the stores must use a variety of strategies to successfully market their own labels.

One way of marketing the lines is to associate them with a well-known personality. Borrowing from its success with such personalities as Jaclyn Smith for knitwear and Martha Stewart for home furnishings, Kmart is using Kathy Ireland for its intimate apparel collections. By using a wealth of in-store signage, the private brands are able to distinguish themselves and attract attention. At Sears, the private label innerwear collection, Personal Identity, is housed in a separate department with a special look.

In-Store Shops

The popularity of the in-store shop extends to retailers, too. Most find that shoppers who are attracted to a particular designer will immediately head to that area, making their selection quickly. With less time for shopping, many women find the store-within-a-store concept a helpful time saver. The popularity of these separate shops can best be understood by their numbers. Calvin Klein has about 1,500 innerwear shops in major stores; Ralph Lauren shops number about 1,400; and Donna Karan has about 800 units.

INC is a private label innerwear line produced by Federated Department Stores. The private label is merchandised in what the company calls "value-driven" shops with customized fixtures. Stores in the Federated organization, such as Macy's and Bloomigndale's, feature the collection. Through their use of well-designed signage and graphics, the INC shops have helped promote the private label products, which have been selling extremely well.

CHAPTER HIGHLIGHTS

- The intimate apparel of modern times evolved from the undergarments worn in Crete, Egypt, Greece, and Rome as early as 2000 B.C.

- At the beginning of the 20th century, couturiers such as Paul Poiret and Madeleine Vionnet created new fashion silhouettes that required a totally different approach to innerwear.

- Calvin Klein startled the intimate apparel market in the 1980s by introducing boxers for women.

- Most decades have featured innerwear designs that were necessitated by the creations of the apparel designers. The one-piece corselet with a low back was the perfect companion for the bias-cut crepe evening dresses in the 1930s, as was the wired half-cup bra for wear under the designs of the 1970s that showed a woman's cleavage.

- Throughout the years, many intimate apparel styles have also influenced apparel designs. The slip dress by Calvin Klein and the bustier popularized by Madonna are just two examples.

- Several relatively new fibers have given intimate apparel designers new ammunition for their creations. Most notable is Lycra® spandex, which is the ultimate stretch fiber.

- Apparel designers and manufacturers brought their recognizable talents and labels to intimate apparel products through licensing agreements. Today, such talents as Calvin Klein, Ralph Lauren, Donna Karan, Tommy Hilfiger, Oscar de la Renta, Valentino, and Mary McFadden are all in the innerwear game.

- Many retailers market their designer intimate apparel collections through in-store shops, just as they do for apparel collections.

- Private label intimate apparel is promoted by stores throughout the United States. The success of the private label concept in apparel and other products appears to be a trend that will stand the test of time.

IMPORTANT FASHION TERMINOLOGY AND CONCEPTS

Antron®	CoolMax®	panties
baby doll	corselet	peignoir
bed jacket	corset	petticoat
body stocking	crinoline	pajamas
boxers	drawers	shapers
bra-slip	farthingale	sports bra
brassiere	girdle	Supplex®
bustier	innerwear	Tactel®
bustle	intimate apparel	teddy
cami	Lycra®	thong
cami-knickers	Micromattique®	undergarments
camisole	negligee	
chemise	pantalettes	

FOR REVIEW

1. What was the name of the first article of clothing recorded in ancient times that supported women's breasts?
2. When was the chemise first introduced in England as an undergarment, and what did it look like?
3. Why was the body stocking introduced?
4. Who was the designer at the turn of the 20th century to focus on the natural look and forgo the need for the corset?
5. Which designer revolutionized underwear for women in the 1980s?
6. Which fiber was the most important invention for the innerwear market?
7. Why were intimate apparel designers quick to enter into licensing agreements with apparel manufacturers?
8. How did Calvin Klein help spread the name of his innerwear lines in Europe?
9. What type of merchandising have retailers used to distinguish their innerwear collections?
10. Which retailer is the largest merchandiser of intimate apparel, and how does it kick off each season's new collection?
11. According to Iris LeBron's Point of View, how is the outerwear market making use of intimate apparel?

EXERCISES AND PROJECTS

1. Visit an intimate apparel department at any major store in your area to determine the merchandising mix of its various products. For each product classification, such as bras, sleepwear, and so on, list the manufacturer brands, designer labels, and private labels.

2. Contact three well-known apparel designers to determine their participation in licensing agreements in the innerwear market. For each designer, create a list featuring each of the products that he or she licenses, such as panties, bras, and so on, and the name of the licensor of those products.

3. From the various fashion magazines and consumer newspapers, collect photographs of the different types of innerwear products featured. Mount each photograph on fomeboard and note the fibers that are used in each product.

4. In Monday issues of *Women's Wear Daily* innerwear is given broad attention. Use one of these issues to write a report on the state of the market, complete with style trends, the important wholesale and retail players in the industry, and current trends. Use the photographs in *WWD* to highlight your findings.

WEB SITE

By accessing this Web site, you will be able to gain broader knowledge and up-to-date information on materials related to this chapter.

Victoria's Secret

www.victoriassecret.com

The Case of Refocusing the Innerwear Merchandise Assortment

Bancroft and Wales is a large, specialized department store that features a product mix restricted to women's, men's, and children's wear. It has 14 branch stores in addition to its flagship store, all of which are located in the Midwest. The retailer has been in business since 1915, and it has generally been a successful venture.

Bancroft and Wales's success is attributed to the management skills of its merchandisers and other key players. Since the founding of the company, the management team has always made the necessary merchandising changes as dictated by the times. During the early 1960s, for example, when the sales of women's sportswear were disappointing, Bancroft and Wales adjusted its merchandising mix to feature more dresses and fewer sportswear items. When sportswear again became popular, the company readjusted its product lines once more. This ability to change with the times has kept the company financially sound.

For many years, women's innerwear had been a small part of the retailer's emphasis. Bancroft and Wales maintained a department but did not give it the same amount of attention as it did other departments in the company. Over the past two years, however, management has noticed an increase in sales of all the intimate apparel categories, with customers regularly requesting a more complete assortment of merchandise. Although store buyers have been increasing their purchases, they have retained the same merchandising concept used in the past. That approach was to utilize the majority of the floor space for name manufacturers' brands and sprinkle it with some of the designer labels.

At the company's semiannual merchandising meeting, the buyers for intimate apparel raised questions about the future of their department and the need to become more competitive in the marketplace. They proposed that the store could significantly increase sales if it took on a more aggressive role in the merchandising of innerwear. The buyers used figures from many of the trade publications to support their views that consumers are looking for more variety.

Several suggestions were made, among them the idea of giving more attention to designer labels and of introducing private brands. The discussion centered on how best to merchandise the various lines if the assortment was expanded, and whether the same concept should be introduced at the branches as well as the flagship store. After a full day of proposals, a final decision had not yet been made. The general merchandise manager was not certain where the additional space would come from if the expansion went forward, and the divisional merchandise manager for intimate apparel was unsure if the private label route was a viable one. It was decided that each buyer for intimate apparel should come up with a plan to be considered.

question

If you were a member of the intimate apparel team, what plan would you suggest for expansion of the department? Make sure that such factors as product diversification, price lines, and space are considered.

I See London, I See France/I See (Famous Designer's) Underpants

What's seen by few but worn by all? Underwear of course. But that may be changing. Utilitarian garments, once worn only for comfort and modesty, are now being purchased for style as well, and intimate apparel may never be the same. As clothes have grown ever more revealing, bras and panties increasingly serve more than a supporting role in wardrobing. Aided by racy ads, rap singers and runway shows, fashion has infiltrated the innerwear market to such a degree that famous designer names now appear as regularly on the waistbands of cotton briefs as they do on dress labels. Why the unprecedented interest in unmentionables?

"It's a new frontier," says Walter Levy, chairman, Levy & Kerson Associates, retail management consultants. "Intimate apparel is a division that has been quiet for a long time so there was a window of opportunity there. It's an area that needed rejuvenation. Plus, designer clothing is not doing as well as it once did because the whole society has turned against conspicuous consumption, so designers have looked at that and decided to move their names and influence into other merchandise categories."

Levy points out that while the sales volume generated by big ticket apparel items is limited, the market for innerwear is much wider. While an outfit from Calvin Klein's ready-to-wear collection can set you back more than $1,000, a pair of his athletic-style sport briefs can be had for less than $15.

"Calvin Klein came in and revolutionized women's underwear and others have followed his lead." Levy reasons that Klein's austere, gray and white, cotton interlock, tops and bottoms struck a chord with consumers because the product filled a need that existed for a comfortable, natural fiber undergarment, but also because their androgynous appearance reflected the new role of women in society. "With men and women all wearing jeans and tee-shirts, unisex underwear was the next logical step." Levy notes that as a result of the line's huge success, the designer is probably better known for his cotton skivvies than he is for his elegantly understated suits.

"There's no question that lingerie today is quite different from the way it used to be even a short five years ago when the bustier became *the garment* to be seen in," recalls Josie Natori. "Daywear used to be half-slips and tap pants. Now it includes bodysuits, and suit camis for daytime dressing. Lingerie in all its forms has truly come out of the closet and is a leading 'must-have' item for the fashion driven customer."

Natori feels the woman of the 1990s lives in a high pressure world and considers the acquisition of pretty lingerie to be a well-earned reward for all her hard work both on the job and at home. Capitalizing on the movement toward a more relaxed form of dressing, Natori has created a separate apparel category for herself by challenging preconceived

ideas about the nature of lingerie and its functions.

"A dramatic re-shaping of sportswear took place in the seventies and eighties," she explains. "What used to be restricted to clothes you wore to participate in sports has been changed forever by the baby-boomer to the highly segmented and highly diversified business it is today. The same kind of redefinition of intimate apparel is taking place now as the line of demarcation between innerwear and outerwear is quickly blurring."

Richard Martin, curator of The Costume Institute at New York's Metropolitan Museum of Art agrees. In a synopsis of the Infra-Apparel fashion exhibition currently on display there, he writes; "One generation's hidden structures are another's conspicuous designs, one generation's undergarments are another's flaunted outer garments." Martin credits Natori with expanding the horizons of intimate apparel and the exhibition represents her as one of the new league of designers who are taking their designs from the "confidential and personal to the public."

One designer who offers the best of both worlds is Donna Karan. One of the most influential names in ready-to-wear and a powerful presence in almost every other fashion category, Karan now solves the problem of what to wear underneath it all with her new lingerie collection. Donna Karan Intimates combines luxury with comfort via simple but sensual shapes, neutral colors and fine, natural fiber fabrics. As the story goes, Karan decided to try her hand at lingerie design for much the same reason as she began many of her other enterprises. She felt there was something missing. Dissatisfied with the fit and feel of most innerwear, she was determined to do better. For example: Karan's cotton/spandex underpants are cut full in back, so they won't ride up, high on the leg to allow ease of movement, and reach the waist, thus providing a measure of tummy control.

One of the major retailers that have opened in-store boutiques for Karan's lingerie line is Neiman Marcus. Joan Kaner, senior vice president and fashion director for the store, is enthusiastic about the venture. "Donna Karan has made a brilliant entry into the marketplace," she says. "She brings a lot to the table. First off, she's a woman, so she knows what women want and need and second she's been able to bring to her intimate apparel the same sensibility that one finds in her clothing collection, and this distinguishes her from many of her competitors."

Ira Livingston, vice president, U.S. marketing for Cotton Incorporated, the fiber company of U.S. cotton growers,

confirms the trend toward increased comfort in innerwear is growing. He says sales of cotton lingerie are on the rise. "In 1992, cotton held a 46% share of the total intimate apparel market, up from 44% in 1991. Our share of the women's panty market climbed from 63% to 66%, while women's bodysuits saw a 1% increase from 56% to 57% during the same time period."

Eileen West, who has been called "the queen of cotton prints," is at the forefront of the comfortable cotton underwear movement. Best known for her soft, romantic women's wear, the San Francisco-based designer now brings her flowering motifs to a variety of licensed products including intimate apparel. Introduced in 1991, her line of foundation garments has a distinctively fresh appeal, and features the same buttons, bows, eyelet and other trims that have become a signature trademark.

Peter Sullivan, National Accounts Manager for Vanity Fair Mills, the licensee for Eileen West Innerwear, says the company chose Eileen West to be their first designer lingerie line because she had the prior association with natural fiber products they were searching for.

The line is comprised almost exclusively of cotton fabrics, half knits, half wovens. Current patterns include gingham checks, madras plaids, stripes and polka dots. Thanks to imaginative styling, the new label has enabled the manufacturer to expand the audience Eileen West traditionally sold to, bringing in a younger, more contemporary customer.

"Updating lingerie looks with novelty cotton fabrics allowed us to offer a visibly different garment. The woven cotton bras and panties were designed to bring a ready-to-wear feeling to foundations," says Sullivan. But, he maintains good looks aren't the only factor. "This is a comfort-oriented product," he adds. "All the bras and bustiers are fully constructed and shirred in the back to give a perfect fit."

Asked to give a prognosis for the future of intimate apparel Ira Livingston notes, "The innerwear market has turned into a veritable who's who of the fashion industry. Recognizable names like Calvin Klein, Josie Natori, Donna Karan, Eileen West, Adrienne Vittadini, Emanuel Ungaro are on the list of cotton lingerie lovers and others like Guess? are still to come. We are forecasting continued growth for the natural fiber in this arena."

Cotton Incorporated, New York, NY

Specialty Chains Get More Intimate

KARYN MONGET

New York—The demand for intimate apparel and related daywear items has consistently been building over the past year at specialty chains, according to store executives, and the potential for growth—especially in fashion items—is strong.

In a spot check at Manhattan units of contemporary chains H&M, Express, Benetton and Gap that cater to the fashion-driven consumer, two trends were highly visible in lingerie areas that ranged from approximately 300 square feet to over 1,000 square feet: an abun-

dance of fashion colors, with prints and fabrics that looked like they walked off a ready-to-wear runway.

One trend in particular came out loud and clear: dual-purpose bras, briefs and bikinis that could be worn on the beach or in the boudoir.

Tristine Berry, apparel merchandising manager for swimwear and intimate apparel at BASF, said, "There certainly is reciprocal styling between intimate apparel and swimwear, and it's a strong influencer for everybody in the market. Everybody wants to do this next season."

Iris LeBron, fashion director of intimate apparel, swimwear and activewear at DuPont, said: "There are so many swimwear looks in lingerie right now. That's what makes it so much fun. These [specialty] stores are doing the things that people want to buy right now."

The taste for exotic colors and prints was also apparent at several Victoria's Secret stores in midtown Manhattan, the Upper East Side and Upper West Side neighborhoods, where the palette of colors ranged from watermelon and coral blush to iris and Saint-Tropez nude. Key prints included a Sixties-inspired pink paisley motif, a Seventies-looking swirl print in coral and burgundy tones, and updated leopard spots.

Seamless ruled at Victoria's Secret, where styles by Body by Victoria were the star groups merchandised in window displays and at the front of each store.

Unlike the sea of traditional solid white, black and pale pink, and blue that continues to glut intimate apparel departments at major department stores, specialty retail operations are editing and merchandising the same lingerie styles for two consumer bases: younger, contemporary consumers they've already captured and the aging baby boomer who wants to look and feel young.

Key examples of crossover intimates-swimwear ideas in the lingerie department of H&M on West 34th Street included a satin beige and ivory reptile-print contour bra and bikini, and a matte Mondrian-inspired multicolored demibra and bikini of woven cotton. Also merchandised alongside the intimates was a red reptile-print sequin bra and panty set that was tagged "swimwear."

When asked if these items were lingerie or swimwear, a sales associate replied, "It goes both ways. Customers are buying the items as intimates and swimwear."

A block down at the Express store, the lingerie area was awash with tropical florals and jungle motifs in bold colors. Printed sheer mesh was a key theme, with coordinating daywear pieces such as sheer skirts, camis and assorted tops.

"Even women who are 40 or older are buying these looks," said one saleswoman, noting that "customers want the lingerie to be seen under a sheer top or an unbottoned shirt."

A spokeswoman for Cleveland, Ohio–based Express, said, "We've been doing Express Underwear since spring 2000. As we speak, we are changing it to Express Lingerie. Sexy is the underlying note. What sets us apart is we've been doing it with what's happening in sportswear, like low-rise thongs and bikinis.

"A lot has been going on," she continued. "We plan to grow the business and are looking at categories like sleepwear and robes. Our new Express swimwear collection was designed by our lingerie designers, and we are considering expanding Express Lingerie stores like the prototype store we have at the Manhattan Mall at Herald Square."

A spokesman for Italian specialist Benetton, said, "Benetton's Undercolors underwear brand was created over 10 years ago. Initially, it was sold in lingerie stores. For the past six years, it has been on sale in the monobrand Undercolors stores.

"Since last year, Undercolors [underwear] has also been present in corners of major departments stores in Europe, and we are expanding in all of Europe, especially Italy. Undercolors is now an international presence, because this brand is in all of our new megastore and new concept stores, including those opening in the U.S."

Crossover ideas between Undercolors' Beach Collection and Women's Underwear Collection include seamless microfiber bras and briefs in bright colors, tubular effects and textures such as ribbing and jacquard weaves, mesh treatments, and a variety of floral prints.

At the Gap unit in Herald Square, a new format merchandises panties on table tops throughout the lingerie area, resembling a department store setup. Gap introduced boxed basic underwear for men and women in the early Nineties, and expanded into Gap Bodywear and related lingerie items two years ago.

In an array of colors, as well as basic black, white and gray, cotton panties at Gap were promoted at "Buy four for $19.95," and nylon panties were "Buy three for $19.95." Wall displays showcased signs saying "My Favorite Bra," which was available in seamless, lace or mesh for $19.99 each.

In a merchandising move similar to that of Gap's sister unit, Old Navy, novelty drawstring pajama bottoms of woven cotton were being sold as key items for $24.

Women's Wear Daily, April 2, 2001

Outerwear Markets Inspire New Trends for Intimate Apparel

IRIS LEBRON

Take a look at what people are wearing as they go by you on the street, on the subway, or in the office. It seems that lingerie doesn't look like lingerie anymore. There are so many influences from other markets that it's difficult to tell whether a dress was a dress from the beginning or whether it was originally a full slip. What used to be luxurious sleepwear has transformed into elegant eveningwear; just add the jewels, and you're ready for a night on the town. It doesn't matter if it was labeled as sleepwear or underwear; as long as it looks good, out the door you go!

Slips double as skirts, camisoles replace blouses, and bustiers are peeking out from underneath jackets as designers borrow ideas from activewear and ready-to-wear markets to freshen up the intimate apparel industry. Simply putting on a suit jacket or sweater twin-set over a slip updates the traditional skirt and feminizes the structured suit. Sportsbras and tailored bras are so clean-lined that they look great under clothes, at the beach, or at the gym.

We used to be embarrassed if our slip was showing; now it's a trend. It's become fashionable to show your underwear. Logoed waistbands peek out from under jeans to show designer names, and bra straps come in colors that are meant to be seen. It's wonderful to layer two bras in contrasting colors as outerwear or have a blue bra strap showing under a brown tank. Markets are not only sharing styles but fabrics as well. Fabrics are no longer locked into a specific market, category, or season. The innovation of comfortable, durable easy-care fabrics make intimate apparel adaptable to more looks and longer wear.

"Anything goes anywhere" is the mantra for the consumer. The point is that consumers want choices, and whether the designers borrow ideas from other markets or the consumer makes her own decision on how to wear what she buys, it all comes down to having the flexibility to do so. Today's woman is multi-faceted and constantly looking for change. Dressing allows us those changes, and it represents the choices we make. Though the marketplace would love a predictable consumer, today's women are far from predictable.

The notion of what is appropriate to wear to a particular event or place is being redefined. Maybe it shouldn't be defined at all. Clothing is a vehicle to express personal values, and today's woman has much to express. She wants to be connected to progress and progress means change.

Iris LeBron, Fashion Director for Intimate Apparel and Activewear, DuPont Fibers

From Corsets to Consciousness

JOYCE BARAN

From the first tug at the lacings on a corset to the bra burning of the 1960s, women's place in society was a direct reflection of her underpinnings.

When we were bound up tight, we were meant to be seen and not heard. Back in the 1860s many a "Scarlett" broke her ribs to achieve a figure that was someone else's ideal. Corsets paid no heed to the body nature made for women. With up to 100 bones and eight yards of lacing the body was coerced into the shape of fashion. Whether it was the wasp waist of the 1860s or the "Kangaroo" stance of the Gibson Girl at the turn of the century, the corset contorted women into their dutiful roles.

The 1920s ushered in a revolution in female manners and morals. The right to vote lifted restrictions on many fronts. The straight, flattened, boyish body look was the liberation of mind and body. However this was still a distortion of "Eve's" torso, and the straight body continued to be engineered by jacquards and boning to flatten and redistribute the tissue.

Finally, in the 1930s came the invention of the first stretchable fabric called Lastex. This extruded rubber allowed the woman and the garment to become one, to breathe together, so to speak. At the same time, movies came into our lives, stretching our imaginations as well. Glamour and satins were molding our lives from the inside out.

World War II created the necessity for women to adopt dual roles. Quickly taking over where the men left off at home, we were forced into functional simpler undergarb by physical work and a somber nation. The fabrics were dull and our lives were dull as we took pause while the world sorted through it's dilemmas.

The war finally ended, and, *God Bless America*, the men returned from war and wanted the women to look like the bombshells they left behind. Out of the factories and up on pedestals, women were sculpted into the most surrealistic shape and lifestyle since the turn of the century. Besides the conical bras, every proper lady wore a girdle—like a statue, nothing was to jiggle as you moved. The female ideal for girls of the 50s was either the June Cleaver picture perfect mom or the Marilyn Monroe sex kitten. As in the past, restrictive foundations inside and outside would eventually implode.

The Age of Aquarius spun us into a mental rebellion. From quietly doing what we were told, we burst into questioning everything. Whether it was the premise of a war or the existence of bras at all, the word *conformity* was history. As the match was lit to the bras at the Miss America contest and panty hose killed the girdle, it was back to nature, mentally and physically. We were in touch with the bodies we were born with. If you didn't abandon bras altogether, there was the "no bra" bra. This was the roller coaster decade that took us from revolution to the camouflage of the 70s.

This camouflage of the next two decades marked the confusion of women trying to fit into a man's world. We were becoming a major factor in the work force, but the rule book was written by and for men. Our femininity was seen as a weakness, so we hid it underneath by flattening our silhouettes. On the outside we were a sea of gray suits with the little bow scarf buttoned tight at the neck. The lingerie departments were pure function as the minimizers became the key to hiding female curves.

Somewhere in the late 80s, we start to recognize our femininity as our strength. Sensitivity, nurturing, intuition, and the ability to juggle multiple tasks have become the exemplary qualities of business leaders today. As we shed our inhibitions, we shed the need to hide in the background.

The Wonderbra, waistnippers, and seat shapers combined with the comfort of DuPont Lycra and high-tech microdenier fabrics were all an acknowledgment of this change. Finally women could be comfortable with the woman they pictured themselves to be. Fashion inside and out have become our individual personality statement.

But most importantly, the irreversible change is attitude. The future of underwear will be dictated by an attitude of looking and feeling good, no matter what we wear. From corsets to consciousness, we are now in control of our own destinies.

Joyce Baran, Vice President of Merchandising/Design, Specialty Intimates Inc.

fashion accessories

Glamorous is a state of mind, a feeling of self-confidence.

BOB MACKIE, DESIGNER

After you have completed this chapter, you will be able to discuss:

- The importance of accessories to the fashion industry.

- The functional and decorative importance of accessories to the wearer.

- The impact made on hosiery with the discovery of nylon and introduction of pantyhose.

- The differences between costume and fine jewelry.

- The differences between functional and decorative belts.

- Why watches, previously just functional accessories, have taken on fashion importance.

Footwear, hosiery, jewelry, gloves, handbags, millinery, belts, watches, scarves, and hair ornaments are the ingredients that lend drama and provide pizzazz to a clothing collection. The excitement generated by a runway designer show is heightened by the accompanying fashion accessories. Once relegated to second-class fashion status, accessories now share the spotlight with apparel designs.

Many U.S. and international creators of fashion apparel collections spend considerable time designing shoes, jewelry, handbags, hats, and other items to coordinate with their lines. Not only do these creations enhance the apparel, but they also bring additional revenue to the companies.

In the accessories market, most of the designers are often the talented but unsung heroes of the back room; recognition goes to the company whose name appears on the items. However, some accessories designers are beginning to receive the recognition they deserve. Robert Lee Morris, for his jewelry designs, and Judith Leiber, for her exquisite handbags, are making fashion headlines just like their counterparts in apparel design. The Council of Fashion Designers of America (CFDA) has helped to promote accessories designers through shows. One is held in facilities adjacent to the tent shows of Seventh on Sixth, which the council sponsors in Bryant Park in New York City. Awards for outstanding achievement of accessories designs are also given at the annual CFDA ceremony.

The accessories industries have also profited from those who are reducing their clothing purchases. Today's consumers often opt to forgo costly apparel purchases and instead choose accessories to spruce up their wardrobes. Often a fashionable necklace or new pair of shoes can transform an old outfit into something new.

The importance of these fashion accessories is highlighted by the increasing number of retailers who have opened accessories-only stores. A walk in any mall or shopping arena immediately reveals the significance of this market to the fashion industry.

The accessories market brings bigger profits to vendors as a result of increased consumer interest.

Accessories can be functional, decorative, or both. For example, a hat or scarf can add colorful accents to a garment while providing protection against a cold, blustery wind. Shoes, belts, scarves, and other small items also serve dual purposes.

FOOTWEAR

The footwear industry takes its signals from other segments of the industry in terms of fashion design. It closely studies the apparel market to make certain that its silhouettes are compatible with what the apparel industry will feature. Through continuous contact with textile mills, fashion forecasters, and colorists, the shoe industry can determine what textures, fabrics, styles, and colors should be produced. Footwear manufacturers play follow the leader so that their designs will blend with the shapes and styles created by the clothing designers.

Characteristics of the Footwear Industry

Much like the fashion apparel industry, the footwear business is seriously affected by offshore production. U.S. companies are confronted with an ever-increasing number of imports. Once limited to fine, expensive Italian designs, imports now include all types of footwear, including shoes, boots, and athletic shoes at competitive prices. As a result many U.S. plants have closed. Although the domestic employment picture remains bleak, the number of shoes purchased in the United States continues to increase.

In the United States, New York City still reigns as the leading center for shoes. Although the factories are located primarily in Maine, Missouri, and Pennsylvania, it is in the New York showrooms that buyers from all over the country make their purchases.

Many companies dot the domestic map, but a few major operations account for most of the production. U.S. Shoe, for example, produces shoes under such distinctive labels as Calvin Klein, Garolini, Cobbies, Famolare, Amalfi, Pappagallo, and Bandolino; it accounts for a large share of the market.

To combine the best of all worlds, U.S. shoe manufacturers have entered into the international production market by participating in joint ventures. In this way, they can capitalize on cost-efficient production in such countries as South Korea and Taiwan.

The leading names in the shoe industry are often the same as those in the apparel industry. Instead of direct participation in a shoe company, many designers are involved through licensing agreements. That is, for a percentage of the sales, they

Doc Marten boots have become a footwear staple.

Boots of every variety are popular items in a man's wardrobe.

permit companies to market a line of shoes under their signatures. The designer's reputation is protected through an arrangement whereby he or she has the right to reject a style before production begins.

The fitness craze also caused changes in the shoe industry. An increasing number of men and women have several pairs of athletic footwear in their wardrobes. Before the 1970s, most consumers owned one pair of Keds or Converse sneakers. Today Nike, Reebok, and other companies produce a large number of styles specifically designed for different activities. Although the athletic footwear business is still larger than it was a few decades ago, its popularity waned in the 1990s, only to catch fire again in the early to mid-2000s. Young people, in particular, had taken to a new breed of shoes inspired by Doc Martens and, in many instances, had redirected their shoe purchases, which it is once again doing in 2007. Today, athletic footwear runs the gamut from the styles that are worn primarily for sporting events to more fashionable styles worn for many occasions and not only to the gym.

Styles

The shoe industry produces a large number of different styles. Some are classics that are popular year in and year out; others make their way through the fashion cycles, reappearing as dictated by the particular apparel styles that are popular.

The men's shoe industry is a little easier to manage, because most of its merchandise is classic. Some men wear the same style of business shoes for many years, replacing them with an identical pair only when they are worn out. Women, on the other hand, are more interested in style. In addition, different heel heights are needed to accommodate pants and various skirt lengths.

Table 12.1

CLASSIC SHOE STYLES FOR MEN AND WOMEN

For Men

Bals	Basic style of Oxford with tongue cut in a separate piece from the vamp of the shoe and joined with stitching across the vamp.
Brogues	A heavy Oxford, usually with wingtip decorated with heavy perforation and pinkings.
Deck shoes	Shoe, now often leather, that uses lacing through the top and sides of the shoe.
Loafers	Slip-on shoe. Popular styles include Gucci and penny loafer. Also worn by women and children.
Sneakers	Canvas or leather athletic wear. Fashion-oriented varieties are generally used for casual wear. Also worn by women and children.

For Women

Classic styles

Pumps	Slip-on shoe with rounded or V-shaped throat usually low-cut, medium- to high heels. Toe shape varies with current fashion styles.
Sandals	Open-type shoe usually held on foot with straps. Also worn by men and children.
Slingback	Open-back pump with a strap around the heel of the foot to hold it in place.

When fashion dictates

Clogs	Shoes with thick platform soles.
d'Orsay pump	Pumps with low-cut sides, closed heel and toes.
Espadrilles	Rope-soled shoe with canvas upper, tied on with long shoelaces threaded through top of shoe and around ankle. Sometimes made without laces as pump cut high and across instep.
Ghillie/gillie	Laced shoe usually without tongue and rounded lacer pulling through leather loop fastened around the ankle.
Hush Puppies	Trade name for casual oxford or slip-on shoe with sueded leather uppers and crepe soles. Also worn by men and children.
Jellies	Molded footwear of soft plastic or rubber with cutouts; made in a variety of colors. Also worn by children.
Mary Janes	Shoes that employ a strap across the instep, sometimes buttoned at side, with a rounded front. Also worn by children.
Spectators	Two-tone pump made in contrasting colors sometimes with stacked heels.

Some of the classic and fashion-oriented styles of shoes for men and women are listed in Table 12.1.

HOSIERY

One of the largest segments of the accessories industry, **hosiery** is produced in mills all over the United States. The available products fall into three categories—**pantyhose**, **stockings**, and **socks**. All three are functional and provide warmth, support, and comfort. However, they are designed and dyed based on fashion trends. The fashion industry decides the colors that will be dominant for a particular season. The assortment of colors range from the darkest blacks to the purest whites, in any shade. Hosiery is produced in a variety of **deniers**, or fineness of yarns, and **gauges**, which define the closeness of the knit.

The greatest boom in the hosiery industry occurred in 1938 when DuPont introduced nylon to the world. Crowds immediately gathered anytime a store announced the arrival of nylon hosiery. With such characteristics as strength and elasticity, nylon quickly replaced silk and rayon.

When stores received nylon hosiery shipments in 1939, eager crowds gathered to purchase the "new fiber stockings."

The introduction of pantyhose in the 1960s was another boom to the industry. This garment was designed to accommodate the miniskirts of that decade.

Socks, once the basic staple of the hosiery industry, have taken on an expanded role. Men and women are making extensive use of socks as fashion items. Men can now purchase patterns such as argyles, geometrics, and woven designs instead of just basic dark, solid tones. The color assortment for men includes every point on the color wheel. Women are also purchasing a range of socks. From the briefest, finest variety to the longer, bulkier types in wool, cotton, and manufactured fibers—the choices are enormous.

The fitness craze significantly expanded the athletic sock from the staple white to a variety of tones and decorative patterns. Many organizations, such as Fila, Ellesse, and Ralph Lauren, that produce activewear also produce socks that bear their logos and sell at prices never before dreamed of.

Selling hosiery is different from selling any other accessories. It is sold in department and specialty stores, but can easily be purchased at supermarkets, convenience stores, vending machines, and pharmacies. It is a merchandiser's dream because try-ons are not necessary and not allowed. Fit by each manufacturer is standard and returns are a rarity.

JEWELRY

With the addition of a dazzling necklace and bracelet, the simplest, most basic black dress can be transformed into an exciting costume. Whether the pieces are genuine diamonds or merely rhinestone, a new look has been created. **Jewelry** is available in an assortment of shops ranging from street vendors and flea market stands to the halls of Tiffany & Company.

Jewelry falls into two categories—fine, or precious, and costume, or fashion. **Fine jewelry** is produced from metals and stones that have intrinsic value. **Fashion jewelry**, on the other hand, has little real value and is purchased more for its usefulness and attractiveness as an accessory.

Fine Jewelry

Fine jewelry has always been looked on as a symbol of achievement. Sometimes a person's importance has been measured in terms of fine jewels. At royal coronations or marriages between aristocratic or celebrity families, the jewels often share the spotlight.

Fine jewelry, like other costly accessories, is available at a wide range of prices. Although two diamonds of comparable size might appear similar to the untrained eye, the actual price differential could be staggering.

The cost of fine jewelry is based on the quality of the precious stones and metals, their size or weight, and the workmanship that goes into its creation. Gemstones include diamond, the hardest natural stone; corundum, more commonly known as ruby; sapphire; emerald; jade; and natural pearl. They are priced according to color, clarity, size, cut, and rarity. Except for pearls, which are measured in millimeters, gemstones are weighed in **carats**. One carat equals 200 milligrams. Precious metals include gold, the most widely used in jewelry, platinum, palladium, and silver. Generally considered too soft to be used in their pure state, precious metals are combined or alloyed with less expensive base metals for strength. Gold is weighed in troy ounces. If jewelry is made from an **alloy** that contains ¹/₂₄ pure gold, it can be described as pure gold. The most popular domestic gold is 14 karat; that produced in other countries is usually 18 karat. If the proportion is less than 10 karats, the term *karat gold* cannot be used.

The most popular silver used in the production of fine jewelry is **sterling silver**. The alloy or combination is 92.5 parts silver to 7.5 parts copper. Not all sterling silver is equal in quality; the thicker the silver, the more valuable the item.

In addition to classic designs in fine jewelry, today's fashion world is increasingly interested in contemporary jewelry design. Tiffany & Company, long a leader in exquisite, priceless fine jewelry creation, has carved out a niche for contemporary fine jewelry. With collections created by Jean Schlumberger, Elsa Peretti, and Paloma Picasso, it has introduced the world of fashion to fresh ideas. The Peretti stylized heart, for example, has become a classic of contemporary design.

Through the imaginative designs of Robert Lee Morris, innovative fine jewelry is receiving significant attention. Additional information on Robert Lee Morris is discussed in a World of Fashion Profile.

Top: Fine jewelry such as these bracelets, necklace, and earrings turn a basic outfit into a statement of high fashion. Bottom: These pieces for Dior are presented in a jewelry box window display.

Costume Jewelry

Costume jewelry ranges from the "fabulous fakes" that simulate fine jewelry to trendy jewelry. Materials that have an appearance similar to precious stones are carefully mounted in gold-filled (thin sheets of gold bonded to a base metal) settings to give the

the world of fashion profile
ROBERT LEE MORRIS

A self-taught jewelry designer, Robert Lee Morris is a major force in the creation of contemporary jewelry. Whether working in a matte gold finish or shiny sterling silver, he has an unmistakable signature that unifies all of his designs. Pieces are immediately distinguishable by their strong, sculptural shape, in which form and function work together.

Morris's designs appeal to the mind as well as the touch, advancing what he calls "Themes of Universal Consciousness." Through powerful allusions to ancient history, religion, myth, and legend, Morris translates timeless symbols into modern forms—daggers, crosses, keys, and fertility symbols. "My recurring theme is the study of man and his artifacts. I want all my work to evoke a warm emotional reaction," states Morris.

After graduating from Beloit College, he established a craft commune in the cornfields of Wisconsin, where he taught himself the basics of jewelry. When the farm in which he lived and worked burned down one winter, he set up shop in Vermont. His work was discovered by Sculpture to Wear, a gallery in New York City's Plaza Hotel. Morris's collection was an instant success amid the work of Picasso, Arp, and Miró. In 1977 he opened Artwear, launching an entire modern jewelry movement.

Through the years he has been showered with such honors as the Coty Award, the Council of Fashion Designers of America Award, the International Gold Award, the FAAB Award for best jewelry designer, and the Woolmark Award. In his many endeavors, he has collaborated with such stars of the fashion world as Geoffrey Beene, Kansai Yamamoto, Calvin Klein, Anne Klein, Donna Karan, and Karl Lagerfeld. His works have been exhibited in such places as the Phoenix Art Museum, the Smithsonian Institution's International Touring Exhibition, and the Harkus, Krakow, Rosen, Sonnabend Gallery in Boston. He is also the subject of a film, *Stripes of a Tiger*.

Design projects by Robert Lee Morris include jewelry, dinnerware, handbags, belts, and containers for Elisabeth Arden.

Today, Robert Lee Morris is busy expanding his designs to handbags, belts, dinnerware, and cosmetics.

impression of the real thing. Many an untrained eye has been fooled by the replicas featured at Ciro's, a company that specializes in spectacular imitations. The majority of costume jewelry, however, is not intended to deceive, but to make a fashion statement. The materials used in their production are as varied as the number of artists who create the pieces. Plastic, beads, wood, metal, rope, ceramic, and stones are commonly used by designers. Their works generally follow trends in the apparel industry and are used to augment the consumer's wardrobe.

Styles

Both precious and costume jewelry come in any number of styles. Each serves a decorative or functional purpose. The popularity of a particular style depends on the materials used, the dictates of the fashion world, and whether or not it is considered standard, traditional wear, as is the case with engagement rings. Table 12.2 lists a representative selection of jewelry categories and styles.

Table 12.2

FINE AND COSTUME JEWELRY STYLES

Bracelet	Ornament that encircles the wrist or arm. Made of metal, plastic, wood, or leather either rigid such as bangle or cuff or flexible with links or chains.
Brooch	Synonym for pin. Jewelry made with pin fastener on back, in all types of materials, including gold and silver; may be set with real or imitation gems.
Charms	Amulets or pendants that depict a variety of images and shapes, such as hearts or disks; may be suspended from bracelets or necklaces.
Cuff links	Decorative closures made of metal, sometimes set in real or imitation gems, in a variety of shapes and sizes used to fasten French cuffs on shirts. Originally worn by men, adopted by women.
Earrings	Jewelry worn in the ear. Available as clip-on, screwback, or pierced varieties, in designs that range from fitting against the earlobes to dropping well below the ear.
Necklace	Jewelry worn around the neck. Available in many lengths from chokers, which conform to the neck, to ropes, which are often 45 inches in length. Made of beads, chains, sometimes with real or imitation gems.
Ring	Jewelry worn on different fingers and made of many different materials and designs. Sometimes there is special significance for particular rings such as engagement, marriage, or graduation.
Studs	Ornamental fasteners used in place of buttons on shirt fronts.
Tiara	Curved head ornament worn from ear to ear, resembling a crown.

GLOVES

Once a fashion accessory worn primarily for decorative purposes, **gloves** have become more functional. Traditionally, department stores offered a wide assortment of gloves ranging from the longest **mousequetaires** to slip-ons. Women owned many pairs to coordinate with specific outfits. Gloves were worn to dinner parties, luncheons, and other social occasions. Beginning in the early 1970s, however, women abandoned the glove as a decorative statement and wore them mainly for protection against the cold. Except for the few, old-line stores that feature a full assortment of gloves, most stores carry only functional gloves. While leather is still a favorite among wearers, knitted styles are also popular.

There are only a few basic styles of gloves, and of those, only two or three are used frequently. Variations in design comes from the different fabrics and trims that adorn them. *Button* is a term used to refer to the measurement of glove lengths. One button is equal to one French inch (approximately ¹⁄₁₂ of an inch longer than the U.S. inch). Measurements begin at the base of the thumb. A one-button glove is wrist length, a six-button glove is about halfway to the elbow, and a sixteen-button glove is a formal length. Table 12.3 lists important glove styles.

HANDBAGS

The handbag industry continues to change. Before the 1970s, **handbags** served functional rather than fashionable needs. Handbag designers were rarely acknowledged by the editorial press or the consumer. The styles and shapes generally fol-

Table 12.3

GLOVE STYLES

Driving glove	Gloves with cutouts on the back of the hand or over the knuckles to increase flexibility. May be knitted or leather, or combination. Originally worn for sports such as golf or race car driving.
Gauntlet	Above-the-wrist glove that flares at the wrist.
Mittens	Separate the thumb from the other fingers; a favorite for children.
Mousequetaire	The longest length glove used for formal occasions. It comes in lengths that measure from eight to sixteen buttons. The glove features a vertical opening above the wrist that allows the wearer to slip her hands out of the glove without the need to remove it.
Shorty	A two-button glove that reaches the wearer's wrist.
Slip-on	Gloves that slip easily over the hand without fasteners or plackets.

This handbag designed by Louis Vuitton is a luxury as well as a functional accessory.

lowed the direction of the apparel industry. That is, handbags had little or no identity of their own. All of this changed in the 1970s, when apparel designers such as Dior and Cardin began to affix their signatures and logos to the bags. Fashion-oriented women quickly purchased them with as much excitement as they afforded the buying of apparel. Soon, the handbag industry reached a new level with the acceptance of signature symbols, such as the now-famous LV logo of a Louis Vuitton design. Constructed of vinyl, the bags sold for upwards of $300 and soon became a symbol for status seekers.

The handbag industry is one in which both famous and unknown designers coexist to bring a wide assortment of styles, at many price points, to consumers. Donna Karan and Paloma Picasso are in the forefront of the higher-priced entries, along with the lines produced by Coach and Dooney & Bourke. Judith Leiber produces a collection in which a single style may sell for as much as $10,000. (Judith Leiber is discussed in a World of Fashion Profile.) Of course, lower-priced lines are also available for those who wish to spend more modest sums.

A walk through any major department store reveals the value of the handbag department to the company. Nordstrom and Bloomingdale's feature a wealth of different manufacturers, but also devote designated spaces to certain lines, such as Louis Vuitton, Fendi, Gucci, and Coach, in much the same manner as they do for special apparel collections. The handbag is no longer just a functional product.

Many styles of handbags are available to the shopper. Some styles are classics; others fall in and out of favor. Some of the typical models are included in Table 12.4.

JUDITH LEIBER

Describing herself as a nice lady from Budapest who prefers cooking and rummaging through antiques as her hobbies, Judith Leiber designs evening bags that are considered art. She began with a $5,000 investment, the price now charged for one of her more elaborate designs. She has received international acclaim and has been the recipient of numerous awards including the Lifetime Achievement Award of the Council of Fashion Designers of America. Her career was the focus of an exhibit mounted at the Fashion Institute of Technology in New York City. The exhibit was titled The Artful Handbag and displayed more than 300 individual treasures ranging from the sophisticated to the whimsical. A book, by the same title, about her life and designs is additional proof of her accomplishments.

To underscore the acceptance of Leiber creations, here are some fashion newsworthy facts:

- Barbara Bush wore her "Millie the dog" to state dinners; Hillary Clinton has sported "Socks the cat" with formal evening gowns.

- The Smithsonian Institution, the Chicago Historical Society, the Dallas Art Museum, and the Los Angeles County Museum of Art include her bags in their permanent collections.
- Beverly Sills, the former international opera star, has a collection of more than 70 bags.
- Ivana Trump admits she has more than she could count.

Leiber has created more than 3,000 styles since she entered the business in the 1960s, with prices beginning at $1,000 for a modest style and ranging upward of $5,000 for more elaborate designs. Before her retirement in 1998, she was not only responsible for creating the patterns but also for overseeing her business operations on an everyday basis. She advised more than 200 factory workers on such matters as how the thousands of individual stones should be adhered to one frame. The "minaudieres," elegantly jewel-encrusted miniatures, receive the greatest attention. Some of her handbags represent fruits and vegetables, such as tomatoes, eggplants, and watermelon; animals; fairy tale characters; and fans of

Judith Leiber handbags are collector's items for her devotees.

the Far East. Her patterns include argyle motifs, stained glass designs, and spider webs. Leiber also produces the finest leather handbags.

She and her husband, a fine-arts artist, admit that they take great pleasure in counting the number of Leiber handbags at each of the social galas they attend.

Table 12.4

TYPICAL HANDBAG STYLES

Backpack	Handbag with straps fitting over shoulder to be worn over back.
Clutch bag	Handbag free of handles that is held or "clutched."
Drawstring bag	Handbag closed by pulling on leather or fabric cord.
Envelope	Long, flat, rectangular-shaped bags that have flap closures. Usually of the clutch type, without handles.
Satchel	Rigid flat bottom with shaped sides closed on metal frames. Similar to doctor's medical bag.
Shoulderbag	Handbag style in any shape or size with a long strap to place on the shoulder. Some straps are adjustable.
Totes	Handbag open on top and held with two straps or handles.

Hats, absent from the fashion market for several years, have been resurrected and now range from simple to one-of-a-kind models.

MILLINERY

There was a time when properly dressed men and women wore hats for both social and business occasions. Since the late 1950s, however, the hat has virtually disappeared from the fashion world. A major blow to the men's **millinery** industry was delivered by President John F. Kennedy, who chose not to wear a hat to his inauguration in 1961. Although Jackie Kennedy revived interest in women's hats, bouffant hairstyles made it difficult for most women to wear them.

Hats are still seen, however, as ensemble enhancements on the European runways. These are generally unique designs created to lend excitement to the events. Few translate into successful sellers. Occasionally, a style or shape may be adapted for widespread use by the millinery industry.

As with gloves, hats have become functional. Women who wear hats generally prefer such casual types as berets and caps made of knits, leather, and straw materials. Men often opt for the soft cap that fits easily into a coat pocket. Young consumers have embraced the baseball cap as their main head covering along with variations on the "trainman's cap," which features a long peaked brim.

BELTS

The belt industry serves both functional and decorative needs. Functional **belts** are essential components of a garment—for example, the belt that comes with a dress as a trim and those that are used primarily by men for their trousers. The greatest impact on the industry, however, is made by decorative belts. They are available in a variety of widths, from ¼ inch to as much as six inches, and in an assortment of materials, including leather, fabric, straw, elastic, rope, yarn, metal, and plastic. As with other fashion accessories, belt styles are dictated by the silhouettes created by the apparel industry. Prices range from a few dollars to several hundred, depending on the materials used and the intricate details of the design.

To observe the impact of today's fashion belt revolution, one need only examine the many offerings at retailers of every price point and structure, as well as the fashion pages of consumer and trade publications. They quickly reveal the broad price ranges as well as the designer names that have climbed aboard the belt bandwagon.

At the top of the scale, belts that run as high as $10,000 can be found in stores such as Neiman Marcus. A Henry Dunay design in crocodile and 18-karat gold sells for $9,216, with a Kieselstein-Cord design in lizard and 18-karat gold priced at just over $1,200. Others in this top-of-the-line bracket include models by Hermes Vendura and Lana Marks. Of course, these are not merely functional "straps" used to hold a skirt or pair of pants in place. They are considered to be works of art by their wearers, worn with the same pride as jewelry, and always in style.

Materials, designs, and workmanship are marks of quality in these belts.

At more moderate price points, names such as Escada, Empirio Armani, Ferragamo, Gucci, and Calvin Klein are making their mark. Their products sell in the $200 to $500 range. Shifting to the lower price points, one finds names such as Ann Taylor, Tommy Hilfiger, and Liz Claiborne.

The New York metropolitan area is the center of all types of belt production. Located within the same geographical area as the apparel industry, manufacturers can quickly and easily respond to the shapes and silhouettes of apparel designers.

WATCHES

Watches are no longer treated just as necessities. They have become fashion-oriented items. Until the late 20th century, the wearer was more interested in performance than appearance, and ownership of more than one timepiece was unusual. Although some women had one watch for everyday use and another for evening wear, one watch served all purposes for most men.

During the early 1980s, watches achieved fashion status with the introduction of the Swatch. For a relatively small investment, consumers could purchase various styles to coordinate with different outfits. Changeable watch bands became popular, enabling users to adapt one watch to different fashion needs.

Many watch manufacturers have capitalized on the acceptance of the watch as a fashion accessory and have entered into licensing agreements with designers. In an era when designer status counts, these names help sell products.

Watches have become fashion items, with many apparel designers creating their own imprint.

At the other extreme of the industry is the fine, jeweled watch. Prices are based on the quality of the instrument, as well as the casing and stones used in its decoration. Timepieces at stores such as Tiffany & Company may sell for as much as $50,000!

Vera, shown working on her designs (above), was the first designer of signature scarves. Her scarf (left) lends an important accent to this blouse.

SCARVES

For added warmth, men, women, and children don knitted and woven **scarves** in rectangular, square, and triangular shapes. This use, however, is by no means the dominant role of the scarf in fashion. Signature scarves, those featuring the logos and names of world-famous designers, play an important role in women's wardrobes. For many years, women have treasured silk scarves in various shapes that display prints, as well as the insignias of Hermès, Dior, Saint Laurent, and Pucci. They are worn with dresses, suits, blouses, and sweaters, draped and tied around the shoulders and neck.

During the 1950s, the U.S. accessories market witnessed the introduction of the first designer or signature scarf. This creation by Vera featured bold designs and imaginative colorations. The scarves sold in impressive quantities.

Hair ornaments are sported by fashionable women.

HAIR ORNAMENTS

Hair accents are an example of an accessory that falls in and out of favor. In one season, flowers may be the choice, in another, the oversized clip, in still another, barrettes in a wide assortment of sizes and shapes. Small companies that manufacture **hair ornaments** look to hair stylists for direction in design.

A variety of materials are used for ornaments. Silks and synthetics are used in flower ornaments; velvet, lamé, and Mylar® are used for bows; hard plastic for combs; metals for clips and barrettes; synthetic stones for decorations; combs for holding ornaments in place; and elastic for attachments.

CHAPTER HIGHLIGHTS

- The special accents or elements that complement apparel are known as accessories.
  As with trimmings, they serve as fashion enhancers and functional necessities.

- Accessories include shoes, hosiery, jewelry, gloves, handbags, millinery, watches, belts,
  scarves, and hair ornaments. Their design and popularity is usually based on the dictates
  of the fashion apparel they are intended to enhance.

- Accessories provide the wearer with the opportunity to alter an outfit's appearance.
  Accessories are used to freshen up wardrobes.

- Many apparel designers, such as Donna Karan, Calvin Klein, Ralph Lauren, and
  Liz Claiborne, are producing accessories through licensing agreements.

IMPORTANT FASHION TERMINOLOGY AND CONCEPTS

alloy	gloves	pantyhose
belts	hair ornaments	scarves
carats	handbags	shoes
costume jewelry	hats	socks
denier	hosiery	sterling silver
fashion jewelry	jewelry	stockings
fine jewelry	karats	watches
footwear	millinery	
gauges	mousequetaire	

FOR REVIEW

1. To what extent are fashion apparel designers entering the footwear market and how are they participating?
2. How has the popularity of athletic shoes affected the shoe industry?
3. Describe the reason for the 1938 boom in the hosiery industry.
4. Discuss how the miniskirt affected the hosiery industry.
5. Differentiate between fine and costume jewelry.
6. What is meant by the term *sterling silver*?
7. What materials, in addition to metals and stones, are used in jewelry designs?
8. What has caused the handbag to become a fashion-oriented accessory?
9. How has the market for gloves changed since the 1950s?
10. What contributed to the decline in popularity of men's hats?
11. Which fashion product changed the market for watches?
12. According to the Point of View article "Crowning Glories," how did a group of independent milliners bring their products to the forefront?

EXERCISES AND PROJECTS

1. Visit a major department store and evaluate, in terms of space, the importance of each accessory category offered for sale. Begin with the one that occupies the greatest amount of space and conclude with that occupying the least. Square footage occupied should be estimated. With this information in hand, compare the amount of attention given to each accessory in the store with the attention it receives from fashion editors.

2. Contact an apparel designer whose name has been associated with a line of accessories. The names can be easily obtained by observing merchandise in a store that carries designer labels. Ask about the merchandising arrangements for the accessories. Are they, for example, owned by the company producing the apparel or are they licensed ventures? Either through the use of a press kit, which many designers publish, or through a company representative, determine the extent of the accessories collections, price points, and methods of promotion.

WEB SITES

By accessing these Web sites, you will be able to gain broader knowledge and up-to-date information on materials related to this chapter.

Footwear Industries of America

www.fia.org

The Hosiery Association

www.hosieryassociation.com

The Case of the Properly Positioned Accessory

questions

1. What are the advantages and disadvantages of the two suggestions for the repositioning of accessories?

2. What other way might the company motivate greater interest in accessories?

As in all department stores, accessories at N.J. Tompkins are divided into specific departments. Shoes, for example, are in their own department; belts, scarves, and handbags share a department; jewelry and hosiery share a common area; and so forth.

The major emphasis at Tompkins has been ready-to-wear. Although the accessories it carries are given great attention, until recently, their sales volume paled by comparison to that in the clothing areas. The increased attention being paid to accessories by the editors of the fashion columns has prompted the company to consider plans that would bolster its sales. One plan is to rearrange the selling floors and place all wearable accessories on the second floor at a point where the various apparel departments converge. This way, the woman purchasing a dress will be in close proximity to jewelry, handbags, hosiery, and other enhancements. Dissident voices argue that such a move would jeopardize "pure" accessories sales that are traditionally main-floor based.

Another suggestion being considered is to establish small accessories "satellites" within apparel departments. Some shoes, handbags, gloves, and so on would be available for sale in each apparel area. Management has yet to give its opinion on these ideas.

With the accessories market expanding through designer licensing agreements and the fashion forecasters heralding these items as wardrobe "musts," N.J. Tompkins must reach a decision on how to better merchandise its accessories.

Crowning Glories

LISA BERTAGNOLI

Shame on Oprah Winfrey. When the talk show maven held a segment on passion a few weeks ago, she brought in as an example a milliner from, of all places, Connecticut.

Chicago hatmakers certainly understand why Oprah chose a milliner for this particular show. With millinery supplies difficult to obtain and the hat-wearing customers hard to come by, passion—not a yen to make a bundle overnight—is what makes these artisans tick.

What they don't understand is why Ms. Winfrey didn't choose a local milliner. Chicago is home to nine of the most passionate hatmakers around, who work under the banner of the Millinery Arts Alliance. These women market the wonder of hats to both dedicated fans and newcomers to the world of chapeaux.

"Women like to dress up, and a hat is the ultimate accessory," said Lisa Farrell, co-president of the alliance and owner of Ooh-La-La, a hat shop in Highland Park, Ill.

The MAA got its start in 1995, when a group of Chicago-area milliners decided to pool their efforts to promote their hats, which are hand-made, often of hand-made materials and can cost up to $700.

"We are offering a couture service," said Loreta Corsetti, co-president and owner of Loreta Corsetti Millinery. Apparently, it's a service more and more women crave. Corsetti expects her sales to double this year, to about $35,000. Farrell, for her part, reports sales of about $5,000 a month. Veronica Chin, who runs Burning Bush Millinery, posts sales of about $1,000 a month, and like Corsetti,

says this year has been phenomenally good.

Custom hats for weddings and events are a huge part of MAA members' business, accounting for 40 percent of Corsetti's business and 50 percent of sales for Susanne Wiesen, owner of Pale Moon Millinery. They agree their clientele are hard to pin down.

"It's hard to say who our typical customer is," Farrell said. "It's younger women who have gone through the baseball hat thing and want something more sophisticated; it's older women who grew up wearing hats. It's a wide range of people."

Chin, for her part, has seen another type of customer, and that's women who are undergoing chemotherapy and are seeking stylish head coverings.

One avid MAA fan is Janice Koerber, a systems analyst in Chicago. Koerber started collecting vintage hats in Chicago and now has over 250, which she displays on pegs hanging about her loft.

Koerber also gives MAA members a boost by marketing hats on her own through Charming Hats in Chicago (CHIC), a hat club she and a friend started five years ago.

"Both of us are hat-wearers, so we started wearing them to restaurants," Koerber said.

Another MAA fan is Dianne Crosell, who works in the wholesale flower business. "I wore hats before I met [MAA members], but now I'm a connoisseur," said Crosell, who spends about $1,600 a year on hats.

MAA members' designs run from simple to ornate. Wiesen's simplest hat on display these days is a taupe sisal cloche trimmed in taupe and finished off with a matching vintage button. Priced at $155, it's a look a woman can dress up or dress down, Wiesen said.

Her most sophisticated hat is a black veiled, heart-shaped cocktail hat trimmed with doupioni silk and festooned with hand-embroidered cherries. The hat took about 12 hours to make: Wiesen does all the work, even embroidery, by hand.

Meanwhile, over at Burning Bush, Chin's favorite hat is what she calls a "Mad Hatter hat": an asymmetrical number made of black silk, banded with a strip of copper Thai silk and decorated with rose and seafoam green silk flowers. Chin calls the $260 creation "a floral fantasia."

While the materials sound simple, hat-making supplies aren't easy to come by in this country. Corsetti, for instance, buys custom-made blocks from Luton, England, and Florence, Italy. "It's difficult for us to find blocks," she said, referring to the forms that are the milliner's equivalent of a dressmaker's dummy.

The alliance's first collaborative marketing effort was called La Fete des Catherinettes, the first American celebration of the traditional French hat-making festival that also honors St. Catherine, the patron saint of milliners.

The celebration began with dinner at Chicago's elegant Brasserie Jo, and continued with a weekend of trunk shows at local boutiques. MAA succeeded in attracting hat devotees and raising about

$6,000 for Y-Me, a national breast-cancer awareness organization.

Richard Melman, owner of Brasserie Jo, part of his Lettuce Entertain You empire of restaurants, was so taken by the hat-wearing women that he invited the MAA to hold a weekly hat dinner at the brasserie. That event, Les Chapeaux at Brasserie Jo, continues to this day. Every Thursday evening, anywhere from 15 to 40 women gather to wear their own creations and perhaps buy a new one from MAA designers, who showcase their hats every week. The hat lovers not only get to show off their latest buys; they also get a complimentary "chapeau au chocolat" dessert, created by Jean Joho, the brasserie's chef.

The yearly Catherinettes show continues as well, changing venues and form every year. In 1999, it was held at Kass-Meridian, a local art gallery. Last year, it returned to Brasserie Jo, and attendees were treated to samples of Beaujolais nouveau to sip as they ogled the latest offerings. This year, the event was held May 15 at the tony Casino Club in Chicago. Loreta Corsetti Millinery were featured, as was a talk by New York socialite Nan Kempner, who brought along some of her hats for millinery show-and-tell. The event was sponsored by the advisory board of the Hope B. McCormick Costume Center at the Chicago Historical Society.

Other hat-marketing strategies are in the works, for instance a Web site. Networking helps immeasurably, noted Corsetti. "We always meet other artisans, and they link us with someone else," she said. "They get new customers, and we get new customers."

Membership has changed some over the years. Founding members who are still active include Corsetti, whose hats are inspired by the art of the Italian Renaissance; Kate Burch of Kate Burch Hat Studio, whose affection for hats grew out of her history of collecting and selling vintage clothing; Eia Radosavljevic of Eia Millinery Design, a graduate of FIT and a hatmaker since 1990; and Laura Whitlock of Laura Whitlock Millinery, who has designed hats for feature films such as "The Hudsucker Proxy" and "My Best Friend's Wedding."

Newer members include Farrell, whose background is in retailing and costume design; Chin, who also teaches millinery at Chicago-area design schools; Holly Lowell, owner of the Queen of H'Arts hat shop in Evanston; Wiesen, a former corporate finance executive who studied millinery with Chin and opened her own millinery business in 1997, and Carmen R. Henry, whose hats are sold at Macy's in Pentagon City, Va., and boutiques around the country.

So far, the alliance's efforts are paying off. "There's more interest in millinery than ever," said Corsetti. "Women have come to not look at hats as something silly, or something their mothers wore."

To find out about current MAA affairs, call their 24-hour "hatline" at 312-409-6311.

WWD Accessories, August 2001

The Doctor's In

KATYA FOREMAN

How an iconic brand found its way back to the heart of youth culture.

Who doesn't remember her first pair of Dr. Martens—the quintessentially British shoes adopted by generations of subcultures from Mods and Skinheads to Goths and the Nineties' unkempt purveyors of Grunge? But while the brand has recently been showing more contemporary shades, including printed, patterned and lasercut styles, its original black boot, according to industry insiders, is headed for a revival. And the more battered, the better. "The classic black style is definitely going to kick off again," predicts London stylist Chloe Beeney, attributing the comeback to fashion's cyclical nature. "That early Eighties feeling of post-romantic, bubble-gum pop is pushing through again and people are dragging their Dr. Martens back out of their closets," she says.

Buyers from Topshop's shoe department say they have stocked up on grungy, beaten-up styles for January. "It doesn't feel like it should be too student-y—that's the new take on them," says senior buyer Marie-Claire O'Sullivan, who suggests a biker/rock vibe, matching high boots with tiny skirts, as a look that works now. But she predicts more sophisticated looks influenced by high-fashion brands will soon eclipse that. "[Dr. Martens] are perfect for that Olive Oyl-skinny legs-big feet look or the longer-line skirts that are looking really fresh again, thanks to houses such as Dsquared, Ann Demeulemeester and Marc Jacobs," she says.

French student Laura Gainche says the current punk rock wave has rendered the boot popular with her peers. "I don't like to wear short skirts or shorts without them," says the 22-year-old, who likes to mix vibrant tights into the formula. "French girls still tend to be a bit reserved, fashionwise, but the boots are really big in Belgium."

"We can definitely sense a resurgence; it's timely," asserts Vicky Wiggins, marketing director for Dr. Martens. The last two years had largely been dormant ones for Dr. Martens, when the brand underwent major restructuring including the relocation of all its factories to Asia. Still, sales have continued rising by around 20 percent per year, predominantly led by women's boots, according to Wiggins. Sales for fall-winter 2006 vaulted 42 percent over the previous year's figures. This included a 180 percent leap in sales in the Ukraine and Russia; 89 percent in Scandinavia, and a 75 percent rise in France. Wiggins attributes the strong growth to a number of factors, such as fashion's return to utilitarian and masculine dress codes. In turn, "weathered" styles in scuffed, grizzly leather and the brand's "Jolie"

boot, a biker version with lacing up to the knee, are very much in demand.

"It's about a tough, sexy look," she says, adding that new takes on the original, such as metallic and laser-etched styles, are also popular.

This fall, the brand launched its first advertising campaign in a year, shot by up-and-coming French photographer Felix Larher, who fuses reportage photography with illustration. The same approach has been used for the upcoming spring campaign. "We used regular people such as DJs, artists and performance artists who fit with our universe," Wiggins explains.

Dr. Martens, which has stores in Europe, Asia and North American—around 1,000 doors worldwide—will add a London flagship in Covent Garden in the next six months.

With a target market of 18- to 22-year-olds, the brand aims to pull in the young crowd with music. Since June, the brand has been the main sponsor of London theater and music venue the Roundhouse, known for its cutting edge gigs. "The idea is to nurture up-and-coming talent," says Wiggins, adding that the venue's studio has been rechristened FREEDM Studio, in keeping with the brand's philosophy.

At New York boutique Trash and Vaudeville, the first American store to get the Dr. Martens license in 1974, the brand's footwear remains in big demand. "A lot of girls are asking for the 1460 Dr. Martens classic," says store manager Jimmy Webb, referring to the first boot that rolled off the production line in England in 1960. "Like the little black dress, it'll never go away."

HOW, *WWD* Fast, October 2006

Specs Appeal

VÉRONIQUE HYLAND

In the 1953 film "How to Marry a Millionaire," Pola, played by Marilyn Monroe, routinely walked into doors and mistakenly read books upside down in an attempt to disguise her nearsightedness. "Men aren't attentive to girls who wear glasses," was Pola's excuse for not wearing her horn-rimmed specs.

Today, though, four-eyed fashionistas are receiving their fair share of attention, poor vision or not. Ashley Olsen, Amanda Peet, Chloë Sevigny, Rosario Dawson and Eva Longoria are just a few of the actresses who have recently been spotted in oversized, professorial eyeglasses. And the nerd look also triumphed on the spring runways. At Dolce & Gabbana, for one, models sported geeky turquoise glasses and severe topknots—a look that's usually more popular at your local branch library.

In Paris, Balenciaga's Nicolas Ghesquière dressed his girls in hefty square-rimmed frames that might do double duty in a high school chem lab. Miu Miu showed teeny glasses in bright colors, while models at Marc by Marc Jacobs wore graphic black or white versions.

So what accounts for this newfound embrace of eyewear? The accessory's popularity can be explained in part by its increasing superfluity. In this era of Lasik surgery and contact lenses, glasses come across as quirky and old-school. Retailers say that women are choosing to buy multiple pairs that reflect their personal style, rather than opting for a single, utilitarian model. Designer Robert Marc uses the term "glasses wardrobe" to describe his customers' changing attitude toward opticals. "More people

have come to the realization that eyewear is just as important of an accessory as shoes and handbags," he says. "Now, you see [fewer] people wearing one pair of glasses as their signature look."

Or as Richard Golden, founder and president of the national chain See Optical, so boldly puts it: "A woman should not wear the same pair of glasses to work every day." He estimates that his average customer buys three pairs a year, although some, he says, buy as many as eight. Retail prices range from $179 to $289 for the store's in-house brand.

According to Blake Kuwahara, creative director of Base Curve, which holds eyewear licenses for Carolina Herrera and John Varvatos, "The more modern thinking is, 'Look, I have 40 pairs of shoes. Why shouldn't I have at least two or three pairs of glasses?'" For fall 2007, Kuwahara is noting a "return to femininity," with eyewear inspired by ready-to-wear. "Looks are decidedly feminine," he says, "with rounder silhouettes—kind of that sexy secretary look." Base Curve's eyeglasses retail from $240 to $300 for John Varvatos styles and from $240 to $325 for Carolina Herrera ones.

Marie Wilkinson, design director of U.K. brand Cutler & Gross, concurs, "The trend for us is definitely for more stylized feminine shapes—real kitten eyes and larger, deeper lens shapes, arching over the perfect penciled brow."

At Morgenthal Frederics, which has boutiques in New York and Boston, the demand continues to grow for small, colorful plastics, notes Jeff Press, the firm's designer and brand manager. His company now sells six optical styles, including the cat-eyed Thelma and the round Puro.

And at Safilo, director of product development Timm Parker, who supervises design for Marc Jacobs, Kate Spade, Juicy Couture, Hugo Boss, JLo by Jennifer Lopez, Nine West and Liz Claiborne, notes that the optical field is still being driven mainly by metal frames. "But we're beginning to see more plastics selling recently in some of the higher fashion brands a la Dior, Gucci, even in Kate Spade, and this has obviously been popular in sunglasses for several years now," he says. Another fall trend, according to See Optical's Golden, who just returned from the European eyewear shows, is the "floating lens" style, which features a gap between the lens and the edge of the frame.

Anthropologie, too, has recently been doing a brisk business in reading glasses, aka "readers." Currently, it carries various styles from four different brands: Eyebobs, A.J. Morgan, Glance and Melissa Eyewear. According to Sarah Wilson, the store's eyewear buyer, three of its top sellers include Eyebobs' Advert, a thick-framed tortoiseshell that retails for $58, and A.J. Morgan's Bunny and Cannes styles, both of which come in brightly colored plastic frames, for $28 each. The biggest eyewear trend at the chain this season is toward a dominant frame, in part influenced by oversized sunglasses. Color is also gaining steam, with red, blue, pink, aubergine and lemon yellow as key shades.

"People definitely have fun with readers because no one has just one pair," notes Anthropologie's chief executive officer, Glen Senk, who owns about 20 pairs himself. "It's rare when people buy one style. Usually, they buy three or four."

Base Curve's Kuwahara perhaps puts it best: "In the past, there was that saying, 'Guys don't make passes at lasses in glasses,'" he says with a laugh. "So women used to be afraid. [But now] they're finding that glasses can be quite sexy, and they can change up your look."

Women's Wear Daily, December 11, 2006

Face Time

SOPHIA CHABBOTT

Alexandre Peraldi, design director of Baume & Mercier

Alexandre Peraldi wears a dark knee-length or floorlength skirt every day. He believes its pure Japanese architectural look will help clear mental clutter in order to design linear, ergonomic and elegant watches for the 176-year-old Geneva-based Baume & Mercier.

"I don't have a precise style, but I have a tendency for things that are quite simple, not the froufrou," said Peraldi, 39, during a visit to New York last month to launch the firm's fall watches.

Peraldi, born in Vetraz, France, became design director of Baume & Mercier in 2001, after working in accessories for Cartier and Yves Saint Laurent. Like many a designer at fashion and accessories houses with rich histories, he has dipped into the company archives, called Studio Design, reviving vintage styles and taking inspiration from the timepieces of the past.

Pieces that are provoking him include a watch with a domed case and the crown on top and an Art Deco-inspired women's bracelet watch with a slanted case and diamond-studded bangle.

"We've been making important changes over the past five years," he said. "We're trying to create a liaison between the creation [the watch] and the wearer. We don't want to be too extravagant nor old-fashioned. There needs to be an equilibrium."

As such, the company launched Diamant, a geometric women's watch with a diamond-laced bezel that is fashionable and comfortable for everyday wear. When designing pieces, Peraldi said he never has a preconceived notion and that inspiration finds him just about anywhere.

"I don't get my inspiration from one moment or one thing," he said. "Like the old Japanese proverb states: If you want to paint a bamboo, you have to observe it first and become a bamboo yourself. Only then can you paint it."

Michael Wunderman, president of Corum

Michael Wunderman lives in Geneva, but the Los Angeles native has a strong connection to his hometown. This comes through in the newest styles from Corum. They include the Golden Bridge watch that was the company's 50th anniversary watch in 2005, for which the functions are visible through a double-sided skeleton case. There is also the sporty Admiral's Cup Competition 48 watch, featuring a 12-sided domed sapphire crystal and an oversize 48-millimeter case made of titanium that launched at the Baselworld Watch & Jewelry Show in April.

"We have so many products that are strong and have a life on their own," said Wunderman, 31, who began working at the Swiss firm his father, Severin Wunderman, acquired in 2000 after having built the Gucci timepiece business. He became president in 2003.

"I was fortunate to be a fly on the wall in the Gucci days. I am a product of my father, but he and I have very strong, passionate ideas that are different," said Wunderman, who will eventually take on the almost $80 million Corum business and is shaking up Corum with youthful, edgy designs.

At next year's fair in Basel, Corum will unveil its redesigned collection, keeping only 20 percent of the tried-and-true classics, like its gold-coin watches and looks with enamel detailing.

"It's going to be much more modern, classy and reliable," Wunderman said. "We're mixing titanium and rose gold with galvanized rubber. We're looking at things in a different way. I know the watch business, but I also know the marketing side of things. I push the engineers outside the box. Technically, we're taking it to another level with the movements."

Wunderman said it's a fruitful and competitive time for the watch industry. The firm is at work on a new tourbillion, a built-in chronograph and an Admiral's Cup watch with a gong that functions like the bell on a ship.

"All the barriers are torn down," he said. "A guy can wear a million dollars on his wrist, and women can wear tourbillions. It's the renaissance period of watches."

Thierry Stern, vice president and member of the management committee of Patek Philippe

As the watch world seems to be in a race to make the world's largest, most tricked-out watch case, Patek Philippe prides itself on going smaller—the tinier, the better.

In order to create women's watches with chronograph and other complications, the company is creating the smallest movements to fit within women's smaller-sized cases.

"You don't want a fashion watch that's in and out in six months," said Stern, 36, who took on the role of vice president and member of the management committee of the firm in 2003. "Some brands are getting too big. I think 42 millimeters is too big."

Stern, like any fourth-generation watchmaker, is also saddened by the fascination by small and new companies with complications like minute repeaters and tourbillions that only a few watch companies have mastered.

"Tourbillion is a fashion victim," he said. "It's difficult to make, and [many brands] are making them now. But the sound of the gong has to be perfect [on a minute repeater], and the tourbillions these companies are making are not accurate. They are destroying the aura."

Stern is focusing on what his company knows and does best: hand-crafted watches and ageless styling.

This year, the firm launched the Gondolo Gemma for women, an elongated rectangular case with a faceted sapphire crystal.

"I'm always amazed that people think that Patek Philippe watches are fragile," he said. "When you're at this level, you can't be fragile."

The company has also ventured into uncharted territory.

"There was never a plan to go into the jewelry business, but our customers asked for it," he said, regarding the introduction of jewelry to complement its 24 watches.

Stern clearly isn't concerned with the profusion of new watch brands, even at its decidedly slow-paced production rate: The 167-year-old firm produces about 38,000 watches per year, even as many of its big-name competitors typically produce as many as 800,000 watches in the same period.

"When business is going well, new brands come in," he said. "When it's bad, they disappear."

details and trimmings

To me, the way forward is a totally couture sequined cape with a pair of jeans or an incredible gown with a denim jacket, mixing luxury with nonluxury.

STELLA MCCARTNEY, DESIGNER

After you have completed this chapter, you will be able to discuss:

- How details are used to differentiate one design from another.

- At least five different details that are used in garment construction.

- The differences between details and trimmings.

- At least six different types of trimmings used as apparel and accessory enhancements.

- The difference between functional and decorative trimmings.

If apparel and accessories were designed without ornamentation or enhancements, they would lose much of their appeal. A dramatic neckline, intricate pockets, and a smocked or pleated bodice are distinguishing features that give a design its character. These and other artistic treatments are known as **details**. They visually enhance fashion merchandise and sometimes increase functionality.

Trimmings, similarly, play an important role in the creation of fashion merchandise. Decoratively, they provide the pizzazz that often transforms the mundane silhouette or shape into something exciting. The intricate beading that brings individuality to a Judith Leiber evening bag and the magnificent flowers that adorn Kökin's millinery creations are just some of the trimmings that help distinguish their designs. These and other adornments provide the fashion designer with "extras" that make the final designs unique.

Some trimmings, known as **findings**, are also functional elements. This category includes zippers, shoulder pads, interfacings, and threads. Although they generally do not play an important visual role, they are necessary for proper fit and appearance.

Some trimmings are both decorative and functional. Buttons, for example, may be used for closure, but unusually shaped or oversized versions also become a design feature. Similarly, colored threads may be used to decorate intricate stitching that enhances a garment's eye appeal.

In the end, it may be the eye-catching quilting, tucks, pockets, buttons, fancy appliqués, braided trim circling the base of a sleeve, little lace collars, rows of colorful ribbons, nailheads, and embroideries that make a particular design successful. Without these tricks of the trade, designs would have less originality.

Trimmings can transform this hat into an exciting fashion design.

DETAILS

The designer picks from a variety of decorative and functional elements when creating a garment, including sleeves, necklines, draped effects, flounces, tucks, seams, collars, pockets, and quilting. It is the manner in which these elements are employed that gives individuality to the garment or accessory. Knowing which and how many to use, and applying them in a manner that highlights the other elements of the design is a constant challenge for designers.

Sleeves

Sleeves are both functional and decorative and come in a variety of styles and lengths. Among the most popular sleeve designs are the **bell sleeve**, which flares into a soft bell-like shape; the **cap sleeve**, which extends on the front and back, covering the shoulders; the **dolman**, featuring a wide armhole that tapers at the wrist; the **kimono sleeve**, cut in one piece with front and back of the garment; the **raglan sleeve**, which extends to the neckline, set in by seams slanting from underarm front and back; and the **set-in sleeve**, which is a fitted sleeve sewn into the armhole.

Necklines

Necklines are an important element of garment design because they highlight the face and neck. The variations are numerous, ranging from high to low to strapless. One is the basic **jewel neckline**, which is a high, round design. It is an opening at the

Dropped shoulders and set-in sleeves regularly appear in fashion collections.

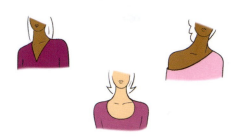

Necklines come in many styles and variations.

top of the garment and fits close to the body. Its name is derived from the idea that it is easily adorned with a strand of pearls or other jewels.

The **bateau neckline** is styled straight from one shoulder to the other. It is sometimes referred to as a boat neckline. Like the jewel neckline, it is collarless.

The **square neckline** employs either a square or rectangular shape that is cut out of the bodice of the garment. It is generally reserved for evening wear or for warm-weather attire.

A **surplice neckline** is one in which one piece of fabric wraps over the other to give a dramatic effect.

The **turtleneck** is a high, rolled-over configuration that fits snugly against the neck and is actually an extension of the body of the garment. It is most often used in knitwear and may be found in apparel worn for daytime and evening. A variation is the **mock turtle**. This is a high neck that simulates the turtleneck but does not roll over. Sometimes it is considered a collar rather than a neckline.

The **cowl neckline** rolls like a turtleneck but does not fit snugly. It drapes down in front and gives a more casual appearance.

A **V neck** resembles the letter for which it is named. It is used in varying degrees of openness, with the most daring plunging to the waistline.

The **one-shoulder design** adds drama to garments. One shoulder is covered; the other is exposed.

A **halter neckline** is high in the front and open in the back. It is used for evening wear and warm-weather apparel. The **keyhole** variety takes its name from a door's keyhole, whose design it imitates.

Designers use these and other types of necklines in a number of ways to emphasize their clothing designs. Necklines may be embellished with a variety of trimmings or left unadorned.

Collars

A collar is a design feature that frames the face and draws attention to it. Unlike the neckline, which is part of the garment, a collar is an extra piece of fabric attached to apparel at the neckline. Although there are many styles to choose from, collars are categorized as either **flat**, like the Peter Pan; **stand-up**, like the Mandarin; or **rolled**, as in the case of the cowl. More specific names are based on their shapes or the costume from which they have been adapted. The **sailor collar**, for example, derives its name from the collar on a sailor's middy.

The following terms are used to describe a collar:

- **Stand**: the part of the collar from the neck edge to the line where it rolls over to the front.

- **Roll line**: the edge at which the stand turns into the front of the collar.

First introduced in the 16th century, collars became popular in the 19th century on men's coats and shirts. In the 20th century, a variety of new styles of collars began to adorn men's, women's, and children's apparel.

A **shawl collar** is a one-piece design that eliminates the seam used on the traditional collar and lapel. It may be single- or double-breasted. It is used in a variety of women's suit and jacket designs, as well as on men's tuxedos. The shawl may be abbreviated and end at the middle of the front of a jacket or extend all the way to the waistline.

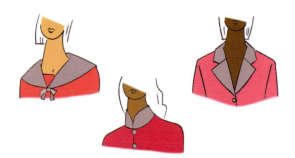

Collars lend individuality to a garment.

Bows are generally used at either the neck or waist, and create a softness to the garment.

The **Mandarin collar** is a stiff, narrow band that fits close to the neck. As its name implies, it is fashioned after the collar detail of an Asian-style jacket. A variation is the **Nehru**, which derives its name from the jacket worn by India's Prime Minister Nehru.

The **Peter Pan collar** is a small, flat type with rounded edges often used in children's apparel.

The **draped collar** consists of two pieces of soft material that fall in folds from the neckline.

The **Eton** is a large collar that is generally made of a stiff fabric. It is fashioned after the collar worn by students at Eton College in Great Britain.

A sailor collar plunges to a "V" in the front, with a tab under the "V," and is square in the back. The collar is finished with an appropriate sailor's tie.

A **convertible collar** can be worn closed at the neck or open. When it is worn open, the finished lapels lie flat against the blouse or shirt. The collar is most often pointed, but sometimes rounded models are used.

Other collars include the **Bertha**, which forms a cape over the shoulders; the **Puritan**, a large collar fashioned after Pilgrim dress; the **Quaker**, a flat, broad collar; and the **funnel**, the shape of which flares out slightly at the top of the neck.

Bows

Although some **bows** may be used as fasteners, their purpose is primarily decorative. They are employed in a variety of sizes and shapes; the choice and placement are left to the creativity of the designer. The result can be floppy, if a sheer such as chiffon is the fabric of choice, or stiff, if a crisper fabric such as taffeta is employed.

For blouses, the placement may be high on the neck, or low, just below a plunging collar. In dresses, an oversized bow may be used as a detail on the back, lending drama to the design. Sometimes bows are formed at the waistline of a skirt where the two ends of a sash are tied together. The fabrics used for the bows are often the same as for the garment itself, but may also be of contrasting material or color.

Pockets

Pockets are both functional and decorative and come in a variety of types. They may be constructed as separate pieces and sewn to the garment, or they may be created as part of the garment. In the latter case, the pocket is concealed. Some of the more commonly used types include the following.

Patch pockets adorn men's, women's, and children's fashions. They are staples on blazer jackets. The construction involves sewing a separate piece of fabric over a portion of the garment. The piece is stitched on three sides, with the top open. The patch pockets that are found on men's jackets serve as the place in which a silk or cotton handkerchief may be inserted for decorative purposes. There are variations of the patch, including one that has a cuff on the upper edge; the kangaroo type, which features an inverted pleat; and the pouch, which employs gathers for decorative fullness. Designers often create variations on patch pockets, using such elements as decorative stitching, zippers, draping, welts, button-down closures, and flaps.

The **slash pocket** is merely an opening in a garment that is finished by machine or hand. An "inside" pocket is then suspended from the finished fabric. This pocket is found in pants and garments where attention to the pocket is not important.

Pleats

Pleats add elegance to silhouettes.

Designers use four basic types of pleats—the accordion pleat, box pleat, inverted pleat, and knife pleat. Each involves folds of fabric that have been either pressed or stitched to form the desired shape. Pleats may be used as the design of an entire skirt or dress, or as accents on almost any part of a garment. Designers such as Fortuny and Mary McFadden use the **crystal pleat**, the tiniest of all pleats, to capture the fashion world's attention.

A more commonly used pleat is the **accordion pleat**, which is often used for an entire skirt. The top is generally stitched to the waistband, with the pleats hanging down. Today's miracle fibers help pleats retain their shapes even after cleaning. The accordion pleat may also be used as neckline accents, in a variety of fabrics. If a stand-up look is required, a stiff material such as taffeta may be pleated.

The **knife pleat** is a pleat that is folded in the desired width and then left to fall straight. Skirts that are pleated often use the **box pleat**, which is created with two knife pleats that face in opposite directions. The **inverted pleat**, generally found on skirts and dresses, in varying lengths, involves the placement of two pleats that face each other. Fabric is available to designers already pleated, in any desired length.

Cowls

The use of **cowls** is a design detail in which the fabric falls in soft folds. It often adds drama to a design and can serve to camouflage the body when it is desired. Certain fabrics, such as matte jersey, chiffon, fine woolen, and velvet, are well-suited for cowls. The draped effect is maximized by cutting the material on the bias, or the diagonal. In this technique, the fabric is cut where the warp or lengthwise yarns intersect with the filling or crosswise yarns.

Cowls may be used for a portion of a garment such as the neckline, for a skirt, or for a whole dress. The latter is generally reserved for evening wear.

Supple fabrics are draped to create cowls.

Gathers

Like cowls, **gathers** are used in a variety of places on a garment to achieve extra fullness. For this purpose, the designer must plan for one to two times the usual amount of material. The fuller the gathers, the more fabric required. When a soft material is used, the fabric falls softly. When a stiffer material, such as taffeta, is the choice, the gathers will produce a stand-away effect.

Gathers are produced by sewing the fabric only on one end of the fabric. The remainder is left to fall loosely, to be shirred down the center of a dress at its waistline for a "corseted" fit, to be draped to one side, or to be attached at the top and bottom of the material—such as from the yoke of a blouse to its waistline—to give a dramatic effect. It is the creative designer who employs gathers in interesting ways.

Quilting

Taken from the various techniques used on bed comforters, **quilting** is used on fashion apparel and accessories. A "puffed up" effect is created by stitching a design on two layers of fabric with padding inserted between them. In quilting, patterned materials often follow a specific design, whereas solids use different types of motifs. A designer may quilt an entire garment, or may quilt just sections, such as collars and cuffs, to create a detail accent.

Seams

Although **seams** are generally used to join two pieces of fabric as unobtrusively as possible, they may also be used as design details. In gloves, for example, **overseaming** is often used to impart a sporty effect. A **piped seam** is another type of detail that provides design interest. The fabric, cut on the bias, covers a cord, the width of which determines the thickness of the piping. Hand-stitched seams are sometimes used on lapel and collar edges for a casual look.

Tucks

These details, which are both functional and decorative, give specific shape to a garment. A strategically placed tuck can help to accentuate the bustling of a bodice. For decoration, several rows of tucks may run parallel to each other, creating an interesting effect. The width of the tucks vary according to the designer's concept.

Miscellaneous Details

In addition to those details already discussed, others used in fashion merchandise include smocking, shirring, rouleau, vents and jabots. **Smocking**, a technique that involves the stitching of small patterns, is used extensively as detail on girl's apparel. **Shirring** is a detail created by using elastic thread that runs row after row on a garment and produces a controlled fullness. **Rouleau** is a decorative detail produced by encircling heavy piping with bias-cut fabric and using the piping in interesting patterns around such places as button closures. **Vents** are openings of various lengths that are used at skirt and dress hemlines and in jackets to provide room for movement. **Jabots** are loosely hanging ruffles at the front of a blouse.

TRIMMINGS

A walk through any well-stocked trimming supplier reveals an endless array of enhancements that can add an extra touch to a designer's creation. Trimmings are so important that many manufacturers and designers have trimming buyers who scout the market for them. In other companies, where trimmings have become the designer's signature, the designer researches the selections personally. In either case, the final choice concerning the trim is made by the designer. The right choice can certainly add to the attractiveness of the garment and its ultimate success in a collection.

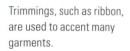

Trimmings, such as ribbon, are used to accent many garments.

The decorative trimmings most frequently used are fabrics, braiding, embroidery, beading, buttons, belts, appliqués, lace, fringes, and buckles. Trimmings that are also functional include thread, interfacings, elastic, and zippers.

Fabric Trims

Every conceivable type of knitted, woven, or crocheted fabric is produced in narrow strips for application as a trim. The lace edging in lingerie, the bands of velvet and ribbons that circle the sleeves and hemlines of a garment, and the contrasting piping—strips of fabrics that are rolled and sewn into narrow bands—are just some examples of **fabric trims**.

Braid

Braiding involves interlacing three or more yarns or strips of fabric to produce a narrow, decorative trim. The process resembles the braiding of hair. Gold metallic braid is a favorite choice when a military look is in fashion.

Appliqué

Small, individual pieces of fabric are often used to create a decoration. When the cutout pieces are sewn or fastened to larger pieces of fabric to form trim, it is called **appliqué**.

Lace

Dresses, intimate apparel, bridal gowns, and sweaters are just some of the apparel designs that are decorated with **lace**. Lace is available from markets all over

Appliqués are decorative elements added to the finished product.

the globe, with choices ranging from the finest, detailed variety to types that are heavily textured. Lace trim is sold on "cards" and is available in widths that usually range from ¼ inch to three or four inches. The use of lace trim varies from season to season. Except for lingerie and bridal wear, it is most popular for summer merchandise.

Embroidery

Various yarns are used to decorate or embroider a garment. **Embroidery** can be hand sewn or produced by machine. The thread used may be in the same coloration as the fabric it enhances or in a contrasting color to create interest. Intricately embroidered designs are produced with schiffli machines that can apply the most intricate pattern in any direction. Organdy and batiste, two widely used sheer fabrics, are often **schiffli embroidered**.

Although the vast majority of the embroidery used today is machine-applied, there has been a resurgence in India with the old tradition of hand embroidery. Techniques that have been used through the ages are appearing once again in fine garments with shoppers from New York to Hong Kong purchasing them.

Beading

In seasons when glitter and sparkle are emphasized, **beading** is a popular method of decoration. Glass and metal beads in a variety of sizes, shapes, and colors are applied by hand or machine. The cost of intricate hand-beading has become prohibitively expensive in the United States. As a result, manufacturers may have the entire garment or accessory manufactured offshore. They may also choose to produce the basic garment domestically and then ship it overseas, where labor costs are lower, for beading. The majority of the beading found on evening wear is produced in Asia.

Beading is a favorite attention-getting decoration.

Sequins

Small, circular, metallic disks that reflect the light are called **sequins**. They come in a variety of sizes and colors and are used extensively for evening wear. Sequins are a particular favorite for holiday collections.

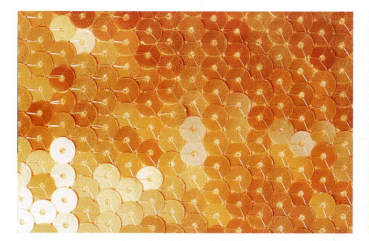

Sequins are often added to designs worn for festive occasions such as holidays and parties.

Rhinestones

Small bits of glass that have been cut to resemble diamonds and other precious and semiprecious stones are called **rhinestones**. Set in *prongs* that are attached to the fabric, they provide a mirrorlike sparkle that reflects the light. Rhinestones come in a variety of cuts and sizes. Evening apparel, handbags, and jewelry make extensive use of rhinestone trim.

Buttons

Although buttons serve as decorative and functional design details, they can also be used to trim a garment. They can easily transform a basic design into one of interest. Buttons are available in pearl, wood, metal, glass, leather, bone, and so on, in all sizes and shapes. Fine garments are usually decorated with buttons made of natural materials. In less expensive garments, natural mother-of-pearl is replaced with plastic, and leather with vinyl. If a self-covered button is required, the apparel producer usually sends fabric to a button contractor who then covers each button with the supplied fabric. Where exposed buttons are to be used as unobtrusively as possible, a covered button is often the choice.

Belts

Belts, other than those purchased separately in accessories departments, are used as functional, decorative additions to dresses, suits, pants, and ensembles. Because it is part of apparel design, the belt is usually inexpensively constructed. Many are made of vinyl, inexpensive leathers, or other contrasting materials, such as rope or chain. In cases where self-covered belts are required, the garment manufacturer supplies the fabric to a contractor for final construction.

Belts for trimmings are either stitched or glued to base materials. The stitched variety produces a more durable product.

Consumers are often attracted to garments with unusual closures.

Zippers

Used primarily as fasteners, **zippers** sometimes add decoration to a design. They come in a variety of lengths and materials. Nylon provides lightness as well as strength, and the major domestic producer is Talon.

Decorative Labels

Labels, usually used on the inside of a garment, came into their own as status-providing identifiers for fashion designers during the 1980s. Designer jeans proudly displayed the creator's name on the back pocket for quick recognition. Today, some companies still use the label on the outside as a means of identifying their garments.

Whether it is used inside or out, the label designs are carefully conceived and produced; woven labels are the choice for quality garments.

Thread

Choosing the appropriate **thread** for a garment or accessory is important to its quality and durability. Thread comes in a variety of thicknesses and basic and fashion colors and is manufactured by the yarn producer. Before the use of manufactured fibers, threads were made of natural fibers, such as cotton and silk. Today, manufactured fibers offer greater choice and more varied characteristics. In addition, the growing use of manufactured fibers requires use of these more flexible threads. With the elasticity of wovens and knits, for example, thread with a more elastic nature is required. The use of polyester thread supplies the strength necessary to withstand the stretch of manufactured and knit fabrics.

Thread comes in cones for use in manufacturing. The cones hold anywhere from 1,200 to 2,400 yards.

Interfacings

Interfacings are functional trimmings used to give shape and support to garments and accessories. They are not seen but are used between the outside layer of the garment and the lining. Collars and lapels on men's suit jackets, for example, are generally enhanced with stable interfacings that can be woven or nonwoven. They may be

Threads, in a variety of types and colors, are both functional and decorative components of garments.

SWAROVSKI

ounded in 1895 in the Alpine town of Wattens, Swarovski has always been a manufacturer of crystal decorative objects and accessories; its distinction is an unequalled level of precision and perfection in the cuts. Through the early 20th century, the company used this skill to produce the highest-quality dressing and grinding tools, the first reflective rear lights for transportation safety, optical devices, and fashion trimmings.

Then, in 1956, Swarovski dazzled the world with its "Aurora Borealis," a stone that shimmers in every imaginable color. As the century progressed, one astonishing success followed another, always maintaining the high standards for which the House of Swarovski is known. In 1965, for example, it launched a line of products for crystal chandeliers. Other landmark developments included the foundation of the Swarovski Collector's Society and, in 1989, the launching of

the Daniel Swarovski line of objects d'art, accessories, and jewelry based on concepts from Ettore Scaottsass, Alessandro Mendini, and Stefano Ricci. The development of the "hot fix" technology made it possible to iron jewelry stones onto material and gave Swarovski a sparkling presence in the trimmings market.

In 1995, Swarovski celebrated its 100th anniversary with a breathtaking crystal exhibition in Wattens. By 1999, it had distributed its first watch collection and marketed the "crystal tattoo," a self-adhesive crystal that can be applied to the skin—a new contribution to the world of body art.

The House of Swarovski has used its skill and ingenuity to create an inspiring range of crystal products. Some are practical; others are simply breathtakingly beautiful. They can be used to decorate your home, your body, and now your fashion wardrobe.

For the 150th anniversary of Marshall Field's in Chicago, Swarovski collaborated with the retail giant to create more than 800 exclusively designed crystal ornaments and a 200-pound tree-topper designed by Andrée Putman to decorate their traditional holiday tree.

held in place by sewing them into the garment or by fusing them. The fused method, which is faster and cheaper, is generally employed in less costly products.

When interfacings are needed for knitwear, stretch-knit interfacings are employed because they are less rigid or stable than the other variety.

Elastic

When gathering is needed at the wrist of a blouse or when shirring is the detail on a bodice, elastic is often used by the manufacturer. Once used primarily to keep the tops of socks from rolling down or for form-fitting swimwear, elastic is now used in a variety of forms for many fashion items. Workout clothing that conforms to the body, bicycle pants, and knit leggings, for example, use elastic thread to sew the components of the garment together.

CHAPTER HIGHLIGHTS

- Details and trimmings can transform a basic garment into one with special appeal.

- Details can be decorative or functional, with some serving in both capacities. They include sleeves, necklines, collars, bows, pockets, pleats, cowls, gathers, quilting, seams, tucks, smocking, and shirring.

- Using one basic body, a designer may create two completely different looks by adding different details to each.

- Trimmings, which further embellish garments and accessories, include embroidery, beading, rhinestones, appliqués, fringes, lace, buttons, and belts.

- Functional trimmings are called findings and include thread, interfacings, elastic, and zippers.

IMPORTANT FASHION TERMINOLOGY AND CONCEPTS

accordion pleat	halter neckline	rolled collar
applique	interfacings	rouleau
bateau neckline	inverted pleat	sailor collar
beading	jabot	schiffli embroidery
bell sleeve	jewel neckline	seams
Bertha collar	keyhole	sequins
bows	kimono sleeve	set-in sleeve
box pleat	knife pleat	shawl collar
braiding	lace	shirring
cap sleeve	Mandarin collar	slash pocket
convertible collar	mock turtle	smocking
cowl	Nehru collar	square neckline
cowl neckline	one-shoulder design	stand
crystal pleat	overseaming	stand-up collar
details	patch pocket	surplice neckline
dolman	Peter Pan collar	thread
draped collar	piped seam	trimmings
embroidery	Puritan collar	turtleneck
Eton collar	Quaker collar	V neck
findings	quilting	vents
flat collar	raglan sleeves	zippers
funnel collar	rhinestones	
gathers	roll line	

FOR REVIEW

1. Describe decorative and functional details. Give examples.
2. Differentiate among the bateau, surplice, and jewel necklines.
3. What are the three basic types of collars used in garment design?
4. In what way does the patch pocket differ from the slash pocket?
5. Which two major designers, one past and one present, have used crystal pleating extensively in their garments?
6. To give greater drapability to a fabric, how must it be cut?
7. Describe the quilting process.
8. Are buttons functional or fashionable?
9. What type of machine is used to embroider intricate patterns in any direction?
10. What fashion trimming was visible on designer jeans in the 1970s?
11. Discuss the importance of interfacings in garment construction.
12. In the Point of View article "Sewing Circle," discuss the highlights of the project.

EXERCISES AND PROJECTS

1. Examine the pages of fashion magazines and select photographs of a variety of necklines used on dresses and blouses. Mount each picture on foamboard, labeling each neckline. In an oral presentation to the class, describe the "mood" of each selected style.

2. Visit a trimmings supplier to examine the products available to fashion designers. Most major cities have such shops that are open to the public as well as to industry professionals. Ask for permission to photograph the different types of trimmings, so that you may report about them to your class. You might concentrate on just one type, such as buttons, or choose to explore the whole trimmings field.

WEB SITES

By accessing these Web sites, you will be able to gain broader knowledge and up-to-date information on materials related to this chapter.

Atlas Embroidery

www.atlasembroidery.com

All About Beading

www.allaboutbeading.com/portals

The Case of the Classic Silhouette

questions

1. Is Amy wise in staying with the concept that has brought her fashion recognition?

2. How else might she add a freshness to her collections without the risk of losing her place in the market.

In her first two years as a designer of bridge fashions, Amy Diamond has made a positive impact on the apparel world. Buyers from the major stores have embraced her collections, which have been profitable for them. Her collections use basic silhouettes with many different fabrics and color harmonies.

Now in her third year of operation, retailers are suggesting that Amy introduce new silhouettes and shapes to attract an even wider market. Although most designers subscribe to regular change, Diamond believes that her strength lies with her basic silhouette, and that there will always be enough business for these classic choices. Her sales manager, however, also believes it is time to try something new. Perhaps, he says, a new silhouette or two should be tried to test the waters. Amy is still shying away from such suggestions and is staying with the concept that has brought success.

Sewing Circle

BETSY LOWTHER

The road between the city of Lucknow and the town of Mahmudabad in northern India bumps past a vivid spectrum of color. Acres of lush fields—bright and green in this especially fertile area in the province of Uttar Pradesh, just east of New Delhi—stretch between tiny towns whose shabby produce stands and busy shops are painted in equally bold blues and yellows. And then there are the saris, in bright shades of deep purple, striking turquoise and an eye-popping pink that's just a shade below Day-Glo.

The 35-mile stretch twists and dips to Mahmudabad Qila—which means *fort* in the Urdu language—the sprawling ancestral home of the Raja of Mahmudabad, whose family has occupied the location for more than 600 years. One only has to squint to envision the decaying palace in its heyday, when the elaborate rose-colored chandeliers were free of heavy cobwebs and the vast library—still stocked with 40,000 tomes, including early editions of Shakespeare—thrived.

But deep inside the fort, there is a treasure of a different sort today—a small, whitewashed workroom, where a group of women from the tiny town gather six days a week to meet and sew. They sit on the floor and chat, their light murmurs mixing with the hum of hand-cranked sewing machines (a necessity, as the electricity only works for about four hours a day). Their fingers move lightly over beautiful creations: hand-spun cotton tunics with delicate embroidery; vibrant, buttoned coats in wool and cotton, and bold patchwork scarves, many

with the exquisite embroidery for which the region is famous. When finished, the pieces will be sold under the name Qilasaaz at private trunk shows in the U.S. and Europe.

The Qilasaaz project is the child, in many ways, of Vijay Khan, wife of the current Raja and known as the Rani. The couple, along with their two grown sons, live most of the year in a crumbling palace in Lucknow, but Khan has traveled to the Qila nearly every week since she started the project almost 15 years ago. Twice a year, she packs up the finished pieces and takes them to cities such as London, New York and Paris for private sales, which earn enough money to keep the operation—and many of the women—afloat for another year.

"Poverty is the biggest problem for these women," says the elegant Khan, who was educated at Smith College and Cambridge University. "They never had any job opportunities before. My purpose was to give them a way to earn a regular income—something they can depend on for the first time in their lives."

More than 30 women are now on the Qilasaaz payroll, and another 30 currently do piecework with the hopes of eventually coming into the workshop full-time. All of the fabric sourced for the pieces comes from local shops specializing in fine linen, pure pashmina and khadi, a hand-loomed cotton, providing even more support to the region's artisans. The operation essentially works as a small cooperative: Because Khan—who has assumed the hefty roles of manager, designer,

public relations representative and sales agent—cannot be at the fort every day, the women of Qilasaaz are responsible for governing themselves. Major decisions are made only after consulting the entire workshop. "These women have more than money now," Khan remarks, "They have a new sense of confidence."

The Qilasaaz collection has earned a loyal following by word of mouth from its society-heavy clientele. "People have a respect for hand-loomed, hand-stitched and hand-embroidered," says Khan, amid the hum of the sunny workroom. "Each piece that is created here is distinct and special, and our customers understand that."

Many of the embroidery techniques used in Qilasaaz pieces are a fading art in rapidly modernizing India, and their unique, high-quality craftsmanship has led two museums—the Calico Museum of Textiles in Ahmedabad, India, and the Whitworth Art Gallery in Manchester, England—to commission samplers for their collections. "These are techniques that have been used and passed down for generations," says Khan, who will cohost the next sale in New York at the end of November. "This work has helped keep such traditions alive."

But while Qilasaaz's pieces have been scooped up by appreciative shoppers from Manhattan to Hong Kong, it's clear they mean the most to the women who make them. When Khan stands to leave, the women smother her with gentle hugs and genuine grins. Their warmth lingers the whole bumpy ride back.

chapter 14

cosmetics and fragrances

Perfume is the unseen but unforgettable ultimate fashion accessory.

COCO CHANEL, DESIGNER

After you have completed this chapter, you will be able to discuss:

- The history of cosmetics and fragrances from ancient times to the present.

- Many of the marketing innovations that helped the cosmetics industry achieve its success.

- The importance of ethnic cosmetics to the industry.

- The role of private branding in the cosmetics industry.

- The various stages of marketing cosmetics and fragrances.

- The distribution of cosmetics.

Companies such as Estée Lauder, L'Oreal, Avon, Shiseido, and Wella dominate the cosmetics industry with a variety of brands; others, with brands such as Obsession, White Diamonds, Chanel No. 5, Opium, Giorgio, and Poison do the same for the women's fragrance industry.

The use of cosmetics and fragrances, however, is not a recent development. As far back as 1500 B.C., stibium pencils and *kohl*, a forerunner of mascara, were used to paint and accent the eyelids. In Egypt and Arabia, it was long stylish to paint the underside of the eye green and the lid, lashes, and brows black with kohl.

The Roman Empire adopted the use of cosmetics on an unparalleled scale in history. Charlemagne's conquests then spread the use of cosmetics throughout Europe. The ingredients used to make the cosmetics were so precious that whole Arabic dynasties were founded on the spoils of hijacking the caravans that carried them. Chalk and white lead were used to lighten the skin, and pumice stone to whiten the teeth. Deep rouges colored the cheeks, and henna tinted the hair and fingernails. Even men made significant use of cosmetic products. In pre-Revolutionary North America, men colored gray hair in beards, mustaches, and sideburns with a product called Mascaro, the name from which *mascara* was derived. In the late 18th century, the French first manufactured cosmetics for commercial use by introducing *Rimmel*, a mascara that was popular for decades.

Similarly, natural aromatic substances have been used since ancient times to cure ailments, enhance and beautify the ordinary, and appease the gods. This indulgence reached its height in ancient Egypt. As Cleopatra prepared to meet Marc Anthony, she bathed in rare and fragrant essences; the sails of her ship were lavishly sprinkled with perfumes; and precious incense was burned in gold and silver censers.

Because bathing was a luxury of the rich and sanitation only rudimentary, perfumes, composed of flower pomades, balms, or roots, appeared in France during the Renaissance to hide odors.

By the late 1800s and early 1900s, the cosmetics and fragrance industries had introduced a host of new products. Jean-Marie Farina introduced *eau de cologne* in 1820. This marked the emergence of Paris as the center of fine perfumery. Companies such as Houbigant and Roger & Gallet made the first synthetic fragrances. In Chicago, a chemist developed a glossy lash darkener in a tube for a company he named after his sister Mabel—Maybelline.

Currently, cosmetics and fragrances are as important to the world of fashion as are the creations of the most famous couturiers. A look at the counters in fashionable retail operations reveal many familiar names, including Calvin Klein, Yves Saint Laurent, Chanel, Ralph Lauren, and Donna Karan. This is a signal that these industries are a huge business with impressive profit potential.

Cosmetics counters are often the busiest areas for retailers.

COSMETICS

In the early 1920s, cosmetics were used primarily by sophisticated consumers. During that time, a Hollywood makeup artist, Max Factor, packaged and sold a cake mascara (an eye-enhancing product that had to be moistened with water) that he had created for the movie industry. From the 1920s through the 1950s, movie stars played an important role in influencing consumers to use cosmetics for everyday use. Some of the products that became popular included foundation, face powder, mascara, eyebrow pencil, cheek color (rouge), lipstick, and nail polish. Movie fans often imitated the looks developed for the screen; the makeup of Grace Kelly and Doris Day, for example, was often copied.

Even at the end of the 1950s, however, many products were still socially unaccepted. In the social climate of that decade, "nice" girls wore few cosmetics. With so little popular interest in cosmetics, the industry spent little time developing new products. A list of the major cosmetic brands prior to 1960 is given in Table 14.1.

Table 14.1

MAJOR COSMETICS BRANDS, PRIOR TO 1960

Aloe Cream	Hazel Bishop
Avon	Helena Rubenstein
Bonne Bell	House of Westmore
Charles of the Ritz	John Robert Powers
Coty	Max Factor
Cover Girl	Maybelline
Cutex	Merle Norman
Dorothy Gray	Natural Wonder
Elizabeth Arden	Princess Marcella Borghese
Estée Lauder	Revlon
Fabergé	Scandia
Fashion Fair	Tussy
Germaine Monteil	Ultima
Hard As Nails	Ultra Sheen
Harriet Hubbard Ayer	Vogue Cosmetics

The loveliest glow of all is yours...with this new liquid make-up!

Revlon 'Touch-and-Glow'

Multimillion-dollar ad campaigns have contributed to the extremely profitable cosmetic market. This Revlon ad is from the 1950s.

Unique packaging and a variety of promotions often launch new products in the cosmetics industry.

Highlights of the Cosmetics Industry

1960s

In the 1960s, the cosmetics industry began a major campaign to reach the mass consumer market. With new and improved items in a wide range of pigments, the cosmetics industry was ready to become a major industry.

As cosmetics became easier to apply and colors looked more natural, the industry offered consumers a more enticing packaging. Suddenly people became interested.

In the 1960s, women began to use cosmetics on a regular basis. A number of breakthrough products were introduced, including powder blusher, for the healthy look; powder eyeshadow for ease in application; powder brow color for a natural look; liquid eyeliner to emphasize eyes; translucent powder to eliminate streaking; gels for a hint of color; lip gloss for a high sheen look; and applicators to help the inexperienced apply cosmetics.

In addition to these new products, packaging designers and marketers played an important role for the industry. Among the many new techniques they developed to influence the consumer are the following:

- *Kits*. Instead of selling items only in single colors, kits offered multiple shades for eyeshadows, lipsticks, pencils, blushers, and in some cases, false eyelashes.

- *Fun Compacts*. Hot color, plastic compacts gave the products a fashion orientation.

- *Megapack Promotions*. Companies packaged total sets of products for eyes, lips, nails, and cheeks, all in a specific color family.

- *Refillable Packaging*. This enabled the consumer to buy a fresh supply of the product without having to spend money on a new package.

- *New Role Models*. Marketers used famous models instead of movies stars in ads.

- *Gift with a Purchase*. Estée Lauder introduced consumers to new products by offering one free item with the purchase of another.

By the end of the decade, sales in the cosmetics industry reached new heights. Preservative-free products became available. Through sales in health stores, they helped capture a segment of the market that had previously shied away from cosmetics. Fragrance-free items also made headlines with the new Clinique line. The new formulas, coupled with sleek, contemporary packaging, opened up yet another segment of the market.

1970s

In the 1970s, cosmetics adapted to the new freedom of choice philosophy of the apparel industry. Women were no longer coerced into wearing just one look. The cosmetics industry followed suit by offering a wide variety of styles from makeup that emphasized the natural look to more exciting and glamorous selections. Instead of using famous models and movie stars as role models in advertisements, the individual woman became the focus of attention.

Key words were now used to emphasize the qualities of various products. Among them were *oil free, nongreasy, waterproof, conditioning, smearproof, smudgeproof,* and *microencapsulated moisture.* Popular products included such new ingredients as NMF (natural moisturizing factor), hydrolyzed protein, vitamins such as pantheol, ph balancers, and polymers. Although these ingredients did improve the quality of many items, it was the use of these names in the ads that attracted the attention of the shopper.

Unique packaging dominated the decade. The curved wand made mascara application easier. Oversized wand applicators were introduced. All-in-one friction feed or gravity-feed packages for blush were introduced. Roll-on applicators increased the sale of lip gloss. Transparent lip caps allowed the consumer to see the color.

New products also contributed to increases in sales. Matte and brush-on lipsticks, combination lipstick and lip gloss, overnight lash conditioner, face tints for sheer coverage, and lip glosses with fruit flavors increased sales to new levels.

Other factors that generated excitement included the offer of a free gift with a purchase, Norman Norell's pairing designer lipstick with designer fragrance, and Helena Rubenstein's use of a computer to personalize customer selection of cosmetics with appropriate coloring.

Because the market for cosmetics and fragrances is highly competitive, advertisers use catchy phrases to gain the attention of consumers.

1980s

The baby boomers, who came to power in the 1980s, were responsible for a new wave of cosmetics—skin-care products that offered treatment benefits. The 1980s were a decade of increased spending, and greater emphasis was placed on cosmetics.

Innovation abounded and new phrases were introduced to capture the market. Claims such as irritant-free, environmentally safe, formulated for contact lens users, safe for sensitive skin, long wearing, fadeproof, and doesn't flake were appearing in every form of advertisement. It was not merely a fashion statement that was being made; now the benefits that the product's use would impart took center stage. To motivate the educated and affluent market, ads identified specific ingredients in cosmetics, such as diamond dust, sunscreens, mink oil, collagen, aloe, and optical diffusers.

Packaging became more sophisticated, with the introduction of double-ended products that combined nail polish and lipstick; self-sharpening, swivel feed pencils for eyelining; super-slim vinyl compacts; and an air-blush system.

New products that made their way to the market included powder pencils, aerosol face powder, multi-purpose items such as an all-in-one nail polish formula containing base and top coat, nail kits for French manicures, brush-on powder lipstick, wet-look nail polish, and the return of cake mascara.

In addition to new products, new technology resulted in point-of-purchase computers for skin and makeup analysis. Private label lines became prominent. Custom-blended colors hit the market for the first time. Price points escalated at the end of the decade. Among the new marketing approaches were **infomercials**, TV programs paid for by sponsors, in which celebrities such as Kathie Lee Gifford extolled the virtues of the product. Unlike the one-minute or 30-second commercial, infomercials run 30 minutes.

1990s

The look of the 1990s was decidedly retro, following the trend established by the apparel designers. With the aging of the baby boomers, skin products became prominent. Once again, fashion models such as Claudia Schiffer, Kate Moss, and Linda Evangelista became the role models for consumers. By the late 1990s, the cosmetics industry turned to actresses such as Elizabeth Hurley, Heather Locklear, and Melanie Griffith to promote its products.

2000s

The cosmetic looks have been varied during the 2000s, with colors following fashion trends. The hot news, especially during 2006, was the focus on antiaging products. Natural and organic ingredients were highlighted in the ad campaigns. Significant attention focused on cosmetics for ethnic markets, along with increases in sales for men's cosmetics.

As the cosmetics and fragrance industry entered the new millenium, its sales figures climbed to new heights. As is the case in other industries, a few leaders continue to make the greatest impact with consumers. Each of these groups manufactures and distributes a host of different brands, with each brand appealing to a distinct market. Table 14.2 lists the top 10 companies according to sales.

Ethnic Cosmetics

One of the fastest-growing segments of the industry has been cosmetics designed for specific ethnic groups. **Ethnic cosmetics** have experienced sales increases of between 50 percent and 75 percent per quarter in most chain stores. Although some attention has been paid to ethnic cosmetics in department stores, such as Fashion Fair Cosmetics, a division of Johnson Publishing Company, little has been done

Table 14.2

THE WHO'S WHO OF COSMETICS TODAY

Top 10 Companies	Selected Brands
1. Avon Products, Inc.	Far Away, Beyond Color.
2. Beiersdorf AG	Atrix, Eucerin, Skin Caviar, Yardley, Ellen Tracy, Tosca, Samatra Rain.
3. The Estée Lauder Cos., Inc.	Clinique, Aramis, Estée Lauder, Jane, Tommy Hilfiger, Bobbi Brown Essentials, Prescriptives, ORIGINS, M.A.C., La Mer, Kiton, Donna Karan, Aveda, Jo Malone, Bumble and Bumble, Michael Kors.
4. Johnson & Johnson	Neutrogena, Clean & Clear, Purpose, pH 5.5, RoC.
5. Kao Corp.	Augu makeup, Jergens personal care products, Sofina cosmetics.
6. L'Oréal Group	Lancôme, Armani, Cacharel, Ralph Lauren, Paloma Picasso, True Illusion, Biotherm, Garnier, Helena Rubenstein.
7. Proctor & Gamble	Oil of Olay, Cover Girl, Pantene, Old Spice, Hugo Boss, Giorgio Beverly Hills.
8. Shiseido	Carita, Jean Paul Gaultier, Issey Miyake, Vital Perfection, Revital, Eizir.
9. Wella Group	Parfum Rochas, Gucci Parfums, Perform, Viva Color, Charles Jourdan, Bogner.
10. Unilever	KL, Innocence, Chloé, Eternity, Obsession, Faberge Brut, White Diamonds, Pond's.

to capture the attention of shoppers through mass merchandising and drugstores. Role models for African American women have included high-fashion model Naomi Campbell and actress Halle Berry.

The Johnson Publishing Company, owner of *Ebony* and *Jet* magazines, has spent considerable time and effort making Fashion Fair Cosmetics the number one selling line for women of color. The line is sold in more than 2,500 department stores in the United States, Canada, the Caribbean, Europe, and Africa. Because this line is sold mainly in department stores, the company introduced another line called Ebone, which is mass-marketed, at lower-price points.

Apparel Headliners and Cosmetics

Before the 1960s, the cosmetics houses bore names that were associated only with the industry. Famous companies, such as Charles of the Ritz, Estée Lauder, Max Factor, Helena Rubenstein, and Revlon, were strictly involved in producing cosmetics and promoted their names as well as the products they produced.

Beginning in the 1960s, a new trend saw an increased use of famous apparel designer names on cosmetics. Because of the recognition bestowed on these designers, consumers were likely to be attracted to any products that bore their names. Givenchy, the famous French couturier; Lilly Daché, the internationally celebrated milliner; and Mary Quant, the London designer, were the first to cross over into cosmetics. The results were so successful that other apparel designers soon joined their ranks.

In 1970, a host of products were introduced with the names of apparel designers, including Calvin Klein, who gained recognition with his designer jeans collection; Halston, one of America's most creative designers; Christian Dior, one of Paris's notables; and Norman Norell, the leading architect of American fashion. In 1980, the list grew even longer with the addition of Ralph Lauren and Yves Saint Laurent.

By the 1990s, fashion designers who wanted to enter this arena had already done so. Competition in the field was so keen that there was a decrease in the number of apparel designers entering the cosmetics industry.

The trend that is currently generating the most excitement is the establishment of companies headed by makeup artists. The practice is not new. In the 1930s and 1940s, Max Factor parlayed his talents into a major cosmetics company. Today, the makeup artist is taking center stage in the industry.

Bobbi Brown, a leading force in cosmetics, was painting faces as recently as 1990. With her considerable knowledge and support from Bergdorf Goodman, which stocked some of the lipsticks she created, she became a leader in cosmetics. In 1995, her wholesale volume was $20 million! Today the figures are well over $30 million with the products in more than 400 stores and 20 countries. Others with similar expertise are getting into the act and blazing new trails for cosmetics.

"It's All About Us" targets the U.S. ethnic beauty market.

Bobbi Brown, whose trendy cosmetics line was founded by makeup artists and is owned by Estée Lauder, at work.

Marketing Lines of Cosmetics

With the different brand names and products in the industry, marketing initiatives have become extremely important. Initiatives include new package design, demonstrations of products, personal appearances, samplings, and giveaways.

Packaging

Knowledgeable industry participants freely admit that only a limited number of ingredients can be used to produce cosmetics. With all of the excitement that surrounds advertising campaigns, the only real difference among cosmetics are the color palettes that each company designs. Yet even the color ranges and emphases for a particular season are not solely decided by the company. The decision is based largely on information from fashion forecasters—the experts who predict what the apparel industry will be featuring. The cosmetics industry then creates colors that will effectively enhance these garments. Because everyone in the cosmetics field focuses on these fashion forecasts, the result is generally a uniform approach to color.

Given these parameters, how can a cosmetics company distinguish its line from the others? The answer often lies with **package design**. In both cosmetics and fragrances, fashionable and functional packaging continues to play a role in helping the shopper choose a particular product. Often, it is the package, rather than the contents, that encourages a consumer to choose one product over another.

In terms of ingredients alone, there is little justification for the price-point spread in the industry. Often, the reason for a higher-priced product is the cost of the package design. Marketers of beauty products spend enormous sums developing unique packaging that will attract the attention of consumers in this competitive field.

Renowned cosmetics and fragrance package designer Marc Rosen is the subject of a World of Fashion Profile.

Demonstrations

The cosmetics departments of most major stores have company cosmetologists, who demonstrate the proper method of makeup application. The **demonstration** usually involves a targeted shopper who will be receptive to and benefit from personalized treatments. After removing any existing makeup from the customer, the cosmetologist professionally applies a range of cosmetics in appropriate colors. This process usually attracts observers who witness the change. Because of the cosmetologist's skill, the customer's appearance is greatly enhanced. As a result, the customer and often the onlookers are motivated to purchase the products that were used in the demonstration.

Personal Appearances

Cosmetics companies attract attention to their products with personal appearances. The makeup artists, who achieve recognition by applying cosmetics to models and theatrical personalities, often appear at the counters in the prestigious stores that sell their lines. Such players as Bobbi Brown, Vincent Longo, François Nars, and Carol Shaw regularly make the rounds of stores such as Bergdorf Goodman, Saks, and Nordstrom, drawing crowds eager to hear them tell about their products. Because these artists were responsible for making up the faces of such movie stars as Demi Moore, Anjelica Huston, and Geena Davis, customers are eager to learn, firsthand, how to improve their appearances.

MARC ROSEN

Marc Rosen has been a leading package designer for many years, working for such giants in the industry as Revlon and Elizabeth Arden. After graduating from Carnegie-Mellon and Pratt Institute, he worked for Revlon for four and a half years. He believes that a "superior, innovative product in beautiful packaging, which can seduce the consumer into wanting to touch it and carry it home, is what it's all about." He says that today's global consumer is buying good design and lifestyle, no matter what the product.

After he left Revlon, Marc further developed his expertise by joining Elizabeth Arden. There he worked closely with such designers as Karl Lagerfeld and the Fendi sisters, for whom he created wonderful packaging. Others for whom he designed unique packaging include Perry Ellis, Oscar de la Renta, Avon, Halston, Princess Marcella Borghese, Chloé, The Limited, and Burberrys.

His designs have gained international attention. Among the most notable are the fan-shaped crystal decanter for Lagerfeld's KL-Women, the Red Door bottle for Elizabeth Arden, the glass sphere-shaped bottle for Perry Ellis 360, and designs for Halston's Catalyst for Men and Ellen Tracy. Six of his designs have won the prestigious FIFI Award, the fragrance industry's Oscar.

Rosen has also been involved in two highly acclaimed museum exhibitions. In 1979 he created the Cosmetic Packaging: A 20th-Century Art Form show at the Fashion Institute of Technology in New York City and cochaired the Fragrance Foundation's Scents of Time exhibit that traveled nationwide.

For 16 years, he has written a column, "On Design," for the influential trade magazine *Beauty Fashion*. He is a trustee of Pratt Institute and an associate professor for package design at its graduate school, where he was presented the prestigious Excellence by Design award and honored with a scholarship fund in his name.

Today he owns his own company, Marc Rosen Associates, which is responsible for many of the package designs seen in the fragrance industry.

In addition to the name players, company representatives, completely knowledgeable about their lines, also appear on the retail circuit. The announcements in the print ads, telling of their visits, usually draw big crowds.

Sampling

Leading cosmetics producers often introduce their products by **sampling**. To implement this strategy, the company creates a promotional package that contains a sampling of its products. When a customer makes a purchase, he or she can purchase an attractive case of these samples for a small price. Not only does this sampling technique encourage purchases, but it also introduces the consumer to other products that might lead to future sales.

Premiums

Many companies use **premiums** as a means of encouraging sales. This marketing technique offers the consumer an attractive item with a purchase. Umbrellas, hand luggage, personalized Christmas ornaments, tote bags, and the like either are given free as a **gift with a purchase** or are available at a modest price. These premiums usually bear the name of the cosmetics company. Thus, when used by the consumer, the premium is a constant reminder of the promotion's product.

These events usually take place during the Thanksgiving-to-Christmas season, the time when stores are busiest.

Direct Mail

Many cosmetics companies provide retailers with flyers and brochures to include in monthly statements to customers. Generally, they announce the introduction of a new product, a special price promotion, a sampling opportunity, or any event that might motivate a purchase either at the store or by phone.

Because the flyer is enclosed with monthly statements, there are no additional postage costs. The only investment is the cost of producing the mailer. Most major retailers realize a significant amount of business through such **direct-mail cosmetics sales**.

Joint Merchandising

Cosmetics merchandising differs from typical merchandising practices in retailing because suppliers and retailers **jointly merchandise** the products. Each manufacturer is assigned a specific counter, or area, and is responsible for inventory taking, stock replenishment, and visual presentation. Members of the sales staff in each area are trained by the producer of the line they represent and are paid salaries that are shared by both the manufacturer and the store. Sometimes the store pays an hourly wage and the cosmetics company pays a commission on sales.

With the manufacturers supplying point-of-purchase displays and presenting individual promotions, each counter takes on a personality of its own, setting it apart from the rest of the field.

Retail Distribution

Intensive distribution is the best description of the cosmetics industry's approach to selling. Except for the private brands and a few exclusive arrangements, the same lines are available in most stores. The prevailing belief is that cosmetics are often impulse purchases. The more visible the product lines, the more merchandise the store will sell. Thus, cosmetics counters are located on the main floor, where customers must pass through when entering or exiting the store.

Various types of retail outlets and distribution practices are employed by the industry, including department stores, cosmetics boutiques, mass merchandisers, discount operations, pharmacy chains, and in-home selling. A new approach to distribution is offered by the megastore format of Sephora, which is the subject of a World of Fashion Profile.

Department Stores

Department stores sell the vast majority of the better lines of cosmetics, including Lancôme, Prescriptives, Clinique, Estée Lauder, Elizabeth Arden, and Ultima II. Because each manufacturer has a separate selling area, each line develops a feeling of individuality. Trained salespeople help solve customers' problems by introducing them to the products best suited to their needs.

Cosmetic Boutiques

Beauty salons and individual cosmetic boutiques often carry their own private brands, a topic that is explored later in the chapter. The success of these operations depends on the service and product knowledge of the cosmetologists. In these environments,

SEPHORA

The limelight in the retail world of cosmetics and fragrances is now centering on a relatively new giant in the industry, Sephora. A division of LVMH Moët Hennessy–Louis Vuitton, Sephora is capturing the vast majority of cosmetics and fragrance headlines in fashion magazines and trade publications. The company shows the promise of soon becoming the single most important retailer of cosmetics in the United States and abroad. Its popularity is primarily due to its innovative format, megastore openings, and enormous advertising campaigns.

As a relative newcomer to the field, the company, Sephora operates approximately 515 stores in 14 countries worldwide, with an expanding base of over 126 stores across North America. Sephora's uniqueness can be seen as soon as one enters its stores. Unlike the traditional cosmetics and fragrance environments, which segment the various product lines into separate counters, Sephora uses a library-style approach that presents its products in an alphabetical arrangement. The shopper can quickly find a favorite under the appropriate letter in the alphabet. For example, Chanel is found in the fragrance section under the letter *C*, Fendi under *F*, and so forth. The selections are there for the taking, with a host of experts always available for assistance. Whenever a specialist shows a product, a single black velvet glove on the hand is used to enhance the presentation. This concept is similar to the one used in the sale of diamonds,

where the gems are shown on a black velvet cloth to make the product look even more exciting. Whether at the magnificent flagship store on New York City's Fifth Avenue or in the numerous outposts found in upscale malls, the visual presentations quickly motivate shoppers to sample Sephora's vast product lines. Testing areas for cosmetics and fragrances are beautifully designed, and experts are always ready when assistance is required.

In addition to its bricks-and-mortar stores, the company provides a Web site, Sephora.com, which features more than 100 beauty brands. Unlike the typical Web sites that are traditionally used by other players in the retailing environment, Sephora uses a host of innovative concepts to gain shopper attention. One of these, called Sephora's Color Library, compares different fashion color looks. It employs a model who is made up to feature several different looks, thus showing the observer how each one will look when applied. The Internet user who wishes to learn more about a particular color can click on that model to see a close-up of the selection along with a description of what the model is wearing. If satisfied, another click or two on any of the items, such as liquid eyeliner or lipstick, for example, enables the user to place an order. The Web site has a

Sephora stores display cosmetics in fixtures that allow customers easy access.

twofold purpose: one is to quickly satisfy the needs of the shopper unable to make a trip to a Sephora store; the other is to motivate in-store shopping.

In another feature on the Web site, roving makeup reporters go to celebrity events and ask the models and actresses what makeup they are wearing. Still another feature is Sephora's interactive Celebrity Makeup Lesson. By clicking on a spot on the screen, the user can quickly learn how the celebrity achieved the particular look. Other equally exciting fare makes Sephora's Web site a place to which fashion-minded women are likely to head.

Based on crowds that are flocking to the bricks-and-mortar stores, the significant numbers using its Web site, and its new arrangement with JC Penney to market its products in their stores, Sephora is becoming a retail cosmetics and fragrance company to reckon with.

an expert usually analyzes the customer's problems and suggests items that will help solve them. The cosmetologists often provide complexion analyses, demonstrations, and makeup applications for special occasions.

Mass Merchandisers

Stores such as Walgreens and Bradlees usually concentrate on lower-priced brands such as Maybelline and require that customers select their own purchases. The items are usually displayed on peg-board walls or shelves that are clearly marked as to

Department stores account for the major business of upscale cosmetic lines.

Mass-merchandisers concentrate on lower-priced lines of cosmetics.

manufacturer and cosmetic category. Point-of-purchase displays are used to draw attention to specific products.

Discount Operations

Companies such as Wal-Mart and Kmart have large sections of cosmetics that are displayed in the same manner as described under mass merchandisers. Their appeal is generally price-oriented, with most items sold below traditional markups. The selections include all price points, with the lower end generating the largest percentage of sales.

Pharmacy Chains

All over the country, pharmacy chains account for a large number of cosmetics sales. In general, these chains have two approaches to sales. One features the merchandise in much the same manner as the mass merchandisers and discount operations; the other employs the services of a cosmetologist who assists the customer in the selection of products. Unlike the department stores, where salespeople represent particular lines and are trained by the manufacturers, the pharmacy chain uses one salesperson to assist customers with all of the products sold.

Direct Selling

Companies such as Avon and Mary Kay Cosmetics sell their products directly to the consumer primarily through individual or group demonstrations. The success of these companies demonstrates that there is a large market for home sales. Representatives carry inventories that are sufficient to satisfy the immediate needs of customers; others carry samples and take orders for future delivery. The keys to success are proper demonstration of the products and personal attention. The direct-sales technique eliminates the obvious distractions of the retail store as well as competition from other brands. The customer's attention is focused solely on the product line being shown.

Private Brands

Although national brands continue to dominate the cosmetics market, more and more retailers are focusing their attention on their own brands. Much as with private label apparel, retailers are marketing their own lines of cosmetics alongside such household names as Revlon and Cover Girl. The purpose, of course, is to provide better profit margins while giving their customers better value.

The success of **private brand cosmetics** became apparent when the industry's trade shows began to feature displays showing all of the elements needed to create such programs. At these annual expositions, for example, the number of suppliers who developed packaging specifically for private brands increased, as did the manufacturers of complete cosmetics lines who were willing to sell their products under a store's own name.

Sears launched a private cosmetics brand called Beautiful Styles. In partnership with the former president of Lancôme, Pierre Rogers, Sears is promoting the new line in many of its stores. It features superior products at quality prices. After a 10-year hiatus from cosmetics, Sears reentered the market in 1993 and hopes to make its profit picture even better with the new private brand.

The Global Nature of Cosmetics

Many cosmetics marketers are expanding their horizons and potential for new business by seeking international markets for their products. By spreading out globally, they reduce the financial impact of adverse economic developments, such as a recession, in one region. Thus, if the United States is experiencing an unfavorable business climate, sales in other parts of the world might still earn profits for the company.

Because cosmetics are in great demand all over the world, it is a natural product for globalization. The approach, however, must be carefully executed; different markets require product variations. Lifestyles and personal characteristics in each market can be different. Marketing research is necessary to make certain that these differences will be addressed. Skin complexion, for example, is different in northern European countries than in other regions and must be assessed so that appropriate colors will be properly marketed.

The regulatory policies of each country must also be evaluated. Some ingredients used in cosmetics are prohibited in certain countries. D & C red number 33, for example, is used fairly extensively in the United States, but is prohibited from use in Japan. Therefore, any product containing that color additive cannot be marketed in Japan. Other colors are more universally accepted and would therefore be better choices for global distribution. If attention is not paid to those details, international marketing will not be successful.

Labeling is another area that must be carefully investigated. Each country has its own rules and regulations governing labels, and they must be studied to avoid problems. Although these and other issues require investigation, the universal use of cosmetics makes international markets a potentially lucrative source of profits.

The cosmetics and fragrance industry is dominated by huge corporations that cater to a global market.

FRAGRANCES

A fragrance is a product that is invisible, available at high prices, and the basis of one of the most profitable international industries. Although it is primarily produced in France and the United States, its appeal is universal. Women are the primary consumers in this multibillion-dollar field, but men purchase a significant number of items for their own use as well as for gift-giving.

For decades, products such as perfume, eau de parfum, toilet water, cologne, and bath coordinates have provided mystery and excitement for their users. Beginning with the essential fragrances extracted from flowers, such as bitter orange, jasmine, and rose, and moving to other ingredients such as grasses, spices, herbs, citrus products, woods, and leaves that come from every corner of the earth, humans have transformed fragrances into products that capture the hearts and minds of most people.

Guerlain and Houbigant were the major players in the fragrance industry until the end of the 19th century. In the early 20th century, the industry slowly started to expand, beginning with François Coty's introduction of Rose Jacqueminot to the public. Discouraged by the refusal of a well-known merchant to sell his new creation,

Coty purposely dropped a small bottle of it on the steps in front of the merchant's store. Passersby, intrigued by the aroma, compelled the merchant to place an order for it. From that moment on, Coty established its position in the world of fragrances.

Today, with its promise of tremendous profits, the field has broadened significantly. The famous couturiers of the past—Chanel, Patou, Lanvin, and Schiaparelli—have been joined by many from the current list of apparel designers, who have entered the market with products bearing their famous signatures. The large number of participants currently makes the fragrance industry one of the world's most competitive.

Highlights of the Fragrance Industry

From 1900 to the beginning of the 1910s, there was the possibility of an increase in the type and production of fragrances, but World War I put a stop to development in this area.

After the war ended, designers created new fragrances—Chanel's Chanel No. 5, Lanvin's My Sin and Arpege, and Jean Patou's Amour Amour and Moment Supreme. In the 1930s, the industry continued to grow. New products, such as Je Reviens by Worth and Tabu by Dana, were successfully launched. Elizabeth Arden made headlines with her introduction of Blue Grass. The world was also treated to what has been billed as the costliest fragrance in the world, Joy.

The occupation of France by Germany during World War II almost destroyed the fragrance industry. But at the end of World War II, fragrance creators brought a rash of new scents to the public. Carven developed Ma Griffe, Christian Dior introduced Miss Dior to celebrate his New Look in fashion, and Nina Ricci brought out L'air du Temps, the great classic floral scent.

In the 1950s, the United States finally became a major player in the fragrance game. Led by Estée Lauder and her Youth Dew, companies such as Revlon and Avon were busy building their empires.

The 1960s witnessed the production and launching of new fragrances in France and the United States. Designers such as Hermés, Guy Laroche, and Yves Saint Laurent introduced product after product to the public. In 1969, however, the first truly great U.S. **designer fragrance**—Norell—took the country by storm with a licensing agreement with Revlon. It was named after the designer Norman Norell, a leading apparel designer in the United States.

During the 1970s, the use of traditional fragrances started to decline. As a result, the industry began to change. In particular, young people, who were disenchanted with the values of the world, sought basic fragrances to replace the costlier products of past decades. Head shops and other specialty outlets appeared on the scene and sold musks, incense, and patchouli in large quantities. The women's liberation movement also affected the industry. Charlie was introduced to augment the masculine pantsuits, ties, and pinstriped fabrics being embraced by the women consumers. At the end of the 1970s, Yves Saint Laurent introduced Opium, with the first megalaunch. It served as the forerunner of such socially controversial fragrance names as Decadence, Obsession, and Poison. By the end of the decade, a record number of new fragrances would be featured. U.S. designers such as Calvin Klein, Bill Blass, Halston, Ralph Lauren, and Diane Von Furstenberg introduced new fragrances to the consumer. Some became major forces in the field; others had little success.

In the 1960s fragrances, such as Chanel No. 5 promoted by celebrity Catherine Deneuve, were major money makers.

This unique bottle is one of many used by the fragrance industry to attract attention.

The 1980s was a decade of comparative ostentation and self-indulgence. Rolex watches, BMWs, designer clothing, and gourmet food were visible everywhere. Status seemed to be the key word, and fragrance producers reacted quickly to fulfill the demands of the market. Prestige packaging and celebrity licensing agreements resulted in price increases, but many consumers had little concern for cost. In addition to the designers from the apparel industry, some of the names adorning new fragrances were from the jewelry, television, music, movie, dance, and art industries.

The economic recession at the beginning of the 1990s caused some concern for the industry. Although some new products entered the market, the introductions were fewer than before. Four years after Passion took the fragrance world by storm, Elizabeth Taylor lent her name to a new fragrance—White Diamonds. It became a best-seller. Donna Karan later introduced her first fragrance, Donna Karan New York. Aside from the fragrance itself, the bottle, designed by her husband, sculptor Stephan Weiss, drew a great deal of attention. By the end of the decade other new scents were marketed by Victoria's Secret, Talbots, Liz Claiborne, Giorgio Armani, and Todd Oldham.

The years from 2000 to 2007 showed a continuation of interest in the fragrance field. Introduction after introduction of new products featured the labels of the tried and true as well as those that bore the names of celebrities, designers, and other well-known personalities. Heading the list as the second half of the decade began were the following:

- Michael Kors's Island Hawaii, part of his Island Fiji brand
- Tom Ford's Black Orchid
- London jewelry designer Solange Azagury-Partrige's Stoned
- Ralph Lauren's Polo Double Black
- Juicy Couture
- Donna Karan's Gold
- Victor & Rolf's Flowerbomb
- Hanae Mori's Magical Moon
- Versace's Crystal Bright
- Celine Dion's fragrance for Coty, Enchanting
- Calvin Klein's Euphoria Blossom

Fragrance Forms

Fragrances are available in four basic types: perfume, eau de parfum, toilet water, and cologne. Each offers the user a different concentration of the scent.

Perfume

Perfume is the strongest, most concentrated, and longest lasting form of fragrance. A blend of natural essential oils and/or aroma chemicals and fixatives makes up each perfume. A truly fine product may contain as many as 300 different elements.

Tom Ford's Black Orchid, Juicy Couture's Fragrance, and Versace's Bright Crystal are three of the industry's "Personality" products.

Perfume balance is achieved by the addition of alcohol, which also acts as the carrier of the fragrance. The amount of alcohol added to the blend determines the scent's strength.

Perfume may be applied directly from the bottle by "splashing" it on. For the most effective and even distribution, however, it should be applied with an atomizer.

Eau de Parfum

One of the newest forms of fragrances found in many producers' collections, **eau de parfum** is used as a preparatory base for perfumes. When it is smoothed or sprayed over the body and enhanced with a perfume of the same scent, the overall effect will last longer.

Toilet Water

Used as a base for perfume or by itself, **toilet water** is lighter and more subtle than perfume. It uses more alcohol and fewer scented oils in its mixture than perfume does. Used in spray form, it might also be used as an accent in the hair, creating a long-lasting scent around the body.

Cologne

The lightest of the fragrance forms, **cologne** may be lavishly applied to all parts of the body. It was initially introduced in the 17th century in Cologne, Germany—thus its name. It is the least concentrated form of perfume.

In addition to these products, a host of others, such as soaps, bath oils, bath salts and crystals, bubble bath, hand and body lotions, bath powder, talc, and deodorants, use fragrances.

The Copycats

In the 1980s, while a large segment of the market treated itself to the expensive designer fragrances, a new breed of product was born. Called **designer impostors**, they mimicked the names that were being heralded by more affluent consumers. In addition to imitating the scents, the packaging was also designed to deliver prestige to the purchaser. The first of these new scents was Ninja, a copy of Yves Saint Laurent's Opium. Ninja ads featured bottles of Opium alongside those of Ninja, with a headline that read, "If you like Opium, you'll love Ninja." The product's success was so quick and profitable that it was quickly followed by others.

By 1995, the new **copycats** were being vigorously marketed to men and women under age 25, at prices that were about half that of the original scents. The leading mimics included U from Parfums de Coeur Ltd., DQI One by Designer Quality Impressionists, QK Too from Deborah International Beauty Ltd., A Man and a Woman by Jean Philippe Fragrances, and Chromosome XX XY from Parfums Vision International Ltd. Each was designed to compete with the highly successful launch of Calvin Klein's CK One, which rang up retail sales of more than $50 million in a few months. Other knockoffs with widespread appeal included imitations of Elizabeth Taylor's White Diamonds, Liz Claiborne's Sunflowers, and Calvin Klein's Escape and Eternity.

Unlike the prestigious stores that sell the original products, the copycats are sold primarily through such mass merchandisers as Walgreens, flea markets, and off-price retailers.

Marketing Lines of Fragrances

As with cosmetics, marketing of scents involves attractive packaging, demonstrations, personal appearances, sampling, and premiums.

The competition is so keen today that the major players often spend enormous sums to launch their new products by a variety of different approaches. Sales for Lancaster Group USA's scent, Zino Davidoff, were boosted by a James Brown concert. Other techniques have included autograph signings and cross-country tours, such as that undertaken by Guerlain's Jean Paul Guerlain to promote Heritage.

The profit potential is so great that some marketing launches, such as those sponsored by Calvin Klein, run more than $40 million.

Men's Fragrances

Although women's scents dominate the marketplace, sales of men's fragrances are also significant. Men's products were first introduced in the 20th century. Until the 1930s, however, the list focused primarily on hair tonics, shaving soaps, and astringent lotions that were used on shaving nicks and cuts.

In the 1930s, some of the products that are still used today were introduced. The two major names were Skin Bracer and Aqua Velva. They dominated the market until

Giorgio Armani's Attitude is
one men's fragrance that is
part of a growing segment of
the fragrance market.

Derek Jeter's Driven fragrance
received significant attention
in the mid-2000s.

Canoe, originally introduced for women, was repositioned as a men's product. It became the best-selling men's scent of the time and is still regarded as one of the classic fragrances.

During the 1950s, additional scents were created for men. For the first time, a French couturier—namely Givenchy—introduced a men's product, called Monsieur de Givenchy, and a women's specialist, Elizabeth Arden, entered the field with Sandalwood.

The widespread introduction of men's fragrances occurred from 1960 to 1970. Estée Lauder's Aramis, Faberge's Brut, and Christian Dior's Eau Savage, became big sellers. From that time on, the race for widespread acceptance included many designers such as Calvin Klein, Hermès, Nina Ricci, Liz Claiborne, Bijan, Chanel, Ralph Lauren, Louis Feraud, and Carolina Herrera.

Today, several hundred brands are competing for men's dollars. The two that were getting the most attention during the mid-2000s were Sean John's Unforgivable and Derek Jeter's Driven. Also high on the list of sellers were L'Homme Yves Saint Laurent, Jean Paul Gaultier's Fleur du Male, and Prada's Prada Men.

Not only are men buying cosmetics and fragrances in record numbers, but beauty treatments for men have become the rage—broadening the market for products originally targeted exclusively to women. This new beauty scene is examined in a Point of View article, "Almond Pedicure: It's a Guy Thing," at the end of this chapter.

CHAPTER HIGHLIGHTS

- The use of cosmetics and fragrances goes back to the civilizations of ancient Egypt and Rome.

- In the early 1920s, cosmetics were used primarily by sophisticated consumers. As late as the 1950s, the industry still had a limited market.

- During the 1960s, cosmetics sales increased dramatically as a result of new products and new marketing techniques.

- Cosmetic sales increased in the 1970s, reaching new heights in the 1980s.

- As the industry grew more profitable, new players entered the arena, including famous apparel designers and cosmeticians from the movie industry.

- Cosmetics are marketed in typical retail outlets as well as through direct sales.

- By the 1990s, one of the fastest-growing segments of the industry was ethnic cosmetics.

- The fragrance industry became big business after World War I, with the launch of Chanel No. 5.

- Although World War II brought the industry to a sudden halt, it was resurrected soon after the war's conclusion, as couturiers famous for their apparel designs joined the fragrance bandwagon.

- Until the 1960s, the field was dominated by the French. In 1969, the first American designer fragrance, Norell, hit the market.

- In the 1980s, fragrance prices began to soar. As demand continued to increase, however, the list of fragrance launches mushroomed, with almost every designer introducing new products.

- Copycat scents also entered the market in the 1980s, offering fragrances at prices that were one-half of the cost of the ones they imitated.

- Beginning in the 1960s, men's fragrances began to gain greater acceptance, and many designers have entered the market with new brands.

- The mid-2000s featured a host of new fragrances for both men and women that featured celebrity names from the theatrical and sports world as well as the designer arena.

IMPORTANT FASHION TERMINOLOGY AND CONCEPTS

cologne	eau de parfum	package design
copycats	ethnic cosmetics	perfume
demonstrations	gift with a purchase	premiums
designer fragrance	infomercials	private brand cosmetics
designer imposters	joint merchandising	sampling
direct-mail cosmetic sales	kits	toilet water

FOR REVIEW

1. When were cosmetics first used?
2. During the 1920s, which group of people served as role models for users of cosmetics?
3. Which decade saw a major increase in the use of cosmetics?
4. With what marketing concept did Estée Lauder help increase cosmetics sales?

5. Who were the first apparel designers to market lines of cosmetics?

6. What role do the fashion forecasters play in the cosmetics field?

7. Describe a joint merchandising program as it relates to the cosmetics industry.

8. Discuss the difference between selling cosmetics in department stores and through mass merchandisers.

9. What are private brand cosmetics?

10. What issues must be addressed to successfully market cosmetics?

11. Which fragrance made its mark by billing itself as the world's costliest?

12. Beginning with the end of the 1970s, what were some of the controversial names given to fragrances?

13. What is the difference between perfume and eau de parfum?

14. What are copycat fragrances?

15. Which celebrity names graced the men's fragrances in the mid-2000s?

16. In Andrea Grossman's Point of View, "Beauty's Great Ethnic Debate," what does the word *ethnic* mean?

EXERCISES AND PROJECTS

1. Visit a department store during the Christmas selling period to gather information on the various promotions offered by the different cosmetics companies. Ask for permission to photograph the promotions. Using the information gathered, present a report to the class.

2. Contact a cosmetics or fragrance company to learn about the various marketing techniques it uses to sell its products. Write a report outlining the specifics of each one.

3. Visit a mass merchandiser or other retailer of copycat fragrances. Make a list of the copycat names and the fragrances they imitate.

WEB SITES

By accessing these Web sites, you will be able to gain broader knowledge and up-to-date information on materials related to this chapter.

Cosmetics, Toiletry, and Fragrance Association
   www.ctfa.org
The Fragrance Foundation
   www.fragrance.org
Sephora
   www.sephora.com

The Case of the Successful Cosmetician

Michelle Sagan worked for five years at the Clinique cosmetics counter in a large southern department store. She was trained to help women with the appropriate selection and application of cosmetics. After a few years, she built an impressive personal following. Many customers came to her for makeup applications whenever they had a special occasion. Although her earnings were substantial, she thought that being in her own business would result in even greater rewards.

As luck would have it, Michelle inherited enough money to open her own cosmetics salon. After careful consideration, she selected an appropriate location. She then shopped the market for the proper fixtures and made arrangements for their installation. The only matter she had not resolved was the merchandise assortment she would carry.

One possibility was to carry an exclusive line of name-brand products, from which there were many to choose. Another was to stock a variety of different brands. The third choice was to go the route of private branding and carry only products that bore her own label—Michelle.

Because she had worked for so many years in the department store, she was able to acquire a list of her regular customers. She planned to contact them about her new operation. The rest of her business, she believed, would come from word-of-mouth recommendations.

questions

Which approach would you suggest Michelle follow? Explain your decision.

Almond Pedicure: It's a Guy Thing

STEPHEN HENDERSON

Not long ago, Elise Berenzweig's mother telephoned to say she'd spotted Elise's husband, Evan, dallying on a weekday afternoon at a suburban New Jersey nail salon. Elise took this news in stride, guessing that Evan had added manicures to what she terms his "going at it full force" beauty regimen.

"I am proud that he wants to look so good," Mrs. Berenzweig said. "Evan is very esthetic. It's important to him."

Just how important, he doesn't hesitate to say. "I'm obsessed about keeping my pants size," said Mr. Berenzweig, 42, a senior vice president at the Rag Shops, a chain of fabric and craft stores. "Nothing will come between my being 170 pounds and a 33 waist. Nothing. I will hurt small children if necessary." His obsession doesn't end with his six-foot-tall physique. He maintains a year-round tan (bolstered in wintertime, he concedes, with a bronzing cream) and schedules frequent "industrial strength" teeth cleanings, massages and pedicures. Some "eye work" may be in his future.

"I am vain, but I'm not conceited," Mr. Berenzweig explained. "Besides, women friends of mine implore their husbands to be more like me."

Attention please, beer-gut Gus, hairy Harry and turkey-neck Tom. Wake up and smell the skin conditioner before women start imploring you to join men across America who are paying more attention to, and more money for, their personal appearance. At all ages and incomes, a steadily growing number of men are tightening their muscles, filing their

fingernails, having their smiles whitened and eyes "undrooped"—or worrying that they should.

Health spas now organize "guys only" nights, and the newest cosmetics stores are designed to be more men-friendly. Cosmetic tooth-whitening appointments were requested by more men in 1997 than ever before, according to the American Dental Association. Face lifts for men more than doubled from 1992 to 1997, and male liposuction patients tripled, says the American Society of Plastic and Reconstructive Surgeons.

"It's O.K. for a man to improve himself in ways that were at one time considered artificial or, even worse, deemed feminine," said Dr. Larry Rosenthal, a cosmetic dentist on the Upper East Side, who offers a one-day "smile lift" for $15,000.

An increase in male vanity is occurring now for a variety of reasons, experts say. Some cite the baby boom generation's fear of aging, coupled with younger men's acceptance that they will be judged by their appearance—a conviction reinforced by the ubiquity of half-naked men in advertisements in the 1990s, hawking everything from soft drinks to Versace jeans.

Others make the point that today's self-reliant women, with incomes of their own, have forced men to shape up because career women can afford to be alone rather than live with a Neanderthal. (Cosmopolitan magazine recently ranked men's back hair as its readers' No. 1 turnoff.)

"Our culture hasn't made sense of either the women's or the gay liberation movement, and as a result, the narcis-

sistic roles are shifting between men and women," said Brian Lathrop, a psychotherapist in Greenwich Village, who said that many of his male clients have body-consciousness issues. "Traditionally, women have expressed their narcissism through sexuality, by being the identified objects of beauty. Men affirmed themselves through aggression, by gaining power and possessions."

He continued: "Now, not only have women gained much more power, but men are allowing themselves, in a way that wasn't possible 20, 10 or even 5 years ago, to display themselves publicly as sexual objects. Most men see this as both exciting and frightening."

The Bliss Spa in SoHo, home of Macho Mondays, has recently doubled in size, partly for its growing male clientele, said Marcia Kilgore, the owner. Offered a plate of peanut butter cookies ("Guys don't like rabbit food," a Bliss staff member said), Allen K. Bernstein declined politely, explaining, "I've got to maintain my girlish figure."

"Girlish" is the last word one would use to describe Mr. Bernstein. At 6 feet 4 inches and 230 pounds, he looks fearsome enough to be the private detective that he is and to play one in movies like *Ransom* with Mel Gibson and *Kiss of Death* with Nicolas Cage. Yet there he lay, hair pulled back in a dainty twist of white terry, getting a $125 double oxygen facial—something he does regularly.

"I'm rough on my body," Mr. Bernstein said, while a beautician daubed chamomile extract onto his cheeks.

"I work crazy hours, run from beeper to beeper, am constantly on airplanes. When I get back from a hard assignment all I want to do is veg out, get a manicure, a pedicure and have my face done. I consider it required maintenance."

Seeing a bruiser like Mr. Bernstein loll his way through a spa day blurs masculine and feminine stereotypes, not unlike the bearded woman in a circus sideshow. An example of a genus as yet unnamed—the Homo narcissus? The Homo fix-him-upper?—this emerging species of male has advanced Darwin's theory from survival of the fittest to survival of the prettiest.

"The perception among men that they are going to be judged, at least initially, by their appearance is quite new," said Dr. James Perlotto, a family physician in New Haven, who is also a professor of medicine at Yale Medical School. "In the baby boomer generation, among men in their 30s, 40s, 50s, it often creates a unique fear of aging. Guys in their teens and 20s, on the other hand, put more value on the surface of things, how they dress, wear their hair."

Dr. Perlotto continued: "Regardless of age, it raises a curious mélange of issues for men, so that discussion of what's good for you tends to blend into what's good for the way you look. I'll be talking about cardiovascular health, and a guy will suddenly ask, "What kind of exercise will firm up my butt?"

The shift in thinking has produced insecurities in some men about their appearance, suggesting that men are now internalizing the same social message that women have suffered under for decades—their worth is based on their looks.

"The average guy is feeling an increasing pressure to be a perfect manifestation of his gender," said Marie Sacco, a clinical psychologist who works with people who have eating disorders at Gracie Square Hospital.

She estimates that one-quarter to one-third of her clients are men. Other eating-disorder specialists note that studies have found an increase in men seeking treatment for anorexia nervosa and bulimia in the last decade.

"There's a healthy indulgence of oneself, be it going to the gym or getting a facial," Dr. Sacco said. "However, when someone works out frantically because they feel inadequate, when people are body dismorphic, that's another story. These men develop the mistaken idea that if they had a perfect body, their lives would be different.'

The perpetuation of this belief may be traced to the ubiquity of bulked, beautiful and unclothed men on magazine covers and in print and television advertisements. "Why do I think men are so body-conscious?" said Joan Kron, a beauty writer. "If I had to blame one thing, I'd say it was the Calvin Klein underwear ads."

In November, Viking will publish Ms. Kron's *Lift: Wanting, Fearing and Having a Face-Lift*. "Look what happened when Sylvester Stallone, this icon of manliness, had his eyes done!" she said. "Guys now feel the same pressure to look young as women do."

Even young men can feel the pressure, as they realize that the results of today's gym routine will demand ever more upkeep as they age. Joseph Panetta, 30, a public relations executive, said that bulking up his body from a "toothpick" into something "bigger and more toned" had given him much greater self-esteem. Yet, he is fearful where his transformation might eventually lead.

"For now, plastic surgery seems like going to the dark side," he said. "It's a philosophical thing. There's a cause and effect that I control at the gym, as opposed to handing over the cause to become the effect. But that line in the sand could change with age, with a loss of my skin's elasticity. I don't know."

If the sands shift for Mr. Panetta, hundreds of plastic surgeons will be waiting with open arms. The five top cosmetic procedures for men, starting with the most popular, are hair transplantation, nose reshaping, liposuction, chemical peels and collagen injections, according to the American Society for Aesthetic Plastic Surgery.

With a growing niche of male clients, Dr. Alan Matarasso has even equipped his office on Park Avenue and 84th Street with a separate entrance for men to insure their privacy. "Men want to reconcile how they feel with how they look," said Dr. Matarasso, who estimated that 25 percent of his patients are men, up from 5 percent a decade ago. "What we do in plastic surgery you can't achieve alone. Even if you go to the gym, you can't take the bump out of your nose, get rid of a turkey neck or that droop in your eyelid."

"There's now a heightened awareness of what guys can do for themselves, of intervention in general," Dr. Matarasso said. "I mean, did we have *Men's Health* 10 years ago?"

Actually, the September issue, now on the stands, marks the 10th anniversary of *Men's Health* magazine (whose average reader, according to MRI Research, is 35 and college educated). That its circulation has soared from 100,000 in 1988 to 1.6 million today is widely seen as reflecting and ratcheting up the American male's growing insecurity about his appearance.

Mike Lafavore, the magazine's editor, bristles at the suggestion that a *Men's Health* cover featuring an Adonis with bulging pectorals and taut abdominal muscles might have any anxiety-producing effect on the male ego.

"Sure, our covers are an ideal, but I don't think men take them seriously as an attainable goal," Mr. Lafavore said. "Our readers need to lose a few pounds and are trying hard. Being perfect is far from their minds."

Dr. Perlotto of Yale Medical School finds that men are extremely susceptible to criticism of their physique, especially when it's an offhand remark from another man. Consider the experience of a 50-year-old New Jersey man. "Eight months ago, I was in Hawaii, and some guy I'd just met said, 'You're such a handsome man, but your eyelids are so heavy,' he recalled. My wife was there, his wife was there, we were talking about general things. Immediately after he said this to me, my eyes felt heavy. I went to the mirror that night, and decided right on the spot to do something about it."

Recognizing that some men are prone to such impulsiveness, Dr. Matarasso, the plastic surgeon, felt compelled to institute a two-day cooling-off period for male clients who are itching to go under the knife.

Taking the opposite approach, Dr. Rosenthal, the cosmetic dentist on the Upper East Side, capitalizes on men's haste by promising same-day service for his "smile lift."

"Guys are trying to get jobs, get women, get other men . . . whatever," Dr. Rosenthal said. "One of the first things that break down as we get older is teeth. Cigars, coffee, drinking red wine, all are the source of major discoloration. People are not only living longer, but they are trying to keep a viable presence for longer, and teeth were not designed to last this long."

A photo album (helpfully emblazoned "Dr. Rosenthal's Celebrity Book") prominently displayed in his offices across from the Carlyle Hotel boasts pictures of clients like Frank Gifford, Michael Bolton and Donald J. Trump. The implication is clear: why wait? If you're in by 8:30 a.m., you can be fitted for custom porcelain veneers and have a celebrity smile by cocktail hour.

"Men want something fast and effective," agreed Simon Cowell, vice president of marketing for the Body Shop, the British-based chain of beauty stores. In October, Body Shop will introduce Of a Man, a line of grooming products like a hair and body wash with conditioner in one bottle. "Women take much more time pampering themselves," Mr. Cowell said. "Men want a quick fix."

And as Dr. Matarasso's secret door suggests, they might not want to be observed getting it—a lesson not lost on Sephora, the large French-owned cosmetics emporium, which opened last month in SoHo. Men's fragrance and skin-care products stretch nearly the length of one wall, all "laid out alphabetically, without any counter in front, since guys can be shy about asking for help," said Steve Bock, executive vice president of merchandising.

Far from shy about anything related to personal beautification, Evan Berenzweig, the gung-ho groomer in New Jersey, would enjoy such unfettered access to the latest skin-care treatments, his wife said. He is now busily passing along a lifetime of trade secrets to his three growing sons.

"When Evan was young, he thought he had blackheads on his nose," his wife said. Determined to spare their eldest son, Addison, a similar fate, "Evan's already prepping him," she said, adding: "He bought Addison cleansing pads and showed him how to use them. Sometimes, they go together to get facials."

How old is Addison?

"He's 12," Mrs. Berenzweig said, with a mother's pride. "And, he's very good looking."

New York Times, August 10, 1998, B7

Beauty's Great Ethnic Debate

ANDREA M. GROSSMAN

New York—The clichéd question "What's in a name?" never rang truer than in discussing the ethnic beauty care category. It's an underdeveloped-but-growing business, which is thought to have significant potential. But the meaning of the term ethnic is a subject of debate, fueled, in part, by cultural sensitivities. The answer to the question could affect how the category is managed, and ultimately how it may grow.

In the Seventies, the word ethnic was adopted by beauty executives as the best term to describe products designed for people of African descent. These days, however, the word tends to take on several meanings, from a replacement for African American, to describing an entire segment of beauty products for a significant swath of the population, including Hispanics, Asians and even those of Mediterranean descent.

Sales of health and beauty aids for people of color now total $5.1 billion,

$1.6 billion of which is generated in food, drug and mass channels, while $3.5 billion comes from sales in salons and beauty and barber stores, according to Segmented Marketing Services, a marketing company based in Winston-Salem, N.C. These sales figures represent double-digit growth over the past decade. More notable, perhaps, is the growing awareness that the specific needs for people of color is just beginning. Take for example the recent commitment by L'Oréal to build the L'Oréal Institute for Ethnic Hair & Skin Research, a facility slated to open in the fourth quarter dedicated to the research and development of products for people of color.

While the growth of the ethnic category—and the research it will receive—may be reaching its highest point of noticeability ever, the use of the word ethnic is also just beginning to be examined.

"The time has come to discuss what it does mean, we really do have to figure this out," said Terri Gardner, president of Soft Sheen/Carson, maker of ethnic hair and skin care products.

The term ethnic and how it is used varies widely from person to person. Some believe the word ethnic has become antiquated, thereby requiring a new term or phrase to replace it. Others believe the word is used correctly only if it is used in conjunction with words that describe the ethnicity of the people in reference. Still others think ethnic is a useful word in the trade since it clearly and quickly communicates what has become to be understood as "products for people of color."

Lafayette Jones, founder of SMSi and publisher of Urban Call, a trade magazine for urban retailers, has frequently written and spoken about the ethnic category and the use of the terminology. Ethnic is a word that he believes is "an industry term that was first used to talk about African Americans, but has developed over time to include Hispanics and other ethnicities." Ethnic, he believes, should be used to describe one's culture, not one's traits. He uses the terms "ethnic food" and "ethnic hair" as examples.

"When we think of ethnic food, we are talking about something that has nothing to do with someone's physicality, it may have the origin of Chinese or Italian but everyone can consume it, everyone can relate to it. With hair care, however, we are talking about something that is physically different, such as a hair texture or skin tone"

Within sales circles, however, the word ethnic sums up an entire category of products that has grown to include people of all ethnicities. "Any sales or marketing person worth their salt knows what ethnic marketing is," Jones said.

On the other side of the coin is the view of Isabel Valdes, a widely known consultant for consumer product and retail companies that are looking to capitalize on the explosive growth of the Hispanic market. Her clients include Target, JC Penney Co., Wal-Mart, Procter & Gamble and Avon Products. Valdes believes the word ethnic connotes a negative message. Instead, she has coined another term, "in-culture," to categorize people from different backgrounds. The words in-culture, she said, help a company focus on a particular person's needs. "The difference for me, from a marketing standpoint, is that if I want to succeed in connecting with my clients and in turn their customers, it has to be within the culture of that particular consumer."

Opinions also differ within the health and beauty aids category.

Ethan Foster, senior vice president of worldwide sales for Soft Sheen, recently explained how the term ethnic came to be used in the beauty industry. 'In the early years, HBA buyers were generally white males, and to walk in and say, "I have some products for black people," wasn't well-received.'

Foster believes that "the time has come" for the industry to change the word "ethnic" to something more politically correct. "[At times] ethnic denotes African American. It is a mistake. It's quite obvious [the word] has to evolve."

For example, when asked how he describes Soft Sheen, Foster explained: "I'm in the business of satisfying the hair and skin needs for people of African descent." Soft Sheen, owned by L'Oréal, makes skin and hair care products under the Optimum Care, Alternatives and Dark & Lovely brands.

Some companies, according to executives, have always tried to focus on how a woman views herself rather than implement terms coined decades ago.

Cover Girl has been reaching out to women of color since 1990, when the company hired its first Latina model for a Hispanic-specific campaign. Marc Pritchard, vice president and general manager of Procter & Gamble Cosmetics North and South America, believes the best way to address our society today is to "try not to identify anyone as 'ethnic' or as part of any minority group—these terms are no longer really relevant in the U.S. in the year 2001."

According to Jeff Rubin, however, HBA buyer for Harmon Drug Stores, the word ethnic is used correctly when applied to classify certain beauty products.

"African Americans, as an ethnic group, have hair texture that is significantly different than any other group." The term ethnic, relating to its more broad definition, doesn't "translate here because it's the special hair care needs" that the word is really being used for.

Rubin points out the frequent use of the word.

"When people ask, 'Who is your ethnic supplier?' I know what they mean. In regard to beauty and hair care, [ethnic] has always been the word."

Others agree. Pat Bailey, vice president of marketing for Pro-Line, owned by Alberto-Culver and maker of the Just for Me brand, believes the word ethnic has its place in the industry, but also has its limitations.

"In talking to consumers, I would never use the word ethnic; they want to know you have a sense of their culture. But if you're talking about communication vehicles to buyers, the term ethnic may be appropriate, only if it's used with other words that qualify which ethnic group you're talking about."

Bailey explained that using and interchanging the word ethnic with black or Hispanic would explain who is being spoken about. "It needs to be co-phrased with some specific identification."

Bailey warns that clustering consumer groups together under the term ethnic can sometimes lead to incorrect methods of gathering consumer data, since consumption patterns are very different from culture to culture. "It's like comparing HBA to electronics," Bailey said.

Ultimately, she believes using a newer phrase, such as "people of color," "better wraps its arms" around the word ethnic when used in combination with African American, black and beauty. "You're talking about the skin and different shade, so using 'people of color' better relates to beauty," Bailey said.

Many companies are using the people of color term now, both in packaging and in their communication messages to consumers.

Colomer USA, for example, uses the phrase people of color on its boxes, which includes the African Pride brand, according to Dennis Smith, senior vice president of sales and marketing for Colomer. Coincidentally, Smith said that "he's recently given some thought" to the use of the word ethnic, especially as to how some people assume it means the same thing as race. "It's like when people think that democracy and capitalism mean the same thing."

However, the word ethnic, Smith believes, is still essential to the business when used correctly. "If you go to the store and a sign says ethnic hair care, you'll see a large section of products used not just by African Americans but also by Hispanics and Asians. It's like when you go to the supermarket and you see a sign for ethnic food, you know that there will be kosher food, Mexican food and Chinese food."

He admits, however, that the word is "probably misused." Since African Americans are one of the largest ethnic groups in the U.S., the term ethnic has led people to use ethnic synonymously with African American. He added that people have been "getting it wrong" for a while and most likely people will continue to use the wrong terms, even if they don't mean to.

'The only correct thing to call me is African American, but some people call me black, even though I'm light-skinned. Please, some people still call me an 'Afro'-American, which is a hair style," Smith said.

Still some can't be convinced tht the term ethnic has a place to modify anything in the beauty world. John Demsey, president of MAC, sees the world as a place that's becoming increasingly small, one that doesn't have room for a word that connotes "the idea of a singular description or class of what an individual is about. In my mind that no longer holds."

Women's Wear Daily, May 11, 2001

Elton John Does Home Fragrance for BBW

MATTHEW W. EVANS

New York—Bath & Body Works is betting that Rocket Man will give it a winning edge in the celebrity beauty fray.

None other than Sir Elton John walked onto the stage at the St. Regis Hotel at a Tuesday morning press conference as BBW unveiled its first celebrity project. Sir Elton was joined by BBW chief executive Neil Fiske and Slatkin & Co. founder Harry Slatkin.

The event marked the launch of the Elton John Fireside Home Fragrance Collection, a holiday line that includes scented candles, fragranced oil and a plug-in device.

BBW began carrying the products Tuesday in 1,700 stores and on its Web site. The retailer's catalogue will also feature the collection, which could generate upward of $10 million in first-year retail sales, according to market estimates. Plans call for 10 percent of this figure, or more than $1 million, to go to the Elton John AIDS Foundation.

"This partnership started because of my personal love of their candles," said John, who struck a serious tone throughout his presentation. "This project will raise urgently needed dollars [for] AIDS research."

Aside from funding for his foundation, John maintained that the Fireside collections' presence across the BBW chain would raise awareness of the work of the foundation, which has raised more than $100 million since its founding in 1992. John added that $1.5 million in new AIDS funding has been awarded for areas in the southern U.S. and Caribbean.

"I'm very proud of the direction the Elton John AIDS Foundation has taken in underserved areas," he said, asserting, "What we have done is far from enough, which is the reason for the [BBW] partnership. This is really an important step for us."

Fiske characterized John and Slatkin as "two great masters; Harry Slatkin is a master of home fragrance and Elton John is a master of rock 'n' roll," he said. "It's home fragrance and music coming together for Bath & Body Works." Fiske added in a later interview that the "Elton John AIDS Foundation is why we're here.

It's more than just a celebrity name on a product."

Slatkin, who began producing Elton John home scents in 1997, said of John, "He has a passion for candles." Slatkin recounted how he once gave John 24 "couture candles" as a gift and added the musician agreed to endorse a collection if the venture would help his AIDS Foundation. "He gets behind what he believes in and that belief turns into a passion," said Slatkin.

Scott Campbell, executive director of the Elton John AIDS Foundation, noted the Slatkin & Co. union is currently John's primary "cause-related marketing relationship." Via the BBW distribution network, "it has the potential to reach an enormous audience."

He noted that a fifth-annual benefit co-chaired by Slatkin and hosted by Whoopi Goldberg at the Waldorf-Astoria Tuesday night, which featured performances by John and Neil Young, would help the foundation. Also benefiting the foundation is an annual event during the Academy Awards. "He does about 40 charitable events a year separate from the Elton John AIDS Foundation," Campbell said of John's humanitarianism.

The Fireside collection, which was inspired by John's estate in the English countryside, features olfactory notes of vanilla bean, cedar wood, Chinese star anise and coriander. The assortment ranges in price from $7.50 for an 8.5-

ml. oil to $16.50 for the primary candle. The plug-in device, dubbed Scentport, is priced at $12.50 and there's a travel candle for $9.50.

Slatkin & Co., a subsidiary of BBW after parent Limited Brands purchased the home fragrance marketer last year, has existing Elton John home fragrances. They are carried at Neiman Marcus, Bergdorf Goodman and Saks Fifth Avenue and have more of a "deluxe" positioning, said Slatkin, who noted candles in the existing line are priced at about $54.

Promotion of the Fireside collection includes a contest called the Legendary Rock Sweepstakes, in which a Daniel K diamond pendant valued at $75,000 will be given away to a registered participant or one who purchases a Fireside candle at BBW.

Plans call for BBW's home fragrance business, which is estimated at $350 million, to include more Elton John products and Slatkin mentioned a formulation for spring 2007 that's in the works. Fiske said he'd "consider line extensions if [Fireside] is as successful as we think it's going to be. I wouldn't rule out personal care, either."

When asked if BBW might begin working with other celebrities, Fiske said it is more about "trying to create brands with great stories." He cited the "oldest apothecary, most famous dermatologist [and] most famous rock star today. They're all great stories."

Beauty Beat, *Women's Wear Daily*, October 4, 2006

home fashions

The images that compose your house can relate to all kinds of symbolic things, ideas that you liked, places you've liked, bits and pieces of your life that you would like to recall.

FRANK O. GEHRY, ARCHITECT

Although the fashion industry focuses on apparel, the home fashions segment is gaining importance. Just as the selection of clothing reflects the mood and personality of the purchaser, so the interior of a home tells the story of the people who live in it.

Home fashions, broadly defined, include upholstered furniture, case goods, and a host of accessory items that encompasses bedding, tableware (dinnerware, glassware, flatware), fabrics, floor coverings, decorative accessories, and decorative ornaments. There are no runway shows or extravaganzas that bring this part of fashion to the public, but many of the world's leading apparel designers are becoming major players in the home fashions field. Significant increases in sales indicate a growing consumer attraction to the products that make up this market.

It is no longer the rule that only fashion apparel changes with great regularity. New and exciting home fashions appear each season, reflecting unique and creative ideas. Although fashion devotees have followed the lead of apparel designers for years by updating their wardrobes to achieve some level of fashion consciousness, until relatively recently, few have paid attention to fashions for the home. With this enormous interest in designer apparel, the creation of home fashions was the next logical arena for apparel designers to enter. Stephen Earle, style director for the magazine *Martha Stewart Living*, believes, "The way clothing is conceived and sold today is not just about a pair of pants, a shirt, a tie, a dress; it's all about a lifestyle." Mr. Earle, who worked for Ralph Lauren in 1983, says that the Lauren furniture, sheets, and tableware are connected to his clothing; together they create a total picture. In Liz at Home, the Claiborne bedding line, the windowpane plaids coordinate with the floral prints in a manner similar to the fabrics of the company's mix-and-match clothing. Designers hope that consumers who are loyal to their apparel lines will purchase their home fashions products as well.

In the past, products for the home were primarily functional. A family furnished a home with necessities that were rarely updated. Two types of dinnerware were selected. The "good set of china" was reserved for festive occasions and a less formal

After you have completed this chapter, you will be able to discuss:

- The evolution of the home fashions industry starting with the mid-1880s.

- Some of the early leaders whose design ideas changed the home fashions field.

- Some of the important styles in home fashions.

- The various products in the home fashions industry and their expanding markets.

- The role of apparel designers in the home fashions industry.

- The changing retail scene for home fashions.

set was used for everyday meals. The variety of table linens was also limited and, except for special occasions, was more functional than decorative. Bed linens were often standard white, sometimes having one color or pattern. As baby boomers began to raise families and furnish their homes, their fascination with designer clothing tempted many to seek the same names for their home products.

Of course, the *designer label* is no guarantee of success. Even such names as Norma Kamali, Karl Lagerfeld, and Yves Saint Laurent—certain tickets for success in fashion apparel—failed with their lines of home fashions. Success in the home fashions field requires careful planning, not just a name on a label. Ralph Lauren's home fashions business is an excellent example of what it takes to market a profitable line. While some companies merely reassign two or three people from their apparel design team to create household products, Lauren employs approximately 130 people solely in his home fashions operation. His showroom includes a **trial apartment** that is refurbished twice a year with a full offering of the next season's look. This total home concept enables buyers and merchandisers to understand the collection's concept and how it should be marketed in the stores. Retail management consultant Walter K. Levy says, "The look of Ralph Lauren's clothing paves the way for logical extension into the home design." Those who follow a carefully developed plan will have a better chance to reap the rewards of successful home fashions merchandising. Given the success of Ralph Lauren and Calvin Klein, other "names" are entering this fast-growing fashion segment. For example, Nicole Miller dinnerware by Sakura is achieving success, and Nautica is entering the market with a line produced by Pfaltzgraff. With Versace, Christian LaCroix, and Christian Dior joining Lauren and Klein at the upper price points, and Jessica McClintock, Liz Claiborne, and Joseph Abboud at more moderate ranges, it seems that every income segment will be targeted.

In addition to the designer phenomenon, two people also had a tremendous effect on the home fashion industry—Martha Stewart and Faith Popcorn. Stewart, a publisher, lecturer, and television personality, brought about an awareness of fashions for the home to the baby-boomer population, showing how to beautify homes and gardens. Faith Popcorn named and predicted the rise of **cocooning**, the stay-at-home phenomenon. This lifestyle change reflected boomers' desire to leave the corporate rat race in search of a better quality of life.

Home fashions combine elements that are as fashionable and trendy as apparel.

Today, the focus in home fashions is on variety. Household products are like wearable fashions, changing with great regularity. No longer will one set of sheets suffice for a few years nor will the same set of dishes be used on a regular basis.

As with the apparel industry, home fashions also has a fascinating history. Many individuals contributed to the transformation of the industry and the beginning of the 20th-century movement toward modernism and the styles that evolved from it.

THE EVOLUTION OF DESIGN IN HOME FASHIONS

Elaborate ornamentation in home fashions was characteristic of the Victorian era. The interiors were overcrowded settings with an excessive use of furnishings. The furniture in affluent homes was handcrafted by skilled workers, who designed and produced the items. Although fine homes still featured quality merchandise, the Industrial Revolution that was taking place resulted in considerable changes in furniture production. Products made in the new factories were no longer designed by craftsmen, but by managerial staffs who knew little about furniture.

It was during this era that the middle class was first able to afford designs once available only to the rich. Because these products were inexpensively mass produced in factories, they did not have the quality of the designs from which they were copied. Although the Victorian era offered a blend of Gothic, Renaissance, Moorish, and Oriental designs in cluttered arrangements, many of these elements led to 20th-century modernism.

In the middle to late 1800s, new industrial machinery produced a variety of crudely made home furnishings. Distressed by the poorly crafted offerings, William Morris, a fine craftsman from England, set out to reintroduce quality products for the home. He led a return to handmade goods that were wrought of fine materials and had less decorative detail. He wrote extensively on his beliefs and lectured about his philosophy on furnishings. This was to be the beginning of the Arts and Crafts movement. His own designs embodied textiles, wallpapers, and other objects. Joining him in the movement were a number of architects and artists who would later be known as interior designers. Simply crafted furniture and accessories were their trademarks. At the turn of the century, another movement emerged to excite the world—Art Nouveau. In Belgium and France, designers Henri Van de Velde, Victor Horta, and Hector Guimard came to the forefront. Their completely new creations featured undulating lines, curved shapes, and oversized flowers. Many of the styles were reminiscent of Japanese design, which featured simple lines and freedom of form. The movement surfaced in the United States after its introduction in France. Louis Tiffany became the master, with his Art Nouveau designs of iridescent glass. These soon became known as Tiffany glass.

Twentieth-Century Modernism

As the world entered the 20th century, four designers emerged as the pioneers and eventual leaders of modernism in architecture and design. They were Frank Lloyd Wright, an American, and three Europeans—Walter Gropius, Ludwig Mies van der Rohe, and Le Corbusier. While they were creating modern styles, other designers were following traditional historical patterns.

Although much of the literature on Wright discusses his architectural genius, less attention is paid to his design elements that enhanced interior spaces. He also

Just as apparel designers look to the past for inspiration so do designers of home fashions. The inspiration for these vases comes from classical shapes in the Arts and Crafts tradition.

designed furniture, lighting, textiles, and rugs, and introduced materials ranging from natural-colored woods to painted steel.

In Germany, Walter Gropius established the Bauhaus school, whose modern designs became primary influences on architecture and interior design. Its popularity continues today with functional products in black, white, neutral, and primary colors. After the closing of the Bauhaus in 1932, Gropius led the architecture department at Harvard University, where he spread his original ideas about modernism.

Mies van der Rohe, also of the Bauhaus school, used an abundance of marble, travertine, steel, and black leather in his modern designs that were void of historical influences or applied ornamentation. Like Gropius, he moved to the United States, heading the Architectural School of Technology in Chicago, where he concentrated on his "less is more" theory of design.

Born in Switzerland, Le Corbusier spent most of his career in Paris where he designed buildings and interior pieces. His approach was cubist, but he used strong primary colors, along with greens and oranges, in a bold new way. His products are characterized by steel tubing, leather cushions, and solid-colored tabletops. Some of his creations have remained popular today and are collectively known as classic modern.

A more fashion-oriented approach to modernism, called Art Deco, originated in France after World War I. It combined primitive art and cubism with modern motifs. The furniture, textiles, glassware, and ceramics industries were greatly inspired by the this style. Examples of the Art Deco styles include Fiesta tableware, the famous perfume bottle designed for Coty by Rene Lalique, and Russell Wright American Modern dinnerware.

After World War II, Gropius and Mies continued to influence the postmodern movement. The most significant styling came from Scandinavia and was called Danish Modern.

During the 1950s, the atomic age played a role in home furnishings. *Sputnik I* and *II* and the testing of the atomic bomb inspired fabric motifs of mushroom clouds and atoms. Asymmetrically shaped tables became popular and Formica became a major material for both furniture and accessories.

The freedom of the 1960s brought further changes in design. Psychedelic colors were as prevalent in home fashions as in apparel. Synthetic fibers made their way into homes, where the best seat in the house was the bean-bag chair.

High Tech, and especially chrome, was popular in the 1970s. The harsh, bright colors of the previous decade were replaced by earth tones. Found objects originally designed for other uses, became standards as home fashions. The orange crate, for example, was now the home's bookcase.

In the 1980s, a new class of consumers evolved. They were the yuppies, whose goal was conspicuous consumption. Evidence of this was the $18,000 price tag for a tea kettle designed by Michael Graves. Lighting took on a new look, with recessed fixtures replacing the traditional lamps in many homes.

The 1990s offered a mixed bag in home fashions. With less money for discretionary spending, consumers' approaches to furnishing their homes changed. Although the affluent still availed themselves of the finest, costliest furniture, others were settling for more practical, functional designs. Most consumers were buying furniture through catalogs and megastores, such as IKEA, and accessorizing them to give style and personality. But designer names were still important. Ralph Lauren expanded his home fashion linens and added paint to his collection. Alexander Julian, once a leader in apparel design, captured a share of the lucrative home market with a line of furniture. Calvin Klein and Liz Claiborne were also making significant inroads into fashion merchandise for the home. Names such as Martha Stewart appeared in value retailers' stores, such as Kmart, to give the budget-minded shopper a taste of luxury at modest prices. Table 15.1 lists some of the designers who have made the transition from apparel to home fashions.

At the start of the 21st century, the interest in home fashions continued to grow. In response to the significant increase in consumer sales generated in the late 1990s and early 2000s, retailers, manufacturers, and designers are making greater efforts to capture a share of the market. More and more apparel designers are entering the field. Retailers are beginning to expand their home fashions offerings, and some department

Table 15.1

APPAREL DESIGNERS AND THEIR HOME FASHIONS AFFILIATES

Designer	Manufacturer
Alexander Julian	Dan River
Tommy Hilfiger	Revman Industries
Laura Ashley	Revman Industries
Calvin Klein	Crown Crafts, Inc.
Joseph Abboud	Bibb Manufacturing
Jessica McClintock	Bibb Manufacturing
Liz Claiborne	Springs Industries
Bill Blass	Springs Industries
Ralph Lauren	WestPoint Stevens
Halston	WestPoint Stevens
Missoni	Ashley McBride
Adrienne Vittadini	Fieldcrest/Cannon
Christian Dior	Sasaki
Christian Lacroix	Christofle
Versace	Rosenthal

Bloomingdales began to focus on home furnishings by opening specialty units.

stores are opening units that are exclusively oriented toward products for the home. By May 2000, JC Penney, which has been very successful in this market, had opened 42 Home Stores averaging 12,000 square feet each. In addition, the company began opening similar stores outside the United States. Bloomingdale's has also begun to focus on home furnishings. Starting with a landmark facility in Chicago, the *Medina Temple*, the company transformed the premises into a multilevel magnificent showcase for everything from furniture and dinnerware to bedding and other products for the home. With its enormous success the next step was to establish a home furnishings emporium in New York City's Soho area. It too was enthusiastically received by the consumer.

Companies that previously restricted their home products to one classification are broadening their merchandise offerings. Villeroy & Boch, a major supplier of tableware from Germany, is now adding glassware, flatware, and home textiles to its merchandise mix.

Value-priced and discount stores are also moving to attract more sophisticated shoppers into their stores. Target is spending considerable sums in magazines such as *Bon Appetit* to show its collections to affluent shoppers. Similarly, Martha Stewart's coordinated line of bedding, paint, and furniture, available at Kmart, is an attempt to reach the upscale shopper.

STYLES OF HOME FASHIONS

Just as there are numerous styles in wearing apparel, so are there in the home fashions industry. Each style has distinct characteristics that distinguish it from the others. As in apparel, the various styles are always available, although the popularity of each changes over time. During the 1960s, for example, micro miniskirts were the rage. Their popularity waned and resurfaced from time to time; however, this style is readily revivable, waiting only for someone to breathe new life into it. Home fashion styles do not fall in and out of favor as quickly as their apparel counterparts; some move in and out of favor while others maintain a steady place in interior design. Of course, some styles ride the waves of acceptance only to see their popularity short-lived. In the early 1990s, Southwestern motifs were featured across the United States. Sales in that style soared nationwide for a few years, but eventually lessened. Similarly, certain colors have successful runs in the home fashions field. Although the color range is enormous, some color harmonies seem to be popular for a only short time, just as they are in the apparel field, whereas others maintain a constant place in home fashions.

In each of the styles that is dominant in home fashions, the merchandise used to complete any setting includes its main element, the furniture, along with the accessories that complement the *case goods* and *upholstered pieces*, and the colors that enhance the environments in which they are placed. As with wearable fashions, the styles selected are generally based on the personal preferences of the individual. Of course, interior designers, home fashions magazines, and settings in stores often help to influence these purchases.

Home furnishings are often categorized by *country* and *period*; a separate category, termed *eclectic*, combines elements of the other two. Some of the more popular styles in each category are described next.

Country Categories

The various styles that comprise country furnishings are distinguished from one another by their furniture designs, accessories, and the characteristic colors, patterns, and textiles used in their soft goods. Popular styles include English, French, Mediterranean, American, and Scandinavian.

English

Old pine furniture, or newly produced pieces constructed with used pine from other sources such as floorboards, is the major type of case goods used in English Country. Floral chintz, featuring an assortment of vibrant grayed blues, greens, and reds, dominates the upholstered pieces, which are typically adorned with needlepoint or tapestry pillows. Often, *throws* are used to accent sofas. Wood floors are generally used in these settings, with Persian rugs defining specific areas. The overall impression imparted by English Country is a lived-in look.

Home furnishing styles are categorized by country and period.

French

The Provence region in France includes such cities as Avignon and Aix-en-Provence as well as a vast number of smaller villages. The style of this region bears a Mediterranean signature. The furniture, whether it is chests, dressers, tables, sofas, or chairs, is generally constructed of pine or chestnut and features curved legs. Many pieces are hand painted. The chair seats are often caned, with cushions added for comfort. The Provençal fabrics give this style its distinctive look. They are generally overall prints, often on polished cotton, and toiles that depict country life. The cottons are usually intensely colored with reds, blues, greens, and yellows dominant. The toiles feature a faded look of pinks and blues. Fabrics are used on the upholstered pieces as well as for bed covers, table toppers, curtains, throw pillows, and other accents. The floors are generally tiled, with terra-cotta the most popular. Ceramic tiles of yellow, blue, and white are used as decorative accents, and dishes appear in the same colors.

Mediterranean

Styles from the countries that border the Mediterranean Sea, such as Italy and Greece, are both functional and decorative. With the intense sunlight of those regions, the windows are often covered with shutters that can be opened or closed, depending on the time of day. Besides providing protection, shutters add a certain amount of charm to a room. Simple wooden designs with painted finishes dominate, and upholstered pieces are often covered in white linen or cotton. Terra-cotta floor tiles are a common feature of this style, and brightly painted ceramics add decorative accents.

American

Although many of the early settlers to North America brought furniture with them from England, a new style developed in this region. The pieces are simple and generally primitively constructed. Small prints, such as calicos (floral and geometric), scenics, and conversationals are generally used on fabrics. Checks, ginghams, and blue resists are also important. Wooden plank floorboards are traditional; these are often adorned with braided rugs. The key to this style is simplicity and serviceability. Among the principal accessories are handmade, patchwork quilts, which are often used on four-poster beds. Folk art pieces play a major part in the American Country look.

The early settlers from Spain and Native Americans contributed different influences in the American West and Southwest. Rough-hewn wooden furniture, along with tribal rugs and pottery, are dominant elements of this style. Large geometric patterns on brightly colored fabrics, often enhanced with black, are typical. New Mexico, particularly Santa Fe, has always been the center for such furnishings.

Scandinavian

Simple lines are the key elements in Scandinavian style. The furniture is usually crafted of pine, with a white paint or wash finish. Furniture may also be stencilled. The dominant colors are blue and white. Simple fabrics with small geometric and floral prints are used. Lace appears as a decorative accent.

Period Categories

Many recognizable styles are identified with specific historical periods. Each period has a personality of its own, and most remain popular today.

Colonial

The style of furniture produced in Britain's American colonies during the mid-1770s was based on the English Georgian style, popular during that period. When the settlers came to America, they brought many pieces with them. Simple, classical lines are evident in the furniture, which is primarily of mahogany. The fabrics used during this period included silk and cotton, in plaids, checks, and prints (both floral and geometric). Crewel work and toiles were also popular. Prevalent colors are dark greens, reds, blues, and golds. Draperies and valances are often used as window dressings to enhance the furniture styles.

Today, the fine, original pieces of colonial furniture are extremely costly and hard to find. Reproductions have become important at prices that are attractive to the general consumer.

Regency

Dating back to the early 1800s in England, the Regency style became popular in the United States, where it was known as the Federal style. Wainscoting, in conjunction with patterned wallpapers, is central to this period. The richest of fabrics, such as brocades, moires, and damasks, were used for draperies that are heavily fringed, accented with tassels, and tied back. Grecian couches and mahogany or lacquered ebony dining chairs and tables are important to the design of this period. Gilt accents on wooden furniture are also prominent. Wall-to-wall carpeting replaced area rugs. This is considered to be one of the more formal periods in home furnishings design.

Biedermeier

The combination of light and dark woods dominates this period, which is neoclassical in design and has German origins. Furniture is simple in form and often used as an accent with furnishings of another period. Most of the original pieces are hard to come by, but reproductions are readily available for those who desire this look.

Victorian

In the late 1880s, Victorian furniture came into prominence. It was the antithesis of simple lines. Very large sofas with overstuffed pillows, pedestal dining tables, dining chairs with curved backs, and fringes are typical of the period. The word *massive* best describes Victorian furnishings. Lace curtains were widely used along with fabrics such as chintz, challis, damasks, brocades, and velvets in a variety of patterns. Beaded fabrics and pillows are central to this style.

Arts and Crafts

In contrast to the elaborate Victorian designs, Arts and Crafts designs were hand-made of fine materials. As previously noted, one of the early contributors to this period, William Morris, is credited with initiating the return of fine-quality offerings to the marketplace. Clean lines and natural materials, such as stone, brick, copper, bronze, and oak woods, are important elements of the furnishings. Small floral, leaf, and geometric patterns in soft colors make up the fabrics.

Modern

In the early 1900s, several different influences emerged that are collectively known as the Modern style. The three main influences are Art Nouveau, Art Deco, and Danish Modern.

Art Nouveau designers emphasized curved lines and patterns, often turning to nature as the source for their designs, which included stylized birds and large flowers. Motifs using lilies, irises, and orchids dominate, but palm fronds and seaweed are also featured. Peacocks and swallows are the favorite birds, and snakes play an important design role as well. Glass vases and art pieces are a significant feature because of their lightness, airiness, and exquisite colors. Stained-glass windows became the focal points of many wealthy homes that featured the Art Nouveau style. Alphonse Mucha, Louis Tiffany, and Jacques Gruber were some of the artists whose work is typical of the style.

Art Deco was fashionable between 1920 and 1940. The name refers to the Exposition Internationale des Arts Decoratifs held in Paris in 1925. From the beginning, Art Deco designs showed great clarity and modernism. Skyscrapers, such as New York City's Chrysler building, theaters, such as Radio City Music Hall, and many exhibition halls were designed in the Art Deco manner. It is difficult to speak of the design as one style because it sometimes was strictly functional, whereas at other times it was decorative and ornamental. Sometimes the designs impart a sense of playfulness, ranging almost on the ridiculous.

The style features aerodynamic curved contours, highly polished surfaces, and vivid colors. A strong feature is the *Ziggurat*, based on the outline of the ancient pyramids. Art Deco introduced the coffee table; it employed cubist motifs for carpets and fabrics. Mirror, chrome, and lacquer are the major surfaces in this design. Satin, leather, velvet, and animal skins are important materials, along with upholstery fabrics replete with strong patterns based on shell motifs, Aztec prints, sunbursts, and fans. The wealth of Art Deco accessories includes ivory, lacquer, bronze, snakeskin, and tortoise shell pieces.

Danish Modern followed Art Deco. It employs clean lines, asymmetrical shapes, and geometric fabrics. Designed originally in Scandinavia, it became a popular style in the United States. Today it is still widely used in homes and offices.

Contemporary

Steel, chrome, and glass, embodied in clean lines, exemplify this style. The look is high-tech. Many materials are used, with industrial carpeting, once reserved for businesses, the preferred flooring in homes designed in this style. The use of white, black, and neutral colors dominates.

PRODUCTS OF THE HOME FASHIONS MARKET

Products made for the home are more plentiful and varied than ever before. Because a complete discussion of furniture would require several volumes, only the products that enhance the furniture and the rooms in which they are featured are examined here.

In response to the sales boom in the **bedding**, or domestics, market—and the fascination of consumers with designer labels—top names in the apparel industry are increasingly joining the home fashions bandwagon. Through licensing agreements with the industry's manufacturing giants, these designers are lending their names, as well as their creative talents, to products for the home. Many major apparel lines, such as Nautica and Esprit, have also entered this market. Table 15.1, earlier in this chapter, lists several designers who now produce bedding as well as other home fashions.

Bedding

Designer bedding has revolutionized the industry into one that is more fashion-oriented.

This group includes sheets, pillowcases, blankets, and comforters. As consumers became interested in creating fashion excitement in their bedrooms, the industry addressed their needs with fashion-related items. Different elements are available in a multitude of designs. These include:

- **Bedskirts**. A decorative edging that covers the box spring and reaches the floor.

- **Duvet cover**. A cover that fits over a comforter and fastens, using Velcro or buttons, at one end. It can be described as a giant pillowcase for a comforter.

- **Pillow sham**. A decorative pillow covering that slips over the pillow.

- **Valance**. A free-standing treatment for the top of a window, often used with draperies or blinds as a decorative piece.

The sheets and pillowcases, as well as the accessories, are constructed of fabrics that vary in quality. The patterns, depending on popularity, can be available for long periods. In this growing industry, new designs are introduced every three to six months. Those patterns that sell in limited numbers last for approximately one year.

Anyone who has purchased bedding is aware of the wide range of prices. As with apparel, price points are determined by quality and designer label. In terms of quality, sheets come in several different classes.

The most expensive types are produced with materials that have high thread counts. A **thread count** is determined by the number of horizontal and vertical threads per square

PORTHAULT

Founded in the 1920s, Porthault established its reputation for producing the world's most luxurious linens. The driving force behind the company was Madeleine Porthault, who along with her husband, Daniel, revolutionized the world of household linens. In 1925 they produced the first truly decorative bed sheets in bright colors printed with impressionistic floral designs. At the time, most people were sleeping on white bed linens.

Porthault's repertoire still includes many of these original designs among its hundreds of prints and embroideries. For example, the Hearts design, now a Porthault classic, evolved from amusing embroidered hearts Madeleine designed for the Duke and Duchess of Windsor.

Throughout the company's development, the Porthault family, which continues to own and manage the firm, has insisted on high quality in both manufacturing and design. Under the direction of Marc Porthault, the son of the company's founders, the firm designs, weaves, dyes, prints, embroiders, and finishes all of its linens exclusively in its own factories and workshops in France. Since the days when Madeleine first visited her clients, personalized customer service has been an important contributor to Porthault's success. Designers visit palaces, embassies, and homes, and work with clients to create the designs that will best complement the customer's decor.

Owing to the exceptional quality of its products and service, Porthault has always had a distinguished list of clients. Pablo Picasso, Charlie Chaplin, the Duke and Duchess of Windsor, Elizabeth Taylor, Jacqueline Kennedy Onassis, Diana Ross, Woody Allen, Lauren Bacall, and Rod Stewart are just a few. The Porthault line is featured in the finest shops around the world, reflecting its emphasis on fine quality and taste.

inch of the cloth. Those classified as **percale** are made of a 180 thread count or higher and are considered fine quality. A coarse type of construction, known as **muslin**, has thread counts of up to 160. In luxury bedding, the count usually runs from a minimum of 200 up to 600. The higher the thread count, the more luxurious the hand, or feel, and the more durable and pill resistant the sheeting. The particular thread count is determined by the manufacturer based on consumer demand. Most retailers carry a broad selection of designs in each thread count.

The majority of sheets come in either blends of cotton and polyester or 100 percent cotton. Although the blend of cotton and polyester affords the user less wrinkling, easy-care applications have now been used to make cottons more resistant to creasing and less dependent on ironing. Sheeting comes in a variety of textures, including the standard smooth types, which have an extremely smooth surface that resembles satin, and flannel, which is made by brushing cotton on one side for softness and warmth.

The price variation is the result not only of the thread count, but also of the color and pattern of the item. Solid-color sheets are more costly to produce than white sheets. Prints on white backgrounds are even more costly because the process requires a separate *screen* for each color application. (See Chapter 8 for an explanation of screen printing.) Embellishments, such as hems and lace, increase the cost even more. One of the costliest and most luxurious collections of linens is produced by Porthault, in France. The company is the subject of a World of Fashion Profile.

Tableware

Tableware encompasses the categories of dinnerware, glassware, and flatware, which are usually displayed together and sold by a variety of retailers, including department stores and specialty shops.

Dinnerware

The dishes we use for our meals are available in a variety of shapes, sizes, and patterns. They come in a range of materials, including **china, stoneware**, glass, and plastics. **Dinnerware** may be purchased as conventional sets, in which the various pieces match, or as individual pieces, which, when combined according to an individual's preferences and creativity, leads to more interesting **table settings**. In stores that feature table displays, the latter arrangement seems to be getting significant attention. The user may mix and match different pieces to suit a specific occasion. Octagonal, oval, and square plates have joined the traditional round shape to provide more fashion interest. As with bed linens, dinnerware designs also reflect historical influences. The styles of the Art Deco period and elegant motifs that have been translated from classical times, for example, are popular with many people.

One of the most important names in china and **crystal** is Rosenthal. The organization is the subject of a World of Fashion Profile.

Glassware

Two major types of glass are used in the production of **glassware**. They are **soda-lime glass**, which is inexpensive but durable, and **lead glass**, which is more expensive and often hand formed. Steuben and Swarovski are examples of the finest lead and crystal glass. The lead variety is the one that has become the more important fashion item. After the pieces are formed, the glass is shaped into a variety of **stemmed pieces**, **footed tumblers**, and **tumblers**. Once this has been completed, the pieces may be enhanced through etching, engraving, cutting, embossing, and sandblasting. Each decorative finish imparts a different appearance.

Flatware

Completing the main pieces found on the dinner table is **flatware**. As with dinnerware and glassware, numerous styles are available in a wide range of materials.

Royalty and the upper class have always used sterling silver to set their tables. Today, sterling silver, in patterns ranging from the ornate baroque to modern designs reminiscent of the Arts and Crafts period, is almost always reserved for special occasions in households that are far less affluent. Sterling silver flatware and serving pieces are often received by newlyweds as gifts and collected until the desired number of pieces have been reached.

Silverplate, a metal that is made up of a small amount of silver that has been adhered to a base metal; stainless steel; bronzeware; metals adorned with ornamental handles; molded resins; and others are used for daily purposes.

The more expensive flatware is often sold in **place settings**, which include four or five different utensils. Less costly flatware is generally purchased in sets, known as service for eight or twelve. Many manufacturers are also selling their products as service for four.

Like many of the other home products, the market is filled with familiar names, such as Gorham and Oneida. New offerings often bear the names of jewelry designers such as Robert Lee Morris.

Fabrics for Home Fashions

One of the most effective ways in which to create a mood or feeling is with fabrics. In every corner of the world, mills are producing patterns and designs in a variety of qualities and price ranges to satisfy everyone's needs. Rich brocades, matalesses,

Table settings run the gamut from formal to informal.

ROSENTHAL

Founded in 1879 in Selb, Germany, the Rosenthal Company has emerged as one of the world's finest porcelain (china) and crystal manufacturers. The original focus on classical-traditional designs took a new turn in 1961 when Philip Rosenthal Jr., son of the founder, launched the Rosenthal Studio-Line. This tabletop collection, which has employed the talents of more than 100 famous artists and designers, gave a day-to-day product a new sparkle lifestyle and an appreciation for master quality. Among those who helped take the company to new fashion heights, with magnificent designs, were Gianni Versace, the internationally renowned fashion designer, and Aldo Rossi, one of the world's leading architects.

Rosenthal's products are internationally marketed. Different assortments of items are produced to reflect the particular taste and style of the different countries in which these items are sold. Originality is a key element in the production of everything Rosenthal makes. The company does not imitate what others have done.

There are three product lines—Rosenthal Classic, the original concept, Rosenthal Studio-Line, and Thomas by Rosenthal, each featuring an assortment of china, stemware, flatware, and giftware. Each is completely different from the others.

- Rosenthal Classic consists of traditional and elegant products that preserve the value of past decades. Classic shapes are merged with deco-

Classical-traditional designs are a key element of the Rosenthal Company.

rative elements and moods of modern times. In this collection, heirloom designs are created and are passed on from one generation to another.

- Rosenthal Studio-Line is design oriented and innovative. Its roster of designers has included Versace, along with Roy Lichtenstein and Dorothy Hafner of the United States, Walter Gropius and Michael Boehm of Germany, Tapio Wirkkala of Finland, Salvador Dalí of Spain, Nina Campbell and Henry Moore of Great Britain, and more than 100 other designers, artists, and architects.
- Thomas by Rosenthal is a function-oriented line with a fresh and youthful appeal and an emphasis on clear shapes and individual items.

By producing these three different lines, the company has retained its standing as a world-class manufacturer, but one that also embraces today's fashion standards.

Before any product is made available to the stores, it must be approved by an independent jury of specialists. This committee name may be affixed to the item. Because of the painstaking attention paid to design, the company has been awarded numerous prizes and distinctions. Its 1,600 individual design prizes include the prestigious honor bestowed by New York's Museum of Modern Art.

The lines are marketed in leading department stores such as Bloomingdale's, Neiman Marcus, and Bergdorf Goodman, in fine specialty stores, and in the company's own "studio-houses." A catalog that features every product in the three lines is available to potential customers so that they may, in the comfort of their homes, make their selections before going to the store to make a purchase.

velvets, and other fancy fabrics are available for those with both traditional and contemporary homes. People with simple tastes based on modern styles can choose from geometric, floral, and plainer styles. Canvas, tweeds, plaids, and others are also available.

Fabrics have many uses in home fashions, including upholstery, curtains, and draperies. The correct fabric selection can immediately transform a mundane room into an exciting one. For example, Missoni, noted designers of elaborate knit fashions, have licensed their patterns for bed and bath products as well as for a line of textiles for interior decorating. Animal skins (leopard, tiger, zebra) continue to be an important part of the fabric business in prints and wovens. This is a basic pattern story that occurs in all looks from traditional to contemporary.

Floor Coverings

Another area of home furnishings in which there are never-ending options is **floor coverings**. Choices abound for every room in the house. In areas where warmth is important, **carpeting** is the mainstay. With today's technological advances, mills are manufacturing increasingly durable products in broader color ranges. Joining the standard wools are polyester, nylon, olefin, cotton, and natural fibers, such as sisal.

The use of **hardwood flooring** has increased in recent decades. The woods may be simply laid in planks or used to form intricate parquet designs. The boom in the hardwood floor market has given greater importance to the use of area rugs. Several types of rugs may be used either to define specific areas in a room or to serve as accents. Each gives a special personality to the setting in which it is used. Some of the popular types are briefly described below:

Fabrics project a mood or feeling in the home fashions market.

- **Kilims**. These are flat woven, woolen rugs. Produced mainly in the regions of Eastern Europe, Turkey, Iran, and Afghanistan, kilim rugs are extremely popular in many regions of the world. Their designs use geometric patterns generally in strong, vibrant colors.

- **Dhurries**. These flat woven rugs come from India. They have a hard surface, due to their cotton base, and their colors are generally subdued. Originally, dhurries

Area rugs from every corner of the globe dress wooden or tile floors.

were produced by prisoners in India, but today, they are manufactured in Indian factories.

- **Persians**. These extremely popular rugs may be hand- or factory-made. The handmade variety can cost more than $50,000. Persian rugs are most often made in the Middle East and Asia. The cost of a rug is often determined by its age and the number of knots per square inch. The designs represent the surroundings of the weaver and tell a story through the representation of trees, flowers, animals, water, and geometrics. These designs have evolved over centuries and reflect regional characteristics—different for every region—in design and color. Rugs that are very tightly woven are usually manufactured in factories. Their designs are created by professionals, and the rug itself is woven by a weaver who follows the plan laid out for him or her.

- **Contemporaries**. A wealth of contemporary designs is available, ranging from those that utilize geometric patterns to those that are more representational. The color range is vast. Most contemporary rugs are machine-made, enabling them to be sold at more modest prices than, for example, Persian rugs.

- **Hand-hooked**. The vast majority of hand-hooked rugs are produced in China, with a lesser number made in India. These rugs are handmade and have the advantage of price points that compare with machine-made rugs. They are quickly produced and come in a vast range of colors and styles. Many simulate the patterns of the more costly Persian rugs. All of them are 100 percent wool. Some of these rugs are micro-hooked, which involves the use of finer yarns, resulting in greater design definition. Because of their excellent quality and relatively affordable prices, hand-hooked rugs are becoming one of the more important types of area rugs in home decor.

- **Rag**. Generally made from cloths that have been recycled, rag rugs date back to the Colonial era. Today's rugs are inexpensive, and the vast majority are produced in developing countries.

- **Braided**. To produce a braided rug, three or more strips of cloth are first braided together to form long strips. These strips are then laced together to form the rug. Braided rugs are generally oval or round in shape. Most of the rugs sold today are machine-made and inexpensive.

In kitchens and bathrooms, floors are usually covered with ceramic tiles. In sizes that range from 9- to 18-inch squares and in designs that range from solids to patterns, the product is extremely serviceable and durable.

For those with more extravagant tastes, marble and granite can be used in just about any room in the house. These floors may be covered with area rugs to complete the design concept.

Decorative Enhancements
Ceramics

In addition to ceramic flooring, ceramic accessories can accent any home decor. The costs range from nominal, for pieces mass produced from molds, to costly, for those made individually by craftspeople who use such methods as a potter's wheel. The glazes, or outer protective coverings, provide the *look* that attracts attention. Large pots for plants, figurines, animals, and table bases are some items that are used as home fashions.

Art Glass

An exciting decorative enhancement to room settings is art glass. Louis Tiffany, considered the leading arbiter of taste in early 20th-century America among the rich and social elite, is one of the leading names in this medium. Many of his creations were a blend of function and design. Tiffany was particularly fortunate to have lived in the age of the lightbulb and the filament lamp developed by Thomas Edison. It was the marriage of the electric light and his magnificent colorful, leaded lampshades that catapulted Tiffany to success. The *Favrile* glass Tiffany used is characterized by multicolored iridescent base colors decorated with applied or enameled designs. Favrile was one of the major movements in the Art Deco period.

Glass created by Rene Lalique was also the rage from the 1890s to 1945, the most important design period for this creative genius. After Lalique was signed by M. F. Coty to design perfume bottles, his reputation soared. He became France's premier glass designer. Lalique's glass figures were usually made of lead crystal and either frosted or enameled. They were either molded or blown. Some were cameo engraved, heavily etched, and featured smooth, acidized, or pearlized finishes.

Today, art glass is extremely popular, and companies such as Orrefors, Kosta Boda, Mikasa, Rosenthal, Waterford, Baccarat, Wedgewood, Villeroy & Boch, and Lenox turn out exquisite pieces.

Basketry

Baskets have always served a functional role, such as holding bread or fruit. Today, baskets have also become design accents that add interest to almost any room in the house. At stores such as Pier 1, row upon row of different styles fill the shelves. At craft fairs, intricate handwoven pieces are featured in an array of natural reeds and other weaving materials. The one-of-a-kind basket often sells for several hundred dollars. Many art galleries feature handwoven baskets from around the world at even greater price points, with some selling for approximately $1,000.

The placement of baskets on shelves, floors, mantels, and window ledges—either by themselves or as holders of plants, towels, accessories—becomes an important part of the interior design.

Accent Pillows

Piled high on sofas, beds, and other upholstered furniture, decorative pillows provide exciting accents to home furnishings. One of the best-known users of **accent pillows** on beds is Ralph Lauren. A look at any Lauren bedding display immediately reveals pillow upon pillow that has been used to create interest.

Pillows come in many designs and shapes. They include needlepoints, scenic brocades, contemporary stripes, velours, velvets, prints, and geometrics. They range in price from $20 to $500, depending on workmanship, size, and fabric.

Accent pillows, in limitless designs and shapes, and beaded frames and mirrors are just some decorative items used to enhance a room's interior.

Plants

Home interiors can be an arena to showcase live and artificial plants. In every room, plants are now used as decorative accents. In the large bathrooms of today's contemporary homes, plants are often used to lend design interest. For example, orchids placed in front of a glass block wall through which diffused light enters, allowing the plants to thrive, provide a dramatic setting to any interior. Large palms of many varieties stand as high as 10 feet tall and majestically create a mood of elegance.

The effect is one of nature brought indoors. For areas in which there is little light, artificial plants of silk and other fibers are used. They require no maintenance and lend the same grace to a living space as do their live counterparts.

Candles

One of the fastest-growing segments of the decorative enhancement market is candles. Once necessary for illumination, before the invention of the lightbulb, today candles are used as accents in homes, gardens, stores, and restaurants. Designs range from the simple to the elegant, including neoclassical forms such as columns and urns. Candles may be produced by dipping, molding, rolling, or hand carving.

Candles may be set in candlesticks that are made from a variety of materials, such as glass, ceramic, metal, or wood; placed in floor-standing candelabras; used in sconces or chandeliers; or set in containers filled with water; or they may be freestanding. Freestanding varieties range from two to six inches in diameter, enabling them to stand without the need for holders. The latter variety is extremely popular in today's decor, particularly at Christmastime.

An infinite range of colors is available, in finishes that include marbling, streaking, hand painting, mottling, stenciling, sponging, and carving. Besides offering an exciting visual effect, candles may be scented to add another dimension to the home setting.

Works of Art

Today, more than ever before, a great deal of the focus of products for the home is on works of art. These include original paintings, limited edition prints, and posters. With the cost of original art out of the reach of the average consumer, more and more are turning to *prints* to ad interest to the walls of their homes. At the lowest price points are posters printed as *open editions*, indicating that they may be reproduced in numbers that are not controlled and retail for as little as $10 each. The other end of the print spectrum are *limited edition* pieces whose numbers are controlled by the artist. Each print is numbered and hand signed and retails for prices that sometimes exceed $2,000 per piece. The price is determined by the rarity of the piece, the artist, the number in the edition, and the printing method used to reproduce it. They are classified as lithographs, serigraphs, and giclees, a relatively new technique that involves the use of the computer. This latter classification is often *hand-embellished* by the artist, giving an appearance that resembles an original piece of art.

Paint

Not long ago, **paint** was available in only a few brands and a limited array of colors. Today, the market has significantly expanded. Augmenting the premixed varieties that bear such labels as Benjamin Moore and Dutch Boy are new colors that include just about any shade or tint. With the aid of computer matching, the consumer can specify any colors as well.

In specialty shops around the country, Martha Stewart is marketing paint that costs $110 a gallon! Her concept is to narrow the field of colors to the ones she deems most appropriate. For example, the typical Benjamin Moore line offers so many shades of white that the shopper is often confused. Stewart sells just one white. In all, her color range includes 80 colors.

Ralph Lauren's approach is to appeal to consumers who are interested in fashion but are not willing to pay Stewart's higher prices. Under an arrangement with Sherwin-Williams, Lauren features more than 400 colors beginning at $20 per gallon. He also sells brushes, tools, and instructional videos to help do-it-yourselfers create fancy finishes. Both Stewart and Lauren group colors that work well together, leaving out the guesswork of matching.

In addition to paint labels and color selection, the paint market has expanded with the introduction of unusual **faux paint finishes**. The finishes are unique, with faux marble heading the list. By applying different layers of paint in different colorations and distressing them with such devices as sponges, the painter can achieve unusual effects. The novice may accomplish a number of different finishes with the purchase of paint kits that include everything necessary to achieve the desired results. Professional painters, using their own techniques, have come up with a wide range of faux finishes. Stores such as Home Depot hold regular seminars for the do-it-yourselfer, while more daring individuals use trial-and-error methods until they come up with the pattern they want.

Limited edition prints are being used extensively in homes and business settings.

Wall Coverings

Papers and fabrics are available as **wall coverings**. Many are available from companies that have been in the business for years. Some wall coverings are made to match the curtains, draperies, and upholsteries used in home design, giving unity to a room's appearance. Fabrics are also made to match wall coverings. The styles range from very formal to simple, and from traditional to contemporary patterns; prices begin at as little as $10 per roll. Consumers who wish to install their own wall coverings can choose among many prepasted versions. For the professional, pastes appropriate to the type of covering are applied separately.

Although the wall covering industry is still flourishing, it is losing some ground to the faux paint industry. Painted walls, when faded or past their prime, can easily be repainted. The removal of wall coverings is considerably more costly and labor-intensive.

Decorative Ornaments

In addition to the previously mentioned accessories, home furnishings include decorative ornaments. Among these are **bifold screens**, which may attractively separate two areas in a small apartment or hide something that the apartment dweller does not want seen. Screens may be in covered fabric, with constructed louvers, or hand painted. The **wine rack** is another functional item that adds interest to a room. Multi-level stands that sit on the floor or on tables may hold numerous objects such as plants, flowers, fruit, or small decorative items. They are often made of wrought iron and come in a variety of heights.

Other examples include **drawer pulls** and **decorative hooks**, used for towel displays. Both are functional as well as pleasing to the eye. **Wall plaques** and **sconces** add excitement to any room. The plaques come in various materials ranging from cement that has been cast to rich handmade glass. The sconces are glass containers that hold bulbs to light a staircase or hallway or are used to accent a part of a room, such as a fireplace. Often it takes a designer's imagination to suggest ornaments others would never think of using.

LICENSING ARRANGEMENTS

For many years, home product lines were marketed by company names. For example, in the bedding field, the appearance of such names as Martex, Westpoint Stevens (a merger of J.P. Stevens and Westpoint Pepperel), and Dan River on labels was important to sales. In dinnerware, Rosenthal and Lenox, with their famous designs, were all that was advertised. The same was true of other home products.

Today, brand marketing is still important, but the names of home furnishings designers are increasingly featured in marketing efforts. These designers, once only known to industry insiders, are becoming well-known to many savvy consumers, who look for their coordinated lines of home furnishings. Among the well-known designers who license products extensively are Raymond Waites, who founded Gear in 1978; Larry Lazlow; Mario Buatta; and Martha Stewart.

To further sales, many home furnishings companies are also entering into **designer licensing** agreements with well-known apparel fashion designers so that they can capitalize on their names and reputations. Consumers who have been satisfied with a Ralph Lauren outfit or a Bill Blass dress are likely to buy the same label when in the market for bedding, dinnerware, and other home items.

Names such as Ralph Lauren, Bill Blass, Joseph Abboud, Alexander Julian, Todd Oldham, and Liz Claiborne of the fashion apparel world are producing home fashions in record numbers. More than once, Bill Blass has said that it is the sheets, and not the suits and dresses, that have made him a millionaire. Alexander Julian, menswear designer, has extolled the benefits of home fashions. Beginning with a collection of sheets, Julian now offers, under the Home Colours label, a selection of lithographs, case goods, upholstery, and lamps. He says it is the biggest success he has enjoyed in years. Not to be left behind, Adrienne Vittadini has also expanded into home fashions. In addition to a line of sheets, wall coverings are sold through the Schumacher Company in New York City. Vittadini's home fashions are marketed in much the same manner as her apparel designs, with coordinated patterns and colors as the central focus. The significant growth in this industry, which has minimal risks when compared to the clothing market, and increased consumer interest can bring substantial profits to a company. As a result, Donna Karan, Calvin Klein, and Mary McFadden have joined the growing list of apparel/home fashion designers.

Unlike their involvement in the manufacture of fashion apparel and accessories, where designers generally participate in decisions concerning fabric purchases, production, marketing, and so forth, in home fashions, designers merely create the patterns and designs used on sheets, tablecloths, dishes, and glassware. The production and marketing are left to the licensors, who have expertise in these areas. For their roles, the **licensees**—the designers whose names will be associated with the products—receive payment in the form of a royalty—a percentage or commission on sales.

The degree of participation by a designer varies from agreement to agreement. In some arrangements, the designer provides the company with design sketches that will eventually be used in the products. In others, the designer oversees a staff that produces the design, with the right to eliminate those that do not meet his or her approval.

No matter which route is taken, the name of the designer takes center stage in the marketing of the product. In many stores, home fashions products are featured on the selling floors as collections, in the same manner as apparel. Ralph Lauren, for example, requires that his bedding collections occupy a particular part of the selling floor, not to be mixed with other brands, exactly as he merchandises his apparel collections.

Some of the major agreements include Springs Industries, which manufactures the Liz sheets and Bill Blass bed linens, and Fieldcrest Cannon, which produces Adrienne Vittadini's home collections. (See Table 15.1 earlier in the chapter for a list of many of the important names in licensing.) These "marriages" have been so successful that many companies have several agreements with designers to create different collections.

Missoni is an example of an apparel designer who has successfully made the transition from apparel to home fashions.

Entertainment Licensing

Not all licenses are designer related. There is a growing trend for characters in the entertainment industry to be featured on all types of home fashions. The majority of these products are directed toward the children's market and include cartoon characters, as well as television and film properties.

Barbie Doll, for example, is a winning name in bedding for young girls; Harley Davidson attracts boys. It is the Disney organization, however, that provides the most important of these entertainment licenses. Mickey Mouse, for example, has had an enormous influence for many years and never fails to appeal to the younger set.

Entertainment licensing agreements for these characters are somewhat different from those for designers. With the exception of the Walt Disney Company, licensors have little, if anything, to do with the designs, except to have the right of approval. They are paid royalties by the manufacturers for the use of their names.

Sports Licensing

Manufacturers of sports apparel and equipment have also joined the licensing explosion, creating lines that bear the names of celebrity athletes. The Palmer Home Collection, introduced in 1995, benefits from the Arnold Palmer name. These licensing agreements are with Lexington Furniture for furniture and Guildmaster for decorative accessories. This **sports licensing** takes advantage not only of the allure of the Arnold Palmer name, but also of the design background of Winnie Palmer, Arnold's wife.

Museum Licensing

The popularity of museum reproductions has opened the way for licensing arrangements among famous museums, manufacturers, and retailers. An example of a major entry into this type of licensing is Museum Treasures by Andrew Cymrot. Beginning first with a few pieces from New York's American Museum of Natural History, the company now licenses products from London's Victoria and Albert Museum, and the Royal Ontario Museum in Toronto. The designs of Daniel Chester French, who designed the Lincoln Memorial, are just some of the items that will be marketed. These **museum licensing** agreements bring a great deal of money to the museums, which otherwise depend on donations, grants, and admission fees to cover their operating expenses.

RETAILING HOME FASHIONS

As with apparel and accessories, a variety of retailers compete in the home fashions market, including department stores, specialty stores, manufacturers, free-standing shops, and catalog companies.

One of the people responsible for developing home fashions merchandising is Terence Conran of Great Britain, who revolutionized retailing by applying the principles of high fashion at low cost in the Main Streets of the world. After a stint as a textile designer and furniture maker, he set up a design conservatory in 1956. He opened his first retail shop in 1964. Its instant success spawned an international chain across the United Kingdom, Belgium, the United States, Iceland, Martinique, Singapore, and Japan. His visual merchandising of the products appealed to the consumers. Before long, many consumers were lining up to purchase home furnishings in a different manner. His early inventiveness led to such operations as Crate & Barrel, IKEA, Pier 1, and Urban Outfitters.

Department Stores

Ever since department stores opened their doors, there has been a department in which shoppers could choose from a selection of dinnerware, bedding, and other home fashions. These items, however, rarely brought the same attention to the store as did its fashion apparel and accessories.

Today, that is changing, and department stores are paying greater attention to home fashions. They are enlarging the selling floors that house this merchandise and are using promotional efforts to publicize them. At Macy's in New York City, table settings are created by celebrities as part of the store's annual Flower Show extravaganza. Personalities from stage, screen, television, and the design world are invited to **dress tables** with dinnerware, glassware, table linens, and silverware. The promotion is very successful and generates a great deal of business for the store.

With all of the attention being paid to home fashions, Macy's has opened its first freestanding store that exclusively features products for the home. This 100,660-square-foot store in Las Vegas is the prototype for others to come.

As previously discussed, Bloomingdale's has also opened stores that exclusively sell home fashion.

Specialty Stores

Many shops that exclusively feature home fashions are opening across the United States. They range from the small independent variety to such major operations as Crate & Barrel, Williams-Sonoma, Linens 'n' Things, Bed Bath & Beyond, Urban Outfitters, This End Up, The Bombay Company, and Pottery Barn. Many specialty chains that heretofore specialized only in wearable fashions, such as Banana Republic and Eddie Bauer, have also joined the home fashions field.

These stores specialize in a limited assortment of merchandise, such as bedding, table linens, bath products, dinnerware, glassware, silverware, and related items. One of the keys to their success is the assortment they offer to the customer. At Bed Bath & Beyond, for example, the merchandise assortment in bed linens is far greater than any department store can offer. The customer is able to choose from a wealth of designs and price points.

Exciting visual merchandising has also been a major factor in attracting customers. Instead of lining the shelves with merchandise in an ordinary manner, stores such

Bed Bath & Beyond, here on New York's Sixth Avenue, is a home furnishings megastore.

as Crate & Barrel and Williams-Sonoma produce magnificent displays that immediately transform mundane items into treasures.

Exclusivity is also an approach taken by many of these stores. Instead of relying on merchandise that may be seen at many different stores, some, such as Crate & Barrel, are combing the globe to bring back goods for their exclusive sale. In this way, the customer cannot comparison shop to get the lowest possible price. Crate & Barrel is featured in a World of Fashion Profile.

Freestanding Manufacturer Outlets

There is a trend in this industry for manufacturers to open shops that feature only their own collections. Companies such as Mikasa, Villeroy & Boch, Waterford, Sheridan, and Royal Doulton operate stores across the country that sell company-produced products. In this way, a customer may see the entire line of merchandise under one roof. Although these manufacturers also sell to department and specialty stores, those retailers have neither the space nor the need to feature every item in a single manufacturer's line. Instead, they select specific designs from a host of companies in the hope that the assortment will motivate shoppers to buy at least one. By entering the retail business, manufacturing companies can eliminate the competition from other lines and offer a full assortment of everything they manufacture.

Catalogs

More and more catalogs that feature home fashions are delivered to households every day. The Bombay Company, Spiegel, The Sharper Image, Garnet Hill, Ballard Designs, Crate & Barrel, and The Company Store are some examples. Some catalogs are produced by traditional department and specialty stores; others represent catalog companies whose method of operation is direct mail. Saks Fifth Avenue, known for its high-fashion apparel and accessories, has entered the home fashions market with a catalog called *Folio Design* for the home. It is published three times a year and features silk throws and pillows from Versace, Calvin Klein's Home Collection, and Ralph

CRATE & BARREL

When people enter Crate & Barrel stores, a visual shopping experience greets them. Unlike the typical stores that sell dinnerware, glassware, giftware, and other products for the home, their selling floors immediately impart a feeling of fashion excitement.

Crate & Barrel began uneventfully in the kitchen of its founder, Gordon Segal, in 1962. As he was washing the dishes, he wondered out loud why nobody in Chicago was selling the type of dinnerware he had just brought back from the Caribbean and New York. At that very moment he decided to open a store to fill this gap in the marketplace. From its opening in 1962, the company has expanded to a 60-store chain in 15 markets with more than 2,000 full-time employees.

The first store was a renovated 1,800-square-foot space in an old elevator factory. By nailing up crating lumber on the walls and spilling products out of their packing crates and barrels, the perfect environment and company name were born. Prices at Crate & Barrel were also better than anywhere else in Chicago. The merchandise assortment was exciting and innovative.

Although Segal knew little about running a retail operation in the beginning, he did have a feeling for good design. The concept was that design did not need to be expensive, but the products had to have a standard of excellence that was evident in showrooms, factories, and stores in Europe.

Following the success of the first store, a team of designers developed

A Crate & Barrel catalog targets their customer with a perfect setting.

the now famous display method that is widely imitated. The concept is to create a "vignette" for specific items to attract attention. And attention and excellent sales have been generated.

In addition to the store operations, Crate & Barrel entered the catalog business in 1973 and turned it into a venture that grossed $600 million in 1999.

Lauren's decoratives for the home. With such a large market for in-home purchasing, catalog sales are constantly growing. Soon, video catalogs will be available that will enable customers to see home furnishing lines. The scope of the home fashions industry may be quickly understood by examining all of the places from which merchandise may be procured and the size of the offerings. A visit to High Point, North Carolina, the home fashions answer to Seventh Avenue for apparel, reveals the level achieved by this market.

Clothing retailers such as Anthropologie are producing specialized home furnishings catalogs, while brick-and-motor home furnishings retailers such as Bed Bath & Beyond are reaching out to customers with their own catalogs.

Online Shopping

With the advent of online shopping, consumers have yet another channel through which to purchase products for the home. As in the case of catalog purchasing, those with limited time can peruse a multitude of Web sites and examine a wealth of home fashions ranging from single items to complete rooms.

Users may search with a particular portal such as www.ask.com that quickly offers numerous choices to access or visit a specific Web site. Most of the retailers who have catalog operations feature their Web addresses on them, making it simple for the shopper to find. For home furnishings, two very popular sites are www.potterybarn.com and www.crateandbarrel.com. The former is particularly well designed in that it not only features a wealth of individual products but also uses a design studio concept that takes the shopper through a virtual showroom of many settings. . The Crate and Barrel Web site features not only the current line of merchandise but also products from its outlet stores.

While the dollar amount spent on home fashions online pales by comparison to in-store shopping, it holds the promise of ever-increasing sales numbers in the future.

CHAPTER HIGHLIGHTS

- Fashions for the home are reaching all-time highs in both interest and sales.

- Home fashions have developed from the elaborate ornamentation of the Victorian period to the trendy products of the 21st century.

- The products of the home fashions market continue to expand, with the use of exciting bedding, tableware, decorative enhancements, and other ornaments in varieties never before available.

- Special licensing agreements with designers and well-known personalities and characters have helped to dramatically increase sales.

- Terence Conran, the British home fashions designer, was the first to retail low-cost, exciting furnishings. His vision spawned new operations such as Crate & Barrel, IKEA, Pier 1, and Urban Outfitters.

- Although home fashions were once marketed primarily in department stores, many different outlets now exist for their sale. They include catalogs, specialty stores, and free-standing designer shops, each of which offers unique merchandise.

IMPORTANT FASHION TERMINOLOGY AND CONCEPTS

accent pillows	cocooning	dress tables
bedding	crystal	duvet cover
bedskirts	decorative hooks	entertainment licenses
bifold screens	designer licensing	faux paint finishes
carpeting	dinnerware	flatware
china	drawer pulls	floor coverings
footed tumblers	percale	table settings
glassware	pillow sham	tableware
hardwood flooring	place settings	thread count
home fashions	sconces	trial apartment
lead glass	silverplate	tumblers
licenses	soda-lime glass	valance
museum licensing	sports licensing	wall coverings
muslin	stemmed pieces	wall plaques
paint	stoneware	wine rack

FOR REVIEW

1. Define the term *home fashions* as it is used in this chapter.
2. Describe the characteristics of home furnishings during the Victorian era.
3. Contrast the Arts and Crafts movement with the Victorian era.
4. Why did William Morris begin a new direction in home fashions, and what was it?
5. Describe some of the highlights of Art Nouveau design.
6. What were some of the highlights of 20th-century modernism?
7. What is Art Deco?
8. What changes in the various segments of the home furnishings industry have resulted in increased sales?
9. List the names of five apparel designers who have entered the home fashions arena.
10. Under what type of arrangement do most apparel designers create bedding and dinnerware?
11. What is meant by the term *entertainment licensing*?
12. How have department stores addressed the growing interest in home fashions?
13. Discuss the impact made by Terence Conran on home furnishings retailing.
14. Currently, which specialty retailers are the leaders in fashion-oriented products for the home?

15. According to Dennis McCafferty's Point of View, "Stop & Smell the Candles," what percentage of the U.S. population buys candles, and which age classification represents the major purchasers?

EXERCISES AND PROJECTS

1. Visit the bedding department in a major department store. Compare the various collections of bed linens in terms of those that feature only the manufacturer's names with those that promote designer labels. With the information gathered, determine the percentage of each category in the department.

2. Contact a dinnerware company, the names of which may be found in any store that specializes in that product line, asking for information about the products it sells. Request information about construction techniques, methods of decoration, price points, and anything else that would be of interest. Obtain photographs of the products and mount them on foamboard according to the classifications they belong to. For each product, list the benefits afforded the user.

3. Contact the office of an apparel designer who also creates home fashions and ask for a press kit. Using this kit, prepare a report telling about the designer's background, and describing how he or she made the transition from clothing to home fashions.

WEB SITES

By accessing these Web sites, you will be able to gain broader knowledge and up-to-date information on materials related to this chapter.

Dan River Inc.

www.danriver.com

Martha Stewart

www.marthastewart.com

The Case of the Designer Dilemma

One of the mainstays of the bedding industry for 45 years has been T.J. Contours, Inc. Its collections have been regularly marketed through stores that cater to people in the upper-lower and lower-middle classes. Sears and Montgomery Ward are typical of the retailers it supplies.

Its strength has been the traditional types of patterns, such as flowers and stripes, which sell at modest price points. The actual designs are created by a team of "unsung heroes," who spend endless hours turning out the patterns. Its packages highlight the names of the company rather than the names of those responsible for the designs.

Alan Santos has been the president of T.J. Contours for the past 10 years. He regularly studies the trade papers for new industry directions and to feel the pulse of the market. In recent years, he has noticed that more and more bedding collections bear designer signatures. Although this had never been considered as an option for his company, he believes the time is right for such a move.

Betsey Peters, the executive vice president of the company, thinks that the move to designer collections would be a mistake. After all, she states, "We've been successful for all of these years without the benefit of designer labels, and the change would be too costly for the company."

At this point in time no decision has been made.

questions

1. With whom do you agree? Why?

2. Are there any other methods by which the company might gain further recognition?

Fashion Designers Go Home

SHARON OVERTON

Once we were content to wear the occasional designer label on our T-shirts or jeans.

Then we discovered the joy of sleeping on designer sheets.

Now everything from soap dishes and cereal bowls to wall paint and mattress covers comes with a designer label. In the nineties, nesting had replaced social climbing and haute couture had led to home couture.

No longer are fashion designers content simply to fill our closets. They're out to fulfill our domestic fantasies as well.

Do you long for a home with the patina of Old Money? To his extensive line of home furnishings—all designed to make you look as if you belong on the social register—Ralph Lauren has recently added wall paints. With names such as Spinnaker Blue and Dressage Red, these Sherwin-Williams hues promise that your walls will bespeak gentility even if you weren't born with a silver spoon in your mouth.

Prefer a sort of stripped-down minimalism that conjures up images of a monastery or Zen rock garden? Check out Calvin Klein's new home collection: austere wooden bowls, sublimely simple china, Italian linen sheets and woven cashmere throws so exquisitely serene, and expensive, you'll have to take a vow of poverty to own them.

Other fashion designers are expanding into the home as well. Alexander Julian's moderately priced Home Colours collection for Universal Furniture Industries features traditionally styled furniture with subtle fashion details, such as argyle-patterned wood veneers and wingtip-style flourishes.

Gianni Versace, whose over-the-top clothing is favored by rock idols and movie stars, does baroque-style home furnishings that might appeal to the Mick Jagger in all of us.

Even Donna Karan has announced that she'll offer a home collection sometime in 1997. (Picture little form-fitting matte jersey slipcovers and cozy chairs that cradle you like a cashmere wrap coat.)

In the meantime, everyone from Joseph Abbound to Liz Claiborne, it seems, has come out with a line of bed sheets and bath towels.

While fashion designers have long lent their names to other types of products, often with mixed results, never before have so many crossed over so completely, extending their aesthetic vision to nearly every corner of our domestic lives, says Richard Martin, director of The Costume Institute of the Metropolitan Museum of Art in New York.

"It's a particularly 1990s kind of phenomenon," says Martin, who has written about Versace's Miami Beach mansion.

As the couture business has slumped, designers have had to look elsewhere for markets to feed the enormous empires they built during the 1980s.

"People do spend more money on shelter now than on clothing," Martin says. "It's very logical to move into that area."

Also, fashion designers have attained an unprecedented celebrity status that gives them greater power to influence the way we think and live.

"I suspect that Donna Karan, Calvin Klein and Ralph Lauren are names that are as familiar as Bill Clinton," Martin says.

"Every street kid now knows the names Giorgio Armani [one of the few designers, it seems, who doesn't have a home collection]. We've come to the point where fashion designers are looked upon with an enormous sense of Faith in a society that doesn't give faith to its political figures or even its spiritual figures."

Naturally, anything that exalted is bound to be ridiculed as well.

Newsweek has poked fun at the idea of pricey designer wall paint as a new "lifestyle fetish."

Starting at $21 a gallon for basic white, Ralph Lauren Paints come in 400 colors grouped in categories such as Thoroughbred, Country, Safari and Santa Fe, which complement his furniture designs. Custom finishing kits are available that will instantly age your freshly painted walls with a patina of "sun-fade, tea-stained, smoke and tobacco effects," according to a Lauren press release.

Perhaps it's not surprising in this age of mind-boggling choices that we look to designers for validation of how we dress and how we live.

Even the Gap, which created a national uniform out of khaki pants and denim work shirts, is said to be considering an expansion into home furnishings. Just imagine: Sofas that are as familiar as a pair of faded jeans and rugs, dishes and lamps all bearing that comforting, generic navy blue label.

The fact that the "Gap Home" rumors persist without confirmation from the company itself shows how eager many shoppers are for the validation of a brand name.

"People are so insecure about what to wear, how to identify themselves," says Deborah Shinn, assistant curator at the Copper-Hewitt National Design Museum in New York. "It gives you a sense of security to wrap yourself up with a name that's sort of sanctioned by the press and popular taste. The same thing goes for the home."

But do the skills that make someone good at shaping a jacket, for instance, necessarily translate into making tables and chairs?

"I think it works when fashion designers have a very, very strong sensibility," Martin says. "But I have a feeling it's the kind of thing that probably will be taken to excess. . . . Do you really need to have Marc Jacobs designing your home?"

Published courtesy of *The Florida Times-Union*, Jacksonville, FL

Stop & Smell the Candles

DENNIS MCCAFFERTY

Somehow, it's comforting. When defining the concept of luxury, we're finding value in a product known more for subtle warmth than for gaudy glitz, a touch of class created when wax meets wick: the candle.

More than flowers, fine jewelry or mahogany furniture. More than expensive kitchenware from Williams-Sonoma or high-powered entertainment centers from Circuit City. The proof? The Unity Marketing research group spent nearly a year tracking consumer spending on discretionary purchases, aka stuff we don't really need but want, aka luxury items.

Here's what they found: In a given year, at least 54% of us will buy candles, behind only books, magazines, videos and music CDs. Young people ages 18 to 34 are the most eager candle shoppers of all, buying every year at a rate of 90%. "What's funny about all of this," says Marianne McDermott, executive vice president of the National Candle Association, "is that not so long ago *nobody* would have thought of candles as a luxury item."

Consumers are drawn to candles with zen-like devotion. It is the scent. The look. The pleasure of striking a match instead of flipping a switch. It is a statement of simplicity amid a universe of digitized chaos. In Mancelona, Mich., don't be surprised to see 30 candles burning at any given time at Phyllis Fries' home. "When I sit at a window seat with a nice book and the candles going," says Fries, 51, "it's like drinking a fragrance into my soul."

In a remarkably thorough 214-page examination of the candle phenomenon, Unity breaks down buyers into a myriad of psychological patterns: There are the decorators and the enthusiasts. There are the "aroma-driven," who are enticed by sublime scents as opposed to eye-catching aesthetics. These people are not to be confused with the "fragrance-averse," who find no appeal in things olfactory. Then, there are the "non-igniters," who can't stand to see a beloved candle wither away into a puddly glop.

Candlemakers are ready to please all. Industry giant Yankee Candle is appropriately named, because it is to candles as the New York Yankees are to baseball—a powerhouse. It commands more than $338 million in annual sales. Some 2.5 million luxury-seeking visitors a year head to the 90,000-square-foot flagship store in South Deerfield, Mass.

"Our guests indulge themselves," says Gail Flood, Yankee Candle's senior vice president of retail. "People are very personal about their choices. The candle is for romance. It's for relaxation. It's for atmosphere. It's for transportation . . ."

Transportation? Er, come again?

"Yes, transportation," Flood explains. "You transport yourself to another place, a fond memory. We have one called Green Grass that takes me back to the first day of spring, playing on the lawn with my sister and taking in the freshly chopped grass after my dad cut it."

Are candles, however, a "chick thing"? Apparently. Women buy no fewer than 96% of all candles purchased. In the split of the sexes, it all makes sense. When the lights go out, a woman blithely strikes a match, shedding warm light on the mystery of night. A man, meanwhile, grumbles, curses the darkness and insists on fumbling around for a flashlight that will provide an appropriately narrow glimpse of his universe. Candles are cats and flashlights are dogs. This division will last for eternity.

Still, men have played a significant role in the candle's emergence. As a 16-year-old in 1969 seeking a Christmas gift for his mother, Yankee Candle founder Mike Kittredge melted some crayons and made his first candle. He opened his first store three years later. The late Amos Ives Root, of the A.I. Root Co., was a beekeeper from Medina, Ohio, whose youngest son started making beeswax candles for chuches in 1929. Such innovation breeds success: Candle sales nationwide have exploded in the past few years, from $1.5 billion in 1996 to a projected $2.3 billion this year. More than a quarter of consumers spend more than $75 a year on candles.

Any candle factory worth its wicks will produce 1,000 to 2,000 varieties. Candles are highbrow horticulture, with creations of Bulgarian Roses and Mexican Orange Blossom. Candles are food, in flavors of Oatmeal Cookie, Candy Corn and Toasted Marshmallow. Appealing to Gen X, there are Jumpin' Java candles with whipped wax "served" in Irish coffee mugs. There are hometown candles with regional flavor: That's not a leafy clump of weeds burning on your coffee table! It's a kudzu candle from Mississippi. And who needs Viagra anyway? Burn a Ylang Ylang instead, one of no fewer than 10 varieties considered aphrodisiacs.

Naturally, when a product seems to serve so many needs, some health-police outfit will come along and say it's dangerous. Candles are no exception. Recently, the federal Environmental Protection Agency warned that burning candles in a home can release possibly harmful pollutants.

Die-hard devotees remain unintimidated. In the case of Faith Pattavina, 44, she and her husband keep as many as 150 candles in use at their home in Palm Beach Gardens, Fla. Gone is the stench from his cigars—washed away with those remarkably vivid, almost spiritually affirming scents. "Candles are my life," Pattavina says. "Did you ever see *Willie Wonka*, where they lick the walls and it tastes like candy? It's the same with candles. Honeydew smells like a fresh melon. Wild Cherry smells like wild cherries. I'll have six candles going and people will walk by and say 'My gosh! What are you baking? An apple pie?'"

It's enough to make you believe that, if you can't go home again, you certainly can buy a piece of it waxed in shrink-wrap.

Pierre Cardin Takes a Step Back in Time

ROBERT MURPHY

PARIS—No visit to Pierre Cardin's cluttered office here would be complete without the futuristic couturier rattling off a litany of his past achievements and dusting off myriad press clippings to bolster his case for greatness.

Cardin brags he was the first—and only—designer to be elected to the Academie Francaise; that he pioneered empire-building by buying hotels, restaurants and theaters, and that his name, splashed on some 800 licensed products, remains one of fashion's best known. Despite his incontestable achievements, one gets the impression the still-sprightly 83-year-old Cardin feels shortchanged in terms of modern prestige.

So it's understandable he's reveling in his latest bragging rights: the Barbarella-worthy furniture he created in the Seventies is garnering serious interest from design cognoscenti and collectors alike. In a survey of Cardin's furniture published in Paris this month (Flammarion), contemporary industrial designer Marc Newson tells an interviewer that Cardin wielded a strong influence on his sensibility.

"He was a major figure turned toward the future," said Newson.

Certainly the surge in appeal in Seventies designs, from Joe Colombo to Maria Pergay, has brought Cardin a new cool factor. But experts also stressed he was a pioneer in blurring the lines between fashion and broader design. That, they said, assured his important status in the development of lifestyle branding.

"Remember, Cardin is really the forerunner to all of the home lines that are everywhere today," said auctioneer Richard Wright, the founder of Wright auction house in Chicago. "He was the first to cross over from fashion to a wider design statement," not just a few pieces for the elite, but a true line meant for real distribution. Wright added that, while prices at auction for Cardin-designed pieces are rising, his furniture remains undervalued. For example, in June the auction house sold a Cardin dining table for $1,800 and a large cabinet for $1,400, although prices in Paris already are starting to climb well above those levels.

"While the look is becoming fashionable, it remains on the cutting edge of collectibility"—a good thing for buyers—Wright said.

For his part, Cardin is treating the interest as he always does: as an opportunity to repeat that he always has been ahead of the curve.

"People are afraid of newness," he said in an interview in his office overlooking the French presidential palace. "Much of what I did was scandalous at the time."

Stacked pell-mell around Cardin are old magazines, books, photographs and other relics of his past glories. The walls are painted green; electric wires coil wildly about the floor. For a design maverick, the atmosphere is decidedly unpolished.

"Really, I should redo this place," said Cardin, waving his hands in the air. "It needs it, I know. I've been here for 50 years. But I think it has a heart to it and a link to the past. I don't know why I should change it now."

Cardin started designing furniture in the late Sixties in a factory on the outskirts of Paris, where he employed some eight artisans.

"I've always loved furniture," he explained. "I first designed furniture with a friend when I was eight years old. His father had a factory. It's always been a part of my universe."

One of Cardin's hallmarks is his proclivity for geometric shapes, particularly the circle, and his love of lacquer. One Cardin-designed desk, for example, looks like a pair of inverted triangles.

"I've traveled so much—I think there are only a couple of African countries, and North Korea, that I haven't visited," he offered. "I was inspired by the world. The pyramids inspired me. I loved lacquer. It's used a lot in Asia and Japan. It's modern and timeless, a beautiful material."

Cardin also worked in resin and stainless steel, the other hallmarks of the disco decade. In 1978, Cadillac issued a limited-edition Cardin-designed Eldorado with 30 layers of red lacquer. That same year, he applied his hand to decorate a sleek jet.

"We made editions of seven or eight for most of the furniture," said Cardin. "Since they were art pieces, we had to limit the production. I still have a lot of the pieces today."

Cardin said he approached furniture in a similar way to fashion. "It's sculpture, but practical sculpture. I have always been attracted to roundness, the male and female form, the way bodies fit today. Sexuality. Procreation. That was scandalous at the time."

Cardin, dressed in a tan suit, showed off a picture of the theater he designed in Paris, with its ultra-sleek auditorium.

"When you looked down on the seats from the balcony, there was a geometric color pattern," he said. "I was inspired by a Serge Poliakoff painting."

He held out a picture of a multicolored sofa in thick sculpted wool, circa 1977. "The idea for this was ecological furniture," he said. "I've always had my own personality. I've never copied. With these pieces, I wanted furniture that was like a plant. A sofa like a leaf. I wanted to sleep in a leaf.

"Look at this," he continued, plucking from a nearby shelf a multifaceted silver box that unfolds to reveal triangular morsels of chocolate. "I designed this for a chocolate salon. I won a prize. People didn't understand that you could package chocolate like this. I was inspired by Sputnik."

Though Cardin stopped making furniture some 15 years ago, when environmental concerns forced him to close his factory near Paris, he has projects for the future.

"Next year I'm going to open a furniture factory in Vietnam," he said. "They can still do the kind of lacquer that I want."

Women's Wear Daily, September 29, 2006

designing and manufacturing fashion apparel and accessories

Before most designers and manufacturers create their product lines, they consult with fashion forecasters. Chapter 16 describes how these specialists explore the fiber mills and other resources to learn about trends they can pass on to their clients.

Armed with this information from forecasters and their knowledge of elements and principles of design, manufacturers begin the creative process, which is discussed in Chapter 17. One of the most important elements of design is color. To choose the right color combinations, it is necessary to understand color theory. The Prang Color System is the most widely used approach.

After the designer has created the initial samples or drawings for new styles, it is time to begin production. A schedule is established that begins with the creation of a production pattern. Today, that pattern is most often produced by means of a computer-aided design (CAD) system. After the necessary patterns are developed, garments are cut and assembled, either by an inside shop or through outside contractors. Those products that are favorably received by retail buyers continue on to production.

Each accessory follows its own manufacturing plan. As Chapter 18 outlines, accessory buyers must understand the many manufacturing methods to accurately assess the quality of the final product.

In today's fashion arena, a wealth of merchandise produced under American labels is designed and manufactured offshore. The concept is known as outsourcing and is discussed in Chapter 19.

Once the garments and accessories are produced, they are ready to be sold to the retailers and then to the consumers. The merchandising of fashion is the focus of Part Five.

fashion forecasting for designers and manufacturers

Fashion is born by small facts, trends, or even politics, never by trying to make little pleats, by trinkets, by clothes easy to copy, or by the shortening or lengthening of a skirt.

ELSA SCHIAPARELLI, DESIGNER

After you have completed this chapter, you will be able to discuss:

- The various ways the fashion forecaster aids the designer, product developer, and retailer.

- The process by which forecasters ultimately make their predictions.

- Why those who forecast fashion must begin as early as 18 months prior to the selling season.

- Why fiber producers use fashion shows as part of their forecasting campaigns.

Manufacturers and designers are very knowledgeable about their industry, but they must also be attuned to changes that will shape their future design decisions. At one time, designers did not need to be familiar with lifestyles, social values, culture, ecology, and other aspects of living to produce a new line. Consumers were followers, not leaders in the world of fashion. Today, designers and manufacturers must understand the needs and values of consumers before they begin to create a design. Consumers are better educated than ever, and they no longer follow the dictates of manufacturers and designers. They accept or reject fashion for a variety of reasons. Although the haute couture runways in Paris still feature innovative and extreme styling, the shows are held more to garner attention than to sell fashion. How many consumers enjoy a lifestyle in which these extravagant designs will find a place? It is the prêt-à-porter collections in France and Italy and the ready-to-wear lines in the United States that are profitable to their companies.

Those in the industry who are responsible for deciding what should be produced must be aware of consumer preferences and determine which materials best serve their needs. Major companies often employ stylists, merchandisers, colorists, and other experts to research the markets and inform their companies about what's hot and what's not. Although this is a solid approach to learning about the latest in fabrics, coloration, and other trends, the globalization of the fashion industry makes it impossible for a few employees to adequately explore the market, discover everything that is available, and fully inform the creative teams who design the merchandise. As a result, a growing number of fashion manufacturers, designers, and product developers of private label collections are employing fashion forecasters.

This service is so important that many segments of the industry operate their own forecasting divisions. In addition to independent firms that forecast women's, men's, and children's wear trends, forecasters in the home products industry, the fiber industry, resident buying offices, color associations, and other specialized areas advise

Fashion forecasters meet regularly to discuss the trends they will ultimately transmit to their clients.

manufacturers on a more limited range of products. Each provides a variety of services for its clients.

Because fashion is such an international business, forecasters are often based throughout the world so that they can bring a broader perspective to the industry. Many companies, no matter where they are headquartered, operate branches in important fashion capitals. For example, Promostyl, one of the major players in the forecasting game, has offices in Paris, London, Tokyo, and New York, each interfacing with the others so that clients will be informed immediately about fashion news throughout the world. By working with textile fiber producers, weavers, colorists, and fashion researchers, and by observing the people on the street wherever there is potential for a new fashion direction, forecasters digest what they have learned and transmit the information to the clientele they serve.

Forecasting companies offer a variety of services ranging from one to unlimited consultations. Each company uses a specific format to disseminate the information it has garnered. Such formats include forecast reports, fabric and color libraries, slides and videos, and individual conferencing.

FORECAST REPORTS

Fashion forecasters may use reports to keep their clients informed. These reports may range from a one-page flyer or brochure to entire books, with supplements added throughout the year. Major companies publish these books twice a year. Some companies offer one all-purpose edition that discusses important developments in each segment of the fashion industry. Others take a more specialized approach and prepare individual books that concentrate on specific segments of fashion. Promostyl uses the latter approach. Through the publication of **trend books**, it alerts its customers to color direction, prints, silhouettes, and style 18 to 24 months in advance of each season. To keep abreast of any new developments that occur between the publication

Silhouettes, fashion trends, and other important newsworthy predictions are presented to clients in trend books. Pictured are spreads from Promostyl's trend book.

of editions, Promostyl prepares supplements that are sent directly to its subscribers. Because fashion is an ever-changing business, new ideas must be properly communicated in a timely fashion to those responsible for design and manufacturing. A skilled fashion forecaster can adapt an idea that might be extreme, such as the designs of Gaultier, into a product that serves a specific market, manufacturer, or retailer.

The basic format of fashion reports, such as Promostyl's trend books, is a series of **fashion directions** for the season. Drawings created by the company's artists accompany photographs from which the design inspirations were taken. Color chips and fabric swatches accompany and enhance each presentation for such apparel and accessories classifications as women's, men's, and children's wear. They clearly outline the direction in which the forecasters feel that industry segment is headed. In addition to the trend books, the company is now preparing online products for their clients sometime in 2007.

Promostyl is the subject of a World of Fashion Profile.

Fabric and Color Libraries

The textile industry is truly international. No manufacturer or designer can research all of the world's fiber and fabrics. Of course, they travel to many global fiber shows a year, but often they need reinforcements and reminders of what they saw, what is available, and what they might have missed at these expositions. **Fabric** and **color libraries** can serve this purpose.

Major fashion forecasters offer complete libraries of the fabrics and fibers available to the fashion industry. By subscribing to these services, designers can review the materials as often as they like and can compare the offerings of different fabric producers to determine which ones best suit their needs. Because the fabric is often the inspiration for a particular style, it is the fabric library that is most valuable to designers.

Design Services

Many major retailers develop their own private label merchandise. Unlike the traditional design houses and manufacturers, which are primarily engaged in creating lines of merchandise for their clients, the retailers focus on buying and merchandising. Those who enter the private label arena might choose to use a team of in-house product developers. Macy's does this for a great many of the items featured under its own labels. Others, however, find an alternative approach best serves their needs.

PROMOSTYL

In 1966, Promostyl began what has become one of the most successful global fashion forecasting organizations. With main offices in Paris, London, New York, and Tokyo, and agents in such places as Australia, Belgium, Brazil, California, Italy, Germany, and Spain, it has been able to keep its clients informed of news on the international fashion scene. The company's client list numbers more than 2,500 designers, apparel and accessories manufacturers, fiber producers, and major retailers.

Through the use of trend books, clients are able to learn as far as 18 months in advance of a coming season what styles, colors, silhouettes, and fabrics have the potential for success. Twice a year, clients also receive specialized books that provide invaluable information for merchandise planning. These publications fall into two categories: Premiere books and Shape books.

The Premiere books are offered under the following titles:

- **Influences**. A compilation of what will be the up-and-coming trends in design, fashion, and interior decoration.
- **Colors**. An analysis of color ranges and harmony suggestions for the women's, men's, and children's sectors, complete with swatches and international color references.
- **Fabrics**. An overview of the future of wovens, knits, and prints, illustrated with samples and developed by theme, photos, and references.
- **Active Sportswear**. A study on this dynamic sector offering beach wear trends in summer and ski wear in winter, plus an overview of the outdoor wear and running gear markets.

The Shape books include the following titles:

- **General Trends for Women**. Individual stories that include shapes, color, and fabric predictions. An important part of this book is the inclusion of fabric samples.
- **General Trends for Men**. Focuses on the various masculine types and the shapes appropriate for each. Special attention is paid to urban, sportswear, and casual wear trends, offering suggestions on detailing and fabric choices for each.
- **General Trends for Children**. Addresses the shapes and trends for children aged 4 to 12 years. Mini-stories are offered and are accompanied by fabric suggestions.
- **Fabric Update**. The latest in fabric innovation and suggestions for incorporation into the client's lines.
- **Shoes**. Men's and women's shoe trends, along with material swatches and theme strategies.
- **Accessories**. An overview of bags, belts, and other accessories, and how they should relate to the fashion silhouettes.

To anticipate the fashion trends, Promostyl undertakes research in the following areas:

- Lifestyles, attitudes, values
- Leisure and sports
- Street fashion, as well as designer fashion and haute couture
- Architecture, design, painting, literature
- Music, film
- Shops, catalogs
- Media
- Sports
- Ecology

With the broad range of services offered to its clients, Promostyl's place in fashion forecasting continues to gain international recognition.

They contract with a **forecaster design service** that designs entire collections for a fee. In this way, the retailer is assured that knowledgeable people are creating new merchandise, without the need to maintain year-round, in-house creative teams.

Audiovisual Packages

To communicate the latest developments for each season, some fashion forecasters develop DVD and video packages that cover trends in silhouettes, styles, colors, fabrics, and patterns. Each client receives a visual program of each season's predictions, along with a narration. For those clients too far from the forecasting company's headquarters to come in for individual conferencing or for those who need to review what was learned from personal meetings, these packages are excellent tools.

In 2007, Promostyl embarked on another venture to provide information to their clients. A variety of products were made available that could be accessed online,

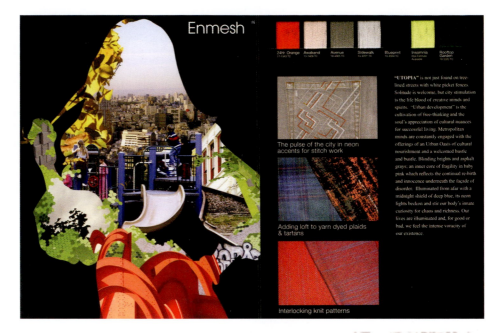

Fabric swatch cards help clients assess availability.

making it easy for users to get up-to-the-minute happenings regarding fashion trends, hot items, and so forth. With their clients located around the world, the online service can connect them to pertinent information as quickly as they can access the Internet Web site.

For retailers interested in private labeling, for example, the entire merchandising team can use these presentations to learn about industry trends.

Individual Conferences

The larger forecasting companies maintain a staff of experts who are prepared to discuss a client's specific problems and needs at an individual conference. A retailer, for example, who plans to enter the private label arena, might want an in-depth conference to determine the best route for producing the desired goods. Similarly, a designer might want to learn more about the best way to promote his or her line. Material sourcing is yet another area that may need special attention. As part of their contractual arrangements, fashion forecasters offer these special consulting conferences.

RESIDENT BUYING OFFICES

The group of market consultants known as **resident buying offices** has expanded its advisory services. At one time, these agencies dealt primarily with bringing retail buyers and manufacturers together. Because many of their retail accounts now develop their own merchandise, resident buying offices provide fashion forecasting services to assist them in determining what items to produce.

One of the major resident buying offices in the forecasting arena is The Doneger Group. A World of Fashion Profile of The Doneger Group appears in Chapter 20. The services offered by resident buying office forecasting divisions include:

- *Color Forecasts*. Seasonal color charts group specific colors into merchandise palettes. Dyed yarns and color photos generally accompany the color forecasts.

- *Trend Forecasts*. Design trends are usually depicted with photographs, drawings, colored yarns, and fabric swatches to help the user obtain an overview of the market.

- *Personal Consultations*. Whether it is to plan a new merchandise collection, choose specific colors and fabrics for incorporation into a line, plan promotions and visual presentations, or make fashion-related decisions, these companies have trained staffs ready to answer client questions and solve specific problems.

- *Newsletters*. One method used to convey information to clients is print or online **newsletters**. They may concentrate on news of fibers and fabrics, shapes and silhouettes, the importance of a new color, hot items that should help generate future business, and color updates.

- *Workbooks*. In-depth publications cover the designs of haute couture. These **workbooks** are presented so that designers and manufacturers at lower price points can use the styles as guides for their own creations.

- *Slide Library*. A complete library of slides of all of the major collections is kept for each season so that they can be used for research.

- *Video Library*. Many of the major designers and manufacturers provide DVDs and video presentations of their seasonal collections. These can be used not only to see what is currently being offered, but also for research purposes.

- *Multimedia Presentations*. At the beginning of each season, a **multimedia presentation** consisting of videos, in-person fashion shows, and other tools is used to bring a broad fashion perspective to the customer.

- *In-Person Reviews of Street Styles*. With so much of today's fashion based on what people are wearing in the street, many companies visit cities to record their observations.

David Wolfe, a leading international fashion forecaster, is featured in a World of Fashion Profile.

FIBER PRODUCER FORECASTERS

Traditional fashion forecasters cover every aspect of the fashion industry; forecasters in fiber and fabric production specifically provide research on fabric. Because many designer creations begin with appropriate fiber and fabric selection, they must receive

DAVID WOLFE

"Everybody in the world wakes up naked and decides what to wear. That decision, conscious or subconscious, is the result of a great many factors and it is those factors that interest me." That is how David Wolfe explains his lifelong interest in fashion, which he describes as "a fascinating mix of style, economics, history, politics, weather, science, sex, and a sense of humor."

Wolfe has gained international fame in the fashion industry, in which he is known as "America's Foremost Fashion Forecaster." Thirty-five years of experience have earned him this title.

A native of Ohio, Wolfe began his fashion career in a small-town department store, where he worked in a position that combined the responsibilities of fashion coordinator, buyer, copywriter, illustrator, and advertising manager. After gaining considerable experience in these aspects of fashion retailing, he spread his wings and tried his hand at an area for which he had great fondness, fashion art. Because London was an exciting fashion city in the 1960s, he made his way abroad and soon established himself as a leading fashion artist. His sketches appeared in *Vogue*, *Women's Wear Daily*, and *The London Times*. Before long he was sought by and worked for Galeries Lafayette, Liberty of London, Harvey Nichols, and Selfridges. In 1969 he became one of the first to enter the fashion service industry. As creative director of I.M. International, he became one of the world's leading fashion forecasters and authorities. In his tenure at that company, he was among the first to discover such talents as Armani, Lagerfeld, Montana, and Versace. Returning to the United States in the early 1980s, Wolfe helped to form The Fashion Service (TFS) and served as president of the New York operation for a decade.

Today, Wolfe is creative director of D3 Doneger Design Direction, the fashion trend and color forecasting service for women's, men's, and children's wear. His other activities include serving as senior fashion consultant to *Video-Fashion*, whose weekly programs of fashion news and designer interviews are broadcast via satellite to 30 million viewers worldwide. He regularly contributes articles to fashion publications through his affiliation with the Overseas Fashion Press Association and is international fashion editor of *Men Men* and *Mode Couture* magazines, high-fashion publications of the Far East.

Rounding out his busy schedule is the delivering of informative and amusing lectures, slide presentations, and television appearances that make him a popular personality on the fashion scene.

fabric information as much as 24 months before a line actually reaches the selling floor. As with fashion forecasters, those in the fiber business use a variety of publications to disseminate information. DuPont, for example, publishes booklets and bulletins about its Lycra spandex fiber. The booklets list the different properties of the fiber and how it might be used in fashion products.

In addition to the standard written materials, the fiber industry regularly uses the fashion show format to feature designs made with the fibers they are promoting. Invited to these events are fashion designers who will, it is hoped, be inspired to use the fiber in their own collections.

FIBER ASSOCIATION FORECASTERS

Forecasting has become a major function of associations in the fiber segment of the fashion industry. Through printed material and fashion shows, they present the latest news on fabric innovations, color trends, and uses of these fibers to their clients.

Groups such as Cotton Incorporated and the Wool Bureau represent producers of natural fibers. It is their responsibility to promote their respective industries and to show how their fibers may be used to serve the needs of the apparel industry and the ultimate consumer.

Cotton Incorporated, for example, uses a unique program of designer collections made exclusively with cotton. At such fashion events as Seventh on Sixth, designers, merchants, and the editorial press are treated to full-scale fashion shows featuring lines created specifically with cotton. The purpose is to inspire designers to consider cotton in future collections.

Forecasting programs traditionally include creatively designed books of color photographs that are used to extract color palettes for swatches of fabrics and yarns. These books also include fashion drawings and **forecast collages** that combine style, fabric, and color.

COLOR FORECASTERS

Because appropriate color selection is one of the more important aspects of fashion design and merchandising, information about color trends is needed by almost everyone. Although many fashion forecasters offer color predictions, few deal exclusively with this element of fashion design.

Color forecasters include the Color Association of the United States (CAUS) and the Color Marketing Group. The goal for these associations is to predict color at least two years in advance of the retail selling season. At CAUS, a forecasting committee meets to select the shades that it thinks will attract the American consumer.

Manufacturers of women's, men's, and children's fashion who subscribe to these services receive swatched color forecasts; interior designers and home fashions creators receive custom silk-screened charts and color chips. To provide up-to-the-minute fashion news, subscribers also receive newsletters and bulletins. In addition, fashion designers regularly consult the color libraries of these companies, which often date back 90 years, for inspiration in creating new products.

As with all fashion forecasting agencies, those specializing in color maintain hotlines for quick answers to color-related questions and offer individual consulting sessions for clients.

Color forecasters meet to predict color trends at least two years in advance of the selling season.

SPECIALIZED FORECASTERS

As the fashion industry continues to grow, general industry forecasters find it difficult to cover every product classification. All too often, they focus on apparel first, with only a secondary emphasis on accessories. To better serve the needs of manufacturers and designers of accessories, a number of specialized forecasters have been established.

One of the more important is the Committee for Colour & Trends, an international forecasting service specializing in footwear, hats, hair ornaments, jewelry, watches, handbags, belts, and hosiery. Its clients include designers, manufacturers, importers, wholesalers, buying offices, and retailers.

As with other forecasters, the committee tracks the colors of the fiber industry, which is so important in making fashion predictions. However, it does not stop there. It uses these color forecasts to develop color harmonies for leather and shoes, as well as other leather accessory industries.

Color is so important to the leather industry, that the Committee for Colour & Trends produces semiannual books that provide examples of new textures in leather and offer specific color recommendations for each merchandise category.

These specialized forecasters also offer individual conferences to discuss such matters as the way in which color trends relate directly to the client, how deliveries should be timed to coincide with those of the apparel industry, and which products might be best emphasized for the next season.

CHAPTER HIGHLIGHTS

- The fashion designer's creativity no longer dictates style and silhouette. Because the consumer has become more independent, fashion manufacturers and designers need accurate and up-to-date information before creating a new line.

- Product developers must learn about the newest fabrics in the marketplace, the colors that are likely to have the greatest customer appeal, and the silhouettes that merit consideration. Although many companies have staffs that research these areas, others use outside sources to gather pertinent merchandise information.

- This role is filled by different types of fashion forecasters, including the general fashion merchandise forecaster, the fiber association forecaster, a division of a resident buying office, and specialized forecasters in such areas as accessories and color selection.

- Fashion forecasters present their findings in trend books, fabric and color library facilities, the design of a complete collection, audiovisual presentations, individual conferences, and fashion shows.

IMPORTANT FASHION TERMINOLOGY AND CONCEPTS

color forecaster	forecast collages	resident buying offices
color library	forecaster design service	specialized forecasters
fabric library	multimedia presentation	trend book
fashion directions	newsletters	workbooks

FOR REVIEW

1. Why is it important for a designer to use the services of a fashion forecaster?
2. Why are more and more retailers using fashion forecasters?

3. Describe the merchandise classifications usually researched by the general fashion merchandise forecasters.

4. How does the fashion forecasting company come up with its predictions?

5. How far in advance of a selling season is information from the forecasters available to designers?

6. What is a trend book?

7. What purpose does the forecaster's color library serve for the designer?

8. Does a fashion forecaster ever actually design a collection?

9. Why are street fashions sometimes used by fashion forecasters in their predictions?

10. Describe a program that Cotton Incorporated uses to show the fashion world how its fabrics may be employed.

11. What is meant by a forecast collage?

12. Define the term *specialized forecaster*.

13. According to the Point of View article, "On the Licensing Lookout," what is the fastest-growing industry related to the license product field?

EXERCISES AND PROJECTS

1. Select a theme as a possible concept for a children's wear collection. Using photographs, drawings, fabric swatches, and color chips, prepare a collage on foamboard as would a fashion forecaster who is about to present the idea to a client.

2. Create a workbook that features haute couture designs. The photographs may be obtained by writing directly to the major fashion houses or from the various fashion publications such as *Vogue* and *Harper's Bazaar*. Prepare an oral report discussing the styles you have selected and how they might be translated into lower-priced merchandise.

3. Contact a fiber producer such as DuPont for information on its fashion forecasting techniques. Using the material provided, prepare an oral report about how the producer disseminates the information to the industry.

WEB SITE

By accessing this Web site, you will be able to gain broader knowledge and up-to-date information on materials related to this chapter.

Promostyl

www.promostyl.com

The Case of the Undesigned Collection

Linda Fain and Brett Williams have both worked for Encore, a manufacturer of moderately priced women's sportswear, for the past three years. She has primarily been engaged in fabric acquisition; he is the top showroom sales rep.

Last month, the two learned that Encore was going to move its operation from New York City to Los Angeles. Each was invited to follow the company westward but, because of family obligations, declined the offer. With the imminent closing of the company, both Linda and Brett are seeking other employment in the fashion business. Although they have been offered positions with an Encore competitor, they are entertaining the possibility of beginning their own business. Experienced in moderately priced sportswear, they believe this would be the best arena for them to enter. With some money of their own and commitments from family members, they have sufficient capital to get started.

Linda will handle purchase of materials and trimmings; Brett will be responsible for sales. Neither of them, however, is an expert in the all-important area of design. Yet they recognize that to enter this highly competitive field, a solidly designed line is a requirement.

Linda believes that they should employ a designer to create the lines. Although people with creative ability are highly paid, she thinks it is the only way to make their new company competitive. Brett would like to use an in-house designer, too, but he is afraid that the expense would be too great in the beginning. His suggestion is to comb the market for exciting styles and copy them in fabrics of their choice. That would save the expense of a designer.

At this time, they cannot decide if either approach warrants further consideration or if a third approach might better solve their problem.

questions

1. Do you think either approach is a sound one? Why?

2. What other arrangement could the new company make? Would it be a better approach?

Style Gazing

How does it happen? When you walk into a store and everything seems to look the same, do you wonder how such a fashion coincidence could possibly occur? It is no coincidence. What is really afoot almost amounts to a conspiracy.

The mystique of fashion striking like creative lighting within the imagination of a designer in an ivory tower in Paris is the kind of image that the industry wants perpetuated. It makes fashion more valuable and helps to justify the high cost of dressing. But designers do not live in ivory towers and there is not much of a market for genuine, one-of-a-kind, bolt-out-of-the-blue creativity. The real process is, in fact, much more fascinating.

Revealed! The secret starting point of many trends. Fashion forecasting companies are mostly based in Paris, London and Milan, and as might be expected, there are several major firms in New York City. The key players, some of the most important forecasting companies, are Promostyl and Peclers in Paris, Design Intelligence in London, plus D3 Doneger Design Direction and Here and There in New York. There are lesser firms around the world too, but not that many. It is a small, very specialised segment of the industry and its purpose is to help designers and manufacturers make the right thing at the right time.

It is important to remember that as far as the business is concerned, the right thing is not necessarily the most fashionable, but it is the most saleable. A "forecast" is not the result of gazing into a crystal ball, but an analysis of what already exists, what has already been created, that will sell in greater quantities in the future. So much of what is passed off as forecasting is nothing more than business guidance that is based on someone else's creativity (usually a "hot" designer like John Galliano or Anna Sui).

If this is spring, next autumn is already over for forecasters. It is Autumn/Winter 1996 right now as far as fashion forecasters are concerned. These savants of styles are way ahead of the rest of the world. Just as the brand new merchandise for Spring/Summer 1995 is being unpacked in the stores, forecasters are three seasons ahead, predicting the colors and fabrics and even the exact garment designs that will eventually be stocked in shops 18 months from now. They take their work very seriously and are taken equally seriously by their clients who pay dearly for a clear vision of the future. Millions and millions of dollars ride on decisions and plans that have to be made far in advance if fibers are to be dyed, fabrics printed and patterns programmed for mass production. One manufacturer describes his company's faith in their forecaster as "a kind of insurance policy."

Self-fulfilling prophecies make predictions come true. How can anyone be certain of what is going to happen so far in the future? It is impossible to be 100 percent accurate, but the fashion business is so precarious that almost any guidance is worth considering. Here's a typical scenario, one that is repeated over and over again, season after season.

First the staff of the forecasting company meet to formulate their vision of things to come, be it colors or a fabric or even a skirt length. They present that vision to their clients who in turn produce the goods according to that vision. Thus, the prophecy is fulfilled. It is a very simple system. Of course, there is a major glitch possible at the end of this chain. What if the forecasted vision does not sell? What if customers don't want to buy that particular color or fabric or style? If that happens several times, then the forecasters are soon searching for new, more gullible clients. But, as is usually the case, when the customer is confronted by a confident presentation of something—almost anything—he or she becomes a believer in the validity of the presentation and will buy.

Haute couture used to act as the world's fashion forecast. Forecasting was not always a part of the fashion system. Decades ago one only needed to see what was being presented in the present, in the salons of haute couture designers in Paris. Twice a year, a dozen or so very important designers of customer-made creations showed their collections. Christian Dior, Balenciaga and Givenchy were the stars then. The premieres of their collections were totally different from the media frenzies today's fashion shows have become. They were refined little affairs; there was no music, just a voice reading the number of each garment as it was paraded.

The couture collections were kept a deep, dark secret. Several weeks after the shows the world's press were allowed to show the designs to the public. Before that "release" date, only the women who were customers and manufacturers who paid a "caution" (a high fee that allowed them to see the show) were given access. Of course, after the press showed the designs, then anybody could copy the new looks and they did, as closely as possible. But the delayed release date meant that the couture customers could rest assured that copies could not be made before their costly originals had been worn in an aura of expensive exclusivity.

There was a well-established trickle-down theory of fashion in those days. It was said that it took exactly two years for a Paris fashion to reach the masses. It was a system that worked perfectly as long as everyone played fair. (And any manufacturer or reporter who did not was ostracised once and for all.) It was John Fairchild, publisher of *Women's Wear Daily*, the influential New York fashion trade paper who brought the system down. He refused to abide by the release dates and was, of course, denied entry. Undaunted, he had his reporters and artists waiting outside in the streets and after each show, they would whisk buyers to a cafe and quickly get a first hand report from their informants. Those sketches and reports appeared instantaneously and copyists the world over got to work.

How times have changed. Today the couturiers are anxious for publicity, eager to cash in on the sales that can be generated when their fashion shows are hyped in newspapers and magazines as well as seen on television. And besides, most couturiers today copy themselves, making cheaper versions of their creations in "diffusion" ranges.

Street style set the stage for the birth of fashion forecasting. Another force came into play to upset the haute couture applecart and set the stage for the birth

of fashion forecasting. A new generation was making street style into fashion news early in the 1960s. Young designers like Mary Quant, John Bates and Emmanuelle Khan who were not couturiers suddenly became important. Young people wanted to wear the same styles their idols wore and manufacturers realized that haute couture was not the only game in town.

But how was a company in Hong Kong or Los Angeles or Tokyo to know what was happening in the fast-paced youth market when there was a new trend every week appearing on London's Carnaby Street? They needed on-the-spot informants, people with a trained fashion eye. Soon a little subculture of style spies came into being. They would haunt the streets and trendy boutiques, secretively sketching the newest cut or detail and then speeding off their efforts to the trend-hungry manufacturers far away.

That worked for a time until the naturally competitive manufacturers decided they had to get their versions of the new trends out before their competition. They then started asking their London and Paris-based correspondents to second-guess what the next new trend would be. And that is how fashion forecasting began. But it is not the end of the story, it is only the beginning.

How forecasting works. Color is the starting point of any season, and every forecaster begins by creating a range of colors specific to the season. The colors are brand new each and every season, meticulously dyed and redyed until they meet the exacting specifications of the colour specialists. At D3, Gae Marino, the managing director, is also the chief color creator, working with a small team of experts. Her color sense is so uncanny that many of the world's leading retailers regard her color choices as a sure route to commercial success. She is said to have

an "eye" in the same way that parfumiers have a "nose."

Colorists travel to the world's fashion capitals and attend fashion shows. They also research carefully the colors that are currently selling. Once colors have been selected, then the fabrics and designs quickly follow suit. The information that forecasting firms accumulate in order to project fashion forward comes from many diverse areas.

Equally vital in the formation of trends are forces such as the entertainment industry, politics, science, weather, and of course, economics. What is currently being worn has to be taken into account. Shifts in population patterns and demographics changes all influence the movement of fashion.

Firsthand observations are important, so forecasters are a travelling tribe, roaming Paris, London and Milan, but also venturing to far flung destinations like Lapland or even Disneyland with sketchbooks and cameras at the ready. They also go to the theatre and films, attend concerts and hang out in clubs constantly. They read all the best-selling novels and even watch TV to check how the public pulse is coursing. A creative director assimilates all these different aspects and forms them into coherent trends that are then sketched and circulated seasonally. Trend books are big "idea" books, loaded with photos and designs and meticulous fashion illustrations.

Were color charts and trend books all that they did, forecasters would be more akin to magazine publishers. However, the New York based D3 Donegar Design Direction claims, "the published products are just 50 percent of what our clients buy—the other 50 percent is a relationship." And every forecasting firm aims to create a close working relationship that will guarantee ongoing fees and prevent notoriously fickle clients switching from one forecaster to another in their feverish race to get to the right trend fast—and first.

Where next? The future of fashion is certainly not an uncertainty to forecasters. They completed their work on Spring/Summer 1995 (the styles seen in this

issue) way back at the end of 1993 and most of them cannot even "remember" that far back. What do they see ahead for you? For Autumn/Winter 1995?

Couture, Spring/Summer 1995

On the Licensing Lookout

JULEE GREENBERG AND KRISTIN LARSON

New York—What will be the next Harry Potter or Teletubbies?

It might be the Power Puff Girls or Miffy, or maybe Tiger Beat or Gigi that becomes a gold mine of licensing royalties. With recent studies showing that teens and tweens are increasing their consumer spending, companies from a variety of fields are looking to tap into this demographic.

The likes of Universal Pictures, Viacom, Warner Bros. and Sony were promoting their brands at the 21st annual International Licensing & Merchandising trade show, which ended its three-day run last Thursday at the Jacob K. Javits Convention Center in Manhattan.

Many were vying for the next hot property, as larger-than-life-sized movie and TV characters—Scooby Doo, Stuart Little and popular storybook character Miffy—were walking the show.

The exhibit featured about 4,700 properties and 469 vendors versus last year's 4,500 and 431, respectively, according to Diane Stone, group show director for Advanstar Communications, the show's producer. Square footage at the show increased by about 25 percent, to 355,000 square feet, and about 18,000 attendees, including retailers and manufacturers, turned out.

Exhibitors ranged from new apparel brands, such as Field & Stream and Jou

Jou, to travel and destination, home decor and food and beverage brands.

"It always seems that when you thought of every category that you possibly can, here comes some more," said Stone. "The cool thing about this show is that it's about concept and not about product, so the booths are spectacular."

The business of licensing is becoming a much tighter market, noted Charles Riotto, president of the International Licensing Industry Merchandisers' Association.

"Licensors are managing their properties a lot closer now," Riotto said. "They're really conscious of the partnership they have with licensees and retailers, where they understand the best licensing programs are the ones that are successful for all three partners and not just for the licensor. They want to develop properties that have longer life cycles, as opposed to properties that are around for a few months."

According to a study conducted for the association by the Yale School of Management and the Harvard Business School, more than $5.84 billion in royalties were paid to licensors based on sales of licensed products in the U.S. in 2000. That was an increase of $248 million from the previous year and would put retail volume of licensed products at $97.3 billion, from $95 billion in the U.S. last year.

While two of the fastest-growing categories were fashion and music licensing—with royalty revenues from fashion licensing climbing 12 percent, to $980 million, and revenues from music licensing up 10.4 percent, to $138 million—the actual fastest-growing industry was the nonprofit and cause-related licensed product field, which climbed 20 percent, to $36 million.

At the exhibit, Primedia Magazines made its debut appearance and featured licensed accessories from the Seventeen magazine collection. The real reason they were at the show, however, was to promote another magazine: Tiger Beat. The entertainment-based fanzine popular for its colorful posters and centerfolds of dreamy teen stars seems to be an ideal brand to license, said Barbara Deering, president of Primedia Magazines.

"While tweens do have some money to spend, these girls don't shop alone," Deering said of the appeal of this preteen group, noting that since most of them shop with their parents, it increases their buying power.

Deering hopes to license the brand to T-shirts, accessories and possibly some home design items like pillows and blankets.

"But how do I get to that tween [group] who's spending $66 billion on product a year?" Deering posed. "That's a tremendous opportunity, and it's kind of an elusive market, and I think that's why we're getting so much interest in Tiger Beat."

With the Power Puff Girls movie coming out in summer 2002, Warner Bros. is hoping to attract the attention of the tween audience with a full apparel program on track.

"It's very popular because it's very on trend with Japan Animation and the whole trend of girl power," said Karen McTier, executive vice president of domestic licensing for Warner Bros. "Girls have really embraced this and, in a lot of categories, it's the number one girls' license."

Being the fashion plate that she is, Barbie took the licensing show as an opportunity to offer a glimpse into her future endeavors.

Is seems she's much more multifaceted than just a doll with pretty clothes. After launching the Barbie clothing and bath and body line last year, the brand will expand into accessories for both adults and children, as well as a line of clothing for tweens.

Launching in Japan now, the tween line will feature a limited amount of bottoms, but a large variety of tops, said Richard Dickson, senior vice president worldwide of girls' division licensing at Mattel Inc., which holds the license. While Dickson said Barbie has already launched a clothing line for children age 3–8, the new tween line will be more mature to suit the age group.

The younger children's clothes will feature an actual picture of the Barbie doll on the apparel, and as the child gets older, she will find that the doll and logo is removed from the garment, Dickson explained.

Now being sold in Barbie concept shops throughout Japan, the new tween line will be sold in the U.S. beginning in 2002 in a variety of retail environments. Mattel will target department stores, along with specialty stores such as FAO Schwartz and mass chains like Target, Dickson said.

While working on a new print ad campaign and growing its Web site, junior clothing label Dollhouse also appeared at the show and was particularly looking to lend the name to a line of bedding items, said Dana Sheill, director of licensing. The company also has its sights set on electronics.

"I want to approach Sony about a possible video game featuring our mascot, Gigi," Sheill said. "We did a poll on our Web site to see if our customers knew her name and surprisingly enough, many knew it."

Women's Wear Daily, June 20, 2001

elements and principles of design for developing a fashion collection

I believe in design that has integrity, design that lasts. Whatever it is, it must be part of the lifestyle and become more personal with time.

RALPH LAUREN, DESIGNER

There is nothing mysterious about how ideas and concepts take shape to become the next season's line or collection. Each new product represents the collaborative efforts of a team and a plan of activities that will, it is hoped, receive the attention and recommendations of the press, the store buyers, and the public.

As previous chapters have emphasized, many steps must be taken to ensure that those responsible for product development and design are on the right track. Design staff interact with the fashion forecasters, study the various influences on current fashion, and comb the fiber, fabric, and trimmings markets. To create a distinctive line or collection that is suited for consumer use, designers must apply the elements and principles of successful designing. The elements of design include the silhouette, details and trimmings, color, and texture. The principles are balance, emphasis, proportion, rhythm, and harmony, and how they relate to each other.

Once all of these considerations have been addressed, it is time to develop and design the products.

ELEMENTS OF DESIGN

When designers begin work on a new line or collection, they may be motivated by any number of factors. A particular geographic region, such as the South Seas, may provide an inspiration. A trend in movies or theatrical productions, as discussed in Chapter 5, or new trends in fabric may provide the stimulus.

Newly developed fibers continue to inspire and direct designers. When nylon was first introduced in 1938, it gave the fashion industry something new to play with. In the 1950s and 1960s, polyester motivated designers to produce garments that would behave perfectly during travel. Not long after, spandex, with its stretch properties,

After you have completed this chapter, you will be able to discuss:

- The elements and principles of design on which apparel and home fashions are based.
- The numerous color harmonies available to designers.
- The individual stages of developing a designer's line or collection.
- A typical timetable that begins with the design concept and ends with delivering the merchandise to the store.

Ralph Lauren discusses the elements of a potential design with his staff.

gave designers a new material that provided comfort to the wearer. More recently, Micromattique, a microdenier polyester fiber with the fineness of silk, has offered designers yet another fabric for their creations.

No matter where the inspiration or motivation comes from, all designs involve shapes or silhouettes, details and trimmings, colors, and textures. How each is manipulated and interrelated with the others is the designer's challenge.

Silhouette

As described briefly in Chapter 5, women's apparel has five basic silhouettes—tubular or straight model, A-line, hourglass, wedge, and bouffant. In men's tailored clothing, there are fewer silhouette choices—the American or classic cut, or the European model.

Working with these shapes, each women's wear designer chooses one, or perhaps two, that will dominate a collection. In the men's industry, one silhouette appears in a collection. It is the other ingredients, such as fabric and trim, that differentiate one garment from the other.

Left: Women's clothing is based on one of five silhouettes. Here, Zac Posen chose the straight silhouette. Right: In men's tailored apparel, it is the attention to detail, such as Etro's use of pattern on the vest, that distinguishes the style of one designer from that of another. Men's silhouettes are typically limited to either a classic or a European cut.

Details and Trimmings

In women's apparel, a basic shape is individualized by various collars and sleeves and the shortening or lengthening of the hemline. In men's clothing, it might be a notched collar or the six-button, double-breasted closure that differentiates one classic silhouette from another. Other detailing might include shoulder pads, puffed sleeves in a leg-of-mutton fashion, or patch pockets on a jacket.

After deciding on the silhouette, detail, texture, and color of a product, the designer must choose the functional and decorative additions that will transform the garment into something unique and observably different from those with similar characteristics.

Although belts, buttons, and zippers may be classified as functional trimmings, they are often selected for decorative reasons. A plastic button may serve the same purpose as a pearl one, but the latter gives the garment a richer quality. Similarly, zippers are most often functional, but those that are conspicuously oversized and visible might add to the design's character.

A variety of decorative trim serves to embellish and enhance a garment. Intricate beading, fine appliqués, unique embroidery, piping in contrasting colors, handmade flowers, rhinestones, lace edging, and others all "dress up" the basic styles. A complete examination of these various details and trimmings can be found in Chapter 13.

Textures

Many designers choose an identical silhouette and details for several pieces in the collection, the only variation being **texture**. Texture, the look and feel of fabric, plays an important role in a garment's appearance. Bulky yarns, for example, when used in woven goods or knits will make the wearer look heavier. Flat knits or wovens, when applied to the same silhouettes, will give a lighter, more flattering image to the same figure.

Texture also affects how the fabric may be manipulated. A stiff felt does not provide the drapability of a soft chiffon. Tweeds are perfect for rugged sportswear, but do not fit the bill for feminine evening wear.

A shiny satin's surface brilliantly enhances its color because of the way the light reflects off the surface, but a corduroy fabric, employing the same coloration, does not provide the brilliance because of its textural ridges, or wales. Color, therefore, is also affected by the fabric's texture.

The knowledgeable designer must be well versed in textures before selecting fabrics for a particular model or design.

Color

The single element that contributes the greatest visual impact without affecting the cost is color. The choice of specific design details, fabric choice, and trim can considerably increase a garment's cost, but color changes the appearance without adding expense. Color provides excitement, mood, and emotion to a design. To maximize color's effect on apparel, accessories, and home fashions, some basic **color theories** and concepts must be understood by those responsible for design.

Nanette Lepore mixes different textures for this fashionable look.

Color Theory

Designers must choose from a wide assortment of available colors. They must decide which colors work best with their creations and in what harmonies they should be used.

Color combinations may be chosen by understanding the most basic concepts of color or by instinct, which breaks all rules and sometimes provides fantastic results. Although most designers have a sense of which combinations are appropriate, that sense is based on an understanding of color systems.

An understanding of these color systems requires familiarity with terminology associated with color. *Hue, value,* and *intensity* are three frequently used terms in the color vocabulary.

HUE The technical term for the name of a color. Thus, red, green, yellow, and violet are **hues**.

VALUE The lightness or darkness of a color. The lightest colors are achieved by different amounts of white and are called **tints**. The darkest are achieved by the addition of black. The greater the amount of black, the darker the color. These darker colors are referred to as **shades**.

INTENSITY Refers to the color's saturation or purity, brightness or dullness. A color may be dulled by adding gray, or its *complement*, a term that will be discussed later in the chapter.

Color Combinations

Various hues, whether pure or in tints or shades, are combined to add unlimited color interest to fabrics.

Combinations are based on one of two systems: the Prang or the Munsell. The **Prang Color System** is the better known and is used extensively by fashion professionals. Developed by David Brewster, it employs a **color wheel** based on the three **primary colors**, yellow, blue, and red, which are used to produce other colors. **Secondary colors**, also called secondaries, are produced by mixing two primary colors. For example, a mixture of red and yellow, two primaries, produces orange, a secondary color; blue and red result in purple, and yellow and blue provide a green hue. With the three primaries and the **neutrals**, black and white, an endless color array can be achieved.

Although fabrics are generally shown to designers and manufacturers in a wide assortment of color harmonies, those responsible for product development can also suggest different arrangements.

The most commonly used color combinations are as follows:

MONOCHROMATIC COLOR SCHEME In this arrangement, one basic color is selected for a design. Interest in the design can be achieved by arranging different values and intensities of the color and highlighting it with such neutrals as black and white. Thus, a red pattern, with pink (a tint of red) and burgundy (a shade of red) and markings of white or black (neutrals) is considered a monochromatic harmony. Only one actual hue is being used.

ANALOGOUS COLOR SCHEME Colors that are adjacent to each other on the color wheel are used to form analogous schemes. The use of yellow, yellow-orange, and orange, or blue, blue-violet, or violet are examples of this color combination. As with the monochromatic arrangement, neutrals may be used to provide additional interest.

The color wheel serves as an excellent starting point for designers to select their schemes.

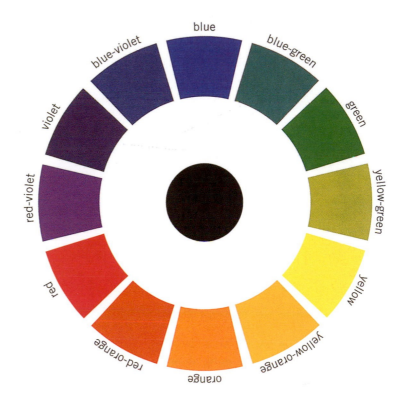

blue
blue-violet
blue-green
violet
green
red-violet
yellow-green
red
yellow
red-orange
yellow-orange
orange

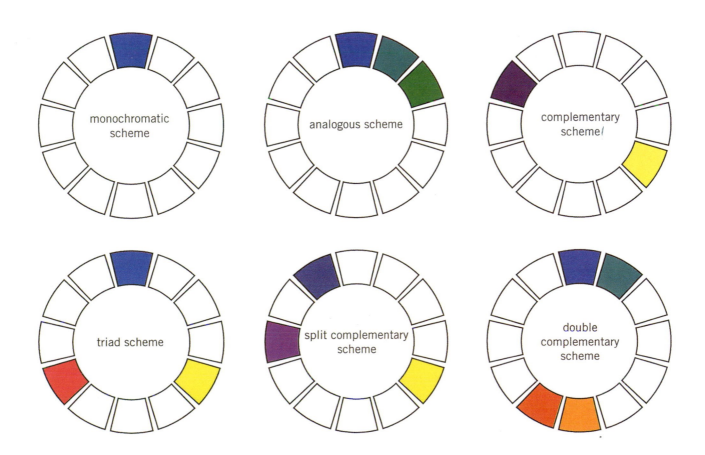

monochromatic scheme

analogous scheme

complementary scheme/

triad scheme

split complementary scheme

double complementary scheme

COMPLEMENTARY COLOR SCHEME Two colors directly opposite each other on the color wheel are referred to as complementary. Red and green or yellow and violet are examples of this arrangement. When designers are looking to enhance the colors in a pattern they often choose the complementary harmony. By placing complements next to each other, the eyes visualize the color as more intense.

SPLIT COMPLEMENTARY COLOR SCHEME A variation on complementary harmony is one that features a basic color along with the two colors on either side of the basic color's complement. Thus, yellow might be used with both blue-violet and red-violet, each of which appears on either side of yellow's complement, violet.

DOUBLE COMPLEMENTARY COLOR SCHEME Another variation on the complementary approach employs two sets of complementary colors. For example, yellow-orange and its complement, blue-violet, may be featured along with yellow-green and its complement, red-violet. Interesting prints often use double complementaries.

TRIADIC COLOR SCHEME In the triadic scheme, three colors, each equidistant from the other two, are used. For example, the three primaries, red, yellow, and blue, are often used in exciting patterns for children's clothing and furnishings.

To understand the various colors, their relationships to each other, and the various combinations or harmonies that can be achieved, see the Color Wheel.

Psychology of Color

Although the basic color theory has a scientific foundation, color selection often involves other considerations. Psychological factors play an important role in the appropriate selection of a particular hue and how it is used in design.

The sense of warmth and coolness projected by color are factors to consider in selecting a color scheme. Although a particular color imparts neither heat nor cold, its presence can create a feeling of warmth or coolness. Blue, green, and violet are considered the **cool colors**; red, orange, and yellow are **warm colors**. A pale blue dress, for example, imparts a cool feeling, while the same dress in red gives off a feeling of warmth.

Another psychological consideration is the emotional effect color has on its observers. Typical reactions to colors include red as a warm, exciting choice; orange as one that provides an earthy feeling; and blue, the favorite of most people, as one with a calming effect. Green generally exudes restfulness, purple drama, and yellow a cheerful atmosphere.

It is up to the product designer to choose from the color combinations available in fabrics that will best serve his or her designs and the effects the designer would like to achieve for the collection.

The intricate manipulation of the various elements creates designs of distinction. Blending fabrics with the right feel and appearance with specific silhouettes, detailing the timely skirt lengths and waistline treatments, perfectly accenting them with decorative enhancements, and coloring them in attractive combinations all contribute to motivating the consumer to purchase.

Designers have always tried to package these various elements creatively. Some have succeeded; others have failed. A few have been lucky enough to create signatures that are immediately recognized by consumers. For example, Fortuny's pleated fabrics made his designs immediately recognizable. Few fashion enthusiasts required label verification for a Fortuny. Of course, not many have achieved such distinction.

YVES SAINT LAURENT

A legend in his own time, Yves Saint Laurent has been one of the most innovative fashion designers. Unlike many designers, Saint Laurent has no single design element as his trademark. He is a master of all design elements.

Born in 1936, he was 17 when he showed his drawings to the editor of *Vogue*, who then selected several for the magazine. After winning his first prize in fashion in the Concours du Secretariat de la Laine for a cocktail dress design, he was introduced to Christian Dior. His initial collection at the House of Dior, which featured the now-famous trapeze design, made him an international success.

In 1961, Saint Laurent left Dior to establish his own fashion house. Since that first collection, the company has grown considerably. Not only does he produce haute couture, but he is also responsible for worldwide distribution of many products bearing his signature, such as hosiery, scarves, ties, shoes, furs, men's apparel, millinery, handbags, jewelry, belts, and fragrances. His work has been recognized by numerous awards, including the Neiman Marcus and Harper's Bazaar awards.

Saint Laurent entered prêt-à-porter in 1966 with the opening of Rive Gauche in Paris. All of the styles sold in the store are designed by him. Today there are more than 100 Rive Gauche shops throughout the world, in such places as the United States, Europe, Canada, Japan, and Australia.

In addition to the much heralded trapeze, Saint Laurent has received accolades for his famous peacoat, his use of the tunic, the abstractions of his Mondrian collection, his pop art dresses, beaded minidresses, Russian peasant look, see-through look, and his dramatic, extravagant ball gowns.

Although designing couture for an adoring public has occupied a significant amount of his time, Saint Laurent has also designed costumes for the theater and for movies. His endeavors include costumes for numerous ballets choreographed by Roland Petit, for whose production he also designed the stage sets; Edward Albee's *A Delicate Balance*; and the revues of the French star Zizi Jeanmaire. His movie credits include costumes for Sophia Loren in *Arabesque*, Claudia Cardinale in *The Pink Panther*, and Catherine Deneuve in *Belle de Jour*.

His achievements have been recognized in the exhibition Yves Saint Laurent, 28 Annees de Creation at the Museum of Soviet Artists in Moscow and in the Costume Institute of the Metropolitan

Yves Saint Laurent gained immediate prominence when he succeeded the legendary Christian Dior.

Museum of Art in New York, by the publication of *Yves Saint Laurent par Yves Saint Laurent* in Russian, and by a retrospective in the Art Gallery of New South Wales in Sydney, Australia.

In 2002, Saint Laurent retired from haute couture designing with a retrospective runway show and closed his couture house. In the words of his partner, Pierre Bergé, Saint Laurent's retirement was "the end of a miracle."

Yves Saint Laurent has ingeniously employed all of the elements. A World of Fashion Profile outlines his achievements. Table 17.1 features a selection of designers and the specific elements that have brought them recognition.

PRINCIPLES OF DESIGN

Whether designers are developing a collection of dresses or suits, footwear or jewelry, or fashions for the home, they must be properly schooled in the principles of design. To capture the eye of the observer, the product must be properly executed in terms of balance, emphasis, proportion, rhythm, and harmony. Each design must effectively use these principles to create a successful product.

Table 17.1

SELECTED DESIGNERS AND SIGNATURE DESIGNS OR DESIGN ELEMENTS

Designer	Designs or Design Elements
Adolfo (1933–)	Chanel-inspired knit suits.
Armani, Giorgio (1934–)	Menswear tailoring; easy shapes; use of neutrals such as taupe, beige, black, and gray.
Balenciaga (1895–1972)	Architectural construction; cocoon coats; chemise; semifitted suit jackets.
Barnes, Jhane (1954–)	Intricate fabrics; innovative details.
Beene, Geoffrey (1927–)	Emphasis on cut and line; innovative use of fabrics and textures.
Blass, Bill (1922–)	Refined cut, expert tailoring.
Cardin, Pierre (1922–)	Nude look; metal body jewelry; unisex astronaut suits.
Cashin, Bonnie (1915–2000)	Layered separates; use of jersey, leathers, tweeds.
Chanel, Coco (1883–1971)	Chanel suit (collarless jacket, trimmed with braid); wool jersey dresses with white collars and cuffs; pea jackets; bell-bottom trousers; fake stones; multiple strands of pearls and gold chains; quilted handbags with shoulder chain; beige slingback pumps with black tips; flat black hairbows.
Courrèges, André (1923–)	Short, white boots; industrial zippers; sunglasses with slit "tennis ball" lenses; squared-off dresses ending above the knee.
de la Renta, Oscar (1932–)	Romantic evening clothes in opulent fabrics; sophisticated daywear.
Dior, Christian (1905–1957)	New Look (rounded shoulders, tiny waists, voluminous, spreading skirts); H-, A-, and Y-line silhouettes.
Ellis, Perry (1940–1986)	Use of natural fibers; hand-knitted sweaters.
Ferré, Gianfranco (1944–)	Sculptured and fluid evening gowns.
Fortuny (1871–1949)	Pleated fabrics; Delphos dress; Peplos (two-piece version of Delphos dress).
Gaultier, Jean-Paul (1952–)	Mix of fabrics; overscaled garments.
Gernreich, Rudi (1922–1985)	Stark cuts; striking color combinations; bold graphic patterns; "No-bra" bra; topless bathing suit; multiple cutouts on swimsuits.
Grès, Alix (1903–1993)	Draped silhouette; often cutouts at midriff; jersey day dresses with cowl necklines; deep-cut or dolman sleeves; kimono-shaped coats.
Halston (1932–1990)	Long cashmere dress with sweater tied over the shoulders; combination of wrap skirt and turtleneck; evening caftans; long, slinky haltered jerseys; introduced Ultrasuede.
Johnson, Betsey (1942–)	Body-conscious clothes; clinging T-shirt dress; clear vinyl slip dress.
Julian, Alexander (1948–)	Unusual and intricate fabrics in multiple colors (as many as 16 in some designs).
Kamali, Norma (1945–)	Body-conscious clothes; giant removable shoulder pads; use of sweatshirt fabrics; draped and shirred jumpsuits in parachute fabrics; down coats.
Karan, Donna (1948–)	Simple silhouettes; classic sportswear looks with stylish edge (well-cut pants; strong coats; sarong skirts; easy dresses).
Kawakubo, Rei (1942–)	Asymmetrical shapes; cotton, canvas, and linen fabrics; torn and slashed; neutral tones; some subtle touches of color.
Klein, Anne (1923–1974)	Recognized suitability of sportswear to lifestyle of American women; interrelated wardrobe pieces of blazers, skirts, pants; sweaters with slinky jersey dresses.
Klein, Calvin (1942–)	Spare, sportswear-based shapes; luxurious natural fibers; leathers, suedes; earth tones and neutrals.
Lacroix, Christian (1951–)	Theatrical, witty clothes; fantastic accessories; pouf silhouette.
Lagerfeld, Karl (1938–)	Removes clothes from their usual context (elaborate embroidery on cotton for couture); mixes wearable clothes with dash of wit (silk dresses with tennis shoes).
Lauren, Ralph (1939–)	Classic silhouettes, superb fabric; fine workmanship; creates upper-crust lifestyles.
McCardell, Claire (1905–1958)	Simple, functional clothes with clean lines; menswear detailing; topstitching; rivets, gripper fastenings; cotton denim, ticking, gingham, and wool jersey; monastic dress; popover; draped bathing suit; ballet slippers worn with day clothes.
McFadden, Mary (1938–)	Fine pleating and quilted fabrics.
Missoni (Rosita: 1931–) (Ottavio: 1921–)	Geometric and abstract knit patterns; bold and multiple color combinations.
Mizrahi, Isaac (1961–)	Young and inventive clothing; unexpected use of fabrics and colors; inspired by McCardell; no longer designing for clothing market.
Montana, Claude (1949–)	Wedge-shaped silhouette, leathers.

Table 17.1 (*continued*)

Norell, Norman (1900–1972)	First to show long evening skirts topped with sweaters; cloth coats lined with fur for day and evening; smoking robe; jumpers and pantsuits; long, shimmering sequined evening dresses.
Oldham, Todd (1961–)	Unconventional colors, prints, beading, and embroidery; whimsical; mix of commercial and offbeat.
Poiret, Paul (1879–1944)	Introduced first straight-line dress; invented the harem and hobble skirts (so narrow at hem that walking was almost impossible); minaret skirt.
Pucci, Emilio (1914–1992)	Brilliant signature prints inspired by heraldic banners; chemises of thin silk jersey (wrinkle-resistant).
Quant, Mary (1934–)	Initiated ideas that are now commonplace (denim, colored flannel, vinyl); miniskirts.
Rabanne, Paco (1934–)	Dresses made of plastic discs linked with metal chains; plastic jewelry and sun goggles in primary colors; fur and leather patches.
Rhodes, Zandra (1940–)	Soft fabrics (chiffon, tulle, silk); hand-screened prints; edges finished with pinking shears; glamorized punk designs; flounced hems finished with uneven scallops.
Rykiel, Sonia (1930–)	Sweaters and sweater looks cut close to the body.
Saint Laurent, Yves (1936–)	Fisherman's shirt; trapeze silhouette; Mondrian dress; see-through blouse; longuette; evening tuxedo; peacoat; Russian peasant look, pantsuits; no longer designing for clothing market.
Sander, Jil (1943–)	Pure and sensual; highest quality in materials and craftsmanship; expert tailoring in suits and coats.
Schiaparelli, Elsa (1890–1973)	Workclothes fabrics for evening wear; colored plastic zippers as decorative features; ceramic buttons in the shape of hands or butterflies; shaped hats in lamb chops or a pink-heeled shoe; avant-garde sweaters with tattoo or skeleton motifs; glowing phosphorescent brooches and handbags that lit up or played tunes when opened; fastened clothing with colored zippers, jeweler-designed buttons, padlocks, clips, dog leashes.
Sui, Anna (1955–)	Maintains a moderate price structure; mix of hip and haute couture.
Tyler, Richard (1948–)	Custom tailoring; graceful cut.
Ungaro, Emanuel (1933–)	Soft fabrics; several and different prints in a single outfit; layers; body-conscious clothes.
Valentino (1932–)	Simple, elegant; well-cut sophisticated sportswear; entrance-making evening clothes.
Versace, Gianni (1946–1997)	Vivid, imaginative, sexy clothes.
Vionnet, Madeleine (1876–1975)	Eliminated high, boned collars from dresses and blouses; bias-cut, eliminating need for fastenings; seams finished with fagoting.
Westwood, Vivienne (1941–)	Designs evidence of fierce rejection of polite standards of dress.
Yamamoto, Yohji (1943–)	Asymmetrical hems and collars; holes and torn edges.
Zoran (1947–)	Limited color range (black, gray, white, ivory, and red); prefers not to use buttons and zippers; avoids extraneous details.

Balance

In its strictest sense, **balance** is the equal distribution of weight on two sides. Absolute balance, however, sometimes leads to designs that lack creativity. Of course, some designs benefit from this approach.

To achieve balance, create a central line for the design. This line may be a real dividing point, as in the case of a man's shirt that is open down the middle and uses button closures, or one that the designer's eye imagines as the center. In either case, trim or ornamentation may be used to formally or informally balance the item. **Symmetrical balance**, most often used in apparel design, uses two identical enhancements on either side of the design, such as patch pockets of equal size. **Asymmetrical balance** might be achieved by the garment's pattern. For example, one side of a sweater might use a single large flower, while the other side uses several smaller flowers. If properly used, the eye sees it as a balanced arrangement.

In home furnishings, bedding displays might use two identical pillows to achieve a basic formal balance, with other shapes, more casually placed on either side of the

Left: The trim calls attention to the design. Right: The one-shoulder neckline becomes the focal point of the design.

imaginary line, to provide interest. Ralph Lauren, in room designs that feature his bedding collections, uses different sizes and shapes of pillows to create an asymmetrical balance.

Emphasis

Drawing attention to a particular area of a product is central to its success. Designers generally choose one area of a garment to feature. This is known as the focal point. If too many areas of interest are given equal attention, the eye will not know where to focus and attention will be lost.

Emphasis is achieved in a number of ways. It might be the neckline or the back of a dress that captures the eye, as, for example, when British designer Vivienne Westwood added bustles to her dresses. It could also be the fullness of a skirt enhanced with petticoats that attracts attention, or some trimming, such as intricate beading. Often, emphasis is achieved through coloration, alternating stripes, or the use of an unusual pattern or print. Contrasting fabrics might provide the necessary emphasis or focal point—for example, the collar on a jacket might be in a different fabric from the rest of the garment.

A successful designer must know how to achieve this emphasis without too many confusing elements.

Proportion

The various elements in the design should be scaled in size to fit its overall **proportion**. For example, the size of the trimmings should be in proportion to the dress they are enhancing. A flower that is too large for a dress may detract from the silhouette, neckline, or other detailing. A belt that is too wide or narrow to suit the garment becomes a disproportionate accent that ruins the silhouette.

Contrasting fabrics in designs for haute couture and ready-to-wear.

In room settings, home fashions are used to enhance a setting. Their proportion must be in line with the furniture in the room or the overall appearance suffers. A mirror that is very large will appear disproportionate when placed over a very small chest.

Rhythm

Although focal point is an important part of any design and is used to attract attention, the consumer must observe and evaluate the entire product. If the details and embellishments have been carefully placed, a sense of **rhythm** will move the eye from one element to the other. Rhythm can be achieved through numerous techniques.

ALTERNATION When light and dark colors are contrasted or when stripes of two colors are employed, alternation in rhythm is the result. The eye manages to focus on the alternating colors, eventually leading the observer to view the entire product.

RADIATION With a sunburst effect, the eye moves from the central point of the sunburst to the outer portions of the design. Imagine a circular ornament that is centered on a handbag. The viewer is first attracted to the ornament, and then the eye moves to the outer edges of the design.

The polka-dot pattern moves the eye over the garment.

PROGRESSION The use of a single color that is featured in a gradation of the darkest to the lightest tone imparts rhythmic **progression**. The eye will automatically move from the darkest to the lightest tones, or the reverse, and draw attention to the complete item. Sometimes a design will use a specific shape for its trim in a variety of sizes. The gradation of the shapes will tend to bring the eye from one to the other, and eventually to all of the garment.

REPETITION **Repetition** involves moving the eye in any direction through the placement of many of the same shapes. Dots in a polka-dot fabric, for example, cause the viewer to move throughout the design. Repetition of some enhancements, such as rhinestones, throughout the garment also tends to make the eye examine the entire object.

CONTINUOUS LINE When some of the elements of the design are connected by a linear device, **continuous line** rhythm is accomplished. If flower ornaments that are part of a design are connected to each other with vines, the eye moves from flower to flower and throughout the garment.

Harmony

Achieving a unified effect requires a degree of cohesiveness among all of the elements in the design project. The relationship of the appropriate shapes in the fabric's pattern or the trimmings, for example, must be in harmony with the rest of the elements. Although there is safety when the absolute rules of harmony are followed, it sometimes

KARL LAGERFELD

Karl Lagerfeld has achieved distinction as the creative force behind numerous collections. In addition to his own signature collection, Lagerfeld creates designs for Chanel and furs for Fendi.

Lagerfeld came to the attention of the fashion world by winning the first prize for women's coat design in a contest sponsored by the International Wool Secretariat. With that achievement, he was hired as an apprentice to Pierre Balmain, where he stayed until he became the chief designer for Patou. He became prominent with his affiliation with Chloë, who produced ready-to-wear with an air of haute couture. Completely in

charge of design, he created clothing with an airy look, much of which was hand painted. It was the femininity of his designs that captured the fashion world's attention.

Leaving Chloë after many years, he established a company bearing his now-famous signature, while still designing for some of the most prestigious fashion houses.

His personal charm and extraordinary presence when coupled with his creative genius make Lagerfeld one of fashion's leaders. How many designers are capable of creating simultaneous collections, each with a different focus?

Karl Lagerfeld designs under his own label, for Chanel, and for Fendi.

results in a dull design. This can be avoided by adding elements that lend excitement. A simple black dress might receive more attention if it is trimmed with gold braid rather than black piping. Karl Lagerfeld is a master at introducing surprise elements in his collections. His accomplishments are featured in a World of Fashion Profile.

Creatively using variety or an element of surprise transforms the mundane into something more exciting. A basic blazer, for example, is considered to be a classic in any woman's wardrobe. Although these garments are extremely serviceable, they are not very exciting. In the early 1990s, designer Joannie Criscione transformed the blazer into a high-fashion item and catapulted her company to success. She unconventionally scattered rhinestones on a woolen blazer and made fashion headlines. The item ran for several years, bringing significant profits to her company, and was eventually knocked off at many lower price points. Although this design treatment might not fit the traditional concept of harmony, it proves that creativity often adds appeal to the product.

DEVELOPMENT OF THE LINE OR COLLECTION

In developing every collection, a designer must follow various stages to bring a concept to market. These stages include creating the design, costing the garment, and preparing a timetable for production that begins with selecting fabric and concludes with filling the orders.

Stages of Development

The designer or design team prepares numerous sketches for the line. Many are rejected, but the surviving ones are eventually transformed into patterns and then into samples. After each sample has been constructed, it becomes part of the initial or preliminary line.

The actual designs may be rendered by hand or by means of a CAD (computer-aided design) system. These systems enable designers to create, color, recolor, and modify the designs in a fraction of the time that it takes to do this by hand. There are numerous companies and CAD systems to choose from.

At this point, the line is shown to store buyers. Those items that receive favorable attention and are ordered by the buyers head for the production line. Patterns are made and graded for different sizes, and items that do not generate orders are eliminated. Once the items have been cut and assembled, they are trimmed and prepared for shipment to retailers. If an item is particularly successful, reorders are placed and filled. Items that sell initially but are not reordered are pulled from the line. As production continues during a season, the development of next season's collection is taking shape, and the cycle starts all over again.

In the development of the line, each garment must be costed by determining the expenses of factors such as materials, trimmings, labor, packaging, production, sales, and freight. Only then will the company know how much to charge to turn a profit. The various stages, briefly discussed here, are fully examined in Chapter 18.

Sketches are the basis for every designer's collection.

Timetable

The time it takes to develop a line varies from company to company. Those who create original designs spend more time in the development stages than those who specialize in knockoffs, or copies of items that are already in the marketplace. Such factors as location of production, whether it is domestic or offshore, and fabric sourcing affect the time it takes to produce a line and ship it to the retailers.

A typical interval from design inception to store delivery is six to nine months for domestically produced merchandise. In the case of offshore production, the timetable may be considerably longer.

Working six months or two seasons ahead, a typical calendar for a domestically produced line for the fall season is as follows:

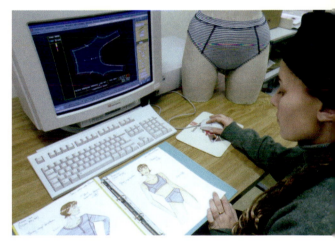

Designs are often created on CAD systems.

JANUARY Fabrics are selected for the new season. Designers prepare their sketches and have them translated into sample garments.

FEBRUARY Samples are adjusted and improved. New designs might be created to broaden the line, while others might be deleted. The new designs are produced as samples.

MARCH Final decisions are made on fabric selection and the full line is readied for buyers. The actual time of store purchasing varies. Some accounts buy early during market week to get the company's first shipments; others wait until the lines have been narrowed and the slow-selling items have been eliminated.

APRIL Early production of ordered garments begins. Sales to the buyers continue in the showrooms and on the road.

MAY This is the heaviest period for placement of orders by buyers. Production continues to fill orders that indicate early delivery dates.

JUNE The major period for production is now in progress. The first orders for early fall delivery are shipped to the stores.

JULY Production is at its peak, and more stores are receiving the merchandise.

AUGUST This is the major shipping period. Production activity varies according to particular style activity. Slower-selling items are taken from the line, and the remainder of the production shifts into full swing for reorders.

SEPTEMBER Reorder activity dominates the production schedule. Most initial orders have been shipped to the stores.

OCTOBER The season ends, and the last store reorders are completed.

Quality Control

One of the major problems faced by manufacturers during the production stages involves **quality control**. If the finished product varies from what was initially expected, customer returns are inevitable. This significantly affects the company's profits. Such elements as construction specifics, material quality, and finished product measurements must be carefully assessed.

The quality control process involves three phases: defining the quality requirements of the company's products in terms of what the customer's expectations will be; determining the methodology used in the assessment of the goods; and setting specific goals and measuring the outcome.

Whether the system employed involves 100 percent inspection, spot checking, or some other technique, it is imperative that checking be an ongoing process. In the aforementioned timetable, quality checking is undertaken during each month that production takes place.

Characteristics of the Line

Designers and manufacturers must determine the scope of their collections; that is, how many individual items should be featured for each season, whether or not a theme will be featured throughout the line, whether specific colors will be exclusively used, and so on. Each company has its own direction for the characteristics of the line.

Themes

A theme is sometimes depicted in terms of the silhouettes that will be featured, a particular color range, or fabric usage. Each season, haute couture as well as lower price point collections generally rely on an overall theme. Carole Little, for example, primarily uses prints as the theme for her collections and has established this as her trademark. Often, there are several themes within a line, which are presented as groups. Several items, generally six to ten, are shown together in a specific fabric, color, pattern, or shape. In this way, the company is able to appeal to a broader group of buyers.

Fashion Direction

In the fashion industry, a designer rarely appeals to every segment of the market. He or she must decide on a fashion direction. For example, the emphasis might be on a fashion-forward innovation or on a more classic design. Whereas fashion-forward ideas often generate excitement, the more classic components of the line generally bring long-term profits.

Single Items

Throughout the industry, many manufacturers produce copies of items that were best-sellers at higher price points. These items are called knockoffs. No relationship exists among the various items on the line. Because these individual styles have proven themselves in terms of sales, the manufacturer is generally assured of winners. The basic style is faithfully copied, using less expensive fabrics and lower-quality production. Companies that specialize in these clones often employ a merchandising stylist who scouts the market looking for hot items. After the stylist selects the style, he or she researches the textile and trimmings suppliers for less costly materials that can be used in production.

The absence of a highly paid designer and the elimination of the costs involved in producing unproven items makes this type of operation relatively low in risk.

Coordinated Items

In the sportswear industry, designers create a variety of items that may be worn together. The separates concept enables store buyers to select those pieces that best suit their customers' needs. Each group of coordinates might feature two skirt silhouettes in different lengths; two or three pants styles in different widths, a variety of waistbands, with or without pleats; several tops; and one or two jackets.

Designer Spec Sheets

Once the designer has selected all of the elements that will be used in his or her design, the final step before production begins is to complete a spec sheet. A spec sheet is a compilation of all of the costs required to transform the design into a finished product.

The form usually contains a flat sketch of the design and the costs of the fabrics and trimmings that will be used. Most spec sheets are now computer generated. When the forms are completed, they are sent to management, which establishes the wholesale prices.

The Point of View article "Computer Spec Sheets Cut Down on Paperwork and Errors" at the end of this chapter examines the use and benefits of today's computer spec sheets.

CHAPTER HIGHLIGHTS

- After the designer has been inspired to move in a particular direction, he or she must focus on selecting the appropriate fabrics and other materials.

- Designers must be fully knowledgeable in the elements that constitute well-designed merchandise. These elements include the silhouette, details and trimmings, texture, and color.

- The designer must also be concerned with the principles of design, including balance, emphasis, proportion, rhythm, and harmony.

- For each individual style, samples must be constructed and evaluated before the product is readied for production.

- A production timetable is established that begins with the selection of fabrics to be used in the samples and ends when the last reorders are filled.

IMPORTANT FASHION TERMINOLOGY AND CONCEPTS

alternation	hue	secondary colors
analogous color scheme	intensity	shades
asymmetrical balance	monochromatic color	spec sheet
balance	scheme	split complementary
color theory	neutrals	color scheme
color wheel	Prang Color System	symmetrical balance
complementary color scheme	primary colors	texture
continuous line	progression	tints
cool colors	proportion	triadic color scheme
double complementary	quality control	value
color scheme	radiation	warm colors
emphasis	repetition	
harmony	rhythm	

FOR REVIEW

1. What are some of the elements that constitute a collection's theme?
2. What are the five silhouettes on which women's apparel designs are based?
3. Define the terms *hue, value*, and *intensity* and explain their impact on a design.
4. What is the difference between a tint and a shade?
5. How can a monochromatic color scheme add interest to its coloration?
6. Which color combination uses two hues that are adjacent to each other on the color wheel?
7. If a designer wants to use two colors that will intensify each other when placed next to each other, which type of combination should be used?
8. Explain and compare the different color schemes used by designers.
9. What is meant by the term *triadic color scheme*?
10. How do symmetrical and asymmetrical balance differ from each other?
11. Describe why it is important for a design to have a focal point.
12. By what means may rhythm in design be achieved?
13. How long is the timetable for domestically produced fashion merchandise?
14. Why has Target started to concentrate more than ever before on color, according to Denise Power's Point of View article?

EXERCISES AND PROJECTS

1. Design a color wheel using color-aid paper or paint chips, available at any commercial paint store. An alternative would be to use colored markers.
2. Bring a man's, woman's, or child's garment to class and present an oral discussion on the various elements that were used in that product's design.

3. Using fashion magazines, select two items that use symmetrical balance in their design and two that use asymmetrical balance. Mount the pictures on foamboard and describe to the class the reasons these designs do or do not work.

4. Bring to class three pieces of fashion merchandise that represent different color combinations. Describe their effects to the class.

WEB SITES

By accessing these Web sites, you will be able to gain broader knowledge and up-to-date information on materials related to this chapter.

Committee for Colour Trends
  www.colour-trends.com

The Color Association of the United States
  www.colorassociation.com

The Case of the Undecided Manufacturer

Amanda Gallop has been working in the fashion industry for 10 years. When she graduated from college, she remained with the company at which she had served an internship. The company, Litt, Inc. has been in business for 35 years and has regularly shown a profit. Its forte was producing knockoffs of best-selling items at significantly lower price points.

Amanda came up through the ranks, beginning as an assistant to the stylist and assuming the stylist role when her supervisor retired. The job involved scouting the marketplace for best-selling products and transforming them into items that could be sold at lower price points. Her daily routine included visiting high-fashion stores that would most likely feature the latest in fashion at upscale prices, calling on the fabrics and trimmings houses to find materials that could be used in the production of the knockoffs, and the rearrangement of some of the design elements to give the products individuality. She was extremely successful in the position and was responsible for many of the "winners" in the Litt, Inc. line.

Three months ago, Gallop inherited a significant amount of money. Her immediate reaction to the inheritance was to open her own manufacturing company. With her experience in the field, she might be a success.

Although her experience was exclusively in the area of cloning best-sellers, she thought that she had sufficient expertise to design original collections. After all, she knew how to recognize good design, had a complete knowledge of the fabrics and trimmings arenas, and knew about manufacturing procedures.

After many discussions with professionals in the industry about the direction the new company should take, she still has not reached a final decision.

questions

Which direction should Amanda take, and why?

Target's Color Story

DENISE POWER

Minneapolis—When Target puts its fall private label apparel collections on the selling floors in a few months, a greater share of the merchandise is likely to get a higher approval rating from shoppers, store buyers and the designers behind the collection.

That's because Target has begun creating garments with a new technology that yields colors that come closer to the original visions of designers, rather than merely being a close approximation.

A garment in the latter category is referred to internally as a "best can do," and it's what retailers must accept when a mill fails to achieve a specified color, and production deadlines close in.

Before Target introduced a new color development process, buyers settled for the off-shade "best can dos" for private label merchandise about 30 percent of the time. Since revamping the process, and leveraging sophisticated color measurement tools, the track record has improved, with only 5 percent of private label merchandise failing to meet exacting color specifications, according to Keith Hoover, manager of color services. Hoover oversees color development for the Target, Mervyn's California and Marshall Field's divisions as well as Associated Merchandising, the New York-based apparel sourcing and product development company. All of these units are divisions of Target Corp.

"Color is the first thing you see when you walk into a store," he said. "And you don't even have to buy anything to get a bad impression if colors are substandard or inconsistent within a collection. By contrast, a product's other attributes, such as fabric shrinkage or color fastness, do not become evident until after the item is purchased and brought home."

The new color development process used at Target not only improved the frequency with which color specifications were met, but it greatly streamlined each stage, from the conception of color palettes for a brand to the often-arduous lab dip approval process. Mills perform lab dips and submit the resulting dyed fabric samples to retailers to demonstrate they can achieve a prescribed color.

Too often, about 70 percent of the time at Target, that initial lab dip had failed to meet color requirements and a second and third round of dyed fabric samples exchanged hands before the exact color was achieved, or the retailer was forced to accept an inferior color. This was as much due to quality control at the mills as it was inadequate color management and communications processes at Target, Hoover said.

The new process resulted in a dramatic improvement in initial lab dip approvals, from 30 percent of first submissions accepted last year to 60 percent of first submissions accepted as of last month.

"This new process puts an emphasis on speed," Hoover said. "'Speed is life' is an internal Target philosophy and the color development process has traditionally been a drag, taking longer than anyone wants," he said.

Hoover outlined some of the key improvements in the process and noted that the system revealed new ways for Target to work with vendors and mills more effectively.

Adding a color coordinator has helped the process, he explained. Under the old method, design teams for each of Target's 15 brand groups developed colors for a collection in a vacuum. Because one team was unaware of the colors created by another team, it was possible for duplication or near-duplication to occur across brands.

Under the new process, a color coordinator reviews all color proposals from designers and eliminates redundancy. At the same time, the color coordinator evaluates each proposed color, from a production standpoint, to weed out those color-fabric combinations that may be almost impossible to reproduce with a high degree of consistency.

New technology has also helped the process. Target invested in a suite of color measurement applications and instruments from Datacolor of Lawrenceville, N.J., that enables it to communicate effectively with international vendors and mills. Because information is exchanged electronically, instead of via fax, approvals and changes can be communicated rapidly and all users' computer monitors are calibrated to the same color specifications.

In addition, analysts are currently tested on visual acuity, to confirm they have the skills to verify whether a lab dip dyed sample meets Target's color specifications.

The mass discounter is leveraging the color measurement technology and simultaneously modifying its process of evaluating lab dip samples. Under the old process, color analysts would visually examine samples and reject those that appeared unacceptable; this practice of relying solely on an analyst's subjective judgment led to some samples being rejected incorrectly, Hoover said.

Now, Target's first step in evaluating a fabric sample is to use color measurement technology to determine whether a sample falls within an acceptable range; if it does, a visual review follows. If the piece falls outside the designated range, the mill is notified and no color analyst's time is wasted examining the piece.

The result, he added, has been that samples that are significantly off shade are identified more efficiently and the vendor is instructed to investigate and resolve the problem with the mill. This frees up Target color analysts to focus their efforts on those samples that are very close to meeting specification.

In the end, it's about speed, Hoover said. With better controls at each stage of the color development process, Target can respond faster to market trends by accommodating shorter time frames for fashion-sensitive apparel. The company expects to extend the new color development process to hardlines this summer.

Women's Wear Daily, February 7, 2001

Computer Spec Sheets Cut Down on Paperwork and Errors

ALISON GRUDIER

In order for a designer or product developer to convey a design idea to a manufacturer, a specification form has to be generated detailing everything from the concept sketch to measurements to fabric and trim information. A new generation of computer software is giving apparel companies the ability to make the process of communication clearer and faster.

The key element in these informational computer-aided design programs is a relational database for recording and recalling the particular details of a garment. Programs also include basic drawing and coloring tools for garment illustrations as well as spreadsheets for capturing and calculating graded measurements.

Where once designers and assistants would spend hours drawing and photocopying sketches and writing measurements, now they are able to recall similar styles from past seasons, make the necessary modifications and transmit the new information electronically to the manufacturer. All of the necessary information can be captured in one location for access by anyone who needs it.

"We have seen greater standardization of information," said Kevin McIntosh, costing manager at the Gap. "It has helped the vendors know where to find the right information on a form whether it is for the Gap, GapKids, Banana Republic or Old Navy divisions."

Bill McMeley, director of product development and production control at Glen Oaks Industries agreed.

"By using a common database, we can quickly populate a new form and get the order in the system faster. We can pull information from our pattern making system to calculate finished garment measurements."

Gui Baltar, designer and program manager at Tail, Inc., a golf and tenniswear manufacturer, notes that his company has been saving time "by a factor of four."

"Before, we had to fill out four forms for each style," he said. "Now, we fill out one set of data and it quickly generates all four forms with more accuracy than our manual methods."

Whether manufacturing domestically or abroad, the ability to transmit data quickly is an absolute necessity. At the Gap, quality assurance inspectors use laptop computers in Hong Kong to call in from the factory to receive the latest version of a spec sheet. The inspection results are available immediately to the merchandiser in San Francisco.

"This has been a tremendous benefit that was only a vision when we started the project four years ago," McIntosh said.

In private-label manufacturing, managing the communications between the customer and the manufacturer can create a huge paper trail. At Glen Oaks, all communications from the customer are scanned in and maintained in the computer specification file.

"Any time we need information on a style, it is immediately available in one central place," McMeley said. "We're eliminating redundancies. The majority of the copies that were distributed on paper were never looked at; only 10% were really needed."

Despite its benefits, users of product data management software say the conversion to the technology is far from painless. Converting from paper files to electronic files can be a long and tedious process. Deciding which information is necessary, how to organize it and doing data entry takes many meetings and manhours.

"A company is being optimistic if they think they can do it in less than two years," McIntosh said.

McMeley agreed.

"We want to create a database of technical 'how-to' drawings but just haven't had the time," he said.

"The first season, we had to work with both hand and computer information," Baltar explained. "This season, we hope to have everything done on computer."

Companies like Reebok, Charming Shoppes and Mast Industries have experimented with developing their own spec sheet programs with varying degrees of success. With off-the-shelf computer pro-

grams like Lotus 1–2-3 and Aldus Illustrator, users can create computerized forms. However, these are sometimes little more than typewritten forms. Though they look more professional, they are no faster or easier to create. Programs written for the apparel industry have easy-to-use features such as topstitching, drawing tools and grade rule tables for measurements in fractions instead of decimals.

Regardless of how the information is computerized, the change is a great management tool, users said.

"This is an ideal time to take a very critical look at what you are doing. We probably changed 50 percent of what we had been creating. Not because we had to, but because when we really looked at it, a lot of what was being done was unnecessary. It's easy to get comfortable in an established system and the computer was just a good excuse to examine those systems."

While the programs are paring paperwork for users, use of paper is up.

"We're actually using more paper. We just have so much more capacity to provide information," Baltar said. "Before, we didn't have a fabrication form. Now, we do. We never gave full measurements on every style. Now we do."

"Merchandisers are reluctant to give up their paper files, but we're hoping that as they grow more used to the electronic files, we can stop printing so much," McIntosh said.

Users are generally pleased with the product specification programs. The programs, they say, make labor-intensive tasks prone to human error much easier to manage.

"Speed is what it's about these days," added Andre Bernard, systems analyst for Reebok. "We can't keep up without using computers to manage all this information."

The Fashion Group International, Inc.

PDM: Simplifying Product Development

DAVID MOIN

With retailers growing their private label assortments, the demands on manufacturers are mounting.

They have to speed production, raise quality standards and work [more closely] with buyers who, during the production cycle, often direct changes in design, whether it's replacing a fabric or a trim, altering a sleeve or giving new instructions on folding garments for packaging.

Communicating this myriad information can be a dilemma, leading to miscommunications, mistakes in production and the dreaded chargeback.

But product data management systems, provided by such companies as Gerber Information Systems and Animated Images, are making life easier for a growing number of apparel suppliers and retailers. Some apparel firms have devised product management systems through their own MIS departments.

In any case, such systems collate all the product data on a single program, forming an "electronic filing cabinet" of a few dozen forms that can be viewed by anyone who needs to have access.

For example, Gerber's Product Data Management (PDM) is a package with

easy-to-read forms, including designer illustrations and notes, grading sheets, cost sheets, cutting tickets, confirmation letters and photographs. The forms are stored in a windows environment, neatly organizing all the fabric, sketch, pattern and labor information.

In the apparel/retail industry, the automation of product development is a relatively new phenomenon. Last September, Gerber Garment Technology acquired Microdynamics, which started developing PDM around 1989. The Gerber Informations Systems division was formed after the acquisition.

It's only been in the past two years that PDM has really caught on, and it's now considered the standard in the industry and an important element of Quick Response.

PDM has been embraced by Macy's, the American Retail Group, the GJM division of Cygne, J. Crew, Eddie Bauer, Bugle Boy and Talbots, among other companies. According to Gerber, roughly 150 companies, with a total of about 2,000 workstations around the world, use PDM.

OshKosh B'Gosh recently bought the system and has installed it in product development, merchandising and design areas, and plans to expand it to factories and contractors. However, many apparel companies still operate manually, with paper spec sheets and other documents that get photocopied and covered with whiteout, as instructions change, and eventually become illegible.

"PDM amounts to accurate and speedier communication, combined with E-mail," said Ken Winer, vice president of MIS, for Winer Industries, a Paterson, N.J.-based $80 million private label supplier to JCPenney Co., Ann Taylor, The Limited and several other retailers.

"There's no paper, no phones, no faxes," Winer said, while noting that PDM files can be printed and faxed to companies that are not on the system. He compared PDM to EDI, which triggers reorders when retailers and suppliers communicate sales data "computer to computer," but added, "PDM communicates person to person through E-mail."

As part of its business, Winer ships blazers, skirts, pants and dresses to the Express division of Limited, which is constantly pushing to develop new products, resetting its selling floors and demanding faster deliveries. Information, including silhouette or fabric changes, sometimes arrives piecemeal, but the data, as Winer

notes, can be sent automatically to all people in the production process, whether it's the pattern maker or a costing executive, giving Winer Industries better control and insuring that the retailer gets what the market demands.

"In a conventional setting, revisions result in duplicate and triplicate copies of paper forms being hand-delivered or faxed, creating a mountain of paper and turning decision makers into file clerks, particularly in the private label business, where the key to success is being flexible to the retailer's demands," Winer said. "PDM handles this by keeping lists of people to notify automatically when a form is changed. If the retailer decides to alter the design, the PDM form affected would be updated by a person. PDM would then automatically send an E-mail to the pattern maker, the purchasing department, the production planning department, etc. The key point is that it's done automatically. No one picked up a phone or made a photocopy or faxed something somewhere. This is 21st-century product."

Discounters, including Wal-Mart, which is expanding its private label Kathie Lee Collection, haven't signed on to PDM. Neither has Dillard Department Stores, May Department Stores, or Sears, Roebuck & Co. Calvin Klein is reportedly phasing it in, but generally major designers are not tuned into the program.

Steve Fineman, director of sales for PDM, said the company expects to double its revenues over the next year, though he wouldn't specify the division's volume.

"What we are trying to accomplish is to speed up the product development cycle, and reduce the time it takes to bring products to market," Fineman said. "In the past, when we talked about Quick Response, that meant faster sewing machines. It takes 10 minutes to sew a

garment, but typically it's an eight-month cycle from conception to going into production."

He contended that PDM can cut weeks out of the cycle.

"We also want to improve the quality through reducing mistakes. Every apparel firm lives in fear of chargebacks," he added.

PDM offers a digital camera, built by Kodak, and priced around $2,000. It provides color snapshots.

Videos can also be transmitted demonstrating how measurements should be taken based on a retailer's preference and other functions.

Penney's tested PDM last year in its men's division, but first installed it in children's wear, after waiting for PDM to make a Windows version available. The chain plans to phase it into women's, men's and home divisions this year. That involves about 100 workstations. On average, it costs $4,000 to $5,000 per workstation, plus ongoing and upgrade costs.

Eric Blackwood, Penney's director of merchandising operations and communications, described the advantages of PDM:

"At Penney's, when our CAD [computer-aided design] fabric, print and design work is done, we put it on the PDM system, filling in the specifications on the preset forms in the system based on type of merchandise. Once that is done, we attach a drawing of the item and also [a picture of] its print, and PDM takes all that information and puts it in one package, which can be transferred by fax or electronically to the supplier. One reason we chose PDM is because it is a PC IBM compatible system, so we can work in most of our mainframe systems with PDM.

"The biggest advantage we see right away is the lack of errors," says Blackwood. "There use[d] to be a lot, when things were faxed or handwritten. On PDM, when a designer makes a correction, they can immediately fax it.

"We might be working with three different companies to produce the same garment or sample. Basically with a punch of a button, a change from a designer can automatically go to those companies.

This is a quantum leap forward. It's a tremendous time saver for designers. This keeps the information correct and flows it to who you want. It used to be done on homemade forms that got faxed. That involved a lot of cutting and pasting."

Blackwood continues, "It also gives our technical designers more capabilities

to do more things than in the past. Before it was the pen and pencil method. Now they can go into the system and retrieve previous designs and make alterations on them [more quickly].

"We hope to have some of our leading partners around the world own this package."

Women's Wear Daily, June 27, 1995

chapter 18

apparel and accessories manufacturing

Designers never made fashion; it's fashionable people who make fashion.

DR. JEAN HOUSTON, RESEARCHER

Before developing a new line or product, a designer researches the concept and takes advice from fashion companies, specialized groups of merchandise fashion forecasters. Once the initial design concepts have been developed, it is time to transform the ideas into salable merchandise.

Each apparel and accessories classification has its own stages of development. Some are fundamental procedures that run across most merchandise products; others are specific to a particular product type. Men's, women's, and children's apparel, for example, generally include the same stages of production, whereas items such as jewelry and shoes require different and specific manufacturing techniques.

The first section of this chapter focuses on the standard procedures used in apparel production. The second section examines the specialized construction techniques used for the production of accessories.

APPAREL MANUFACTURING

The largest segment of the fashion industry produces apparel. To be profitable, manufacturers and designers pay attention to costing the product, the methods used in procuring materials, and the manufacturing process.

Costing the Product

After the designer creates the styles that will make up a collection, the costs of transforming these ideas into products must be determined before any production may begin. Costs for each and every component of the item must be carefully assessed, so that the garment can be properly priced and a profit realized. The slightest error in determining the costs of such items as a garment's lining and its decorative or functional enhancements could result in losses to the company. At first, costs are estimated based on the original sample. Once the decision has been made to go ahead

After you have completed this chapter, you will be able to discuss:

- Production costs for men's, women's, and children's apparel.
- Various production alternatives available to the fashion apparel industry.
- How piece goods are ordered by the manufacturer.
- The stages of apparel production.
- The techniques employed in the manufacture of footwear.
- Some of the manufacturing techniques used in fine and costume jewelry production.
- The four major parts of gloves and how gloves are assembled.
- The stages used in the production of handbags.
- The benefits of quick response.

437

with production, the estimated figures must be transformed into actual costs. In addition to the prices of materials and trimmings, the expenses incurred in production and distribution must also be assessed. Only when these exact figures are calculated will the producer know how much to charge the retailer for the merchandise.

Fabrics

Whether it is the fabric for a dress, leather for a coat, or skins for a fur garment, the exact amount needed for each unit of production must be determined. Very often, several types of materials are used for a garment. In such cases, each must be individually assessed and figured into the total materials cost. In the case of a ball gown, not only will the cost of the primary material be figured, but also the costs of other fabrics and the lining. The cost of the gown's materials might break down as follows:

6 yards chiffon for skirt ($22.00 per yard)	$132.00
¾ yard brocade for bodice ($16.00 per yard)	12.00
4 yards rayon lining ($1.75 per yard)	7.00
Total cost of materials	$151.00

Trimmings

Trimmings or adornments must be individually priced. Such items as buttons, zippers, hooks and eyes, beading, appliqué, flowers, and so forth must be included in the cost assessment. Using the same ball gown as a model, the following trimmings are also figured into its cost:

½ yard satin piping for bodice ($4.00 per yard)	$2.00
3 rhinestone buttons ($2.30 each)	6.90
1 14-inch zipper	8.00
Total cost of trimmings	$16.90

Production Labor

The designer selects the appropriate fabric and manipulates it for the proposed design.

The next step is to calculate the production labor costs. These include making, grading, and marking the patterns and cutting and assembling the garment. If the entire process is accomplished in-house and costs are based on hourly wages, the computa-

tion is relatively simple. This approach to production, however, is less frequently used in the industry. Most manufacturers supply some of the production tasks and engage outside contractors for the remainder of the operations. Cutting, for example, may take place in an **inside shop** that the company owns. Sewing and finishing, however, might be sent to an **outside contractor**, who is paid for services rendered. When an outside contractor is used, the cost is generally based on a predetermined schedule that is specified in a contract that is negotiated for a specific number of garments. To determine the real cost of one garment, the total cost must be divided by the number of pieces to be sewn. Continuing with the example of the ball gown, production labor costs would be as follows:

inside cutting ($28.00 per hour) ¼ hour	$7.00
contracted sewing (500 pieces at $15,000)	30.00
finishing ($30.00 per hour) ½ hour	15.00
Total cost of production labor	$52.00

Garment assembling is a key production cost.

Transportation

The cost of freight must also be included for each unit of production. When an entire garment is produced in-house, the expense of moving it from one contractor to another is eliminated; this brings down the cost. As noted earlier, however, this is the exception rather than the rule.

The distance from one production point to another and the time needed for production dictate the type of transportation that will be used. In some cases, U.S. manufacturers use a combination of domestic and offshore production. This results in considerable transportation costs. Manufacturers negotiate contracts with freight companies based on the number of units that will be transported. The actual cost of transportation for each unit is then calculated, so that it can be accurately figured into the final cost of the product.

Distribution

Once the product has been completed, the manufacturer must sell it to the retailer. In the garment industry, two methods are generally used. One involves the maintenance of an **in-house sales staff**; the other the use of manufacturer's representatives who sell the goods in their own facilities. No matter which approach is taken, the cost of selling each product must be figured.

Wholesale Price

Once all of the costs have been assessed, the manufacturer must decide on a markup that covers any additional expenses of doing business, such as rent, utilities, and advertising, and still brings a profit to the company. The markup is the difference between the cost and the **wholesale price**:

wholesale price − cost = manufacturer's markup
$100.00 − $60.00 = $40.00

The markup is expressed as a percentage of the wholesale price. Thus, in the above example, the markup would be 40 percent.

If expenses are not carefully determined, the actual profit will be less than antici-pated. Even when the proper calculations are made, other factors may affect antici-pated profits. For example, some items might not sell as well as expected and might warrant being sold below regular wholesale prices. Bearing this in mind, manufactur-ers are always at risk, hoping that their initial planning proves accurate.

Materials Procurement

Once samples have been produced and their manufacturing costs calculated, the ma-terials must be purchased. Based on the actual yardage needed for each item, the manufacturer will determine the number of items that need to be sold before a profit is realized. This number is called a **cutting ticket.** The amount of each cutting ticket varies from product to product and manufacturer to manufacturer. A company will begin to earn a profit when the number of items on the cutting ticket is sold. Some companies do not cut a single piece until orders have reached the cutting ticket. Oth-ers take chances by cutting and assembling before orders are received.

The size of the manufacturing company and its potential volume determines how materials are purchased. Large companies buy fabrics directly from the major textile mills so that they can get the lowest prices. Smaller companies, unable to satisfy the minimum ordering requirements of major textile companies, are usually restricted to smaller textile producers or wholesale fabric suppliers. Other factors that determine which suppliers to use include delivery time, reliability of supply, and methods of payment.

Trimmings must also be purchased. Most of these purchases are made through wholesalers who deal specifically with decorative and functional enhancements.

Manufacturing Process

The designer creates a pattern for each garment either through draping or flat pattern-making. Some companies adjust or correct these standard patterns and use them in ac-tual production. In most cases, however, individual production patterns are created.

Production Pattern

The process for creating **production patterns** is similar to that used to design actual garments. A production pattern has all of the exact details, including sizing; sample patterns do not. Production patterns may be rendered by hand or prepared with the use of computer-aided design (CAD) systems. Manufacturers of mass-produced items prefer CAD systems because of their efficiency and accuracy. At this stage, strict ad-herence to size standardization is important. Anyone who has tried on several dresses or suits of the same size made by different manufacturers will quickly notice that they often do not fit exactly the same way. Some feature narrow cuts, while others might be fuller fitting. Whereas all refrigerators that offer 20 cubic feet have the same hold-ing capacity, not all size-10 dresses fit the same way. The patternmaker must address the needs of the manufacturer's clientele before any patterns are prepared.

Grading and Marking the Pattern

After the production pattern is completed, it must be graded to fit the range of sizes in which the garment will be produced. Although the samples of misses-sized dresses are often made to fit size 8, a complete assortment of sizes for the garment might range from size 6 to 16.

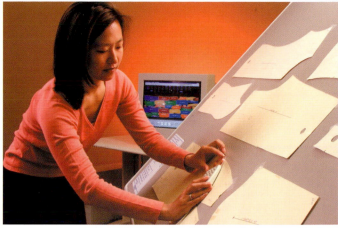

Patterns are created with the use of computers.

Grading is accomplished manually or by computer. The operator creates the full range of sizes by increasing or decreasing the sample pattern. To satisfactorily perform this procedure manually, the grader must have specific skills—it is the hand that performs the actual calculation for each size. However, computer programs use a **digitizer** to mark the key points on the pattern for each size in the range. Once the key points of each design are set in the computer's memory, an accurate pattern for each size is automatically produced. Computerized grading saves so much time that manual grading is being phased out.

Once grading is completed, **production layouts**, or markers, as they are called, are constructed from a piece of paper that measures the same width as the material that will be used for the garment. The purpose is to minimize fabric costs by determining how to cut the maximum number of garment parts from a single piece of fabric. A separate marker is traced from the pattern boards for each of the garment's components, including the bodice of the dress, the skirt, and sleeves. Each of the parts is placed as closely as possible to the next to eliminate fabric waste. Every wasted scrap of fabric contributes unnecessarily to the cost of the garment.

Computers are used for both grading and **marking**. Some of the vendors for such programs include Assyst Inc., Lectra Systemès, and Polygon Software and Technology.

Production patterns comprise the initial line.

Cutting the Garment

After the patterns and markers have been generated, the fabric must be cut. The procedure depends on the number of identical items needed to be produced. In couture manufacturing, one-of-a-kind garments are individually cut by a skilled craftsperson whose trained hands and eyes manipulate the fabric.

In most cases, however, where the key to success is in mass production, layer upon layer of fabric is spread on a cutting table and cut as if it were one piece. As many as 500 layers of material may be cut at one time, either by hand or by the use of a **CAM (computer-aided manufacturing)** system.

Cutting is accomplished in numerous ways, the method being determined by the desired quantities. A cutter carefully cuts the fabric into the necessary component parts.

In hand cutting, the cutter guides a vibrating blade around the edges of the marker. A vertical blade is better than a circular blade because it more accurately follows the curves of some designs. The fineness or coarseness of the blade depends on the thickness and density of the material.

Although traditional hand cutting is still found in many factories, more and more companies use a computer, sometimes to direct a laser beam, to cut the garment. Its speed and accuracy significantly improves production.

If a style is a **staple** item, such as men's dress shirts, dies are developed to cut the pieces of the garment. The dies are constructed of sharp steel edges that easily cut through all of the fabric layers. **Die cutting** is similar to using a cookie cutter.

Because manufacturers are always looking to lower costs, they constantly explore new ways to improve the accuracy and speed of the cutting stages.

Assembling the Garment

Manufacturing a fine men's suit, for example, might require as many as 250 separate assembling operations. Although this is not typical of all apparel manufacturing, it does indicate that the cost of sewing a garment together can be a significant factor in the cost of production.

Two approaches are used to assemble garments. A garment can be assembled by one individual or by an assembly line. The latter is the more common approach in the fashion industry because it is a less expensive way to mass produce apparel. Each individual along the assembly line performs just one task and then passes the garment to the next individual, who performs the next task. This process continues until the garment is completed. Factories using this approach generally locate individuals performing the same task in one area. After a batch of the pieces have been completed, it is moved to the next production area.

Assembling a garment may require as many as 250 steps.

Only very expensive garments are now hand assembled. The majority of apparel is completed with a variety of power sewing machines. Handwork, if used at all, is reserved for the application of decoration or trimmings.

Several types of machines are used, including the lock-stitcher, which sews a straight seam; the chain-stitcher, which produces a looped effect; the overlock, which sews one seam over another to enhance appearance; the blind-stitcher, which is used to hem garments; and the buttonhole machine, which automatically sews buttonholes.

As with every other stage of production, sewing is increasingly automated. This reduces costs by significantly reducing the time needed for sewing. In the manufacture of inexpensive apparel, computer-driven machines are replacing the individuals who previously sewed garments by hand or machine.

Another time-saving technique is fusing, in which two pieces of fabric are bonded together. In the menswear industry, for example, less expensive suits are being produced by fusing rather than sewing parts together. Although costs are reduced, the long-term serviceability of the garment is diminished.

Finishing the Garment

After the garment is assembled, it needs to be finished. This might involve sewing buttons, setting in zippers, applying beading or appliqués, or adding stitching for ornamentation. These finishes can be performed by hand or machine.

Once these finishes have been applied, the garment is ready to be pressed. Pressing not only sets the fabric, as in the case of men's suits, but also readies it for inclusion in a retailer's inventory.

Labeling the Garment

The final stage of production involves labeling the garment. One label identifies the manufacturer or designer. It tells the consumer who was responsible for the garment's creation. If the name is well known, the consumer may make certain assumptions about quality and the retailer may be able to charge a higher price.

Other labels include information on laundering and general care. If not accurately explained, the item might be improperly laundered and ruined, causing unnecessary returns to the vendor. Finally, if merchandise is produced offshore, the country of origin must be identified on a permanently sewn label.

Quick Response

Quick response, as outlined by the Management Systems Committee of the American Apparel Manufacturers Association, is "a management philosophy, since it embraces actions by all functions of a business, working in concert with each other. It also involves working in concert with suppliers and customers in meaningful, in-depth trading partner alliances using uniform, standard procedures. The alliance has mutual objectives of increased sales and profitability and reduced inventory for all the partners." It is a combination of techniques that a business uses during all stages of production, from the procurement of raw materials to the delivery of the finished product to the consumer.

The goals of quick response include reduced production time, lower inventories, and increased profitability. Two technologies that help achieve these goals are **bar coding** and **electronic data interchange (EDI)**. They improve the communication process among manufacturers, materials suppliers, and retailers. Bar coding has simplified the recording of **point-of-sale (POS)** information, which can be quickly sent

Garments making their way through the streets of New York City's garment center.

to those businesses involved in shipping the goods from the production point to the consumption point. EDI has improved communication among all of these businesses. Because information about what is selling can be conveyed quickly to everyone from producer to retailer, inventory replenishment is fast and accurate. Ultimately, quick response results in smaller and more frequent orders, eliminating the need to overstock an abundance of goods. It provides the same advantage for all other segments of the fashion industry.

ACCESSORIES MANUFACTURING

Most people take for granted the number of different fashion accessories available to enhance their wardrobes. Few, however, are informed about how these goods are produced. How many consumers, for example, could guess that it takes as many as 300 individual operations to construct a single pair of fine men's shoes! It is no wonder that companies such as Cole-Haan charge as much as $500 for a single pair of oxfords.

Although accessories manufacturers and apparel manufacturers address many of the same problems, including costing the items, the actual construction of some accessories require specialized production techniques. The lasting of shoes, full-fashioning of hosiery, the hammering of metals in jewelry pieces, piqué seaming of gloves, and hand-blocking of millinery are just some examples of the individual needs of accessories manufacturing.

Knowledge of the manufacturing techniques for accessories, when added to the information in the apparel section of this chapter, is beneficial for both industry professionals and consumers. It better enables those who sell the products to justify the prices by a commanding knowledge of production techniques. For consumers, familiarity with the different stages of production helps them spend their dollars more wisely. Chapter 12 described all of these fashion accessories; this chapter explains how they are produced.

Many steps are required to manufacture footwear—from the design sketch to the creation of the last and model shoe, to transforming the last to the pattern, to cutting the material and stitching the final product.

Footwear

From fine, intricately detailed leather shoes to the various canvas models, literally several hundred types of shoes are available for sale. Within each of these classifications, the price can vary greatly. A man's pair of business shoes may be purchased for as little as $50 or as much as several hundred dollars. The difference is based on the cost of materials and the production techniques.

Parts of the Shoe

Each shoe is composed of three basic parts: the upper, the soles, and the heel.

1. The **upper** is broken down into three separate pieces: the *vamp*, which covers the toes and the front portion of the foot and includes the *tongue*, and the two quarters that encompass the back portion.

2. The **sole** is more than one layer of material. It consists of the *insole*, which is found on the inside of the shoe closest to the foot; the *midsole*, which lies between the insole and the outermost sole of the shoe; and the *outermost sole,* which is the thickest of the sole's components. The thickness is necessary because of the significant amount of friction caused by the shoe touching the ground.

3. **Heels**, or **bottoms** as they are technically referred to in the trade, are available in a variety of styles and heights. They are the last pieces to be attached to the body of the shoe.

After each part has been constructed, shoes are assembled.

Production

From original design concept to finished product requires many steps. As with other products, the complexity of construction is a significant component in the price of the final product. In some aspects of shoe production, the same operation may be completed by hand or machine. If the former is used, the final price will be higher. The shoe manufacturer must choose the production methods necessary to manufacture a shoe that addresses such factors as fit, comfort, and price.

The following stages of development are basic to traditional shoe construction.

DEVELOPING THE DESIGNER LAST. Once the designer has sketched the style, a **form** or **last** is created on which the model shoe is constructed. Each last conforms to the style, size, and fit characteristics of the finished footwear. The last is generally sculpted from wood by skilled craftspeople. When a last is considered worthy of inclusion in the manufacturer's line, it is then transformed into a *production* or *development last*.

CREATING THE DEVELOPMENT OR PRODUCTION LAST. Every style and size that is to be produced requires a separate last. These final lasts are made of polyethylene logs that are placed on duplicating lathes, which turn and copy the designer's last. With the tremendous range of sizes and widths for each style, it is not unusual for as many as 50 individual production lasts to be created. After the lasts have been turned out, they are transformed into flat patterns. Today, this is often accomplished with the use of CAD programs, such as MicroDesign and Artworks.

TRANSFORMING THE LAST INTO PATTERNS. The three-dimensional last or form is transformed into flat patterns—a different one for each part of the shoe. To be certain that the end parts will fit when assembled into a shoe, each pattern's part must be perfectly constructed. The parts include the different pieces that constitute the upper portion of the shoe, the various soles, the heels, and all of the decorative embellishments.

In one method of pattern production, the last is wrapped with adhesive tape. The design and reference points are marked by pencil. The tape is then cut along the design lines and peeled away from the last. It is then flattened on paper and cut into the various pieces. At this point, some manufacturers grade the patterns into the different sizes needed for production.

CREATING DIES. To mass produce shoes, many layers of material must be cut at one time. To do so, dies, which resemble cookie cutters, are produced. Sharp steel strips that will cut through the material are bent to conform to the various shapes needed.

CUTTING THE MATERIAL. The material is cut either by hand or by dies. In the case of synthetic or manufactured goods, an automated die technique is used so that expenses can be reduced. When leather is used, the cutting process is generally

Table 18.1

TECHNIQUES FOR LASTING SHOES

Technique	Description
Goodyear Welt	One of the finest methods of lasting uses two seams to attach the upper shoe to the sole. The first is a hidden chain-stitched inseam that holds a strip called the welt and the inseam together. The second is a lock-stitch outseam that attaches the outersole.
Mackay	This method uses tacking, stapling, or cementing to attach the upper to an insole. The entire piece is then attached to the outersole.
Littleway	In this method the sole is stitched directly to the upper.

performed by hand. This more costly procedure allows the skilled craftsperson to avoid parts of the leather that have blemishes and other unsightly markings.

FITTING AND STITCHING THE SHOE. The largest number of individual operations are performed in an area called the fitting room. Here, all of the components of the shoe are stitched together. Some highly detailed shoes require as many as 60 individual processes during this stage of production. Linings, for example, must be attached to such parts as the vamp and quarters; the quarter is then sewn onto the vamp; the tongue, if used, is attached; "eyelets" are made; and decorative stitching is applied.

LASTING. This stage of construction may be performed by a number of different techniques. Basically, they all require that the fitted upper is pulled over the last in a series of operations that makes the upper conform to the shape of the last. The decision to use one lasting technique over another depends on such factors as quality, appearance, and function.

Some of the commonly used methods, including the Goodyear Welt, are listed and defined in Table 18.1.

ASSEMBLING THE REMAINING PARTS OF THE SHOE. As the upper is being assembled, various other parts, such as the counters, sock linings, shanks, and heels, are also being assembled.

BOTTOMING. The lasted upper receives the shanks and fillers, and is ready for **bottoming**, the permanent attachment of the outer sole to the shoe upper. The heels are then nailed through the insole for strength.

FINISHING THE SHOE. The final operations include buffing the bottoms to achieve a smooth finish, polishing the shoe to enhance its luster, and *treeing*, which entails placing the shoe on a form to make certain that it is properly shaped. If laces or ornaments are part of the design, they are attended to at this time.

Hosiery

Full-length stockings, knee-highs, pantyhose, and socks are both functional and decorative accessories for all individuals. All of these items are knitted to conform to the shape of the legs and feet. Dress hosiery may be made of nylon, microfibers, or spandex, whereas socks are usually made from a variety of natural fibers such as cotton, wool, and cashmere, and manufactured fibers such as rayon, acrylic, and polyester.

Production

Although the introduction of new knitting machines has made production faster, the construction techniques used in the hosiery industry are much the same as they have been for years.

Some stockings are manufactured using the **full-fashioned technique**, which produces a flat form in the desired size and shape. A back seam is then used to finish the product. After the basic hosiery has been completed, it is dyed, placed on forms, and heat-set for shape retention.

Seamless hosiery, a mainstay in the industry, uses a one-piece construction arrangement that forms the hosiery with the use of circular knitting machines. As with full-fashioned hosiery, it is made according to size and shape, then dyed and heat-set.

Pantyhose, the largest-selling type of dress hosiery, may be made in one of two ways. One method involves sewing individual stockings to a panty to form the product. The other involves the creation of a one-piece item on special machines. In both cases, the products are dyed and heat-set.

Socks follow the same general principles of construction as stockings and pantyhose. They are knitted on circular machines, usually in a natural color that may be dyed at a later time when the fashion colors have been determined. If patterns are to be used in the design, different colored yarns are used at the time of construction to generate the desired motif.

Jewelry

The cost of jewelry ranges from a mere dollar or two to several thousands for a single piece. Obviously, the materials used in construction significantly contribute to the final price. However, cost is also affected by different production techniques.

Production

Metals are transformed into materials for use in jewelry by a number of methods. Some are accomplished by machine; others are the work of skilled craftspeople. The various techniques for producing jewelry, including **annealing** and **casting**, are listed and defined in Table 18.2.

Once the metals have been processed, they can be used alone or combined with stones to create various types of jewelry.

Gloves

The type of construction used in making gloves depends on the materials used, the desired appearance, and the final price of the product. The easiest gloves to produce are those that are knitted. Because the entire product is generally one piece, little assembly is needed. The only sewing required is to close the tips of the fingers and to add enhancements. It is the construction of leather gloves that requires a series of different operations.

Parts of the Glove

Generally, gloves are comprised of four parts: trank, fourchettes, quirks, and thumb.

1. The *trank* is the rectangular shape that constitutes the front and back portion of the glove.

2. The *fourchettes* are the narrow oblong pieces that are inserted between the fingers to improve the wearer's comfort.

Table 18.2

VARIOUS TECHNIQUES FOR PRODUCING JEWELRY

Technique	Description
Annealing	Heating the metals to make them more pliable.
Antiquing	Applying chemicals to darken the metal so that an old look is achieved.
Casting	Liquefying and pouring metals into casts that represent different designs.
Die-striking	Reproducing many of the same pieces through the use of a mold or form. Materials are placed between the dies and squeezed into shape by means of a hydraulic press at extreme pressures.
Drawing	Softening and forcing metals that are to be woven into designs through a series of holes, each slightly smaller than the previous one, until the desired thickness has been achieved.
Embossing	Using pressure to apply a three-dimensional effect onto metal.
Engraving	Scratching a design into metal by hand or machine.
Etching	Producing a design by applying acid to unprotected areas of a metal.
Florentining	Producing a series of fine scratched lines by engraving.
Forging	Heating and then hammering metals to achieve a desired shape.
Fusing	Joining two pieces by liquefying the metal under extreme heat.
Rolling	Pressing metals into sheets so that they can then be cut or bent to required shapes.
Soldering	Joining two metals by using a third metal that has a lower melting point. The solder must be of the same color and strength as the two metals to be joined, so that it will be undetectable on inspection. The two pieces to be joined are held in place by wire, steel pins, or plaster, depending on the type of solder to be used.
Repoussé	Hammering a flat piece of metal into a three-dimensional piece.
Welding	Using heat and pressure to join together two or more metals.

3. *Quirks*, small triangular inserts that are used at the base of the fingers, provide extra comfort and movement.

4. The final part is the *thumb*, of which there are two varieties. The *bolton* is a bulky design that provides freedom of movement; the *quirk thumb* is a sleeker style that allows for a snug fit.

Production

To construct gloves composed of leather or woven goods, two stages are required—cutting the material into its various components, and sewing them together.

CUTTING The method used for cutting leather depends on its quality. For finer gloves, a skilled cutter dampens and stretches the leather to assure proper fit and cuts each piece one at a time. This method is called *table-cutting*. In lesser quality leathers and woven fabrics, the glove is constructed by the pull-down method. This involves using dies that cut the material in a cookie-cutter fashion.

ASSEMBLING Generally, one of the following four techniques is used to assemble a glove:

1. **Inseaming**. The least expensive technique. The seams are sewn together on the outside of the glove and then turned inside out. This leaves no visible seam.

2. **Outseaming**. The opposite of inseaming. The seams are stitched along the edges and left exposed.

3. **Overseaming**. A technique that involves stitching over the edges.

4. **Piqué Seaming**. The most expensive technique. Piqué seaming requires a special machine that sews one edge of the material over the other, both on the front and back, exposing only one raw edge. It is used for producing sleek gloves.

In some constructions, a third stage, called *pointing*, is applied. This is the application of decorative stitching on the back of the glove.

Handbags

Handbags serve both functional and decorative purposes. They have become one of the more important parts of a wardrobe. They range in price from a few dollars to thousands of dollars for the most intricate designs, as discussed in Chapter 12.

Parts of the Handbag

Using as few as three or four parts, or as many as 30, the basic components of a handbag are the *frame*, or *body*, over which the design is constructed; the *gussets*, which are side panels that allow for expansion of the piece; the *lining*, which covers the stitching or gluing that has been used; the *handles*, which come in a variety of lengths and make carrying easier; and closing devices, such as zippers, clasps, locks, snaps, and drawstrings.

Although all of these components are necessary to create the handbag, it is the material that gives each item its individuality. The different types include leather, which still dominates the marketplace, vinyl, plastic, wood, straw, lucite, and metallics. Finally, ornamentation further distinguishes one product from another. It might be appliqués, fringe, buttons, sequins, beads, stones, or flowers.

As with other apparel and accessories classifications, the process begins with the designer. Most often, the design is created on paper.

Production

After the design has been completed, it is first assembled in a material such as muslin or felt and fitted with the necessary closing devices and enhancements. Each style is then assessed in terms of potential sales. Those deemed to have the best chances for success will enter production.

Initially, a pattern is constructed for each part of the design. This may be done by hand or by the use of a CAD system. In either case, the completed patterns are used as the guides over which the materials will be cut. In the case of fine leather handbags, each part is individually cut to avoid scars and blemishes. Skilled craftspeople are well paid to perform this hand-cutting task. The actual cutting may be accomplished by means of a sharp knife or, in some cases, with dies that stamp out the pieces. When fabric bags are produced, the fabric is generally layered so that many pieces may be simultaneously cut, saving time and money.

The pieces are assembled by hand or machine. They are then ready to receive any stiffening materials that may be used between the body of the bag and the lining to lend support. In soft bag construction, stiffening materials are unnecessary. Other parts, such as plastic strips or stays, may provide support. Foamlike fillers can give the product a softer feel. The body is now fitted to the frame and readied for the addition of closures, handles, and any decorations indicated on the original design.

After the bag is finished, it is ready for inspection. In cases such as the Judith Leiber handbags and other high-quality products, the inspection process is carefully carried out for each item. When customers are asked to spend large sums of money

Quality control is assured at all levels in a Louis Vuitton factory. Here Vuitton products are assembled.

for such products, only the finest quality makes it to the stores. In the case of costly bags, each one is individually boxed. For lower-priced items, bulk packing is typical.

Belts

As with many other fashion accessories, belts are enjoying new popularity, as discussed in Chapter 12. Apparel designers are now creating belts in styles that are expensive to produce. Although the final products take on many different appearances, the methods of belt construction are rather simple. It is the choice of material and ornamentation that creates the interest.

Production

Many different materials are used to construct belts, such as leather (still the most popular), fabric, straw, metal, vinyl, lucite, and elastic. The material generally dictates the method of construction.

For leather belts, each piece is cut to the desired length and width either by hand or using a strap-cutting machine. If a shaped belt is required, such as one that fits the contour of the body, a die is usually produced that stamps out the shape. In producing quality leather belts, the cutter needs to avoid unsightly markings.

Some belts are then affixed with a backing, which is attached either by means of a walking-foot machine, which sews the two pieces together, or by gluing. When fabric belts are produced, layer upon layer is stacked so that the fabric can be cut in batches by means of dies. Because the materials are manufactured, blemishes are not a problem.

After the body of the belt has been completed, decoration such as stitching or nailhead inserts is applied. If holes are needed, they are punched into the pieces by hand or machine. Finally, the buckles are inserted and closed by sewing or gluing.

Cinch or elasticized belts are constructed by a different method. The material is cut to size and sewn around the edges. Closures such as snaps or hooks are then attached. For chain belts, the links are fastened one to another, until the desired length is achieved; a final link is used as a closing device. The easiest belt to construct is the sash. It merely requires cutting fabric to the appropriate length and width and sewing the edges. Because there are no formal closing devices, the process is quickly completed.

Hats

Although the number of men and women who wear hats today pales by comparison with years ago, some people still consider them essential parts of a fashionable wardrobe. Of course, in cold weather, hats are a popular form of functional attire. For those who want to wear hats, a few manufacturers continue to produce them.

Production

As with all accessories, the method of production for hats is based on the ultimate selling price and the various materials required for each style. The less expensive variety is machine made; the finer entries are crafted by hand.

After the designer sketches the model, it is transformed into a sample. The basic components of each sample include the body of the hat and the ornamentation with which it will be enhanced. After the samples have been evaluated in terms of their sales potential, production is ready to begin. Sometimes, milliners are called on to create one-of-a-kind hats that cost several hundred dollars, but most often, the items are mass produced.

For the fall and winter months, felt hats are still the mainstay of men's and women's collections. The felt is cut, either by hand or by machine, and then shaped by using **cones**. The felt is repeatedly steamed under pressure on the cones. The **crown**, or body, of the hat, and the **brim** are then formed. After another round of steam is applied, the brim of the hat is trimmed until the desired width is achieved. Hats are now ready for trimming. Men's hats usually include a fabric band around the crown and sometimes a small feather for decoration. Women's hats are trimmed following the designer's concept.

In the spring and summer, straw is the most popular material for hats. Sometimes these hats are made of woven mats that are shaped on wooden forms called **blocks**. Each style has its own block. The straw material is repeatedly steamed on the blocks until the shape of the hat has been achieved. Once the moisture from the steaming has been removed, a stiffening material called *buckram* might be added underneath to help maintain the hat's shape. In some straw hat designs, the construction involves overlapping narrow strips of straw until the appropriate shape is achieved. This plaiting process is accomplished with the use of sewing machines. After the plaiting has been completed, the material is placed on blocks for shaping and is stiffened for shape retention.

Other hat styles that have less rigid formations use soft materials, such as velvet, velveteen, and velour. To produce these unstructured models, the operator cuts the fabric to size and shape, drapes it, and sews it into a soft style.

Fashionable hat designs are important elements in today's fashion scene. Some of the production steps are shown here.

Knitting, by machine or hand, and crocheting are also used to construct many of the functional hats worn by children and adults seeking protection from the cold weather. The production is generally a one-piece affair without the need for any sewing.

A final touch that distinguishes one model from another is ornamentation. Feathers, flowers, veils, bows, ribbons, appliqués, and beads can be applied by sewing or gluing. The finished products are then either individually boxed or shipped in bulk cartons to the store.

Scarves

Scarves are made in a variety of sizes and shapes. Once considered only as a functional product, scarves have become a favorite fashion accessory.

Production

The construction of scarves is simpler than that of other fashion accessories. They are often made from rolls of fabric that are cut to the appropriate sizes and shapes, then hemmed by machine or by hand. Hand-rolling is reserved for the more expensive varieties.

Designer scarves are usually made as individual pieces. They begin with solid colors that are then silk-screened to create a pattern. Some of these scarves have become collectibles and command hundreds of dollars.

In addition to the exquisite colorations and silk-screened motifs, decorative elements such as fringe, beading, and sequins are used as enhancements.

Watches

Although watches are basically functional timepieces, many styles are now available to serve different fashion purposes. Men and women often have more than one, with each serving different wardrobe needs.

Production

The oldest variety is the mechanical model that uses jeweled movements for precision. Jewels are inserted into tiny holes to act as friction points. Although expensive watches use precious jewels, today's inexpensive variety substitutes synthetic stones.

When the electronic watch was introduced, it was quickly accepted as a more functional product. The mainspring barrel used in mechanical watches is replaced by a power cell that usually lasts for approximately a year. Instead of the common "ticking" generated by mechanical watches, the electronic watch features a soft hum. With fewer parts than the other watches, it is more serviceable.

By substituting solid-state components for the moving parts used in the mechanical and electronic models, a new generation of watches was born. Instead of hands that moved to indicate time, digital numbers were displayed whenever a button was pushed. Before long, anyone could own a reliable digital watch for as little as $15.

With the use of quartz crystals, the watch industry was further revolutionized. The quartz timepiece is 10 times more accurate than conventional models. With the addition of microcircuitry, these watches also display dates and days of the week. Other features include stopwatches, temperature readings, and information storage capabilities.

Watch casings, which are designed to protect the mechanisms, serve as attractive bracelets. Made from precious metals, such as gold and platinum, and functional materials, such as stainless steel, they are the work of specialty designers.

CHAPTER HIGHLIGHTS

- Many of the production operations used in the manufacture of apparel goods are basic to all products. Specialized procedures become necessary, however, in the production of accessories.

- Before production begins, each product must be costed so that an appropriate wholesale price can be established.

- Fabrics are bought in quantities that reflect the predetermined sales potential for each garment or accessory item.

- Apparel manufacturing requires the creation of a production pattern, grading and marking the pattern, cutting the fabric, and assembling the garment.

- Many operations are now computerized to increase accuracy and profits.

- Each garment or accessory is finished with functional and decorative embellishment and then labeled to indicate the company's name, product care, and country of origin if produced offshore.

- Many accessories require specialized manufacturing techniques.

IMPORTANT FASHION TERMINOLOGY AND CONCEPTS

annealing
bar coding
blocks
bottoming
brim
CAM (computer-aided manufacturing)
casting
crown
cutting ticket
die cutting
digital watch

digitizer
electronic data interchange (EDI)
full-fashioned technique
grading
heel
in-house sales staff
inseaming
inside shop
last
marking
outseaming

outside contractor
overseaming
piquè seaming
point-of-sale (POS)
production layouts
production pattern
quick response
sole
staple
upper
wholesale price

FOR REVIEW

1. What is the first step that must be considered before actual production takes place?
2. List the various factors that determine a product's cost.
3. Differentiate between inside shops and outside contractors.
4. In what ways do manufacturers sell their goods?
5. Define the term *cutting ticket*.
6. How have computers affected the manufacturing process?
7. Why must patterns be graded?
8. Describe the two methods of assembling garments used in the fashion industry.
9. What purposes do labels serve on fashion products?
10. What are the three basic parts of a shoe?
11. Describe the role played by lasting in shoe production.
12. What are two methods used to produce pantyhose?
13. List and define four techniques employed in jewelry construction.

14. Why is it easy to produce a cinch belt?

15. On what type of form is a felt hat shaped?

16. Differentiate between the two types of watches.

17. In the Point of View article, "Fashion's Best-Guarded Secret, the Assistant, Emerges," which assistant designers have emerged as superstars?

EXERCISES AND PROJECTS

1. If you live in the vicinity of an apparel manufacturer, inquire about the possibility of visiting the plant to learn about production. Take a camera along to record the various operations. Mount the photographs on a foamboard and use them in an oral report that outlines the various stages of production at the company you visited.

2. Carefully take apart a garment you are ready to dispose of and try to assess the following:

   • The yardage of material used

   • The functional and decorative trimmings

   • Special finishes

   Then determine the approximate cost of each of the elements by visiting a materials and trimmings supplier. Try to determine the actual cost of the goods in the product.

3. Consult a watch manufacturer about the different production techniques used in watch making and prepare a written report.

4. Disassemble a used shoe to uncover all of its basic components. Each component should be mounted, labeled, and described in terms of the purpose it serves.

WEB SITES

By accessing these Web sites, you will be able to gain broader knowledge and up-to-date information on materials related to this chapter.

Garment Contractors Association of Southern California

   www.garmentcontractors.org

American Apparel Producers' Network

   www.aapn.net

   www.usawear.org

SEAMS online

   www.seams.org

The Case of the Production Dilemma

Jan Rogers and Peter English are considering forming a partnership to manufacture moderately priced women's dresses. Each has had previous experience in the field. Jan was the production manager for Artway, a dress company that has been in business for 40 years; Peter was the assistant production manager for Bell Sportswear, makers of inexpensive skirts, pants, and tops. Jan used in-house production and Peter used outside contractors.

For a designer, they have agreed on Renée Philips, who, while carrying the title of assistant designer, actually created many of her own styles. She is capable of preparing both the design and production patterns, and is familiar with computer-aided design technology.

The new company has limited financial resources, but nevertheless the principals want to see their dreams come true. They expect to begin their year with four collections, one for each season.

Together with Renée, the two are planning their production methodology. Jan believes the in-house approach is the most appropriate, whereas Peter favors the use of outside contractors. Renée is not certain which route would be most beneficial to the fledgling company.

questions

Which approach would you suggest the new company take in terms of contracting versus in-house production? Why?

Fashion's Best-Guarded Secret, the Assistant, Emerges

RUTH LA FERLA

In the din of applause that followed Bill Blass's runway show for spring 1999, the designer emerged at the end of the catwalk, one arm around each of his two chief assistants, a gesture of acknowledgment as generous as it was rare.

In an industry famous for its seething rivalries and titanic egos, Mr. Blass's decision to take his bows last month with the two assistant designers—Laura Montalban and Craig Natiello—was so unusual that Mr. Natiello, a dry-spoken man with a distinctly jaded air, was momentarily giddy. "I feel like a deb," he said afterward. "Maybe I should have worn white."

If Mr. Natiello's instant in the limelight turned his head, you really couldn't blame him. He and many of his counterparts at other fashion houses have long toiled in obscurity, their contributions recognized only by close associates and a handful of fashion insiders. Until relatively recently, the assistant designer was an employer's best kept secret, generating ideas and sometimes executing them, sketching models and draping mannequins.

"I don't think there's a designer in the world who doesn't have an assistant or a design team behind him," said the designer Carolina Herrera. "But few people talk about it. And the team is always hidden."

Lately, however, the veil of secrecy has begun to lift, if only by degrees. It may be because so many former assistants have succeeded in what almost all aspire to: emerging as stars themselves, appointed to lead houses. They include Tom Ford, the designer for Gucci; Alber Elbaz, formerly an apprentice with Geoffrey Beene and recently named Yves Saint Laurent's designer of ready to wear, and Narciso Rodriguez, who has his own line, and also designs for Loewe.

In the past, only a handful of well-known designers—mostly notably Giorgio Armani and Nino Cerruti in Europe and Mr. Beene in New York—introduced their backup team on the runway and to the press, bluntly declaring that a fashion collection is not the product of a single mind.

"You are bound to be influenced by the esthetics and the technological expertise of the people who work for you," said Mr. Cerruti, Mr. Rodriguez's former employer. Pretending otherwise is disingenuous, if not archaic, he continued, adding, "It reminds me of the time young girls were kept as virgins in a castle until they got married."

Still, in a business built largely on image, such candor is exceptional. The question of just who designs a collection remains so sensitive that many designers declined to discuss it at all. A spokeswoman for Calvin Klein did not return calls about the matter, and a spokeswoman for Ralph Lauren, declining comment, said, "This is too complicated a subject, because there are so many people who work as assistants in our company." A spokeswoman for Richard Tyler said that the designer and his creative director, Simon Holloway, were both too busy last week to talk about it.

At the root of their reticence may be the need to reinforce the public perception that a single individual is responsible for the clothing with a designer's name on it. Matt Nye, a former assistant to both Mr. Lauren and Mr. Klein, who recently created his own collection, said: "Smaller houses can generate notoriety and revitalize their image by attaching themselves publicly to a youthful designer. But in a bigger company, a designer doesn't want that association. It does him no good. People like Ralph and Calvin are huge personalities. They're still viable factors in the credibility game."

Moreover, in fashion, as in other highly competitive industries, young talent is jealously guarded. "Fashion is incestuous," Mr. Nye said. "So if you have a very gifted designer, you keep him under wraps."

Just as often, however, it is the assistant who elects to stay behind the scenes, mastering the role of understudy. Damiano Biello, a Paris-based consultant, who collaborated with Mrs. Herrera on her latest collection, isn't fazed by his near-anonymith. "I'm ambitious and working hard so that one day I can open my own business," he said. "But first there is a price to pay, and I am willing to pay it."

Part of that price includes persisting in a job with hazy outlines. "Being an assistant can mean a lot of things—you can go get the coffee or you can help make a dress," said Robert Funk, a New York designer and former sample cutter, designer and sounding board for Zoran, Jackie Rogers and Marc Jacobs.

Whether called associate designer, creative director or designer, the designer's assistant, working alone or as part of a team of 4 to 40, juggles a roster of jobs, from scouting fabrics, cutting sample garments and sketching models to running interference between the design studio, where ideas germinate, and the sample room, where they take shape.

But the heart of the job is to serve as antennae, picking up design and cultural signals that one's employer may be too busy, or too secluded, to note. "As you get older, you need fresh blood—you want to look at the world through another pair of eyes," said Diane Von Furstenberg, who named Catharine Malandrino, 35, a Frenchwoman 16 years her junior, as designer of the DVF Signatures collection this year.

Established designers like Ms. Von Furstenberg draw on an ever-changing pool of talent, feeding on the visions their associates inspire.

"If you are an entry-level assistant, the more naive you are, the more the designer likes it," said Mr. Nye, who worked for Mr. Lauren in the early 1990's. "You might come in one day dressed like Annie Oakley and on another dressed like a rock climber, and it was, 'Where did you get those cargo pants, that shirt?' You knew that Ralph would literally like to strip you, physically, mentally and even emotionally to find out where your heart is at."

In the climate of relative candor and intimacy that flourishes at smaller houses, the exchange between designers and assistants is more like a tennis game, a volley of ideas so spontaneous that it's hard to be sure where each originates. But it's still the designer who has the last word. "Nothing gets out of here without Mrs. Herrera seeing it," said Mr. Biello. He nevertheless pushes through an idea of his own from time to time, like the

leather jacket that opened Mrs. Herrera's last spring collection. It was made, at Mr. Biello's daring suggestion, in a shade of Barbie-doll pink.

The role of the assistant is often to play provocateur, espousing quirky or daring ideas that may not fly. But outside the studio, the assistant acts as chief advocate for an employer's point of view. "The assistant is the voice of the designer in the designer's absence," said Lillian von Staufenberg, Bergdorf Goodman's fashion director of women's apparel. "It's up to him to make sure that we get the designer's vision."

The design process is often a collaboration among specialists. "Every one of us has an area of expertise, and the designer draws on that," said John Nickleson, who heads Oscar de la Renta's design studio.

Tiong Tan, who works for Jackie Rogers, describes the procedure as a progressive experiment. "We began last year with one of the previous season's most successful models, a dress that was gently draped at the neck," he said. Next, Mr. Tan, whose specialty is draping, transformed the garment in stages, drawing a swath of fabric across the waist, tweaking it and, finally, as Ms. Rogers beamed approval, letting it fall in a tier to the floor. "When we pinned it, we agreed it worked," he said. Another hit was born.

Not every garment to reach the runway is the child of such happy consensus. Mr. Natiello recalled surprising his boss, Mr. Blass, with a pair of black lace cargo pants, an item trendier than the designer might have chosen on his own. "I knew it!" Mr. Natiello remembers Mr. Blass bellowing with displeasure when he saw the pants. "Do you hate it?" the assistant asked, borrowing one of Mr. Blass's pet

phrases. Well no, the designer admitted. And the trousers survived, appearing on the runway last month.

The assistant may also be responsible for working with influential private customers. Mr. Natiello "can make or break what you are wearing," said Marin Hopper, the fashion director of Elle magazine, who often defers to him during private fittings of Mr. Blass's clothes. Such trust is the outgrowth of a camaraderie that extends beyond the studio. "We all know each other past 5 o'clock," said Mr. Natiello, who fits members of the junior social set by day and parties with them after hours.

They, in turn, attend Mr. Blass's collections. "We're Craig's cheering section," said Brooke de Ocampo, a friend and one of the house's youngest clients, adding that she could sometimes detect Mr. Natiello's influence on the runway. "It might be a square neckline or just a simple strapless dress," she said. "He understands what we want: elegant and uncomplicated clothes."

Inevitably some assistants feel emboldened to strike out on their own, opening their own businesses. But the move is always fraught with professional risk.

Robert Funk, who opened his own design business in 1997 after a 20-year apprenticeship, acknowledges that he was apprehensive. "It's an adjustment," he said. "I'd been used to expressing myself through somebody more fabulous. Now, it's like the floor has fallen out."

"Being able to reach a customer with my ideas directly is exciting he added, brightening. "But you do feel exposed. As an assistant, I was always hiding in plain sight."

New York Times, Fashion, December 15, 1998, B15

The Private Label Gold Mine

SAMANTHA CONTI

Private label manufacturers are among the best-kept secrets of Italy's fashion industry, supplying millions of pieces of clothing each year to major retailers in the U.S., Europe and Asia, and helping to determine the way many American women dress.

For more than 30 years, little-known manufacturers whose identities are jealously guarded by their top-drawer clients have been producing private label collections for the U.S., European and Asian markets.

Companies such as The Limited Group and Federated Department Stores, retail chains like Talbots and The Gap and catalogs like Lands' End do a vigorous business here, especially in knitwear and leather accessories.

U.S. retailers meet regularly with their Italian manufacturers swapping sketches, choosing fabrics and surveying samples. They also work closely with buying offices which act as liaisons between Italian companies and their foreign clients.

Industry experts say Italy's private label business is changing rapidly because clients around the world, and especially in the U.S., have become more demanding: increasing their private label orders and asking for more sophisticated, diverse products.

As a result, manufacturers and buying offices say they are working harder than ever to increase their productivity, creativity and cost-efficiency in what is becoming a highly competitive market.

"The business has changed considerably in the past 10 to 15 years. Today, there is more interest in private label than ever before and more hard work involved in producing collections," said Francesco Diaco, owner of the Florence-based buying office IBS Italia, which represents The Limited Group.

"It used to be that buying offices just made sure the merchandise was ordered and delivered to the client on time. Today we work very closely with the client and the manufacturer and do everything from scratch. We start with the fabric and yarn fairs and follow the process through to the end," he said.

Diaco does 75–80 percent of his business with The Limited Group, which IBS has been working with since 1963. "We have a very solid history with The Limited Group—ever since Leslie Wexner came here in the 1960s, we have been coordinating their private label collections in Italy," he said.

Diaco has teams dedicated to each of the Limited stores he represents, including Henri Bendel, The Limited, Express, Victoria's Secret, Lane Bryant and Lerner's. When they are working on a collection, Diaco's teams meet at least once a month with their counterparts from The Limited stores to review fabrics, sketches and samples.

The Henri Bendel team works chiefly on accessories, knitwear and jackets. The Limited team helps create accessories, skirts, shirts, pants and knitwear, and the Victoria's Secret group spends much of its time researching fabrics that might then be cut and sewn in another country.

Diaco said he is optimistic about the future of the private label business in Italy. "Each year, for example, Bendel's increases its volume of private label items sourced here. But it is not alone. In general, I think department stores are moving increasingly toward private label because it sets them free. They can market and manage the collections the way they want, and they can express their individuality through a private label collection," he said.

Bloomingdale's, which produces cashmere sweaters in Italy, is one store that is looking to boost its private label production here. "We'll be looking at Italy with an eye to increasing our private label business," said Kalman Ruttenstein, senior vice president of fashion direction at Bloomingdale's.

Manufacturers say they are willing to go to the ends of the planet to make their customers happy and drum up more business.

Quadro, a manufacturer based in Montale, Italy, makes knitwear for The Limited Group in collaboration with IBS and for May Co., in addition to producing three of its own labels for the Italian domestic market.

In 1995, some 60 percent of its turnover, which the company would not divulge, was generated by private label business with U.S. customers. "About three years ago, the U.S. market all of a sudden became very interested in private label, and each year our clients increase their volumes," said Cosetta Innocenti, who oversees production of private label collections.

Last year, Quadro turned out more than 600,000 units for shipment to the U.S. About one-third of those were twinsets destined for the shelves and racks of The Limited stores. Among the rest were classic merino wool sweaters for May Co.

Innocenti said her company works hard to please its demanding U.S. clients. "Americans often want to place their orders late and want delivery as soon as possible, and we are willing to meet those needs. If it means working on Saturday and Sunday, then that's no problem," she said. "The Limited stores ordered 130,000 twinsets in September, and the delivery was made by November."

Alberto Danti, the owner of Maglificio Fiesole, another Tuscan knitwear manufacturer, said his American clients, which include Federated Department Stores, Talbots and Lands' End, have become pickier and more demanding over the years.

"They have become more demanding because the market is so much more difficult today. "The Made in Italy label just isn't enough anymore," he said. "Today, we do a lot more research on color, styling and fabrics because our clients want their products to stand out. For example, we pay a lot of attention to padding, stitching and collars."

Danti said he is convinced the key to success in the U.S.—which generated 60 percent of his company's $40 million turnover last year—is developing close working relationships with clients. Fiesole

has an office in New York to keep an eye on the market and react quickly to clients' needs.

Italian manufacturers and the buying offices say that while competing with the Far East is becoming increasingly difficult because of Italy's high labor costs, they are confident about the future.

"Italians can compete with the prices in the Far East because they are willing to lower their prices and make a deal," said Maureen Skelly Bonini, who owns one of the biggest buying offices in Italy and has been in the business for 25 years.

"For the manufacturers, continuity and loyalty are very important. Relationships are important, and once you have those, you can work well over here. Italy is also the strongest country for fabrics. In many cases, it's just easier to do the work over here," said Bonini, whose U.S. clients include The Gap, Banana Republic and Old Navy.

Diaco of IBS Italia agreed. "Outside competition is becoming more and more important, and even some Italian companies are choosing to move some of their

operations outside the country because of labor costs," he said.

"But, in the end, what saves this market is Italians' knack for inventing new styles, finishes and fabrics. Foreign clients need Italians for fresh ideas," he added.

The private label business is becoming just as popular inside Italy as it is outside—increasing numbers of Italian companies want to get in on the act.

"There was a time when many well-established companies turned their noses up at the idea of producing private label collections," said Armando Branchini, vice president of InterCorporate, a consulting firm here.

"But that began to change in the early 1990s, when manufacturers began to reevaluate their priorities due to the changing economy. Now, producing private label is no longer an embarrassment. If companies already have the manufacturing muscle, they know they can boost their turnover considerably by producing private label," he added.

Women's Wear Daily, Italia '96, February 1996

chapter 19

outsourcing fashion design, production, and management

One of the greatest victories you can gain over someone is to beat him with politeness.

JOSH BILLINGS, HUMORIST

Outsourcing has become one of the hottest topics in today's business arena. Rarely does a week go by that the print and broadcast media are not discussing the latest company to join the outsourcing bandwagon, how its decision to go this route will affect employment in the United States, and what the ramifications will be for consumers. Just about every business segment, to some extent, has embraced the concept, citing its pros and cons. Arguments ranging from the reduced cost of doing business and benefits to the consumer to the displacement of workers and harm to the U.S. economy are regularly debated. Each side presents a number of different rationales to underscore its position, with one generally not being able to convince the other of its advantages or disadvantages.

The fashion industry is no stranger to outsourcing. Where a manufacturer was once involved in the various stages of bringing a design to its completion, such as creating the silhouette, patternmaking, cutting the fabrics into the various components, assembling them into garments, and trimming them with enhancements, today's producers are rarely involved in all of these procedures. Instead, the industry has seen manufacturers relinquish their production involvement in favor of using outside resources to handle some or all of these chores. The company that actually manufacturers the entire item from conception to conclusion is a dying breed. The vast majority have reassigned not only production but also many other business activities, such as accounting, quality control, and sometimes even product design, to third parties.

In their quest to involve others in their operations, fashion manufacturers have gone one of three routes. They may use outside contractors in the United States, known as **onshore outsourcing**; may go to distant countries such as China and India, in what is called **offshoring**; or may use **nearsourcing** or **nearshoring**, in which closer countries such as Mexico and Costa Rica are their partners.

Whatever the arrangement, to understand the rationale behind the ever-growing outsourcing phenomenon, one must study its benefits and detriments, the state of the concept both domestically and internationally, the cross-cultural skills necessary for

After you have completed this chapter, you will be able to discuss:

- Why cultural awareness is necessary for success in business abroad.

- How to properly dress for business meetings in foreign countries.

- The advantages and disadvantages of outsourcing.

- How workforce displacement may affect the economy in the United States.

- Why local customs can affect production and delivery of merchandise.

- The importance of the proximity of fabricating materials.

- The use of domestic outsourcing.

- The major centers for overseas outsourcing.

India has become an important outsourcing center for fashion production.

its implementation, and the appropriate etiquette needed when entering into contractual agreements with overseas participants.

CULTURAL AWARENESS IS VITAL FOR SUCCESS IN BUSINESS ABROAD

Before examining the pros and cons of outsourcing, considering and selecting the outsourcing venue or venues, preplanning the meeting with potential partnerships, and finally making the visit to their headquarters, the manufacturer and designer must carefully address a few general areas of concern.

Such aspects as cultural differences, the avoidance of faux pas, the appropriateness of gift giving at business meetings, and appropriate dress are just some of the considerations with which outsourcers should be familiar. The following concepts are general in nature; more specifics are discussed later in the chapter.

Cultural Differences

Doing business within the United States is similar no matter where the **outsourcing partner** is based. Of course, subtle differences are found between the North and South, but none are so unusual that real adjustments in business dealings must be addressed.

When offshore or nearshore involvement is the choice, however, cultural differences among the options must be considered. For example, not only are the languages different, but women may not have the same place in business as their male counterparts, greetings may not include touching such as a handshake, the eating of meat may be frowned upon, use of alcohol may be taboo, and gift giving may not be appropriate. For business deals to go smoothly, these faux pas must be avoided.

Avoiding a Faux Pas

Some words have different connotations in different parts of the world. Even some English words, when spoken in the United Kingdom, may have different meanings than what Americans intend. This language barrier becomes even more difficult when business associates are speaking foreign languages. A slight mispronunciation may result in a very different meaning. Such a faux pas can make the host country representative uncomfortable. Intensive study and the use of an interpreter can help minimize such occurrences.

Gift Giving

In some countries, the giving of gifts is a common part of doing business, while in others it is frowned upon and considered to be a bribe. In Indonesia the recipient of a gift will not open it in public because doing so is looked upon as greedy; in Mexico a gift is not expected by a business associate, but a small token of one will be appreciated by a secretary; and in Hong Kong a gift is an important part of business practice. Learning what is expected and what is frowned upon will be an advantage for the visiting businessperson.

Appropriate Dress

What is appropriate in one part of the world might be improper in another. While conservative dress is generally safe, it is not always a uniform standard. In the sections on the various countries, later in the chapter, the topic is fully covered to show the differences around the globe.

In the United Kingdom, some English words have different meanings from what an American speaker might intend.

THE PROS AND CONS OF OFFSHORE OUTSOURCING

The benefits and shortcomings of farming out some of a fashion organization's operations are numerous. Those actively involved in offshore outsourcing, as well as business managers and consultants, regularly offer their opinions regarding the practice. The following is a summary of some of the arguments industry experts make.

Advantages

LOWER LABOR COST generally heads the list of the benefits. By partnering with outside contractors or other companies that perform business management functions, savings are usually realized. Countries such as India, China, Costa Rica, and many other developing nations are capable of performing many different operations at lower costs. For apparel manufacturers, in particular, the cost of garment assemblers is considerably less than that attributed to onshore workers, with hourly rates unacceptable in the United States.

CONCENTRATION ON SPECIFIC TASKS such as design and selling allows the company to perform these activities more efficiently, as they do not have to spend time on other operations. Once the collection is created, the cutting, sewing, and trimming chores are given over to outside contractors who follow the instructions set forth by

The World of Fashion Profile

EXECUTIVE PLANET

Offering invaluable tips for the business executive who is ready to travel abroad to make deals with companies in offshore venues is the focus of Executive Planet. Through its Web site, www.executiveplanet.com, an invaluable set of guidelines are available without cost.

A wealth of information regarding appropriate business etiquette, customs, and protocol necessary for the inexperienced executive to use is prepared by experts in global business. By choosing the country to which the executive will travel, specific information regarding that country can be found. Especially important to fashion companies wishing to pursue manufacturing contracts are countries such as South Korea, Indonesia, Malaysia, and others that are home to outsourcing producers.

In addition, the Web site provides information on the preparation and usage of business cards, the expected paces of the impending meeting, preferred presentation styles, recommended appointment scheduling, venues for business lunches, the appropriateness of gift giving, the use of names and titles, proper business dress, the manner in which women are treated in business situations, the tone of voice to expect, and welcome topics of conversation before the purpose of the meeting is reached.

The Web site also features related links that are invaluable to the international businessperson.

In China, an important fashion-producing country, it is necessary for visiting business-people to understand proper etiquette.

the company. Without these responsibilities, a company can pay more attention to areas such as marketing and product development.

BUDGET CONTROL becomes more manageable because costs such as rent can be established and figured into the expenses. If all of the operations are performed in-house, it is more difficult to plan for unexpected expense increases such as utility costs that may arise.

AVAILABILITY OF SKILLED MANAGEMENT is a reality. In addition to the work-force that performs the cutting and sewing functions, a wealth of management individuals are available in many countries. India, in particular, has a significant number of highly educated and skilled management personnel who work at much lower pay levels than their U.S. counterparts. **Quality control**, customer service, and accounting expertise are, in particular, the duties they perform at high levels of efficiency and lower expense to the company at home.

MATERIALS ACQUISITION is also a plus for apparel manufacturers. Although the United States was once a leader in textiles production, the domestic industry has almost disappeared. Relatively few fabrics are made in the USA because of the increase expense of production. With the industry now based in other countries, designers and product merchandisers regularly visit offshore regions for their garment needs. Once the materials have been chosen, it is often easier to enter into arrangement with contractors in these same textile-producing countries to produce the garments. This results in much lower shipping expenses.

FLEXIBILITY in terms of facing potential changes in business is often a plus. If, for example, a downturn in the U.S. economy is predicted, a U.S. company that performs all of the tasks of operation will likely have commitments, such as union contracts that disallow a decrease in staff, that will prevent the company from stemming its losses. With outsourcing, the ability to curtail production, and thus minimize expenses to meet the expected decreased product demands, is generally simpler.

SMALLER INVESTMENTS IN STARTUP COSTS are a reality because the company need only to fund such activities as designing and selling the collection. When a host of other functions are performed in-house, the new company must cover expenses for space, machinery, and so forth.

BETTER TECHNOLOGY for equipment is often a benefit because the outsourcing partner is more likely to have the latest in equipment. Manufacturers are often strapped for funds needed to bring out a new collection, and sometimes must make do with less advanced equipment such as cutting and sewing machines. The outsourcing contractor, on the other hand, often invests in state-of-the-art technology because he or she is not saddled with many other expenses.

The naysayers also make excellent points in regard to outsourcing. The following are some of the points they offer in defense of their positions against the practice.

Disadvantages

WORKFORCE DISPLACEMENT is the major complaint of those against the spread of outsourcing. In many fashion and fashion-related industries the craze has caused the shutdown of plants that produced textiles and manufactured the garments. For decades families have worked in factories turning raw materials into fabrics, or assembling the components into apparel. With the enormous popularity of outsourcing, what seems like limitless numbers of workers have been relieved of their duties.

ADVERSELY AFFECTING THE ECONOMY is another cry that many critics are voicing. With the layoffs in the textile mills, for example, the towns in which they were located have witnessed shuttered doors of stores that catered to the needs of these workers. Many have become ghost towns no longer benefiting from the customers' patronage due to their unemployment. While the call for retraining of the displaced personnel is repeated every day, it is often impossible for those aged 55 or over to do so.

INCREASE IN EXPENSES FOR GLOBAL TRAVEL is a reality. Product developers, merchandisers, and other management individuals must make regular trips to offshore destinations to oversee the efficiency of the outsourcing partner. While savings may be attributed to lower labor costs, this expense could possibly offset the savings.

LOCAL CUSTOMS that are different from practices in the United States could adversely affect production. In Mexico, for example, the siesta, or rest period in the middle of the day, could hamper production and cause longer manufacturing periods. In the fashion industry, time is of the essence for the proper merchandising of goods. Each lost day could mean less selling time for retailers.

Purchasers of Louis Vuitton products expect them to be produced in France, and not in China, where more and more fashion items are produced.

DELIVERY DELAYS are also a possibility if the offshore contractor is far from the merchandise destination. Akin to production slowdowns, as discussed above, timeliness is also important when it comes to delivering the goods to the merchant. To make up for slower deliveries, the alternative might be express shipping, but this is an additional expense that many companies cannot afford.

MISCOMMUNICATION is another potential problem. Although e-mailing and faxing are often adequate in discussing problems, **language nuances** can lead to misunderstandings and cause harm to the process.

LUXURY BRAND LABELING that identifies a less prestigious venue as the actual place of production than the country from which the consumer believes the item was manufactured can lead to loss of credibility and lower sales. When shoppers spend large sums for Armani, Vuitton, and Valentino, they expect the product to be made in France or Italy, not China where many of these items are actually produced. The labeling laws are very specific in the United States, demanding that the country of origin be clearly visible on the labels. How many will balk at this practice is still not yet known, but it must be considered by the designers.

CONSIDERATIONS FOR ESTABLISHING AN OFFSHORE OUTSOURCING PARTNERSHIP

The decision to outsource operations involves a great deal of investigation by the company. Many areas must be researched before a company can enter into a contractual agreement with an outsourcing partner. Just as manufacturers have numerous choices, such as textile suppliers, trimmings and findings resources, and so forth, when in-house production is the method of operation, so too do they have multiple options when going the outsourcing route.

The following are some areas of concern that will need to be investigated.

LOCATION OF THE OUTSOURCING PARTNER is especially vital to the fashion producer. When merchants are involved in call centers, it doesn't really matter how far away the outsourced company is. Communications are such that whether the "voice" is in India, China, or the United States, the result will be the same. On the other hand, when manufacturing is the primary task, location is important. Being far from the fashion operation's headquarters often requires extra time for shipping the goods. A delay with fashion merchandise could shorten the selling season. While China may offer cost-saving production terms, its distance could be prohibitive.

QUALITY AND SERVICE offered by the partner must be compatible with the company's expectations. A fashion designer or manufacturer who has captured the attention of his or her clientele with creative designs and workmanship when he or she was involved in all of the aspects of production must expect the same levels of competence from the outsourcing partner. If the established standards that brought consumer recognition to the brand are compromised, future business can be adversely affected.

COUNTRY REPUTATION is often a factor that plays a role in a consumer's assessment of the product. When a designer name, for example, implies that the garment was made in a country like Italy, known for its fine workmanship, but the label indicates the actual production has been accomplished in a less "prestigious" country, there might be a negative response from the ultimate consumer. While this would not generally cause concern for moderately priced goods, the marquee designer must exercise caution before going ahead with such outsourcing.

PRODUCTION CAPABILITY of the outsourced company must be assessed to make certain that orders of significant size may be accommodated. It is especially important if some orders are larger than those typically placed. In such instances, multiple suppliers could be the answer. Orders may be divided among several partners who can cumulatively handle product needs.

ONGOING PERFORMANCE EVALUATION is a necessity to determine if the outsourcing partner is producing the goods as promised. Quality controllers, for example, should make regular visits to the partner's premises to evaluate production in terms of established standards.

COST ASSESSMENT should be realistic and compare the expected savings with the cost of in-house production. Costs may be underestimated by the partner or hidden to gain the business of the fashion operation. Such expenses as shipping and handling, communication, and so forth must be accurately established with ceilings placed on the costs.

LOCAL LAWS in outsourced countries may carry certain restrictions and should be addressed before any contracts are signed. These might range from taxes and tariffs to the terms that deal with ownership.

EXPERIENCE OF THE PARTNER'S MANAGEMENT TEAM is vital because the company that has outsourced production is generally very far from the partnering operation. Being unable to oversee the day-to-day activities requires on-the-job expertise that will assure the highest level of performance.

PROXIMITY OF THE FABRICATING MATERIALS to the garment production plant is a consideration. If the materials used in the manufacturing process are far from the production point, not only might there be considerable costs in transporting them, but the time it takes for the transfer could be unacceptable. Finding partners that have all of the qualities necessary to manufacture items that meet company standards and are located closer to the production facility would be the best choice.

ASSUMPTIONS AND "GUESSTIMATES" should be avoided. While businesses have general notions about conditions in the United States, they cannot take chances concerning the same in overseas venues. This is especially true in developing countries where political unrest and government restrictions could affect the partner's daily operation.

DOMESTIC OUTSOURCING

For many years fashion manufacturers in the United States have chosen the option of outsourcing some of their operations to third parties that are domestically located. Those who perform these operations are called **contractors**. Most often their activities are cutting and sewing.

Although this form of outsourcing has been a popular option in the past, the practice has been steadily diminished and replaced with offshore outsourcing. **Domestic outsourcing** offers the benefits of proximity, but labor and other costs are generally greater than with offshore outsourcing. Some of the major reasons for the higher costs are the following:

- **Unionization**. Just like manufacturers who use in-house staffs to produce their garments, contractors are also faced with the rules and regulations set forth by union contracts. The end result of these arrangements is higher costs.

- **Fixed expenses**. With rental and utility expenses ever-increasing, the domestic contractor must continuously raise prices to compensate for these costs. In turn,

Many American manufacturers outsource their production to domestic contractors.

the manufacturers who have gone this route must raise their prices to cover the increase.

- **Labor shortages.** For many years, the industry had a greater number of experienced workers than the demand for them. Recent years have seen a change in the number of experienced people capable of doing the job right. Today's employment climate has drastically changed, with fewer and fewer people opting for this type of career. This, coupled with the problems of illegal immigrants, has made labor shortages a reality.

HIGH-PROFILE OFFSHORE OUTSOURCING VENUES

When we examine the labels in the garments produced by American fashion manufacturers, the appearance of "Made in the USA" is almost nonexistent. While marquee designers and manufacturer's brands are the hallmarks of most fashion products sold in the United States, there is little actual domestic production taking place on their part. As discussed in the preceding sections of this chapter, the trend has been for the manufacturers to move production offshore by partnering with other companies, leaving the U.S. companies to primarily engage in the marketing of the fashions they have designed. Some have even gone to outside sources for creating the styles, simply operating sales offices and using "road" staffs to sell their collections.

The reality of offshore outsourcing is underscored by examining Tables 19.1 and 19.2.

Table 19.1

SELECTED FASHION DESIGNERS WITH OUTSOURCED PRODUCTION

Designer	Selected Partnering Countries
Ralph Lauren	Malaysia, Hong Kong, Philippines, Sri Lanka
Donna Karan	China
Calvin Klein	China
Anne Klein	China
Liz Claiborne	China

Table 19.2

SELECTED RETAILERS WITH OUTSOURCED PRODUCTION

Retailer	Partnering Countries
Gap	Dominican Republic, China
Banana Republic	India, China
Macy's	Poland, China
Saks Fifth Avenue	India
Nordstrom	Canada, China

Donna Karan outsources some designs to be made in China.

Banana Republic uses Indian and Chinese firms for some production.

PREPARATION AND MEETING WITH POTENTIAL OUTSOURCING PARTNERS

Once manufacturers choose their outsourcing partner, they must prepare themselves before any meeting takes place. If the choice is a domestic contractor, the task is less challenging in terms of behavioral approaches, etiquette, and so forth. If, however, the decision is to contract with an offshore or nearshore outsourcing partner, language and the nuances of business dealing might be quite different from what the U.S. business community is accustomed to.

Besides language differences, each country has certain customs and expectations that must be properly handled. Where a shake of the hand is appropriate in the United States when greeting a business counterpart, this is not necessarily the case in Japan, where a bow of the head might be better appreciated.

The following countries, while not the only ones used as outsourcing partners, are examples of those generally involved in production for U.S. designers. The areas that must be addressed before any trip abroad is made, along with what might be expected during the meetings, are examined separately for each country.

China

The People's Republic of China has become one of the more important outsourcing partners for U.S. fashion designers in terms of merchandise production. Before entering the actual negotiations for a commitment to a manufacturing partnership, the following measures should be addressed:

- The use of an interpreter is preferred so that both parties understand the subtleties of the discussion.

- If the dialogue is undertaken without an interpreter, simple sentences, spoken with frequent pauses, will facilitate comprehension.

- Business cards should be printed in English on one side and Chinese on the other. The use of gold printing is a plus because this indicates prestige and prosperity.

- Chinese culture and history should be studied and used during the meeting.

- If a group is used to represent a company, be prepared for only the senior members to lead the discussion.

- Prepare proper dress for the occasion. Conservative suits with subdued ties for men, and conservative suits or dresses for women should be chosen.

Once the preliminary preparation has been completed, it is likely that the following will take place at the time of the meeting.

- A bow is the traditional Chinese approach, but in some situations a handshake is in order. The cue should be taken from the host.

- Be prepared for little smiling because emotions are generally repressed in business situations.

- Casual conversation regarding such areas as health is typical. The avoidance of politics is appropriate.

- In place of the word "no" to a question, expect "perhaps," "I'm not sure," or "we'll see" to be used. These really mean "no."

- Extended periods of negotiation or delays are typical and should be expected as normal procedure.

- Even when a deal seems to be struck, the meeting may be extended.

- A break for lunch is typical.

- Even when the deal seems to have been consummated, the Chinese have been known to try to make last-minute changes to improve their positions.

India

In addition to their ever-increasing presence in call centers, India has become an important contracting agent for U.S. designers and manufacturers.

Preliminary preparation before the actual trip abroad to seek out production partners includes the following:

- Learn some commonly used phrases in Hindi, one of the two major languages spoken in India. For most business dealings, however, English, the other official language, will suffice.

In China, where many American companies are outsourcing production, bowing is a traditional custom.

- Prepare a business wardrobe that will include suits and ties for men, and suits and dresses with high necklines and long sleeves for women. Leather apparel should be avoided since Hindus revere cows and do not use leather products.

- The hiring of an Indian lawyer will help maneuver through the details of contracts with companies. Legislation varies considerably among the various parts of India, thus making this an essential aspect of the prenegotiation.

- If your team has a high-ranking woman, expect this to require extra efforts because India is not generally comfortable with working women.

- The use of an Indian representative could help minimize any potential for negative dealings.

- PowerPoint presentations and detailed proposal plans should be prepared before the actual meeting takes place to give the participants a better knowledge of the company's background and needs for the business relationship.

Business suits, shirts, and ties are the preferred style of dress for international businesspeople.

After addressing the preliminaries, the actual negotiation will more than likely include some of the following:

- A delay in the actual starting time of the negotiation may take place because Indians are generally rather lax about time. This should not be considered an affront, just a typical occurrence.

- Small talk generally precedes direct negotiation. Talk of such mundane topics as the weather and one's trip to the country are common.

- A show of hospitality, such as serving tea, is often part of the negotiating process.

- Open disagreement with the terms is typically avoided. The negotiation may include comments stating a desire to discuss disagreements at a later time.

- A final decision is unlikely after a first meeting. Time is often necessary to discuss details with those who might not be present at the meeting.

- The use of a direct "no" is not appreciated in India; more vague statements of dissatisfaction, such as "we'll try," are more acceptable during a negotiating session.

- Many meetings are likely before a final arrangement is finalized.

Indonesia

Many U.S. companies are using Indonesia as partners in manufacturing their fashion products. Like other countries, they maintain certain principles in their carrying out of business practices. Before the actual negotiation takes place, some of the following should be expected or addressed:

- The nation is primarily made up of Muslims whose Islamic beliefs make them different from other countries. Studying their beliefs would be helpful in making long-standing business relationships.

- Women's positions are quite different from those of other Muslim countries, often making them participants in business dealings.

- When making preliminary arrangements for meeting with potential contractor partners, it is essential to make certain that the participants are high-ranking individuals who can make decisions.

- Indonesians are typically slow decision makers, and pressure to make quick decisions will more than likely hamper the proceedings.

- Conservative dress should be carefully prepared. Suits and ties are preferred for men, although a sport jacket and tie is acceptable. Women should make certain their arms are covered and skirts should be worn knee-length or longer. Suits or dresses are appropriate, but pantsuits should be avoided.

- An Indonesian representative should be employed, if possible, to advise on potentially delicate matters.

Once the preliminaries have been thought out, the actual meeting may involve the following:

- A delay of the meeting's expected starting time is typical. Being hurried is not expected in Indonesia.

- The use of a business card, printed in color and embossed, will be looked on favorably. Business cards should be carefully examined and not just stuffed into a pocket.

- Decision making is usually a group effort, so presenters should address the group and not an individual.

- Anger or causing embarrassment is strictly unacceptable. Losing faith can cause a deal to be lost. Respect and trust are essential to any negotiation.

- Expect the final decision to take many meetings, perhaps over months.

- Politeness is essential but will not determine the meetings outcome.

- Patience must be exercised during negotiations, the length of which may be longer than that generally experienced in the United States.

- No matter how long the actual meetings take, avoid showing impatience through loudness or body language.

Malaysia

Of late, Malaysia has become a very important offshore outsourcing center for U.S. manufacturers and designers. Before a meeting with an outsourcing partner in Malaysia, preplanning should be undertaken to address the following:

- A wardrobe comprised of linen clothes is important because of the hot and humid climate. Suit jackets and ties are safe bets, with the jacket likely to be removed once the meeting begins. Women should choose long-sleeved blouses and skirts that cover the knees and should not wear pants suits.

- Business cards should be prepared using English on one side and Chinese on the other because most businesspeople in Malaysia are Chinese.

Linen is the fabric of choice for businesswear in Malaysia, where the climate is hot and humid.

- The employment of a Malaysian rep would be beneficial to help understand the customs of the country.

The actual meeting will probably involve some of the following:

- Business cards will be exchanged and carefully examined.

- Long negotiating periods are typical with no decisions made until many trips to the country have been completed. The initial visit is primarily for the purpose of getting acquainted.

- Even though English is spoken, the grammar and pronunciations could imply different meanings, making a representative an important part of the negotiation.

- Losing face could be a disaster; courtesy is a must or the deal may be lost.

- If a question seems to be deliberately avoided, this is a way of saying "no" and should be an indication that it is time to move on to another topic.

- Expect long periods of silence during which time responses are being formulated. As much as 15 seconds could elapse before answering a question.

- It is not unusual for negotiations to continue even after a contract has been signed.

Mexico

Ever since NAFTA was passed, Mexico has become an important outsourcing partner for U.S. companies, particularly in the fashion industry. With inexpensive labor costs and its proximity to the United States, Mexico is very important in the manufacturing process.

Before embarking on a trip to enter into a contractual arrangement, U.S. fashion manufacturers must be aware of the following:

- The details of a contract, in terms of time, might not be met. Mexicans are known to take their time even if specific time frames have been established. Their use of the word *mañana*, which literally means "tomorrow," actually may mean longer.

- "No" is generally not used in negotiation. "Maybe" is used to mean the same thing.

- Be prepared to answer questions regarding prices for the same services in the United States so they can use them as points in the discussion.

- Learning about their culture, and showing interest in it, often gives extra credibility to the visiting business representative.

- Most business meetings will be interrupted for lunch or siesta, which may last several hours, so time must be allocated for it.

- Men should prepare a business wardrobe that features a conservative dark suit and tie. For women, the standard is conservatism in either dresses or classic suits.

Once these parameters have been established, and the meeting time set, the actual appointment should include the following:

- Make conversation that exhibits enthusiasm for the country and touches on Mexican culture and learning about it. Talking about one of the country's museums will give sufficient information to discuss before the actual business topics.

- Be ready to talk about recent company innovations because Mexicans are often accepting of them.

- Cultivating a personal relationship is generally important and may make the terms of the deal easier to achieve.

- Stress the importance of time, especially with fashion merchandise that is "perishable," and how lateness in production and shipping will affect business. Although this may be stressed, there is no telling if the time constraints will be met.

- A slow negotiating pace is the norm. Trying to rush details will not be welcome.

It should be emphasized that the countries discussed here are not the only ones engaged as outsourcing manufacturing partners for U.S. businesses. Through discussions with trade associations, examining trade papers, and utilizing governmental agencies, other countries will emerge as potential outsourcing nations.

Due to low labor costs and its proximity to the United States, Mexico has become an important outsourcing partner for U.S. companies.

CHAPTER HIGHLIGHTS

- U.S. businesses are reaching out to offshore outsourcing partners to produce their fashion merchandise in ever-increasing numbers.

- Contracting with fashion-production companies outside of the domestic markets requires significant attention to cultural differences in order to make the relationships proceed properly.

- Appropriate business dress is an essential part of the negotiating process.

- Prior to making the trip abroad, business executives must prepare themselves in terms of customs, language usage, and other cultural factors.

- Reduced labor costs, although often given as the main reason for outsourcing, doesn't always merit the practice.

- Outsourcing can adversely affect the U.S. economy by forcing the shutdown of manufacturing plants, creating ghost towns.

- Location of the outsourcing partner for fashion merchandise must be carefully considered to avoid extra shipping time.

- Cost assessment of outsourcing is necessary to determine if the anticipated savings warrant the arrangement.

- Domestic outsourcing is sometimes very costly due to union expenses and labor shortages.

- Many major retailers have gone the outsourcing route in the production of their private label collections.

- Among the leading outsourcing partnering countries for fashion merchandise production are China, Malaysia, Indonesia, and Mexico.

IMPORTANT FASHION TERMINOLOGY AND CONCEPTS

Contractors	Nearshoring	Outsourcing
Domestic outsourcing	Nearsourcing	Outsourcing partner
Fabricating materials	Offshoring	Quality control
Language nuances	Onshore outsourcing	Workforce displacement

FOR REVIEW

1. To what extent are today's fashion manufacturers actually producing their own collections?

2. What is meant by the term *onshore outsourcing*?

3. Explain why cultural differences must be explored by U.S. companies wishing to enter into offshore outsourcing.

4. How important is appropriate dress for those entering into negotiations with foreign producers, and how might they learn about the dos and don'ts?

5. What is generally conceded as the main reason for U.S. businesses to use outsourcing?

6. Is workforce displacement really a result of offshore outsourcing? Explain.

7. How might local customs affect outsourcing outcomes?

8. Are language nuances ever a reason for miscommunication between outsourcer companies and their counterparts in the United States?

9. Can the location of the potential outsourcing partner affect the U.S. manufacturer's bottom line? In what way?

10. Is it necessary for a U.S. manufacturer to visit his or her outsourcing partner to assess quality control?

11. What are the traditional procedures performed by domestic contractors in the production of fashion apparel?

12. Even if discussion with offshore outsourcers are in English, why might it be important to use an interpreter in the negotiation?

13. Why has Mexico become an important country for outsourcing?

14. Although the word *mañana* literally means "tomorrow," what might it actually mean when used in negotiations in Mexico?

15. Why shouldn't leather products be worn during negotiations with companies in India?

EXERCISES AND PROJECTS

1. Search the Internet to find companies that prepare executives for meetings with companies in foreign countries. Draft a summary of the important points of preparation.

2. Visit any major retailer in your area to examine the labels of the products in their merchandise assortments to discover which countries are producing the products. Make a list of five brands along with the countries that produce their products.

WEB SITES

By accessing these Web sites, you will be able to gain broader knowledge and up-to-date information on materials related to this chapter.

Connections Magazine
   www.connectionsmagazine.com

Executive Planet

www.executiveplanet.com

Cyborlink

www.cyborlink.com

Linguarama

www.linguarama.com

The Case of the Fashion Designer Who Wishes to Improve Company Profitability

Young and vibrant, with five years of experience as an assistant designer for a major fashion label, Paul Jefferies has had his share of raves from the fashion industry. Although the label for which he designs doesn't carry his signature, the fashion editorial press has singled him out as the driving force behind the resurgence of his company as a major player in the industry. His ability to assess the needs of the fashion-forward 25- to 35-year-old female, and create clothing, to which they most favorably respond, has given him thoughts about designing his own collection.

Although his talents are mainly in the creative arena, Paul believes he has enough overall knowledge of the industry to bring a collection to market that will prove to be a financial success. After a year of scouring friends, relatives, and acquaintances in the industry for backing, he has amassed a sufficient amount of money to mount a collection bearing his name on the label.

Planning has included taking a small space in an off-the-beaten-path section of Greenwich Village in New York, which will include a design studio, space for selling, and room for bookkeeping duties. The only area of concern that still requires a decision is the choice between offshore outsourcing, nearsourcing, or domestic contracting. The one decision that has been made in terms of production is not to handle it in-house. Together with his investors, Paul is involved in a discussion of the pros and cons of each possibility.

questions

1. What are the advantages of each of the choices for production?

2. Which option would you suggest as the logical choice? Defend your answer with factual criteria.

To Outsource or Not to Outsource

WILLIAM MCKINNEY, THERESA ENEBO, AND MICHAEL RINGMAN

Outsourcing and offshoring are two words that have become staples in household conversations across the United States and are part of daily life for more than 350,000 people who are employed in U.S. contact centers today. According to the National Association of Software and Services Companies, the outsourcing industry is responsible for nearly $5.1 billion in annual revenues in the United States. According to the research and analyst firm Gartner, the industry will exceed $12.2 billion by 2007. With so much discussion and conjecture about contact center outsourcing, how do you cut through the clutter and determine if outsourcing is right for your company?

There are considerable benefits to outsourcing your contact center services, including increased cost efficiency, access to cutting-edge technology, improved customer satisfaction, and greater functionality. There are also some crucial factors to consider when making the decision to outsource, such as internal transition challenges, the potential for lost jobs, and cultural differences in some offshore contact centers.

When making the decision to outsource or keep contact center operations in-house, it is imperative that you take a realistic look at your organization, its current operations, and where it's headed. As you decide what the right choice is for your company, consider the following list of dos and don'ts for successful outsourcing. They might be the difference between just hiring an outsource supplier or gaining a trusted, comprehensive outsource partner who makes your business more productive and profitable.

Doing it Right: The Rules for Successful Outsourcing. To ensure success with your company's outsourced contact center services, consider the following:

Do Consider the Big Picture. Most companies interested in outsourcing their contact center services look to decrease the costs associated with labor and technology, but outsourcing helps your company do more than just cut costs. Enlisting the help of an outsource partner can give your company access to the latest contact center technology without incurring the costs of purchasing, maintaining or upgrading expensive equipment. Technologies such as Voice-over-IP (VoIP), computer telephony integration (CTI), and interactive voice response (IVR) may not be affordable for in-house contact centers, but they add great value in the customer relationship management chain. Outsourcers can offer this technology at a favorable cost because of their scale, allowing for greater functionality and efficiency in the contact centers.

Also, most companies who outsource have core competencies that are distinctively different from customer care and contact center technology, ranging from manufacturing and retail to financial services. When they partner with an outsourcer, they gain the freedom to focus on their core competencies.

Finally, the decision to outsource can mean lost jobs within your company as you cut staff to avoid job duplication; however, outsourcing doesn't always have to translate into inevitable layoffs. Companies might choose to outsource only the technology component, keeping their current staff intact. Also, when companies outsource their contact center services, they have the ability to more accurately predict their staffing needs so they can avoid overstaffing or duplicating job functions.

Do Look for the Latest and Greatest. One of the key benefits of outsourcing is deferring the costs of expensive, state-of-the-art contact center technology to your outsource partner. Make sure to find a partner who employs the latest technology. Companies can see substantial cost savings when their outsource partner has the latest and most powerful technology.

Do Ensure Company-Wide Support. Before outsourcing your contact center services, ensure that you have as much internal acceptance and support for the change as possible. The number one factor in determining how well the transition to outsourced operations goes is the way the change is communicated and supported internally. Here are some tips:

1. Communicate openly with all employees, from executives to contact center and technology staff, about the transition and how it will help better serve customers, improve the company's performance, and make their jobs easier.
2. Establish clear and realistic objectives, goals, and expectations for

the transition. Depending on the number of call types and complexity of services, a gradual, phased approach will help ensure success.

3. Build a partner relationship with your outsourcer, as opposed to a supplier relationship. The relationship will be most successful if you openly share all information, policies and tools to thoroughly train new agents, familiarize them with your company, and better serve customers.

4. Know that you will face some challenges during the transition process, but, with the proper framework in place, internal support, and a trusted outsourcing partner, the benefits of outsourcing will certainly outweigh the challenges.

The Don'ts: Maximizing Your Outsource Partnership. Now that you know what you should consider when making the decision to outsource, here are a few equally important things to avoid:

Don't Consider Only Cost: As with any other product or service, cost is a critical factor. However, in the outsourcing business, the old adage, "You get what you pay for," rings true. Though most companies are looking to reduce contact center costs, companies should also look for an outsource partner who

can help identify and open additional revenue opportunities, provide technology that improves efficiency and lends more insight into your business processes, and help serve your customers better.

Though it's sometimes difficult for companies to trust an outsource partner with their customers, the customer experience is almost always improved. When companies are ill-equipped to handle customers efficiently—when customers are on hold too long, are transferred several times, have to repeat information, or their problems aren't solved—is when customer satisfaction suffers most.

Don't Give Up Control. The thought of giving up control of an integral part of your business, such as the contact center, may be a bit worrisome. However, many companies find that when they outsource their contact center services, they actually gain more control of the operations because of the measurability outsourcing provides. The contact center industry is likely one of the most measurable industries in the world and with advanced technology, companies can literally see how every minute in the call center is spent.

In the traditional in-house model, companies tracked according to budget and service level. By using an outsourcing partner, companies can track these areas and how their contact center operations

align with business metrics and objectives, providing a higher-level, full-scale view of how contact center operations affect the business as a whole.

Don't Outsource Just to Outsource. Outsourcing doesn't make sense for every company in every situation. If a company is planning to retain contact center staff along with an outsource partner, the job duplication usually cancels out any significant cost savings. If the existing staff is essential to the business, outsourcing is probably not your best option.

One of the greatest challenges companies face when deciding whether or not to outsource is the human element—the potential for lost jobs and the cultural differences in some offshore contact centers. Though outsourcing companies are taking numerous steps to improve these situations, even implementing accent neutralization programs, these concerns are very real and should be carefully considered in the decision process.

For companies around the world in virtually every industry, outsourcing can mean significant cost savings and increased efficiencies that directly impact the bottom line. However, companies must be in the right position, choose the right partner, and properly manage the transition process to truly achieve outsourcing success.

part five

merchandising fashion

Before retailers purchase merchandise, many look for expert assistance from outside sources. The largest of these information and advisory services are called resident buying offices. These offices, which are the focus of Chapter 20, provide information to the buyers, who can then make educated buying decisions.

Fashion retailers operate from a variety of locations, including downtown, central districts; malls; festival marketplaces; and high-fashion centers. Each store provides services in order to gain a competitive edge on its neighbors. Increasingly, these retailers, including department stores, specialty stores, and direct merchants, are selling directly to consumers through catalogs and online services. An overview of this constantly evolving area is found in Chapter 21.

To differentiate their operations from their competitors and to attract more shoppers into their stores, many retailers engage in advertising, special events, and visual presentations. Each segment of the fashion industry promotes itself through a variety of means, as described in Chapter 22. The fashion show is the most typical approach for designers. If their methods of operation are in line with customers' needs and if the right promotions are undertaken, success will probably follow.

resident buying offices and other fashion information sources for retailers

Fashion is not something that exists in dresses only. Fashion has to do with ideas, the way we live, with what is happening.

COCO CHANEL, DESIGNER

After you have completed this chapter, you will be able to discuss:

- The terms *resident buying office* and *commissionaire*.

- How a private office is different from an independent office.

- The services resident buying offices provide to their clients.

- Trade associations and trade publications as sources of fashion information, and the roles they play in the fashion industry.

- The importance of trade exposition to designers and manufacturers.

Decision making in the world of fashion is an ongoing process. Those involved must understand the consumers' needs and how best to accommodate them. At every stage of the process, fashion professionals need accurate information on fashion trends and consumer preferences. Chapter 16 discussed how designers and manufacturers acquire such information. This chapter focuses on sources for retailers.

The road from the point of production to the point of consumption is long and complicated. Successful fashion decision makers do not operate in a vacuum or make decisions on a whim. They rely on countless resources to gather accurate information so they can meet their goals.

The fashion industry has many institutions that provide information and advisory services to retailers, including resident buying offices, reporting services, trade associations, and trade publications. The astute fashion retailer uses the services of many of these resources before purchasing merchandise. Some services require annual membership contracts; others require relatively inexpensive dues.

RESIDENT BUYING OFFICES

In Chapter 16, we discussed the relationship of resident buying offices, or fashion merchandising and consulting groups, as some like to be called, to designers and manufacturers. Resident buying offices, the term that is still used by most people in the industry, also provide the *fashion retailer* with a significant number of services. They are located in wholesale fashion markets, where they have representatives who help store buyers with purchasing decisions.

Most offices are independent, serving the needs of their retail clients for an annual fee and commission. Those that are classified as store-owned, or private, provide services exclusively to their retail owners.

Independent Offices

A few hundred resident buying offices are found in the United States and abroad. In the United States, most are based in New York City. The larger ones have branch offices in regional whole-sale markets; some also maintain branches in the more important global fashion centers. With so many to choose from, retailers must decide which office best suits their needs. One of the best known of the independent resident buying offices is The Doneger Group, which is the focus of a World of Fashion Profile.

Selecting an Independent Office

If a company does not manage its own office, it must choose from the **independent offices** by analyzing a number of factors.

First is the roster of stores already represented by the office. Because the fashion business is highly competitive, it is unlikely that two competing merchants would want market representation by the same company. With information regularly disseminated to member stores on such topics as merchandise recommendations, new resources, and fashion direction, it is easy to understand how competitors could simply become clones of one another and eventually present the same fashion image. If care is taken to choose a market representative that has no competing stores as clients, ideas and information can be freely exchanged without concern for direct competition. This exchange of ideas is commonplace during market week, a period when merchants travel to their wholesale markets to preview the new lines at the resident buying office facilities.

Second, the cost of membership must be considered. The expense involved in market representation is based on a number of factors, including the size of the office, number of branches available, scope of global representation, types of services, and amount of direct purchasing undertaken for the client.

A review of typical contracts and fee schedules of numerous resident buying offices indicates that the following expenses are charged to the member stores:

1. An annual fee, generally paid in equal monthly installments, for the services provided by the office

2. A percentage of all merchandise purchased by the resident office for the store

3. A flat charge for postage

Finally, the prospective client should be certain that the services provided truly fill his or her needs. Not every retailer has the same requirements. Some might merely want a representative to place reorders or special orders, check delivery dates, and follow up on orders. Others who deal in off-price merchandise might only want to be directed to those vendors who have closeouts. Still others might want the full complement of services, including handling complaints with vendors, direction in fashion forecasting and promotion, and suggestions on visual presentation.

Store-Owned Offices

Some major department stores in the United States enjoy the advantage of having a **store-owned** office that works exclusively for them or a small group of affiliated

The resident buyer communicates with clients concerning decision-making policies.

THE DONEGER GROUP

Henry Doneger began his business in 1946, serving the needs of the fashion retailer. Today, The Doneger Group, located in New York City's garment center, is the largest resident buying office and market consulting firm in the United States.

Doneger's team of experts stands ready to solve the merchandising problems of small retailers as well as such giants of the fashion world as Nordstrom. The concept has been extremely successful because of the way Doneger's custom tailors and personalizes its services to fit individual needs.

To accomplish the many different tasks required by its clients, The Doneger Group is organized into several different divisions, including:

- *Doneger Buying Connection.* Emphasis is placed on the purchase of sportswear, apparel, and outerwear for the large-sized woman.
- *Doneger Kids.* Focus is children's wear in all price categories.
- *Doneger Menswear.* Men's tailored clothing and sportswear in all price points is the emphasis.
- *Price Point Buying.* The focus is on the off-price retailer.
- *D3 Doneger Design Direction.* This group is actively involved in fashion forecasting.
- *HDA International.* This import-export division addresses the major global markets.

- *Fashion Service.* This division is a trend forecasting service for women's wear.
- *Doneger Online Services.* The focus is on the Internet as a tool for creating an improved business environment.

Each division communicates with its clients in many ways. Typical publications are print and online newsletters that give clients a look at current and future fashion trends, private label announcements, seasonal planning guides, and trends booklets.

With experts in every aspect of the company's operation, Doneger has become the hallmark of the industry.

---

stores. Because they require considerable attention, their needs cannot be served by an independent who represents many clients. These offices are referred to as **private** (or corporate) **offices**.

Few companies are large enough to warrant an office that works exclusively for them. If, however, the company is sufficiently large or its degree of specialization is sufficiently unique, it might choose to establish an office for its exclusive use.

The Federated Department Store organization operates its own office called Macy's Merchandising Group. It primarily serves the more than 800 Macy's units across the United States and Bloomingdale's, the other department store in the organization. Its main responsibility is to develop private brands such as INC, Alfani, Charter Club, and others. Its role is to supply this type of merchandise that augments the independent brands that the store buyers choose for their inventories. Sears also has a private office because of the size and complexity of its business operations; Neiman Marcus, always in search of unique merchandise, also maintains a private office.

Independent Buying Office Services

The types of services provided by the independent resident buying offices vary from company to company. Some, such as The Doneger Group, offer every service that might possibly improve the performance of their member stores. The smaller establishments often restrict their services to market representation that places special orders and reorders, checks on the status of orders already placed, and makes recommendations on best-selling items.

The following discussion represents the scope of resident buying office operations and explains how they assist retailers to become more profitable.

Purchasing Merchandise

Although the store buyer is responsible for the purchase of merchandise, the resident office may be called on to place reorders or special orders, or, in some unusual cases, may be the sole purchasing agents for the store. For example, a store might have numerous requests for $150 white dresses and not have any in stock. With the store buyer far away from the market tending to store duties and responsibilities, he or she may authorize the resident buyer to scout the market for appropriate white dresses.

Reorders are merchandise requests that need immediate attention. Because the merchandise might also be reordered by other stores, its availability may be limited to just a few retailers. With time of the essence, the reorders are often placed by the resident buyers, who, because of their clout in the market, get better delivery time than the store buyer could.

Whenever an order is placed by the resident buying office, the client is charged a commission for the service.

Preparing for Market Week

The busiest time for resident buying offices is the period preceding and including market week. A market week is a time when manufacturers in a specific industry introduce their new collections to retailers. Buyers and merchandisers visit the wholesale market to purchase for the coming season.

Because the store buyers come to town for such short periods of time, every hour must be carefully spent. The resident buying office plays an important role by researching the market before the store buyer's arrival. The resident buying office staff prescreens the lines, investigates new resources, determines styling and color trends, and does any preliminary work necessary to make the store buyer's visit more productive. Some offices prepare fashion presentations during market week so that their clients will know what to expect in the market. Representatives often accompany store buyers to the manufacturer's showrooms to help formulate purchasing plans.

Resident buying office staff work very closely with buyers during market week.

Product Development

With the enormous growth of private label merchandise in major retailers' merchandise assortments, they have been able to sell items that are unique to their stores. For a retailer to develop a private label, there must be a need for a large quantity of the merchandise. Thus, only the largest of merchants have been able to participate in such programs.

Today, many resident buying offices are in the business of offering the same opportunity to their members. By employing **product developers**, the offices design and produce specific styles for the exclusive use of their customers. Because the membership of the office is restricted to noncompeting stores, the use of this private label merchandise will, in effect, be available only at the stores represented by the office. Under this arrangement, smaller retailers can now purchase private label merchandise in small quantities, something they were unable to do alone.

Best-Seller Notification

When the season opens, retailers hope for a few items that will generate constant reordering. It is difficult to predict which, if any, of the original purchases will become a best-seller, or hot item. Through their constant interaction with manufacturers and their member stores, resident buying offices are made aware of the season's best-sellers. Most offices regularly communicate such news to their customers through print and online product updates. In this way the retailer is made aware of what's "hot" and can purchase that merchandise. Most retailers will agree that it takes only a few best-sellers to make a season profitable.

Communications

For many years, one of the mainstays of communication between the buying offices and their retail members was the use of brochures and flyers. The vast number of items that were earmarked for dissemination took a great deal of time to produce and distribute. First, the information had to be written up by a buyer. Next, it was sent to the word-processing department to be produced as a typewritten piece. Finally, it was mailed to the client roster. At best, this process required two weeks, and the information was often received too late for prompt reaction.

Today, a giant step forward has been taken with the development of resident buying office Web sites. Using the Internet, these fashion services can now provide timely information to their customers. The Doneger Group, the largest of the resident buying offices, is accessible 24 hours a day at its Web site, Doneger Online. Many of the company's written reports are generated online, including information on color trends and promotional opportunities. Other newsworthy fashion items are featured as well. Having this information available instantaneously enables retailers to avail themselves of merchandise in a timely fashion.

Importing

Examination of the labels on apparel and accessories sold in the United States reveals that much merchandise is manufactured offshore. Major retailers regularly visit foreign markets and purchase goods that ultimately yield a higher profit than domestically produced goods. Small retailers, by virtue of their size and sales potential, cannot take advantage of this source of purchasing. Because the outlay of cash necessary for such an undertaking is out of their reach, they generally purchase their merchandise from the manufacturers' standard offerings. Most of the larger resident buying offices, however, now put such purchasing within the reach of the smaller merchants. With branches in foreign countries, or through affiliation with *commissionaires* (foreign resident buying offices), the procurement of imported items is made easy.

Group Purchasing

Many vendors have minimum order requirements that are too high for the smaller retailer. Some resident offices make such merchandise available by pooling these smaller orders into a larger one that complies with the purchasing regulations of the vendors. Not only do small retailers now have access to otherwise unavailable goods, but they might even receive a discount if the group order is large enough to qualify for a quantity discount. The end result of such **group purchasing** is desirable merchandise at a discounted price.

Promotional Activities

An important key to success for any retailer is recognition. Few if any stores can boast freedom from competition. To attract attention and motivate shoppers to visit their stores, major retailers spend large sums on sales promotion and advertising. Without the advantage of an in-house staff or the dollars needed for participation in promotional activities, most smaller retailers are unable to participate in such sales campaigns.

Some of the full-service resident buying offices have sales promotion departments to plan and develop brochures that can easily be adapted for store use, provide expertise on advertising layouts, recommend directions for every aspect of visual merchandising, and prepare mailers for insertion into customer monthly billing statements.

Off-Price Purchases

Vendors must often dispose of merchandise in their inventories to make way for the next season's goods. They might have styles that did not sell as well as anticipated, colors that did not seem to capture the consumer market, or broken size ranges. Much like their retail counterparts, vendors run sales to turn over their inventories. One of the best deal makers in these situations is the resident buying office. It negotiates with the manufacturers for a rock-bottom price and makes the goods available to member stores. Many retailers take advantage of the situation by buying off-price products and mixing the recently acquired goods with their regular merchandise. They might choose to sell these new items at regular prices, actually reflecting a very high markup for a while, reaping the benefits from the reduced prices they pay, or they may sell them quickly at bargain prices. Many promotional retailers perceive this as the most important service offered by resident buying offices. In fact, some offices have separate off-price divisions, and some are strictly organized as an off-price resident buying office. By utilizing this type of merchandise procurement, the smaller retailer can compete more easily with the giants in the industry, who are able to negotiate these closeout deals for themselves.

Checking on Delivery

Once an order has been placed, it is never safe to assume that the shipment will be delivered by the specified time. Manufacturers are notorious for shipping goods after the order's scheduled completion date. Their excuses run the gamut from employee slowdowns to late delivery of the materials needed for production. Although these might sometimes be valid explanations, they are frequently just excuses. Some manufacturers simply make promises they cannot keep or even sell merchandise earmarked for one store to another.

Whatever the reasons for the delays, retailers are the ones who suffer. They buy according to specific purchase plans and must have sufficient goods on hand to do business. Otherwise, customers will simply go elsewhere to satisfy their needs.

Most resident buying offices constantly check on the status of their customers' orders. In fact, this is one of the major duties of the resident assistant buyer. Because the offices have considerable clout by virtue of the number of stores they represent, they can apply pressure to have the goods shipped on time. If they discover that the merchandise will not be delivered as promised, they can attempt to find replacement goods for their clients.

Making Adjustments

Substitution shipping is as commonplace in the fashion industry as late delivery. Manufacturers sometimes substitute another color for the one that was ordered, send sizes that were not ordered, use a different fabric in the construction of a garment, or even send styles not ordered in place of those that were.

These occurrences are not just bothersome, they can cause serious problems for the store. The retailer now has merchandise that might not suit the store's needs. Merchandise that has been substituted for other items may be returned, but that leaves the retailer with a void in the inventory. Resident buyers are most often called on to handle such adjustments. They might persuade the vendor to give the store a discount on the unordered merchandise they keep or make arrangements for price reductions on the next order. Whatever the solution, the resident buyer can represent the store in such negotiations.

Other adjustments for problems such as minor damage, returns for discoloration in laundering, shrinkage, and improper fit are often handled by the resident office.

Resident buyers, busy at their desks, are always ready to communicate market news to the stores.

Whereas an individual retailer might receive unsatisfactory responses, the resident office is usually successful.

Merchandising

Although the store buyer is ultimately responsible for quantities, promotional endeavors, and visual presentation on the selling floor, outside help is often needed to solve some of these problems. Resident offices are generally available to assist with specific problems. Because they deal with so many manufacturers who make suggestions on how to merchandise their lines and so many clients who address these problems on a daily basis, they are excellent resources for such advice.

Making Store Supplies Available

The initial establishment of a retail operation and the improvement of an existing one involve the planning of store designs, acquiring fixtures, planning and procuring of proper lighting, purchasing of props and mannequins, developing appropriate packaging needs, and purchasing of everyday supplies.

In this complex field, merchants, who are more attuned to merchandising and management decisions, use full-service resident buying offices to address and solve such problems.

Direct-Mail Programming

Retailers are increasing their sales volume through catalogs. Although larger merchants have the facility for such endeavors, the smaller retailer is often unfamiliar with the direct-mail arena. More and more full-service resident offices are developing catalogs for their clients. They might be specific merchandise booklets directed at a specific market or more general merchandise catalogs. These catalogs feature the merchandise the office believes will generate the most business. The office makes arrangements to have the proper assortment delivered to the store in anticipation of customer orders.

FOREIGN RESIDENT BUYING OFFICES

With fashion truly a global industry, merchandise is now produced in every part of the world. The fascination with foreign-produced goods is no longer limited to the prestige and quality associated with them. Now, lower prices coupled with excellent design also make merchandise imports desirable.

Major fashion retailers regularly visit international markets in pursuit of merchandise. Many have corporate or cooperative resident buying offices that maintain foreign branches to purchase merchandise. Some of the larger, independent resident offices also have representation through their own foreign branches.

In addition to these arrangements, countries all over the world have independent resident buying offices known as **commissionaires**. Although the word *commissionaire* is French, it is used wherever foreign offices function.

Top: Resident buyers and store buyers regularly cover trade shows all over the world. Bottom: Manufacturer's booths are featured at trade shows so that buyers can view the lines under one roof.

As with their U.S. counterparts, commissionaires are service specialists. Working either on a fixed fee or for a percentage of the purchase cost, these agents provide the expertise needed for Americans to participate in the fashion importing arena. Not only do they make arrangements for merchandise selection, but they are also knowledgeable about quotas, tariffs, shipping arrangements, price negotiations, and storage. Because the acquisition of such goods is more complicated than that of goods domestically purchased, the store buyer must provide detailed information about the items to be imported. Dealing with a foreign vendor is often complicated by poor communication. The commissionaire's ability to speak the country's language often results in better terms for the American purchaser.

Just as domestic resident buyers assist their clients with market visits, commissionaires also accompany buyers to visit manufacturers abroad. They can make any purchasing visit more productive by screening lines and taking buyers directly to the most promising vendors.

REPORTING SERVICES

Retailers interested in keeping informed about developments on the fashion scene may subscribe to a reporting service. These companies are in business only to provide industry-wide information in a variety of reports.

One of the major companies in this field is the Retail Reporting Corporation. It publishes a number of informational pieces that assist the fashion retailer in merchandise planning and acquisition. Among their offerings are the following regular reports:

- *New Resources*. Published weekly, this report alerts buyers to new companies and the merchandise they produce.

- *Hotline*. This weekly presentation highlights merchandise that appears headed for success.

- *Retail Executive Digest*. This weekly analysis of retailing covers every aspect of the business.

- *Editor's Overview*. This analysis of the market highlights resources of importance, designer collections, accessories information, and retailers of distinction.

- *Reorder Report*. This report is a compilation of the week's hottest items and the names of retailers experiencing success with these items.

- *Merchandise Report*. An individual analysis of a particular item, this report is complete with the resource, price, and store that is featuring the item, and where it has been advertised.

- *Accessories*. This weekly publication covers the latest in shoes, hosiery, jewelry, hats, gloves, and handbags, suggesting where selected styles may be purchased.

TRADE ASSOCIATIONS

Throughout the fashion industry, at home and abroad, organizations have been formed to serve specific fashion groups. Their goals are primarily to publicize the specific industry component they serve to those who have the potential use for their products. Collectively, they plan seminars, prepare informational reports, conduct studies, confer awards, and disseminate information on trends.

Most segments of the fashion industry are served by these **trade associations**. Among the better known are the Chambre Syndicale, the Council of Fashion Designers of America (CFDA), the National Retail Federation (NRF), Cotton Incorporated, the Wool Bureau, Fashion Group, the Fashion Footwear Association of New York (FFANY), the Footwear Industries of America, and the Leather Apparel Association. CFDA is featured in a World of Fashion Profile in Chapter 10.

National Retail Federation

The largest of the trade associations representing the retail industry is the **National Retail Federation (NRF)**, headquartered in Washington, D.C., and previously known as the National Retail Merchants Association (or NRMA).

Representing the major department stores and specialty chains in the country, the NRF holds its annual national meeting every January in New York City. At that time, the industry leaders make presentations examining the vital areas of retailing. Regional meetings are also held throughout the year to deal with specific areas of retail concern. The various meetings provide fashion merchants, as well as others, with information on trends, pricing considerations, offshore sources of supplies, consumer motivation, and visual merchandising. In addition to professional topical seminars, numerous trade suppliers are on hand to introduce the retailing industry to the latest available technology and products for the merchandising, management, and operations of their stores.

In addition to informative meetings, the NRF publishes a variety of journals and periodicals that enable retailers to get a glimpse of the market. Of particular importance is *Stores* magazine, which presents articles on retailers, designers, product development, and innovative trends. The magazine provides information that readers can adapt to their own situations.

The National Retail Federation is the largest retail trade association.

Trade Publications

One of the best sources of information about the fashion industry is the **trade publication**. Published on a daily, weekly, or monthly basis, trade publications provide up-to-the-minute details on what is current in the industry and what can be expected. For a nominal cost, designers, manufacturers, retailers, and anyone with an interest in fashion can quickly learn about the industry. Some periodicals are directed toward a specific market segment; others provide a general market overview.

The principal player in fashion-oriented trade publications is Fairchild Publications. Based in New York City, it publishes such influential newspapers as *Women's Wear Daily* (*WWD*), which covers both the domestic and international scene on women's and children's clothing, accessories, and textiles. *Daily News Record* (*DNR*) is another Fairchild publication for the menswear and textile industries. Other U.S.-produced trade periodicals include *Fashion International*, *Fashion Showcase Retailer*, and the *California Apparel News*.

An excellent monthly publication for retailers is *Stores* magazine, which features every aspect of retail management and merchandising from industry trends to current interests. It is published by the National Retail Federation.

VM&SD (*Visual Merchandising and Store Design*) is a monthly publication of particular importance to people responsible for visual merchandising and display

Periodicals for every segment of the fashion industry are published by the Fairchild Fashion Group, a division of Condé Nast Publications.

programs. It features articles on display innovation, prop acquisition, new materials, and lighting and general store design.

Trade publications from abroad help decision makers in the United States keep abreast of what is happening all over the world. Excellent sources of information about the international fashion scene include *Style* from Canada; *Gap* from France; *Textile Forecast, Fashion Forecast, Fashion Update, Fashionews, Fashion Record, Fashion Weekly,* and *Fashion Extras* from Great Britain; *Femme Elégante* from Spain; *Mode* from Australia; and *Italian Design Fashion* and *Sposabella* from Italy.

CONSUMER PUBLICATIONS

Some fashion magazines, such as *Harper's Bazaar, Elle, GQ, Essence, Vogue,* and *Glamour,* are produced for consumers. *W* is a bimonthly Fairchild publication for the consumer that explores the fashion scene, from the designer's collections to who is wearing what fashions. Because buyers, manufacturers, and designers should be aware of what fashion news the consumer is being fed, they regularly study these **consumer publications**. Editors of consumer fashion publications wield considerable power in the industry because their readers often follow their suggestions. A knowledgeable fashion buyer can evaluate the fashion emphasis for a particular season in these publications and adjust inventory to reflect what the consumer is being shown.

In addition to the domestic consumer magazines, more and more foreign publications grace this country's newsstands. Such magazines as *Linea Italiana, L'Official,* and *Paris Vogue* are read consistently by the U.S. fashion industry for inspiration and information.

CHOOSING INFORMATION RESOURCES

The fashion professional can choose from a wide range of information and advisory resources. If there are no budgetary restraints, the motto is the more the merrier. Everyone connected with fashion is constantly seeking newer and better ways to reach as many customers as possible. By subscribing to these resources, a total overview of the fashion market can be developed.

Companies with less to spend on information must be more selective in choosing resources. Is the resident buying office a better choice than the reporting service? Only careful exploration of individual needs will provide the appropriate answer.

If financial resources are very limited, the best route to take is the trade publication. For very little money, a subscription to a publication such as *Women's Wear Daily* will bring relevant information that can be used in making retail decisions. One trade paper, supplemented by the consumer periodicals, could supply just enough to keep those in the industry aware of what is happening.

CHAPTER HIGHLIGHTS

- One of the keys for success in the fashion industry is current information. It takes only a few errors in judgment to lead a company into bankruptcy.

- Knowledgeable fashion practitioners seek as much industrial advice as possible before making fashion decisions.

- The sources available for information and advisory services include the resident buying office, reporting services, trade associations, and trade publications.

IMPORTANT FASHION TERMINOLOGY AND CONCEPTS

commissionaires	National Retail Federation	substitution shipping
consumer publication	(NRF)	trade association
cooperative office	private office	trade publication
group purchasing	product developers	
independent office	store-owned office	

FOR REVIEW

1. What advantage does the private resident office afford its stores that independent offices do not?
2. Briefly describe the costs of resident buying office membership.
3. To what extent do resident buying offices perform actual purchasing services?
4. Describe market week.
5. How important is the best-seller notification by resident offices to their members?
6. How can resident offices make available goods that are otherwise unavailable to retailers whose requirements are comparatively small?
7. Why have foreign resident buying offices become increasingly important?
8. What is a reporting service?
9. How does a trade association help retailers learn about industry trends?
10. How can a consumer publication help fashion buyers improve their positions?

EXERCISES AND PROJECTS

1. Contact an independent resident buying office requesting information on its operation and the forms it uses for client communication. Prepare an oral presentation on the information received, highlighting such aspects as costs for members, services available, and markets served.
2. Select a trade publication, such as *Women's Wear Daily*, *DNR*, or *California Apparel News*. Discuss the publication's various features. How much space is devoted to trend columns, hot items, manufacturer advertising, and classified advertising?
3. Make an appointment with a fashion buyer or assistant buyer from a large department store to learn about the information and advisory resources they use in the selection of merchandise. Present the information in a report to the class.

WEB SITES

By accessing these Web sites, you will be able to gain broader knowledge and up-to-date information on materials related to this chapter.

The Doneger Group
   www.doneger.com

Forecast and Reporting Services
   www.fashionindex.com

The Case of High-Fashion Competition

The Female Connoisseur is a specialty retail organization that epitomizes haute couture. Designer collections from all of the world's fashion centers grace its selling floors. The company has grown. In its present position, it operates a flagship store and six branches. The clientele for the Female Connoisseur is extremely affluent and is willing to pay any price for unusual fashion designs.

In its quest for high-fashion merchandise, the store uses a resident buying office specializing in upscale merchandise. The office assists the store buyers, who have the actual purchasing responsibility. The office has excellent coverage of the U.S. and international fashion markets. The ever-increasing annual profit margin is indicative of the store's acceptance by the high-fashion consumer.

With the emphasis on international fashion merchandising, the store has started to feel competition it has never before experienced. In particular, Raleighs, a major department store, has just expanded its designer offerings. Because Raleighs and the Female Connoisseur flagship stores are located opposite each other, the newly expanded fashion collection at Raleighs is resulting in intense competition. What was once an ideal, unique retail situation has now become a challenge to maintain. The Female Connoisseur is being aggressively challenged.

Amanda Baker, the store's fashion director, believes the time is ripe for the introduction of an exclusive private label collection of designer-quality dresses and sportswear. If quality and design could be the hallmark of their own line, they could slowly motivate their customers to buy private label merchandise and concentrate less on lines that both stores feature. Her suggestion that the retailer hire its own design staff to create its own line has met with opposition from management, which contends, "We are retailers and should stick to what we know best." Furthermore, the experiment could be extremely costly, requiring a large capital expenditure for workrooms and equipment.

While the challenge of producing private labels still intrigues the company, no one has come up with a plan that satisfies management.

questions

1. Is a high-fashion couture private label a reasonable approach?

2. Do you agree with management's decision not to hire a design team and build a design facility? Explain.

3. How would you suggest the Female Connoisseur confront this new competition?

Doneger Group at 60: Adapting is Key

DAVID MOIN

New York—It's an odd time for Abbey Doneger, president of The Doneger Group, to discuss acquisitions. It's not that another one is imminent. It's just that there's nothing on the table at the moment, which is unusual for him.

In any event, he'd much rather discuss his son's lacrosse game, or his staff, which he considers family. Several have been on board for a decade or longer, including senior merchants Roseanne Cumella and Kathy Bradley-Riley, and Joan Rivera, the spunky lobby receptionist who greets visitors with, "Hello, gorgeous." It's a company that's attracted talent from fallen retailers and by absorbing other firms.

"We've acquired businesses that provided us with new clients, that have expanded our services, and we've added industry expertise. All of that has helped reposition the company. But number one, an acquisition is for talent," Doneger said during an interview, after arranging photos of his father, his wife and three sons so they're in the view of a photographer taking his picture.

"I always think about change and positioning the company as a one-stop shop for any retailer, manufacturer or designer."

The Doneger Group has been on a prolonged buying spree, acquiring 18 companies since 1980—buying offices, consultants, trend forecasters and publications have been gobbled up. The strategy has not only eliminated competition, it's helped Doneger transcend a dated image of a traditional buying office,

a format that's virtually extinct now, and evolve into a more modern and rounded fashion merchandising, consulting and trend-forecasting organization that now does little actual buying on behalf of retailers. Instead, "We are doing a lot of the kinds of activities that determine what retailers will be buying, in terms of research and analysis," the 55-year-old Doneger said. "Retailers are looking for expertise. And if you ask me what they have to do, they need to attract talent and stay fresh with their merchandise presentations. Apparel stores are not just competing against other apparel stores. They're competing against Apple and Starbucks for consumer dollars."

His last acquisition was Here & There, a provider of fashion information and trend publications, in September. Again, Doneger is quick to point out talent was the driver and the key asset is Kai Chow, creative director of Here & There. Chow visits 14 cities around the world each year shopping stores, mills and textile companies to build up a veritable library of swatches and styles into which product developers from such stores as Target, Wal-Mart and J.C. Penney, as well as designers, can tap.

Tonight, The Fashion Institute of Technology will honor The Doneger Group on its 60th anniversary at FIT's John E. Reeves Great Hall. It's a benefit for the Henry Doneger Scholarship Fund for FIT students enrolled in the baccalaureate fashion merchandising management program, expected to draw more than 600 people. The privately held Doneger Group

was founded in 1946 by Abbey's father, the late Henry Doneger, whose name is still on the front door to the offices at 463 Seventh Avenue here.

"I worked side by side with my father for over 20 years," Abbey said. "We actually shared an office early on. For him, family was numbers one, two and three in priority. I learned about leadership from him and how to lead by example. He was a strong personality, but always treated people fairly. He took pride in opening the office every morning at 7:30. His style was different from mine; he could be a little rough-and-tumble. My style is a little bit softer on the outside," and associates say the younger Doneger is very hands-on management in a way that's more paternal than demanding.

The Henry Doneger Associates division remains the heart and soul of the company, consisting of 60 market analysts who shop the fashion markets and counsel retailers on items, trends, key resources and emerging classifications. They visit the stores to help fill the merchandise voids and regulate the inventory excesses, and work with clients on specific projects, such as product development. They save store buyers time in the market by previewing lines in advance and weeding out those that are not right for the store. "Even for the most experienced professional, Seventh Avenue can be overwhelming," Doneger said.

"Every retailer is trying to figure out how to differentiate themselves, and at the same time, [is] trying to generate more sales," observed Tom Burns, another Doneger veteran who serves as senior vice president for developing new businesses and clients and oversees the creative services unit. "They want to add value in their product offerings. They want to build powerful brands within their four walls and build the store into a brand itself. We are an enabler. It's our job to have an opinion and make recommendations. If we make 10 and only one gets accepted and works, that's great. It's our responsibility to be able to drill down, really examine a store and determine what will work."

"We are very 'roll-up-your-sleeves' consultants," added Leslie Ghize, senior vice president for strategic initiatives and day-to-day operations. "We are not just sitting and talking. All of our merchants are in the stores. They know what's in there. They become very much part of the store team."

Regarding what stores are angling for, "Everybody is looking to be better, better, better," Ghize said. "Nobody wants to buy a plain tube of toothpaste anymore."

Other Doneger's clients include Nordstrom, Dillard's, Belk, Kohl's, TJ Maxx, Overstock.com, ShopNBC, Home Shopping Network, Bon-Ton and Boscov's. International clients include Almacenes Paris in Chile, the Suburbia specialty division of Wal-Mart Mexico; Sears Mexico; House of Fraser in the U.K.; Edgar's and Woolworth's in South Africa, and Robinson's in Singapore. About 20 percent of the 350 clients are major chains; the bulk are smaller specialty chains and mom-and-pops. Doneger publications under the names Style Insight, West Coast Insight, Euro Insight, First and Investments are geared to reinforce information learned from visits to the office.

The group also includes the Carol Hoffman division, a buying office purchased in 2001. It has 75 retail clients selling contemporary, better and designer-priced women's clothes, giving Doneger an upscale orientation.

Tobe, publisher of The Tobe Report, was acquired last year. "Tobe is a well-established brand with an international following," including Neiman Marcus and Gap, Doneger said. "We're running it as a separate division and will give it its own new space. Tobe does a big-picture analysis of industry trends with some consulting services wrapped around that, while Doneger is a service organization with some publications wrapped around its services," he explained.

There are also the Price Point Buying off-price division and the Doneger Consulting unit for special projects, such as product development and strategic initiatives.

The other dimension to Doneger is called Creative Services. It provides trend and forecasting publications and advice. Creative Services has 450 subscribers and clients including retailers, designers and manufacturers.

Walking into the 45,000-square-foot Doneger offices here, there are thousands of samples on racks in the halls. To the unfamiliar, it appears to be a serious case of clutter. But each garment on each rack has a purpose—to illustrate a trend, a bestseller or a hot label.

"Here's a blouse attached to a sweater; we show it to a buyer, tell them what it means and they get it," said Cumella, senior vice president of merchandising, overseeing dresses, outerwear, suits, intimate apparel and accessories. In this case, the blouse illustrates a fashion story on layered looks and black on white. Items end up on wall grids in meeting rooms where fashion presentations to retailers take place. The information is reinforced with Doneger publications, which are available online, and by preliminary macro overviews of what's happening in the world of fashion by the creative services team.

"A store like Nordstrom comes in and wants to see what's new. Any of our specialists has to have more information than anybody she talks to," added Cumella. "If Nordstrom has a question about a line, I better know the answer."

For higher-priced fashion-forward retailers, such as Nordstrom, the objective is to spotlight new resources and designers. For lower-priced stores, it's about highlighting the tried-and-true looks and labels. They don't necessarily want to be first out with trends. "We drill down the information and customize it for retailers," said Kathy Bradley-Riley, senior vice president of merchandising for sportswear. "There have been major categories of business that we had a pulse on early on, like premium denim, contemporary sportswear. It's our job to see it and understand it and translate it to our clients."

Between all the racks, the product stories, the publications and the trend information, Doneger is a kind of a microcosm for what's happening on Seventh Avenue. Currently, it's a combination of merchandise representing Christmas reorders, spring and fall. A visit to one room revealed a presentation demonstrating proportion shifts, to skinnier bottoms, high-waisted looks and loose tops with some volume. "Skinny-legged jeans will be more of a fall 2007 story than this fall, and overalls with bibs will be an important look in the junior market. The overalls are more feminine and less farmer than the past," said Cumella.

Industry sources estimate The Doneger Group generates about $25 million in annual revenues through retainer fees collected from retailers based on the scope of services provided, and manufacturers can advertise in Doneger publications and on its Web site.

The company is a small operation with industry sway. "We consider Doneger an excellent source for global market trends," said Liz Sweeney, president of women's apparel for J.C. Penney. "Their considerable services are important to our trend, merchant and design organization."

"I've been in business for 44 years and with Doneger for 43 years," said Joseph Dugan, owner and president of the Colony Shop Inc., a moderate-to-better-priced, nine-unit women's specialty chain in Arkansas, and perhaps Doneger's longest-standing client. "We visit Doneger a minimum of seven times a year. When we are in the market, we start and finish each day at Doneger. They know the vendors that are performing, what's coming in the future and what happened in the past. I've seen a lot of the other [buying offices] go out of business. They are the only one I know doing a complete job. Without their services, we could not have made it all these years."

Women's Wear Daily, November 6, 2006

chapter 21

the fashion retailer

Good taste shouldn't have to cost anything extra.

MICKEY DREXLER, J. CREW CEO

The hopes and dreams of fashion designers are ultimately in the hands of the fashion retailers. The design team can create an exciting new silhouette or coloration, but it is their retail counterparts who determine which products will be offered for sale. Retail buyers and merchandisers screen all available merchandise before deciding which lines to display.

Fashion retailers are motivated by the needs of their specific consumer markets. Some stores concentrate on fashion-forward merchandise at very expensive price points. Others cater to the fashion-conscious consumer, who wants the latest designs at affordable prices. Between these extremes, there are shoppers with other motivations. Because fashion is an ever-changing industry, retailers must determine which new ideas and concepts will satisfy the needs of specific consumer groups.

These retailers are responsible for the successful distribution of fashion. What organizational structures govern their activities? In what types of settings are these fashion retailers found? How do these retail operations confront increasing competition to gain their fair share of the market? How are fashion retailers using the Internet and online shopping services to generate additional sales of their merchandise? These are some of the questions addressed in this chapter.

After you have completed this chapter, you will be able to discuss:

- The differences among flagship, branch, and spinoff stores.

- The reasons off-price retailers sell at lower prices but achieve significantly higher markups.

- Why many fashion manufacturers have opened their own retail outlets.

- The different ways in which retailers are using the Internet to promote sales of their products.

- Five services that large fashion retail operations offer to customers.

- The various participants in the merchandise selection processes at most department stores.

CLASSIFYING THE RETAILERS

Retail organizations in the 21st century bear little, if any, resemblance to the trading posts and general stores of earlier days. In the highly specialized and very competitive environments of today, retailers with fashion orientations cannot rely on the techniques of their predecessors.

There are many types of retailers, each with a specific formula for attracting customers. Some are industrial giants; others, small entrepreneurs. Although there are

specific classifications of retailers, consumers are often confused by the groupings. For example, Saks Fifth Avenue and Macy's are both department stores. The former, however, is technically a specialty department store because its merchandise is primarily concentrated in one major category—apparel. Macy's, on the other hand, is a traditional department store. It carries a wide assortment of both apparel (**soft goods**) and nonapparel (**hard goods**) lines, such as electronics and furniture. The following discussion describes the different types of retail classifications, based on merchandise assortment and methods of operation.

Department Stores

An outgrowth of the general store, which featured an assortment of merchandise in a casual or, more accurately, a disorganized array, department stores present a wide range of merchandise in defined areas or departments. As described previously, traditional department stores sell hard goods and soft goods; specialized department stores sell only one major type of merchandise. Both groups operate from a **flagship**, or main store; they expand their operations by opening **branches** that carry a representative sampling of the flagship's offerings.

Top: Bergdorf Goodman epitomizes upscale American retailers. Above: Fashion-oriented malls are among the most successful venues for retailers.

Macy's annual Flower Show is just one major event sponsored by the department store.

Many department stores are starting to compete with specialty stores by opening smaller units that restrict their assortment to one narrow type of merchandise. They are called spinoff, or twig, stores. Macy's is a leader in such operations, with spinoffs of some of its more successful lines. For example, Charter Club operations, which carry private label merchandise, can be found across the country. This trend appeals to customers who increasingly prefer to shop in smaller surroundings. By selling products that have already proven successful, these spinoff stores satisfy many shoppers' needs and earn profits for their companies.

Even if a department store features both soft goods and hard goods, consumers are mainly attracted by fashion merchandise. For example, Sears, which built its reputation on appliances and tools, has undertaken promotional campaigns to underscore its shift toward more fashion merchandise. Profitability is the major factor in the disproportionate assortment of fashion items to hard goods.

Department stores with strong fashion orientations are the most aggressive in terms of advertising and promotion. Macy's, Bloomingdale's, and Lord & Taylor have almost daily fashion promotions in newspapers to capture the customer's attention. The final chapter of this text explores the department store's concentration on promotion. Department stores also try to develop a retailing image that sets them apart from the competition. For example, customer service and attentive selling are features that customers associate with Nordstrom, the subject of a World of Fashion Profile.

Department stores generally feature a category of apparel at many price points, each presented in a different area of the store. Thus a store might sell sportswear in three different locations—main floor, third floor, and sixth floor—but each concentrates on a separate price range or price point. In the past, stores differentiated departments by such terms as better, moderate, or budget. Today, the progressive retailer has eliminated these obvious price designations and has assigned catchy names to each area. Consumers, however, soon come to understand what prices each name stands for. Bloomingdale's, for example, houses its moderate dress collection in Boulevard Dresses.

Many department stores are now involved in a new concept of separation called **collection merchandising**. More and more shoppers are looking for merchandise from the collections of specific designers. Therefore, instead of grouping merchandise by product category, stores are establishing departments that feature the merchandise of a well-known designer. DKNY, Tommy Hilfiger, Giorgio Armani, Liz Claiborne, and Ralph Lauren are merchandised in this manner. Sometimes, the designer makes this arrangement mandatory and may also determine how the collection will be visually presented on the store's selling floor. Ralph Lauren, for example, requires that his merchandise be featured in separate shops that use the Lauren "lifestyles" approach to fixtures and props.

In a related trend, some department stores are leasing floor space to outside businesses. **Leased departments** often include the cosmetics, furs, and fine jewelry departments. If the merchandise warrants specialized retailing ability, it is better to lease the space to an outside expert for a portion of the profits. To the consumer, it is another department in the store; to the department store, it is a department that follows the store's rules, but operates independently.

Department stores are a global phenomenon, but the majority are in the United States. Although London boasts Harrods, and Paris, Printemps, the United States' entries are significantly more numerous. Examples include Bloomingdale's and Macy's, with the latter now operating more than 800 units all over the country, and Filene's in the Northeast.

NORDSTROM

A Seattle-based department store, Nordstrom is becoming the envy of department stores across the nation. After opening its doors in 1901 as a shoe store, it initially expanded its merchandising mix by adding apparel to its offerings. The philosophy of carefully assisting shoe customers at the time of purchase was carried over to the store's newer divisions. With service becoming the benchmark on which it would build a reputation, sales per square foot rose to a level twice the national average.

At a time when many department stores are closing their operations, Nordstrom is moving ahead with opening after successful opening. Not only is the company expanding in the West, where it is based, but also on the East Coast.

Although Nordstrom carries exciting merchandise, that is not the only reason for its success. Most industry professionals agree that the retailer's attention to customer convenience is what separates Nordstrom from the rest of the field. In many of the stores, a formally attired pianist sets the tone by playing a grand piano in the center of the selling floor. Many departments have upholstered chairs for tired customers, changing rooms for parents tending to babies, and tables where children can use coloring books. These are just some of the touches that make Nordstrom unique.

Attentive selling is also a Nordstrom forte. Paid on the basis of straight commission, sales associates do everything to make the customer's experience a

Nordstrom is considered the nation's most service-oriented fashion retailer.

pleasant one. Shoppers may be assisted throughout the store by one salesperson instead of having to search for a different one in each department. This gives the shopper a feeling of personal attention. Little extras, such as snacks for the shopper, are also commonplace. This superlative personal shopping service makes the Nordstrom sales associate one of the highest paid in retailing, with annual earnings reaching as much as $75,000 per year!

Nordstrom's merchandising borrows from the past. Markdowns occur only three times a year—two at the season's end and one for its anniversary celebration. The constant markdown philosophy subscribed to by most American depart-

ment stores tends to confuse shoppers, but Nordstrom's customers know exactly when prices will be lowered.

Nordstrom is also using the Internet to complement its bricks-and-mortar business. At its Web site, the company now stocks more than 20 million pairs of shoes, enough to meet the needs of shoppers with specific needs that might not be filled even in the retailer's well-stocked stores.

All of these factors, plus a positive image that seems to improve year after year, makes Nordstrom one of the world's most dynamic retail operations.

Nordstrom is considered the nation's most service-oriented fashion retailer.

Specialty Stores

As merchandise became more varied, some early retailers moved away from the general merchandise concept and pioneered the first limited line stores, which concentrate on one merchandise classification. Today, these specialty stores are a major force in retailing. And specialize they do! Whether it is the upscale Ann Taylor or

Designers such as Ralph Lauren merchandise their collections in retailers' stores-within-a-store.

Cosmetic departments are generally leased arrangements between retailers and manufacturers.

the downscale Limited, specialty store retailing captures the attention and money of fashion-minded consumers.

This type of retail organization has two advantages. Because merchandise is restricted to one classification, the stores often feature the widest assortment available. In addition, shopping is faster and more convenient. With more people holding full-time jobs, the quick purchase has become a necessity.

The specialty store designation indicates nothing more than a merchandising philosophy. This store might be a single-unit operation or part of a chain organization.

Two members of The Limited organization: Victoria's Secret (top) and Express (bottom).

Physically, specialty stores run the gamut from under 1,000 square feet to several thousand square feet.

So successful were the early specialty store entrepreneurs that many opened additional units in other locations. Thus, the concept of the chain was developed. Chains are retail organizations with two or more units operating from a central headquarters or home office. In the present retail environment, they continue to expand. The largest of the fashion apparel chains is The Limited, Inc. Beginning as a four-unit chain in Columbus, Ohio, it has developed into a major retailer through expansion and the acquisition of such names as Express, Victoria's Secret, Bath & Body Works, and Henri Bendel. The Limited's roster now boasts more than 4,000 units!

At the same time, however, there are independents who compete successfully by carving out a share of the market.

Specialty store operations are so successful that a number of designers and fashion manufacturers have opened retail specialty shops to feature their own designs. These include Liz Claiborne, Ralph Lauren, and Nine West. Even couture designers such as Armani, Chanel, and Missoni are operating their own specialty stores.

Whether they are independents or parts of chain operations, specialty stores have become the major force in fashion retailing. More and more specialty stores are deciding to concentrate entirely on a brand that the retailer has developed. The Gap organization, with such stores as Gap, Gap Kids, Baby Gap, and Banana Republic; The Limited group, with names such as Express and Victoria's Secret; and Benetton are examples of this type of retailing. Instead of relying on other manufacturers' brands, they establish their own products and place them in their retail environments. In this way, the brand and the store are thought of as one. The advantages of such operations are numerous. They include the elimination of price cutting (which is often the practice in traditional retailing formats), the exclusivity of merchandise, the development of products designed especially for their own clientele, the elimination of middlemen, and the control of merchandise delivery dates.

If the shopper's needs are satisfied at these types of retail organizations, a loyal customer base is developed. With the significant expansion of such retail operations in the past few years, it is safe to assume that both customer and retailer are receiving what they expect from the arrangement.

Boutiques

A variation on the typical specialty store is the **boutique**. It is most often a one-unit operation that features upscale, fashion-forward merchandise. The assortment is generally restricted to just a few pieces of each item, with custom-tailored apparel some-

times featured. Customers frequent boutiques because they are usually guaranteed the latest in fashion innovation and are individually assisted by trained salespeople. In many of these operations, success depends on individual salespeople who develop their own clientele. They call customers when special merchandise arrives, notify them of special sales, and act as personal shoppers for those who want such attention.

Designer Boutiques

In all of the major cities around the world, fashion designers are opening units of their own. Names such as Versace, Giorgio Armani, Prada, Calvin Klein, Donna Karan, Ralph Lauren, Hugo Boss, Sonia Rykiel, Chanel, Fendi, and Yves Saint Laurent are gracing the marquees. Although the products of these world-famous designers are featured in fashion emporiums other than their

Designers such as Ralph Lauren (top) and Chanel (bottom) operate individual specialty shops in stores.

own, the growth of designer boutiques is accelerating for several reasons. One is the space constraints inherent in the traditional department store and specialty retailer formats. Given the limited space, only a few of the designer's offerings may be merchandised. Another reason is the amount of money a store has available to purchase such merchandise. With so many designers in the field, only a fraction of a store's budget may be spent on a single designer, therefore limiting purchases to just a few items. In contrast, in a designer boutique, the entire collection may be featured. Yet another reason, and perhaps the most compelling, is that by featuring only a designer's own collection, the temptation for customers to comparison shop is eliminated at the site of purchase. In traditional stores, shoppers may go from one designer department to another before making a selection. From every report in the trade papers, this concept has been extremely profitable, and it can be expected to gain strength in the future.

Indie Boutiques

Different from both the traditional boutiques that shoppers have come to know for many years and the designer boutiques are the **indie boutiques**. The name is an abbreviated form of the word *independent*. Indie boutiques began in 1997 in Tokyo and quickly spread to New York's offbeat shopping streets and other locations throughout the world.

These stores—such as DDC Lab on Orchard Street and Wearmart on Elizabeth Street, both in New York City—set their own moods by designing and selling merchandise for which they expect to create a following. Unlike the more popular designers who create just a few lines each season, these fashion operations continuously bring out new designs as the need arises. They can react very quickly to consumer demand.

Off-Price Retailers

Among the most successful retailers are the **off-price merchants**. The off-pricers buy late in the season, when manufacturers are forced to close out their lines at reduced prices, and can sell the merchandise at reduced prices to consumers.

Companies such as T.J. Maxx, Marshall's, Stein Mart, Daffy's, Loehmann's, Syms, and Burlington Coat Factory are continuously expanding to meet the needs of the consumer who looks for fashion bargains. Many prestigious labels are found in the off-price stores. In fact, the most successful stores are those that feature such renowned names as Baby Phat, Max Studio, Marc Jacobs, Elie Tahari, Theory, Jones New York, DKNY, Calvin Klein, Kenar, August Silk, and Liz Claiborne.

Factory Outlets

Across the United States, fashion manufacturers are opening their own units to dispose of season leftovers and current, slow-selling items. In places such as St. Augustine, Florida; North Conway, New Hampshire; Freeport, Maine; Woodbury Commons, New York; and Secaucus, New Jersey—and far from the traditional stores—top fashion names are liquidating their inventories. Stores bearing such prestigious fashion names as Coach, Geoffrey Beene, Calvin Klein, DKNY, Anne Klein, and Tahari are clustered in centers that group as many as 100 or more stores.

Whereas retailing in the 1980s reflected the values of a generation that cared more about status than price, the picture in the 1990s shifted to reflect consumers' concern with value, even for the most upscale merchandise. From every indication, the trend for this type of **value shopping** keeps growing. These **factory outlets** attract not only individual families, but also busloads of people who come on shopping sprees arranged by the center's merchants. The demographics concerning these outlet centers are interesting: 65 percent of the shoppers are married, and 74 percent are female, with household incomes from $25,000 to $75,000. Most shoppers are between 35 and 54 years of age. Furthermore, a telephone survey indicated that 9 out of 10 Americans have visited an outlet center located anywhere from half an hour to more than two hours away from their homes.

Off-price retailers, such as Marshall's (top) and Burlington Coat Factory (center) are excellent outlets for manufacturer overruns and closeouts. Loehmann's (bottom) is credited with being the first women's off-price specialty operation.

Direct Retailers

Just about every U.S. household receives numerous catalogs filled with fashion merchandise that is theirs for the purchase with only a phone call to the **direct retailer**. Once the domain of the major department stores with their seasonal offerings, direct retailing has spread to companies that sell by this method only. With a wealth of fashion products in apparel, shoes, jewelry, cosmetics, handbags, and home furnishings, at every conceivable price point, the shopper at his or her leisure may peruse these publications, selecting what best suits his or her needs.

The popularity of direct retailers is a result of several factors. One is the increased time spent by families in the workplace. Women, in particular, once the shoppers of the world, are now busy in careers that leave little time for shopping. Another factor is the improved quality of the merchandise being offered in terms of fabric, styling, and fit. A third factor is the ease with which returns may be made if the selections chosen are found not to be suitable.

In addition to the traditional retailers, companies that are not really in the business of selling goods may mail catalogs to their clients. American Express, for example, sends its cardholders a catalog that features a large assortment of fashion merchandise, including precious jewelry, apparel, watches, and accessory items. Many airline companies include catalog offerings within their in-flight magazines. While customers are waiting to reach their destinations, they are shown many different items that may be ordered in flight.

Category Killers

Stores such as Toys "R" Us, Kids "R" Us, and Bed Bath and Beyond are known as **category killers**, or specialty discounters. They carry large selections of one merchandise classification, and generally sell at discount prices. With the attention they generate, category killers take a great deal of business away from other stores that carry some of the same merchandise. Some department stores have found it financially sound to eliminate some of the merchandise categories, such as toys and home fashions, and concentrate on fashion apparel.

Subspecialty Stores

A new breed of retailer, the **subspecialty store**, is having a significant impact on consumers. As with specialty stores, they restrict their offerings to one classification, but the classification is even narrower. For example, the typical men's specialty store carries an assortment of tailored clothing, sportswear, activewear, and accessories. The subspecialty store selects only one of these products to sell. The Knot Shop, a store that carries only ties, is an example of subspecialty retailing. Its rapid expansion across the country indicates that this is yet another retail direction for the future.

Flea Market Operations

All across the United States, shoppers are flocking to **flea markets**. These markets can be found in outdoor locations, such as movie parking lots, and in indoor facilities that once housed single retail operations. Many operate only on weekends; others, such as one of the nation's largest, The Swap Shop in Sunrise, Florida, is open seven days a week.

The emphasis in these places is price. Merchandise runs the gamut from household to fashion-oriented items. For manufacturers seeking to dispose of leftovers and

All across the United States, flea markets attract great numbers of shoppers seeking bargains. They often operate in outdoor parking lots and other large spaces.

sometimes seconds, the flea market is a perfect venue. Flea markets have many vendors, each with comparatively limited retail space and lower operating costs than traditional retailers. Vendors work on very low markups and are able to sell at considerably reduced prices.

Many a manufacturer has been saved by being able to dispose of unwanted merchandise to flea market vendors.

Franchises and Licenses

Many companies prefer to expand their retail operations by inviting qualified individuals to open their own **franchises** or **licensed units**. The company often provides specialized training for the individual, who benefits by opening a unit with an established name and recognized product line. In return, the company receives a fee, a percentage of sales, and the individual's guarantee to buy all merchandise from the parent company. Unlike a franchising agreement, licensing arrangements do not include an initial fee for participation.

Although these agreements have long been used by fast-food vendors, such as McDonald's, Burger King, and Carvel, fashion retailers, including Lady Madonna, Benetton, Ralph Lauren, and Bellini, are now offering similar arrangements.

Mass Merchandise Discounters

Perhaps the greatest impact on retailing today has been the **mass merchandisers**, including Wal-Mart, Kohl's, and Target. Although they sell much more than fashion merchandise, their role as fashion merchandisers continues to expand. Manufacturers find these outlets, with their enormous volume, very attractive.

The emphasis is on price and value. There are few frills and limited personalized sales help. Customers generally make their own selections. The reward is lower prices.

Wal-Mart is the largest mass merchandiser.

With the increasing cost of living, more and more people are heading for these stores. These companies are now expanding into other parts of the world in impressive numbers.

Catalogs

The number of catalogs that make their way into the consumer's home grows every year. Some are divisions of companies that are primarily bricks-and-mortar operations, while others are solely direct marketing companies. Most sell fashion apparel for men, women, and children, accessories such as jewelry, handbags, and shoes, and home furnishings. The price points range from modest to upscale. The latter merchandise offering is perhaps best exemplified by the Neiman Marcus Holiday Book, the granddaddy of the catalogs aimed at the affluent that was launched in 1959. In addition to traditionally fashionable apparel and accessories, the book features a host of eye-catching items that are merely there for shock value, and not to sell quantities of the items. However, these unique items do sell, albeit in very limited numbers. The 2006 catalog, for example, featured a $3.8 million lifetime membership to Massimo Ferragamo's private Tuscan resort of 16th- and 17th-century villas, a $1.8 million short flight in space, and the complete archives of couturier Jacques Fath for $3.5 million.

Of course, the bulk of the catalogs feature merchandise that is likely to sell in quantities that make the ventures profitable.

Interactive Retailers

Traditional retailers, which operate from the stores mentioned in the preceding section and through catalogs, are confronted by several new types of competition. Most important are the cable television stations, called **interactive retailers** because sellers and consumers may communicate with one another directly during a purchase.

Everyone who subscribes to cable television has witnessed the growth of channels that sell merchandise. The biggest of these are the Home Shopping Network (HSN) and QVC, each boasting as many as 20,000 transactions per hour!

At first, these channels limited merchandise to lower-priced items, generally in jewelry and accessories. Today, they sell high-fashion apparel, accessories, and cosmetics at every price point. With such high-profile names as Joan Rivers, who markets her own jewelry collections on the air, the "shows" attract people who are intrigued with celebrity affiliation. The latest marquee name to join the fray is Sephora, who joined forces with HSN in December 2006. Using personalities to hawk its wares, the company will focus on nine core brands and its own label.

Online Retailers

During the decade of the 1990s, words such as *Web site*, *online*, and *Internet* began to take center stage in the marketing of merchandise. Initial fears and hesitation about the security and viability of Web-based selling have given way to a focus on the Web as a means to generate more business for retailers' operations. Although the numbers have not yet reached significant proportions in terms of overall sales, especially in

These sketches represent the Couture Merchandise focus of the Neiman Marcus Holiday Book.

J. Crew and Anthropologie offer seasonal catalogs of their merchandise.

fashion merchandise, the outlook for **online retailers** appears to be positive.

Companies that previously restricted their selling to retail stores or catalogs now have an Internet presence. They include just about every department store, specialty organization, discounters, off-pricers, and cataloguers. Even luxury operations such as Neiman Marcus market upscale products, such as a $2,000 Gucci handbag and a $7,000 David Yurman bracelet. Brandan Hoffman, president and CEO of Neiman Marcus Direct, reported in 2006 that the most recent fiscal year's revenues exceeded $400,000 and that internal projections call for sales to exceed $1 billion in the next few years.

Also included is a new wave of online retailers—the small boutiques. In addition to operating from their stores, more and more are reaching out via the Internet to shoppers who would otherwise be unable to visit their stores. The following table features a representation of these fashion emporiums, their store locations, their Web sites, and the merchandise they offer.

By combining traditional store-based sales with 24-hour Internet availability—the bricks-and-clicks concept—retailers are able to expand their reach to consumers, increasing customer convenience and in many cases providing a broader range of items for purchase than could be featured in their space-limited stores. A number of companies have emerged that function only as online retailers, including Bluefly.com,

Cable shopping networks, such as QVC, attract huge audiences.

Table 21.1

Company Name	Location	Web Site	Merchandise Offered
Hejfina	Chicago, IL	www.hejfina.com	Menswear, custom furniture
La Garçonne	Fairfield, CT	www.lagarconne.com	Mod outfits
Creatures of Comfort	Los Angeles, CA	www.shop.creaturesofcomfort.us	Sculptural clothing, shoes
Blaec	Santa Barbara, CA	www.blaec.com	Boutique clothing
Oak	Brooklyn, NY	www.oaknyc.com	Mostly black-and-white clothing, some prints
Azalea	San Francisco, CA	www.azalealine.com	Jeans, organic beauty products
Milk	West Hollywood, CA	www.shopatmilk.com	Retro-inspired clothing

which features high-end fashion at heavily discounted prices; Yoox.com, based in Milan, which sells out-of-season designer apparel and accessories at discounted prices; and E-dressme.com, which features fashion at regular prices.

Traditional bricks-and-mortar chains are increasingly relying on the Internet to enable their customers to research items before driving to a store for purchase. A 1999 survey by the Internet research firm Jupiter Communications found that consumers spent more than $135 billion in stores and catalogs as a direct result of research they did online. In fact, 68 percent of shoppers contacted in a May 2000 survey reported that they had used the Internet to evaluate goods online before purchasing these items in a physical store.

With retailers expending significant money to develop their Web sites, and more and more fashion merchandise being offered online each day, the Internet is becoming an important retail outlet. Many industry watchers believe that the traditional bricks-and-mortar chains that will fare best in this new environment are those that use the Internet to drive traffic between their stores and Web sites, or provide unique merchandise or discounts that are unavailable in their physical stores.

If the holiday shopping of 2006 is a barometer of the future, Internet purchasing is certain to become an arena for retail business. With online spending increasing by

The Internet has become an excellent source for luxury merchandise.

26 percent over 2005 for the first 50 days of the holiday season, to $26.1 billion, the outlook seems to be extremely bright. Summed up by Marshall Cohen, NPD Group's chief industry analyst, "Online continues to grow at alarming rates."

RETAILER LOCATIONS

At the beginning of the 20th century, the only viable place to establish a retail operation was in a downtown area. Together with community general stores, found mostly in rural areas, and mail-order catalogs, these were the only retail outlets for customers. Times have certainly changed! Malls of every size, shape, and image now serve the needs of consumers. Some are enclosed, others open; some are vertically constructed, others expand horizontally. Festival marketplaces, which revitalize urban areas, are also very much in fashion. Abandoned places that were once thriving seaports, breweries, railroad terminals, or historic districts are developed into combination tourist attractions and retail centers. In more affluent areas, centers have been developed that cater exclusively to the upper-class shopper. Although downtown is still a vital retail location, retailing is no longer relegated to the traditional downtown shopping district.

Downtown Central Districts

Most major department stores still operate from their downtown flagship stores. The executive headquarters for Macy's is in Herald Square, a downtown shopping area in New York City. Likewise, Filene's is in downtown Boston. Not only are most merchandising and policy decisions made in these locations, but the parent stores generally account for a significant part of the company's sales volume.

From the 1950s through the 1970s, the downtown areas of many cities underwent significant changes. As people moved to the suburbs, flagship stores experienced declining sales. The middle class was now shopping at suburban branches. Although this was a serious situation, most retailers maintained their main stores.

In the past 20 years, cities across the United States have been gentrified. Large sums have been expended to revitalize urban America. Once again, downtown is alive and well and doing considerable retail business.

Shopping Malls

Across the United States, shoppers find that enclosed shopping facilities are the perfect places to satisfy their needs. In the 1950s, the first malls were built as outdoor shopping arenas. One of the first enclosed shopping malls to be built in the United States was the Walt Whitman in Huntington, New York. It was so successful that it became the prototype for future malls. Outdoor malls reacted by enclosing their facilities to offer a climate-controlled shopping environment. Today, the **enclosed mall** is the dominant type of retail location. The majority are horizontally constructed in suburban areas where land is plentiful and less expensive than in the downtown urban areas. To accommodate the large number of consumers, many have added floors, doubling and tripling their original size. The magnitude of this type of expansion is obvious at Roosevelt Field, a suburban shopping center outside New York City. Originally built in 1957 as an outdoor

Macy's in Herald Square, New York, is home to the retailer's largest store and the company's executive offices.

Old malls such as Roosevelt Field are modernizing and expanding to meet consumers' needs.

center, it first enclosed its facilities and then added another level to become the nation's fifth largest center. By 1997, with the completion of another extension that included Nordstrom's, it had become one of the largest malls in the United States.

Based on the success of suburban malls, developers have begun creating downtown malls in urban centers. Because real estate costs are significantly higher and land is often less readily available, the direction has been toward the **vertical mall.** An early example is Chicago's Water Tower on fashionable North Michigan Avenue. Flanked by a prestigious hotel, the Ritz Carlton, and movie theaters, this shopping facility boasts an atrium and seven selling floors occupied by such major stores as Macy's and Lord & Taylor. In addition to these **anchor stores**, there are 125 specialty shops, including Gap, Louis Vuitton, Banana Republic, Henri Bendel, and The Limited.

Another type of mall combines an entertainment center with shopping facilities. Mall of America in Bloomington, Minnesota, has attracted record crowds to its premises. With shops surrounded by rides and attractions, the entire family can enjoy the experience.

Where malls were once moving only in the direction of enclosed facilities, the mid-2000s witnessed a return to the outdoor format. Based on the success of Old Orchard in a Chicago suburb in the early 1990s, Simon Properties has started to move in that direction with other locations. One of the most successful is Town Center in Jacksonville, Florida. In just one year, the first phase that included Dillard's and many specialty stores and restaurants, such as the Cheesecake Factory and P.F. Chang's, was completed and work began on a second phase.

Many of these expanded retail and entertainment properties are owned by the Simon Property Group, which is the subject of a World of Fashion Profile.

Festival Marketplaces

South Street Seaport in New York City, Inner Harbor in Baltimore, Quincy Market in Boston, and Union Station in St. Louis are just a few examples of **festival marketplaces**. These centers are built on abandoned properties that have been resurrected and transformed into tourist attractions boasting a considerable number of fashion operations. Through the creative genius of numerous developers, including the Rouse Company, which transformed Boston's historic landmark building, Faneuil Hall, into Quincy Market, these areas have become exciting and profitable places for tourists to satisfy their shopping needs.

Unlike other shopping facilities, festival marketplaces are not anchored by giant department stores; they are basically clusters of specialty stores. Typical tenants are Gap, Express, Talbot's, The Sharper Image, and Banana Republic.

Clearance Discount Centers

A number of extremely large shopping facilities are springing up all across the United States. Some are outdoor facilities that include outlets of traditional retailers that sell unwanted items at greatly reduced prices. Several, however, have been built as enclosed environments. They feature as much as two miles of storefronts under one roof. The most famous of these are called the **mills**. Sawgrass Mills in Fort Lauderdale, Gurnee Mills outside of Chicago, Franklin Mills near Philadelphia, and Potomac Mills in northern Virginia are examples of these complexes.

The tenants of these supershopping arenas, whose forte is bargain merchandise, include giants such as Off 5th (a division of Saks Fifth Avenue), Nordstrom Rack (a division of Nordstrom), Spiegel, and Macy's, and chains such as Ann Taylor, Nine West, Lillie Rubin, and others, which were unable to sell out their inventory in traditional stores. With prices reduced as much as 75 percent, the cumulative sales are astounding.

High-Fashion Centers

Many major cities boast fashion centers that are not located in malls, congested downtown areas, or festival marketplaces. These are generally shopping streets dotted with upscale fashion retailers. Their target markets are affluent consumers who seek the latest in both domestic and international styles, with price not a factor. Some of these areas feature branches of such well-known fashion organizations as Neiman Marcus and Saks Fifth Avenue, but the majority of the shops are small, boutique-like operations that feature designer merchandise from Yves Saint Laurent, Ungaro, Armani, Sonia Rykiel, Louis Vuitton, Hermès, Norma Kamali, and Calvin Klein.

These high-fashion centers include Madison Avenue and Fifth Avenue in New York City, Rodeo Drive in Beverly Hills, Worth Avenue in Palm Beach, and Oak Street in Chicago.

SIMON PROPERTY GROUP

Founded in 1960, Simon Property Group has become the country's largest owner, developer, and manager of market-dominant real estate. It has more than twice the market share of its nearest competitor, and employs almost 7,000 people. Today, the company manages a retail network that drives more than $30 billion in annual sales. The company owns or has an interest in 256 properties, comprising regional malls, community shopping centers, and specialty and mixed-use properties.

The company's holdings cut across the entire bricks-and-mortar spectrum. Its tenants include high-fashion merchants such as Nordstrom and Saks Fifth Avenue; specialty chains such as Gap and Banana Republic; department stores such as Dillard's, Belk, and Bloomingdale's; and a host of mass merchants, category killers, discounters, and manufacturers' outlets.

Among Simon's most productive and recognizable properties are the Forum Shops of the Twelve Caesars in Las Vegas, Nevada, a shopping arena that replicates a Roman environment, and the world-famous Mall of America in Bloomington, Minnesota, which offers a wealth of entertainment facilities along with scores of famous retailers. The Mall of America concept features attractions such as Knott's Camp Snoopy, Lego Imagination Center, Golf Mountain, and theme restaurants such as RainForest Café. It is an innovation that attracts people from all over the United States and Canada. Other important properties

St. John's Town Center, in Jacksonville, Florida, is drawing record crowds.

include Lenox Square in Atlanta, Georgia; Roosevelt Field on Long Island; and Town Center in Boca Raton, Florida.

Like many retailers, Simon is establishing its name as a brand. The program is expected to make Simon a household name, similar in recognition to Gap, Coca-Cola, and Tommy Hilfiger. What makes Simon so unique is that no other retail developer has taken this route.

The program begins with the coupling of the Simon name to the name of the mall on entry doors, parking lot banners, and signs. There is also a "pledge" that is visible in each mall that has been signed by every member of the mall staff promising to provide superior shopping and special amenities in a meticulously maintained environment.

To make the public aware of the program, an extensive television and radio campaign delivers a message designed to intensify shopper identification.

The slogan is, "Simply the best shopping there is."

Like many major retailers, Simon has established a Youth Foundation that fosters economic and career development among youth through the implementation of focused and appropriate educational programs. Its goal is to give back to the community that supports its retail efforts. Education Resource Centers are opening in malls all over the country that are used for community-based initiatives such as GED programs, accelerated learning, college-credit courses, and certificate programs in retail management and operations for mall employees.

Through the vast expansion of its properties, and its recognition of its role as the major player in retailing environments, Simon has revolutionized the approach to sales arenas in retailing.

Faneuil Hall became the centerpiece for Quincy Market in Boston and the first festival marketplace in the United States.

Outlet malls are excellent arenas for manufacturers to sell leftover merchandise.

Power Centers

Throughout the country, small shopping arenas, known as power centers, offer customers merchandise at highly discounted prices. The stores are usually very large retailers, known for competitive pricing and capable of drawing large crowds. Many are fashion-oriented retailers such as Filene's Basement and Burlington Coat Factory. In

High-fashion centers, such as New York's Trump Tower, attract upscale consumers.

these cavernous facilities, they dispose of merchandise purchased from other retailers and manufacturers. The one limitation is that a power center must be located sufficiently far from traditional malls so as not to plague them with unfair competition.

Miscellaneous Centers

Other types of shopping environments include **mixed-use centers** that combine shopping, office space, hotels, and permanent residences; **strip centers** that feature about 20 stores, with a few fashion-oriented retailers interspersed among the grocers and service-oriented retailers; and **transportation terminals**. The latter group is gaining importance in the United States. Taking their cue from London's Heathrow Airport, where fashion shops such as Harrod's and Bally serve the crowds waiting to make connections, transportation hubs such as USAir's Pittsburgh air terminal and Washington, D.C.'s Union Station offer waiting travelers an abundance of fashion merchandise retailers.

INTERNATIONAL EXPANSION OF U.S.-BASED FASHION RETAILERS

Today, many U.S. fashion retailers are involved in global expansion in addition to their efforts at home. With travel to the United States at an all-time high and store recognition gained through international exposure via the editorial pages of fashion magazines, the global community is more aware of U.S. stores than ever before. Many people abroad recognize the United States as the center for retail fashion and want to purchase merchandise from its well-known stores.

Some of the countries in which American retailers have opened units are those one would expect. Canada, for example, is a major center, where companies such as Gap, Kmart, Pier 1, Original Levi's Stores, Spiegel, Talbots, Tiffany & Company, and Wal-Mart have branches. Shoppers in Japan are also able to shop at branches of several American stores, including Barneys, Brooks Brothers, Nicole Miller, Saks Fifth Avenue, Tiffany & Company, and Williams-Sonoma, among others. Other countries that have embraced U.S. retail operations include France, Germany, China, Mexico, and the United Kingdom.

Global expansion is also underway in many places that might seem unlikely, such as Abu Dhabi/U.A.E. (JC Penney and Tiffany & Company), Argentina (Levi-Strauss and Wal-Mart), Bulgaria (Levi-Strauss), Dubai (Polo Sport), Indonesia (Calvin Klein and Oscar de la Renta), Russia (Calvin Klein), and South Africa (Gant).

Facing considerably less competition abroad than they do at home, many American retailers have stepped up their overseas expansion plans in order to gain a share of the generally untapped global marketplace.

RETAIL ORGANIZATIONAL STRUCTURES

The 1990s saw a few giants emerge in the retailing industry. The May Company purchased Lord & Taylor, Federated Department Stores bought Macy's, Dayton Hudson acquired Marshall Field's, and what was once a very small, five-unit chain, Proffitt's, with its takeover of Carson Pirie Scott and Saks Fifth Avenue, became a giant in fashion retailing. The benefits of size that these industrial giants gain enable them to obtain better wholesale prices and merchandise exclusivity.

Just as the 1990s witnessed changes in retail ownership, so did the 2000s. By the middle 2000s, major changes had taken place. Most notable was the activity in the Federated organization. The company went on a buying rampage and purchased the May Company as well as Marshall Field's, changing the names of those stores to Macy's. Each of the other Federated divisions such as Burdines and Rich's were renamed Macy's, placing the Macy's signature on more than 800 doors. Today, all Federated stores are either Macy's or Bloomingdale's.

Some of the other notable changes that have taken place from the early to middle 2000s include:

- Sears Holding now owns Kmart in addition to the Sears stores.
- The Neiman Marcus Group has added Horchow.
- The Limited Corporation has disbanded the Structure division and now operates Express, Bath & Body Works, Victoria's Secret, The Limited, C.O. Bigelow, White Barn Candle Company, and Henri Bendel.
- Target no longer owns Marshall Field's, Mervyn's, or Dayton Hudson, and only operates Target stores.

No matter how large or small their operations are, retailers must establish organizational structures that maximize efficiency. The structures employed vary from company to company. Small stores are often negligent in this area. Many of the duties and responsibilities performed by the employees are not specifically assigned, and the actual tasks required of store personnel are accomplished in an unstructured format. This haphazard approach often leads to confusion on the part of the employees and lower profits for the company.

Larger stores, on the other hand, subscribe to a more formal, structured approach. In department stores, a divisional plan segments the store into major functions or divisions of the operation. The plan typically is a four- or five-function arrangement; the major areas are merchandising, management, operations, advertising and promotion, and control. Each division is supervised by a manager who often enjoys the title of vice president and supervises numerous middle-management subordinates. In addition to the heads of these divisions, who are the major decision makers for the company, and the people who work for them, other employees function primarily as advisory or support people. This organizational structure is known as **line and staff**. The line people are the decision makers; the staff personnel serve in an advisory capacity.

Chain organizations are similar in structure but operate from a home office or central headquarters, away from the individual stores. They often have more divisions than department stores because of frequent expansion. This necessitates new locations, centralized warehouses, and constant research and development.

Although most retail operations have a formal structure that delineates lines of authority, an informal structure may also exist within a company's framework. Thus, certain key people have a greater voice in the management of a company than do others.

Whatever the structure of the company, it should be regularly assessed and changed to make the organization function more efficiently.

SERVICES OFFERED BY THE FASHION RETAILER

Few retailers believe customers shop in a particular store solely because of its merchandise assortment. The retail business is highly competitive; merchants must distinguish themselves from the competition to attract enough customers to turn a profit. One way to achieve this goal is by providing customer services. The nature of the company and its philosophy dictate the types of services they will offer. As a rule, those with price as the chief attraction offer the fewest services; those with traditional, fashion retailing operations provide the most.

Personal Shopping

Every upscale fashion emporium offers some kind of **personal shopping**. Every major retailer has its own program that includes a number of different approaches. Most provide telephone assistance for shoppers who call the store with merchandise requests. The caller might ask the personal shopper to assemble items from different departments to be reviewed by the customer at a designated time. This is the concept followed by the Macy's by Appointment (MBA) program. At Bergdorf Goodman, an upscale fashion retailer, customers are invited into a salon to view and try on merchandise. Lunch and refreshments are also served to each client. In the Bloomingdale's men's department and at Nordstrom, the personal shopper may visit the customer's home or office with the merchandise in hand.

Corporate Purchasing

Many upscale retailers have consultants who assist businesses in the purchase of presents for employees and clients. At peak gift-giving times, such as Christmas, this is an excellent program for generating increased sales. Popular items sold through these **corporate purchasing** programs include perfume, silk scarves, small leather goods, and home products. The store wraps the gifts and sends them to designated clients with very little customer involvement.

Interpreters

Tourists are a major source of revenue for retail establishments. To attract their business, retailers in the major cities employ interpreters to accommodate foreign-speaking visitors.

Gift Registries

People who are engaged to be married and those who are prospective parents are excellent markets for fashion retailers. To eliminate the purchase of unwanted or duplicate merchandise by gift givers, these individuals select the items they would like to receive and register their preferences with an appropriate store.

Large department stores and specialty stores have established such **gift registries**. The store records the selections on a computer so that well-wishers may purchase one of these gifts on a visit to any branch store. Purchasers outside of the store's trading area may handle the transaction by phone. Items ranging from bed and bath linens and dinnerware for the bridal couple to layette items for the expectant parents are bought in this manner. Gift registries are advantageous for the retailer, because the potential for returns is minimized.

Service is the key to success for many retailers.

Beauty Salons

Many retailers include a beauty salon on the premises. Although this service is a leased department, its purpose is to bring shoppers into the store. Once there, they might be motivated to make an unplanned purchase. Some fashion retailers provide informal modeling in the salons, so customers can view the range of the store's apparel and accessories. Because shopping time is at a premium, this hour or two can generate business for the store.

Travel Services

Some retailers also operate leased travel departments. Although this service does not directly sell merchandise, it does provide an opportunity to familiarize potential travelers with the store's merchandise. As with beauty salons, these departments attract additional consumers to the store. Sometimes, the travel department works in conjunction with the store's personal shoppers, who are able to tailor selections to travelers' needs in a short period of time.

Restaurants

Dining facilities do more than feed hungry shoppers. They give shoppers an opportunity to relax within the store's environment. Many retailers provide a variety of dining services, from snack bars to elaborate restaurants. In Bloomingdale's New York City flagship store, Le Train Bleu, a fine French restaurant, is a popular place for upscale shoppers to satisfy their appetites. During the meal, some retailers offer modeling of store merchandise. Afterward, the refreshed customer may be sufficiently motivated to continue to shop.

Gift Wrapping

Most major fashion retailers provide **gift-wrapping services**. Some are free; others cost the customer a nominal amount of money. A gift that is beautifully wrapped always makes a positive impression. Not only does the recipient feel special, but he or she will remember the store when in need of a gift for someone else.

Alterations, delivery of merchandise, charge accounts, child care, and other services are also provided by the retail industry. Each store must decide which services will generate enough business to warrant their inclusion, and which will help distinguish them from their competitors.

PURCHASING FASHION MERCHANDISE

All merchants make buying decisions; however, none are as complex as the purchase of fashion merchandise. Just deciding what skirt length will be acceptable to customers is enough to drive most buyers crazy. Making the decision six months or more in advance of sales complicates matters further. In addition, the buyer must evaluate color decisions, price points, silhouette preferences, and fabric selections.

Responsibility for the Purchase

At the helm of the fashion merchandising hierarchy is the store's general merchandise manager (G.M.M.). This person determines dollar allocations for each division's purchases and heads the team that will create the store's fashion image. Major stores divide the merchandising responsibility into divisions, each having a divisional merchandise manager (D.M.M.). For example, stores may have divisions for menswear, fashion apparel, accessories, and other products. The D.M.M.s are responsible for dividing their purchasing budgets among the various departments within their jurisdiction. Menswear, for example, might be divided into tailored clothing, sportswear, activewear, outerwear, and haberdashery. Each department has a buyer who actually purchases the merchandise. Most stores have a check on their buyers and require that significant purchases be approved by the appropriate D.M.M., but it is the buyer who plays the major role in the store's purchasing.

Merchandise Selection

The actual selection of specific styles is the result of research and planning. Qualitative and quantitative decisions are based on such sources as sales records, trade publications, shopping the competition, various advisory services, fashion show presentations, and trade associations. Each buyer must carefully study all available information before making purchasing commitments. Decisions concerning specific merchandise selections, which resources are most suitable, and when goods should be delivered are then built into a purchasing plan that evaluates styles, colors, sizes, and fabrics in the right quantities at the desired price points. In practice, this is known as the development of a **model stock**.

Today's fashion buyers face more complicated challenges than their predecessors. With the enormous amount of competition and the recent growth of off-price merchants, the buyer can no longer purchase only nationally advertised labels. Although fashion customers still purchase designer and brand-name merchandise, they can easily find this merchandise at greatly reduced prices in off-price stores. As a result, retail giants have called on many of their buyers to become product developers and help create private label merchandise exclusive to their stores. A seasoned buyer knows the proper mix of well-known fashion brands and private label merchandise to satisfy customer needs.

A major contribution to determining merchandise selection can be made by a fashion director. Those stores with fashion-forward images often employ these highly paid individuals to help buyers with fashion decisions. Fashion directors often carry the title of vice president, indicating the importance of the position. Their multifaceted job includes researching the industry before the buyers make purchasing decisions. They typically visit the fiber mills to learn about what is new on the textile horizon, consult fashion forecasters to learn about new trends, attend fashion events that give an overview of the coming season, and meet with the editorial staff of influential fashion publications to "pick their brains." The information is then disseminated to the buyers, who are now better equipped to make purchasing decisions.

DEVELOPING A FASHION IMAGE

A retail organization's **fashion image** can be determined from a review of its ads in newspapers and magazines. If every retailer had the same image, it would be difficult for the shopper to decide which one to patronize. A major responsibility of the fashion-oriented retailer is to develop an image that will motivate shoppers to become customers. Those who successfully do this become the major players in the game of fashion.

Over the past two decades, many stores that were household fashion names have disappeared. Although it is difficult to assess what went wrong in each case, the lack of a fashion image that met with customer approval certainly played some role. Stores such as Marshall Field's, Dayton Hudson, Gimbel's, Bonwit Teller, and B. Altman & Company, all giants at one time, are now just memories. They have been replaced by retailers who have done a better job in relaying their fashion messages to the public. Only those who continue to properly assess their customers' needs will be around to reap the benefits and rewards.

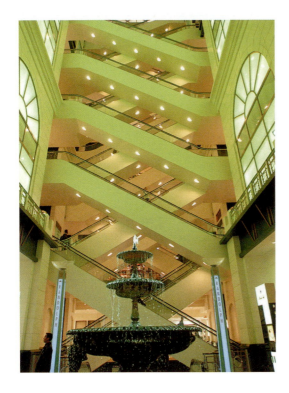

Fashion images are often established by constructing elegant premises.

Retailers advance their fashion images through promotion. Using a variety of techniques that include fashion shows, special celebrity appearances, fashion workshops, and visual presentations, the retailer tries to motivate the customer to come and see what all the excitement is about. The next chapter focuses on how the retailer makes use of special promotional tools.

CHAPTER HIGHLIGHTS

- Traditionally, fashion retailers operate department and specialty store organizations.

- An increasing number of retailers function as off-pricers, flea market vendors, discounters, subspecialists, franchisees and licensees, mass merchandisers, direct merchants, and interactive salespeople.

- Online services are increasingly important as a way for fashion retailers to facilitate customer shopping. Traditional retailers, from specialty stores to discounters and direct merchants, are expanding their services to include Web sites where shoppers can research and purchase merchandise or receive additional discounts beyond those offered in bricks-and-mortar stores. A smaller number of retailers function only online.

- The most popular of the traditional shopping areas was usually the downtown central district. Their popularity waned for a time, but these stores are now experiencing a revival.

- The most preferred shopping environment is the enclosed shopping mall.

- Other types of retail centers include festival marketplaces, outlet centers, and notable fashion streets.

- To overcome increasing competition, retailers offer such services as personal shoppers, corporate purchasing, interpreters, gift registries, and gift wrapping.

- Merchandise selection is typically accomplished by a team headed by a general merchandise manager, but the ultimate purchasing decision is in the hands of the buyer.

- Retailers of apparel and accessories must develop fashion images that distinguish them from their competitors.

IMPORTANT FASHION TERMINOLOGY AND CONCEPTS

anchor stores	flea market	mixed-use center
boutique	franchises	model stock
branch	gift registries	off-price retailer
category killer	gift-wrapping services	online retailer
collection merchandising	hard goods	personal shopping
corporate purchasing	indie boutiques	soft goods
direct retailer	interactive retailers	strip center
enclosed mall	leased department	subspecialty store
factory outlet	licensed unit	transportation terminals
fashion image	line and staff	value shopping
festival marketplace	mass merchandiser	vertical mall
flagship	mills	

FOR REVIEW

1. In what ways are department stores competing with specialty stores?
2. How have the early malls been transformed to meet the needs of today's shoppers?
3. Why do some fashion retailers subscribe to collection merchandising?
4. What is a leased department?
5. How does the boutique differ from the specialty store operation?
6. Explain the principal reason for the popularity of direct retailing.
7. In what way does the subspecialty store differ from the specialty shop?
8. Differentiate between franchises and licenses.
9. How do fashion retailers use the Internet to increase merchandise sales?
10. What is a festival marketplace?
11. Describe the operations at the Mills.
12. What is meant by the term *interactive retailer*?
13. Distinguish between line people and staff people.
14. Why is the personal shopper such an important part of the fashion retailer's staff?
15. Define *corporate purchasing*.
16. Explain how an in-store restaurant helps the retailer.
17. Why has product development become so important for some buyers?

EXERCISES AND PROJECTS

1. Visit two retail operations in your community, one a traditional store and the other an off-price retailer. Compare their operations in terms of services offered, merchandise available, and price points.
2. Contact a major fashion-oriented department store or, if possible, visit one in person to determine the scope of its personal shopping services.
3. Interview a fashion buyer, store manager, or department manager. Prepare a report on their company's involvement in private label merchandise.
4. Visit a festival marketplace and a traditional shopping mall to compare the environments. Take photographs and mount them on foamboard. Identify and list their differences.

WEB SITES

By accessing these Web sites, you will be able to gain broader knowledge and up-to-date information on materials related to this chapter.

Federated Department Stores

   www.federated-fds.com

National Retail Federation

   www.nrf.com

Stores magazine

   www.stores.org

The Case of the Friendly Competitors

The downtown area of a major midwestern city has been home to two large department stores for more than 50 years. Although each has a core of regular customers, they are in competition with each other. Both have fashion orientations, but Goldens is a little more fashion forward than the more traditional Baker & Foster. Like most fashion retailers, both organizations feature services for their shoppers and initiate regular promotions and special events to increase customer traffic. They do not share company secrets with each other; however, their relationship has been amicable. Although several lines of merchandise are featured in both stores, they never seem to be involved in pricing disputes. Each works on the traditional retail markup, reducing prices only when items fail to sell or at the conventional sales periods.

Yesterday's lead story in major local newspapers centered on the ground breaking for a new retail operation. Lamberts, a well-known off-price retailer, announced that it will be opening a new unit three miles from the downtown area. Although the new business is not within walking distance of the old-line department stores, it is within easy reach via public and private transportation. Known for its shrewd merchandising practices, Lamberts features well-known fashion merchandise at 20 to 50 percent below regular retail. Although Goldens and Baker & Foster receive their goods early in the season and Lamberts purchases later to gain a price advantage, Lamberts does pose a threat to the traditional retailers.

Management at both Goldens and Baker & Foster have called senior staff meetings to discuss plans for dealing with this potential new competitor. Several possible approaches have been suggested:

question

Which of the possible solutions should be employed to meet the challenge of the new retailer? Defend your answer.

1. Merchandise bearing the same labels should be discounted to meet the competition.
2. New services should be offered to capture customers' attention.
3. Service should be curtailed so that prices can be reduced throughout the store.
4. Private labels should be increased.
5. Lines carried by Lamberts should be discontinued.

Automating Markdowns: The Keys to Success

DAVID MOIN

One of retailing's hottest new technology tools isn't for every merchant.

A survey of 18 retailers that implemented the software, known as markdown optimization, concluded that not all stores should use it. Less than 50 percent of the retailers were able to quantify a return on investment. However, those that could calculate sums reported margin gains of 2 to 3 points and a majority believed the technology benefited the bottom line.

The study concluded that retailers generating the most ROI from markdown optimization systems were selling fast-turn, short-life-cycle products, and operating a promotional strategy built around mark-downs that were specific to items or clusters of stores with similar performances on the items. They also had a disposition for embracing analytics. Almost half the companies surveyed had 100 percent of their merchandise incorporated in the markdown optimization initiative.

"If you look at markdown optimization as a technology strategy, you are not going to be very successful," said Antony Karabus, founder and chief executive officer of Karabus Management, a Toronto-based retail consulting firm that has implemented the software and related coaching at 12 retail companies including 10 in the U.S. "It has to also be part of your marketing strategy and embraced by those working on the selling floors."

Among those participating in the survey were American Eagle Outfitters, The Northern Group Retail, Bloomingdale's, Casual Male, Ann Taylor, Nordstrom, Loehmann's, J.C. Penney and Gap. Oracle and SAS are among the handful of suppliers of markdown optimization. Oracle in 2005 bought ProfitLogic, which pioneered a software suite for merchandise optimization including markdowns.

Seeking to learn how much value retailers were getting from markdown optimization, Karabus commissioned the Bloom Group, a research firm, to conduct the survey. The study is timely considering that the technology has been gathering steam since being introduced in 2001.

Pricing used to be done more by gut instinct, when retailers could be involved in all aspects of their businesses. But many retailers have expanded to different regions and climates, making it difficult to determine when and by how much merchandise in each store should be marked down.

The survey's results also coincide with next week's National Retail Federation expo and convention at the Jacob K. Javits Center in Manhattan, which attracts about 30,000 retailers and suppliers and promotes emerging retail technologies. It's also clearance time at retail, so markdown systems are in full gear.

Karabus said about two-dozen retail companies in North America have implemented markdown optimization that has had an impact on several merchandise categories or are chainwide. Typically, the installation process takes 20 weeks or so, and costs, including hands-on coaching and software training, range from $3 million to $5 million or more, depending on the size of the company, Karabus said. "It's not cheap, but the payback can be incredible."

The survey found that seven retailers could quantify the technology's impact on gross margin; eight perceived benefits but were unable to quantify them, and three saw little or no benefit. The results depend on the character and culture of the company and its product lines. Replenishment systems are more worthwhile for businesses selling more basic merchandise with long shelf lives.

However, "If the life cycle of product is 10 to 16 weeks, that is the sweet spot," Karabus said. "If you're selling predictable, slow-turning stuff, what do you need optimization for?"

The system has been successful at chains such as American Eagle, Bloomingdale's and Northern Group. Every Monday morning, it could be a planner, buyer or pricing analyst who receives markdown recommendations via computer on the items for which they are responsible. "They can accept the markdown recommendation, reject it or modify it," Karabus said. "The trick is to take the markdowns when there is still demand on the upward curve of the life cycle of the item. That's counterintuitive. But you want to extend the peak demand before it starts waning."

Web Is Growing Mecca for Designer Discounts

SHARON EDELSON

Designers have always been coy on the subject of liquidating unsold merchandise, and off-pricers have played along by keeping brand names out of their advertising and marketing efforts. But the Web has removed the mystery from discounted designer clothing. Now, anyone with a computer and an Internet connection can immediately see a plethora of marked-down designer apparel.

Choosing a channel for unloading leftover styles seems to be a matter of personal preference—and economics. Some designers can't stand the idea of their garments dangling on wire hangers at off-price stores. For them, fashion e-tailers have become new retail accounts.

Shoppers logging onto Bluefly.com will see a large selection of contemporary fashion from Twelfth Street by Cynthia Vincent, A.B.S., Tufi Duek, Shoshanna, Jill Stuart, Vera Wang and BCBG Max-Azria at discounts of 20 to 75 percent. The Web site conveniently calculates the savings for each item. "You save 52 percent," informs a listing beneath a Michael Kors dress discounted from $2,800 to $1,344.99. Chloé's popular Edith handbags are available in six colors for $1,328, a 20 percent savings off the original $1,660. Styles from Gucci, Prada, Hermès, Tod's and Ferragamo are featured at similar discounts.

"Everyone knows that every brand today has products offered on sale at some point in their life cycle," said Bluefly.com chief executive officer Melissa Payner. "You're not going to hide it by sending it to Loehmann's or TJ Maxx or Daffy's. There's no ability in the off-price stores to maintain the integrity of a brand. You send to Century 21 and, at the very best,

it's placed on a rounder, but half of it falls on the floor with other brands. Our photography style is upscale.

"We're not only buying merchandise that's off-price, we're specifically buying into the trends of the season," added Payner. "We're going to only take what's really important and present it in the most upscale presentation. We're not the low-price leader. If we were, we'd have to take everybody's junk."

Yoox.com, based in Milan, sells out-of-season designer apparel and accessories at a discount, but that's not its whole business. The company also carries current merchandise at full price, acts as an incubator for emerging talent and is partners with designers on special projects such as a lingerie collection from Dolce & Gabbana made from excess fabric. "We take products that we feel are still viable and that we think we can sell," Hilary Bowers, a Yoox spokeswoman, said. "It can be products they had in their stores that didn't sell through."

Bowers said Yoox, which features Roberto Cavalli, Prada, Balenciaga and Missoni, has been the beneficiary in recent years of larger production runs. "The more [garments] designers make, the less expensive it gets," she said, adding that having a partner like Yoox allows designers to order more garments than they normally would. "They can have a space that allows them to maintain their brand's image and achieve sell-throughs."

Nicole Miller sells a variety of designs to e-commerce sites. Online is a growing part of the company's business. "They're additional retailers," Bud Konheim, ceo, said of fashion Web sites. "They're really good retailers." Miller has a strong pres-

ence on discounters such as Bluefly .com and at full-price online stores like E-dressme.com, nordstrom.com, blooming dales.com and neimanmarcus.com.

Online specialty stores buy current-season merchandise directly from manufacturers and sell it at full price, taking markdowns at the same time as their brick-and-mortar counterparts. Some of the more developed online businesses, such as saks.com, have their own buying teams that function exactly like the ones for physical stores. Denise Incandela, senior vice president of Saks Direct, said 70 to 75 percent of the merchandise on saks .com is the same as that in the company's stores. The rest could be items from existing brands aimed at a younger customer, or different brands or different categories. Incandela said saks.com will be the company's second-highest grossing "store" this year, after the Manhattan flagship.

"We regard everybody as an equal buyer," Konheim said. "The advantage of e-commerce is that you can shop from the comfort of your home, and the photography is very good. But you don't have instant gratification and you don't get to touch the product with e-commerce. Also, everybody gets to look at a Web site and see the discounts. You want to protect your regular-price business. This is a very careful kind of distribution. We don't want to cannibalize our [department and specialty store] business."

Richard Jaffe, a retail analyst at Steiffel Nichlaus, said selling to brick-and-mortar off-price stores was preferable to liquidating online. He questioned the ability of e-tailers "to pay and pay regularly and command the highest price," and said designers might better protect their images by selling to off-pricers rather than exposing their excess inventory to a much larger audience online. "If you go on the Web, it's public information that you're selling your goods at a discount," said Jaffe. "If you sell it to TJX, it disappears into the maw."

But many designers object to the maw, where shoppers ransack racks for bargains, leaving garments all the worse for the wear.

"We used to sell to Century 21, Loehmann's and a couple of others, but we don't intend to do that any more," said Bernard Aiden, ceo of Catherine Malandrino. "We have our own stores and an e-commerce site. Off-price stores really are not good for the brand. I prefer e-commerce or opening more stores. I'd even rather have an outlet store. I'm working on opening one at Woodbury Commons [in Harriman, N.Y.]. Designers are emotional about the way their clothes are treated. There's no respect at off-pricers. The clothes are thrown on the racks. I want to see the collection treated the way it was designed to be treated."

Consolidation in the retail industry has left designers with fewer department stores with which to do business. Selling to off-pricers is no longer just a means of disposing unwanted goods; it can become another much-needed profit center.

"You used to have two major department store customers, Federated Department Stores and May Department Stores," Jaffe said. "Now, there's only one—Federated. Whatever leverage you had, wherever you could have played one off the other, that's gone."

According to Jaffe, Federated closed 78 stores after the merger, which has resulted in $2 billion to $2.5 billion in lost inventory.

"How do you make it up?" he asked. "With off-pricers. Because of the lack of costs associated with department stores, you sell highly profitable additional units. The economics are very intoxicating. Name a designer who doesn't want to grow the top line."

TJ Maxx has found enough willing suppliers to "execute a more upscale merchandising approach in which the merchants aggressively seek out the most exciting product at prices reflecting excellent value," said Todd Slater, a retail analyst at Lazard Capital. Selected stores have been selling designers such as Dolce & Gabbana and Jil Sander at 50 to 60 percent off.

DKNY, Baby Phat, Max Studio, Jones New York and Ellen Tracy are staples at TJ Maxx, which also has a limited selection of Marc Jacobs, Elie Tahari, Ralph Lauren and Theory. The off-pricer's marketing approach has become more sophisticated; e-mails go to top customers announcing arrivals such as Dooney & Bourke handbags at 50 percent off.

Off-pricers buy much of their inventory directly from manufacturers and have been making exclusive deals with brands the same way department stores do. TJ Maxx obtained the license to sell Willi Smith's WilliWear label in 1996 and carries it exclusively. The stores sometimes score big quarry. Several years ago, TJX bought excess inventory from Blackglama. Mink coats were sold in about 50 TJ Maxx locations for $4,999 to $12,000. Every store had a velvet rope around the coats and an armed guard.

"We're all in the same business because we're all looking for a piece of the same pie," said Marsha Wilson, ceo of Daffy's, which operates 18 stores in New York, New Jersey and Pennsylvania. "Because we're so fashion conscious and so value conscious, our position is basically the same today as it's always been. There are a lot of manufacturers that cut specifically for the outlet stores. It's not necessarily the same merchandise. They'll take last year's fabric for the outlet or off-price stores. The stores don't care if it's dated fabric as long as they get the label because that's what's important to them. We're not big enough to have clothes made for us. I don't have hundreds of stores to fill. We're just opportunists. For us, there's enough to go around. We haven't had a tremendous amount of difficulty" finding merchandise.

"We're pretty much buying directly from [manufacturers] what they have available at the best available price," said Fred Forcellati, vice president of advertising and creative at Loehmann's. "Why is there so much merchandise out there? When things are good, everyone's producing more and there's always excess on hand. But there always seem to be goods available. We're there for the consumer and we're there for the industry. The industry likes us to be there, but they'd never admit it."

Web merchants that sell discounted designer fare are sensitive to a designer's conundrum: wanting to liquidate leftover fashion, but doing so in the quietest way. "Some manufacturers use us as a discreet channel to clear inventory out," said Jacob Hawkins, senior vice president of online marketing at Overstock.com, which offers Ferré leather jackets for $149.99, an 80 percent savings from the original price. "You can get great brands at discounted prices. Out of courtesy to the brands, we don't discuss the names [in print]."

While sales at Bluefly.com rose more than 30 percent in the last quarter and the company expects to do $60 million in sales in 2006, Payner said she was still rebuffed by some designers. "Some brands say they'll sell you everything," she explained. "Other designers say, 'As soon as you're big enough, I'll sell to you exclusively.' We carry a lot of contemporary designers, but no misses'. We have 150 new styles coming in every day."

Like all retailers, Bluefly.com looks for exclusive products to give it an edge over the competition. "For the most part, designers aren't manufacturing specifically for us," Payner said. "If we're very successful with something, we might ask a designer to make it for us again or we might ask them to make it for us in other colors. The more we do that, the more we differentiate ourselves. Whenever we do those kinds of things, we're very successful."

But Payner has no illusions about the reasons people shop at Bluefly.com. "It's been a long time since anyone wanted to brag about paying top dollar," she said. "Last year, we had waiting lists for discounted Fendi Spy bags."

Natalie Massanet, founder of Net-a-porter.com, designed the e-commerce site to resemble a fashion magazine with editorial content. It's about as close as you can get to a high-end specialty store, restricting markdowns to carefully defined sale periods. "In the beginning, we were fighting the perception that the Internet was low-frills, discounted goods," said Massanet. "Quite a few companies operating in the online fashion space are focussed on previous-season discounted goods. Our proposition is getting the products at the same time as the stores and ordering directly from the brands." When merchandise on Net-a-porter goes on sale, it's usually marked down 35 percent. "We're not known as aggressive discounters," Massanet said.

"Net-a-Porter approaches us as any other retailer would," said Aiden. "They look at the collection at the same time as Bergdorf Goodman and Neiman Marcus. It's really another distribution channel, except they look at certain criteria, like items with more visual interest and details rather than more basic pieces."

"Retail is working and e-commerce is working," Konheim said. "Which one gets stronger in the future? Who knows. The convenience factor of the Internet is unbelievable. E-commerce is a growing part of the business."

Women's Wear Daily, January 7, 2006

Retail Development Enters New Era

DAVID MOIN

John Bucksbaum, chief executive officer of General Growth Properties Inc. and chairman of the International Council of Shopping Centers, has strong opinions about what consumers and communities want from him and other developers.

"They are encouraging densification," he said in an interview. "They don't want more 'greenfield' in development."

By densification, he means redeveloping malls with offices, hotels, theaters, parks, outdoor dining and other elements beyond the traditional menu of department and specialty stores and fast-food courts. It often means reclaiming abandoned department stores and other spaces and rebuilding and upgrading properties to be more in touch with current lifestyles.

The mixed-use phenomena will be a major theme in Bucksbaum's state of the industry address and a special session at the ICSC New York National Conference & Deal Making meeting, Dec. 4 to 6 at the Hilton New York.

Mixed use emerged as a trend in development in the Eighties, but in many cases flopped because the market demand for certain elements contained in the projects was absent, Bucksbaum said. "Now we are able to pick and choose and bring more of the art of science" to densifying malls, he said. "We can understand what other uses [beyond retail] can be successful in a marketplace. Going forward, you will see much more mixed use. People don't want to commute 90 minutes to work. Consumers don't want to drive 30 minutes to go shopping."

Bucksbaum returned from a mixed-use conference in Hollywood, Fla., last month convinced that it's the way of the future.

"This was a remarkable conference in the sense that it was the first [of its kind] put on by five different trade organizations." ICSC was the lead organizer; others hosting the event were the National Association of Industrial and Office Properties, the National Multi Housing Council, the American Resort Development Association and the Building Owners and Managers Association.

"They were expecting maybe 400 people," Bucksbaum said. "We had 1,100. That shows you the interest in what's happening in real estate. Mixed use is very much front and center today. We have the room on our sites to bring it in. Retail is a wonderful hub to build around. You can take back [vacated] department store space, and do other retail formats, residential, offices or hotels, depending on what's the greatest demand for that space. . . . In the Eighties, people were building all four components on Day One," and that sometimes led to failure, he noted. But now there's a greater chance of success since developers have a better understanding of the market demands at properties that have been around for awhile.

General Growth's Natick Mall in Massachusetts is being renovated and expanded with what Bucksbaum described as a second, more upscale center that will be anchored by Nordstrom and Neiman Marcus, and two, 12-story residential buildings with luxury condominiums. The 40-year-old site has about 1.6 million square feet of gross leasable space and is anchored by Macy's, Lord & Taylor and Sears.

"We expect it to become the South Coast Plaza of the New England region," Bucksbaum said. The 40-year-old South Coast Plaza, in Costa Mesa, Calif., has 2.8 million square feet of gross leasable space and is the biggest in the country, for retailing, though Mall of America has more total square footage when you add in its entertainment features.

On a smaller scale, General Growth operates mixed-use centers such as

Mizner Park in Boca Raton, Fla., which is 15 years old and includes retail, residential and office space, along with an art center and a performing arts center. "It's a highly productive center," Bucksbaum said, with about 175,000 square feet for retail, about 800 or 900 residential units, and more than 150,000 square feet of office space.

"There is a lot of complexity to mixed use," Bucksbaum continued. "There are more opportunities to fail when you start getting involved in more than one type of use. It's got to be well planned and that's not easy."

There's a lot of construction and architectural considerations, he noted, such as with residential coexisting in a retail project, entrances and parking locations for residents must be thought through, as well as what the view from the apartments would be.

Developers also must update their retail space. Market demands are changing and consumers want revamped formats, whether it's open-air settings, stores with entrances and facades facing mall exteriors for easier access from their cars, retail "streetscapes" or outdoor retail villages with cafes, fountains and parks.

"The way malls are being designed and built is much different today," Bucksbaum said. "It's as an exciting period for our industry as we ever had."

Retailers are starting to understand if they want to continue to expand, they have to rethink their real estate for different settings, such as urban markets. "There is real business to be done in urban markets," he said. "More and more retailers are exploring them."

Also, developers are going upscale in terms of tenants, ambience and amenities. "This is very much a trend," Bucksbaum said. "All customers have aspirations to move up. Retailers have done a good job of adjusting their selections. Coach is probably the best example of [a retailer] who has brought a luxury name to a level of affordability. Neiman Marcus is doing that with Cusp," a new division with two units and a contemporary assortment. "Apple is a great example of an upscale product within reach of the masses. There is a belief that upscale retail is a little more recession proof. With department store consolidation, Nordstrom is being given new opportunities in markets that didn't exist for them before. Neiman's, too."

Women's Wear Daily, November 27, 2006

Sephora's World Grows: Home Shopping Network Latest Channel for Chain

PETE BORN

Sephora's drive to extend its reach is being beamed across the television airwaves with the debut today of a series of one-hour shows on Home Shopping Network.

The French-based beauty retail chain is broadcasting four shows today—at 1 A.M., 9 A.M., 1 P.M. and 4 P.M.—from its

Fifth Avenue store near 48th Street in New York. A trio of personalities—Julie Redfern, the Sephora beauty editor, and Dianna Perkovic and Collen Lopez from HSN—will pitch Sephora's top picks for holiday gifts and beauty tips to navigate a season of partying. The initial program

will focus on bestsellers from nine core brands and its own label.

"Our hosts are there to editorialize," said Betsy Olum, senior vice president of marketing at Sephora. "They are not there to hawk products; they are there to describe trends and show new product."

She described the broadcasts as the preview shows, with a regular schedule starting in February and plans calling for five hours of programming per month from a permanent set that will be built in HSN's headquarters in St. Petersburg, Fla. It will be complete with prominent Sephora signage and fixtures designed to create an in-store ambience.

"We believe there is a huge market out there," Olum said, "with more demand than we can satisfy by building 30 or 40 new stores a year."

While Sephora has steamed ahead with store openings, the retailer also has relentlessly pursued what Sephora president David Suliteanu calls "brand enhancement opportunities." First, the company, which is owned by LVMH Moët Hennessy Louis Vuitton, struck up a partnership in March with Klinger Advanced Aesthetics to tap into the burgeoning consumer demand for spa treatments. Then in late September, J.C. Penney Co. unveiled new and renovated stores containing sizable Sephora store-within-store boutiques. "Penney's gave us the opportunity to reach out to a new clientele who may not have previously shopped us before," Olum said, adding the reduced and edited assortment in the Penney's boutiques "allows them to shop for beauty in a different way. The assortment is smaller and more focused and isn't overwhelming."

And there seemed to be no objections from Penney's to Sephora's latest move. "Anything that Sephora does to raise brand awareness is a benefit to J.C. Penney," said Darcie Brossart, vice president of corporate communications.

The appeal of HSN has become apparent to Sephora. "Whenever any of our brands would go on TV there would be a lift in our store business," Olum said. The appeal of the shopping channel is evident from the statistics Olum ticked off: HSN reaches 89 million households, 75 percent of customers are female, the average age is 25 to 54, and the average household income is $61,000 a year.

Olum underscored the potential and discussed why Sephora decided on HSN, rather than QVC, and alluded to the apparent desire to move the network's programming forward by Mindy Grossman, chief executive officer of the parent IAC/Interactive Corp., headed by Barry Diller.

"First and foremost, HSN did not have a broad beauty offering, so there was an amazing and immediate opportunity for us," Olum stated. "Additionally, with their great demographics and Mindy Grossman at the helm, the partnership promises to be even more exciting."

Today's Sephora preview will feature bestsellers from nine of the retailer's core brands, including Make Up For Ever, Cargo, Dior, The Balm, T3 hair dryers, Oscar Blandi, Urban Decay, Lip Fusion and the Sephora brand of bath and body care and accessories and implements. These brands also are expected to return in the February lineup, which currently is being put together by Nicole Frusci, director of brand marketing for Sephora. Spokesmen, experts and in-house makeup artists also will make appearances on the shows; for instance, Oscar Blandi was scheduled to appear in the 9 A.M. segment.

Michael Henry, vice president of merchandising for beauty at HSN, noted that Ken Pavés appeared on a show in October selling hair extensions. The show rang up four times the expected sales and the customer age was seven years younger than the average, he said.

Scott Sanborn, senior vice president of marketing, said the emphasis in the Sephora-HSN shows will be "on new discoveries in products and new ideas on how to use products." For instance, Dior is featuring a new mascara and Lip Fusion has a holiday set. Olum said that as in the case of Penney's, Sephora is offering its best picks of its core vendors, not slanting its assortment for TV.

HSN now has core beauty business, with its major brands consisting of Susan Lucci, Lauren Hutton and Marilyn Miglin.

Henry said he sees opportunity to build up the color cosmetics and hair categories. He said skin care now does about 50 percent of the portfolio, and he would like it to represent only 40 percent. Conversely, makeup now claims 25 percent, and Henry would like it to be 35 percent.

Sanborn said the hookup with Sephora was attractive because the specialty chain's image as "the beauty authority" provides a platform of credibility for the network. But HSN apparently has built up its own following in beauty. Sanborn noted the channel has had no problem selling beauty serums priced over $100 apiece. White noted the market perceptions have changed dramatically since the Eighties, when home television shopping was first introduced. The mass-class divide has completely blurred and so have the boundaries between price points.

The HSN executives also expect the Sephora shows to have a ripple effect. Two of the Sephora brands, Lip Fusion and Go Smile, have been scheduled for their own shows in January. The promotional theme running through that month will be "the new you." The HSN approach is highly editorial with tightly edited offerings and live demonstrations that can be very persuasive. Sanborn noted, "What works on TV is being able to show dramatic results, and that can really drive sales."

Henry added, "We are curating the assortment" and picking up marketing materials from the Sephora Web site.

With the explosion in lifestyle retailing, the HSN-Sephora pitch will be: "'Here are the five things you need to buy,' and that is how we get into the homes." He added, "We really are presenting the product to the customer in more of a problem-solving way than as marketing."

News is also a factor. Sanborn pointed out that Clever Carriage Co. sold out of 11 styles of handbags by showing different looks. It took 40 minutes, well short of the hour that was allotted.

Sephora's Olum sees the opportunity of entering so many households. "This is a destination for them. They flip on the TV and are ready to shop."

White also sees a chance to acquaint his customer with the world of Sephora. "Probably what will happen is that there will be a customer who will be educated about Sephora."

Women's Wear Daily, December 13, 2006

Warehouse Clubs Aim for Frugal and Fancy

SHARON EDELSON

Warehouse clubs, not content to sell bulk toilet paper and giant bottles of ketchup, are trying to reinvent themselves as destinations both for wholesale bargains and luxury products. Their aim: attract affluent consumers who spend more with each visit.

In June, Sam's Club held a press event in a rented penthouse apartment in Manhattan to tout its luxury offerings for the holiday season. There were diamond necklaces in weights of 1 carat to 5 carats, priced from $2,700 to more than $8,000, and designer handbags, including a Prada style for $395.

"We've been recognized as a bulk seller and as catering to small businesses," Greg Spragg, executive vice president of merchandising for Sam's, told the crowd, adding that the retailer wants to become known for selling affordable luxury items.

Sam's and its rival Costco have much to overcome in terms of strengthening luxury offerings. First and foremost is the difficulty in buying designer apparel, handbags and accessories directly from manufacturers. At the summer press event, Dee Breazeale, vice president and divisional merchandise manager for the jewelry division of Sam's Club, said the Prada handbag on display was just one of many designer brands Sam's carries.

"There are always about 12 handbag styles available at Sam's," she said. "It's always a treasure hunt. You never know what you're going to find."

Designers have been aggressively bringing legal action against unauthorized retailers such as warehouse clubs and off-pricers, which will further limit the product flow. Fendi filed a complaint in June against Wal-Mart Stores, Sam's parent, in U.S. District Court, Southern District of New York, alleging that Sam's had been selling counterfeit handbags with the Fendi logo. A Wal-Mart spokesman said that the complaint was without merit and that the company would show the products were acquired properly.

One indication of the direction Sam's may be moving in is the recent hiring of Patty Warwick as senior vice president of apparel. Warwick, who was senior vice president and general merchandise manager of home at May Merchandising Corp., has extensive experience in private label development.

In her résumé, Warwick wrote: "Succeeded in developing and delivering the first private-label brands to May Company's home store." She also has ties to designers. As senior vice president and general merchandise manager, of home, intimate apparel and hosiery at the Meier & Frank division of May, she "transformed the division to an upscale fashion-oriented business," according to the résumé.

Costco, with $57 billion in annual sales and 488 stores, is known for selling caviar and gourmet foods, expensive wines, handbags, jewelry, household appliances and personal care products. Merchandise varies from market to market, but Costco's Web site offers a glimpse: handbags by Dolce & Gabbana, Carlos Falchi, Fendi, Coach and Furla; Chip & Pepper boot-cut stretch jeans for $119.99; watches from Bulgari, Bedat, Breitling, Cartier, Chopard and Concord, as well as a Patek-Phillippe Twenty-4 style for $21,999.99; and Diesel, Ralph Lauren, Marc Jacobs, Giorgio Armani and Versace sunglasses.

Costco said it goes about buying fashion the way any department store would. The assistant merchandise manager for apparel, Shannon West, listed fall trends in Costco Connections magazine such as aged and worn denim in skinny cuts, jeans with pockets embellished with stitching and rhinestones, ruffle shirts, bell and flutter sleeves, cardigans, cowlnecks and crochets, and coats in cotton velvet, faux shearling and quilted micro fiber.

"Shannon and her team keep the clothing tables at Costco up-to-date with trips to New York several times a year to meet with suppliers and see the latest trends," the magazine said.

Costco is forging ahead in the fragrance and beauty area. Stores sell Baby Phat Goddess, Burberry Brit Red, Estée Lauder's Tom Ford Amber, Salvatore Ferragamo Subtil and Chanel No. 5. The retailer recently launched Kirkland Signature by Borghese beauty products. Georgette Mosbacher, Borghese's chairman, chief executive officer and president, said the line is almost identical to the signature Borghese brand, but the prices are not. For example, the Age Defying Eye Cream, which costs $19 at Costco, would be priced at $125 to $175 in department stores, Mosbacher said.

The company also plans to expand the test of its concierge service, available in Southern California, to the rest of the state. Shoppers can call an 800 number to get advice about merchandise, which the company said is perhaps better than consumers would receive from the manufacturers' toll-free numbers.

More than half of Costco's members, 64.7 percent, earn in excess of $50,000 annually, according to Retail Forward. Almost half of all Sam's Club members, 48.8 percent, earn less than $49,500 a year; however, the retailer said the number of members with higher incomes is growing.

"Selling high-margin discretionary products to its customer base has become a lucrative enterprise, but the clubs need to focus on high-velocity items," said Todd Slater, a retail analyst at Lazard Capital Markets. "Upscaling too much can prove dangerous."

Sam's Club, which does $40 billion in annual sales, emphasizes fresh produce, bakery goods, organics, wine, office supplies for small business owners, electronics and fine jewelry, especially engagement rings. Apparel makes up a relatively small fraction of sales, and the retailer rarely sells designer labels.

Like its larger sibling, Wal-Mart, Sam's has been making overtures to upscale customers for some time. Several years ago, Sam's ran an ad in In Style magazine with the tag line "Expect the Unexpected" and an image of a 20-carat fancy yellow-gold diamond ring for $1 million, which was featured on its Web site. These days, Sam's offers what it calls "Dream Jewelry": a 10-carat heart-shaped diamond for $721,233, a 31.90-carat cushion-cut cognac diamond ring for $343,000 and a necklace with 82 carats of pear-shaped diamonds, $263,574.

Slater said such jewelry is basically window dressing. "If the clubs didn't carry jewelry, I doubt it would significantly impact the business model one way or the other," he said. "It's an impulse category and can contribute high margins, and in the case of a big diamond, a high average ticket. It adds cachet and even differentiation, but it's probably not a huge category. Watches are probably an important piece of the jewelry category.

"It's important for the clubs to focus on high-velocity items," Slater continued.

"They are geared for a low number of high-velocity items [and stockkeeping units] that can sell in the millions of units, that can fit on a palette and that are self-service and don't require a lot of labor to sell. The club is a low-cost model that has paper-thin margins, so the club model is not very well suited to low-velocity, high-average-priced retail unit items."

The key to generating higher sales may be location, location, location.

"Sam's grew up in the South, and its stores are located, on average, in smaller, more rural markets than Costco, which grew up on the West Coast," Slater said. "The average Costco club is located in larger and more affluent markets, so it tends to appeal to a higher-end demographic and generates higher average club volumes."

Costco has been actively looking for real estate in Manhattan. The company was planning to open a unit in a new retail development, East River Plaza, between 116th and 119th Streets, but it was replaced by Target. Robert Futterman, chairman of the real estate company that bears his name, said finding another site for Costco will be difficult but not impossible. "I know they want to be in the city," he said. "They need to be on one level. But where are you going to get 150,000 square feet in Manhattan?"

Futterman said he hasn't "heard much buzz about Sam's Club" looking for space in Manhattan.

Women's Wear Daily, October 16, 2006

advertising, special events, publicity, and visual merchandising

People ask me if I run out of ideas. I don't run out of them; I run after them.

GENE MOORE, VISUAL MERCHANDISER

Capturing the attention of potential customers, whether individuals in the trade or household consumers, is the responsibility of fashion promoters. The most beautifully designed and manufactured product is a success only if it finds a receptive audience. Promotional teams develop marketing strategies and events designed to motivate consumers to buy.

Everyone in fashion recognizes the importance of effective promotion. Designers, manufacturers, and retailers of fashion merchandise pay as much attention to promoting their products as they do to designing and merchandising them. Elaborate runway shows, video presentations, and multimedia advertising campaigns are just some of the methods that can be used to introduce new collections, seasons, styles, and designs to an eagerly awaiting audience. The cost of these promotional undertakings sometimes run into the millions. Calvin Klein, for example, spent $40 million to launch a new fragrance.

Many fashion organizations take a four-pronged approach to promotion: advertising, special events, publicity, and visual merchandising.

ADVERTISING

"That paid-for form of nonpersonal presentation of the facts about goods, services, or ideas to a group" is the American Marketing Association's definition of **advertising**. Traditionally, advertisers have used both broadcast and print media to get their messages across. Today, electronic advertising is also being carried over the Internet. In the fashion industry, advertising sponsors include trade organizations, mills, designers, manufacturers, and retailers. Each sponsor attempts to address the target market for his or her products.

After you have completed this chapter, you will be able to discuss:

- Some of the promotional methods used in the fashion industry.

- How manufacturers and retailers approach advertising.

- How designers, manufacturers, and retailers use consumer publications.

- The differences between promotional and institutional advertising.

- The benefits of cooperative advertising to the manufacturer and retailer.

- Five types of special events and how they help their sponsors.

- The differences between advertising and publicity.

- The role of the visual merchandiser in promoting fashion.

535

Eye-catching displays are a retailer's silent salesperson.

The development of a new yarn, the opening of a designer's collection, the introduction of an innovative fashion concept, or the personal appearance of a designer all require some form of promotion. Advertising is often the form chosen by the fashion industry. A timely, carefully crafted advertisement usually gets the message to the appropriate audience. Each company establishes an advertising budget and chooses the media best suited to its particular product. A new women's apparel manufacturer hoping to capture retail store buyers' attention would probably select *Women's Wear Daily* (*WWD*) for advertising, a men's furnishings company would probably concentrate on *DNR* (*Daily News Record*) for its advertising to potential trade purchasers, and a retailer, hoping to capture a share of the market, would select the consumer newspaper that best typifies the market in which the store operates.

The responsibility for advertising varies from company to company. Those with significant sales volume usually have separate in-house advertising departments responsible for such activities as campaign preparation and production. Small companies may simply rely on outside agencies as the need arises. Others might assign the chore to a marketing executive who has numerous other tasks to perform. There is no industry norm. Each company meets its advertising needs in the manner that best suits its particular operation.

Fashion Advertisers

The industry is segmented into numerous parts. Each establishes its objectives and then attempts to gain the attention and respect of potential purchasers. The group to which each addresses its offering dictates the format and outlets to be used in advertising.

Designers

Many designers have advertising needs that are twofold in nature. One is to make the trade aware of their creations—that is, to capture the attention of the store buyers and merchandisers who make selections for their particular clientele. The other is to reach the ultimate consumer. By informing the ultimate purchaser of their designs, they are attempting to presell their lines to those who will wear them. Thus, designers advertise in particular trade periodicals to motivate store buyers and in consumer magazines and on television to appeal to ultimate users.

In the era of licensing, many world-famous designers have their own promotional divisions that coordinate the advertising of all their licensed products. It is not unusual for a designer such as Donna Karan to have a 10-page spread in a fashion magazine featuring many of the products he or she makes available through licensing arrangements.

Manufacturers

The producers of fashion merchandise spend significant sums on advertising. Their targets are generally the retailers who are their potential customers. Advertising of this nature usually appears in trade papers and magazines or through direct marketing. Many manufacturers secure the names of potential accounts from marketing research organizations and then mail brochures, flyers, and videos that depict their offerings to them. Those with nationally recognized labels might take the same route as designers and place ads in consumer fashion magazines, such as *Harper's Bazaar*, *GQ*, *Elle*, *Ebony*, and *Glamour*, to keep their names in the public eye.

Retailers

The major share of the retailer's promotional budget is earmarked for advertising; the major portion of the advertising budget is spent on newspaper ads. A review of any newspaper will quickly underscore this medium's importance to the retailer. For comparatively little cost per reader, a store can quickly announce a sale, promote its image, notify customers of an impending promotion, or communicate any messages that might motivate consumers to buy.

Many of the major retailers have large staffs that are responsible for advertising. Specialists in copy, artwork, production, layout, and research work together to produce the scores of advertisements that appear in newspapers. The giants in the industry have additional personnel who specialize in direct-mail catalogs, television, and radio advertising. Many retailers have invested in computer hardware and desktop publishing software so that they can create their own catalogs. This has cut production expenses considerably in this area of advertising.

Preparing ads requires the skills of many individuals.

Trade Associations

These groups or organizations use advertising to alert members to special events. The National Retail Federation uses direct mail to notify members of meetings, the National Association of the Display Industry might use an ad in a trade publication to announce an industrial show, and MAGIC might use *Women's Wear Daily* to advertise its trade presentations. These organizations are concerned only with trade members and use the media most closely associated with the trade represented.

Media

Selecting the appropriate print and broadcast media in which to advertise requires careful assessment of the product and its target audience. Although the newspaper wins hands down for retailers, many stores choose to allocate their advertising dollars to several media.

Many designers use trade advertising to reach their retailers. This ad from Eileen Fisher appeared in *WWD*.

Trade associations advertise
upcoming shows in trade
journals.

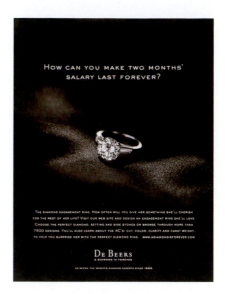

An eye-catching style or
signature attracts consumer
readership.

Each fashion advertiser must examine all of the choices within each medium before deciding where to advertise most effectively.

Newspapers

The newspaper allows an advertiser to reach most readers on a daily basis. It gets its point across quickly and efficiently. Retailers, to establish customer continuity, use newspapers as their chief means of communication. With very little notice, a store can quickly capitalize on an event. A sudden accumulation of snow, for example, might tempt the footwear buyer to do a spread on the latest styles in water-resistant boots. The **lead time** needed for magazines or television advertising eliminates them as a source of last-minute advertising.

Many fashion retailers develop a style or signature for their newspaper advertisements. A particular type of fashion illustration or photography might catch the reader's attention. If used regularly over a period of time, it could be a device customers will look for when reading the paper.

Placement of ads also plays an important role for advertisers. Many papers charge additional money for locations the reader is more likely to see. For example, some companies have contracts with newspapers that reserve a **regular position** (that is, the same place in every issue) for their ads, so that their customers can quickly locate the ad. Others pay for **preferred position**, placement in a particular part of the paper. The least expensive placement is **run of press**, a term used to indicate placement wherever the publisher decides. Run of press does not offer the advantages of the other types of placement.

Although newspapers offer such advantages as diversified readership, low ad cost per reader, ease of acquisition, and leisurely reading, they also present some drawbacks to the advertiser. The life of the message is limited, only lasting until the next issue is published. The poor quality of the paper stock does not provide for attractive reproduction, and color is sparsely used except in magazine supplements.

Magazines

Unlike newspapers, which cover relatively regional areas, magazines are excellent for national exposure. For that reason, most manufacturers and designers prefer them for their ads. In addition, the fashion industry has magazines in which offerings can be promoted. Some are trade publications such as *Style*, produced in New York, and *Gap*, published in France; these give producers exposure to wholesale purchasers. Designers, manufacturers, and retailers opt for national advertising in consumer-oriented magazines such as *Harper's Bazaar*, *Glamour*, *Vogue*, *Ebony*, and *Seventeen*.

The magazines offer a variety of benefits, including the finest quality reproduction in both black and white and color; an audience that generally reaches from coast to coast, although regional editions are available; and a readership life that surpasses every other medium. Unlike newspapers, readers often keep magazines for extended periods of time or pass them to others. The latter makes them even more valuable.

Some limitations on magazine ads are the high cost, geographically dispersed markets, and the long lead time necessary between preparation of the ad and its publication. Among the 30 leading fashion magazines, *Better Homes and Gardens* is the most successful. It is followed by *Southern Living*, *Glamour*, and *Vogue*.

Direct Mail

One of the most effective methods of reaching a particular market segment is direct mail. Manufacturers often send hard-copy or electronic press kits, brochures, or pamphlets that feature their newest offerings to their regular accounts or potential customers. Retailers are the primary users of direct mail. Whether it is catalogs that alert customers to the company's new merchandise or flyers inserted with end-of-the-month credit card account statements, direct mail generally brings significant additional revenue to the retailer.

Some retailers offer merchandise in their catalogs that they do not stock in the stores. Victoria's Secret, for example, limits its store inventory to intimate apparel and some fragrances, but sells an abundance of sportswear in its catalog.

Unlike other ads, direct mail earmarked for a particular household or company receives the reader's undivided attention and can be examined at the reader's leisure. One important requirement of a good direct-mail program is the updating of the mailing list. If customers have moved, or the list incorrectly states the address, the mailer serves no purpose.

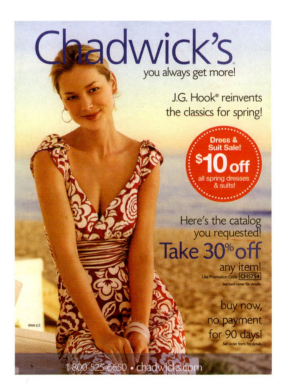

Direct-mail catalogs are reaching more and more consumers each year. They capture the reader's attention.

Television and Radio

Although some companies, such as Gap, have successfully incorporated television into their promotional programs, neither the garment industry nor the majority of fashion retailers use television and radio as advertising mainstays. The major exceptions are the cosmetics and fragrance industries. Calvin Klein's many fragrances are marketed on television, as is White Diamonds, by Elizabeth Taylor. The drama and sexual appeal of these products, coupled with television's ability to create a mood, has resulted in increased sales.

One advantage of television is its ability to quickly expose vast numbers of people to a particular message. Some companies, however, find that the tremendous production costs and air-time expenses are too high for a message that disappears in a matter of seconds. To make the ad worthwhile, it must be shown many consecutive times.

Some retailers use limited amounts of television time. Because their trading areas are relatively small, they generally opt for **local spots**—ads that are aired only in specific geographical areas. This significantly reduces the cost of the commercial and delivers the message to those who are within reach of the store.

Because radio must rely solely on sound to capture an audience's attention, the fashion industry is not a big customer. In cases where a store wishes to announce a sale or publicize a special fashion event, radio is sometimes used.

The Internet

Joining the list of other advertising media is the Internet, although in comparison to the other long-established media it is still in its infancy. Subscribers who "surf the Net" will find various Web sites with a wealth of products that may be ordered directly from their home or office computers.

Internet sales pale in comparison with other types of advertising offerings. However, the statistics related to online shopping show its potential as another outlet that retailers can use to reach customers. Consider the following statistics about Internet use:

- Median age of users: 33 years

- Average household income: $65,000

- Number of online shoppers: 50 million

The Internet's unparalleled ability to reach consumers worldwide ensures that many other retailers will soon join the ranks of companies such as Eddie Bauer, Lands' End, and Spiegel that already have active Web sites.

Advertising Classifications

Two distinct types of advertisements are used to gain customer attention. Whether the ads are trade oriented and directed toward the industry or consumer based and focused on the ultimate consumer, the formats are either promotional or institutional. **Promotional advertising**, or product advertising as it is sometimes called, is used to sell specific items. **Institutional advertising**, on the other hand, directs its efforts toward projecting a particular image, achieving goodwill, or announcing special events.

Fashion organizations often use both formats. A manufacturer might wish to alert store buyers to a particularly hot item and will focus advertisement specifically on that style. When the aim is to advance the company's image or reputation, the institutional approach is used.

Similarly, retailers may elect to sell specific goods or to improve their fashion images. If the former is the goal, a particular item or group of items is carefully presented. If image building is the objective, then attention might concentrate on the store's roster of designer resources, its commitment to service, or anything else that will present it in a good light.

Sometimes the advertiser uses a combination of both approaches. At Lord & Taylor, for example, ads very often call the customer's attention to its loyalty to American

Retailers sometimes combine both promotional and institutional messages in one ad.

designers. In the same advertisement, the store features specific designs by these people. The emphasis on American designers is the institutional portion of the combination ad, with the specific styles the promotional portion.

The use of promotional or product advertising far outweighs that of institutional advertising. Its positive effect can be quickly measured by increases in sales for the advertised items. The results of institutional advertising cannot be measured as scientifically or as quickly. Because the store's image is the focus of such ads, success can only be judged over a long period of time.

Cooperative Advertising

When two companies share the cost of an advertisement, they are participating in **cooperative advertising**. Fiber producers who wish to motivate a designer to use their fabric in apparel collections often provide promotional assistance to the designer for the product's advertisement. Retailers are often the recipients of advertising allowances when their ads feature a particular manufacturer. In both situations, the end results should be beneficial to both participants.

With the cost of advertising always increasing, businesses increasingly look to their suppliers for promotional dollars. The cooperative arrangement makes the cost of advertising a dual responsibility. Each party generally pays 50 percent of the cost, based on a predetermined formula. For example, a manufacturer may establish that it will give a retailer an advertising allowance based on up to 10 percent of purchases. This allowance will then be used to cover one half of the cost of the ad.

Institutional ads promote a store's image and goodwill.

Creative professionals in ad agencies produce attention-grabbing advertisements.

In addition to producing an incentive to purchase from a particular resource, such cooperation also gives the user the potential for more advertising space than the company can afford on its own.

Advertising Agencies

Although many fashion organizations maintain their own advertising staffs, they often use the services of experts for special campaigns. They, along with those who do not have in-house staffs, may employ an **advertising agency** to handle their print and broadcast advertisements.

Advertising agencies employ professionals who are expert in every aspect of advertisement preparation and also have a complete understanding of the media. The agency receives a commission—usually 15 percent of the cost of the ad—from the media in which they place their clients' advertisements. For specialized services, agencies may charge their clients an additional fee.

The choice of an agency depends on the needs of a client. Some agencies specialize in fashion layouts for manufacturers; others in retail-oriented work; and still others in only one medium. The user should carefully select the agency that best meets his or her needs.

SPECIAL EVENTS

To bring attention to the fashion organization, many schedule happenings—**special events**—that are not typical day-to-day operations. Retailers, manufacturers, designers, trade associations, and mills each have many avenues for reaching both regular audiences and potential users of their products or services. These special events may be major attractions that cost significant amounts and last for several weeks, or they may be less-costly one-day affairs. Fashion shows, celebrity appearances, theme parades, demonstrations, charitable celebrations, and special sales are just some of the events in which the fashion industry participates.

Fashion Shows

Few special presentations offer the drama and excitement of **fashion shows**. Whether the audience is composed of professional industrial purchasers or consumers, the live production seems to excite everyone. Budgeting considerations, space, audience size, and purpose play a role in deciding the format of a fashion show. Once these factors have been addressed, the production will follow one of two forms.

The **runway show** is the most elaborate type of fashion show. These shows require music, either live or recorded, choreography, scripts, and models. **Informal modeling** is the second format used. As the name implies, models walk informally among customers to show off selected outfits. In store restaurants and beauty salons, models parade the latest fashions in the hope that consumers will be motivated to buy the merchandise.

At one time, formal productions were commonplace in the fashion industry. Fiber producers, such as Monsanto, staged elaborate productions that rivaled the most original theatrical events. Original musical scores, special choreography, creative stage sets, imaginative lighting, and scripted dialogue were used in these industrial extravaganzas. Professional actors, dancers, musicians, and models spent countless hours rehearsing for the big event. Today, however, this type of show is extremely rare on the fashion scene. Although it generates a great deal of excitement in the industry, the expense generally outweighs the benefits. On July 13, 1998, in Paris, France, one of these amazing fashion show extravaganzas took place. A World of Fashion Profile features the Yves Saint Laurent World Cup fashion show.

The runway show is a major industry promotion used to generate excitement.

Many segments of the fashion industry use the fashion show as one of their special events. Some use their own premises for the event; others contract for grand ballrooms, restaurants, theaters, or other arenas. In addition to selecting the proper environment, care must be exercised in inviting the members of the audience. Fashion shows are usually sponsored by the fiber industry, garment manufacturers, retailers, trade associations, and trade expositions.

Fiber Industry

The runway show has replaced the earlier extravaganzas. Companies such as DuPont, for example, rent auditoriums or other arenas for the presentation of fashions that utilize their fibers. Its Lycra® spandex show is a major event to which apparel designers are invited to inspect garments made from the fiber.

Garment Manufacturers

Seasonal shows are the norm for the garment industry. During market week, in particular, the major garment producers kick off the season with a fashion show. Many designers regularly feature runway productions on their own premises or in rented

YVES SAINT LAURENT'S WORLD CUP FASHION SHOW

Following France's triumph over Brazil in the 1998 World Cup soccer championship, another show of equal magnitude took center stage. The event was a fashion extravaganza with 300 models wearing haute couture gowns designed by Yves Saint Laurent during his 40-year career.

As 100 drummers furiously banged their wooden sticks on red oil drums to a recording of Ravel's *Bolero*, the models took the field in front of 80,000 screaming soccer fans. The crowd soon became silent, as most witnessed their first couture show. The models crisscrossed the field in V-shaped lines—like birds flying in formation—across a deep blue skyscape, complete with clouds, painted on an enormous drop cloth. Yves Saint Laurent looked on from his corporate box high above the field.

At the end of the show, a 15-minute presentation, all 300 models formed the YSL logo in the center of the field. Filled with pride and excitement, Saint Laurent waved to the cheering crowds. He said, "Watching the show made me want to continue with couture. . . . For me, this represents a great deal of emotion. I didn't imagine it could be so spectacular."

A look at the costs and planning underscores the immensity of the production. The price was $4 million—the most ever spent on a fashion endeavor—for the festivities at the newest stadium in France, Stade de France, an outdoor arena. In addition to the spectators who were present, it was estimated that 1.7 billion people saw the event on worldwide television.

Among the 300 high-fashion models were the world-famous models Carla Bruni, Alek Wek, and Laetitia Casta. In addition, 600 hair stylists, makeup artists, and assistants spent six hours preparing the models and helping them with their costumes. Did the expense justify the production? To judge from the attention paid by the hordes of fashion editors present and the coverage given by the press, the publicity generated was greater than that of any other conceivable event. It will probably stand out as the single most exciting fashion show ever to be mounted anywhere in the world.

spaces. These shows concentrate primarily on the merchandise, not on the scenic backdrops. Most often, the only prop is a back wall that features the designer's name or logo.

The runway is either cluttered with several models displaying a particular design group or has only one or two models at a time. Some productions use commentary, but the trend is to use printed programs to identify each style. In most shows, manufacturers carefully accessorize each garment with compatible shoes, hats, millinery, and jewelry.

A trend in the middle price point is to have in-house fashion shows. Showrooms are now designed so that the selling floor may be transformed into open spaces that can be used for fashion shows. Liz Claiborne's menswear showroom can quickly hide the partitions and racks that generally fill the room to make way for its runway presentations.

Many manufacturers of men's and women's apparel are choosing unusual, off-premises, centralized facilities to present their shows. The tents at Bryant Park in New York City have been the successful home of many runway shows for women's wear. Places such as Sony's sound stage have become a venue for featuring men's fashions.

Garment industry productions are directed toward two specific groups. One is the professional buyers and merchandisers, who actually purchase the garments for their stores. The other is the editorial press, whose positive comments in their columns and on the air can bring enormous attention to a line.

Many designer and upscale manufacturer's lines are promoted through **trunk shows**, which bring a designer's entire collection to a store for a day or two for customers to view. The designer or a company representative accompanies the collection to answer questions from consumers. Because stores rarely carry a vendor's entire line, it is an opportunity for customers to view an entire collection and special-order specific items. Sometimes, shoppers are able to have certain styles customized for their special needs. A color not usually offered, a longer-length skirt, or a different trim might be made available. The St. John Knit stores' trunk shows offer customizing at no additional cost to customers.

Ads in the newspapers and direct-mail brochures are used to notify potential attendees of such events.

Retailers

Many store organizations also use fashion shows to motivate customers. The shows might be regular features at the store's restaurant or special productions that highlight a particular manufacturer, designer, charitable event, or promotion.

A number of the retail operations jointly sponsor fashion shows with garment manufacturers. Generally, these are informal in-house runway shows that feature a particular company's collection. The production's costs are usually divided between the store and the sponsoring vendor. In cases where the retailer is a significant client of the manufacturer, the designer may be on hand to attract more attention.

Shows of this nature usually take place in or near the selling area of the department that features the show's merchandise. In this way, at the event's conclusion, immediate sales might take place.

Trunk shows are used to show a designer's entire collection to interested consumers. Here Stella McCartney is fitting a customer at a trunk show.

Trade Associations

Most of the fashion industry's components have a trade organization or association for its members. The fashion show format is used by the Chambre Syndicale in Paris, which sponsors the couture and prêt shows in a centralized environment, and Hair America, the fashion branch of the National Hairdressers and Cosmetologists Association. The trade associations use the shows to make the press aware of their field's latest offerings and to enable their membership to view the fashion directions being taken by their colleagues.

Trade Expositions

Throughout the world, producers of fashion showcase their new collections to the retail market in large arenas. Such groups as Salon de'Habillement Masculin (SEHM), which features European menswear in Paris, MAGIC, and the National Association of Men's Sportswear Buyers (NAMSB), which is a major trade show for American men's fashions, all participate in trade expositions. These informal shows are directed toward the press and the retail buyers. The merchandise is a representation of some of the lines featured at the trade show.

Resident Buying Offices

When buyers visit the garment center during market week, many first visit their resident buying office. These offices use fashion shows to make buyers aware of trends for the season. Buyers are given programs that list the names and addresses of the featured resources so that the buyers can visit them to see entire collections.

Fashion Magazines

Some magazines sponsor shows for fiber producers, retailers, manufacturers, designers, and the press. One of their goals is to develop industry relationships that can result in the purchase of advertising space.

Personal Appearances

One of the surest ways to bring an audience to a store is to advertise a personal appearance by a celebrity. Each industry, including the fashion industry, has charismatic personalities whose very presence will guarantee large crowds. Whether it is Calvin Klein or Karl Lagerfeld promoting a fragrance, Betsey Johnson talking about her newest collection, or Anna Sui showing her latest line, the results are usually successful. In addition to the celebrities associated with fashion, popular entertainers also draw crowds. Although the customer's initial intention is to get a glimpse of the celebrity, the increased traffic usually translates into sales throughout the store.

Parades

The most famous of all retailer-sponsored parades is Macy's Thanksgiving Day Parade in New York City. Not only does it provide enjoyment for the people who line the parade route, but it is also enjoyed by people across the country on national television. The parade signifies the official opening of the Christmas shopping season. The parade has been so successful for Macy's that stores all across the nation now have parades in their own cities.

A World of Fashion Profile features Macy's and its use of special events.

Demonstrations

Capturing the shopper's attention sometimes necessitates a **demonstration** of how a product may be used. The cosmetics industry often uses the demonstration technique to entice customers to purchase its products. Cosmetics manufacturers periodically send a cosmetologist to demonstrate proper use of their products on the faces of willing participants and to explain the procedures to the audience that has gathered. Not only does the participant generally buy some of the items, so do those who watch the demonstration.

Mobile Presentations

Unlike the typical designer special events, which require attendees to come to a company's own venue or a space that it has rented for the occasion, this new format enables the event or promotion to move from one place to another in a mobile vehicle. These **traveling road shows** are akin to libraries on wheels or medical clinics that look to disseminate information.

In fashion, two such entries were the brainstorms of designers Ron Chereskin and Claiborne (menswear). Chereskin used a double-decker bus that moved into areas of

MACY'S

One of the reasons for the enormous interest in Macy's is the wealth of promotions it produces. As a leading world fashion retailer, its fashion shows range from introducing a new designer collection to charity benefits. The company, however, does not stop there. It is Macy's institutional promotional events that separate the store from most others.

By now, the Thanksgiving Day Parade is legendary. With helium-filled balloons floating toward the sky, the marching bands making their way through streets lined with thousands of spectators, the celebrities who are regular participants, and the ultimate arrival of Santa Claus, it is an experience for both the eyes and ears. The treat is extended to millions of television viewers all across the United States who faithfully watch the extravaganza each year. Produced by Macy's own special productions department, which works an entire year on its preparation, the parade involves 3,000 employees, who volunteer to march as clowns, dancers, and balloon handlers.

Macy's Fourth of July fireworks display is another exciting event that is viewed by thousands of people from New York City's waterfront or on board local boats. Eleven thousand display shells and effects are exploded to create more than a million bursts of color and light, playing against a specifically written musical score. Like the parade, it is syndicated on television to 150 stations. This production brings Macy's a great deal of publicity.

For two weeks every spring, the Flower Show has become another Macy's tradition. Its Herald Square flagship main floor of 265,000 square feet is filled with exotic plants. A major spectacle, it is planned more than a year in advance. Floral experts throughout the world collect their finest specimens for showing. An additional feature consists of home fashion displays designed by celebrities.

Tap-O-Mania is an event that grows in size every year. For one Sunday each August, a time when shoppers are not accustomed to enthusiastically filling the store, Macy's puts on the largest tap dancing festival in the world. Participants, with or without tapping experience, are invited to join in the fun. Each year, the event attracts more than 6,000 tap dancers, who perform in front of the flagship's entrance, attracting scores of shoppers. Unlike the other promotions, which cost large sums of money, this one is relatively inexpensive.

Through such unusual undertakings, Macy's has established itself as the country's premier retail promoter.

The Macy's Thanksgiving Day Parade is one of the store's major annual attractions.

New York City frequented by tourists, such as Lincoln Center and the Empire State Building, to assist potential customers with fashion advice. The goal was to reach the "everyman." Claiborne made use of an 18-wheel truck with a changing room in which visitors to the city could try on the latest fashion innovations from the company. Familiarizing their consumer audience with the company's merchandise, it is hoped, will encourage individuals to become customers when they shop for clothing after their return home.

Sampling

This type of promotion requires giving away products to prospective users. As with demonstrations, the cosmetics and fragrance manufacturers use this type of promotion most often. In the retail stores where their products are sold, the manufacturers provide sample items or kits that are given free with a purchase or provided at a minimal cost. The brainchild of Estée Lauder, the practice is now followed by most major cosmetics producers.

This practice is particularly prevalent from the period between Thanksgiving and Christmas, when stores are the busiest. If the sample meets with positive results, the customer may be motivated to become a regular user of the item.

Premiums

Sometimes fragrance and cosmetics vendors reward purchasers of their products with premiums that are free or comparatively inexpensive. The items include umbrellas, luggage, carrying cases, T-shirts, and other items that generally bear the vendor's name. In this way, the recipient will continue to publicize the vendor whenever the premium is used.

One inventive premium, offered at little cost, came at the hands of CK Calvin Klein jeans. Customers who purchased a pair of CK jeans were offered an MTV pager that was different from others available in the marketplace. It weighed 1.5 ounces, was less than two inches in size, and had a black, rubberized finish. The pagers gave the wearer a chance to win MTV merchandise, prizes, and trips while providing behind-the-scenes updates on MTV news and music information.

Personal Improvement Sessions

Many fashion retail operations present seminars on personal grooming and proper dress. These events are usually held in a store's special events center or community room and feature a fashion consultant who discusses the "dos and don'ts" of appropriate dress. What to wear to the office or to that special occasion is often the main topic. Preselected outfits are shown during the presentation in the hope that shoppers will decide to purchase them. Beauty experts who talk on topics ranging from skin care to hairstyles are also featured. These talks and demonstrations turn lookers into purchasers.

PUBLICITY

The goal of any designer, retailer, manufacturer, or trade organization is to make itself known to its public. As we have learned, enormous sums are spent on advertising and promotional events to turn potential customers into real purchasers. Most major fashion organizations hope that these paid promotional activities will earn them additional recognition from the press. Such coverage is the most cherished form of promotion, free **publicity**.

Technically, the term *free publicity* is correct. The media print or air on radio or television, without cost to the company, newsworthy stories about a company's accomplishments. For example, the New York City tent shows provide an additional boost for those designers lucky enough to be singled out for their creations by a television show, a consumer newspaper, or a trade periodical. Sometimes, the publicity is negative. A glaring headline on the fashion pages might also spread information about a disappointing collection!

Although the word *free* is used, such publicity usually results from a company's expenditure on a special event or promotion. A designer's expenses for producing a special fashion show could reach as much as $200,000. Thus, although the publicity is free, it comes as a result of a real dollar investment.

People who are responsible for liaising with the fashion press or media are known by a variety of titles, including publicist, public relations person, marketing specialist, promotion director, and fashion director. They and their staffs are responsible for exploring all possible avenues for publicizing their companies, but they generally use two major tools—press releases and press or media kits.

Press kits are excellent vehicles for communication in the fashion industry.

Press Releases

Most companies use **press releases** to communicate with the media about interesting fashion activities. The standard format of a press release, generally sent via e-mail, offers the company's logo, name, address, telephone and fax numbers, e-mail address, and the name of the person to contact for additional information. The first line indicates the date the company wants the information to be disseminated. Often the word *immediate* is used.

The text of the release should have a headline in bold type, and the information should be factual and free of the writer's opinion. It should also include enough information so that the newspaper, magazine, or broadcast media can use all of the piece or only that part it finds most appropriate for its audience. Copywriters carry a heavy workload, and the press release can save a great deal of time.

If a photograph or drawing is appropriate for the release, it can be downloaded as a separate attachment to be used at the fashion editor's discretion.

Press Kits

The major publicity tool a designer, manufacturer, retailer, or trade association uses is the **press** or **media kit**. Press kits are used to entice media coverage and alert the potential market to a special event or happening.

To attract the press to an opening of a designer's collections, in-house publicists or public relations specialists develop press kits and coordinate the activities that are necessary for its production. Included in the typical designer kit are a biographical sketch that emphasizes the designer's past achievements, a release highlighting the theme or emphasis of the collection, and photographs representative of the designer's latest efforts. Copywriters, photographers, artists, and graphic designers work together to make certain that the kit will motivate attendance and provide enough factual information to make the media's task easier.

Retailers use press kits to announce the opening of a new department or a new branch store, introduce a philosophical change in the company's direction, or publicize a special event or celebration.

When Macy's announces its many special events, such as its annual Flower Show, the Thanksgiving Day Parade, the Tap-O-Mania promotion, or its fireworks display on the Fourth of July, to the media, it does so with a press kit. Replete with photographs, statistical figures of the event, and written information, its purpose is to encourage favorable publicity.

The National Retail Federation (NRF) and NAMSB need to inform their markets about special meetings or market openings. They too produce press kits in the hope of motivating the fashion media to cover their events. The majority of the press kits today are sent via e-mail.

Visual merchandising promotes both the store image and the merchandise.

VISUAL MERCHANDISING

If a company's advertising and special events have been on target, potential customers will be motivated to examine the products available for sale. Upon arrival at a retail operation or a manufacturer's showroom, customers should be greeted with an environment carefully designed to further arouse their interest. Designed to capture on-premises attention, visual presentations enhance a company's selling and display areas by establishing a climate in which sales will be made. This is an integral part of the areas of promotion already explored.

Retailers play the dominant role in **visual merchandising**; however, manufacturers are also capitalizing on the favorable impressions made by visual presentations. Manufacturers of apparel, accessories, and home fashions carefully display their products in their showrooms in a manner that will immediately put the professional buyer in a positive shopping mood. Westpoint Stevens, in its 20,000-square-foot showroom, features products in various room settings that express different lifestyles. Sheets and towels are no longer routinely stacked, but are displayed in bedrooms and bathrooms decorated with furniture, fixtures, and other attractive household accessories.

The design and execution of visual presentations may be coordinated by full-time company teams headed by visual merchandising directors, many of whom carry the title of vice president, an indication of the position's importance. The presentation can also be produced by consultants, who are paid by companies to design settings and execute display installations, and by freelancers, who periodically install visual presentations.

In retailing, visual merchandising is generally broken down into two areas—windows and interiors.

Window Displays

The silent sellers for many retailers are the windows that line the streets and malls. In the downtown flagships, careful attention is paid to **window displays**. Usually changed once a week, the themes might include a holiday such as Christmas, a special salute to a designer's new collection, a specific sale period, the introduction of a store's new private label, or anything that might attract the attention of passersby. These visual stories range from the unique, such as the animated presentations at Christmastime, to the traditional. Whatever the event or occasion, they must be executed with props and lighting that enhance the display.

The major department stores plan their window presentations many months in advance. The visual merchandising director develops a *window schedule* that outlines, week by week, the window displays that will be executed. Stores such as Lord & Taylor, Neiman Marcus, Tiffany & Co., Henri Bendel, Bloomingdale's, and Macy's prepare these calendars for six-month periods and spend considerable sums on window displays that will, they hope, generate in-store traffic.

Interior Displays

Inside the stores, visual merchandisers are regularly installing displays and improving the general appearance of the store. With the enormous cost of retail rentals, many merchants are reducing the amount of space for formal windows. Particularly in malls, the

Interior self-service displays show the merchandise and allow customers to make their own selections. Attentive housekeeping is required to enable customers to find the styles, colors, and sizes they want.

Mannequins often generate interest for the merchandise they feature.

windows are often merely glass fronts. In such cases, **interior displays** are given greater attention.

One of the trends in interiors is the elimination of props that depict particular seasons or holidays. For example, Gap merely changes its merchandise displays in the store, without using any holiday or seasonal symbols.

To meet the challenge of visual presentation, both the participants who engage in the actual installations and the company's management, which must approve the expenditures, must be fully versed in the company's policies and practices. Just as apparel designs must be based on sound elements and principles of design, so must visual presentations.

Elements of Visual Presentation

First and foremost, the merchandise must take center stage in any visual presentation. The excessive use of props may detract from the merchandise, making the displays less effective than originally intended. By carefully employing fixtures, props, mannequins, lighting, signage, materials, and color as enhancements of merchandise, the visual effort should be successful.

The choice of these enhancements must be left to the experts. Selecting the appropriate mannequins, for example, is a difficult decision. Those in a position to purchase them must not only have an understanding of the available vari-

ADEL ROOTSTEIN

When Adel Rootstein mannequins appeared on the fashion scene, the world of visual merchandising was reshaped. Although display mannequins were readily available in a variety of materials and designs at a wide range of prices, none provided the uniqueness and quality of a Rootstein. It is not simply a matter of putting new makeup and a new wig on the same old form; her figures always reflect the changes that take place from one decade to another. The shapes of the bodies, the poses, and the facial expressions are details that reflect today's individuals.

The painstaking process begins with finding a real person from whom a model can be fashioned. Theatrical stars, celebrated personalities, beauty queens, internationally famous models, and anonymous people have all served as models for Rootstein mannequins. Next, a staff sculptor shapes a clay replica of the individual chosen. From the clay form, a mold is prepared from which a cast is created. Skin texture, color, makeup, and wigs are then fashioned to complete the mannequin. Although the company manufactures traditional as well as stylized models, the realistic form is the company's forte.

A visit to most mannequin showrooms reveals a series of unadorned forms available for purchase. Not so at Rootstein's. In keeping with its individuality, the company stages a new mannequin presentation twice a year in its showrooms. Each season's presentation is the equivalent of a new Broadway production. A theme is developed, a special costume collection is designed specifically for the mannequins, and the display is magnificently illuminated. It is visual merchandising at its best.

With more than 300 mannequins in its collection, this London-based company provides visual merchandisers all over the globe with a particular fashion image.

eties, but must also know which type best serves their specific needs. At the top of the mannequin field is Adel Rootstein, the London-based company that is the subject of a World of Fashion Profile.

Professional display houses offer visual merchandisers a wealth of **props**. Those with special talents also look to unusual places for their props. The "junk pile" often turns up interesting pieces that may be restored with some ingenuity and paint. Household items, such as chairs and ladders, also make useful merchandise holders. A creative visual merchandiser can produce a display for a minimum of dollars.

Color is also important to the visual team. Without any additional expense, the right colors transform the ordinary presentation into a showstopper.

A knowledge of lighting is also necessary in order to maximize its benefits. Today's visual merchandiser has access to such forms of lighting as high-intensity discharge (HID) and halogen/quartz lights, in addition to traditional light sources. Few elements are as effective at quickly transforming unimaginative presentations into exciting ones as lighting.

Signs and **graphics** have also become more varied. They are available in a host of materials and are used to identify specific departments as well as to describe the merchandise. One of the more exciting types is the backlit transparency, which incorporates light with the sign. It gives a three-dimensional effect and draws attention wherever it is used. A great deal of signage is now produced in-house, with the aid of computer software. As a result, signage is available more quickly and less expensively than ever before.

Visual merchandising is not used merely to describe formal displays. The way in which merchandise is featured on the selling floor is equally important. Many retailers have created customer interest by the use of attractive visual merchandising. Crate &

Barrel and Williams-Sonoma, both in the home products arena, use exciting visual presentation throughout their stores. By artistically arranging typical merchandise in an eye-appealing manner, they have increased their sales volume. It is that aspect of promotion that turns lookers into buyers.

Only when all of the components of a fashion promotion program are carefully executed will successful results be achieved. In this era of stiff competition, fashion organizations must pay as much attention to promotion as they do to product design and merchandising.

CHAPTER HIGHLIGHTS

- Fashion organizations of every type and size develop a variety of promotional programs, including advertising, special events, publicity, and visual merchandising, to enhance their images and sell merchandise.

- Manufacturers, designers, trade organizations, and retailers use all of the media to advertise, with retailers relying on the newspaper as their primary tool.

- Special events are periodic presentations, such as fashion shows, personal appearances, demonstrations, mobile presentations, premiums, and sampling.

- If a special event is enthusiastically received by the press, free publicity may be an eventual by-product.

- Visual merchandising chiefly is used by retailers to give their offerings more eye appeal and to motivate purchasing.

IMPORTANT FASHION TERMINOLOGY AND CONCEPTS

advertising	lead time	regular position
advertising agency	local spot advertisements	run of press
cooperative advertising	media kit	runway show
demonstration	preferred position	signs
fashion shows	press kit	special events
graphics	press release	traveling road show
informal modeling	promotional advertising	trunk show
institutional advertising	props	visual merchandising
interior displays	publicity	window displays

FOR REVIEW

1. Describe the four components of fashion promotion.
2. How does advertising differ from publicity?
3. In what way does the fashion designer's advertisement differ from the fashion retailer's?
4. For what purpose do trade organizations participate in advertising campaigns?
5. Of all the available media, which is most extensively used by fashion retailers and why is it their choice?
6. What advantages does the magazine afford the advertiser that the newspaper does not?
7. Why is direct mail such a positive force in advertising?
8. Differentiate between promotional and institutional advertising.
9. To which market is the manufacturer's fashion show directed?
10. Briefly describe the typical press kits created by fashion designers, retailers, and trade associations.

11. What is a trunk show?

12. Which fashion component makes the most use of visual merchandising?

13. In Lisa Lockwood's Point of View article, what is the theme of "Hot and Bothered"?

EXERCISES AND PROJECTS

1. Contact a designer, manufacturer, or retailer and request a company press kit. From the materials obtained, prepare an oral report on the particular kit and use the elements as visual aids when presenting the information. If an overhead projector is available, use it to show the parts of the press kit.

2. Using fashion magazines as a resource, select one designer's clothing and prepare a press release for that designer's collection. Make sure all of the essentials of a good press release, as discussed in the text, are present.

3. Make arrangements with a local store to use its merchandise for a school-sponsored fashion show. Small committees should be formed and given separate responsibilities for the show's production. One could work on coordination, another on publicity, another on music and commentary, and so on.

4. Visit a shopping mall to photograph five of its tenants' windows. Using the photos as visual aids, discuss the various elements that comprised each display.

WEB SITES

By accessing these Web sites, you will be able to gain broader knowledge and up-to-date information on materials related to this chapter.

Visual Merchandising and Store Design

www.visualstore.com

Advertising Age

www.adage.com

American Advertising Agencies

www.americanadagencies.com

The Case of the Cost-Free Advertising Campaign

Major manufacturers and retailers set aside large sums of money promoting their merchandise and their companies. They recognize the value of such investments and make certain that their budgets are sufficient to reach potential customers.

Barbara Simms fully understands the need for promotion. In college she learned all about the benefits, and she witnessed, firsthand, the returns realized from such activities when she worked for a major department store. The store, Atlees, Ltd., spent a great deal of money on advertising and extravagant special events. It reaped extra benefits from the publicity derived from the special presentations. The company not only invested heavily, but it also had a large in-house staff that could create professional ads, build props, and create exciting promotional themes.

Recently, Barbara left Atlees, Ltd., and opened a small neighborhood fashion boutique. The initial costs of opening the shop were more than she anticipated and little was left for promotion. She would like to spend her limited resources wisely for a good advertisement and also present a cost-free special event that would make her trading area aware of her boutique. Her problem is how to coordinate an ad and special event without straining her budget.

question

Describe a special event that would be virtually cost-free and an advertisement that would be inexpensive and compatible with the event.

Hot and Bothered

LISA LOCKWOOD

Heavy breathers, rest assured: fashion's sex-obsessed advertising ways are probably here to stay.

Spring proved to be one of the most explicit seasons in years, with elements of autoeroticism, lesbianism and voyeurism alongside the bare breasts, backs, legs and various other uncovered body parts featured in campaigns from some of fashion's most powerful houses.

Such pervasive flashing of flesh—and other racy depictions—can, however, lead one to wonder whether fashion has finally overheated. The answer isn't as simple as prude versus libertine. Fantasy and fun aside, some ad experts are beginning to question whether so much steam works: Does it attract the real customer or alienate her? And then there's the boredom factor: When is too much simply too much?

Lighten up, say the free spirits; these images are meant to show women in full command of their sexual powers, to be entertaining and to titillate. The counterpoint: It's time for a nice cold shower.

"At the end of the day, everyone wants to look sexy and attractive," says Doug Lloyd, owner of Lloyd & Co. (One of Lloyd's key accounts is Gucci, which, along with Versace and, of course, Calvin Klein, set the industry standard for sexually aggressive advertising.) "There are degrees by which these envelopes get pushed," Lloyd points out. "The tones get set by designers and the entertainment industry and work their way down to the print medium. When I work with Tom [Ford, creative director of Gucci], everything's always

sexy. Versace definitely pushed that; Dior pushed it for a couple of seasons."

Lloyd, as well as other ad executives, believes the approach is more effective with European women, who are a lot more comfortable with nudity and sexual imagery than Americans. "I think it's more accepted within the European culture. Those brands [such as Gucci, Versace and Dior] are from a leadership position. They're more open than an American brand."

"European women go topless, and there's a different cultural attitude," agrees Richard Kirshenbaum, co-chairman of Kirshenbaum Bond & Partners. "I think there's the sense of the female form, of femininity and allowing oneself to enjoy being a woman. It's an important factor to European women.

"The people who respond to these ads are not necessarily the mainstream. When you take a look at Versace, the customer is more specific than Banana Republic," said Kirshenbaum. "They [Versace] are leading, not following. They need to appeal to a customer who needs to be out there."

But there are detractors. In fact, some maintain that the ads this season not only miss the mark, they're demeaning to women. "We're at a real low point," says Jean Kilbourne, author of *Can't Buy My Love: How Advertising Changes the Way We Think and Feel* (Touchstone Books, 2000) and the video series "Killing Us Softly," about the advertising industry's image of women. She singles out Dior's grease-and-dirt-smeared models and Versace's garter-belted bunch for criticism.

"It's a cultural climate where women are often portrayed as victims of violence and often are turned into objects or things," Kilbourne contends. "It contributes to a climate where women are seen as objects. Violence is normalized, and it trivializes violence against women and eroticizes it."

Kilbourne says images that used to belong to the world of pornography have crossed over to the mainstream, pointing to the Versace ads that show only the lower back and legs of a naked woman wearing a garter belt and high heels, along with another clothed woman, strewn across an unmade bed.

"These sexy images are trying to get the attention of men, but on a deeper level, they want to get the attention of women, who want to get the attention of men," she says. "It's hard to know where it's going to go. We've had sexual intercourse, sado-masochism, kiddie porn, bondage. In my book, I talk about the next big thing is having sex with products."

Donatella Versace, meanwhile, maintains that, while her ads may have sexual overtones, they're not really to be taken so literally. What some might see as lesbian imagery is far from it. Rather, the dressed woman is gazing toward a figure that is her own naked self, according to Donatella. "There is the idea that below the surface of fantasy and luxury lies something complicated and powerful, which is not so easy to identify on first glance," says Versace. "It's an interpretation of a woman, and her sexuality, that is more challenging and more complex."

Dior says comments, particularly about its latest campaign, miss the point entirely. A Dior spokesman says the images, which include two models posing inside and beside a vintage Cadillac, have nothing to do with violence or the suppression of women. Rather, the house says the ads depict a woman who is not only sexy, feminine and beautiful, but also able to change a tire or adjust the carburetor. "She's authentic and independent—a symbol of freedom."

In fact, Dior credits the ads for fuelling a 70 percent sell-through of its camouflage dresses in two months and stoking demand for its "trailer-park" handbags with Cadillac door handles.

Aside from the debate over subjective interpretation, an odd alliance of sorts could be forming—at least in theory—between conservatives and feminists. Or, as some call it, the George W. Bush factor: Could the conservative spirit in the White House, not to mention a hesitant economy, unleash a backlash against the overt and the edgy?

"There's a movement that's becoming a little more conservative. [However] there's also a reactionary effect," says Kirshenbaum. "People are dedicated to controversy and to rebelling. Opinion leaders and style leaders are taking more of the rebelling side."

Some contend that the politically minded should really pay no mind, arguing that most ads actually fail to achieve their goal of mixing the seamier qualities of X-rated fare with a glam factor.

"I do think it's oversaturated, but I don't think it's overheated," says Harold Koda, curator of the Costume Institute at the Metropolitan Museum of Art. "The problem with the sexy ads is they don't live up to the imagery that exists in other places. In TV, you see all that sexiness, but in motion. The [print] ads

themselves are very consistent with each other."

He believes that, eventually, people will get bored and advertisers will move on. "Fashion feeds on novelty. People who gravitate to novel experiences have a lower threshold for it. The very people they're targeting will become bored with it.

"The worst thing you can say about a fashion ad is it's neutral or boring," Koda adds. "All of this stuff was really visceral when it was in *Dutch* magazine. Since then, it just seems old. It's been going on too long. I think a Sixties *Playboy* magazine is much sexier in its coyness than this stuff."

Koda argues that fashion houses that rely on provocative, sexy images aren't really targeting people over 30. "The libido requires upping the ante. The ads relate to people of a generation who basically have to wear a Latex suit to go out on a date. For them, [sex] is more cerebral. The edginess, toughness and aesthetic. The chill runs through them and registers with people liberated by penicillin and STDs. This is more cyber-sexy. Sex is so conceptual to people. It's so fraught with other issues. This registers with men and women below 30, in their early to mid-20s. That group is dealing with all this stuff in a different way."

Do the ads ever titillate?

"Very skinny girls wearing arch clothing designed by homosexuals is intrinsically not sexy," says Barneys New York creative director Simon Doonan. "Construction workers and Pamela Anderson are sexy. The ads don't seem sexy, they just seem gritty. It's arguably effective. The Dior ads seem very camp. But it does get your attention. Fashion people always try to make fashion sexy, and it never is and never was. Azzedine Alaïa was able to marry high fashion and sex. Everything

else is some desperate attempt to compensate for the fact that it's not sexy.

"What you see is a desperate attempt to imbue it with sexuality, which always feels very phoned in. Sex is not a function of high fashion. It's the opposite of high fashion. Fashion is a self-absorbed quasi-intellectual process, opposed to raw sexuality," says Doonan.

"There's good sexy and bad sexy," says Peter Arnell, chairman, AG Worldwide. "A lot of what's been done is bad sexy. The work, in my opinion overall, might be displaying sexy imagery, but not sexy ideas. The work lacks objectivity. It's very stylistic and decorative, but it's without meaning. It doesn't drive the consumer toward a focus. It drives them toward a trend and, in doing so, homogenizes the effort. It never gets them into the brand, only the advertising.

"Sexy has always been there. It's nothing new. I think they're not intimate, they're not real. They're contrived, and in most cases you can get much better stuff on the Internet."

Over the years, fashion advertisers have been criticized for photographing a gorgeous woman and slapping on a logo, without any thought to a concept or big idea. The same holds true with the new wave of provocative poses, according to some advertising executives.

"It hasn't gone far enough in the conceptual arena," says Paul Meany, art director of TBWA/Chiat/Day New York. "It doesn't shock anymore, when you see every ad has the same thing. They hire a good photographer and put a logo in the corner. What's really missing is the concept. What would be really shocking would be if there was an idea to it."

Rich Silverstein, co-chairman of Goodby Silverstein & Partners, a San Francisco ad agency that handles clients such as eluxury.com, Got Milk, Isuzu, eBay and Budweiser, says: "The lines have been crossed between what's advertising and what's editorial. It's highly sexually charged. It's sexier than pornography, because you think you know these people. Porn is like a lampoon of something, but here you put people who are very attractive in provocative clothes.

"I think the quality of the photography is so high now, the makeup and the styling. It used to be if a woman sat on a chair with her legs wrapped around it, it was amazingly provocative," continues Silverstein.

He points out that sexy images work for fashion companies, but not for other product categories. "The whole rule of fashion is to be shocking and provocative. 'Let's see how far we can push it so people are bothered by it.' That's what art has always been. It's always been shocking and then it becomes the norm. Nudity and provocation and showing breasts is the norm now. It's normal now to have two women kissing or two men kissing."

Such imagery can actually help sell certain fashion brands, but misfire in other, less appropriate categories. "I think

it builds fashion brands and cosmetic brands," he says. "It does not build nuts-and-bolts products like Life cereal or shaving cream." And it can make for some strange moments in public. "I'm on an airplane and don't know if I should close the magazine," Silverstein confessed. "Years ago, [these images] would be in a publication you wouldn't be reading in public. I find the pages of *Vogue* more provocative than *Playboy*."

"Using sexy imagery is the oldest trick in the book to get people to notice your advertising," says Madonna Badger, principal, chief creative officer, Badger, Kry & Partners. "I think women react to great clothes, and great ads that are smart. Look at the sexuality of Helmut Newton. There's an intellectual quality.

"The sexiest ads are not necessarily great advertising. Calvin is a terrific example of great, sexy ads. The Obsession ads told a story, instead of being exploitive. [Today] it's 'Who can be the most outrageous?' Women are smart and see through it. I love a great, sexy ad. I just question if it's not a race of who can outdo the next."

Then there's the school that feels advertising is simply answering a consumer need—a question of providing the right stuff at the right time.

"Advertising is totally driven by what it believes the audience wants," says Ingrid Sischy, editor in chief of *Interview*. "I'm fascinated by the idea that advertising is going into the 'under the bed' stage. In the Eighties, that's where art went. At the time, sex stopped being a dirty secret. For me, the fact that advertising is really using sex as a subplot is extremely optimistic. People who analyze what the audience wants are listening to people. It's a great moment, instead of being a repressive moment." In other words, it's better to get sex out in the open and talk about it.

"I think, culturally, it's very optimistic," Sischy states. "But it all could change because of Bush. However, if people do it to be trendy, then I'm bored. When people are doing it with real consciousness, then I'm interested. Then it can go hog wild. We can all be blushing."

Women's Wear Daily, The Magazine, July 9, 2001

Art and Commerce: Top Directors Go Commercial—Literally

ELLEN GROVES

Paris—An advertising executive's dream checklist may once have included a Hollywood star, a big budget and a much-lusted-after product to plug. Now a celebrated director has been added to the mix.

Luxury brands are scrambling to recruit big-name Hollywood filmmakers.

Just this week Lancôme revealed it has hired "2046" director Wong Kar Wai to make a fragrance commercial with Clive Owen and Daria Werbowy, while last fall Christian Dior tapped "Chicago" director Rob Marshall for a film starring Monica Bellucci; Agent Provocateur recruited "Leaving Las Vegas" director Mike Figgis

to shoot four mini films featuring Kate Moss, and Brett Ratner, famed for "X-Men: 3," shot Quincy Jones and Molly Sims for a Jimmy Choo campaign.

While luxury houses have a history of teaming up with movie directors, the trend has accelerated as brands try to broaden their consumer base, according to advertising executives. The brands, of course, get the imprimatur of a major director—who might be able to attract equally big-name actors and actresses. Such filmmakers are especially important with stars like Nicole Kidman, who are protective of their images and who sign on because they know they'll be working with someone they trust. As for the directors—they get money.

Sources said the amount a director can earn varies widely, but generally is in the $50,000- to $100,000-a-day ballpark (as one agent said, "pretty good money"). A commercial can take up to two weeks to prep and shoot. Sources said Baz Luhrmann, for instance, got about $1 million for the Chanel No.5 commercial with Kidman, who was paid $10 million over three years. Similar amounts were paid to director John Woo for his BMW campaign and Michael Mann for his Mercedes-Benz commercial, sources said. They estimated the Chanel film cost about $15 million in all, as did Woo's BMW movie "Hostage" in 2002, which also starred Clive Owen.

"Luxury brands are seeking to differentiate the way they advertise," said Sarah Musgrave, account director at Saatchi & Saatchi. "What's different is that normally companies have not had the budgets, but now more luxury brands are going democratic and reaching out to mass audiences."

Film directors obviously have the ability to entertain the masses, but they also bring something more to the advertising mix than just technical proficiency.

"Filmmakers are storytellers," said Ratner, whose next project is a campaign for Revlon makeup. "Brands want something more than just pictures of clothes. I love fashion, I deal with it in movies and with hair and makeup."

Similarly, Dior chose Marshall to lens the Bellucci-fronted campaign for its

Rouge Dior lipstick because of his ability to convey more than simply a product plug, according to Stephanie Ravillion, business manager for Dior makeup.

"It's not at all a simple ad for a lipstick," she said. "It shows luxury as a promise of happiness, it's a message to women and I think women feel happy once they see this film."

The LVMH Moët Hennessy Louis Vuitton-owned beauty firm also has worked with Wong in the past, as well as directors David Lynch, Ridley Scott and Claude Chabrol, on campaigns for fragrance and skin care. But the Marshall movie is the first such spot for color cosmetics.

Marshall, whose route into film was via Broadway shows rather than commercial work, had previously turned down advertising offers.

"I had heard that you're a slave to the powers that be, to the client and to the agency, and I wasn't sure if that would be something fun artistically," he said, adding, however, that Dior managed to win him over. "They just said, 'Paris, Dior, and Monica Bellucci.'"

Indeed, since the majority of luxury brands are at some point fronted by major celebrities, it seems a logical progression for big-name directors to follow suit.

"There's lots of respect between an actress and a movie director," said Ravillion. "There's a kind of fusion that doesn't happen so easily if it's an art director."

"We spoke the same language," said Marshall of Bellucci. "We could talk about the character and the story."

And like Nicole Kidman and Baz Luhrmann for Chanel, brands are creating the ultimate dream teams by recruiting directors and actors who've worked together in the past.

For its Hypnôse Homme scent, Lancôme reunited Wong and Owen—the

pair first worked together on a BMW campaign featuring James Brown in 2001. Wong's involvement was a major draw for Owen. "Lancôme came and said Wong Kar Wai and there is nobody better in the world than Wong Kar Wai," he said at a Paris press conference earlier this week. "When I saw 'In the Mood for Love'— the word cool is overused—but it is one of the coolest things. He conveys this restrained sexuality and sensuality. There is not a living director I would rather work with on a campaign like this."

Owen lauded the director's attention to detail. "He is really, really specific. For an actor to work with someone that's that on top, it's a real privilege. . . . I wasn't Clive Owen in that film [for Lancôme], I was directed, it's acting."

In addition, luxury brands can lure top directors because of the financial and creative freedom a short film can allow, since it's unhindered by budget battles with studios and generally is shot in a short period of time.

"If you think about the per-second luxurious budgeting, it's a dream job," Musgrave pointed out.

"Films take two years, [the Dior shoot] was a matter of weeks," said Marshall, adding he had complete free creative rein.

"A director can have artistic freedom with nobody questioning," agreed Musgrave.

But that freedom can sometimes bring more than a hint of controversy. Jimmy Choo's fall-winter campaign sparked consumer reactions as sharp as the spiky stilettos being advertised, since it shows legendary music producer Quincy Jones pictured sitting next to model Molly Sims' seemingly lifeless body with a shovel in his hand.

"I think Quincy looks like a gangster, so to end the story we show her [Sims] in the trunk and him digging a hole—that doesn't mean he killed her," insisted Ratner. "But they got a lot of hate mail over at Jimmy Choo for that."

Jimmy Choo president and creative director Tamara Mellon chose Ratner for his vast experience as a director.

"So many of the big fashion campaigns look the same and are very static," she said. "Using a director gives the images a sense of energy and movement, like stills from a movie, that really makes them stand out in the magazines."

And while many of the big luxury brands are collaborating with big-time movie directors, others are tapping rising stars.

To freshen up its image, 76-year-old French leather goods brand Lamarthe tapped model Elettra Rossellini, daughter of Isabella Rossellini, and young director Zoe Cassavetes, daughter of John Cassavetes, to make an Internet film. After its debut on Lamarthe's Web site, the black-and-white movie, dubbed "Elettra in the City," landed in e-mail inboxes this month.

"It was the duo [Rossellini and Cassavetes] that we were interested in," explained Diane Lepel Cointet, Lamarthe's marketing and communications director, adding the combined power of two well-known names was an edgy way to give the brand the "glamour of cinema."

Advertising executives warn, however, that striking the right relationship between brand and director is crucial. "It will be interesting to see how low people will go, whether it's the right match for the right director," Musgrave said. "It's one thing to say, 'Fine I'll do Chanel or Bulgari, but, I'm going to do Polo or Lacoste,' is that going to be as interesting? There is a need on behalf of directors to keep themselves to exclusive brands."

For Ratner, however, the role of the director is straightforward. "I'm either selling a performance or selling a product," he said.

Women's Wear Daily, January 12, 2007

Show Me the (Luxury) Products

VALERIE SECKLER

Forget about provocative sexual imagery. Don't even think about waiflike models. People's lust for luxury fashion is best stirred by hot shots of the goods themselves, based on a recent survey.

Despite fashion's longtime use of sexual innuendo and the vogue for marketing that strikes an emotional chord, wealthy adults responded most favorably when luxury goods themselves were portrayed front and center in the print ads of 20 fashion brands. The ads were shown to them in August by the Luxury Institute. "Less is more," said the institute's chief executive officer, Milton Pedraza. "The consumer is looking for the product as hero."

Not that this desire makes a product-centric take a breeze to pull off.

"It's easy to show products in a way that is boring," said Reed Krakoff, president and executive creative director at Coach, whose ads were most favored

among those of the 20 brands consumers considered. "A lot of times, people look for a gorgeous image and wonder, *does it show enough of the product?*" added Krakoff, who leads the development of Coach's ads, created entirely in-house. "We look at [product] as a way to create excitement."

For example, in a bid to stand out in a sea of color fashion ads, Coach chose a black-and-white palette for its spring print campaign featuring a pair of pumps and a handbag—the first time it had used black-and-white photography in its ads in seven years. "We thought, when it's not in color, it's going to catch people's attention, and we were going for a romantic, vintage-y feel," Krakoff recalled.

While many luxury ads have long highlighted the products themselves, people may want more of the same because it's hard to buy into an extravagant fantasy without a strong portrayal of the

particulars, observed Raul Martinez, chief executive officer at ad agency AR, whose clients include D&G, Versace and Calvin Klein. "Whether you're buying a $5,000 bag or a $29.99 bag, you want to see it," Martinez said. "Luxury is a dream, and you want to buy into that world. There's an allure to that."

The tactic apparently has not been used to its greatest effect, however, as the top-ranked advertising (by Coach) scored a 6.58 on a scale from zero to 10, in the Luxury Institute study. The ratings of the affluent crowd's 10 favorite campaigns declined on a gentle slope, bottoming at the 5.24 accorded the ads of the Calvin Klein Collection, ranked 10th by those adults.

Part of the problem, Pedraza said, is that "there is not a great deal of consumer feedback that goes into creating these ads. Many of the companies said they are not doing ad testing."

Affluent adults who were asked what main message they took from a Dolce & Gabbana ad picturing women in suggestive poses amid haystacks made comments ranging from "funky, fresh, fun fashion" to "It comes across as way too much sex among women." The ad was not among the group's top 10 favorites.

For the popular Coach ad, in contrast, there were numerous interpretations of its message, such as "Coach sells (or has or makes) shoes" and more than a dozen references to the portrayal as either classy, classic, elegant, expensive or fine.

Neither Coach, nor Polo Ralph Lauren, whose Polo Jeans G.I.V.E. ads rated as the second favorite among the affluent adults, solicit opinions from consumers about ads while the spots are being developed or after they have been seen.

"Our philosophy here is that we are the consumers, and we use our own gut instincts," said David Lauren, senior vice president of advertising, marketing and corporate communications at Polo Ralph Lauren, which seeks to address an aspirational sensibility with all of its brands. "Sometimes the product is the hero. Other times, it's a lifestyle shot with no product or with product and a model," Lauren added.

Style and design were the biggest influence on people who purchased luxury fashion goods in April through June, reported 610 of the 1,000 consumers who bought such things, in Unity Marketing's second-quarter Luxury Tracking Study. "So ads [mostly] featuring products are zeroing in on that," noted Unity president Pamela N. Danziger.

While acknowledging it's difficult to measure a print ad's sway over consumers' purchases given the many possible influences, Krakoff said Coach's black-and-white campaign was probably effective since the bag, the brand's priciest ever at $798, "sold out twice." (Previously, Coach's highest-priced bag was $498.)

Celebrities featured in ads—such as Halle Berry's turn in the Versace campaign—did not make people any more or less likely to buy the brand advertised, the Luxury Institute found, but the celebs did heighten people's awareness of them.

Consumers signaled how effective they found the print ads for the 20 luxury fashion brands by considering their relevance, clarity, distinctiveness and appropriateness for the label being marketed. In the case of seven of their 10 top-rated ads, people considered it equally likely they would buy those brands after seeing the ads. The notable exception was Calvin Klein Collection, which placed as the seventh most-likely brand they would buy, after seeing ads that ranked as only their tenth favorite.

Women's Wear Daily, October 4, 2006

Newspapers' Future: Think Like a Magazine

AMY WICKS

While it's no news circulation is slipping at major metropolitan newspapers such as the *New York Times*, the *Wall Street Journal* and the *Los Angeles Times*, observers are asking why these publications are continuing to raise ad rates as some subscribers head for the door.

But the *L.A. Times* has a bone to pick with those who wonder whether it is still a viable avenue in which to advertise and obtain news. Looking ahead, a spokeswoman indicated the paper will start thinking more like a magazine when it comes to readers and focus on growing its individual paid circulation. The Audit Bureau of Circulations Fas-Fax report showed that for the six months ended in September, the West Coast paper fell 8 percent in daily circulation, but the spokeswoman countered that ABC's number included "other paid circulation," such as copies delivered to hotel rooms. Incidentally, ABC's statistics also showed that the *L.A. Times* individual paid circulation is up. "Individually paid copies deliver a more engaged reader to advertisers and therefore a more favorable return on investment," she said—in other words, newsstand.

And that's not the only magazine trait the Times will start exhibiting. Looking forward, the newspaper will offer more options for advertisers, including front-section strips in several sections, innovative ad units and multimedia packages. On the edit side, the *Times* is ramping up its fashion and lifestyle coverage. Late last year, Elizabeth Snead, who has covered fashion for *USA Today* and E! Online's Fashion Police, joined its online awards Web site, The Envelope, for its "Styles & Scenes" coverage. The paper also recently unveiled a redesign of its Sunday Calendar. The two-part section was renamed "Movies-TV-Style" and "Arts & Music."

"The intensified editorial ranges from society events and fashion trends to pop culture and Web discoveries and the rich arts scene," said a spokeswoman.

But fashion advertisers may really start to take notice once the paper introduces a new weekly fashion and lifestyle section, for print and online. Sources close to the *L.A. Times* confirmed plans are under way, but no timetable has been set.

Meanwhile, the *Wall Street Journal* has also expanded its style coverage. Journal publisher L. Gordon Crovitz previously told *WWD* that female *Journal* readers purchase "more women's fashion items than do all the readers of the women's magazines—combined."

As the *L.A. Times* and the *Journal* continue to chase those stylish ad dollars, some advertisers are seeking ad rate cuts, especially since newspapers are cutting deals like never before. "I suspect that many, but not all, newspaper publishers are running scared," said Gene Willhoft, president of Absolute Media. Still, Willhoft said, there is a major hurdle for advertisers who seek lower ad rates. The *L.A. Times* and *New York Times* "are very important papers in their respective DMAs [designated market area] and are tough to buy around if the target is an upscale, educated audience," he said. "Advertisers must be prepared to walk away or the negotiations may not be successful."

George Janson, managing partner and director of print at mediaedge:cia, said he is open to negotiating rates but isn't happy about the fact that even though newspaper circulation drops every year,

ad rates still rise (the *L.A. Times*, *New York Times* and the *Journal* are all planning increases for 2007). Janson works with clients including Chanel and Xerox.

Regarding its ad rate increase, a *New York Times* spokeswoman contended the paper "remains one of the best places to reach an influential, educated, high-quality audience. Advertisers continue to value that reach and are willing to pay a premium for it."

One executive who agrees with that philosophy is Ruediger Albers, president of jewelry firm Wempe. He advertises in the *New York Times* and the *Wall Street Journal* and partially attributes Wempe's success to his regular exposure in both papers. "What's the alternative to reaching one million people that have the spending power of *New York Times* readers?" he asked.

As for the *Journal*, Albers is partial to its value-added opportunities, such as being invited to an event where he can mingle with other advertisers and consumers. At one event, a chance meeting with S. Epatha Merkerson led to the actress wearing (and being photographed in) Wempe jewelry at major award shows. Albers is considering increasing his schedules in both papers, but negotiations aren't finalized. Presumably rates and placement remain an issue.

Amid weakening ad trends, the Internet seems to offer more hope. The *New York Times* Co. recently reported that its Internet revenue might increase 30 percent next year, and a source said

the *L.A. Times* "is in the same ball-park, if not slightly ahead of" the *New York Times* projection. A spokeswoman said Dow Jones Online isn't reporting forecasts for 2007, but this year online revenues were up 20 percent.

Ad-tracking firm TNS Media Intelligence projects advertising budgets to stall next year, but the silver lining will be growth in online media (including search), which is coincidentally expected to grow up to 30 percent. Sarah Baehr, vice president of media at Avenue A | Razorfish, said the company predicts that online will outpace other media growth for three main reasons: The share of online media is still disproportionately small compared with offline media, several marketers haven't maximized their fullest potential online, and the accountability and tractability of online (compared to other media) are compelling.

While speaking at a *New Yorker* breakfast, Sir Martin Sorrell, group chief executive at WPP Group, said people spend approximately 20 percent of their time online, but advertising online budgets are still in the single digits. He cited News Corp. owner Rupert Murdoch as an excellent example of utilizing the Internet (MySpace, for one) and said most established agencies aren't moving fast enough to gain a foothold in this arena. Sir Martin contended the delay is partially due to the fact that top executives at agencies are nearing retirement and want to coast in their jobs and leave the Internet issue to their future replacements.

Women's Wear Daily, December 15, 2006

selected examples of color and fashion trend forecasting services

The Color Association of the United States (CAUS)
315 West 39th Street
New York, NY 10018
(212) 947-7774
Fax: (212) 594-6987

The Doneger Group
463 Seventh Avenue
New York, NY 10018
(212) 560-3760
Fax: (212) 560-3971

Here & There
104 West 40th Street
New York, NY 10018
(212) 354-9014
Fax: (212) 764-1831

International Colour Authority
(for American agent, see
Color Association of the United States)

Margit Publications
1412 Broadway, Suite 1102
New York, NY 10018
(212) 302-5137
Fax: (212) 944-8757

Pantone Color Institute
590 Commerce Boulevard
Carlstadt, NJ 07072
(201) 935-5500
Fax: (201) 896-0242

Pat Tunsky Inc.
1040 Avenue of the Americas
New York, NY 10018
(212) 944-9160
Fax: (212) 764-5105

Promostyl
250 West 39th Street
New York, NY 10018
(212) 921-7930
Fax: (212) 921-8214

RTW Review
P.O. Box 27688
Milwaukee, WI 53227
(414) 425-6503
Fax: (414) 425-2501

The Tobé Report
50 East 42nd Street
New York, NY 10017
(212) 867-8677
Fax: (212) 867-8602

selected trade associations for the world of fashion

APPAREL

American Apparel & Footwear Association
1601 North Kent Street
Arlington, VA 22209
(800) 520-2262

Associated Corset & Brassiere Manufacturers Inc.
1430 Broadway, Suite 1603
New York, NY 10018
(212) 354-0707

Clothing Manufacturers Association
730 Broadway
New York, NY 10003
(212) 529-0823

Council of Fashion Designers of America (CFDA)
1412 Broadway
New York, NY 10018
(212) 302-1821

The Fashion Group International Inc.
597 Fifth Avenue
New York, NY 10017
(212) 593-1715

International Association of Clothing Designers and Executives
475 Park Avenue
New York, NY 10016
(212) 685-6602

International Swimwear & Activewear Market and the Swimwear Association
110 East Ninth Street
Los Angeles, CA 99079
(213) 630-3610

The Intimate Apparel Council
c/o The Bromley Group
150 Fifth Avenue
New York, NY 10011
(212) 807-0978

Men's Apparel Guild of California (MAGIC International)
6200 Canoga Avenue
Woodland Hills, CA 91367
(818) 593-5000

National Association of Men's Sportswear Buyers (NAMSB)
60 East 42nd Street
New York, NY 10165
(212) 856-9644

National Knitwear & Sportswear Association
386 Park Avenue South
New York, NY 10016
(212) 683-7520

Underfashion Club Inc.
347 Fifth Avenue
New York, NY 10016
(212) 481-7792

United Infants & Children's Wear Association
1430 Broadway
New York, NY 10018
(212) 244-2953

Young Menswear Association
47 West 34th Street
New York, NY 10001
(212) 594-6422

ACCESSORIES

Fashion Footwear Association of New York (FFANY)
811 Seventh Avenue
New York, NY 10019
(212) 767-0160

Fashion Jewelry Association of America
Regency East
1 Jackson Parkway
Providence, RI 02903
(401) 273-1515

Headwear Institute of America
1 West 64th Street
New York, NY 10023
(212) 724-0888

Jewelers of America
52 Vanderbilt Avenue
New York, NY 10036
(212) 658-0246

National Association of Fashion and Accessory Designers
2180 East 93rd Street
Cleveland, OH 44106
(216) 231-0375

National Fashion Accessories Association
350 Fifth Avenue
New York, NY 10001
(212) 947-3424

Neckwear Association of America
151 Lexington Avenue, Suite 2F
New York, NY 10016
(212) 683-8454

The Hosiery Association
3623 Latrobe Drive, Suite 130
Charlotte, NC 28211
(704) 365-0913

TEXTILES

Acrylic Council
1285 Avenue of the Americas
New York, NY 10016
(212) 554-4040

American Association for Textile Technology, Inc.
347 Fifth Avenue
New York, NY 10016
(212) 481-7792

American Association of Textile Chemists and Colorists
One Davis Drive
P.O. Box 12215
Research Triangle Park, NC 27709
(919) 549-8141

American Fiber Manufacturers Association
1150 17th Street NW
Washington, DC 20036
(202) 296-6508

American Printed Fabrics Council
469 Seventh Avenue
New York, NY 10018
(212) 744-4111

American Textile Machinery Association
11 Park Place
Falls Church, VA 22042
(703) 538-1789

American Textile Manufacturers Institute
1130 Connecticut Avenue NW, Suite 1200
Washington, DC 20036
(202) 862-0500

American Wool Council
6911 South Yosemite Street
Englewood, CO 80112
(303) 771-3500

American Yarn Spinners Association
P.O. Box 99
Gastonia, NC 28053
(704) 824-3522

Carpet and Rug Institute
310 South Holiday Avenue
P.O. Box 2048
Dalton, GA 30722
(706) 278-3176

Cashmere and Camel Hair Manufacturers Institute of America
230 Congress Street
Boston, MA 02110
(617) 542-7481

Fur Farm Animal Welfare Coalition, Ltd.
225 Sixth Street East
St. Paul, MN 55101
(612) 222-1080

International Linen Promotion Commission
200 Lexington Avenue
New York, NY 10016
(212) 685-0424

International Silk Association
c/o Gerli & Co., Inc.
41 Madison Avenue
New York, NY 10010
(212) 213-1919

Leather Industries of America
1000 Thomas Jefferson Street NW, Suite 515
Washington, DC 20007
(202) 342-8086

Mohair Council of America
516 Norwest Bank Building
P.O. Box 5337
San Angelo, TX 76903
(915) 655-3161

National Cotton Council of America
1918 North Parkway
P.O. Box 12285
Memphis, TN 38182
(901) 274-9030

Polyester Council of America
1675 Broadway
New York, NY 10019
(212) 527-8941

United Textile Association
386 Park Avenue South
New York, NY 10016
(212) 689-3807

Wool Bureau Inc.
330 Madison Avenue
New York, NY 10017
(212) 986-6222

RETAIL

American Management Association
1601 Broadway
New York, NY 10019
(212) 586-8100

Footwear Industries of America
1420 K Street NW
Washington, DC 20005
(202) 789-1420

National Mass Retail Association
1901 Pennsylvania Avenue NW, 10th Floor
Washington, DC 20006
(202) 861-0774

National Retail Federation
100 West 31st Street
New York, NY 10001
(212) 244-8780

National Shoe Retailers Association
9861 Broken Land Parkway
Columbia, MD 21046
(410) 381-8282

Shoe Retailers League
275 Madison Avenue
New York, NY 10016
(212) 889-7920

HOME FASHIONS

American Furniture Manufacturers Association
P.O. Box 14P-7
High Point, NC 27261
(336) 884-5000

Carpet and Rug Institute
P.O. Box 2048
Dalton, GA 30722
(706) 278-3176

Decorative Fabrics Association (DFA)
950 Third Avenue
New York, NY 10022

International Home Furnishings Representatives Association (IHFRA)
209 South Main
High Point, NC 27261
(336) 889-3920

National Association of Decorative Fabrics Distributors (NADFD)
3008 Millwood Avenue
Columbia, SC 29205
(800) 445-8629

National Association of Floor Covering Distributors (NAFCE)
410 North Michigan Avenue
Chicago, IL 60611
(312) 321-6836

National Home Furnishings Association (NHFA)
P.O. Box 2396
High Point, NC 27261
(800) 888-9590

Upholstered Furniture Action Council (UFAC)
Box 2436
High Point, NC 27261
(336) 885-5072

credits

TEXT

Chapter 1: Page 24, Clark, Evan. "Global Marketplace Expands Landscape of Counterfeiting," *WWD*, October 3, 2006, p. 17. Reprinted with permission from *Women's Wear Daily*. *WWD* is a registered Trademark of Advance Magazine Publishers, Inc. ©2006 Fairchild Fashion Group. All rights reserved. **Page 25,** Groves, Ellen. "Ethical Fashion Goes Mainstream," *WWD*, October 31, 2006, p. 12. Reprinted with permission from *Women's Wear Daily*. *WWD* is a registered Trademark of Advance Magazine Publishers, Inc. ©2006 Fairchild Fashion Group. All rights reserved. **Page 27,** Murphy, Robert. "Pierre Cardin Museum Chronicles a Legend," *WWD*, November 15, 2006. Reprinted with permission from *Women's Wear Daily*. *WWD* is a registered Trademark of Advance Magazine Publishers, Inc. ©2006 Fairchild Fashion Group. All rights reserved.

Chapter 2: Page 59, Luther, Marylou. "Why Women Designers Really Matter, 1930–1995," The Fashion Group International, Inc.

Chapter 3: Page 85, "What Ever Happened to Customer Loyalty?" *Retail Futures,* Vol. 1, No. 1. **Page 87,** Power, Denise. "Customers Turn Reviewers," *WWD*, December 13, 2006, p. 10. Reprinted with permission from *Women's Wear Daily*. *WWD* is a registered Trademark of Advance Magazine Publishers, Inc. ©2006 Fairchild Fashion Group. All rights reserved. **Page 88,** Colavita, Courtney. "Acting on impulse, men's shopping habits have become more spontaneous, opening up new opportunities for retailers," from Made In Italy, Retail Strategies, *DNR*, January 8, 2007. Reprinted with permission from *Daily News Record*. *DNR* is a registered Trademark of Advance Magazine Publishers, Inc. ©2007 Fairchild Fashion Group. All rights reserved.

Chapter 4: Page 107, Gelsomino, Jerry. "Arriba! Are you reaching out to the multiethnic consumer base?" From The Planning Stages, VM & SD, April 2005, p. 12. Reprinted by permission from ST Media Group. **Page 108,** Harper, Rhonda. "Vision 2020, Integrating Hispanic Marketing into the DNA of Your Company," Ketchum South, January 15, 2007.

Reprinted by permission from Rhonda Harper, TopRight, Atlanta GA. **Page 112,** Fine, B. Jenny. "Iman in Charge," from Beauty Biz Column, *WWD*, December 2006, pp. 39–41. Reprinted with permission from *Women's Wear Daily*. *WWD* is a registered Trademark of Advance Magazine Publishers, Inc. ©2006 Fairchild Fashion Group. All rights reserved.

Chapter 5: Page 133, D'Innocenzio, Anne. "Fashion's Fast Cycle," *WWD,* June 15, 2000. Copyright ©2000 Condé Nast Publications. All rights reserved. Reprinted by permission. **Page 134,** Wolfe, David. "Street Style," courtesy of DE Doneger Design Direction, The Color and Trend Forecasting Division of the Doneger Group. **Page 137,** Conte, Samantha. "Hilfiger signs French soccer star: Tommy to design capsule line inspired by Thierry Henry, who will also appear in formal and underwear ads," from Newsfront, *DNR*, December 11, 2006, p. 12. Reprinted with permission from *Daily News Record*. *DNR* is a registered Trademark of Advance Magazine Publishers, Inc. ©2006 Fairchild Fashion Group. All rights reserved. **Page 138,** Greenberg, Julee. "Stars on the Wane: Celebrity Fashion Lines Lose Their Mojo," *WWD*, December 18, 2006, p. 6, 7. Reprinted with permission from *Women's Wear Daily*. *WWD* is a registered Trademark of Advance Magazine Publishers, Inc. ©2006 Fairchild Fashion Group. All rights reserved.

Chapter 6: Page 161, Ellis, Kristi. "Congress to tackle trade issue: Democratic controlled legislature expected to be skeptical about deals this year," *DNR*, January 8, 2007, p. 9. Reprinted with permission from *Daily News Record*. *DNR* is a registered Trademark of Advance Magazine Publishers, Inc. ©2007 Fairchild Fashion Group. All rights reserved. **Page 162,** Marsh, Emily. "Read and React: Organizers adapt their show to attract customers in a changing market," *WWD*, November 26, 2006, p. 2. Reprinted with permission from *Women's Wear Daily*. *WWD* is a registered Trademark of Advance Magazine Publishers, Inc. ©2006 Fairchild Fashion Group. All rights reserved.

Chapter 7: Page 189, Seckler, Valerie. "Advice to Aspiring Designers: Get Smart Before Getting Started," *WWD,* March 27, 1995. Copyright

Chapter 21: Page 527, Moin, David. "Automating Markdowns: The Keys to Success," *WWD* January 12, 2007, p. 14. Reprinted with permission from *Women's Wear Daily*. *WWD* is a registered Trademark of Advance Magazine Publishers, Inc. ©2007 Fairchild Fashion Group. All rights reserved. **Page 528,** Edelson, Sharon. "Web is Growing Mecca for Designer Discounts," *WWD* January 7, 2007, p. 22–23. Reprinted with permission from *Women's Wear Daily*. *WWD* is a registered Trademark of Advance Magazine Publishers, Inc. ©2006 Fairchild Fashion Group. All rights reserved. **Page 530,** Moin, David. "Retail development enters new era: ICSC Chairman John Bucksbaum homes in on mixed use and densification," from Section II, *WWD*, November 27, 2006, p. 6. Reprinted with permission from *Women's Wear Daily*. *WWD* is a registered Trademark of Advance Magazine Publishers, Inc. ©2006 Fairchild Fashion Group. All rights reserved. **Page 531,** Born, Pete. "Sephora's World Grows: Home Shopping Network Latest Channel for Chain," *WWD*, December 13, 2006, p. 12. Reprinted with permission from *Women's Wear Daily*. *WWD* is a registered Trademark of Advance Magazine Publishers, Inc. ©2006 Fairchild Fashion Group. All rights reserved. **Page 533,** Edelson, Sharon. "Warehouse Clubs Aim for Frugal and Fancy," From Section II, *WWD*, October 16, 2006, p. 6. Reprinted with permission from *Women's Wear Daily*. *WWD* is a registered Trademark of Advance Magazine Publishers, Inc. ©2006 Fairchild Fashion Group. All rights reserved.

Chapter 22: Page 557, Lockwood, Lisa. "Hot and Bothered," *WWD*, The Magazine, July 9, 2001. Copyright ©2001 Condé Nast Publications. All rights reserved. Reprinted by permission. **Page 559,** Groves, Ellen. "Art and Commerce: Top Directors Go Commercial—Literally" from Media/Advertising, *WWD*, January 12, 2007, p. 10–11. Reprinted with permission from *Women's Wear Daily*. *WWD* is a registered Trademark of Advance Magazine Publishers, Inc. ©2007 Fairchild Fashion Group. All rights reserved. **Page 561,** Seckler, Valerie. "Show Me the (Luxury) Products" from Marketing, *WWD*, October 4, 2006, p. 14. Reprinted with permission from *Women's Wear Daily*. *WWD* is a registered Trademark of Advance Magazine Publishers, Inc. ©2006 Fairchild Fashion Group. All rights reserved. **Page 562,** Wicks, Amy. "Newspapers' Future: Think Like a Magazine" from Media/Advertising, *WWD*, December 15, 2006, p. 10. Reprinted with permission from *Women's Wear Daily*. *WWD* is a registered Trademark of Advance Magazine Publishers, Inc. ©2006 Fairchild Fashion Group. All rights reserved.

PHOTO

Part One Opener: Condé Nast Archives/Fairchild Publications, Inc. Giovanni Giannoni/Fairchild Publications, Inc.

Chapter 1: Illustrated by Erin Fitzsimmons/Fairchild Publications, Inc.: The Metropolitan Museum of Art: 3; Bettmann/CORBIS: 4, 5 (bottom), 5 (right), Courtesy of Marshall Fields: 6 (top); © The Granger Collection, New York: 6 (bottom); © Chien-min Chung/Getty Images: 7; David Turner/Fairchild Publications, Inc.: 9; Erin Fitzsimmons/Fairchild Publications, Inc.: 10; © Bill Pugliano/Getty Images: 11; © 20th Century Fox Film Corp. All rights reserved, Courtesy: Everett Collection: 13; Fairchild Publications, Inc.: 14, 15, 18 (left), 20 (top left); Courtesy of Lands End: 17; George Chinsee/Fairchild Publications, Inc.: 18 (right); Hans

Deryk/Reuters/Landov: 19; Peter Parks/AFP/Getty Images: 20 (right); Karl Prouse/Catwalking/Getty Images: 20 (bottom).

Chapter 2: Illustration by Erin Fitzsimmons/Fairchild Publications, Inc.: 29; Hulton Archives/Getty Images: 30 (left); Library of Congress: 30 (right); The Metropolitan Museum of Art: 32 (left); 37 (right); 44 (top); Kent State University: 32 (right); Bettman/CORBIS: 33, 34, 36 (bottom), 37 (left), 39, 40 (top), 40 (bottom), 41, 44 (bottom left), 44 (bottom right), 45, 49; Courtesy of Fairchild Publications, Inc.: 35, 43, 46 (right), 48, 51, 54 (left), 54 (right); Los Angeles County Museum of Art: 36 (top); Time & Life Pictures/Getty Images: 38 (bottom); Condé Nast Archives: 42; © Quadrillion/CORBIS: 47; New York Times Pictures: 48 (left); © Paramount/The Kobal Collection: 50; Mattei Michele/Corbis Sygma: 52 (top); © Pierre Verdy/AFP/Getty Images: 52 (bottom); Stan Honda/AFP/Getty Images: 53 (left); Pam Francis/Getty Images: 53 (right).

Chapter 3: Illustration by Erin Fitzsimmons/Fairchild Publications, Inc.: 62; Fairchild Publications, Inc.: 63 (top), 64; U. S. Census Bureau: 63 (bottom); © Andrew Paterson/Alamy: 66; © Tracy Kahn/CORBIS: 68; © CORBIS: 70; © Pierre Vauthey/CORBIS SYGMA: 71; © Mary Kate Denny/PhotoEdit: 73; © David Montford/Photofusion Library/Alamy: 76; Focus Suites of Philadelphia: 80.

Chapter 4: Illustration by Erin Fitzsimmons/Fairchild Publications, Inc.: 90; © Gabe Palmer/Alamy: 91; © Carlos Barria/Reuters/CORBIS: 92 (bottom); Alexander Tamargo/Getty Images: 92 (top left); © Rune Hellestad/CORBIS: 92 (top right); Photo by Emerito Pujol, courtesy of Chiqui Cartagena: 94; © Joson/zefa/CORBIS: 95 (left); David Turner/Fairchild Publications, Inc.: 95 (right); © Christian Simonpietri/SYGMA CORBIS: 96; Steve Eichner/Fairchild Publications, Inc.: 97 (left) © 2007 AP Photo: 97 (right); © Burke/Triolo Productions/Brand X/CORBIS: 98 (bottom); Robert Amador/Getty Images: 98 (top); Steve Eichner/Fairchild Publications, Inc.: 99 (top); © Bill Aron/PhotoEdit: 100 (top); © Jason Szenes/epa/CORBIS: 100 (bottom); © Gary Conner/PhotoEdit: 101; Fairchild Publications, Inc.: 102, 103 (bottom); Frank Mullen/Wireimage.com: 103 (top); Zack Seckler/Fairchild Publications, Inc.: 104.

Chapter 5: Illustration by Erin Fitzsimmons/Fairchild Publications, Inc.: 115; John Aquino/Fairchild Publications, Inc.: 116; Erin Fitzsimmons/Fairchild Publications, Inc.: 117; David Hogan/Hulton Archives/Getty Images: 121 (top); © Neal Preston/CORBIS: 121 (bottom); Underwood & Underwood/CORBIS: 122; Bettmann/CORBIS: 123, 127 (left), 128; Everett Collection: 124 (left); © Universal Television/courtesy Everett Collection: 124 (right); © Anat Givon/AP Photo: 125 (bottom); Everett Collection: 125 (top left); HBO/Courtesy Everett Collection: 125 (top right); Dave Hogan/Getty Images: 126 (bottom); Timothy A. Clary/AFP/Getty Images: 126 (bottom); © Tim Graham/CORBIS: 127 (right); © Michael Caulfield/AP Photo : 129 (bottom); David Hume Kennerly/Getty Images: 129 (right); Yuri Gripas/Reuters: 130.

Chapter 6: Illustration by Erin Fitzsimmons/Fairchild Publications, Inc.: 142, 146 (left), 146 (right), 164; © 2007 AP Photo: 143; Garrige Ho/Reuters: 145; Fairchild Publications, Inc.: 150, 151 (left), 151 (right), 153, 156; Janet Schwartz/AFP/Getty Images: 154; © Lester Lefkowitz/CORBIS: 155.

Chapter 7: Illustration by Erin Fitzsimmons/Fairchild Publications, Inc.: 164; © Dex Images, Inc./CORBIS: 166; ©Larry Mangino/The Image

Works: 168; ©Norbert Schiller/The Image Works: 169; Fairchild Publications, Inc.: 167, 171; © Osman Orsal/AP Photo: 173; © Index Stock Imagery, Inc.: 174; George Gerd/GettyImages: 175; ©Larry Mangino/The Image Works: 176; Robert Mitra/Fairchild Publications, Inc.: 177; Fairchild Publications, Inc.: 178, 181; Eamonn McCabe/CAMERA PRESS/Retna Ltd.: 179; Robert Mitra/Fairchild Publications, Inc.: 180.

Part Two Opener: Fernando Bueno/Photographer's Choice/Getty Images: 198; Giovanni Giannoni/Fairchild Publications, Inc.: 199.

Chapter 8: Illustration by Erin Fitzsimmons/Fairchild Publications, Inc.: 200; © Oberto Gili/Beateworks/CORBIS: 201 (right); Fairchild Publications, Inc.: 201 (top), 212; © Radius Images/Alamy: 204; © Malcolm Case-Green/Alamy: 205 (bottom); © BIOS LorgnierAntoine/Peter Arnold, Inc.: 205 (top); © Chris Howes/Wild Places Photography/Alamy: 206; Kevin Phillips/GettyImages: 207 (bottom left); © Tim Wright/CORBIS: 207 (bottom right); American Fiber Manufacturers Association: 207 (top right); Dennis Novak/Photographers Choice/Getty Images: 210 (top); Ron Giling/Peter Arnold, Inc.: 210 (bottom). © The Print Collector/Alamy: 211; Drawings by Fairchild Publications, Inc.: 213 (all); © Image Source Pink/Alamy: 213 (bottom); © Dynamic Graphics Group/Creatas/Alamy: 215; © Jeremy Horner/CORBIS: 216; © Maximillian Stock LTD/PHOTOTAKE Inc./Alamy: 217 (top); © Expuesto—Nicolas Randall/Alamy: 217 (bottom); Courtesy of Cotton Incorporated: 220 (bottom), 220 (bottom left), 220 (bottom right), 220 (top left), 220 (top right). Courtesy of Pantone, Inc.: 220 (bottom right).

Chapter 9: Illustrattion by Erin Fitzsimmons/Fairchild Publications, Inc.: 227; Fairchild Publications, Inc.: 228 (right), 231, 242 (top right), 242 (bottom right); MN Chan/Getty Images: 228 (left); Hiroko Masuike/AFP/Getty Images: 229; © Douglas Peebles/CORBIS: 230; John Chiasson/Getty Images: 233 (top), 233 (bottom); John Calabrese/Fairchild Publications, Inc.: 234; © Tina Feinberg/AP Photo: 237; Chris Moore/Catwalking/Getty Images: 238; © Stephanie Maze/CORBIS: 239 (top); © Sucheta Das/AP Photo: 239 (middle); © Danny Lehman/CORBIS: 239 (bottom); Pasha Antonov/Fairchild Publications, Inc.: 242 (bottom left).

Part Three Opener: Fairchild Publications, Inc.: 248; Karl Prouse/catwalking/Getty Images: 249.

Chapter 10: Illustration by Erin Fitzsimmons/Fairchild Publications, Inc.: 250; Fairchild Publications, Inc.: 251, 253, 261 (top), 261 (bottom), 262 (top), 263, 265 (right); Robert Mitra/Fairchild Publications, Inc.: 252 (right); Talaya Centeno/Fairchild Publications, Inc.: 256 (bottom left), 256 (bottom right); John Aquino/Fairchild Publications, Inc.: 256 (top left); Thomas Iannoccone/Fairchild Publications, Inc.: 256 (top right), 264; Keystone/Getty Images: 252 (bottom); Robert Mitra/Fairchild Publications, Inc.: 265 (left); Pasha Antonov/Fairchild Publications, Inc.: 266 (left), 266 (right), 267 (right); John Aquino/Fairchild Publications, Inc.: 267 (left); Kyle Ericksen/Fairchild Publications, Inc.: 271; Kyle Ericksen/Fairchild Publications, Inc.: 272 (left); David Turner/Fairchild Publications, Inc.: 272 (right).

Chapter 11: Illustration by Erin Fitzsimmons/Fairchild Publications, Inc.: 282; Tortora, Phyllis and Eubank, Keith: *Survey of the History of Costume: A History of Western Dress*, 3rd edition, Fairchild books, ©1998 p. 306: 285; Kyle Ericksen/Fairchild Publications, Inc.: 286; Fairchild Publications, Inc.: 287; Courtesy of Fairchild Publications, Inc.: 288;

DuPont: 291; James Keyser/Time & Life Pictures/Getty Images: 293; Donata Sardella/Fairchild Publications, Inc.: 295; Tim Jenkins/Fairchild Publications, Inc.: 296.

Chapter 12: Illustration by Erin Fitzsimmons/Fairchild Publications, Inc.: 306; Fairchild Publications, Inc.: 307 (left), 311 (bottom), 314, 316 (right), 317 (top); © Cindy Charles/PhotoEdit: 307 (right); John Aquino/Thomas Iannoccone/Fairchild Publications, Inc.: 308 (bottom); Ethan Miller/Getty Images: 308 (top); DuPont: 310; George Chinsee/Fairchild Publications, Inc.: 311 (top); Photograph by Carl Scheffel/Courtesy of Robert Lee Morris: 312; New York Times Pictures/Andrea Mohin: 315; Giovanni Geannoni/Fairchild Publications, Inc.: 316 (left); George Chinsee/Fairchild Publications, Inc.: 317 (bottom); © 2006 Christopher Moore Limited: 318 (bottom); The Vera Company: 318 (top left), 318 (top right); William West/AFP/Getty Images: 326 (bottom).

Chapter 13: Illustration by Erin Fitzsimmons/Fairchild Publications, Inc. 326 (top); Illustrations by Kichisaburo Ogawa: 327, 328, 329, 330; Francis Guillot/AFP/Getty Images: 332 (bottom); © Patrick Byrd/Alamy: 332 (top); Fairchild Publications, Inc.: 333 (bottom left), 333 (bottom right), 333 (top), 334, 336, 341; © Jacqui Hurst/CORBIS: 335.

Chapter 14: Illustration by Erin Fitzsimmons/Fairchild Publications: 340; Advertising Archives: 342 (top); Thomas Iannoccone/Fairchild Publications, Inc.: 342 (bottom); *WWD* NACDS insert April 2007 pg./Fairchild Publications, Inc.: 343; Courtesy of Marc Rosen: 345; Fairchild Publications, Inc.: 345 (top), 345 (bottom), 349, 350 (top), 350 (bottom), 352, John Aquino/Fairchild Publications, Inc.: 354; 355 (bottom); Robert Mitra/Fairchild Publications, Inc.: 355 (top left); Thomas Ionnoccone/Fairchild Publications, Inc.: 355 (top right); George Chinsee/Fairchild Publications, Inc.: 357 (left); Talaya Centeno/Fairchild Publications, Inc.: 357 (right).

Chapter 15: Illustration by Erin Fitzsimmons/Fairchild Publications: 367; Target: 368 (left), 368 (right); © Tim Street-Porter/Beateworks/Corbis: 370; Tim Boyle/Getty Images: 372; Haanel Cassidy/Condé Nast Archives: 373; Fairchild Publications, Inc.: 376, 387; © Fernando Bengoechea/Beateworks/Corbis: 379 (bottom); © Mika/zefa/Corbis: 379 (top); © Lourens Smak/Alamy: 380; © Michel Arnaud/Beateworks/Corbis: 381 (bottom); © AP Photo: 381 (top); Target: 383; Ellen Diamond: 385; Erin Fitzsimmons/Fairchild Publications, Inc.: 387; Courtesy Crate & Barrel: 390.

Part Four Opener: Courtesy of Zac Posen: 398; Mark Mainz/Getty Images: 399.

Chapter 16: Illustration by Erin Fitzsimmons/Fairchild Publications, Inc.: 400; The Donegar Group: 401; Colour Association of the United States: 402 (right), 404 (top); Cotton Inc.: 402 (left), 404 (bottom); Image Source Photography: 407.

Chapter 17: Illustration by Erin Fitzsimmons/Fairchild Publications, Inc.: 415; Mark Mainz/Getty Images for IMG: 416 (bottom left); Karl Prouse/Catwalking/Getty Images: 416 (bottom right); Courtesy Fairchild Publications, Inc.: 416 (top), 421, 426; Robert Mitra/Fairchild Publications, Inc.: 417; Giovanni Giannoni/Fairchild Publications, Inc.: 424 (bottom left), 424 (bottom right); Kyle Ericksen/Fairchild Publications, Inc.: 424 (top left); Top Shop: 424 (top right); Peter J. Origlio/Fairchild Publications, Inc.: 425; © Annebicque Bernard/CORBIS SYGMA: 427

(bottom); © Jens Bpttner/dpa/Corbis: 427 (top); Guiseppe CacaceAFP/ Getty Images: 432 (bottom), 432 (middle).

Chapter 18: Illustration by Erin Fitzsimmons/Fairchild Publications, Inc.: 437; Fairchild Publications, Inc.: 438 (bottom left), 438 (right), 451 (left), 451 (right); Kyle Ericksen/Fairchild Publications, Inc.: 439; Erin Fitzsimmons/Fairchild Publications, Inc.: 441; © Kirsty McLaren/ Alamy: 441 (bottom); Gerber Technology, Inc.: 441 (top left), 441 (top right); © Jean Pierre Amet/BelOmbra/Corbis: 442 (bottom); Aizar Raides/AFP/Getty Images: 442 (top); Mark Ralston/AFP/Getty Images: 445 (bottom left), 445 (right), 445 (top left); Guiseppe Cacace/AFP/ Getty Images: 452 (top).

Chapter 19: Illustration by Erin Fitzsimmons/Fairchild Publications, Inc.: 461; Fairchild Publications, Inc.: 462, 466; Tim Graham/Getty Images: 463; China Photos/Getty Images: 464; David McNew/Getty Images: 468; Zack Seckler/Fairchild Publications, Inc.: 470 (right); John Aquino/Fairchild Publications, Inc.: 470 (left); Dave & Les Jacobs/Blend Images/Blend Images/Getty Images: 471; Zubin Shroff/Stone+/Getty Images: 472; Brad Rickerby/Reuters: 474.

Part Five Opener: Serra Akcan/NAR Photos: 480; Pascal Le Segretain/ Getty Images: 481.

Chapter 20: Illustration by Erin Fitzsimmons/Fairchild Publications, Inc.: 482; The Donegar Group: 483, 485; Courtesy of Fairchild Publications, Inc.: 488, 489 (top), 489 (bottom), 492; National Retail Foundation: 491.

Chapter 21: Illustration by Erin Fitzsimmons/Fairchild Publications, Inc.: 499; Fairchild Publications, Inc.: 500 (bottom left), 500 (top), 502, 504 (bottom), 507 (middle), 511 (top), 511 (bottom left), 511 (bottom center), 511 (bottom right), 514 (bottom), 516, 517 (bottom left), 517 (bottom right), 524 (left), 524 (right); © Jennifer Graylock/AP Photo: 500 (bottom right); Talaya Centeno/Fairchild Publications, Inc.: 503 (top); Pasha Antonov/Fairchild Publications, Inc.: 503 (bottom); Kyle Ericksen/Fairchild Publications, Inc.: 504 (top), 505 (top); Sharon Donovan/Fairchild Publications, Inc.: 505 (bottom); Tim Boyle/Getty Images: 507 (top); John Aquino/Fairchild Publications, Inc.: 507 (bottom); © JTB Photo Communications, Inc./Alamy: 510 (top); Jeff Greenberg/PhotoEdit, Inc.: 512 (left); Courtesy Shopbop.com: 512 (right); Erin Fitzsimmons/Fairchild Publications, Inc.: 514 (top), 518 (top), 518 (bottom); © Bob Krist/CORBIS: 517 (top); John Lund/Paula Zacaharias/Blend Images/Getty Images: 521.

Chapter 22: Illustration by Erin Fitzsimmons/ Fairchild Publications, Inc.: 535; Talaya Centeno/Fairchild Publications, Inc.: 536; © RubberBall/Alamy: 537 (top); *WWD*/Fairchild 537 (bottom); Fairchild Publications, Inc.: 537 (bottom), 539; Lord & Taylor: 541; Courtesy United Colors of Benetton: 542 (top); © SuperStock/ Alamy: 542 (bottom); Giovani Giannoni/Fairchild Publications, Inc.: 543; Steve Eichner/Fairchild Publications, Inc.: 545; © AP Photo: 547; The Doneger Group: 549; David Turner/Fairchild Publications, Inc.: 550; Gareth Jones/Fairchild Publications, Inc.: 551 (top); Talaya Centeno/Fairchild Publications, Inc.: 551 (bottom); David Turner/Fairchild Publications, Inc.: 552 (top); Kyle Ericksen/Fairchild Publications, Inc.: 552 (bottom).

index